CIPM® PROGRAM LEVEL I VOLUME 2

2018

ISBN 978-1-946442-01-7 (print)
ISBN 978-1-944250-98-0 (ebk)

September 2017

CONTENTS

◙ indicates an optional segment

Investment Performance Presentation

◘ indicates an optional segment

◘ indicates an optional segment

How to Use the CIPM Program Curriculum

Congratulations on your decision to enter the Certificate in Investment Performance Measurement (CIPM®) Program. This exciting and rewarding program of study reflects your desire to become a serious portfolio evaluation professional. You are embarking on a program noted for its high ethical standards and the depth of knowledge, skills, and abilities it develops. Your commitment to the CIPM Program should be educationally and professionally rewarding. CIPM certificants are dedicated to life-long learning and maintaining currency with the ever-changing dynamics of a challenging profession. The CIPM Program represents the first step towards a career-long commitment to professional education.

To begin your study:

1 Schedule your examination.

2 Access the CIPM Learning Ecosystem and access your study materials.

EXAM SCHEDULING

Examinations are provided online by our testing partner, Pearson VUE. We suggest you schedule your exam appointment with them as soon as possible, because appointments are first-come, first-served. With 24 hours notice, Pearson VUE allows you to reschedule your exam to another available time and place within the same exam window. Rescheduling your exam appointment must be completed within the exam scheduling window. When you schedule or reschedule your exam appointment with Pearson VUE, you will receive an e-mail confirmation. Contact Pearson VUE www.pearsonvue.com/contact/ if you do not receive a confirmation of your appointment.

CIPM LEARNING ECOSYSTEM

The Learning Ecosystem is a customized learning program that makes studying for the CIPM Exam enjoyable, efficient, and effective. The Learning Ecosystem is an online portal that adapts to your needs, strengths, and weaknesses, serving you the right material at the right time and focusing on the areas you need to focus on the most. It helps you stay focused, engaged, and on track while you study.

TIP

Everything you need is in one place. We provide an eBook version of the curriculum for your convenience should that be your preferred method of study. The Learning Ecosystem contains the exact same content. There is no need to do both. If you elect to use the eBook, you may still log into the Learning Ecosystem to take advantage of study tools, such as flashcards, practice tests, and the mock exam.

FEATURES OVERVIEW

The Learning Ecosystem is web-based and accessible through all common browsers.

- The Learning Ecosystem is designed to work well on whatever device is convenient at the moment, whether your desktop, tablet, or smartphone.
- Your progress through the course is automatically recorded so you can seamlessly switch between devices.

TIP

If you are accessing the Learning Ecosystem on a mobile device, it is possible to preload some content for times when you will not have continuous internet access. While you still have Internet access, log in to the Learning Ecosystem and launch your next study activity. This content will remain available when internet access is cut off, for example if you are on mass transit.

Home: Dashboard

Here you will find a summary of your progress through the material and a summary of your strengths and weaknesses with the content.

Study Plans

There are two kinds of study plans from which to choose: structured and adaptive.

- The structured plan will help you keep track of the time remaining before your exam and will suggest the number of activities to complete each day to stay on track. The structured plan will take you through the content in the same order as it appears in the eBook.
- The adaptive plan will begin with a short pre-test to establish a baseline for your existing knowledge. From that point forward, the system will track and adapt to your strengths and weaknesses with the content each time you interact with it. For example, it may adjust your pace through the material to spend less time on content where you are strong and more time on content where you comparatively weaker.

TIP

You are not stuck with your choice of study plan. You can switch back and forth between the structured and adaptive plans. When you switch from one study plan to the other your progress is not lost, and you do not need to start again at the beginning.

TIP

Whichever study plan you choose, studying consistently is the key to success.

Study Tasks

Whichever study plan you are using, the Learning Ecosystem will always let you know which study task is next. Study tasks can include reading a lesson, completing practice questions, completing chapter review questions, reviewing flashcards, or taking a mock exam.

- Lessons are composed of the same content found in the eBook.
- Practiced questions help you review and make sure you understood what you have learned.
- Flashcards test your understanding and recall of important terms and definitions.
- The mock exam is of similar length and weight as the live examination and can help gauge your overall readiness for the live exam.

TIP

As you work through lessons, practice problems, and flashcards, the Learning Ecosystem will frequently ask you to assess your confidence in knowing the material being covered. This information is tracked and presented to you in your Learning History. In the case of the adaptive plan, this information may supplement the system's understanding of your relative strengths and weaknesses.

TIP

If you are studying primarily from the eBook, you can still access the study tools in the Learning Ecosystem without working through a study plan. All of the study tools are accessible directly through the tabs within the menu bar on the left side of the Learning Ecosystem screen.

Other Study Resources

The Learning Ecosystem provides resources that supplement your study tasks.

- The Game Center makes reviewing your flashcards more enjoyable by presenting them within the context of a game in which you may compete with fellow candidates.
- Discussion boards are a place where you can confer with fellow candidates when you need a little extra help or a motivational nudge.

TIP

Discussion boards are **not** actively monitored or moderated by CFA Institute; please use them with that caution in mind. Our vendor monitors the boards for vulgarity and inflammatory language; to speak with a CFA Institute representative please contact us at **info@cfainstitute.org**.

> **TIP**
>
> For technical support assistance or to give us feedback on the Learning Ecosystem or course of study, you may also use the messaging feature.

- The Learning History tab reports trends in your performance over time with tracking on how you have done on practice tests and the mock exam. Additionally, the learning history summarizes your confidence in the topics within the program.

CURRICULUM DEVELOPMENT

The CIPM Program curriculum is grounded in the practice of the portfolio evaluation profession. CFA Institute performs a continuous practice analysis with investment professionals around the world to determine the knowledge, skills, and abilities that are relevant to the profession. Regional expert panels and targeted surveys are conducted to verify and reinforce the insights from practice analysis. The practice analysis process ultimately defines the CIPM Candidate Body of Knowledge (CBOK™).

The examinations are written by practicing certificants and are designed to allow you to demonstrate your mastery of the CBOK as set forth in the CIPM Program curriculum. As you structure your personal study program, you should emphasize mastery of the CBOK and the practical application of that knowledge. For more information on the practice analysis, CBOK, and development of the CIPM Program curriculum, please visit www.cfainstitute.org/programs/cipm/courseofstudy/Pages/index.aspx.

ORGANIZATION OF THE CURRICULUM

The reading assignments are the basis for all examination questions, and are selected or developed specifically to teach the CBOK. These readings are drawn from CIPM Program-commissioned content, textbook chapters, and professional journal articles. Learning outcome statements are listed with each lesson. These LOS indicate what you should be able to accomplish after studying the lesson. We encourage you to review how to properly use LOS, and the descriptions of commonly used LOS "command words," at www.cfainstitute.org/programs/cipm/courseofstudy/Pages/cipm_learning_outcome_statements.aspx. The command words signal the depth of learning you are expected to achieve from the reading. You should use the LOS to guide and focus your study, as each examination question is based on an assigned lesson and one or more LOS. However, the lessons provide context for the LOS and enable you to apply a principle or concept in a variety of scenarios. *Candidates are responsible for the entirety of all required material in the curriculum.*

CANDIDATE RESOURCES

CFA Institute provides a web page that contains numerous resources to help in your successful completion of the CIPM Program. On this page you will find links to testing policies (calculator policy, ID policy, and others); exam details and logistics; testing accommodations; curriculum errata; and a detailed glossary of terms. You should visit this site often to obtain current information: www.cfainstitute.org/programs/cipm/Pages/index.aspx.

FEEDBACK

At CFA Institute, we are committed to delivering a comprehensive and rigorous curriculum for the development of competent, ethically grounded investment professionals. We rely on candidate and member feedback as we work to incorporate content, design, and packaging improvements. You can be assured that we will continue to listen to your suggestions. Please send any comments or feedback—or perceived errors—to info@cfainstitute.org. Ongoing improvements in the curriculum will help you prepare for success on the upcoming examinations, and for a lifetime of learning as a serious investment professional.

Performance Evaluation

Measurement, Attribution, and Appraisal

Study Session 2	Overview and Return Measurement
Study Session 3	Return Attribution and Benchmark Analysis
Study Session 4	Risk Measurement, Risk Attribution, and Security Characteristics
Study Session 5	Performance Appraisal
Study Session 6	Manager Selection

TOPIC LEVEL LEARNING OUTCOME

The candidate should be able to calculate rates of return; explain and apply analytical techniques to determine the sources of returns relative to appropriate benchmarks; and calculate and interpret basic risk measures.

PERFORMANCE EVALUATION

STUDY SESSION 4

Risk Measurement, Risk Attribution, and Security Characteristics

Having covered return measurement and return attribution in earlier study sessions, the first reading of this study session introduces risk measurement and risk attribution.

The second reading explains how performance professionals can use portfolio characteristics analysis in monitoring managers' implementation of their equity investment mandate, conducting holdings-based style analysis, and determining the sources of return.

READING ASSIGNMENTS

7 Risk Measurement and Risk Attribution
by Frances Barney, CFA, C. Mitchell Conover, PhD, CFA, CIPM, and Philippe Grégoire, CFA

8 Equity Portfolio Characteristics in Performance Analysis
by Stephen C. Gaudette, CFA, and Philip Lawton, PhD, CFA, CIPM

READING

7

Risk Measurement and Risk Attribution

by Frances Barney, CFA, C. Mitchell Conover, PhD, CFA, CIPM, and Philippe Grégoire, CFA

Frances Barney, CFA (USA). C. Mitchell Conover, PhD, CFA, CIPM, is at the University of Richmond (USA). Philippe Grégoire, CFA (Canada).

LEARNING OUTCOMES

Mastery	*The candidate should be able to:*
☐	**a.** distinguish between non-financial and financial risk and explain types of each kind of risk;
☐	**b.** describe the objectives of risk measurement and risk attribution;
☐	**c.** contrast the following classifications of market risk: *ex ante* versus *ex post*, stand-alone versus portfolio, idiosyncratic versus systematic, absolute versus relative, and symmetric versus asymmetric;
☐	**d.** describe and interpret return data sets with respect to their implications for market risk;
☐	**e.** calculate, interpret, and critique the following measures of dispersion: variance, standard deviation, mean absolute deviation, and tracking risk;
☐	**f.** calculate and interpret beta;
☐	**g.** calculate, interpret, and critique the following measures of downside risk: semi-variance, target semi-variance, semi-standard deviation, and target semi-standard deviation;
☐	**h.** calculate, interpret, and critique drawdown, average drawdown, maximum drawdown, and largest individual drawdown;
☐	**i.** describe and interpret value at risk and stress tests and explain the strengths and weaknesses of each;
☐	**j.** describe approaches to estimating value at risk;
☐	**k.** describe equity and bond characteristics and valuation metrics that are related to risk;
☐	**l.** recommend appropriate risk measures with respect to specified objectives;
☐	**m.** interpret risk attribution analyses;
☐	**n.** describe the relationship between risk attribution and return attribution and explain considerations in selecting a risk attribution approach.

1 INTRODUCTION

This reading is about the measurement of risk and risk attribution. **Risk** is exposure to uncertainty.[1] Risk attribution, formally defined later, is concerned with analyzing and describing the components of a portfolio's risk.

We can view risk in a forward-looking or a backward-looking sense. The primary focus in this reading is on the measurement of variability that has occurred in the past. Risk measurement and risk attribution are important concerns for investment managers and their clients.

This reading will survey many aspects of risk and provide answers to the following questions:

- How do non-financial and financial risks differ? What are their subtypes?
- What are the objectives of risk measurement and risk attribution?
- How can market risk be visually represented, and how are these representations interpreted?
- What are the advantages of risk measures that quantify only downside risk?
- How are drawdown and value at risk measures used?
- What are the equity and bond characteristics related to risk?
- How is risk attribution analysis interpreted?
- How are risk and return attribution analyses related?

The balance of the reading is organized as follows. Section 2, after providing needed background on risk, presents an overview of the most common ways market risk is measured. Section 3 introduces security characteristics as measures of risk. Section 4 discusses risk measure selection. Section 5 introduces risk attribution, and Section 6 presents conclusions and a summary.

2 RISK AND RISK MEASUREMENT

The concept of risk is applied in various settings with distinctive risk characteristics. Companies and investors face two broad categories of risk: non-financial and financial. Non-financial risks include such things as the death of key executives and the failure of computer systems. These risks are not usually the concern of performance analysts. Certain financial risks are. **Financial risks** are those due to events in external financial markets. Financial risks are further delineated into three major types: market risk, credit risk, and liquidity risk.

The focus in this reading will be on market risk. **Market risk** is the risk that results from unexpected changes in share prices, interest rates, currency exchange rates, and commodity prices, as discussed below. The factors responsible for market risk are numerous. For equities, these factors include changes in the outlook for countries, changes in industries in which the company competes, and factors specific to the company. Interest rates can shift abruptly because of unexpected changes in central bank policy and/or the demand for loanable funds (the latter can change quickly as macroeconomic prospects change). Currencies fluctuate due to variability in floating exchange rates, as well as (in the case of fixed exchange rates) the chance that a government will devalue or revalue its currency. Commodity prices are often volatile due to supply shocks, changes in inflation, and other factors.

1 Grégoire (2007, p. 309).

Credit risk refers to the risk of loss caused by the failure of a counterparty (**counterparty risk**) or a debtor to make a payment (e.g., the default of a bond issuer). Note that credit risk can arise from either inability or unwillingness to make a payment. Furthermore, a loss may be incurred from an increase in credit risk that is not associated with actual default; the increase in risk could be due to deterioration in the counterparty's financial position.

Liquidity risk results from the inability to trade an asset quickly without making price concessions.[2] Liquidity risk increases as market depth declines, and it is accentuated during market crises when there is insufficient trading. At the extreme, liquidity risk means that an asset cannot be traded at all. More frequently, liquidity risk results in higher trading costs. For assets that are less liquid and harder to resell, the dealer will require a higher profit. To increase the profit, the dealer will widen the spread made from trading the asset, referred to as the bid–ask spread. The bid–ask spread is the difference between the price the dealer will pay for the asset (referred to as "the bid") and the price at which the dealer will sell the asset (referred to as "the ask"). From the investor's perspective, a widening bid–ask spread results in a loss in value, because higher prices are paid when the asset is bought and lower prices are received when the asset is eventually sold.

In addition to financial risks, companies and investors also encounter non-financial risks. **Non-financial risks** include operational risk, model risk, and settlement risk. **Operational risk** is the risk of loss from failure in a company's systems or procedures or from external events, such as "acts of God" or terrorist action. **Model risk** results when a model is incorrect or misapplied. For example, many believe that mortgages and related securities were misvalued in the late 2000s, precipitating the 2008 financial crisis. **Settlement risk** results from a breakdown in the settlement of a trade. More specifically, once an investor has fulfilled one side of a trade, there is a risk that the counterparty will not fulfill the other side of the trade. Settlement risk increases when the counterparty is in a different time zone and the final settlement of a trade does not occur until the next business day.

Other non-financial risks include regulatory, legal/contract, tax, sovereign/political, and accounting risks. **Regulatory risk** results from changes in regulations that adversely affect valuation. For example, new regulations governing trading could reduce the affected assets' values. **Legal/contract risk** arises from contract terms that are not clearly specified, a scenario that results in potential litigation. **Tax risk** results from unexpected changes in tax rates or rulings. **Sovereign/political risk** stems from government action. For example, a government may decide to suspend convertibility of its currency, so that investors cannot exit its market. **Accounting risk** arises from uncertainty about how a transaction should be recorded and the potential for accounting rules to change.[3]

A summary of the types of financial and non-financial risks is provided in Exhibit 1.

2 Note that the term *liquidity risk* is sometimes used to refer to the inability to readily obtain funding, also referred to as **funding risk**. As an example of funding risk, during the credit crisis of 2008, many financial institutions could not obtain the external financing needed for their daily operations and had to urgently sell assets at steep discounts.

3 For a more detailed discussion of risks and their management, see Chance, Grant, and Marsland (2007); Christopherson, Cariño, and Ferson (2009); Jorion (2009).

Exhibit 1 Types of Financial and Non-Financial Risks

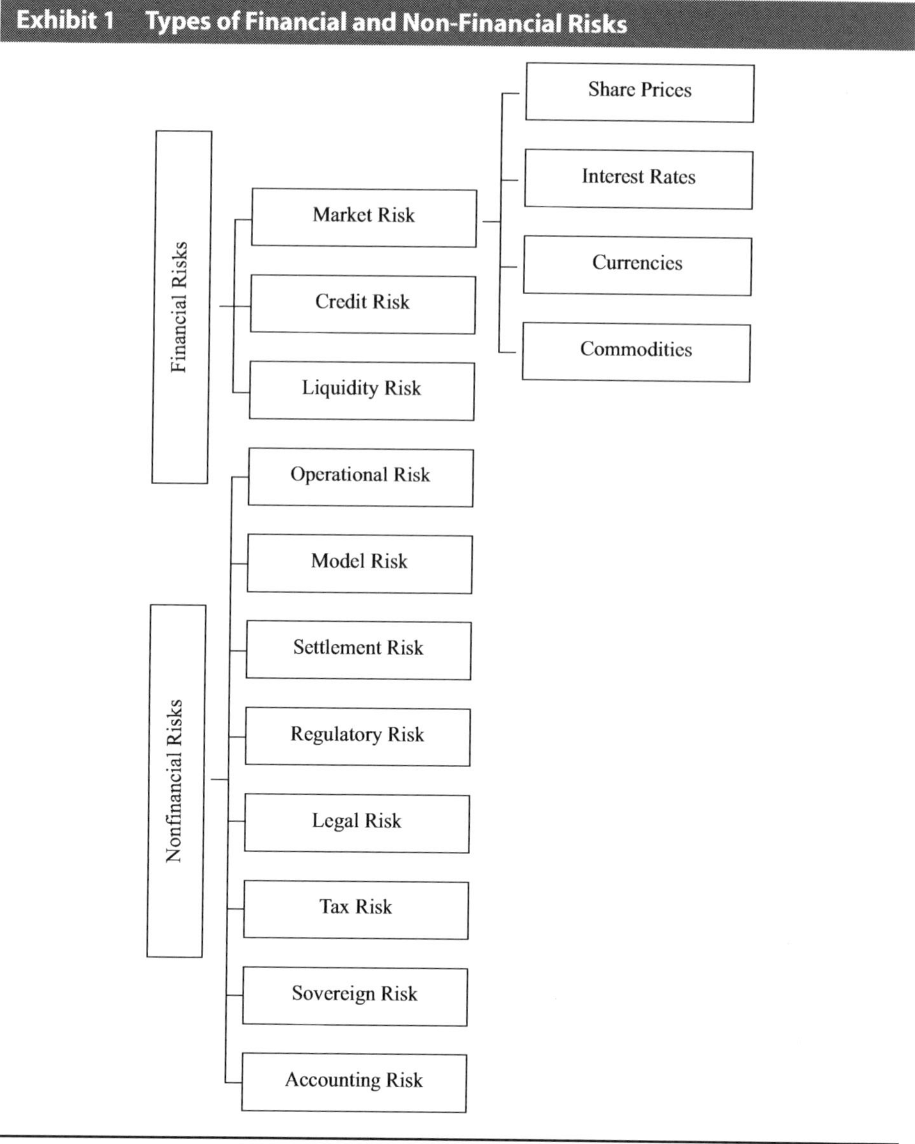

In the discussions to follow, we will further delineate market risks and examine methods of measuring market risks.

EXAMPLE 1

Types of Risk

1 A US investment fund purchases US Treasury bonds. Which of the following *best characterizes* the risk from this investment?

   A Credit risk

   B Market risk

   C Liquidity risk

2 A performance analyst uses fictional (made-up) prices for an asset that trades infrequently. The reported performance for the fund misstates its true performance. Which of the following *best characterizes* the risk in this example?

   A Model risk

B Liquidity risk

C Operational risk

3 To improve market liquidity and confidence during crises, a government decides to limit the trading of over-the-counter contracts. Which of the following *best characterizes* the risk from this limitation?

A Financial risk

B Regulatory risk

C Legal/contract risk

Solution to 1:

B is correct. Because US Treasury bonds have minimal risk of default and are very liquid, their primary risk is from unexpected changes in interest rates. Unexpected changes in interest rates are a component of market risk.

Solution to 2:

C is correct. The use of fictional prices by the performance analyst is best characterized as operational risk. Operational risk is the risk of loss from failure in a company's systems or procedures. In this example, no immediate loss resulted from the analyst's actions, but the misreporting does create potential liability for the fund.

There was no stated misapplication of a model, so the risk in this case is not model risk. Although the asset is illiquid, liquidity risk refers to the inability to trade an asset. So the analyst's use of fictional prices is best characterized as operational risk.

Solution to 3:

B is correct. The action by the government to limit the trading of over-the-counter contracts is best characterized as regulatory risk. Regulatory risk arises from changes in regulations that negatively affect asset valuation. In this case, the investors who currently hold over-the-counter contracts would likely see their value diminish.

Although liquidity will diminish for the over-the-counter contracts and liquidity risk is a component of financial risk, the government action is best characterized as regulatory risk. Legal/contract risk results when contract terms are not clearly specified, so it is not applicable in this example.

2.1 Objectives of Risk Measurement and Risk Attribution

Investors accept some risk of loss in order to earn the chance for investment gains. The investment monitoring process includes evaluation of the risks taken as well as the returns achieved. This evaluation of risk and return is part of the feedback loop that provides input into the investment management process, as well as into manager selection and retention decisions.

The objective of risk measurement and risk attribution is to enable the investor to understand the relevant risks involved in the investment under evaluation. Advisers, portfolio managers, consultants, and other fiduciaries hired by the investor may also use risk measures in their investment or advisory roles. Risk measurement is also a key component of a risk control framework; such a framework involves the identification of relevant business objectives, risks to achieving those objectives, measures of risk, and associated controls to manage those risks. Managers responsible for monitoring the risk of a company or an industry use risk measures to evaluate current strength and anticipate potential issues.

Just as return attribution reveals the sources of returns within a portfolio that are associated with different factors or decisions, risk attribution reveals the sources of risk associated with those same factors or decisions. For example, consider a manager with broad investment discretion measured relative to a published benchmark. If return attribution reveals that this manager outperformed the benchmark as a result of investing outside the benchmark, the investor might be concerned about the unanticipated risk from that active position. However, if risk attribution revealed that the decision to invest outside the benchmark reduced the volatility of the overall portfolio returns, the investor might be more comfortable with the manager's active investment decisions. Risk attribution in combination with return attribution enables a more comprehensive analysis of the effects of management decisions on the portfolio.

Risk measurement and risk attribution provide information useful to performance appraisal (which is concerned with identifying investment skill). The evaluation of risk-adjusted returns first requires the identification and analysis of an appropriate risk measure to represent a unit of risk. The selection of an appropriate risk measure can vary depending on the risk preferences of the investor, the purpose of the risk analysis, and the asset class or investment strategy under review.

The following is a list of some of the ways that risk measurement and risk attribution may be used by different participants in the investment industry or for different types of investments.

Investment Policy Definition:

- Investors may choose particular risk measures as a way of defining their individual risk appetites.
- An investment adviser may specify risk limits in drafting an investment policy for a private wealth client.

Portfolio Construction:

- A portfolio manager may use risk measures as part of mean–variance portfolio optimization or another asset selection and allocation process in the construction of a portfolio.
- A corporate treasurer may use *ex ante* risk measures to estimate potential scenarios in forecasting cash flow requirements. For example, a firm managing fixed-income portfolios to support its operating cash needs may select investments that minimize risk under different scenarios of changing interest rates and credit ratings.

Portfolio Analysis:

- An investment consultant may use risk attribution analysis of a portfolio to evaluate whether or not the manager is taking risks consistent with the manager's stated investment philosophy.
- An institutional investor may evaluate risk characteristics of the composite of all portfolios in an asset class relative to the benchmark stated in the investment policy. The objective might be to determine whether, in the aggregate, the portfolios delivered the benchmark's level of risk.
- A hedge fund manager may use *ex ante* risk measures to analyze a potential strategy change under different market scenarios.

Enterprise Risk Analysis:

- A risk manager responsible for multiple portfolio managers may use risk attribution to evaluate which strategies have the greatest contribution to increasing or hedging overall firm risk exposures.
- A corporate executive may review risk measures of the corporation's pension assets compared to its pension liabilities to understand the potential impact of different market scenarios on the financial strength of the corporation.[4]
- A regulator may review risk reporting to estimate potential systemic risks to an institution or industry. For example, some regulators request specific stress tests intended to evaluate the strength of financial institutions or investment vehicles under conditions such as credit or liquidity crises or extreme changes in markets or interest rates.

There are many different definitions of risk and many different measures available, depending on the objectives of the investor. Risk measures may be applied to a single investment or to all of the investments in an economic sector, region, country, or other grouping. Risk measures can also apply to a composite or asset class, to a total fund or benchmark, or to an entire company or industry.

Risk measurement and risk attribution are useful tools for helping the investor understand the risks inherent in any investment strategy. It is important to understand the different risk measures in order to manage the risks that are most appropriate to the investment goals and concerns of the investor.

EXAMPLE 2

Objectives of Risk Measurement

1 Reporting risk characteristics to regulators is associated with which stage of the investment process?

  A Enterprise risk analysis

  B Performance evaluation

  C Investment policy definition

2 If a manager incorrectly describes the volatility of a particular investment strategy, the investor who selects that manager is *most likely* to experience:

  A lower returns.

  B higher volatility.

  C unanticipated risks.

3 What kind of analysis is *most likely* to reveal that an equity portfolio has more exposure to value factors than to growth factors compared to the portfolio benchmark?

  A Risk attribution

  B Portfolio construction

  C Performance evaluation

4 In this reading, *pension plan* refers to *defined benefit pension plan* in which the benefits to a participant on retirement are determined by a formula rather than by investment returns.

Solution to 1:

A is correct. Regulators require enterprise risk reporting in order to monitor the enterprise risk of an institution and the contribution of the institution to the systemic risks of an industry. Performance evaluation is the review of portfolio managers' results relative to the stated investment mandates and is less relevant to regulatory reporting than enterprise risk. Investment policy definition is the first part of the investment process, preceding other types of reporting and review.

Solution to 2:

C is correct. One of the purposes of evaluating risk measures is to enable the investor to understand the risks of potential investment decisions. If a manager incorrectly describes any risk measure, such as volatility, the investor who selects that manager will be exposed to unanticipated risks, which could mean higher or lower returns, as well as higher or lower volatility.

Solution to 3:

A is correct. Risk attribution analysis could reveal the tilt of a portfolio toward value factors or growth factors.

2.2 Contrasting Perspectives on Risk

Risk may be viewed in many different ways. In this section, we compare the following classifications of market risk: *ex ante* versus *ex post*, stand-alone versus portfolio, idiosyncratic versus systematic, absolute versus relative, and symmetric versus asymmetric.

In addition to decomposing market risk into risk from share prices, interest rates, currency exchange rates, and commodity prices, we can examine market risk using classification perspectives.

The first classification is that of *ex ante* versus *ex post* risk. *Ex ante* is a Latin term meaning "before (in time or place)." The ***ex ante* risk** is that anticipated for the future. For example, the *ex ante* risk is typically thought to be higher for emerging market stocks than for developed country stocks. Accordingly, investors would typically pay less for the same level of future cash flows from an emerging market stock than they would for a developed country stock in the same industry.

Of course, when we look back over a period of time, the returns for emerging market stocks may turn out to have less variability than those for developed country stocks. The variability in investment returns after the fact is referred to as ***ex post* risk**, or more literally, the variability that lies behind. The *ex post* return variability can be quite different from that expected *ex ante*.

In performance measurement, we focus on measuring *ex post* returns. However, *ex post* returns can affect our estimation of *ex ante* risk. The predictive power of *ex post* risk measurements for *ex ante* risk declines as the investor's portfolio changes composition. For example, a manager who recently replaced bonds with stocks would not be expected to maintain the same level of risk.

Stand-alone risk measures the variability of an asset's return, independent of the performance of other assets. **Portfolio risk**, on the other hand, measures the variability of a collection of assets. If an investor is viewing one asset in isolation from other assets, stand-alone risk would be a suitable measure. Most investors, however, are also concerned with portfolio risk, because they typically hold more than one asset. Portfolio risk is almost always less than a weighted average of the components' stand-alone risk because the individual asset price movements will offset one another.

For example, assume that competitors Siemens and General Electric (GE) have the same stand-alone risk and an investor invests half his wealth in each. If GE's stock price declines due to a major product recall, the Siemens stock should benefit. Assume that, to some degree, the stock price movements of GE and Siemens will offset one another. Therefore, a portfolio of GE and Siemens would have less variability than the average of GE's and Siemens's stand-alone risks.

The concept that investing in a portfolio of assets will reduce risk is referred to as diversification. Although the concept of diversification is often explained by using the proverb "Don't put all your eggs in one basket," it has a richer context in the investment world. In our example, the investor's loss from GE's stock price decline is mitigated because the investor has also invested in Siemens, and also because Siemens will increase in value as GE falls. In the real world, Siemens and GE do not need to move in opposite directions to cause a reduction in portfolio risk; it is required only that the two stocks not move together perfectly.

The total stand-alone risk for an asset can be decomposed into idiosyncratic risk and systematic risk. **Idiosyncratic risk** is that due to unexpected changes in company-specific factors, whereas systematic risk is that originating from broad financial market conditions and the macroeconomy (i.e., the system). For example, if fraud occurs at a company, the resulting loss in value would be termed idiosyncratic risk. If, however, a company faces increased financing costs because of central bank actions, we would refer to this as **systematic risk**. Other examples of systematic risk factors would be changes in economic growth forecasts, changes in consumer confidence, and any other factor that affects the majority of securities.

Some companies are more sensitive to the macroeconomy than others. For example, the auto industry is typically more sensitive to system wide factors than the food industry. The auto industry flourishes when the economy does well and suffers as economic prospects decline. On the other hand, the food industry's product is a necessity, so demand is not as variable.

In a well-diversified portfolio, idiosyncratic risk is negligible because company-specific events will cancel one another out. In our example above, the decline in the GE stock price was offset by an increase in Siemens' stock price. However, both GE and Siemens will suffer to some degree if there is a global recession; that is, systematic risk cannot be diversified away. So for a well-diversified investor, systematic risk is more relevant than idiosyncratic risk. Idiosyncratic risk is often referred to as company-specific or unsystematic risk.

Our next risk distinction is that of absolute versus relative risk. **Absolute risk** measures return variability without comparison to a benchmark, whereas **relative risk** measures the variability of returns relative to a reference point. Hedge funds are sometimes said to be absolute return funds because they employ nontraditional strategies and therefore cannot be measured against common benchmarks. Mutual funds, however, are often measured against a market index, with the difference in returns referred to as the excess return. The variability of the excess returns is relative risk.

For some investors, the distinction between absolute and relative risk is paramount. For example, a pension fund manager must satisfy future payments owed to retirees. In this case, the absolute variability of the portfolio isn't as important as its variability relative to the retirement liabilities. The portfolio must fluctuate with retirement liabilities so that the necessary payments will be satisfied. The potential difference between assets and liabilities is relative risk and is often referred to as **surplus risk**.

Relative risk is also important to investors whose performance is expected to track that of a market benchmark. When manager returns deviate from the benchmark, the variability of the deviations is referred to as **active risk** and measured by tracking risk.[5] Note that a manager's portfolio could increase in value but still underperform its benchmark, thus performing well on an absolute basis but poorly on a relative basis. From this perspective, we can see that absolute risk measures two components: the risk

5 This concept is known by several names, including tracking error and tracking error variance.

of the benchmark and the risk of the active management return. In contrast, relative risk measures only the risk of active management. In performance measurement, we often use relative risk to scale a manager's active return.

For many investors, the risk of losing money is more important than the risk of gaining money.[6] Therefore, the variability from upside returns is much less of a concern than the variability from losses. Instead of focusing on all variability in a portfolio (**symmetric risk**), some investors focus just on the part of variability that reflects losses by using **asymmetric risk** measures. In other words, whereas symmetric risk measures examine the variability of both positive and negative performance, asymmetric risk measures are typically used to quantify only underperformance. Note, however, that if an asset has historically had high, predominantly upside variability, then it is likely that this variability reflects the potential for losses in the future.

Asymmetric risk measures become useful when examining investment strategies that are specifically designed to avoid losses. For example, some strategies will sacrifice some upside to pay the costs of hedging to reduce the likelihood and extent of losses. These strategies will have limited downside risk but reduced upside potential. In the questions below and in the next section, we will examine methods to describe and visualize investment risk.

EXAMPLE 3

Risk

Exhibit 2 provides the growth of $100 invested on 1 January 2008 using monthly returns from January 2008 to October 2009, a period of great turbulence in the global financial markets. The stocks shown are the US companies Clorox, Goldman Sachs, and Eastern American Natural Gas.

6 Investors with this characteristic are said to be loss averse (Kahneman and Tversky 1979).

Exhibit 2 Growth of $100 Invested 1 January 2008 to 10 October 2009

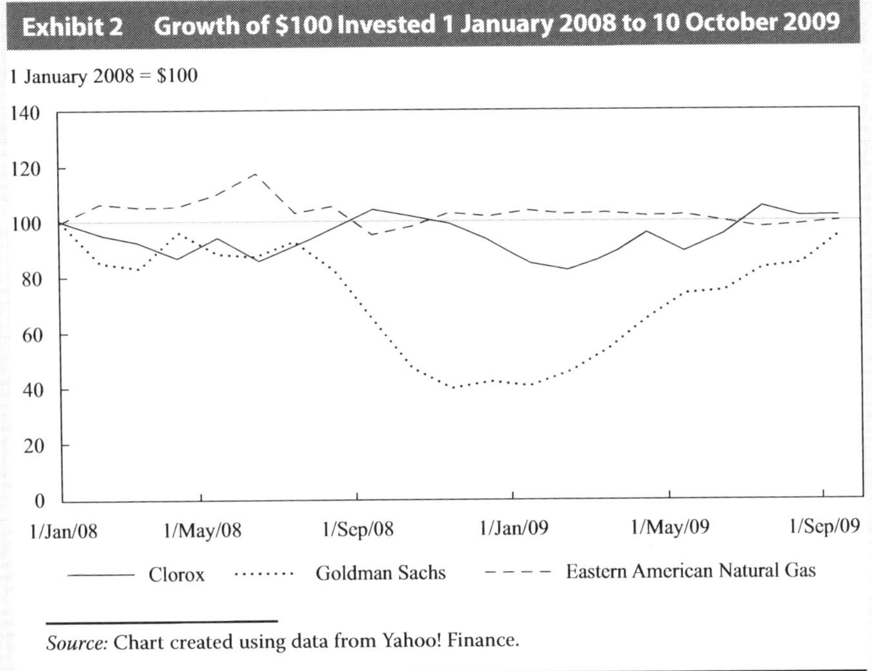

Source: Chart created using data from Yahoo! Finance.

1 The *ex post* risk of Goldman Sachs during the first half of 2008 was *most likely:*

A lower than its *ex post* risk during the second half of 2008.

B the same as its *ex post* risk during the second half of 2008.

C greater than its *ex post* risk during the second half of 2008.

2 Suppose an investor specifies a minimum return target of 0%. For which of the following stocks will the divergence between asymmetric and symmetric risk be the greatest in 2009?

A Clorox

B Goldman Sachs

C Eastern American Natural Gas

3 An investor composes a portfolio of equal parts Eastern American Natural Gas and Clorox. For the year 2008, the investor's portfolio risk is *most likely:*

A less than the stand-alone risk of Eastern American Natural Gas.

B the same as the stand-alone risk of Eastern American Natural Gas.

C greater than the stand-alone risk of Eastern American Natural Gas.

Solution to 1:

A is correct. As illustrated in Exhibit 2, during the second half of 2008, Goldman Sachs's stock price fell sharply, whereas during the first half of 2008, its stock price was more stable. Therefore, Goldman Sachs's *ex post* risk (its variability in returns after the fact) during the first half of 2008 was lower than its *ex post* risk during the second half of 2008.

Solution to 2:

B is correct. In this case, the investor has specified a minimum return target of 0%. Asymmetric risk measures downside variability, whereas symmetric risk measures both upside and downside variability. An asymmetric risk measure would consider only returns below 0% as risk. Notice that of all the stocks,

Goldman Sachs has the strongest performance in 2009. It does have returns that are somewhat volatile, but these returns are predominantly positive; that is, most of its variability is upside variability. Its asymmetric risk will be lower than its symmetric risk because in most 2009 months it will have outperformed the 0% target return; that is, it does not have much downside variability.

Clorox's stock experienced some losses during 2009, so its asymmetric risk will be more similar to its symmetric risk, relative to Goldman Sachs. Eastern American Natural Gas was fairly stable in 2009, so its asymmetric risk will be more similar to its symmetric risk, relative to Goldman Sachs.

Solution to 3:

A is correct. In 2008, the returns for Eastern American Natural Gas are generally positive until June, then turn generally negative, and end the year positive. For Clorox, the returns are generally negative until June, then turn positive, and end the year on a negative trend. Thus, for much of the year, the returns for the two stocks move in opposite directions. Combining them in a portfolio would result in lower portfolio risk than investing in Eastern American Natural Gas alone. So the investor's portfolio risk will be less than the stand-alone risk of Eastern American Natural Gas.

2.3 Interpreting Data Sets

With several basic risk concepts in hand, it is appropriate to introduce the specific concepts and tools for analyzing investment data sets. In this section, we introduce the concepts of frequency distributions, histograms, and measures of central tendency.

One way to examine the performance of a portfolio manager is to summarize the manager's holding period returns into a frequency distribution. A **frequency distribution** uses intervals of returns into which each period's return is placed.

As an example, we will use the historical monthly returns for the Argentina stock market from January 1976 to March 2011, calculated in US dollars. Upon sorting the returns, the smallest return is –64.95%. We will use interval values from –65% to +65%, with interval widths of 5%. After each monthly return has been placed in an interval, some intervals will have more than one observation. The resulting frequency distribution table is shown in Exhibit 3.

Exhibit 3 Frequency Distribution for Argentina Stock Returns

Interval	Frequency of Observations
–65% to –60%	2
–60% to –55%	0
–55% to –50%	1
–50% to –45%	1
–45% to –40%	2
–40% to –35%	1
–35% to –30%	4
–30% to –25%	5
–25% to –20%	16
–20% to –15%	17
–15% to –10%	26
–10% to –5%	54

Exhibit 3 (Continued)

Interval	Frequency of Observations
−5% to 0%	61
0% to 5%	70
5% to 10%	65
10% to 15%	32
15% to 20%	18
20% to 25%	13
25% to 30%	7
30% to 35%	7
35% to 40%	4
40% to 45%	2
45% to 50%	2
50% to 55%	1
55% to 60%	2
60% to 65%	2
65% and above	8

Source: Frequency distribution created using data from Datastream.

The table would be read as follows: In the first interval, there are two return observations greater than or equal to −65% and less than −60%. There are no observations between −60% and −55%. The interval with the highest frequency of observations is 0% to 5%. There are eight returns that are greater than the highest interval value of 65%.[7]

Another method of summarizing data is to use the frequency distribution to plot a bar chart, with the resulting figure in Exhibit 4 referred to as a **histogram**.

7 A standard frequency distribution and histogram would plot all the intervals that returns reside in, but to simplify the presentation, we categorize the eight highest returns in the interval "65% and above."

Exhibit 4 Histogram of Argentina Stock Returns

Source: Histogram created using data from Datastream.

The histogram provides a visual confirmation of the frequency distribution, where again the interval with the highest number of observations is 0% to 5%, with 70 returns in that range. If an investor believed that these *ex post* return frequencies were indicative of the future, he or she might conclude that the *ex ante* return was between 0% and 5%.

However, instead of providing only a range of *ex post* returns, we can also calculate the average, or **arithmetic mean return**, for a historical time period. Given returns R_i, from $i = 1, \ldots, n$, the arithmetic mean of returns, $\bar{R}$, is:

$$\bar{R} = \frac{1}{n}\sum_{i=1}^{n} R_i \tag{1}$$

These *ex post* Argentina stock market returns consist of 423 monthly returns. The sum of the returns is 1,463.71%. The arithmetic mean is then 1,463.71%/423 = 3.46%. The investor might then conclude that the most likely return in the next month would be 3.46%.

Instead of using the arithmetic mean return as a measure of central tendency, the investor may instead want to use the median return. The **median** is the "middlemost" observation; i.e., in a set of observations that has been ranked from highest to lowest, the median will lie in the middle. The advantage of the median is that it is not affected by the magnitudes of extreme values, as is the mean. However, this advantage can also be viewed as a disadvantage in that the median does not incorporate the magnitudes of values, only the relative ranking of the data.

In our example, there are 423 observations. To find the middle observation, we calculate $(n + 1)/2$, where n is the total number of observations. The median is then the $(423 + 1)/2 = 212$th observation. When we rank the returns from highest to lowest, the 212th return is 1.55%.[8]

8 Note that if there were an even number of observations, the median would be the average of the $n/2$ and $(n + 2)/2$ observations.

Being simply the "middlemost" value, the median is not affected by the magnitudes of extreme values on either end of the histogram. The arithmetic mean, on the other hand, is affected because those extreme values are included in calculating the sum. If the arithmetic mean is greater than the median, it is usually the case that there are extreme positive values pulling the arithmetic mean up. This generally results in **positive skewness**. When large losses weigh down the arithmetic mean, **negative skewness** generally results.[9] Investors generally prefer positive skewness because it indicates the opportunity for large positive returns.

As shown in Exhibit 5, a positively skewed distribution is asymmetric, as there are more large gains than large losses. As a result, the right tail is longer than the left tail. In a negatively skewed distribution, there are large losses that lengthen the left tail.

Exhibit 5 Positively and Negatively Skewed Distributions

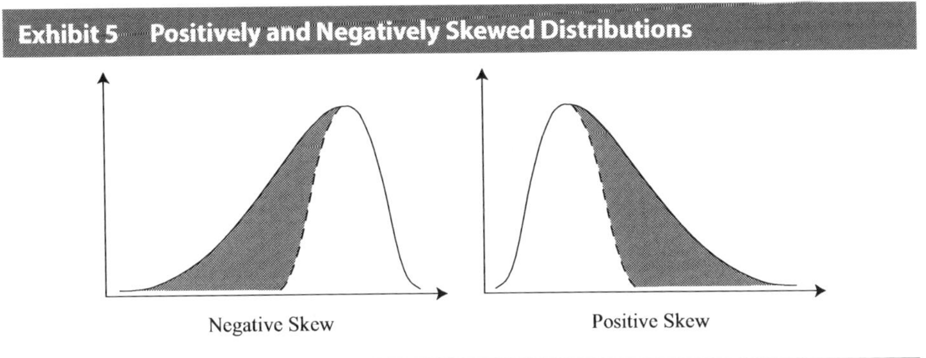

The analysis we have used so far is **time-series analysis**, in which the returns for an asset are examined over time. The returns for the Argentina stock market are clustered around the middle values, but there also appears to be a fair amount of variability. This variability represents risk to the investor because it indicates that large losses are possible. But how variable are they relative to some other investment? To address this question, we turn to **cross-sectional analysis**, where we compare the returns for one asset against those for another.

We next examine the US dollar returns for the Morgan Stanley Capital International (MSCI) Europe/Australasia/Far East (EAFE) Index. EAFE is an index that includes the returns for more than 20 developed country markets. We would expect EAFE to have less variable returns than Argentina because it is composed of more mature countries and because it is diversified across many countries. Argentina is often classified as an emerging market, and emerging markets usually entail greater return variability. The histogram of EAFE returns, using the same return intervals and time period as for Argentina, is shown in Exhibit 6.

9 It is sometimes said that if the distribution is positively skewed, the mean will be greater than the median, and with negative skewness, the mean will be less than the median. However, this is not always true, especially in the case of discrete distributions. For more information, see von Hippel (2005).

Exhibit 6 Histogram of EAFE Index Returns

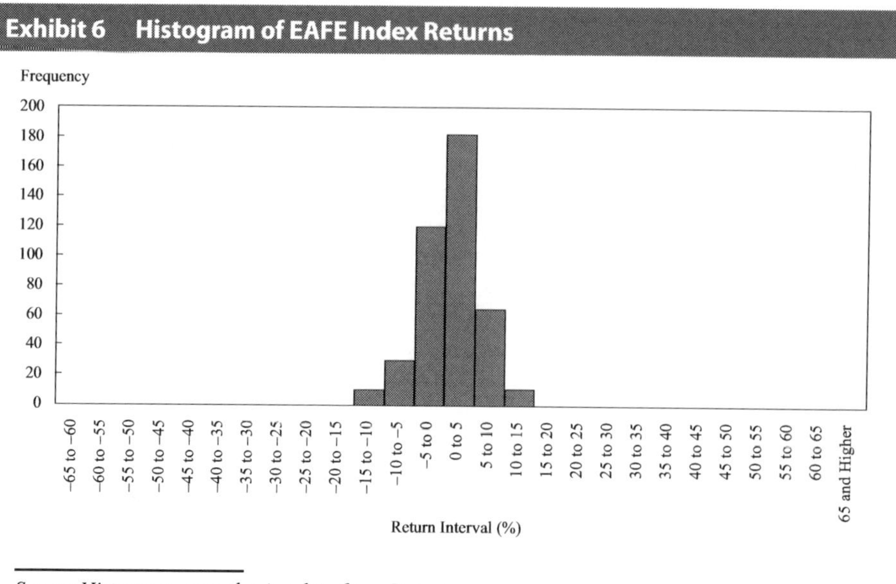

Source: Histogram created using data from Datastream.

It is obvious that the returns for EAFE are much less variable than those for Argentina. Although the highest frequency of returns is again in the 0% to 5% range, there are no returns less than −25% or greater than 20%. We would conclude that the dispersion in EAFE returns is relatively low.

There is also very little skewness, as the return distribution is fairly symmetric. The arithmetic mean and median are quite close at 0.98% and 1.07%, respectively. If an investor had invested in the EAFE Index, there would have been no opportunity to earn returns of 65% or greater, as there was during eight months for Argentina.

However, there was also no month in which the investor lost more than 25% of EAFE value. In the case of Argentina, there were 16 months during which the loss was greater than 25%. The possibility of extreme losses, referred to as **tail risk** (in reference to the left tail in a distribution), results in much more value destruction in the case of Argentina. The lowest return in Argentina was almost −65%, whereas it was −20% for EAFE. The potential for a loss, often referred to as **downside risk**, is 45% for Argentina, as 190 of the 423 monthly returns are negative. For EAFE, this statistic is lower at 39%, as 163 returns are negative.

Previously, we used the median to separate the Argentina returns into halves. Another method of examining the returns would be to divide the data into four sections, or **quartiles**. The three values that separate the returns into fourths are referred to as the first quartile, the second quartile (the median), and the third quartile. We rank the returns from lowest to highest to determine each quartile value. Doing so for both Argentina and EAFE, we would obtain the values shown in Exhibit 7.

Exhibit 7 Quartile Values for Argentina and EAFE Index Returns

	Argentina	EAFE
1st Quartile	−7.46%	−1.73%
2nd Quartile	1.55	1.07
3rd Quartile	9.66	4.00

Source: Quartiles created using data from Datastream.

The quartile statistics confirm the results from the histogram. The potential for high returns is much greater for the Argentina stock index than it is for the EAFE Index. A quarter of the returns for the former index are greater than 9.66%, as opposed to 4.00% for the EAFE Index. But again, there is also a greater potential for losses. A quarter of the returns for Argentina are lower than –7.46%, as opposed to –1.73% for the EAFE Index. We could also divide the data into **quintiles** (fifths) or **deciles** (tenths) or **percentiles** (hundredths) to make comparisons.

Using visual comparisons and rankings of returns, it is easy to determine that the returns for EAFE are much less variable than those for Argentina. Some comparisons aren't quite as obvious. In these cases, more exact risk measures are needed. We now examine other methods of quantifying return variability.

EXAMPLE 4

Interpreting Histograms

The histogram below provides the percentage changes in the value of the Brazilian real (BRL) relative to the US dollar from February 2007 to February 2012. There were 259 weekly observations. Reflecting the appreciation of the real over this time period, the sum of its weekly returns during the measurement period was 23.31%.

Exhibit 8 Histogram of Changes in the Value of the Brazilian Real Relative to the US Dollar

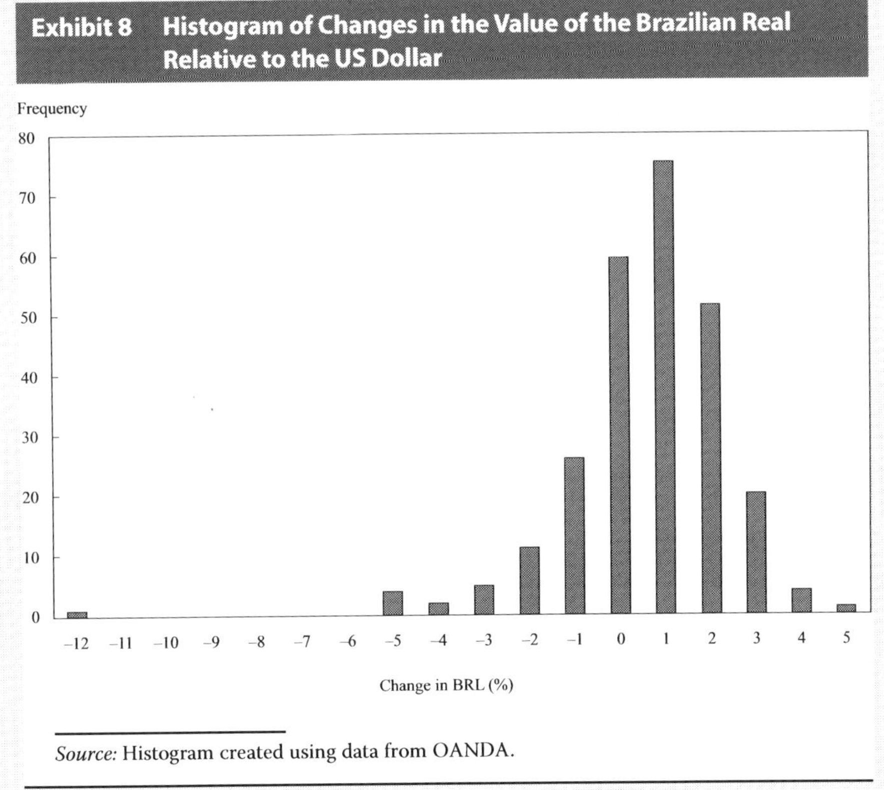

Source: Histogram created using data from OANDA.

Using the information provided, address the following:

1 Determine how the median observation would be found for these data.
2 Calculate the arithmetic mean of the weekly percentage changes in the value of the real.
3 Discuss the presence of tail risk in the data.

Solution to 1:

To determine the median, calculate $(n + 1)/2$, where n is the total number of observations. For these data, the median is equal to the $(259 + 1)/2 = 130$th observation. If we had the original data for the exchange rate changes and ranked the returns from highest to lowest, we would find that the 130th return was equal to 0.28%.

Solution to 2:

The arithmetic mean is the sum divided by the total number of observations. In this case, we calculate 23.31%/259 = 0.09%.

Solution to 3:

There is one extreme value in the −12% interval, which is in the far left tail of the distribution. This change in value of the real was −12.6% and occurred during the week of 12 October 2008, a period of heightened market variability.

We refer to the possibility of extreme losses as tail risk, and we would characterize changes in the value of the real as being subject to this risk. The extreme loss of −12.6% represents negative skewness and helps "pull" the mean (0.09%) down below the median of 0.28%.

2.4 Measures of Dispersion

This section introduces variance, standard deviation, and mean absolute deviation as measures of dispersion, which are often used to represent absolute risk. Also discussed is tracking risk, a counterpart to standard deviation for measuring dispersion relative to a benchmark. Other measures of relative risk—correlation, covariance, and beta—are discussed in the next section.

One method of quantifying risk is to calculate the **variance** for a set of returns. The formula for the variance (σ^2) is:

$$\sigma^2 = \frac{\sum_{i=1}^{n}\left(R_i - \overline{R}\right)^2}{n} \quad (2)$$

The formula says that to obtain the variance

1 Calculate the arithmetic mean, $\overline{R}$;

2 Calculate the difference between each periodic return, R_i, and the mean;

3 Square the differences;

4 Sum the squared differences; and

5 Divide by n, where n is the number of observations.[10]

In the formula, greater differences from the mean will result in a greater variance. Therefore, a larger variance indicates greater risk. The variance will equal zero only when all the returns are the same.[11]

10 If this formula were used for statistical inference, the goal would be to provide a sample estimator of the population variance. In this case, we would divide by $n - 1$ instead of n to provide an unbiased estimate of the variance. In performance measurement, however, the goal is to describe the variability of a given set of returns. For that purpose of pure description rather than inference, n is the appropriate divisor (see Hubert (1972)); practice indicates that $n - 1$ would also be acceptable as the divisor in the calculation. Regardless of which divisor is used, the performance analyst should use consistent calculations when comparing one set of returns to another.

11 The variance is usually calculated using the arithmetic mean; however, the geometric mean can also be used. See Feibel (2003, p. 141).

The variance treats positive deviations from the mean the same as negative deviations because squaring the difference removes the sign of the deviation. For this reason, the variance is referred to as a symmetric risk measure. It is also an absolute risk measure because its calculation does not require a benchmark.

If the variable is stated in terms of percentage, the variance of the variable is in percent squared, that is, (%). Percent squared has no natural interpretation. By taking the (positive) square root, we return to percentage as the unit of measurement. For this reason, many practitioners prefer the **standard deviation** of returns, σ, which is the square root of the variance:

$$\sigma = \sqrt{\sigma^2} \tag{3}$$

As with the variance, higher values of the standard deviation indicate greater risk. The standard deviation is probably the most widely used risk measure, because of its comparability with the mean return and its use in portfolio analysis. When it is plausible to assume the variable being examined follows a normal (bell-shaped) distribution, we expect that approximately 68% of the observed values will fall within plus or minus one standard deviation of the population arithmetic mean value and 95% will fall within two standard deviations. (Roughly speaking, the population mean is the mean calculated from a complete set of values for the variable.) If the population mean is known (or is reliably estimated), these facts may allow the analyst to state (or estimate) the range of values around the population mean within which 68% and 95% of values are likely to be found.

Another property of the standard deviation is that it can be easily converted to an approximate annualized figure when returns are independent over time.[12] If t is the number of holding periods in a year, then the annualized standard deviation from a periodic standard deviation σ is:

$$\sigma_{annualized} = \sigma\sqrt{t} \tag{4}$$

For example, if the quarterly standard deviation is 5%, then the annual standard deviation is approximately $5\% \times \sqrt{4} = 10\%$.

Variance and standard deviation are probably the most important risk measures for investments. They are widely used and have many useful properties. However, they do possess some disadvantages. First, recall from our previous discussion that idiosyncratic risk can be diversified away, with systematic risk remaining in the well-diversified portfolio. The variance and standard deviation quantify total standalone risk; they do not provide a clear picture of an asset's systematic risk and how it responds to market conditions.

Second, if an asset is illiquid, then these risk measures will be underestimated. The reason is that if an asset has not traded lately, the pricing for it will be stale. So the last traded price or an appraisal price will be used in place of a current trade price in the risk calculation. If the asset had been traded, the trade price might show considerable discrepancy from the previous price or appraised value. This problem often occurs with hedge funds, private equity, real estate, and other alternative assets.

Third, these risk measures assume that returns are symmetrically distributed about the mean return. They are particularly susceptible to outlier returns because in calculating the variance, the differences from the mean are squared. In the example of Argentina, there were several large positive returns that resulted in positive skewness. The variance and standard deviation will be inflated by skewed returns. Skewness is usually present when a portfolio contains options or has option-like returns.

12 Another way of stating that the returns are independent over time is to say that there is no serial correlation.

Our third measure of risk, the mean absolute deviation, is not as influenced by skewness in returns. The **mean absolute deviation** (MAD) calculation measures variability but does not square the differences from the mean. Rather, it utilizes the sum of the deviations. Because summing the deviations would result in zero, the MAD calculation uses the absolute value of the deviations:

$$\text{MAD} = \frac{\sum_{i=1}^{n} \left| R_i - \bar{R} \right|}{n} \qquad (5)$$

The MAD can be interpreted as the average amount by which a single return will deviate from the mean return. As with variance and standard deviation, a higher MAD indicates greater risk. The MAD is not used as much as the standard deviation because the latter is more readily applicable in portfolio analysis and utility functions.

The variance, standard deviation, and mean absolute deviation are absolute risk measures, where a benchmark return is not used in the calculation. Our next measure, **tracking risk**, is a relative risk measure because it is calculated relative to a benchmark. The tracking risk (TR) is the standard deviation of the difference between portfolio returns, R_p, and benchmark returns, R_B, over time:

$$\text{TR} = \sigma(R_p - R_B) \qquad (6)$$

The smaller the tracking risk, the more closely a portfolio tracks its benchmark. If the difference between portfolio and benchmark returns follows a normal distribution and the tracking risk is, for example, 50 basis points, then 68% of the time, the return difference will be within plus or minus 50 basis points of the benchmark. Tracking risk increases as the manager's risk profile deviates from that of the benchmark. If a portfolio's style and risk exposures change over time, then the tracking risk will also likely change.

Tracking risk is usually used for portfolio returns, as opposed to individual asset returns, because it measures the ability of a portfolio manager to mimic the risk of an index. The tracking risk is sometimes referred to as the tracking error, tracking error volatility, or active risk. The last term follows because tracking risk is the standard deviation of the active return, which is the difference between portfolio and benchmark returns.

Active managers are less concerned about active risk than are passive or enhanced indexing managers. A passive manager that is tracking an index usually has tracking risk of 1% or less, an enhanced indexing manager usually has a goal of 2% or less, an active large-cap US equity manager has tracking risk between 2% and 6%, and an aggressive manager has risk in the range of 6% to 9%.[13] Tracking risk is a useful measure for enhanced indexing, where the goal is to provide a return similar to that of a benchmark but to deviate from the benchmark when opportunities present themselves. The investment policy statement for a portfolio typically specifies the allowable tracking risk.

The tracking risk measure is useful because the manager could be generating the same mean return and standard deviation as the benchmark but deviating from the benchmark over various time periods. The tracking risk would reflect these deviations, indicating that the portfolio and the benchmark have different risk exposures and that, going forward, the portfolio may not satisfy its intended purposes. On the other hand, both the benchmark and the manager's portfolio could have high variability, but the tracking risk could be low if the manager closely tracks the index. This level of risk might be perfectly acceptable to the portfolio owner.

13 DeFusco, McLeavey, Pinto, and Runkle (2007, p. 655).

A disadvantage of the tracking risk is that it measures both upside and downside deviations. Tracking risk could be high when a manager has outperformed the benchmark. Note, however, that outperformance or underperformance does not necessarily imply that a manager has tracking risk, because tracking risk is measured as volatility relative to a benchmark. A manager who consistently underperformed the benchmark by 1% each month would have zero tracking risk, despite having negative active return.

A second disadvantage of the tracking risk measure is that it is very sensitive to the benchmark chosen. Tracking risk can be quite high when measured against one benchmark and low against another.

2.5 Beta

Beta (or sensitivity to market movements) is another risk measure, one with linkages to theoretical models of how assets are priced. To develop the expression for beta, we need to introduce the concepts of covariance and correlation. Whereas the tracking risk specifically examines the relationship between a portfolio and a benchmark, the **covariance** is a measure of how any two assets move together over time. Analysts are particularly interested in how one asset's returns change relative to another's when forming portfolios. In equation form, the covariance between returns R_A and R_B is:

$$\text{Cov}(R_A, R_B) = \frac{\sum_{t=1}^{T}(R_{A,t} - \bar{R}_A)(R_{B,t} - \bar{R}_B)}{T} \tag{7}$$

The formula says that to calculate the covariance between two assets:

1 calculate the arithmetic mean for each asset;

2 calculate the difference between each periodic asset return ($R_{A,t}$ and $R_{B,t}$) and its mean $(\bar{R}_A$ and $\bar{R}_B)$;

3 calculate the product of the periodic differences;

4 sum the products; and

5 divide by T, where T is the total number of observations over time.[14]

A positive covariance indicates that the assets move together; that is, when one asset appreciates in value, the other also tends to increase, and when one asset declines, the other usually does the same. A covariance value near zero indicates that the assets tend to move independently of one another. Lastly, a negative covariance indicates that the assets tend to move opposite to each other.

The covariance is a useful tool when considering portfolio risk. All else equal, assets with negative covariance are preferred in a portfolio because they will move opposite to one another, thereby reducing overall portfolio variability. An asset may have high stand-alone risk as measured by its variance, but if its covariance is sufficiently low, adding the asset to a portfolio could actually reduce portfolio variability.

The magnitudes of covariances are, however, not readily comparable. For example, it is easy to see that a covariance of 0.1132 is lower than a covariance of 0.1282, but there is no intuitive interpretation of how much lower it is. Furthermore, the covariance is affected by the magnitudes of the individual asset variances. Examining the formula's numerator above, if the periodic deviations from the mean are large for each asset, both the variance and the covariance will be large. Therefore, a larger covariance does not necessarily mean that there is a closer association between the two asset returns.

14 A $T - 1$ divisor is used if this formula is employed for statistical inference.

The correlation between two assets ($\rho_{A,B}$) provides a more intuitive and comparable measure of how interrelated the assets are. The **correlation** is the covariance scaled by the product of the individual asset standard deviations (σ) and is bounded by minus one and plus one:

$$\rho_{A,B} = \frac{\text{Cov}(R_A, R_B)}{\sigma_A \sigma_B} \tag{8}$$

$$-1.0 \leq \rho_{A,B} \leq +1.0 \tag{9}$$

The correlation thus improves upon the covariance because it adjusts for each asset's volatility. In contrast to the case of covariance, we can definitively say that a correlation of larger magnitude indicates a stronger association between the two assets.

The correlation also allows for intuitive interpretations and comparisons. If an asset pair has a correlation of one, their returns always move together in unison. If an asset pair has a correlation of minus one, the two always move opposite to each other.[15] If the correlation is zero, the assets move independently of each other.

When constructing a portfolio, assets with negative correlations are preferred (all else equal) because their opposing movements will reduce portfolio risk. In reality, it is difficult to find assets with negative correlations because almost all assets are affected to some extent by macroeconomic conditions.[16] Example 5 shows the calculation of various risk measures.

EXAMPLE 5

Calculating Variance, Standard Deviation, Mean Absolute Deviation, Tracking Risk, Covariance, and Correlation

Exhibit 9 provides four monthly returns for Stock A and an index.

Exhibit 9 Data for Calculation of Covariance and Correlation

	Stock A	Index
1 Jan 2012	–0.80%	1.20%
1 Feb 2012	7.20	4.20
1 Mar 2012	–2.20	0.80
1 Apr 2012	5.80	3.80

1 Calculate the variance for Stock A and the index.
2 Calculate the standard deviation for Stock A and the index.
3 Calculate the mean absolute deviation for Stock A and the index.
4 Calculate the tracking risk for Stock A against the index.

15 The correlation between two assets will be one when there is a constant positive relationship between them. The correlation between two assets will be minus one when there is a constant negative relationship between them. If the relationship is not constant, then the absolute value of the correlation will not equal one.
16 The exception is that in markets that allow both long and short positions (e.g., derivative markets), the correlation between the positions should be close to minus one. In a world with arbitrage, a portfolio consisting of a long position and its respective short position will provide a return close to the risk-free rate.

5 Calculate the covariance between Stock A and the index.

6 Calculate and interpret the correlation between Stock A and the index.

Solution to 1:

To obtain the variance and standard deviation for the stock and index, first calculate the arithmetic mean return.

For Stock A, it is $\frac{-0.80\% + 7.20\% - 2.20\% + 5.80\%}{4} = \frac{10.00\%}{4} = 2.50\%$.

For the index, it is $\frac{1.20\% + 4.20\% + 0.80\% + 3.80\%}{4} = \frac{10.00\%}{4} = 2.50\%$.

Notice that the stock and index have the same mean return.

To calculate the variance (σ^2) for the stock, calculate the deviations from the mean, square the deviations, sum them, and then divide by four (the number of observations). We show the calculation in detail to make clear the use of percentages.

σ^2 for Stock A:

$$\frac{(-0.80\% - 2.50\%)^2 + (7.20\% - 2.50\%)^2 + (-2.20\% - 2.50\%)^2 + (5.80\% - 2.50\%)^2}{4}$$

$$= \frac{(-0.008 - 0.025)^2 + (0.072 - 0.025)^2 + (-0.022 - 0.025)^2 + (0.058 - 0.025)^2}{4}$$

$$= \frac{(-0.033)^2 + (0.047)^2 + (-0.047)^2 + (0.033)^2}{4}$$

$$= \frac{0.001089 + 0.002209 + 0.002209 + 0.001089}{4} = \frac{0.006596}{4} = \frac{0.6596\%}{4}$$

$$= 0.1649\%$$

The variance calculation is repeated for the index.

σ^2 for the index:

$$\frac{(1.20\% - 2.50\%)^2 + (4.20\% - 2.50\%)^2 + (0.80\% - 2.50\%)^2 + (3.80\% - 2.50\%)^2}{4}$$

$$= \frac{0.0916\%}{4} = 0.0229\%$$

Solution to 2:

The standard deviation (σ) is the square root of the variance. For the stock and index, the calculations are as follows:

For Stock A: $\sqrt{0.1649\%} = 0.0406 = 4.06\%$

For the index: $\sqrt{0.0229\%} = 0.0151 = 1.51\%$

The variance and standard deviation calculations indicate that, although the mean returns are the same, the stock has a higher return variability than the index.

Solution to 3:

To calculate the mean absolute deviation (MAD), calculate the absolute value of the deviations from the mean in each period, sum the deviations, and then divide by the number of observations.

For Stock A, the MAD is:

$$\frac{|-0.80\% - 2.50\%| + |7.20\% - 2.50\%| + |-2.20\% - 2.50\%| + |5.80\% - 2.50\%|}{4}$$

$$= \frac{16.00\%}{4} = 4.00\%$$

For the index, the MAD is:

$$\frac{|1.20\% - 2.50\%| + |4.20\% - 2.50\%| + |0.80\% - 2.50\%| + |3.80\% - 2.50\%|}{4}$$

$$= \frac{6.00\%}{4} = 1.50\%$$

Again, the variability measured for the stock is greater than that for the index.

Solution to 4:

To calculate the tracking risk (TR), first calculate the difference between the stock and index returns in each period and determine the mean difference:

$$\frac{(-0.80\% - 1.20\%) + (7.20\% - 4.20\%) + (-2.20\% - 0.80\%) + (5.80\% - 3.80\%)}{4}$$

$$= 0.00\%$$

Note that because the arithmetic mean returns are the same, the mean difference in returns is equal to zero.

The tracking risk is the standard deviation of the differences. So, first calculate the variance of the differences, which is the sum of the squared deviations from the mean divided by four:

$$\frac{(-2.00\% - 0\%)^2 + (3.00\% - 0\%)^2 + (-3.00\% - 0\%)^2 + (2.00\% - 0\%)^2}{4}$$

$$= \frac{0.2600\%}{4} = 0.0650\%$$

The tracking risk is the square root of the above variance:

$$TR = \sqrt{0.0650\%} = 0.0255 = 2.55\%$$

Solution to 5:

The first step in calculating the covariance is to determine the differences between the periodic stock and index returns and their respective means. The periodic differences are then multiplied, the products are summed, and the result is then divided by the number of observations to calculate the covariance. The mean returns for both the stock and index are 2.50%, so the covariance calculation is:

$$\frac{\begin{bmatrix}(-0.80\% - 2.50\%)(1.20\% - 2.50\%) + (7.20\% - 2.50\%)(4.20\% - 2.50\%) \\ +(-2.20\% - 2.50\%)(0.80\% - 2.50\%) + (5.80\% - 2.50\%)(3.80\% - 2.50\%)\end{bmatrix}}{4}$$

$$= \frac{0.2456\%}{4} = 0.0614\%$$

Notice that the covariance is positive because the stock and index tend to move together. More specifically, all four terms in the numerator are positive. When the stock is above its mean, so is the index (the second and fourth terms), resulting in a positive product of differences. When the stock is below its mean, so is the index (the first and third terms), resulting again in a positive product of differences.

Solution to 6:

The correlation (ρ) is the covariance divided by the product of the Stock A and index standard deviations. The standard deviations above, presented as percentages with four decimal places, are 4.0608% for the stock and 1.5133% for the index.

$$\rho = \frac{0.0614\%}{(4.0608\%)(1.5133\%)} = 0.9992$$

The correlation indicates that the stock and index move together in almost perfect unison. Notice that the correlation here is more readily interpretable than the 0.0614% covariance calculated previously because the correlation is bounded by positive one.

Although Stock A has more than twice the variability of the index (as indicated by the standard deviations), its return pattern closely mimics that of the index. This is illustrated in Exhibit 10. The stock essentially amplifies the return pattern of the index.

Exhibit 10 Returns for Stock A and the Index over Time

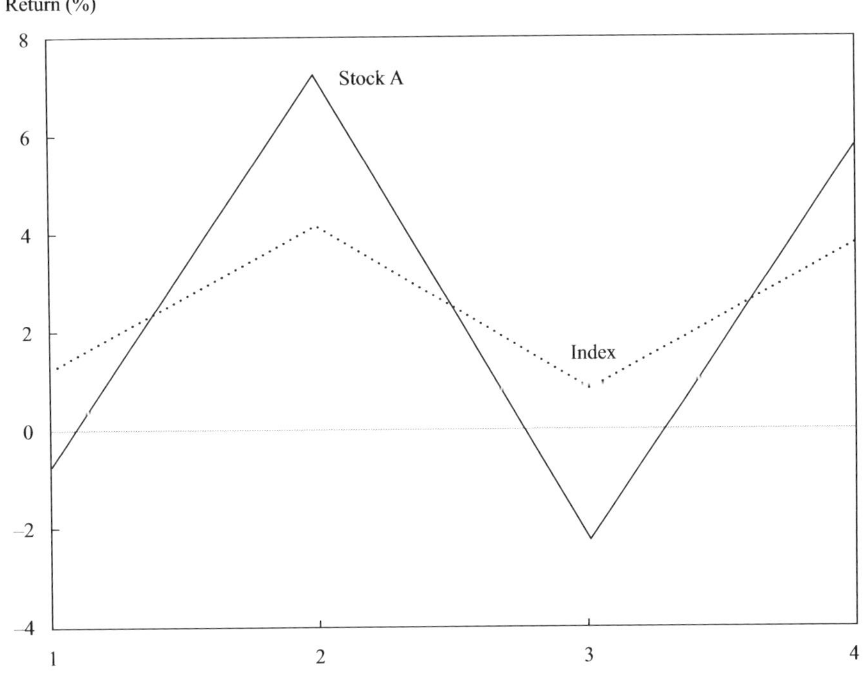

EXAMPLE 6

Calculating and Interpreting the Variance, Standard Deviation, Mean Absolute Deviation, and Tracking Risk

Exhibit 11 shows monthly returns in US dollars for McDonald's and the S&P 500 Restaurants Sub-Industry index.

Exhibit 11 Restaurants Data

	McDonald's	S&P 500 Restaurants Index
1 Jan 2011	−3.39%	−1.95%
1 Feb 2011	−4.09	−3.29
1 Mar 2011	2.77	2.51
1 Apr 2011	1.47	4.32
1 May 2011	3.49	2.43
1 Jun 2011	3.75	2.72
1 Jul 2011	5.77	6.85
1 Aug 2011	0.86	−0.78
1 Sep 2011	4.96	1.86
1 Oct 2011	−4.50	−5.86
1 Nov 2011	6.85	9.05
1 Dec 2011	4.68	4.74

Source: Datastream.

1 Calculate the variance for McDonald's.

2 Calculate the standard deviation for McDonald's, annualize it, and comment on the advantage of the standard deviation relative to the variance.

3 Calculate and interpret the mean absolute deviation for McDonald's.

4 Calculate and interpret the tracking risk for McDonald's using the S&P 500 Restaurants index as the benchmark.

Solution to 1:

We first must calculate the arithmetic mean return for McDonald's, which is a simple average of the 12 monthly returns:

(−3.39% − 4.09% + 2.77% + 1.47% + 3.49% + 3.75% + 5.77% + 0.86% + 4.96% − 4.50% + 6.85% + 4.68%)/12 = 1.8850%

In the table below, we then calculate the deviations from the mean and the square of those deviations.

	McDonald's Monthly Return	Deviations from Mean	Squared Deviations
1 Jan 2011	−3.39%	−5.28%	0.2783%
1 Feb 2011	−4.09	−5.98	0.3570
1 Mar 2011	2.77	0.89	0.0078
1 Apr 2011	1.47	−0.42	0.0017
1 May 2011	3.49	1.61	0.0258
1 Jun 2011	3.75	1.87	0.0348
1 Jul 2011	5.77	3.89	0.1509
1 Aug 2011	0.86	−1.03	0.0105
1 Sep 2011	4.96	3.08	0.0946
1 Oct 2011	−4.50	−6.39	0.4077
1 Nov 2011	6.85	4.97	0.2465
1 Dec 2011	4.68	2.80	0.0781

	McDonald's Monthly Return	Deviations from Mean	Squared Deviations
Sum of squared deviations			1.6937%
Variance			0.1411%

We sum the squared deviations and obtain 1.6937%. There are 12 monthly observations, so we divide by $n = 12$ and obtain a variance of 0.1411%.

Solution to 2:

The standard deviation is the square root of the variance, so it is $\sqrt{0.1411\%} = \sqrt{0.001411} = 0.0376 = 3.76\%$.

There are 12 months in a year, so the annualized standard deviation is $3.76\% \times \sqrt{12} = 13.01\%$.

Whereas the variance is in percent squared and is therefore not directly comparable to the arithmetic mean return, the standard deviation, as the square root of the variance, has the advantage of being in the same units as the mean return.

Solution to 3:

In the fourth column of the table below, the absolute value of the deviations from the mean are presented.

	McDonald's Monthly Return	Deviations from Mean	Absolute Value of Deviations
1 Jan 2011	−3.39%	−5.28%	5.28%
1 Feb 2011	−4.09	−5.98	5.98
1 Mar 2011	2.77	0.89	0.89
1 Apr 2011	1.47	−0.42	0.42
1 May 2011	3.49	1.61	1.61
1 Jun 2011	3.75	1.87	1.87
1 Jul 2011	5.77	3.89	3.89
1 Aug 2011	0.86	−1.03	1.03
1 Sep 2011	4.96	3.08	3.08
1 Oct 2011	−4.50	−6.39	6.39
1 Nov 2011	6.85	4.97	4.97
1 Dec 2011	4.68	2.80	2.80
Sum of deviations			38.15%
Mean absolute deviation			3.18%

Summing the absolute value of the deviations, we obtain 38.15%. Dividing by 12 provides the mean absolute deviation for McDonald's of 3.18%. This result can be interpreted to mean that, on average, McDonald's stock return will differ by ± 3.18% from the mean return of 1.8850%.

Solution to 4:

To calculate the tracking risk, first calculate the difference between McDonald's stock return and the S&P 500 Restaurants index, as in the fourth column of the table below.

	McDonald's	S&P 500 Restaurants Index	Difference in Returns	Deviations from the Mean Difference	Squared Deviations
1 Jan 2011	−3.39%	−1.95%	−1.44%	−1.44%	0.0208%
1 Feb 2011	−4.09	−3.29	−0.80	−0.80	0.0064
1 Mar 2011	2.77	2.51	0.26	0.26	0.0007
1 Apr 2011	1.47	4.32	−2.85	−2.85	0.0813
1 May 2011	3.49	2.43	1.06	1.06	0.0112
1 Jun 2011	3.75	2.72	1.03	1.03	0.0106
1 Jul 2011	5.77	6.85	−1.08	−1.08	0.0117
1 Aug 2011	0.86	−0.78	1.64	1.64	0.0268
1 Sep 2011	4.96	1.86	3.10	3.10	0.0960
1 Oct 2011	−4.50	−5.86	1.36	1.36	0.0185
1 Nov 2011	6.85	9.05	−2.20	−2.20	0.0485
1 Dec 2011	4.68	4.74	−0.06	−0.06	0.0000
Mean difference			0.0017%		
Sum of squared deviations					0.3325%
Mean of squared deviations					0.0277%
Tracking risk					1.66%

We then calculate the average of these differences over the 12 months. The result is an arithmetic mean of 0.0017%. In the fifth column of the table, the deviation of each difference from the mean difference is calculated. In the last column, these deviations are squared, and the sum of the squared deviations is 0.3325%. Dividing by 12 months, we have 0.0277%. The square root of this result is the tracking risk, 1.66%.

Although tracking risk is most commonly used with portfolios, here it is used with an individual stock. Because McDonald's is a large part of the S&P 500 Restaurants index, the tracking risk is very small at 1.66%, which is similar in magnitude to the tracking risk for an enhanced indexing manager.

Recall from our earlier discussion that although idiosyncratic risk can be diversified away, the systematic risk component of total risk cannot. The most widely used measure of systematic risk is referred to as beta. To determine beta, we examine how an asset's returns move with the overall asset market. More formally, **beta** is the covariance between the asset and market returns divided by the variance in market returns:

$$\beta_A = \frac{\text{Cov}(R_A, R_M)}{\sigma_M^2} \tag{10}$$

The equation states that the beta, β, for asset A is equal to the covariance between asset A returns, R_A, and the returns on the market, R_M, divided by the variance in market returns, σ_M^2. Because it is impossible to measure the returns of all the assets in an economy, a broad market index, such as the MSCI World Index, is often used to measure market returns.

By dividing by the variance in market returns, beta provides a standardized measure of risk, where systematic risk is gauged relative to one. If the asset return moves in synchronicity with the market return, the covariance will be the same as the market's variance and the beta will equal one.[17] An asset whose returns amplify the market's will have a beta greater than one, whereas a relatively less variable asset will have a beta less than one. We would expect a company in the cyclical auto industry to have a beta greater than one but a company in the less volatile food industry to have a beta less than one. For example, Ford Motor Company is estimated to have a beta of 2.53, whereas the estimated beta for Kraft Foods is 0.49.[18]

Beta is also useful because it indicates the risk an asset contributes to a well-diversified portfolio, where higher-beta stocks increase portfolio risk by a greater amount than lower-beta stocks. Generally speaking, more-risk-averse investors will prefer lower-beta assets.

Earlier, we said that for a well-diversified investor, systematic risk is more relevant than idiosyncratic risk. Because it measures only systematic risk, beta is a very important and widely cited relative risk measure.

EXAMPLE 7

Calculating and Interpreting Beta (1)

Using the calculations from Example 5, determine the beta for Stock A against the index and interpret its value.

Solution:

To determine the beta for Stock A, divide the covariance between the stock and index by the variance for the index:

$$\beta_A = \frac{0.0614\%}{0.0229\%} = 2.68$$

The beta is greater than one, indicating that the asset returns are more cyclical than those of the average stock, as represented by the market. Although the correlation between Stock A and the index is almost one (0.99) and Stock A's mean return is the same as that for the index (2.50%), the stock is highly cyclical and its periodic returns amplify the market returns. Stock A has more systematic risk than the average stock.

EXAMPLE 8

Calculating and Interpreting Beta (2)

1 In which of the following scenarios would a company's beta be *most likely* to increase?

- **A** A technology company's chief financial officer is accused of manipulating the company's quarterly earnings.
- **B** A biotech company's research department has discovered a cure for a widespread genetic disorder.
- **C** A producer of household necessity goods branches out into luxury products with higher profit margins.

17 More specifically, to have a beta equal to one, as we can see from the numerator of the covariance calculation, the deviations of the asset's periodic return from its mean must be the same as those for the index.
18 Yahoo! Finance.

Use the data below for Questions 2 and 3.

The data below are for the same index as in Exhibit 9 but for a new stock, which we will refer to as Stock B. The mean return for both Stock B and the index is 2.50%. The standard deviation is 0.6403% for Stock B and 1.5133% for the index.

	Stock B	Index
1 Jan 2012	1.60%	1.20%
1 Feb 2012	3.00	4.20
1 Mar 2012	2.20	0.80
1 Apr 2012	3.20	3.80

2 Calculate the covariance, correlation, and beta for Stock B against the index.

3 Compare the beta for Stock B against that calculated for Stock A in Example 7.

Solution to 1:

C is correct. If a producer of household necessity goods branches out into luxury products, then the company's profits will likely become more cyclical, so that the company will sell more during economic expansions and less during economic recessions. Therefore, its returns will amplify market returns more than previously and its systematic risk and beta will increase.

If a company's chief financial officer manipulates the company's earnings, this action is unrelated to the market at large and the company's systematic risk and beta should not be affected. This scenario would result in an increase in the company's *unsystematic* risk. The same is true if a biotech company discovers a cure. This scenario is also unrelated to market wide movements.

Solution to 2:

To calculate the covariance, first determine the difference between the periodic stock and index returns and their respective means. Multiply the periodic differences, sum the products, and then divide by the number of observations to arrive at the covariance.

The mean returns for the stock and index are both 2.50%, so the covariance calculation is:

$$\frac{\begin{bmatrix}(1.60\% - 2.50\%)(1.20\% - 2.50\%) + (3.00\% - 2.50\%)(4.20\% - 2.50\%) \\ +(2.20\% - 2.50\%)(0.80\% - 2.50\%) + (3.20\% - 2.50\%)(3.80\% - 2.50\%)\end{bmatrix}}{4}$$

$$= \frac{0.0344\%}{4} = 0.0086\%$$

The correlation (ρ) is the covariance divided by the product of the standard deviations for Stock B and the index:

$$\rho = \frac{0.0086\%}{(0.6403\%)(1.5133\%)} = 0.89$$

To determine the beta, divide the covariance between Stock B and the index by the variance for the index, which is the square of its standard deviation:

$$\beta_B = \frac{0.0086\%}{(1.5133\%)^2} = 0.38$$

Solution to 3:

The mean return is the same for Stock B and the index, and the correlation between them is close to one at 0.89, indicating that the returns for Stock B and the market move together. However, the beta for Stock B was less than one, indicating that it has less cyclicality and less systematic risk than the average stock. This result is in contrast to Stock A, which had a beta greater than one and more systematic risk than the average stock. As illustrated in Exhibit 12, Stock A amplifies the return of the index whereas Stock B dampens the index return pattern.

Exhibit 12 Returns for Stock A, Stock B, and the Index over Time

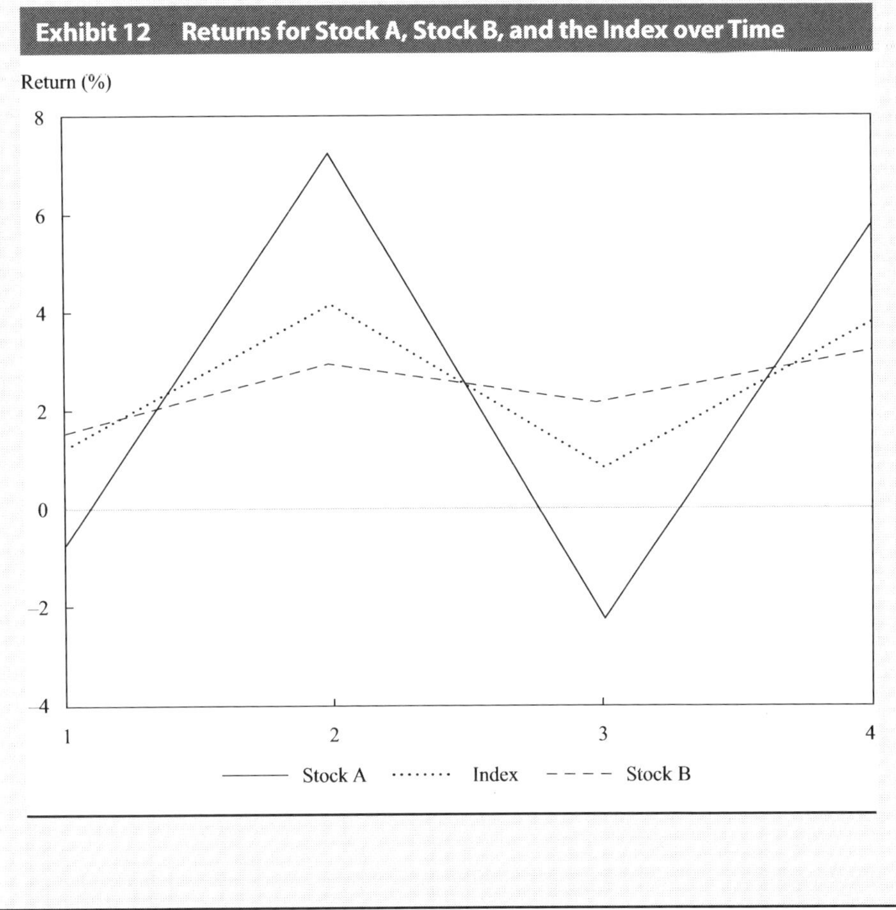

2.6 Measures of Downside Risk

One problem with the aforementioned symmetric risk measures is that gains (positive deviations from the mean or benchmark) are weighted the same as losses (negative deviations from the mean or benchmark). Most investors would consider only losses to constitute risk. We therefore now turn to asymmetric risk measures that can be used to quantify downside risk. These measures include semi-variance, target semi-variance, semi-standard deviation, and target semi-standard deviation.

The **semi-variance** is similar to the variance except that only deviations below the mean are used. The steps in calculating the semi-variance are as follows:

1 Calculate the arithmetic mean return;

2 Calculate the deviations from the mean, but only for those returns less than the mean;

3 Square the deviations;

4 Sum the squared deviations and divide by n, where n equals the total number of returns (both returns less than the mean and returns greater than the mean).

The formula for the semi-variance is:[19]

$$\text{Semi-variance} = \left[\sum_{\text{for all } R_i < \bar{R}} \left(R_i - \bar{R}\right)^2 \right] / n \tag{11}$$

The **target semi-variance** is the same as the semi-variance except that a specified target return is used instead of the mean return.

If the target return is B, the formula for the target semi-variance is:

$$\text{Target semi-variance} = \left[\sum_{\text{for all } R_i < B} \left(R_i - B\right)^2 \right] / n \tag{12}$$

The target return may be zero (for clients concerned about losing money), a constant positive return, the risk-free rate, a market benchmark return (for those evaluated against an index), or an actuarially determined return necessary to satisfy liabilities. If the target return is the arithmetic mean return, the target semi-variance equals the semi-variance.

The **semi-standard deviation** is simply the square root of the semi-variance, and the **target semi-standard deviation** is the square root of the target semi-variance. The target semi-standard deviation is sometimes referred to as the downside deviation, with the target return referred to as the minimum acceptable return. If the target return is equal to the manager's benchmark, the target semi-standard deviation provides a downside perspective on tracking risk.

The advantage of the target semi-variance and the target semi-standard deviation is that some investors may consider returns below a target return as risky, whereas the semi-variance and its square root consider only returns below the mean as risky.

Although downside risk measures better represent most investors' concept of risk by focusing on losses, there are several problems with them.

First, the variance and standard deviation are more familiar to investors and their statistical properties are well established. The variance and standard deviation are used in the calculation of beta, the Sharpe ratio, and other popular performance evaluation measures.

Second, because downside risk estimates use information from only half the distribution of returns and omit information from upside returns, they are not as statistically accurate as the symmetric risk measures.

Third, if returns are symmetrically distributed about the mean, then the semi-variance and the semi-standard deviation do not add any information beyond that already provided by the better-understood symmetric risk measures of the variance and standard deviation. The semi-variance will be half the variance when returns are

19 See Josephy and Aczel (1993) for an unbiased and consistent estimator for the semi-variance that can be used for statistical inference.

symmetrical, and the measures are essentially the same in this case.[20] If, however, returns are *not* symmetric, then forecasting downside risk is problematic because asymmetric risk is less stable over time than symmetric risk.

Fourth, when measuring portfolio risk using individual asset risks, it is much easier to determine the portfolio variance and standard deviation than the portfolio downside risk. There is no straightforward method of aggregating individual assets' semi-variance and semi-standard deviation into portfolio semi-variance and semi-standard deviation.[21]

Lastly, the target semi-variance and target semi-standard deviation require the specification of a target return and so are ambiguous because they are dependent on investor preferences. For example, some investors might specify a target equal to the risk-free rate and others a constant 5%.

EXAMPLE 9

Calculating and Interpreting Semi-variance, Target Semi-variance, Semi-standard Deviation, and Target Semi-standard Deviation

The following are daily stock returns in Korean won for Kumho Petrochemical and Korea Line during 12 days in 2010 and 2011.

Exhibit 13 Two Korean Share Issues

	Kumho Petrochemical		Korea Line
23 Dec 2010	1.01%	13 Oct 2010	0.42%
24 Dec 2010	0.67	14 Oct 2010	0.11
27 Dec 2010	−0.55	15 Oct 2010	1.16
28 Dec 2010	−1.22	18 Oct 2010	−0.73
29 Dec 2010	2.25	19 Oct 2010	−1.26
30 Dec 2010	0.44	20 Oct 2010	−1.07
31 Dec 2010	0.00	21 Oct 2010	−1.83
3 Jan 2011	−0.22	22 Oct 2010	−1.65
4 Jan 2011	5.21	25 Oct 2010	−13.07
5 Jan 2011	3.06	26 Oct 2010	1.67

(continued)

20 The reason that the semi-variance and semi-standard deviation do not provide any additional information over the variance and standard deviation is that return deviations are still measured relative to the arithmetic mean. For example, consider two assets, Good and Bad. Good has a mean return of 10%, and Bad's is −10%. If they both have the same symmetric return variation about the mean, then their variances and standard deviations will be equal. Their semi-variances and semi-standard deviations will *also* be equal because the histograms are identically centered on the mean, with the only difference being that Bad's is shifted to the left. The semi-variance and semi-standard deviation will differ from the variance and standard deviation only when returns are skewed, because one side of the return distribution will have greater variation than the other. See the Kumho Petrochemical and Korea Line example for an illustration of this situation. Note, however, that the *target* semi-variance and *target* semi-standard deviation for Good and Bad will not be equal, because the deviations are measured relative to a target return, *not* the arithmetic mean. For example, if the target return is 5%, Bad will have underperformed the target more than Good, resulting in a higher target semi-variance and a higher target semi-standard deviation for Bad.

21 The semi-variance and semi-standard deviation also cannot be differentiated for portfolio optimization purposes.

Exhibit 13 (Continued)

	Kumho Petrochemical		Korea Line
6 Jan 2011	10.43	27 Oct 2010	−0.38
7 Jan 2011	−0.46	28 Oct 2010	0.51

Source: Datastream.

1 Calculate the semi-variance for Kumho Petrochemical and Korea Line.

2 Calculate the semi-standard deviation for Kumho Petrochemical and Korea Line.

3 The variance for Kumho Petrochemical is 0.0989%, and the standard deviation is 3.14%. The variance for Korea Line is 0.1360%, and the standard deviation is 3.69%. Compare the variance and standard deviation for each stock to its semi-variance and semi-standard deviation. Comment on the differences for each stock.

4 Compare the risk of Kumho Petrochemical to that of Korea Line.

5 If the investor specifies a daily target return of 0.17%, what are the target semi-variance and target semi-standard deviation for each stock?

6 Compare the risk of underperforming the target return for Kumho Petrochemical and Korea Line using the target semi-variance and target semi-standard deviation.

7 Compare the semi-standard deviation for Kumho Petrochemical to its target semi-standard deviation. Compare the semi-standard deviation for Korea Line to its target semi-standard deviation. What accounts for the differences for each stock?

Solution to 1:

We first calculate the arithmetic mean return for Kumho Petrochemical:

(1.01% + 0.67% − 0.55% − 1.22% + 2.25% + 0.44% + 0.00% − 0.22% + 5.21% + 3.06% + 10.43 − 0.46%)/12 = 1.7183%

We do the same for Korea Line and obtain an arithmetic mean return of −1.3433%. In the table below, we then calculate the deviations from the mean when the daily return is less than the mean for Kumho Petrochemical and the square of those deviations. The deviations are not calculated when the daily return is greater than the mean return, and those rows are blank.

	Kumho Petrochemical	Underperformance from Mean	Square of Underperformance
23 Dec 2010	1.01%	−0.71%	0.0050%
24 Dec 2010	0.67	−1.05	0.0110
27 Dec 2010	−0.55	−2.27	0.0515
28 Dec 2010	−1.22	−2.94	0.0863
29 Dec 2010	2.25		
30 Dec 2010	0.44	−1.28	0.0163
31 Dec 2010	0.00	−1.72	0.0295
3 Jan 2011	−0.22	−1.94	0.0376
4 Jan 2011	5.21		

	Kumho Petrochemical	Underperformance from Mean	Square of Underperformance
5 Jan 2011	3.06		
6 Jan 2011	10.43		
7 Jan 2011	−0.46	−2.18	0.0475
Sum of squared deviations			0.2847%
Semi-variance			0.0237%

We sum the squared deviations and obtain 0.2847%. Dividing by $n = 12$, we obtain the semi-variance of 0.0237%. We then do the same for Korea Line.

	Korea Line	Underperformance from Mean	Square of Underperformance
13 Oct 2010	0.42%		
14 Oct 2010	0.11		
15 Oct 2010	1.16		
18 Oct 2010	−0.73		
19 Oct 2010	−1.26		
20 Oct 2010	−1.07		
21 Oct 2010	−1.83	−0.49%	0.0024%
22 Oct 2010	−1.65	−0.31	0.0009
25 Oct 2010	−13.07	−11.73	1.3751
26 Oct 2010	1.67		
27 Oct 2010	−0.38		
28 Oct 2010	0.51		
Sum of squared deviations			1.3784%
Semi-variance			0.1149%

Using the same process, the calculated semi-variance for Korea Line will be 0.1149%.

Solution to 2:

The semi-standard deviation is the square root of the semi-variance, so for Kumho Petrochemical it is $\sqrt{0.0237\%} = 1.54\%$. The calculated semi-standard deviation for Korea Line is 3.39%.

Solution to 3:

The semi-variance will be half the variance when returns are symmetrical because the semi-variance measures variability on only one side of the histogram. Both the variance and semi-variance are affected by outlier returns. But because the semi-variance considers only returns below the mean, the semi-variance will be greater than half the variance when returns are negatively skewed. The semi-variance will be less than half the variance when returns are positively skewed because the largest return variability is on the right-hand side of the histogram.

The Kumho Petrochemical returns are positively skewed because of the 10.43% return on 1/6/2011. As a result, the semi-variance is 0.0237%/0.0989% = 0.24 of the variance. The semi-standard deviation of 1.54% is also less than the standard deviation of 3.14%.

In the case of Korea Line, there is a negatively skewed return on 10/25/2010 of –13.07%. The semi-variance is 0.1149%/0.1360% = 0.84 of the variance. The semi-variance is more than half the variance because it measures the half of the distribution with the larger deviation. The semi-standard deviation of 3.39% is also close to the standard deviation of 3.69%.

Solution to 4:

The standard deviation of 3.14% for Kumho Petrochemical is similar to that for Korea Line of 3.69%. Using symmetric risk measures, it would appear that the risk for these two stocks is similar.

However, the variance and standard deviation for Kumho Petrochemical are inflated by positive skewness. These measures are misleading in this case because most investors favor positive skewness. When we compare semi-standard deviations, we have 1.54% for Kumho Petrochemical versus 3.39% for Korea Line. The semi-standard deviations reflect the greater downside risk of Korea Line and would be better indicators of past performance in this case.

The value of the semi-variance and the semi-standard deviation is that they reflect that the downside risk of Kumho Petrochemical stock is not as great as the variance and standard deviation indicate. It is important to note, though, that return asymmetries are not constant through time and, thus, past return asymmetries do not necessarily imply future return asymmetries.

Solution to 5:

In the table below, we calculate the deviations from the target return when the daily return is less than the target return for Kumho Petrochemical and the square of those deviations. The deviations are not calculated when the daily return is greater than the target return, and those rows are blank.

	Kumho Petrochemical	Target Return	Underperformance from Target	Square of Underperformance
23 Dec 2010	1.01%	0.17%		
24 Dec 2010	0.67	0.17		
27 Dec 2010	–0.55	0.17	–0.72%	0.0052%
28 Dec 2010	–1.22	0.17	–1.39	0.0193
29 Dec 2010	2.25	0.17		
30 Dec 2010	0.44	0.17		
31 Dec 2010	0.00	0.17	–0.17	0.0003
3 Jan 2011	–0.22	0.17	–0.39	0.0015
4 Jan 2011	5.21	0.17		
5 Jan 2011	3.06	0.17		
6 Jan 2011	10.43	0.17		
7 Jan 2011	–0.46	0.17	–0.63	0.0040
Sum of squares				0.0303%
Target semi-variance				0.0025%

We sum the squared deviations from the target return and obtain 0.0303%. Dividing by n = 12, we obtain the target semi-variance of 0.0025%. The target semi-standard deviation is the square root of the target semi-variance, so for Kumho Petrochemical it is $\sqrt{0.0025\%}$ = 0.50%. The calculations for Korea Line are below.

	Korea Line	Target Return	Underperformance from Target	Square of Underperformance
13 Oct 2010	0.42%	0.17%		
14 Oct 2010	0.11	0.17	−0.06%	0.0000%
15 Oct 2010	1.16	0.17		
18 Oct 2010	−0.73	0.17	−0.90	0.0081
19 Oct 2010	−1.26	0.17	−1.43	0.0204
20 Oct 2010	−1.07	0.17	−1.24	0.0154
21 Oct 2010	−1.83	0.17	−2.00	0.0400
22 Oct 2010	−1.65	0.17	−1.82	0.0331
25 Oct 2010	−13.07	0.17	−13.24	1.7530
26 Oct 2010	1.67	0.17		
27 Oct 2010	−0.38	0.17	−0.55	0.0030
28 Oct 2010	0.51	0.17		
Sum of squares				1.8730%
Target semi-variance				0.1561%

Summing the squared deviations and dividing by 12 results in a target semi-variance of 0.1561%. The target semi-standard deviation is then 3.95%.

Solution to 6:

The risk of Kumho Petrochemical underperforming the target return is much lower, as the target semi-variance is 0.0025% versus 0.1561% for Korea Line. The target semi-standard deviation for Kumho Petrochemical is only 0.50% versus 3.95% for Korea Line.

Another way of viewing Korea Line's underperformance is that its return was lower than the target in 8 of the 12 days whereas Kumho Petrochemical underperformed the target in just 5 days. These day counts confirm the conclusions we reached using the target semi-variances and target semi-standard deviations.

Solution to 7:

From above, the semi-standard deviation for Kumho Petrochemical is 1.54% and the target semi-standard deviation is 0.50%. The semi-standard deviation examines downside deviations from the arithmetic mean return for Kumho Petrochemical of 1.7183%. The target semi-standard deviation examines downside deviations from the target return of 0.17%. Because the target return is lower than the mean return, the risk of Kumho underperforming the mean return is greater. Therefore, the target semi-standard deviation is lower than the semi-standard deviation.

For Korea Line, the opposite is true. The target return of 0.17% is greater than the arithmetic mean return of −1.3433%. Therefore, the risk of underperforming the target return is greater than the risk of underperforming the mean. Accordingly, the target semi-standard deviation of 3.95% is greater than the semi-standard deviation of 3.39%.

2.7 Drawdown Measures

Another class of risk measures is known as drawdown measures. **Drawdown measures** capture various aspects of peak-to-trough value declines. Common measures include drawdown, average drawdown, maximum drawdown, largest individual drawdown, and drawdown duration. An **individual drawdown**, or simply a **drawdown**, is a decline in value (represented by a series of negative returns only) following a peak valuation.

Consider the return stream in Exhibit 14. To determine the drawdowns in this return stream, calculate the percentage drop in value relative to a higher preceding value. The initial return is negative, so the first drawdown is equal to the first month's negative return. Following periods quickly regain the initial loss to reach higher values. The next loss begins in the fifth month with a series of four negative returns, for a cumulative drop of:

$$[1 + (-4.2/100)] \times [1 + (-0.7/100)] \times [1 + (-1.2/100)] \times [1 + (-3.4/100)] - 1 = -9.2\%$$

Subsequent months exhibit positive returns, so they do not affect the drawdown calculations in this return series. For ease of reference, the two individual drawdowns in Exhibit 14 are shown in bold text to distinguish the individual drawdowns from the component returns within the multi-period drawdown in this example.

Exhibit 14 Monthly Fund Returns

Month	Return	Unit Value	Individual Drawdowns
0		1.000	
1	−2.4	0.976	**−2.4**
2	1.4	0.990	
3	2.3	1.012	
4	3.2	1.045	
5	−4.2	1.001	−4.2
6	−0.7	0.994	−4.9
7	−1.2	0.982	−6.0
8	−3.4	0.949	**−9.2**
9	2.7	0.974	
10	7.9	1.051	
11	6.6	1.121	
12	2.1	1.144	

By itself, measuring a single drawdown does not provide much insight unless we can determine the drawdown relative to some additional information. To gain a better understanding of the context of losses experienced by the investors of a given fund, we can calculate additional measures: The **average drawdown** is the average of a specified number of the largest drawdowns over a given period, the **maximum drawdown** is the largest peak-to-trough loss within a period, and **drawdown duration** is the time it takes to experience and then recover from the maximum drawdown. Of these, the most commonly used measure is maximum drawdown.

According to the US Commodity Futures Trading Commission, worst peak-to-trough drawdown (**maximum drawdown**) means the greatest cumulative percentage decline in month-end net asset value due to losses sustained by a pool, account, or trading program during any period in which the initial month-end net asset value is not equaled or exceeded by a subsequent month-end net asset value. Such a decline must be expressed as a percentage of the initial month-end net asset value, together with an indication of the months and year(s) of the decline from the initial month-end net asset value to the lowest month-end net asset value of the decline.[22]

Exhibit 15 shows two years of monthly returns[23] for two hedge funds, along with the unit values and individual drawdowns.

Exhibit 15 Two Hedge Fund Return Series

	Fund A				Fund B		
Month	Return (%)	Unit Value	Individual Drawdowns (in bold) (%)	Maximum Drawdown (in bold) (%)	Return (%)	Unit Value	Individual Drawdowns (in bold) (%)
0	0.00	1.000			0.00	1.000	
1	2.6	1.026			−1.3	0.987	**−1.3**
2	9.7	1.126			3.2	1.019	
3	6.5	1.199			1.1	1.030	
4	−3.8	1.153	**−3.8**	−3.8	−5.4	0.974	**−5.4**
5	1.6	1.172		−2.3	9.3	1.065	
6	−0.7	1.163	−0.7	−2.9	−13.2	0.924	−13.2
7	−3.4	1.124	−4.1	−6.2	−3.7	0.890	−16.4
8	−11.3	0.997	−14.9	−16.8	−2.5	0.868	**−18.5**
9	−2.3	0.974	**−16.9**	−18.8	8.1	0.938	
10	2.9	1.002		−16.4	0.7	0.945	
11	4.6	1.048		−12.5	−0.5	0.940	−0.5
12	9.2	1.145		−4.5	−10.1	0.845	**−10.5**
13	−7.1	1.063	**−7.1**	−11.3	3.8	0.877	
14	0.6	1.070		−10.8	12.2	0.984	
15	−2.1	1.047	−2.1	−12.6	−5.1	0.934	−5.1
16	−5.0	0.995	−7.0	−17.0	−0.2	0.932	**−5.3**
17	−1.3	0.982	−8.2	−18.1	4.3	0.972	
18	−4.1	0.942	**−12.0**	**−21.4**	11.9	1.088	
19	9.5	1.031			−5.3	1.030	**−5.3**
20	5.6	1.089			2.1	1.052	
21	10.2	1.200			6.5	1.120	
22	−5.4	1.135	−5.4		0.8	1.129	
23	−1.6	1.117	**−6.9**		−2.9	1.096	**−2.9**
24	0.4	1.122			2.3	1.122	

22 17 CFR 4.10.

23 To simplify the exhibit, two years of monthly returns are shown, but three years of monthly returns is a more common and more statistically robust time period for calculating drawdown measures.

Two-Year Total	Fund A	Fund B
Cumulative return	12.2%	12.2%
Annualized return	5.9	5.9
Standard deviation	5.6	6.2

Both funds earned the same cumulative return over the two-year period, but their drawdown measures and standard deviations are different. Standard deviations in this example are calculated as the standard deviation of the population of two years of monthly returns, rather than as an annualized standard deviation.

As stated earlier, an individual drawdown is the cumulative loss represented by a series of negative returns only. The largest individual drawdown is different from the maximum drawdown in that a positive return will determine the end of the series of returns for an individual drawdown, but the maximum drawdown may include positive returns between the peak and subsequent trough.

Individual drawdowns in Exhibit 15 are shown in bold to distinguish them from the negative returns for any specific month within a drawdown series. The largest individual drawdown experienced by Fund A during the period was –16.9%, followed in order of decreasing magnitude by –12.0%, –7.1%, and –6.9%. The number of drawdowns can vary greatly across funds within the same time period, so to enable comparability among funds, the average drawdown is usually stated in terms of a specific number of the largest individual drawdowns during a given period. For example, the average drawdown (3) within the two-year period for Fund A is calculated as the average of the three largest individual drawdowns, or (–16.9% – 12.0% – 7.1%)/3 = –12.0%. In calculating the largest individual drawdowns, large cumulative drawdowns that are components of larger cumulative drawdowns cannot be included without double counting. For example, –14.9% in Exhibit 15 is not counted as one of the three largest individual drawdowns because it is a component of the –16.9% drawdown.

The maximum drawdown for Fund A is illustrated in Exhibit 16. The maximum drawdown includes periods of positive and negative returns, as it defines the maximum peak-to-trough percentage loss experienced by the fund during the period. Exhibit 16 shows the relative values for Fund A represented by the peaks and troughs. In this example, the peak that begins the maximum drawdown period is not the highest peak during the period; there is a later, higher peak that represents the high-water mark, the highest value achieved by the fund during the entire period. The drawdown that occurred after the high-water mark was only –6.9%, while the maximum drawdown for Fund A was –21.4%.

Exhibit 16 Peaks and Troughs, Fund A Drawdowns

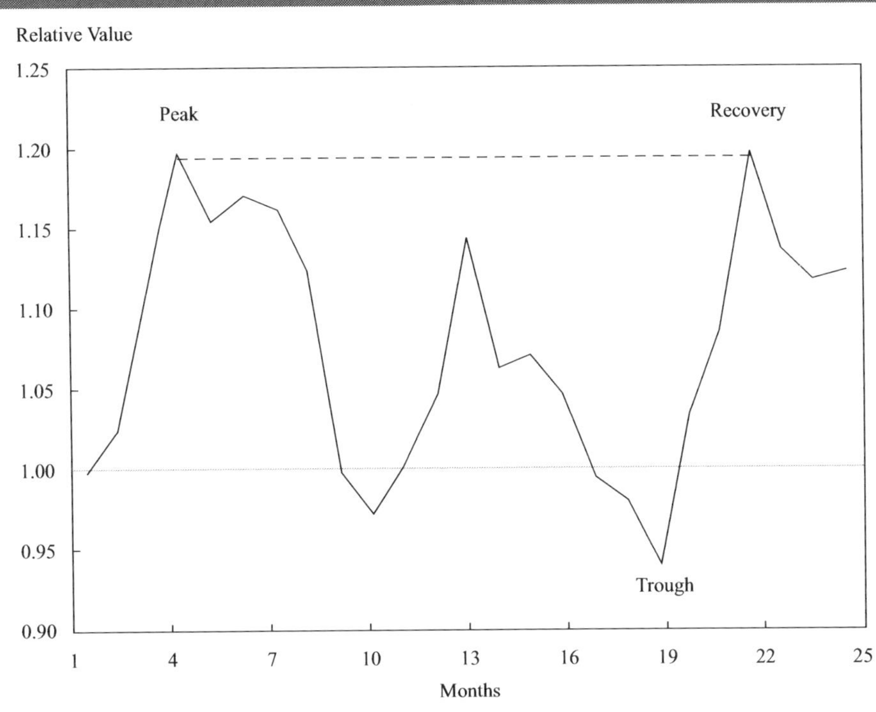

To calculate the maximum drawdown, we identify the highest and lowest unit values during the period and calculate the percentage decline from one of the highest values to a subsequent low value. We repeat the process until we have found the largest percentage drop during the period. For example, in Exhibit 15, the highest unit value for Fund A is 1.200 (Month 21), but the lowest value after that peak is 1.117, which represents a drawdown of –6.9%. The next-highest peak is 1.199 (Month 3), and the lowest value after that peak is 0.942. The drawdown from the peak of 1.199 to the trough of 0.942 is (0.942 – 1.199)/1.199 = –21.4%. This is the maximum drawdown for Fund A for the period.

The drawdown duration is a measure of the length of time a fund experienced the maximum drawdown before recovering. In Exhibit 15, Fund A started to experience the maximum drawdown after the peak at Month 3 (1.199) and didn't recover full value until Month 21 (1.200). The drawdown duration for Fund A was 21 – 3 = 18 months.

All else equal, a fund with a larger (more negative) maximum drawdown is considered to be "riskier" than a fund with a smaller (less negative) maximum drawdown.

Drawdown measures are frequently used in analyzing the returns of hedge funds and commodity funds. Hedge funds are generally lightly regulated pooled investment vehicles with high investment minimums. Hedge funds represent many different strategies, but they are generally characterized by more investment flexibility, less transparency, less regulation, and less frequent valuations than more traditional equity and fixed-income investment fund structures.

There are two major reasons for the popularity of drawdown measures in the analysis of hedge fund risk.

First, many hedge funds' return streams depart from the normal distribution to a greater extent than those of traditional investments. As a result, traditional volatility-based risk measures may be less useful. Some hedge fund strategies, particularly those that include less liquid investments, may exhibit lower return volatility than traditional strategies with more frequently priced investments. Investors who perceive relatively lower hedge fund return volatility as equivalent to lower risk may not recognize that many hedge funds also include significant risks of loss. Drawdown measures do not rely on the assumption of a normal distribution of returns.[24]

Second, drawdown measures may be informative about the business risks of hedge funds because of the way these funds compensate the investment manager. Hedge funds often compensate the investment manager with a fixed asset management fee (such as 2% of average assets under management) and an additional incentive fee equal to a substantial percentage (e.g., 20%) of the increase in value above the previous high level, known as the high-water mark. If a hedge fund earns high returns leading to a high valuation in an early period and subsequently has negative performance with generally lower valuations, hedge fund staff may believe it is unlikely that they can erase the losses and earn the incentive compensation that is only possible above the earlier high valuation. This situation may present business risks for an investor because the investment team may take more risk in an attempt to exceed the high-water mark and earn the incentive fee. Furthermore, the investment team may experience key staff turnover if compensation declines with performance, decreasing the chances that the fund can recover the losses. Drawdowns are often also associated with fund redemptions, because investors tend to withdraw money after periods of negative performance, sometimes leading to the liquidation of the hedge fund. Note that the fund may have experienced a maximum drawdown in some historic period and have already recovered and hit new high-water marks, so the presence of a large maximum drawdown somewhere in the fund's return stream may or may not indicate the current risk of staff turnover.

A disadvantage of maximum drawdown relative to other measures of risk is that it is a single observation based on a time-dependent data series. More data, in the form of more frequent returns or a longer track record, tend to generate larger maximum drawdown calculations, so it is important to compare consistent time periods and return frequencies when evaluating the maximum drawdowns of multiple hedge funds.

EXAMPLE 10

Hedge Fund Drawdown Measures

1 An analyst evaluating two hedge funds is considering increasing the number of drawdowns used in calculating average drawdown from three to five. The new average drawdown calculated from five drawdowns would be:

A less negative.

B unchanged.

C more negative.

2 Exhibit 15 shows the return stream of Fund B. The maximum drawdown of Fund B is:

A −20.6.

B −18.5.

C −13.2.

3 The largest individual drawdown of Fund B is:

A −20.6.

B −18.5.

C −13.2.

24 Rogers and Van Dyke (2006).

4 The drawdown duration of Fund B in months is:

A 5.

B 7.

C 13.

Solution to 1:

A is correct. Increasing the number of drawdowns included in calculating the average drawdown will always result in a smaller (less negative) average drawdown. The drawdowns used in the average drawdown calculation are the largest (most negative) individual drawdowns, so the additional observations included in the calculation will be smaller (less negative) individual drawdowns.

Solution to 2:

A is correct. The highest value of Fund B is in Month 22 (1.129), but the lowest value after that high-water mark represents a drawdown of only –2.9%. The next-highest peak earlier in the return stream before a decline is in Month 18 (1.088), but the subsequent drawdown is only –5.3%. The lowest value during the period was in Month 12 (0.845). The highest peak before that low point was in Month 5 (1.065), which represents a drawdown of –20.6%. This is the maximum drawdown during the period.

Solution to 3:

B is correct. The largest individual drawdown is not the same as the maximum drawdown; the largest individual drawdown must be a series of unbroken negative returns. The largest cumulative loss represented by an unbroken series of negative returns is –18.5.

Solution to 4:

C is correct. The drawdown duration includes the period of decline from the peak (Month 5) to the trough (Month 12), and it also includes the period until full recovery (Month 18). The duration from Month 5 to Month 18 is the drawdown duration, 13 months.

2.8 Value at Risk and Stress Tests

In the following sections, we describe value at risk and stress tests and explain the strengths and weaknesses of each.

2.8.1 *Value at Risk*

Value at risk is one of the most common forward-looking risk measures, but it is also possible to calculate as a measure of historic returns. Value at risk is a probability-based measure of loss potential—expressed by convention as a positive number either in units of currency or as a percentage—that can be applied to an investment, a portfolio, a strategy, or a company. More formally, **value at risk** (VaR) is an estimate of the loss that we expect to be exceeded with a given level of probability over a specified time period.[25] In the definition, "that we expect to be exceeded" indicates that VaR is a *minimum*. The statement "The portfolio's daily 1% VaR is €3 million" means that there is a 1% probability that over a day the portfolio will lose at least €3 million. Equivalently,

25 In the terminology of statistics, VaR with an x percent probability for a given time interval represents the xth percentile of the distribution of outcomes (ranked from worst to best) over that time period.

we can state that with 99% confidence the portfolio's daily VaR is €3 million.[26] VaR is sometimes misunderstood to represent the maximum amount at risk of loss; this error could lead an investor to underestimate the amount of risk within a portfolio.

VaR is usually a forward-looking or *ex ante* risk measure, and any estimation of VaR is calculated within a probability or confidence level. The probability statement for a 95% confidence level is that 95% of the time, the loss in the portfolio will be less than the calculated VaR. An alternative view of the same information is that 5% of the time, the loss in the portfolio is expected to be at least as great as the VaR. A wider confidence level would lead to a greater VaR calculation and the assumption of a less frequent loss of the VaR amount or more. A 99% confidence level is a more conservative VaR calculation because it focuses the user on evaluating more extreme outcomes than does a 95% level. The most commonly used confidence levels are 95% and 99%.

The simplest way to calculate a VaR measure is to sort a series of returns to identify the worst returns and then identify the return representing the desired probability level. For example, consider the series of expected monthly returns in Exhibit 17.

Exhibit 17 Value at Risk

Monthly Return Observations	Return (%)
1	8.9
2	3.2
3	–7.8
4	2.1
5	–13.7
6	11.0
7	5.7
8	–8.2
9	15.2
10	9.4

To identify the VaR with a 90% confidence interval and a one-month time horizon, sort the returns from highest to lowest. The worst return in this series is –13.7, and the next worst is –8.2. Nine times out of ten, or 90% of the time, if this return series is representative of expected returns, we would expect to lose no more than –8.2% in a given month. In practice, a much larger set of observations would be appropriate, but this simple example illustrates the concept.

The time horizon is another critical element to any VaR description. The time horizon measures the amount of time over which returns will be calculated. In our example above, we considered a portfolio with a 90% confidence level, a time period of one month, and a VaR of 8.2%. In this example, the portfolio could be expected to have a single monthly loss worse than 8.2% only 10% of the time. This measure does not describe the probability of consecutive monthly losses, which might produce losses that were significantly greater than 8.2%.

The selection of the time horizon is dependent upon the characteristics of the investor. VaR was developed by investment banks as a way of measuring their daily earnings at risk. Some financial institutions that currently report VaR show a daily VaR calculation, representing an actively traded investment portfolio. Some pension

26 This discussion draws heavily on Chance, Grant, and Marsland (2007).

funds report weekly or monthly VaR, reflecting the lower frequency of reporting that may correspond with a longer investment horizon. All else equal, a longer time horizon will lead to a larger calculated VaR measure.

There are three common approaches to estimating VaR, each with different assumptions, data requirements, advantages, and disadvantages:

- analytical (sometimes called "variance–covariance" or "parametric"),
- historical, and
- Monte Carlo.

The analytical approach to estimating VaR is relatively easy to calculate, requiring only an expected return and standard deviation of returns. The analytical approach has a significant disadvantage, however, in its reliance on the assumption of a normal distribution of returns. Depending upon the strategy analyzed, the assumption of a normal distribution may be appropriate or inappropriate. For example, a developed markets equity portfolio would be more likely to exhibit a normal distribution of returns than a fixed-income arbitrage hedge fund. A portfolio utilizing options as a significant portion of the strategy is more likely to exhibit returns that have significant differences from the normal bell curve distribution, so the analytical approach to estimating VaR would be inappropriate for this portfolio.

Another approach to estimating VaR is the historical method. For example, if there are 100 observations of historical returns, an estimated historical VaR with a 99% confidence level is the second-to-worst return in the entire series because it was exceeded by 1% of the observations.

One advantage of the historical method is that it does not require assumptions about the distribution of portfolio returns. The data required are a series of historical returns for the portfolio or security being analyzed. However, the historical method does make the assumption that historical returns are an appropriate representation of the likelihood of future returns. This assumption may or may not be true depending upon the time periods under evaluation. A historical time period that lacked a market crash, for example, would not incorporate the risk of a crash in simulations. A disadvantage of the historical method of estimating VaR is that it is extremely unlikely that the specific set of circumstances that occurred during a given historical period will occur again with exactly the same effect.

One complication with the use of the historical method to estimate VaR is the requirement that the current investments be associated with a relevant historical return stream. New stock or debt issuances, for example, may not have existed for the entire period under analysis. In this case, it may be possible to identify a proxy investment and consider the historical period of relevant returns. VaR calculations can be very sensitive to the accuracy and completeness of the input data.

The Monte Carlo method of estimating VaR might be appropriate for a portfolio that displays a return distribution significantly different from the normal distribution. Many hedge funds are characterized by return distributions with fat tails, indicating a relatively higher percentage of return outcomes in the outer ranges of observed returns. The Monte Carlo method uses a random number generator to estimate potential return outcomes, making it easier to incorporate the effect of options and other derivatives into the analysis. A disadvantage of the Monte Carlo method of estimating VaR is that as the number of individual investments increases, the complexity of the calculations requires significant computer resources.

One criticism of VaR is that it sounds like the maximum value that could be lost, when it is more accurately defined as the minimum value that can be expected to be lost over a specified period and with a given probability. Extensions of VaR have been developed to address estimates of the magnitude of expected losses in excess of the VaR amount. For example, **tail value at risk** (TVaR; also known as conditional VaR, conditional tail expectation, and expected shortfall) is equal to VaR plus the expected loss in excess of VaR, given that such excess loss occurs. For example, for 99% VaR, TVaR would capture the average of the worst 1% of outcomes. In this context, the condition relevant to conditional tail expectation or conditional VaR is that returns are worse than the VaR.

Contribution to VaR is a useful adaptation of the VaR measure, although the different methods of calculating contribution to VaR are beyond the scope of this reading. Contribution to VaR is a measure of the relative volatility of the different segments of a fund compared to the volatility of the total fund. Consider the pension risk analysis in Exhibit 18, illustrating contribution to VaR across different asset classes of a pension fund.

Exhibit 18 Pension Risk Analysis (% of total fund)

	Contribution to Value at Risk	Asset Allocation
Global equities	75%	61%
Treasuries	–4	11
Hedge funds	2	4
TIPS	1	8
Real assets	17	9
Commodities	9	5
Cash	0	2

Exhibit 18 shows that the global equities segment represents 75% of the VaR of the total fund but only 61% of the assets. In this example, the Treasuries segment is a powerful risk diversifier within the total fund, representing 11% of the assets but offsetting 4% of the total fund VaR. This implies that increasing the allocation to global equities would tend to increase the total fund VaR and increasing the allocation to Treasuries would tend to decrease the total fund VaR.

In addition to the parameters described above (confidence level, time horizon, and methodology), there are several types of VaR measures that can provide different information about portfolios. For example, the VaR at an overall portfolio level can be calculated in many ways, but exploring the relationships within the component segments provides insights into relative risks that can help support investment allocation decisions. Within an overall portfolio, the contribution to VaR can be calculated as the amount a given segment contributes to the calculated VaR, without showing the cross-asset-class diversification benefits separately. Another way to show such an analysis would be to report the benefits of diversification as a separate segment, or to show an alternative calculation of undiversified VaR for each segment separately. The calculated VaR can be reported as a percentage of market value, as a percentage of total VaR, or as an absolute market value. Incremental VaR can be shown as the effect of simply removing one or more segments, with or without re-allocating the market value to the remaining segments. There is no single standard way to estimate VaR or the different extensions of VaR, and in each case, it is important to clarify which calculation is reported simply as "VaR."

The choices in calculating VaR have a material impact on the numbers reported, so it is important to understand the assumptions that were used in calculating the VaR measures before making investment decisions based on such estimates. Once VaR is calculated for a total portfolio and its underlying segments, reviewing the relative risk of the segments compared to the total portfolio, of the portfolio compared to the benchmark, and the various measures over time provides useful insights.

EXAMPLE 11

Analysis of VaR

Assume the following:

- Portfolio value = €1,000 million; total VaR = €100 million
- Equity allocation = €500 million; equity contribution to VaR = €80 million
- Treasuries allocation = €500 million; Treasuries contribution to VaR = €20 million (or 4% of €500 million)

If €100 million is moved from equities to Treasuries, holding all else equal, total VaR would be *closest* to:

A €80 million.

B €88 million.

C €100 million.

Solution:

B is correct. The equity and Treasuries contributions to VaR as a percentage of the amount invested in equity and Treasuries were, respectively, €80 million/€500 million = 16% and €20 million/€500 million = 4%. After the movement of €100 million from equities into Treasuries, the equity contribution to VaR is 16% of €400 million = €64 million; the Treasuries contribution to VaR = 4% of €600 million = €24 million. Total VaR = €64 million + €24 million = €88 million.

2.8.2 *Stress Tests*

Another application of forward-looking risk analysis is stress testing. Many regulators are now requiring firms to report the results of stress testing, in some cases with very specific parameters and in other cases with broad guidelines allowing room for interpretation. Stress testing is a process by which we can estimate the expected impact on a portfolio of changes in different parameters, such as changes in equity markets, commodity prices, or interest rates. Scenario analysis is related to stress testing in that it illustrates the expected portfolio impact of specific historic scenarios were they to happen again.

Stress testing and scenario analysis usually incorporate factor analysis to simplify the computational requirements. Each investment or portfolio is affected by changes in relevant market factors, which can be represented by different indexes or securities. Once we know the correlation of the investment returns to the factor returns, we can calculate the expected impact on the investments of changes in the factors. Stress testing involves selecting the specific factors or combinations of factors that we want to analyze and identifying the effects of large unfavorable movements in the values of those factors. For example, the US Securities and Exchange Commission requires money market funds to review the impact of changes in interest rates, credit quality, and fund liquidity separately and in combination and to identify the point at which the fund cannot maintain a constant per share value.

Historical scenario analysis has some of the same disadvantages as the historical method of calculating VaR. The investments in the current portfolio may not have been in existence during the historical period considered in the scenario. Historical scenarios are usually selected for memorable periods of dramatic loss or volatility. The use of factor exposures enables an estimate of the probable impact on a current portfolio if past changes in factors were to repeat. A disadvantage of historical scenario analysis is the fact that history tends not to repeat itself with precisely the same effects. One advantage of historical scenario analysis is that it is intuitive and can help to show the importance of managing investment risk.

EXAMPLE 12

Value at Risk and Stress Testing

1 Which methodology for estimating VaR would *most likely* be appropriate for a portfolio that includes a significant number of options and other derivatives?

A Historical

B Parametric

C Monte Carlo

2 Given a one-month value at risk number of $1 million with a confidence interval of 99%, an investor would be expected:

A not to lose more than $1 million in any given month.

B to lose more than $1 million in a month 1% of the time.

C to lose approximately $1 million in a month 1% of the time.

3 What kind of adjustment in calculating value at risk would be an example of stress testing?

A Increasing the confidence interval from 95% to 99%

B Decreasing the time horizon from one week to one day

C Increasing the correlation of returns across investments to one

Solution to 1:

C is correct. The Monte Carlo methodology uses a random number generator to predict a large number of possible return outcomes, and this approach is less reliant than the other methodologies on the assumption of normally distributed or stable returns.

Solution to 2:

B is correct. The VaR calculation is an estimate of the minimum loss expected with a given confidence level over a specified time horizon.

Solution to 3:

C is correct. Adjusting the confidence level or time horizon used to calculate value at risk will change the resulting value, but these parameters do not describe any change to the risk of the current portfolio or market. Adjusting the assumed correlation is an example of stressing a parameter that describes the risk of the market, so the resulting value would describe the impact on the portfolio of changing conditions in the market.

ANALYSIS OF INVESTMENT CHARACTERISTICS

3

Most of the risk measures discussed in earlier sections describe movement in portfolio returns, reflecting volatility or loss of capital. As a complement to analysis of investment returns, analysis of investment characteristics can provide additional insight into the underlying investments. This insight can enable an investor to understand exposures to different factors within and across portfolios.

Types of investment characteristics include valuation measures, interest rate sensitivity, geographic exposure, type of issuer or investment structure, liquidity estimates, and credit quality. General descriptions of these categories are included in Exhibit 19.

Exhibit 19 Categories of Investment Characteristics

Category	Description
Valuation measures	Most relevant for equities, these measures relate the price of a security to one of the factors affecting company valuation. Price/earnings (P/E), price/book (P/B), and price/cash flow (P/CF) are examples of valuation measures. These measures are used in analyzing investment style and also in estimating risk. Generally, higher valuation measures indicate riskier investments.
Interest rate sensitivity	Relevant for fixed income and interest rate derivatives, this characteristic describes the expected effect of changes in interest rates on the value of the investment.
Economic sector or industry classification	Primarily applicable to equity and corporate bonds, this characteristic associates the company that issued the equity or debt with the economic sector or specific industry in which that company operates. Industry or sector exposure across geographies has risen in importance with the increasing globalization of world economies and investment strategies.
Geographic exposure	Relevant for any asset class, the geographic exposure of investments is a factor that can dominate other aspects of investment risk, particularly in times of geopolitical uncertainty. Concentrated geographic exposure is generally associated with increased risk.
Type of issuer	Relevant for most asset classes. For example, fixed-income investments can be issued by companies, countries, states, or other governmental agencies. This characteristic is useful for concentration analysis based on types of issuers and can highlight related measures that may be relevant (such as credit quality or geographic exposure).
Investment structure	Relevant for all asset classes. Examples include common or preferred stock, bonds, asset-backed securities, swaps, and private equity. For a portfolio with a concentration in asset-backed securities, for example, an analysis of the underlying assets might help explain the risk profile of the portfolio.
Credit quality	Relevant for fixed income, publicly traded equity, and credit derivatives, this characteristic concerns the likelihood that the issuer, issue, or counterparty will be able to meet obligations.

(continued)

Exhibit 19 (Continued)

Category	Description
Liquidity	This characteristic is relevant across asset classes. All else equal, low-liquidity investments are riskier than high-liquidity investments. Liquidity estimates the ability to purchase or sell investments quickly without impacting prices. Low levels of market liquidity may mean that investors will find it hard to liquidate a bond or common share position in a timely way without accepting a discount to the security's intrinsic value. In the case of private equity and hedge funds, liquidity is determined by the contractual provisions of the investment documents rather than by market factors. For example, hedge funds often require waiting periods or charge additional fees to withdraw funds.
Leverage	Relevant across asset classes. All else equal, high-leverage investments are riskier than low-leverage investments. The use of derivatives generally includes a notional exposure that is often different from the market value of the investment, effectively leveraging the exposure that is the subject of the derivative. Leverage may also be created by short positions or borrowing. Generally, portfolios with more leverage are considered riskier.

These characteristics are calculated at the security level initially and can be rolled up to the portfolio level or analyzed at the level of a grouping or segment within a portfolio or composite. Portfolio or composite characteristics may be compared with benchmark characteristics.

Some characteristics are specific to the investment strategy, and some are relevant across asset classes. Characteristics specific to equity investments include measures that evaluate the health of the underlying company, such as debt-to-equity ratio, return on equity, and free cash flow. Many of the same characteristics that are used to understand the investment style of a manager or portfolio (e.g., value versus growth, large capitalization versus small capitalization) can also be used to estimate risks within a portfolio. For example, investors analyzing the risk of a growth strategy could consider measures of earnings per share growth over several years compared to measures of sales growth over the same period to develop an opinion of how sustainable the growth in earnings might be. Exhibit 20 describes the relationship between security characteristics and investment risks. (Panel A illustrates the analysis possible with specific pairs of characteristics, and the definitions of the referenced characteristics are given in Panel B.)

Exhibit 20 Comparing Security Characteristics

Panel A: Pairing of Characteristics

Characteristics	Rationale
P/E (ex negative EPS) vs. % negative earnings surprise	The higher a portfolio's valuation levels (P/E, P/B, P/CF, etc.), the higher the earnings expectations and the greater the risk of having a significant amount of negative earnings surprise. This analysis is also relevant for highly earnings-focused market-oriented managers.
I/B/E/S one-year growth mean vs. falling estimate revisions	Companies with high expected growth are generally riskier because they often sell at higher valuations. Thus, the higher the expected growth, the more important it is that the exposure to negative EPS revisions be limited.
Cash flow five-year growth vs. EPS five-year growth	This is essentially a measure of earnings quality. The best situation would be for a manager's cash flow growth to be close to or above its EPS growth. EPS growth well above cash flow growth would be undesirable.

Panel B: Definitions of Terms

Characteristic	Definition
P/E (ex negative EPS)	This characteristic measures the P/E ratio of the entire portfolio; it is equivalent to summing the holdings' prices and dividing that result by an approximation of "normalized" EPS (earnings per share). For companies with volatile earnings patterns, this measure can be more meaningful than other earnings ratios that are subject to cyclical peaks and troughs. For example, economically sensitive stocks exhibit their lowest P/E ratios when their EPS levels are highest, and vice versa; the P/E ratio of a portfolio invested in such stocks could be misleading when compared to the P/E ratios of other portfolios. Using a normalized earnings proxy helps offset such potential distortions.
I/B/E/S one-year growth mean	The long-term growth forecast statistic indicates the consensus outlook for a portfolio's EPS growth. I/B/E/S provides means of research analysts' estimates for companies' one-year growth rates.
% Negative earnings surprises	This statistic measures negative earnings surprises in the most recent quarter. The market generally rewards investors holding stocks with greater-than-expected reported earnings.
Falling estimate revisions	These statistics indicate the trends in earnings estimates based on I/B/E/S data by comparing current estimates for each stock with the previous month's estimates.
Cash flow five-year growth	This statistic measures a holding's cash flow growth over the previous five years. It is a useful alternative measure of growth for companies which do not have earnings, have weak earnings, or whose book values do not reflect intangible assets (e.g., service companies or high-technology companies). The statistic indicates the overall business growth and financial stability of companies (even when the growth is not flowing through to the bottom line).
EPS five-year growth	This statistic measures the trailing five-year EPS growth of a portfolio's holdings.

Source: Degroot and Greenwood (2009/2010)

Characteristics specific to fixed-income investments include measures of interest rate sensitivity, such as duration and convexity, as well as credit quality of the issue. Duration is one of the most commonly used measures to represent the relevant risks of fixed-income investments. Specifically, duration estimates the percentage price change in a bond or a portfolio of bonds with a 100 basis point change in yield. A bond with a duration of 4.6 would be expected to experience a change in price of 4.6% when yields change by 100 basis points. A change in yield of 50 basis points would likely change bond prices by 2.3%.

Duration calculations assume that when yields change, they make a parallel shift, changing the same amount at each point in time on the relevant yield curve. In practice, the relationship between yields and bond prices is not completely linear, so the shape of the curve is described by a measure of convexity.

Duration of a portfolio is calculated as the weighted average of the individual security durations. A portfolio with a higher overall duration than the relevant benchmark could be expected to experience greater return volatility associated with interest rate changes than a portfolio with lower duration. We can also analyze a portfolio by dividing it into different duration ranges and then reviewing weights, returns, or other measures for each of those duration segments separately.

Evaluating fundamental risk characteristics is an approach to monitoring risk in cases where investors have limited or infrequent precise information about the underlying investments of alternative assets, such as hedge funds, private equity, or real estate. Alternative investments are often less liquid and valued less frequently than other investments. Infrequent valuations complicate returns-based volatility measures, so evaluating factor exposures and the risks associated with those exposures is an approach to understanding risks across asset classes.

Some characteristics can be aggregated to evaluate exposures across asset classes, including alternative investments. For example, economic sectors and industries are traditional equity characteristics but are also applicable to corporate debt and private equity. Credit quality is often viewed as a fixed-income characteristic, but it is possible to evaluate credit exposures to the counterparties to derivative contracts. Country and regional exposures are relevant across asset classes and are particularly relevant for real estate investments.

These characteristics and other equity and fixed-income characteristics can also be used to evaluate the investment style of a manager relative to a benchmark. More simply, examination of the exposures of investments to regions, sectors, and macroeconomic factors can be used broadly to evaluate concentration risk.

EXAMPLE 13

Analysis of Investment Characteristics

1 What type of characteristic associates the price of a common stock with the underlying company's financial statistics?

   A Valuation

   B Liquidity

   C Economic industry

2 What type of characteristic can highlight the concentration risk of geopolitical uncertainty within an investment portfolio?

   A Sector exposure

   B Industry exposure

   C Geographic exposure

3 What type of characteristic is potentially relevant across asset classes?

A P/E ratio
B Convexity
C Geographic exposure

Solution to 1:

A is correct. Valuation characteristics relate the price of common stock to elements of company valuation, such as earnings, book value, and cash flow.

Solution to 2:

C is correct. Geographic exposure characteristics identify the concentration risk associated with investments in a particular geographic region or country. Geopolitical risks generally affect a particular geographic region or country.

Solution to 3:

C is correct. Geographic exposure characteristics can apply equally to equities, fixed-income investments, real estate, and currencies, as well as underlying holdings within private equity and hedge fund structures.

RISK MEASURE SELECTION

4

The selection of risk measure is affected by many things, including investor preference, the stage of the investment process, the role of the person analyzing risk, the purpose of the analysis, and the strategy being analyzed. Many different risk measures are available, and no mechanical procedure will ensure that appropriate measures are selected in a particular circumstance. However, addressing the following questions can be useful:

- What are the goals against which success is being measured?
- What investment constraints (e.g., time horizon, liquidity, regulation) are applicable?
- Do characteristics of the investment strategies or holdings' return distributions affect the validity of given risk measures?

We have defined risk as exposure to uncertainty. The answer to the first question should help to identify the nature of the uncertainty involved in attaining specific investment goals. For example, the goal of a defined-benefit pension plan's sponsor is frequently to be able to pay current and future retiree benefits with a high degree of confidence. The sponsor faces the risk of not being able to meet those pension liabilities, given current assets and planned contributions; therefore, measures of surplus risk are relevant and measures of risk relative to a custom benchmark representing liabilities might also be relevant. The goal of a UK domestic large-capitalization equity fund may be to outperform an index of large-cap UK shares. Because the fund manager's mandate is to deliver excess return over a benchmark, the manager faces uncertainty about whether deviations from the benchmark will be compensated by additional returns. Thus, tracking risk can be a relevant risk measure for the fund manager and for investors in the fund. Investors with that portfolio manager may also be interested in additional risk measures related to their own investment goals. For example, for measuring the impact of investing in the fund on the systematic risk of the investors' overall portfolios, the fund's beta is relevant. Indeed, the determination of appropriate risk measures depends upon who is performing the analysis and the particular questions to be answered.

Investment constraints can be relevant to risk measure selection. Future liquidity needs may suggest the need for monitoring volatility and downside risk measures. Various regulations may effectively require banks to monitor VaR and to perform stress testing. Some bank regulators require reporting on duration, credit quality, or other material exposures. A bond fund mandate with specific concentration limits will often have limits on sector exposures, duration, or credit quality variance relative to the benchmark.

Characteristics of strategies and asset holdings can affect the validity of risk measures. Volatility measures such as standard deviation are most appropriate for symmetric return distributions. The use of options generally introduces return asymmetries. Certain strategies may involve the risk of infrequent but extremely large losses; for such strategies, risk measures addressing tail risk, such as VaR and TVaR, may be relevant.

The following are additional examples of risk measure selection:

- Insurance companies have the investment goal of supporting liabilities; thus, asset/liability management and measures of risk relative to expected liabilities are important.
- Endowments and foundations often focus on the need for long-term capital growth after inflation to meet required spending minimums. These types of institutions, because they are long-term investors, are often relatively well situated to earn any return premium that may be associated with low-liquidity investments. They generally have larger allocations to illiquid investments.
- Some hedge fund strategies enable broad investment authority across asset classes such that there is no meaningful benchmark. In that case, absolute risk measures, such as VaR or maximum drawdown, are likely to be more appropriate than benchmark-relative measures. Hedge funds often use VaR measures to manage their strategies dynamically, without reference to benchmarks or client reporting.

Every risk measure has both advantages and disadvantages, so there are benefits to considering multiple approaches to estimating risk.

EXAMPLE 14

Selection of Risk Measures

1 Which of the following risk measures would be *most* appropriate for evaluating a passive index manager?

A Beta

B Volatility

C Tracking risk

2 Which of the following measures would be *most* appropriate in analyzing the relevant risk of a broad fixed-income portfolio?

A P/E ratio

B Convexity

C Drawdown duration

3 Which of the following measures would be *most* appropriate in analyzing the risk of a hedge fund without a viable benchmark?

A Surplus risk

B Tracking risk

C Value at risk

4 Which of the following approaches to monitoring risk would be *most* appropriate for regulators of financial institutions interested in understanding the risk of extreme outcomes?

A Stress testing

B Credit quality analysis

C Liability benchmarking

5 An investor concerned with the effect of an investment on the systematic risk of a portfolio is *most* likely to be concerned with the investment's:

A beta.

B volatility.

C value at risk.

Solution to 1:

C is correct. The mandate of a passive index manager is to track the performance of the benchmark index; the relevant measure for that objective is minimal tracking error, or tracking risk.

Solution to 2:

B is correct. Convexity is a measure of the sensitivity of the duration of a bond to changes in interest rates. In general, the higher the convexity, the more sensitive the bond price is to a change in interest rates.

Solution to 3:

C is correct. Absolute risk measures such as VaR are appropriate in cases in which a viable benchmark is not available.

Solution to 4:

A is correct. Stress testing analyzes the potential impact of extreme outcomes on portfolios or institutions.

Solution to 5:

A is correct. Beta is a measure of systematic risk.

RISK ATTRIBUTION

5

Risk attribution provides an understanding of the sources of risk, identifying the sources of portfolio volatility for absolute mandates and the sources of tracking risk for relative mandates. In an ideal world, all investors would hold very well-diversified portfolios, face only systematic risk, and adjust their exposure to systematic factors to match their appetite for risk. However, in the real world, managers seek opportunities for profit by taking specific exposures to risk. Risk attribution identifies the risks taken and, together with return attribution, helps complete the picture of the investment manager's active decisions.

Risk attribution should reflect the investment decision process being analyzed. Exhibit 21 classifies risk attribution approaches and serves as a road map to our coverage of the topic by matching investment decision processes with risk attribution models. The columns indicate whether the focus is on absolute or relative risk. The rows categorize investment decision processes as bottom-up, top-down, or factor-based. A bottom-up approach starts with and is focused on individual security selection. Top-down approaches focus first on macro decisions, such as allocations to economic sectors, and then on security selection within sectors. A factor-based approach looks for profits by taking different-from-benchmark exposures to risk factors driving asset returns.

Exhibit 21 Selecting the Appropriate Risk Attribution Approach

Investment Decision Process	Type of Attribution Analysis	
	Absolute	Relative (vs. Benchmark)
Bottom-up (individual security selection)	Marginal contribution to risk **Section 5.1.1**	Marginal contribution to tracking risk **Section 5.1.2**
Top-down (allocation then security selection)	Not covered	Top-down risk attribution **Section 5.2**
Factor exposure	Factor's marginal contribution to risk and specific risk **Section 5.3.1**	Factor's marginal contribution to tracking risk and active specific risk **Section 5.3.2**

To explain the risk dimension further, for absolute mandates where the manager does not refer to a benchmark, the risk of the portfolio is explained by exposures to the market, size, and style factors and by the specific risk due to stock selections. The attribution model seeks to quantify the contribution of each exposure and of specific risk.

A manager who refers to a benchmark will attempt to beat the benchmark return by taking active factor sensitivities (different-from-benchmark exposures) and by selecting stocks. A risk attribution model will decompose the tracking risk (TR) into an active factor risk and an active specific risk (or asset selection risk).

Suppose that the manager follows an absolute bottom-up process. As the manager does not refer to a benchmark, the standard measure of risk is the volatility (standard deviation) of returns. The objective of an attribution model will be to measure the contribution of selection decisions to portfolio risk. To calculate these contributions, we need the marginal contribution of each asset to the portfolio risk—that is, the increase (decrease) of the standard deviation due to a small increase in holdings. Having the marginal contribution of a security to portfolio risk will allow us to calculate the contribution of stock picking for bottom-up processes.

For portfolios that are managed against benchmarks, the standard measure of risk is tracking risk (the standard deviation of active return). The objective of an attribution model will be to quantify the contribution of active decisions to tracking risk. For bottom-up processes, the central concept will be the marginal contribution to tracking risk, which when multiplied by the associated active weight gives the contribution to tracking risk. For top-down processes, as the active return is explained by allocation and selection, risk attribution will identify the contribution of allocation and selection to tracking risk.

In the first section below, we will present risk attribution for portfolios that are active in allocation and/or stock selection. The second section will develop a risk attribution model that explains the tracking risk in terms of allocation and selection decisions. The third section will cover risk attribution for portfolios that use factor models for active management.

5.1 Marginal Contributions to Risk and Tracking Risk

As explained, standard deviation is an appropriate measure of risk for portfolios that are managed on an absolute basis. Risk attribution aims at decomposing the level of risk to identify the largest contributors to risk. Before we present formally the calculation of risk contribution, let us illustrate the intuition.

Suppose Manager A holds a long-only portfolio that is well diversified in European equities. Afraid of a possible recession, Manager A decides to add some gold to the existing portfolio. We have the intuition that this move lowers the risk of the existing portfolio, although on a stand-alone basis, gold is a risky asset. This intuition is correct, as gold generally displays a negative correlation with the stock markets. We can say that gold has helped to lower the risk of the existing portfolio because gold is often negatively correlated with the equity returns. The variables that explain the marginal contribution to risk are the standard deviation and the correlation.

5.1.1 *Marginal Contribution to Risk*

Risk attribution aims at identifying the decisions that explain the level of portfolio risk; hence, it is necessary to know the marginal contribution of an asset class to calculate its total contribution. As an example, let us suppose that the marginal risk contribution of the banking sector to the portfolio is 15%; that is, the total risk will increase by 0.15% as the weight in the banking sector increases by 1%. If the total weight in the banking sector is 10%, the contribution of this sector to the portfolio risk is 1.5%. The total risk of the portfolio is then equal to the sum of the contributions—that is, the weighted sum of the marginal contributions. Exhibit 22 illustrates how to break down the total risk of a portfolio. The contribution of a sector to the portfolio risk is equal to the weight times the marginal contribution. The numbers show that the largest contributor to the standard deviation is the financial sector. The second-largest contributor is the telecommunication sector, with a contribution equal to 1.92%.

Exhibit 22 Marginal Contribution to Risk

GICS®	Marginal Contribution	Weight	Contribution
Energy	12.00%	6.00%	0.72%
Materials	10.00	8.00	0.80
Industrials	13.00	14.00	1.82
Consumer discretionary	15.00	12.00	1.80
Consumer staples	14.00	7.00	0.98
Health care	16.00	6.00	0.96
Financials	18.00	14.00	2.52
Information technology	18.00	8.00	1.44
Telecommunication services	16.00	12.00	1.92
Utilities	8.00	13.00	1.04
Total risk			**14.00%**

The marginal contribution of an asset (or an asset class)[27] measures the sensitivity of the portfolio's volatility to a small change in the asset's holding. To illustrate this point, let us assume that the manager increases by 1% its holding in the "consumer discretionary" sector. As the marginal contribution of this sector is 15%, the total volatility of the portfolio will increase by 1% × 15% = 0.15%. Formally, the marginal contribution is:[28]

$$MC_i = \frac{\Delta\sigma_P}{\Delta w_i} = \rho_{iP} \times \sigma_i \quad (13)$$

where

$\Delta\sigma_p$ corresponds to a small change in the portfolio standard deviation that follows a small change in weights, Δw_i

ρ_{iP} is the correlation between the asset class i and the portfolio, P

σ_i is the volatility of the asset class i

As explained, the contribution of an asset class is equal to its weight times the marginal contribution. The sum of contributions (C_i) gives the total risk (σ_p) of the portfolio:

$$C_i = w_i \times MC_i \quad (14)$$

and

$$\sigma_P = \sum_{i=1}^{N} C_i \quad (15)$$

To break down the risk of a portfolio, we should first calculate the correlation between each asset class and the portfolio, as well as the volatility of each asset class. Correlation and standard deviation are estimated on a set of historical returns that contains a sufficient number of data points—that is, three years of monthly data or one year of weekly data.

EXAMPLE 15

Marginal Contribution to Risk

Assume that we observe portfolio returns over a period of one year on a monthly basis. Exhibit 23 gives the returns of two asset classes, bonds and equities. Assuming that the portfolio is rebalanced monthly and that the allocation has been constant over the year, we can calculate the portfolio return as the weighted sum of monthly returns. The portfolio monthly return is equal to the weighted sum of returns; that is, for Month 1, R_P = 0.4(−0.80%) + 0.6(4.50%) = 2.38%. As the portfolio rebalances each month, monthly returns are calculated using the same weights. The total return over one year (equivalently, the time-weighted rate of return) is found by linking monthly returns: [(1.0238)(0.9575) ··· (0.9991)] − 1.00 = 0.1434 or 14.34%.

27 In the text, we will always use "asset class," which is to be understood to cover the case of "individual asset" as well.

28 The demonstration of Equation 13 can be found in either Grinold and Khan (2000) or Menchero and Hu (2006).

Exhibit 23 Bond and Equity Returns[29]

Month	w_{Bond}	w_{Eq}	R_{Bond}	R_{Eq}	R_P
1	40%	60%	−0.80%	4.50%	2.38%
2	40	60	1.32	−7.96	−4.25
3	40	60	2.49	3.06	2.83
4	40	60	0.41	−1.57	−0.78
5	40	60	1.40	5.63	3.94
6	40	60	−0.90	0.88	0.17
7	40	60	0.54	9.95	6.19
8	40	60	0.29	1.50	1.02
9	40	60	1.99	8.34	5.80
10	40	60	1.06	−6.34	−3.38
11	40	60	2.30	−1.17	0.22
12	40	60	−0.29	0.05	−0.09
		Annual TWR:	10.19	16.42	14.34

The standard deviations for each asset and the portfolio are then needed. To calculate the standard deviations, we first calculate the arithmetic means.

The arithmetic mean returns for bonds, equities, and the portfolio are:

$$\overline{R}_{Bond} = (-0.80\% + 1.32\% + \ldots - 0.29\%)/12 = 0.82\%$$

$$\overline{R}_{Equity} = (4.50\% - 7.96\% + \ldots + 0.05\%)/12 = 1.41\%$$

$$\overline{R}_{P} = (2.38\% - 4.25\% + \ldots - 0.09\%)/12 = 1.17\%$$

Using these results in the expression for standard deviation, we calculate the volatility for bonds, equities, and the portfolio:

$$\sigma_{Bonds} \sqrt{\sum_{t=1}^{12} \frac{\left(R_{Bonds,t} - \overline{R_{Bonds}}\right)^2}{12}} = 1.093\%$$

$$\sigma_{Equity} = \sqrt{\sum_{t=1}^{12} \frac{\left(R_{Equity,t} - \overline{R_{Equity}}\right)^2}{12}} = 5.136\%$$

and $\sigma_P = \sqrt{\sum_{t=1}^{12} \frac{\left(R_{P,t} - \overline{R_P}\right)^2}{12}} = 3.107\%$

To calculate the correlation of bonds and equities with portfolio returns, we must first calculate the covariance:

$$\text{Cov}_{Bond,P} = \sum_{t=1}^{12} \frac{\left(R_{Bond,t} - \overline{R_{Bond}}\right) \times \left(R_{P,t} - \overline{R_P}\right)}{12} = 0.000044$$

and $\text{Cov}_{Eq,P} = 0.00158$.

29 The reader's calculations may differ slightly from those shown because of rounding error.

We now calculate the correlation of each asset class with the portfolio:

$$\rho_{Bond,P} = \frac{0.000044}{0.0109 \times 0.0311} = 0.128 \text{ and } \rho_{Equity,P} = \frac{0.001579}{0.0513 \times 0.0311} = 0.99$$

With these numbers, we are able to calculate the marginal contribution and the contribution of each asset class.

- Marginal contribution for bonds is 0.128 × 1.093% = 0.140%
- Marginal contribution for equities is 0.99 × 5.136% = 5.085%

The calculation of contributions is straightforward; as the weight for bonds is 40%, the contribution is 0.4 × 0.140% = 0.056%. Similarly, for equities, we obtain 3.051%. The total risk of the portfolio is then 3.107% = 0.056% + 3.051%.

	Bonds	Equities
Correlation with portfolio	0.128	0.99
Weight	40%	60%
Marginal contribution	0.140%	5.085%
Contribution	0.056%	3.051%

The marginal contributions show that an increase of 10% in equities will increase the portfolio risk by 0.508% while a decrease of 10% in bonds will lower the volatility of the portfolio by a small amount, 0.014%. Approximately, after this rebalancing (+10% in equities, −10% in bonds), the risk of the portfolio would be 3.107% − 0.014% + 0.508% = 3.602%.

This example shows that the change in asset allocation has increased the volatility of the portfolio by 0.495% = 3.602% − 3.107%. To appraise the efficiency of the active management decisions, we have to verify that the increase in volatility (0.495%) is compensated by a sufficient risk premium. Portfolio theory tells us that it is possible to compare the annual performance of two portfolios by using the Sharpe ratio. Let us call P1 and P2 two portfolios that allocate, respectively, 40% and 30% to bonds. Exhibit 23 gives the returns of P1, and Exhibit 24 gives those of P2. For a 4% annual risk-free rate, the Sharpe ratios of the two portfolios are:

$$\text{Sharpe(P1)} = \frac{14.34 - 4}{3.107\sqrt{12}} = 0.96 \text{ and Sharpe(P2)} = \frac{14.91 - 4}{3.602\sqrt{12}} = 0.87$$

The analysis of the Sharpe ratio suggests that the excess return (0.57%) is not large enough to compensate the increase in volatility.

Exhibit 24 Bond and Equity Returns

Month	w_{Bond}	w_{Eq}	R_{Bond}	R_{Eq}	R_P
1	30%	70%	**−0.80%**	**4.50%**	**2.91%**
2	30	70	**1.32**	**−7.96**	**−5.18**
3	30	70	**2.49**	**3.06**	**2.89**
4	30	70	**0.41**	**−1.57**	**−0.98**
5	30	70	**1.40**	**5.63**	**4.36**
6	30	70	**−0.90**	**0.88**	**0.35**
7	30	70	**0.54**	**9.95**	**7.13**
8	30	70	**0.29**	**1.50**	**1.14**
9	30	70	**1.99**	**8.34**	**6.44**
10	30	70	**1.06**	**−6.34**	**−4.12**

Exhibit 24 (Continued)

Month	w_{Bond}	w_{Eq}	R_{Bond}	R_{Eq}	R_P
11	30	70	2.30	−1.17	−0.13
12	30	70	−0.29	0.05	−0.05
	Annual TWR:		10.19	16.42	14.91

In Example 15, we have assumed that the portfolio rebalances every month to keep weights constant in each asset class. Although this assumption is convenient for calculation and presentation, it is not often the case in actual portfolio management. Asset allocations are generally not constant. When allocations change over time, the calculation of the contribution of a given asset class must take account of the changes. The solution to this problem is quite straightforward; instead of calculating the standard deviation and the correlation of each asset class using unweighted historical returns, $R_{i,t}$, we calculate both using historical contributions to return, $w_{i,t} \times R_{i,t}$.[30] The contribution (C_i) of asset class i to the portfolio risk (σ_P) is

$$C_i = \rho(w_i R_i, R_P) \times \sigma(w_i R_i) \quad (16)$$

where $\rho(w_i R_i, R_p)$ is the correlation of the historical contribution to return with the portfolio return and $\sigma(w_i R_i)$ is the volatility of the contribution to return.

EXAMPLE 16

Contributions to Risk: Analysis of Tactical Allocator

Manager A is active in tactical asset allocation. Changes in allocation are given in Exhibit 25. Bond and equity returns are the same as in the previous example. Given weights and returns, we can calculate the contributions to return for each month. Contributions over one year are obtained by linking monthly contributions.

Exhibit 25 Tactical Asset Allocator[31]

	Weights		Returns		Contributions		Total
Month	w_{Bond}	w_{Eq}	R_{Bonds}	R_{Eq}	$w_{Bond} \times R_{Bond}$	$w_{Eq} \times R_{Eq}$	R_P
1	10%	90%	−0.80%	4.50%	−0.08%	4.05%	3.97%
2	40	60	1.32	−7.96	0.53	−4.78	−4.25
3	20	80	2.49	3.06	0.50	2.45	2.95
4	30	70	0.41	−1.57	0.12	−1.10	−0.98
5	10	90	1.40	5.63	0.14	5.07	5.21
6	20	80	−0.90	0.88	−0.18	0.70	0.52
7	20	80	0.54	9.95	0.11	7.96	8.07
8	20	80	0.29	1.50	0.06	1.20	1.26

(continued)

30 Note that "contribution to return" is weighted return.
31 The reader's calculations may differ slightly from those shown here because of rounding.

Exhibit 25 (Continued)

	Weights		Returns		Contributions		Total
Month	w_{Bond}	w_{Eq}	R_{Bonds}	R_{Eq}	$w_{Bond} \times R_{Bond}$	$w_{Eq} \times R_{Eq}$	R_P
9	30	70	1.99	8.34	0.60	5.84	6.44
10	40	60	1.06	−6.34	0.42	−3.80	−3.38
11	40	60	2.30	−1.17	0.92	−0.70	0.22
12	40	60	−0.29	0.05	−0.12	0.03	−0.09
			10.19%	**16.42%**	**3.22%**	**17.72%**	**20.94%**

Using data in the "Contributions" columns, we calculate the standard deviation of historical contributions to return. The arithmetic mean returns for contributions of bonds and equities are:

$$\overline{w_{Bond}} \times \overline{R_{Bond}} = \frac{(-0.08\% + 0.53\% + \cdots - 0.12\%)}{12} = 0.25\%$$

$$\overline{w_{Equity}} \times \overline{R_{Equity}} = \frac{(4.05\% - 4.77\% + \cdots 0.03\%)}{12} = 1.41\%$$

Using these results in the expression for standard deviation, we calculate the volatility for the contributions to return of bonds and equities:

$$\sigma(w_{Bond} \times R_{Bond}) = \sqrt{\sum_{t=1}^{12} \frac{\left(w_{Bond,t} \times R_{Bond,t} - \overline{w_{Bond} \times R_{Bond}}\right)^2}{12}} = 0.323\%$$

$$\sigma(w_{Equity} \times R_{Equity}) = \sqrt{\sum_{t=1}^{12} \frac{\left(w_{Equity,t} \times R_{Equity,t} - \overline{w_{Equity} \times R_{Equity}}\right)^2}{12}} = 3.681\%$$

Before calculating the contribution of each asset class, we need to calculate correlations between contributions to return and portfolio return.

For bonds:

$$\text{Cov}(w_{bond} \times r_{bond}; R_P)$$
$$= \sum_{t=1}^{12} \frac{\left(w_{Bond,t} \times R_{Bond,t} - \overline{w_{Bond} \times R_{Bond}}\right) \times \left(R_{P,t} - \overline{R_P}\right)}{12} = -0.000017$$

$$\rho(w_{Bond} \times r_{Bond}; R_P) = \frac{Cov(w_{Bond} \times r_{Bond}; R_P)}{\sigma(w_{Bond} \times r_{Bond}) \times \sigma(R_P)} = -0.145$$

For equities:

$$\text{Cov}(w_{Equity} \times r_{Equity}; R_P)$$
$$= \sum_{t=1}^{12} \frac{\left(w_{Equity,t} \times R_{Equity,t} - \overline{w_{Equity} \times R_{Equity}}\right) \times \left(R_{P,t} - \overline{R_P}\right)}{12} = 0.00133$$

$$\rho\left(w_{Equity} \times r_{Equity}; R_P\right) = \frac{Cov\left(w_{Equity} \times r_{Equity}; R_P\right)}{\sigma\left(w_{Equity} \times r_{Equity}\right) \times \sigma\left(R_P\right)} = 0.996$$

1 Based on the information just given, calculate the contributions to risk of bonds and equity.

2 Describe the contributions of bonds and equity to return and volatility.

3 Judge whether Manager A was a successful tactical asset allocator.

Solution to 1:

The contribution to risk is equal to the correlation times the standard deviation of contribution to return. We can summarize the risk and return analysis in the following table:

	Contribution to Risk
Bonds	−0.047% = −0.145 × 0.323%
Equity	3.667% = 0.996 × 3.681%
Portfolio	3.620% = 3.667% − 0.047%

It is straightforward to verify that the sum of contributions is exactly equal to the portfolio standard deviation.

Solution to 2:

Bonds have positively contributed to the return (3.217%) while reducing the volatility by −0.047%. Equities have contributed 17.72% to the return and 3.667% to volatility.

	Contribution to Risk	Total Return	Contribution to Return
Bonds	−0.047% = −0.145 × 0.323%	10.19%	3.22%
Equity	3.667% = 0.996 × 3.681%	16.42%	17.72%
Portfolio	3.620% = 3.667% − 0.047%	20.94%	20.94%

Solution to 3:

The portfolio total return, 20.94%, is higher than the return for either bonds or equities. This results from good tactical allocation decisions. For example, during Month 7, the equities return was 9.95% and the allocation in equities was 80%, whereas the allocation was only 60% during Month 2, when the return was −7.96%.[32]

Because benchmarks are used more often than theoretical pricing models to appraise the performance of portfolios, we will now review the contribution to tracking risk, which is the standard risk measure for portfolios that are managed against benchmarks.

32 To gauge whether the active allocation produced alpha (i.e., delivered higher returns than needed to compensate the risk), we need a reference, either a theoretical pricing model (CAPM, APT) or a benchmark. Using the results of this example—that is, a contribution to risk for bonds that is close to zero—we could compare the contribution of bonds to the contribution that results from a risk-free rate investment.

5.1.2 *Marginal Contribution to Tracking Risk*

In the previous section, we focused on portfolios that are managed on an absolute basis. In this section, we focus on relative management and will explain how to calculate the contribution of each asset class to tracking risk. Contributions to tracking risk are useful information especially for mandates that include tracking risk limits. For example, suppose the objective assigned to a manager is to deliver an excess return of 200 basis points with a tracking risk that does not exceed 300 basis points on an annual basis. It is then important for the manager to know the contributions of active decisions to the actual level of tracking risk.

To calculate the marginal contribution to tracking risk, it is useful to write the tracking risk (TR) as a function of the active weights ($w_{i,P} - w_{i,B}$) and the pairwise asset covariance $\sigma_{ij} = \text{Cov}(R_i;R_j)$, with "P" and "B" denoting the portfolio and benchmark, respectively:

$$\text{TR} = \sigma(R_A) = \sqrt{\sum_{i,j=1}^{N} dw_i \times \sigma_{ij} \times dw_j} \quad (17)$$

where R_A is the active return of the portfolio and $dw_i = (w_{i,P} - w_{i,B})$ is the active weight in stock i.

To measure the contribution of active investments to the tracking risk, we first need to estimate the marginal contribution to tracking risk—that is, the increase (decrease) of the tracking risk that follows a small change in the active weight in asset i, dw_i.

The marginal contribution to tracking risk[33] is given by the following equation:

$$MC_i(\text{TR}) = \frac{\Delta TR}{\Delta dw_i} = \rho(r_i;R_A) \times \sigma(r_i) \quad (18)$$

The covariance in Equation 18 is between asset i and the active portfolio return. Let us assume that the active weights remain constant. Under this assumption, the level of tracking risk is equal to the weighted sum of the marginal contributions:

$$\text{TR} = \sum_{i=1}^{N} dw_i \times MC_i(\text{TR}) \quad (19)$$

Equation 19 highlights that it is possible to explain the tracking risk as the sum of the contributions of each of the active investment decisions. Whereas return attribution models give the contribution of active decisions to the active return, Equation 19 adds a risk dimension to the attribution process.

EXAMPLE 17

An Active Equity Portfolio of ETFs

To calculate the contribution of active investment decisions to the tracking risk, consider an equity portfolio actively managed against a benchmark that includes 40% of the S&P 500 Index and 60% of the S&P MidCap 400 Index. The manager is not a stock picker and so decides to invest in ETFs that track the S&P 500 and S&P MidCap 400 indexes. Exhibit 26 gives the return of each ETF as well as the active weights. Note that active weights are always constant over the period. The S&P 500 Index is overweighted by 10%, while the S&P MidCap 400 Index is underweighted by 10%. The manager rebalances the portfolio at the start of each month.

33 See Menchero and Hu (2006) and Grégoire and Van Oppens (2006).

Using the data in Exhibit 26, we will calculate the following risk indicators:

- Tracking risk
- Standard deviation of each ETF
- Correlation of each ETF with the active return
- Marginal contributions to TR and contributions of each ETF

Exhibit 26 ETF Portfolio Results

Month	w^P_{500}	w^B_{500}	w^P_{400}	w^B_{400}	R_{500}	R_{400}	$R_{P,t}$	$R_{B,t}$	$R_{A,t}$
1	50%	40%	50%	60%	–0.80%	4.50%	1.85%	2.38%	–0.53%
2	50	40	50	60	1.32	–7.96	–3.32	–4.25	0.93
3	50	40	50	60	2.49	3.06	2.78	2.83	–0.06
4	50	40	50	60	0.41	–1.57	–0.58	–0.78	0.20
5	50	40	50	60	1.40	5.63	3.52	3.94	–0.42
6	50	40	50	60	–0.90	0.88	–0.01	0.17	–0.18
7	50	40	50	60	0.54	9.95	5.25	6.19	–0.94
8	50	40	50	60	0.29	1.50	0.90	1.02	–0.12
9	50	40	50	60	1.99	8.34	5.17	5.80	–0.64
10	50	40	50	60	1.06	–6.34	–2.64	–3.38	0.74
11	50	40	50	60	2.30	–1.17	0.57	0.22	0.35
12	50	40	50	60	–0.29	0.05	–0.12	–0.09	–0.03
					10.19[a]	16.42	13.73	14.34	–0.61

[a] The time-weighted return is used to calculate one-year returns.

Tracking risk

$$\text{TR} = \sqrt{\sum_{t=1}^{12} \frac{\left(R_{A,t} - \overline{R_A}\right)^2}{12}} = 0.526\%$$

Standard deviation

$$\sigma_{500} = \sqrt{\sum_{t=1}^{12} \frac{\left(R_{500,t} - \overline{R_{500}}\right)^2}{12}} = 1.093\%$$

$$\sigma_{400} = \sqrt{\sum_{t=1}^{12} \frac{\left(R_{400,t} - \overline{R_{400}}\right)^2}{12}} = 5.136\%$$

Correlations

To calculate the marginal contribution to TR, we need the correlation between each index and the portfolio active return. Let us first calculate the covariance:

$$\text{Cov}\left(R_{500}, R_A\right) = \sum_{t=1}^{12} \frac{\left(R_{500,t} - \overline{R_{500}}\right) \times \left(R_{A,t} - \overline{R_A}\right)}{12} = 0.000013$$

$$\mathrm{Cov}(R_{400},R_A)=\sum_{t=1}^{12}\frac{\left(R_{400,t}-\overline{R_{400}}\right)\times\left(R_{A,t}-\overline{R_A}\right)}{12}=-0.000265$$

Correlations are the covariance divided by the product of the standard deviation:

$$\rho(R_{500},R_A)=\frac{Cov(R_{500},R_A)}{\sigma_{500}\times\sigma_A}=\frac{0.0000127}{0.01095\times 0.00526}=0.220$$

$$\rho(R_{400},R_A)=\frac{\mathrm{Cov}(R_{400},R_A)}{\sigma_{400}\times\sigma_A}=\frac{-0.000264}{0.05135\times 0.00526}=-0.978$$

1 Based on the information provided, calculate the marginal contribution to tracking risk of each ETF.

2 Interpret the results of Question 1.

Solution to 1:

Marginal contribution to tracking risk is equal to the correlation between the ETF and active return times the ETF's standard deviation (Equation 18):

$$MC_{500}(\mathrm{TR})=\rho(R_{500};R_A)\times\sigma(R_{500})=0.220\times 1.093\%=0.240\%$$

$$MC_{400}(\mathrm{TR})=\rho(R_{400};R_A)\times\sigma(R_{400})=-0.978\times 5.136\%=-5.024\%$$

We can now summarize the attribution results that explain tracking risk.

	Active Weights, dw_i	$\sigma(r_i)$	$\rho(r_i\,;R_A)$	MC_i(TR)	C_i(TR)
S&P 500	10%	1.093%	0.220	0.240%	0.024%
S&P MidCap 400	−10	5.136	−0.978	−5.024	0.502

Solution to 2:

The results show that overweighting the S&P 500 has contributed to the tracking risk by 0.024% while underweighting the S&P MidCap 400 has contributed a larger amount (i.e., 0.502%). As the marginal contribution of the S&P MidCap 400 is negative, overweighting this asset class would have resulted in lower tracking risk. We can verify that the sum of the contributions is equal to the tracking risk.

Example 17 assumed that weights remained constant over a year. Usually, portfolio managers change their allocations over time; the calculation of contributions to tracking risk has to take account of such changes. To take the changes into account, we simply need to calculate the correlation and the standard deviation of active contributions to return (active weights times returns) instead of absolute returns. The contribution to tracking risk is:

$$C_i(\mathrm{TR})=\rho(dw_iR_i,R_A)\times\sigma(dw_iR_i) \quad (20)$$

Contributions sum up to the tracking risk:

$$\sigma(R_A)=\mathrm{TR}=\sum_{i=1}^{N}C_i(\mathrm{TR}) \quad (21)$$

Using Equation 21, a performance analyst can break down TR and attribute the actual level to each active investment decision. To achieve this task, the first step is to collect portfolio historical data over a period with a chosen frequency (daily, weekly, monthly). The second step is to calculate the standard deviation of active contribution to return and the correlation. Example 18 illustrates data collection and calculations.

EXAMPLE 18

A More Actively Managed Portfolio

To calculate the contributions of several active management decisions to the tracking risk, we consider the same portfolio as in Example 17 but with active weights that change frequently, as illustrated in Exhibit 27. To attribute the tracking risk to active weights in each ETF (S&P 500 and S&P MidCap 400), we have to calculate

- standard deviation of active contributions to return;
- correlation between active contributions and active returns; and
- contributions to tracking risk.

Exhibit 27 A More Actively Managed Portfolio

Benchmark Weights		Active Weights		ETF Returns		Active Contributions		Active Return
w_{500}	w_{400}	dw_{500}	dw_{400}	R_{500}	R_{400}	$dw_{500} \times R_{500}$	$dw_{400} \times R_{400}$	R_A
40%	60%	−30%	30%	−0.80%	4.50%	0.24%	1.35%	1.59%
40	60	0	0	1.32	−7.96	0.00	0.00	0.00%
40	60	−20	20	2.49	3.06	−0.50	0.61	0.11%
40	60	−10	10	0.41	−1.57	−0.04	−0.16	−0.20%
40	60	−30	30	1.40	5.63	−0.42	1.69	1.27%
40	60	−20	20	−0.90	0.88	0.18	0.18	0.36%
40	60	−20	20	0.54	9.95	−0.11	1.99	1.88%
40	60	−20	20	0.29	1.50	−0.06	0.30	0.24%
40	60	−10	10	1.99	8.34	−0.20	0.83	0.63%
40	60	0	0	1.06	−6.34	0.00	0.00	0.00%
40	60	0	0	2.30	−1.17	0.00	0.00	0.00%
40	60	0	0	−0.29	0.05	0.00	0.00	0.00%
				10.19%	**16.42%**			

Tracking risk

The mean active return is the sum of active return divided by the number of observations (12).

Tracking risk is the standard deviation of the active return.

$$TR = \sqrt{\sum_{t=1}^{12} \frac{\left(R_{A,t} - \overline{R_A}\right)^2}{12}} = 0.673\%$$

Standard deviation of active contributions

$$\sigma\left(dw_{500} \times R_{500}\right) = \sqrt{\sum_{t=1}^{12} \frac{\left(dw_{500,t} \times R_{500,t} - \overline{dw_{500} \times R_{500}}\right)^2}{12}} = 0.205\%$$

$$\sigma\left(dw_{400} \times R_{400}\right) = \sqrt{\sum_{t=1}^{12} \frac{\left(dw_{400,t} \times R_{400,t} - \overline{dw_{400} \times R_{400}}\right)^2}{12}} = 0.707\%$$

Correlations between active contributions and active returns

As in Example 16, to calculate the correlation, we need first to calculate the covariance:

$$\text{Cov}\left(dw_{500} \times R_{500}, R_A\right) = \sum_{t=1}^{12} \frac{\left(dw_{500,t} \times R_{500,t} - \overline{dw_{500} \times R_{500}}\right) \times \left(R_{A,t} - \overline{R_A}\right)}{12}$$
$$= -0.0000003$$

$$\text{Cov}\left(dw_{400} \times R_{400}, R_A\right) = \sum_{t=1}^{12} \frac{\left(dw_{400,t} \times R_{400,t} - \overline{dw_{400} \times R_{400}}\right) \times \left(R_{A,t} - \overline{R_A}\right)}{12}$$
$$= 0.0000455$$

By dividing the covariance by the product of the standard deviations, we obtain the correlation:

$$\rho\left(dw_{500} \times R_{500}, R_A\right) = \frac{cov\left(dw_{500} \times R_{500}, R_A\right)}{\sigma_{dw_{500} \times R_{500}} \times \sigma_A} = \frac{-0.0000003}{0.00205 \times 0.00673} = -0.0217$$

$$\rho\left(dw_{400} \times R_{400}, R_A\right) = \frac{cov\left(dw_{400} \times R_{400}, R_A\right)}{\sigma_{dw_{400} \times R_{400}} \times \sigma_A} = \frac{0.0000455}{0.00707 \times 0.00673} = 0.957$$

Calculate the contributions to tracking risk based on the information given.

Solution:

Contributions to tracking risk are equal to correlations times the standard deviations (Equation 20).

$$C_{500}(\text{TR}) = \rho\left(dw_{500} \times R_{500}; R_A\right) \times \sigma\left(dw_{500} \times R_{500}\right) = -0.0217 \times 0.205\%$$
$$= -0.0044\%$$

$$C_{400}(\text{TR}) = \rho\left(dw_{400} \times R_{400}; R_A\right) \times \sigma\left(dw_{400} \times R_{400}\right) = 0.957 \times 0.707\%$$
$$= 0.677\%$$

Exhibit 27 highlights that, on average, the manager has underweighted the S&P 500 Index and overweighted the S&P MidCap 400 Index. The actual level of tracking risk is explained by the decision to overweight the S&P MidCap 400 Index. As this decision explains 100% of the tracking risk, it is useful to add to the risk analysis a return attribution to verify whether the active return covers the risk. Underweighting the S&P 500 did not increase the tracking risk; it has even contributed to a small decrease in the tracking risk.

Although these results are the output from a series of calculations, we may want to investigate them further. Why does underweighting an index by the same percentage as the other index is overweighted have a contribution that is so different? Intuitively, it might seem that the contributions should be of about the same magnitude. The next example will illustrate this.

EXAMPLE 19

Investing Outside the Benchmark (1)

The objective of this example is to illustrate that calculating the tracking error contributions by using absolute contribution to return ($dw \times R$) leads to non-intuitive results; that is, investing in the benchmark contributes to tracking risk!

Let us say that the benchmark is invested 100% in the S&P 500 Index. The portfolio allocates 60% to an ETF that tracks the S&P MidCap 400 Index and 40% to one that tracks the S&P 500. The active weights are +60% for the S&P MidCap 400 and −60% for the S&P 500.

We expect that the 40% allocated to the S&P 500 will not contribute to tracking risk. This expectation is intuitive, as the benchmark is the S&P 500. However, suppose we apply Equation 20 to explain tracking risk. Exhibit 28 gives monthly returns for each index as well as active weights.

Exhibit 28 Investing Outside the Benchmark

Active Weights		ETF Returns		Active Contributions		Portfolio	Benchmark	Active
dw_{400}	dw_{500}	R_{400}	R_{500}	$dw_{400} \times R_{400}$	$dw_{500} \times R_{500}$	R_P	R_B	R_A
60%	−60%	4.50%	−0.80%	2.70%	0.48%	2.38%	−0.80%	3.18%
60	−60	−7.96	1.32	−4.77	−0.79	−4.25	1.32	−5.57
60	−60	3.06	2.49	1.83	−1.49	2.83	2.49	0.34
60	−60	−1.57	0.41	−0.94	−0.24	−0.78	0.41	−1.18
60	−60	5.63	1.40	3.38	−0.84	3.94	1.40	2.53
60	−60	0.88	−0.90	0.53	0.54	0.17	−0.90	1.07
60	−60	9.95	0.54	5.97	−0.32	6.19	0.54	5.65
60	−60	1.50	0.29	0.90	−0.17	1.02	0.29	0.73
60	−60	8.34	1.99	5.00	−1.20	5.80	1.99	3.81
60	−60	−6.34	1.06	−3.80	−0.64	−3.38	1.06	−4.44
60	−60	−1.17	2.30	−0.70	−1.38	0.22	2.30	−2.08
60	−60	0.05	−0.29	0.03	0.18	−0.09	−0.29	0.21
		16.42%	**10.19%**			**14.34%**	**10.19%**	**4.15%**

The level of tracking risk is:

$$TR = \sqrt{\sum_{t=1}^{12} \frac{\left(R_{A,t} - \overline{R_A}\right)^2}{12}} = 3.159\%$$

The table below shows the results of risk attribution:

	$\sigma(dw_i r_i)$	$\rho(dw_i r_i\,;R_A)$	$C_i(TR)$
S&P 500	0.656%	0.220	0.144%
S&P MidCap 400	3.082	0.978	3.015
Tracking risk			**3.159%**

Surprisingly, in Example 19, the allocation to the S&P 500, which is the benchmark, appears to have contributed to tracking risk. This result contradicts the intuition that investing in the benchmark does not contribute to the tracking risk. The solution to this puzzle lies in the definition of contributions to return. Contributions can be relative to the benchmark return or absolute. Relative contributions are equal to the active weight (dw_i) times the active return, while absolute contributions are equal to the active weight times the absolute return:

$$AC_i = dw_i \times r_i$$

Relative contributions are defined relative to the benchmark return:

$$RC_i = dw_i \times (r_i - R_B),$$

where R_B is the benchmark return.

In Example 19, absolute contributions were used to calculate the contributions to tracking risk, which explains why the allocation to the S&P 500 contributed to the tracking risk.

EXAMPLE 20

Investing Outside the Benchmark (2)

Example 20 uses the same data as Example 19; that is, the benchmark is invested 100% in the S&P 500 Index and the active portfolio allocates 60% to an ETF that tracks the S&P MidCap 400 Index and 40% to an ETF that tracks the S&P 500 Index. We now use the relative contributions to return to calculate the tracking error contributions. We expect that investing in the S&P 500, the benchmark, will not contribute to the tracking error.

Exhibit 29 gives the relative contributions to return as well as active weights and active returns.

Exhibit 29 Investing Outside the Benchmark (2)

Active Weights		ETF Returns		Active Contribution, Relative to the Benchmark				
dw_{400}	dw_{500}	R_{400}	R_{500}	$dw_{400} \times (R_{400} - R_B)$	$dw_{500} \times (R_{500} - R_B)$	R_P	R_B	R_A
60%	−60%	4.50%	−0.80%	−3.18%	0.00%	2.38%	−0.80%	3.18%
60	−60	−7.96	1.32	5.57	0.00	−4.25	1.32	−5.57
60	−60	3.06	2.49	−0.34	0.00	2.83	2.49	0.34
60	−60	−1.57	0.41	1.18	0.00	−0.78	0.41	−1.18
60	−60	5.63	1.40	−2.53	0.00	3.94	1.40	2.53
60	−60	0.88	−0.90	−1.07	0.00	0.17	−0.90	1.07
60	−60	9.95	0.54	−5.65	0.00	6.19	0.54	5.65
60	−60	1.50	0.29	−0.73	0.00	1.02	0.29	0.73
60	−60	8.34	1.99	−3.81	0.00	5.80	1.99	3.81
60	−60	−6.34	1.06	4.44	0.00	−3.38	1.06	−4.44
60	−60	−1.17	2.30	2.08	0.00	0.22	2.30	−2.08
60	−60	0.05	−0.29	−0.21	0.00	−0.09	−0.29	0.21
		16.42%	**10.19%**			**14.34%**	**10.19%**	**4.15%**

Based on the information provided, calculate the contribution to tracking risk of each ETF.

Solution:

Because the relative contribution to return of the active investment in the S&P 500 is 0, the standard deviation of this active allocation is 0; hence, the contribution to tracking risk is 0. Exhibit 29 shows that the contribution of active investment in an ETF that tracks the S&P MidCap 400 Index is equal to the total active return (R_A). If we read the first row of Exhibit 29, we verify that the contribution of active investment in the ETF that tracks the S&P MidCap 400 Index is −3.18%, which is exactly the active return, −3.18%. Thus, the allocation to the S&P MidCap 400 ETF explains the tracking risk. Tracking risk attribution for this example is summarized in the following table.

	$\Sigma[dw_i(r_i - R_B)]$	$\rho(dw_i(r_i - R_B) ; R_A)$	$C_i(TR)$
S&P 500	0.000%	0.000	0.000%
S&P MidCap 400	3.159	1.000	3.159
			3.159%

5.1.3 *Section Summary*

- Marginal contribution to risk measures the variation of standard deviation caused by a small change in weights.
- Marginal contribution to tracking risk measures the variation of standard deviation of active returns caused by a small change in active weights.
- Contribution to risk is equal to weight times marginal contribution when allocation remains constant over the period. When allocation changes over the period, the contribution to risk is calculated by using historical contribution to return.
- Contribution to tracking risk is equal to active weight times marginal contribution when active allocation remains constant over the period. When active allocation changes, the contribution to tracking risk is calculated by using historical active contribution to return.
- Active contributions to return are either absolute or relative. Tracking risk attribution gives more intuitive results when relative contributions are used.
- Attribution models that decompose standard deviation are appropriate for investment decision processes that seek absolute return through active allocation and stock picking (top-down) or through stock picking alone (bottom-up).
- Attribution models that decompose tracking risk are appropriate for investment decision processes that seek excess return relative to a benchmark through active allocation and/or stock picking.

5.2 Top-Down Risk Attribution

In this section, we consider top-down investment processes that consist of allocation decisions and then stock picking. Our objective is to measure the contribution of each decision in this two-step process. When we analyze active return, the most frequent models are Brinson style models—that is, models that isolate an allocation and a selection effect. An interaction effect, as well as currency effects, can be added to the model. In such processes, managers add value through allocation decisions (by instrument classes, sectors, geographic zones, etc.) and, within each class, through stock picking. The objective is to deliver active return while keeping the tracking risk within some predefined restrictions. As an example, a mandate might ask for an excess return of 200 basis points over the benchmark with a tracking risk that does not exceed 300 basis points. Return attribution models decompose the active return to identify the contributions of allocation and selection decisions, while risk attribution models measure the contributions of these active management decisions to the tracking risk. In section 5.1, we reviewed models that decompose standard deviation of return and tracking risk. In section 5.2, we will attribute tracking risk to allocation and selection decisions.

For a top-down, two-step process, the active return over period t is the sum of allocation and selection:

$$R_A = \sum_{i=1}^{N}(A_i + S_i)$$

where the allocation effect is

$$A_i = \left(w_i^P - w_i^B\right)\left(R_i^B - R_B\right)$$

and the selection effect is

$$S_i = w_i^P\left(R_i^P - R_i^B\right)$$

Tracking risk is the standard deviation of the active return:[34]

$$\text{TR} = \sigma(R_A) = \sum_{i=1}^{N}\left[\sigma(A_i)\times\rho(A_i;R_A) + \sigma(S_i)\times\rho(S_i;R_A)\right] \quad (22)$$

This expression shows that the sources of tracking risk are the volatilities of allocation and selection as well as their respective correlations with the active return. Let us suppose that the manager is passive in stock picking and active in allocation. Active returns are totally explained by allocation decisions; hence, the correlation of the allocation effect with active return is one. Tracking risk is equal to the volatility of the allocation effect. Similarly, if the manager is passive in allocation and active in selection, the correlation of selection effect with active return is 1 and the tracking risk is equal to the volatility of the selection effect. For portfolios that are active in both allocation and selection, the tracking risk will depend on the volatilities of both effects and on the correlations of these effects with the active return.

EXAMPLE 21

A Top-Down Manager

The benchmark of a portfolio is invested in bonds (40%) and stocks (60%). Benchmark weights remain constant over the year; hence, the weights are not displayed in Exhibit 30. The manager is active in both allocation and selection. Exhibit 30 displays active returns as well as allocation and selection effects over 12 months.

Exhibit 30 A Top-Down Manager

Portfolio Weights		Portfolio Returns		Benchmark Returns					Allocation		Selection*	
w^P_{Bonds}	w^P_{Eq}	R^P_{Bonds}	R^P_{Eq}	R^B_{Bonds}	R^B_{Eq}	R_P	R_B	R_A	A_{Bonds}	A_{Eq}	S_{Bonds}	S_{Eq}
10	90	−0.8	4.5	0.09	−0.68	3.97	−0.37	4.34	−0.14	−0.09	−0.09	4.66
40	60	1.32	−7.96	0.79	3.79	−4.25	2.59	−6.84	0	0	0.21	−7.05

34 Menchero and Hu (2006).

Exhibit 30 (Continued)

Portfolio Weights		Portfolio Returns		Benchmark Returns					Allocation		Selection*	
w^P_{Bonds}	w^P_{Eq}	R^P_{Bonds}	R^P_{Eq}	R^B_{Bonds}	R^B_{Eq}	R_P	R_B	R_A	A_{Bonds}	A_{Eq}	S_{Bonds}	S_{Eq}
20	80	2.49	3.06	0.03	0.5	2.95	0.31	2.63	0.06	0.04	0.49	2.05
30	70	0.41	–1.57	0.99	3.24	–0.98	2.34	–3.32	0.14	0.09	–0.17	–3.37
10	90	1.4	5.63	0.26	6.92	5.21	4.26	0.95	1.2	0.8	0.11	–1.16
20	80	–0.9	0.88	0.41	–0.51	0.52	–0.14	0.67	–0.11	–0.07	–0.26	1.11
20	80	0.54	9.95	–0.46	–0.97	8.07	–0.77	8.83	–0.06	–0.04	0.2	8.74
20	80	0.29	1.5	0.21	8.16	1.26	4.98	–3.72	0.95	0.64	0.02	–5.33
30	70	1.99	8.34	0.03	–9.58	6.44	–5.74	12.17	–0.58	–0.38	0.59	12.54
40	60	1.06	–6.34	0.55	4.59	–3.38	2.97	–6.35	0	0	0.2	–6.56
40	60	2.3	–1.17	–0.49	–2.45	0.22	–1.67	1.88	0	0	1.12	0.77
40	60	–0.29	0.05	–0.2	1.97	–0.09	1.1	–1.19	0	0	–0.04	–1.15
		10.19	**16.42**	**2.22**	**14.64**	**20.94**	**9.82**	**11.12**	**1.46**	**0.98**	**2.82**	**5.86**

* The smoothing methodologies are not covered in this reading. GRAP chaining methodology is used to calculate 1-year allocation and selection effects.

We verify that allocation and selection effects over the first month are:

$$A_{Bonds} = \left(w^P_{Bonds} - w^B_{Bonds}\right)\left(R^B_{Bonds} - R_B\right)$$
$$= (0.1 - 0.4) \times (0.09 - (-0.37)) = -0.14\%$$

$$A_{Eq} = \left(w^P_{Eq} - w^B_{Eq}\right)\left(R^B_{Eq} - R_B\right) = (0.9 - 0.6) \times (-068 - (-0.37)) = -0.09\%$$

$$S_{Bonds} = w^P_{Bonds} \times \left(R^P_{Bonds} - r^B_{Bonds}\right) = 0.1 \times (-0.8 - 0.09) = -0.09\%$$

$$S_{Eq} = w^P_{Eq} \times \left(R^P_{Eq} - r^B_{Eq}\right) = 0.9 \times (4.5 - (-0.68)) = 4.66\%$$

Effects are calculated every month. To obtain total allocation and selection, we link (chain) monthly effects. Allocation and selection effects are summarized in Exhibit 31, which shows that allocation decisions have added 2.44% over the benchmark return while selection has delivered an excess return of 8.71%. The question that arises is, How much have these decisions contributed to the level of tracking risk? To answer this question, let us first calculate tracking risk and then, using Equation 22, attribute TR to allocation and selection decisions. Tracking risk is the standard deviation of the active return:

$$\text{TR} = \sqrt{\sum_{t=1}^{12} \frac{\left(R_{A,t} - \overline{R}_A\right)^2}{12}} = 5.491\%$$

To attribute TR to allocation and selection, we need first to compute the standard deviation of these effects. Results are summarized below:

Standard Deviation of Allocation and Selection Effects		
	Allocation	**Selection**
Bonds	0.46%	0.37%
Equity	0.31	5.73

Although selection in stocks has delivered an excess return of 5.88%, which is about 50% of the total excess return (11.15%), it has a cost in terms of risk, as the volatility of selection is 5.73%. If the selection effect is highly correlated with the excess return, it means that the selection effect's volatility increases TR almost one-for-one. If the selection effect has a low correlation with the active return, TR will increase by a very small amount even if the selection effect's volatility is high. In this example, we see that the selection effect of equity (Exhibit 31) explains 50% of active return, and a closer look at each month (Exhibit 30) shows that the stock selection effect often has the same sign as the active return. Based on this observation, we expect that the correlation between the selection effect of equity and the active return will be close to 1.

Let us now calculate the correlations between effects and active return. Results are summarized in the following table:

Correlation between Allocation/Selection Effects and Active Returns		
	Allocation	**Selection**
Bonds	−0.40	0.32
Equity	−0.40	0.99

Correlations for the allocation effect are equal because, in this example, we have only two asset classes.[35] Now we have all the data to calculate the contributions of allocation and selection to tracking risk:

$C(A_{Bonds}) = \sigma(A_{Bonds}) \times \rho(A_{Bonds},R_A) = -0.40 \times 0.46\% = -0.18\%$

$C(A_{Eq}) = \sigma(A_{Eq}) \times \rho(A_{Eq},R_A) = -0.40 \times 0.31\% = -0.12\%$

$C(S_{Bonds}) = \sigma(S_{Bonds}) \times \rho(S_{Bonds},R_A) = 0.32 \times 0.37\% = 0.12\%$

$C(S_{Eq}) = \sigma(S_{Eq}) \times \rho(S_{Eq},R_A) = 0.99 \times 5.73\% = 5.68\%$

Let us now compare these results with the volatility of each effect:

	Allocation		**Selection**	
	Volatility	**Contribution**	**Volatility**	**Contribution**
Bonds	0.46%	−0.18%	0.37%	0.12%
Equity	0.31	−0.12	5.73	5.68

These numbers show that although allocation effects are volatile, their contribution to tracking risk is negative; that is, allocation decisions have contributed to lowering the level of TR. Selection effects, especially equity selection decisions, have increased TR.

35 The correlations are equal because the bond weights are known once the weights in stocks are defined. It is the same for returns, as the benchmark return is the weighted sum of the bond and stock returns.

Tracking risk contributions improve the return attribution analysis. Adding contributions to allocation and selection effects gives a better view of the risk–return profile of the active management.

Exhibit 31 Summary

	Returns			Return Attribution		Risk Attribution	
	R_P	R_B	R_A	Allocation	Selection	Allocation	Selection
Bonds	10.19%	2.22%	7.99%	1.46%	2.82%	−0.19%	0.12%
Equity	16.42	14.64	1.80	0.98	5.86	−0.12	5.68
Total	20.94%	9.82%	11.12%	2.44%	8.68%	−0.31%	5.80%

As Exhibit 31 shows, equity selection has a contribution (5.86%) greater than 50% of total active return (11.12%) while it has contributed almost all the selectivity tracking risk (5.68% of 5.80%). Is a selection effect of 5.86% large enough to compensate a 5.68% increase in tracking risk? To answer this question, we should express all numbers in relative terms—that is, as a percentage of the total active return and total tracking risk (5.80% + −0.31% = 5.49%).

Such an analysis reveals that bond selection represents 2.2% (0.12/5.49) of tracking risk for an active return equal to 25.4% (2.82/11.12) of total active return. For equity selection, this percentage is 103.5% (5.68/5.49) of tracking risk for an active return equal to 52.7% (5.86/11.12) of the active return.[36] From a risk return perspective, bond selectivity investment decisions have a better contribution than equity selectivity investment decisions.

5.3 Factor-Based Risk Attribution

Traditional portfolio theory states that investors should be compensated for taking risk; that is, they should capture a risk premium associated with risks that cannot be removed through diversification. While the capital asset pricing model (CAPM) identifies a single return source, the market risk premium, other models—such as the international capital asset pricing model (ICAPM) and arbitrage pricing theory (APT)—allow for multiple return sources or factors. For instance, Fama and French (1992) found empirical evidence that small-cap and value stocks tend to outperform. To capture these premiums, a manager could go long a value index and a small-cap index while shorting a growth index and a large-cap index. Such a strategy is a factor-based investment.

In Section 5.3.1, we will consider absolute portfolio risk and attribute the total risk of the portfolio to each factor exposure. We will also attribute tracking risk to active exposure to each factor. The latter type of analysis, explored in Menchero and Hu (2006), is presented in section 5.3.2.

36 Because the selection has contributed 5.80% to the tracking risk and the allocation has a negative contribution, −0.31%, we obtain a percentage that is more than 100% for the contribution of the selection to the tracking risk.

5.3.1 *Marginal Contribution to Risk*

Let us suppose that the Fama and French (1993) three-factor model explains stock returns. The only sources of return are the market risk premium, the small-cap premium, and the value premium. All other risk factors can be removed through diversification; hence, these factors are not priced on the market.

The Fama–French model is:

$$R_P - R_f = \alpha_P + \beta_{P1} RMRF + \beta_{P2} SMB + \beta_{P3} HML + \varepsilon_P$$

where

R_P and R_f = the return on the portfolio and the risk-free rate of return, respectively

$RMRF$ = the return on a market value–weighted equity index minus the return on one-month Treasury bills

SMB = small minus big (a size factor), the return of a small-cap portfolio minus the return of a large-cap portfolio

HML = high minus low (a value style factor), the return of a high book-to-market portfolio minus the return of a low book-to-market portfolio

Under the assumptions of the model, it is possible to invest in a portfolio that is market neutral ($\beta_{iM} = 0$), that is not sensitive to the value factor ($\beta_{iHML} = 0$), and that captures the risk premium associated with small caps ($\beta_{iSMB} > 0$). If the portfolio is well diversified, the volatility of the portfolio is $\sigma_P = \beta_{PSMB} \times \sigma_{SMB}$.

However, most portfolios are not exposed to a single source of risk, and it is of interest to decompose the total volatility of the portfolio into the contributions of the different risk factors. Moreover, if the manager selects some specific stocks to deliver alpha, he or she bears another risk, asset-specific risk.

The decomposition of portfolio volatility into the contributions of systematic factors and specific risk is given by the following equation:

$$\sigma_P = \frac{\sigma^2\left(\sum_{i=1}^{N} w_i R_i\right)}{\sigma_P}$$

As we assume that asset returns, R_i, have three factors in common (the Fama–French factors), the portfolio volatility is:

$$\sigma_P = \frac{\sigma^2\left(\sum_{i=1}^{N} w_i \left[\alpha_i + \beta_{iM} R_{RMRF} + \beta_{iSMB} R_{SMB} + \beta_{iHML} R_{HML} + \varepsilon_i\right]\right)}{\sigma_P}$$

It is then possible to develop the variance to obtain an expression of the portfolio volatility as a function of the factors' volatilities, the sensitivity of each asset to these factors, and the correlation of the portfolio with each factor:

$$\begin{aligned}\sigma_P = {} & \sum_{i=1}^{N} w_i \beta_{i,M} \sigma_M \rho_{M,P} + \sum_{i=1}^{N} w_i \beta_{i,SMB} \sigma_{SMB} \rho_{SMB,P} \\ & + \sum_{i=1}^{N} w_i \beta_{i,HML} \sigma_{HML} \rho_{HML,P} + \frac{1}{\sigma_P} \sum_{i=1}^{N} w_i^2 \sigma_\varepsilon^2\end{aligned} \quad (23)$$

Let us note that the sensitivity of the portfolio to factor $K = M$, SMB, or HML is the weighted sum of the securities' sensitivities; that is,

$$\beta_{P,K} = \sum_{i=1}^{N} w_i \beta_{i,K}$$

which gives

$$\sigma_P = \beta_{P,M}\sigma_M\rho_{M,P} + \beta_{P,SMB}\sigma_{SMB}\rho_{SMB,P} + \beta_{P,HML}\sigma_{HML}\rho_{HML,P} + \frac{1}{\sigma_P}\sum_{i=1}^{N} w_i^2\sigma_\varepsilon^2 \quad (24)$$

where

σ_M, σ_{SMB}, and σ_{HML} = volatility of the market, size, and style factors return

$\rho_{M,P}$, $\rho_{SMB,P}$, and $\rho_{HML,P}$ = correlation between the market, size, and style factors return and the portfolio

$\beta_{i,M} \times \sigma_M \times \rho_{M,P}$ = marginal contribution of the market risk factor

$\beta_{i,SMB} \times \sigma_{SMB} \times \rho_{SMB,P}$ = marginal contribution of the size factor

$\beta_{i,HML} \times \sigma_{HML} \times \rho_{HML,P}$ = marginal contribution of the style factor

$\frac{1}{\sigma_P} \times \sum_{i=1}^{N} w_i^2 \times \sigma_\varepsilon^2$ = specific risk contribution

Equation 24 shows that the portfolio volatility is the sum of the contributions for each factor plus a specific term.

EXAMPLE 22

A Value Investment Style

Let us consider a well-diversified portfolio. The portfolio invests in different ETFs that represent investments in medium-size companies with different book-to-market ratios. Each ETF belongs to a specific book-to-market bucket. Exhibit 32 gives the sensitivity of each ETF to the three factors—the market factor (*M*), the size factor (*SMB*), and the style factor (*HML*). ETFs are given in order from the lowest book-to-market bucket to the highest one. Let us consider a portfolio that is short –80% in the ETF representing investments with a low book-to-market ratio and that invests 10%, 30%, 20%, and 40% in the other book-to-market ratio buckets. The sensitivity of this portfolio to each factor is given by the weighted sum of the ETFs' sensitivities. For example, the portfolio sensitivity to the market factor is:

$$\beta_{PM} = \sum_{i=1}^{5} w_i\beta_{iM} = -0.8\times1.1 + 0.1\times1.02 + 0.3\times0.98 + 0.2\times0.97 + 0.4\times1.07$$
$$= 0.138$$

Exhibit 32 Sensitivity of Each ETF to Each Factor

	Book-to-Market					
	Low	2	3	4	High	Portfolio
α	–0.08	0.04	0	0.06	0.07	**0.108**
β_M	1.1	1.02	0.98	0.97	1.07	**0.138**
β_{SMB}	0.75	0.63	0.59	0.47	0.64	**–0.01**
β_{HML}	–0.39	0.03	0.32	0.49	0.68	**0.781**

The portfolio is characterized by sensitivities to the market, size, and style factors of 0.138, –0.01, and 0.781, respectively. This portfolio has a clear bias toward the value factor and is neutral toward the size factor.

Let us consider the following correlation matrix between the return factors:[37]

Exhibit 33 Correlation Matrix

	M	SMB	HML
M	1	0.32	–0.37
SMB	0.32	1	–0.1
HML	–0.37	–0.1	1

The volatilities of the return factors are shows in Exhibit 34:

Exhibit 34 Factor Volatility

M	16.33%
SMB	15.44
HML	13.11

Let us assume that the correlations between each factor and the portfolio return are given:[38] $\rho_{M,P} = -0.164$, $\rho_{SMB,P} = -0.047$, and $\rho_{HML,P} = 0.977$. The coefficients show a strong bias toward the value style, as the correlation is close to 1. The marginal contribution of each ETF and each factor is given by $\beta_{i,K} \times \sigma_K \times \rho_{K,P}$; *K* represents a factor (*M*, *SMB*, or *HML*). All coefficients of sensitivity ($\beta_{i,K}$), correlation, and factor volatility are given in Exhibits 32, 33, and 34, respectively. The marginal contribution of the market factor of an ETF that has a low book-to-market ratio is the product of that ETF's market beta, the market's standard deviation of returns, and the ETF's correlation with the market factor: $1.1 \times 16.33\% \times (-0.164) = -2.95\%$. Exhibit 35 gives all marginal contributions of all factors and ETFs.

Exhibit 35 Marginal Contributions

	Low	2	3	4	High
M	–2.95%	–2.74%	–2.63%	–2.60%	–2.87%
SMB	–0.55	–0.46	–0.43	–0.34	–0.47
HML	–5.00	0.38	4.10	6.28	8.71

Because the contributions of each ETF and each factor are equal to the marginal contribution times the weight invested in each ETF, we are now able to calculate the contribution of each factor to the portfolio volatility. The contribution of the market factor to the portfolio volatility is $-0.37 = -0.8(-2.95) + 0.1(-2.74) + 0.3(-2.63) + 0.2(-2.60) + 0.4(-2.87)$.

37 Fama and French (1996, p. 73).

38 Although we assume that these correlations are given, it is possible to calculate these correlations.

Exhibit 36 Contribution of Each Risk Factor

	Low	2	3	4	High	Portfolio
M	2.36%	−0.27%	−0.79%	−0.52%	−1.15%	−0.37%
SMB	0.44	−0.05	−0.13	−0.07	−0.19	0.01
HML	4.00	0.04	1.23	1.26	3.48	10.00

The market factor contribution of the ETF that has a low book-to-market ratio is 2.36% = (−0.80) × (−2.95%).

The analysis shows that the main contributor to the total volatility of the portfolio is the style factor. A more detailed analysis shows that the style factor explains most of the portfolio volatility. Moreover, the bias toward the value factor, obtained by shorting the low-book-to-market ETF and investing 40% in the high-book-to-market ETF, is highlighted in the first and last columns of Exhibit 36.

Although all calculations have been realized within the Fama and French three-factor framework, all results are generalized to *N*-factor models.

5.3.2 *Marginal Contribution to Tracking Risk*

Actively managed equity portfolios deviate from their benchmarks by overweighting (underweighting) either particular sectors or individual securities within sectors. Viewed in terms of risk factors, actively managed portfolios take different-from-benchmark exposures to risk factors such as size, style, and market. Both approaches to active management aim at delivering active returns while keeping risk within acceptable limits. Although models such as those presented in sections 5.1.2 and 5.2 are useful for the former approach, the latter approach calls for models that identify the contributions of taking active exposures to risk factors. In this section, we consider a portfolio that holds constant active exposure to risk factors. We begin with the expression of the active risk within the Fama–French three-factor model framework.

$$\sigma(R_A) = \beta_{A,M}\sigma_M\rho_{M,A} + \beta_{A,SMB}\sigma_{SMB}\rho_{SMB,A} + \beta_{A,HML}\sigma_{HML}\rho_{HML,A} + \frac{1}{\sigma_P}\sum_{i=1}^{N}\left(w_i^A\right)^2\sigma_\varepsilon^2 \quad (25)$$

where

$\beta_{A,M} = \sum_{i=1}^{N} w_i^A \beta_{i,M}$ = the active exposure to the market factor

$\beta_{A,SMB}$ and $\beta_{A,HML}$ = the active exposures to the size and style factors

σ_M, σ_{SMB}, and σ_{HML} = the volatilities of the market, size, and style factors

$\rho_{M,A}$, $\rho_{SMB,A}$, and $\rho_{HML,A}$ = the correlations between the market, size, and style factors and the active return

w_i^A = the active weights

σ_ε^2 = the specific variance

$\sigma_M\rho_{M,A}$, $\sigma_{SMB}\rho_{SMB,A}$, and $\sigma_{HML}\rho_{HML,A}$ = the active risk sensitivities for the market, size, and style factors

The first three terms of Equation 25 represent the factor risk contribution to tracking risk (FR_A), and the last term is the specific risk contribution (SR_A). Therefore, the tracking risk can be expressed as

$$\sigma(R_A) = FR_A + SR_A \tag{26}$$

Each term of the factor risk contribution corresponds to the active exposure to a factor times the active sensitivity for the same factor.

To calculate the active risk sensitivity for each factor, we begin with the standard expression for the tracking risk within a factor model:

$$\sigma(R_A) = \frac{1}{\sigma(R_A)} \sum_{k,l} \beta_{A,K} \sigma_{kl} \beta_{A,l} + \frac{1}{\sigma(R_A)} \sum_i \left(w_i^A\right)^2 \sigma_\varepsilon^2 \tag{27}$$

$\sigma_{K,L}$ is the covariance between the factors K and L. For an explanation of how the first summation in Equation 27 is to be calculated, see the appendix to this reading.

The active risk sensitivity, Γ_K^A, for the factor K is given by

$$\Gamma_K^A = \sigma_K \rho_{K,A} = \frac{1}{\sigma(R_A)} \sum_L \beta_{A,L} \sigma_{KL} \tag{28}$$

Using these equations, it is then possible to decompose the tracking risk and quantify the contribution of each factor to the actual level of the tracking risk. The following example illustrates tracking risk attribution.

EXAMPLE 23

Active Value Investment Style

Let us consider a portfolio invested in five ETFs similar to those presented in Example 22. The benchmark is also invested in the five ETFs. Weights and active weights are as follows:

	Low	2	3	4	High
Portfolio	40%	30%	10%	20%	0%
Benchmark	10	10	10	20	50
Active weights	30	20	0	0	-50

Let us assume that the specific variance is zero—in other words, that the portfolio is perfectly diversified. The tracking error comes exclusively from the factor risk.

The coefficients of the Fama–French three-factor model are as follows:

	Book-to-Market				
	Low	**2**	**3**	**4**	**High**
α	−0.08	0.04	0	0.06	0.07
β_M	1.1	1.02	0.98	0.97	1.07
β_{SMB}	0.75	0.63	0.59	0.47	0.64
β_{HML}	−0.39	0.03	0.32	0.49	0.68

Source: Fama and French (1996)

It is now possible to calculate the active exposures to the market, size, and style factors using the sum of the active weights and factor betas.

$$\beta_{A,M} = \sum_{i=1}^{N} w_i^A \beta_{i,M} = 0.3(1.1) + 0.2(1.02) + 0(0.98) + 0(0.97) - 0.5(1.07)$$
$$= -0.001$$

$$\beta_{A,SMB} = 0.3(0.75) + 0.2(0.63) + 0(0.59) + 0(0.47) - 0.5(0.64) = 0.031$$
$$\beta_{A,HML} = 0.3(-0.39) + 0.2(0.03) + 0(0.32) + 0(0.49) - 0.5(0.68) = -0.451$$

These results show that the portfolio differs from the benchmark essentially by its active exposure to the style factor. This is a direct consequence of the active weights, as the portfolio is mainly invested in ETFs that have low book-to-market ratios while the benchmark is invested in high-book-to-market ETFs.

Tracking risk

To calculate the tracking risk, we need the correlation between the risk factors as well as the volatility of these factors. The correlation matrix between the return factors[39] is as follows:

	M	***SMB***	***HML***
M	1	0.32	−0.37
SMB	0.32	1	−0.1
HML	−0.37	−0.1	1

And the volatilities of the return factors are:

M	16.33%
SMB	15.44
HML	13.11

As the portfolio and the benchmark are well diversified, it is possible to calculate the tracking risk using Equation 27 with the specific term equal to 0:

$$\sigma^2(R_A) = \sum_{i,j} \beta_{A,i}\sigma_{ij}\beta_{A,j}$$

where $i,j = M, SMB$, and HML and σ_{ij} is the covariance between the factors. The covariance matrix is as follows:

	M	***SMB***	***HML***
M	$(0.1633)^2$ = 0.02667	0.32 × 0.1633 × 0.1544 = 0.0807	0.37 × 0.1633 × .1311 = −0.00792
SMB	0.0807	$(0.1544)^2$ = 0.02384	−0.1 × 0.1544 × .1311 = −0.00202
HML	−0.00792	−0.00202	$(0.1311)^2$ = 0.01719

39 We use figures from Fama and French (1996, p. 73) for this example.

It is now possible to calculate the tracking risk of the portfolio. The calculation involving summation over two variables is explained in the appendix.[40]

$$\sigma^2(R_A) = \sum_{i,j} \beta_{A,i}\sigma_{ij}\beta_{A,j}$$

$$= [(-0.001)(0.02667) + (0.031)(0.0807) + (-0.451)(-0.00792)](-0.001) + [(-0.001)(0.0807) + (0.031)(0.02384) + (-0.451)(-0.00202)](0.031) + [(-0.001)(-0.00792) + (0.031)(-0.00202) + (-0.451)(0.01719)](-0.451) = 0.003568$$

Tracking risk is $\sigma(R_A) = \sqrt{0.003568} = 5.97\%$.

Tracking risk attribution

The objective of tracking risk attribution is to quantify the contribution to the tracking risk of each risk factor. In our example, these risk factors are the market, size, and style factors. The first step is to calculate the active risk sensitivity for each factor using Equation 28:

$$\Gamma_M^A = \frac{1}{0.0597}(-0.001 \times 0.02667 + 0.031 \times 0.0807 - 0.451 \times -0.00792) = 0.06355$$

$$\Gamma_{SMB}^A = \frac{1}{0.0597}(-0.001 \times 0.0807 + 0.031 \times 0.02384 - 0.451 \times -0.00202) = 0.02752$$

$$\Gamma_{SMB}^A = \frac{1}{0.0597}(-0.001 \times -0.00792 + 0.031 \times -0.00202 - 0.451 \times 0.01719) = -0.1307$$

It is now straightforward to calculate the contributions of the market, size, and style factors to the tracking risk.

$$\text{Market} = \beta_{A,M} \times \Gamma_M^A = -0.001 \times 0.06355 = -0.01\%$$

$$\text{Size} = \beta_{A,SMB} \times \Gamma_{SMB}^A = 0.031 \times 0.02752 = 0.09\%$$

$$\text{Style} = \beta_{A,HML} \times \Gamma_{HML}^A = -0.451 \times (-0.1307) = 5.89\%$$

These results show that the style factor explains almost 100% of the tracking risk, which is what we expected, as the portfolio is tilted toward low book-to-market ratios whereas the benchmark is tilted toward high book-to-market ratios.

---

40 The solution shown, 0.003568, is based on full precision. For those with a background in matrix algebra, the calculation involved can also be represented using matrix algebra as:

$$\begin{pmatrix} -0.001 & 0.031 & -0.451 \end{pmatrix} \begin{pmatrix} 0.02667 & 0.0807 & -0.00792 \\ 0.0807 & 0.02384 & -0.00202 \\ -0.00792 & -0.00202 & 0.01719 \end{pmatrix} \begin{pmatrix} -0.001 \\ 0.031 \\ -0.451 \end{pmatrix}$$

CONCLUSIONS AND SUMMARY

6

This reading has explored the critical topic of market risk. Among the observations made in the course of the reading are the following:

- Investment risk can be categorized as non-financial or financial risk. Financial risks are those due to external capital markets, whereas non-financial risks include operational, model, settlement, regulatory, legal/contract, tax, sovereign/political, and accounting risks.
- Financial risks are further delineated into market risk, credit risk, and liquidity risk. Evaluation of risk and return is part of the feedback loop that provides input into the investment management process, as well as into manager selection and retention decisions.
- The objective of risk measurement and risk attribution is to enable the understanding of risks involved in the investment under evaluation.
- *Ex ante* risk is the return variability anticipated for the future, whereas *ex post* risk refers to past variability in investment returns. Stand-alone risk measures the variability of an asset's return by itself, and portfolio risk measures the variability of a collection of assets. Stand-alone risk can be decomposed into idiosyncratic risk, that from unexpected changes in company-specific factors, and systematic risk, that from the macroeconomy.
- Absolute risk measures return variability without comparison to a benchmark, whereas relative risk utilizes a reference point. Symmetric risk refers to all variability, whereas asymmetric risk is most often used to measure the part of variability reflecting losses.
- A frequency distribution can be used to summarize investment performance by placing periodic returns into intervals. The resulting graphical illustration is referred to as a histogram.
- The arithmetic mean return is the average return, and the median return is the "middlemost" value. Positive skewness pertains to the presence of extreme positive values, whereas negative skewness pertains to the presence of extreme negative values. Downside risk is the potential for a loss, and tail risk is the possibility of extreme losses.
- Common measures of risk are the variance, standard deviation, mean absolute deviation, and tracking risk. The variance is the average of squared deviations from the mean, and the standard deviation is the square root of the variance. The mean absolute deviation is the arithmetic average of the absolute value of deviations from the mean, and tracking risk is the standard deviation of return differences from a benchmark.
- The covariance is a measure of how any two assets move together over time, and the correlation is its standardized form, bounded by minus one and plus one.
- Beta measures how an asset's returns move with the overall market and is the corresponding covariance divided by the variance in market returns.
- Asymmetric risk definitions that quantify only downside risk include the semi-variance, target semi-variance, semi-standard deviation, and target semi-standard deviation.
- The semi-variance is similar to the variance except that only deviations below the mean are calculated. The target semi-variance measures only deviations below a specified target return. The semi-standard deviation is the square root of the semi-variance, and the target semi-standard deviation is the square root of the target semi-variance.

- Drawdown risk measures capture various aspects of peak-to-trough value declines. Common measures include drawdown, maximum drawdown, and largest individual drawdown.
- Drawdown risk measures are especially common in analyzing hedge funds, because incentive fees are typically not payable to management when fund value is below the prior peak value.
- Value at risk is an estimate of minimum expected loss, calculated with a given time horizon and level of confidence. Stress testing is a process that estimates the expected impact on a portfolio of changes in various parameters.
- Three methods of estimating value at risk are (1) analytical (sometimes called variance–covariance or parametric), (2) historical, and (3) Monte Carlo. Each method has different data requirements and assumptions that affect the calculation of the estimated risk.
- Return attribution models decompose the excess return to identify the contribution of allocation and selection decisions, while risk attribution models measure the contribution of these active management decisions to the tracking risk.
- Risk attribution models must reflect the different investment decision processes. In attributing risk, it is convenient to classify the different models in two dimensions: absolute versus relative and factor exposures versus an allocation method.
- Risk attribution models that decompose standard deviation (tracking risk) are appropriate for investment decision processes that aim at delivering absolute return (active return).
- For absolute mandates, marginal contribution to volatility gives the variation of standard deviation of returns caused by a small change in weights. Volatility of asset (asset class) returns, as well as their correlation with portfolio returns, explains the level of marginal contribution.
- Factor-based risk attribution explains the active exposures to style factors that have contributed to the level of the tracking risk.
- For benchmark mandates, risk attribution shows that the sources of tracking risk are the volatility of the allocation and selection and their respective correlations with the active return.

OPTIONAL SEGMENT

APPENDIX TO RISK MEASUREMENT AND RISK ATTRIBUTION

This appendix[41] explains and illustrates background concepts for the Return Attribution and Risk Measurement and Risk Attribution readings.

1 Mathematical Notation

The summation operator Σ was explained in the Appendix to Return Measurement. This section covers double summation.

1.1 Double Summation

The summation operator, represented by the Greek letter sigma, Σ, is used to represent addition (summation) of variables. Thus,

$$\sum_{i=1}^{3} x_i = x_1 + x_2 + x_3$$

Consider the following double summation:

$$\sum_{i=1}^{3}\sum_{j=1}^{3} x_i y_j = x_1(y_1 + y_2 + y_3) + x_2(y_1 + y_2 + y_3) + x_3(y_1 + y_2 + y_3)$$

The operators direct you to set the value of x to x_1 and then multiply x_1 by the sum of the y's indicated by the inner summation sign; then add to that x_2 multiplied by the sum of the y's; then add to that x_3 multiplied by the sum of the y's. Another more compact notation for this double summation is:

$$\sum_{i,j=1}^{3} x_i y_j = (x_1 + x_2 + x_3)(y_1 + y_2 + y_3)$$

2 Describing Returns

The following subsections review several basic concepts of descriptive statistics.

2.1 Return as a Random Variable

A random variable is a quantity whose numerical value is determined by a chance event, that is, the value of the random variable is uncertain. Random variables contrast with constants, numerical quantities with certain or fixed values. The return on a risky security is a random variable. Although an investor may be uncertain about the specific return for the risky security it may be possible to assign a probability to a specific return outcome. Exhibit 1 provides an example of a discrete random variable (*discrete* means the possible outcomes are countable).

Exhibit 1 Probability Distribution of Security Returns

Security Return	Probability
15%	0.10
9%	0.20

(continued)

41 Prepared by Murli Rajan, CFA. Rachel Siegel, CFA, assisted in editing.

Exhibit 1 (Continued)

Security Return	Probability
5%	0.55
–6%	0.15

Note that each outcome for the random variable, security return, has a specific probability of occurrence; for example there is a 10% chance that the security return will be 15%.

2.2 Mean and Median of a Set of Returns

Data may be summarized using measures of central tendency such as the mean and median. Measures of central tendency are intended to describe typical or common values for the random variable. The mean has several variations, including the arithmetic mean and the geometric mean. Calculations of these statistics are illustrated using the data in Exhibit 2.

Exhibit 2 Time Series of Returns

Year	Return
2006	15.65%
2007	12.53%
2008	1.50%
2009	3.70%
2010	11.46%
2011	18.57%

EXAMPLE 1

Calculating an Arithmetic Mean

The arithmetic mean of a set of values is the sum of the values divided by the number of values summed. The arithmetic mean (average) of the return series presented in Exhibit 2—the arithmetic mean return—is calculated as follows:

$$\text{Arithmetic Mean Return} = \frac{\sum_{t=1}^{6} R_t}{T}$$

where R_t is the return for each year and T is the number of years of data available.

$$\text{Arithmetic Mean Return} = \frac{15.65\% + 12.53\% + 1.5\% + 3.7\% + 11.46\% + 18.57\%}{6}$$

$$= 10.57\%$$

EXAMPLE 2

Calculating a Geometric Mean

The geometric mean (average) of the return series presented in Exhibit 2 is calculated as follows:

$$\text{Geometric Mean Return} = \left[\prod_{t=1}^{6}(1 + R_t)\right]^{1'T} - 1$$

where R_t is the return for each year and T is the number of years of data available. Representing the annual returns in decimal form (i.e., 15.65% is 0.1565 in decimal form), the geometric mean return is:

$$\begin{aligned}\text{Geometric Mean Return} &= [1.1565 \times 1.1253 \times 1.015 \times 1.037 \times 1.1146 \times 1.1857]^{1/6} \\ &\quad - 1 \\ &= [1.8103]^{1/6} - 1 = 0.1040 = 10.4\%\end{aligned}$$

EXAMPLE 3

Calculating the Median

The median is the middle term in a time series after the series has been sorted into ascending or descending order. Exhibit 3 shows the data from Exhibit 2 after the series has been sorted into descending order.

Exhibit 3 Data from Exhibit 2 Sorted in Descending Order

Return
18.57%
15.65%
12.53%
11.46%
3.70%
1.50%

When a series has an odd number of data points, the middle term is readily located. When a series has an even number of data points, by convention the median is calculated as the average of the $n/2$ and the $(n+2)/2$ terms, i.e., as an average of the values of the two middlemost data points. In Exhibit 3, the $n/2$ term is the 3rd term, 12.53%. The $(n+2)/2$ is the 4th term, 11.46%. The average of these two terms is the median, 12.00%.

2.3 Normal Distribution

Until now we have been discussing discrete random variables for which there are a fixed or countable number of possible outcomes. In contrast, a continuous random variable has an infinite number of possible outcomes. Continuous random variables may be described by one of a number of continuous probability distributions such as the uniform distribution, the normal distribution, or the lognormal distribution. In finance, one of the most commonly used distributions is the normal distribution. For example, the variance–covariance (or analytical) version of the well-known risk metric Value at Risk (VaR) assumes security returns follow a normal distribution.

The univariate normal distribution is symmetric, bell-shaped, and completely described by its mean and variance (or standard deviation). Exhibit 4 depicts two normal distributions, both with an underlying mean, μ, of 0; one has an underlying standard deviation, σ, of 1 and another has an underlying standard deviation of 2.[42]

Exhibit 4 Normal Distribution

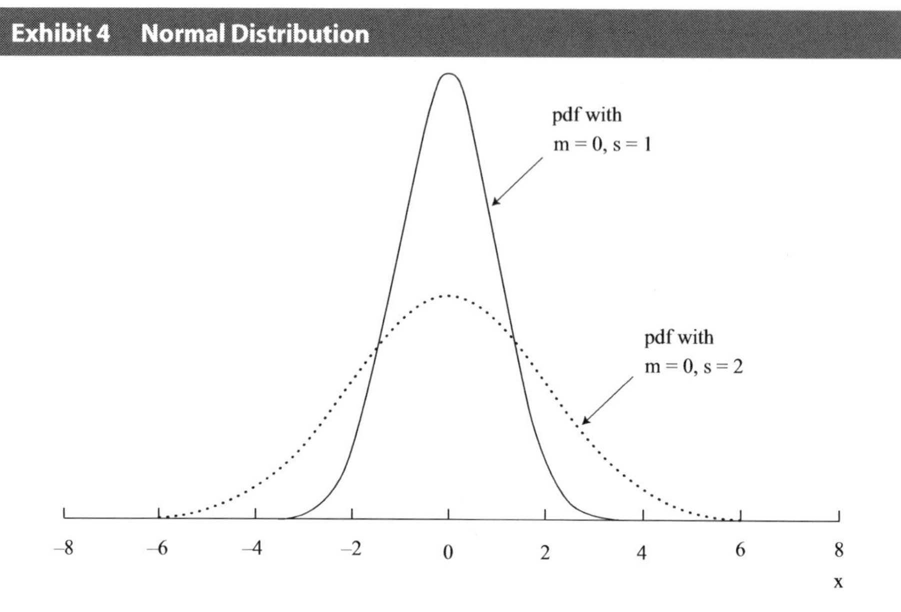

If the security return follows a normal distribution it is possible state that, roughly speaking, 68% of observed returns will be within one standard deviation of the mean, that is, the mean ± 1 standard deviation; 95% of observed returns will be within two standard deviations of the mean return;[43] and 99% of observed returns will be within three standard deviations of the mean.[44] Here, the "mean" refers to the underlying or population mean, taking into account all possible values of the random variable.

2.4 Confidence Intervals

A confidence interval is a range of possible values for a parameter for which one can assert with a given probability—called the degree of confidence—that the interval will contain the parameter. For example, assume a normally distributed random variable with a mean of 7% and standard deviation of 3%. The interval defined by $\mu \pm 2\sigma = 7\% \pm (2)(3\%)$ or 7% ± 6%: an interval running from 1% to 13%. With 95% confidence—only a 5% chance of being wrong—the interval from 1% to 13% contains the observed return. There is a 2.5% (5%/2) chance that the return will be below 1%, in the left tail, and a 2.5% chance that the return will be above 13%, in the right tail.

Note here the "±." Sometimes, only one side or "tail" of the "bell" is of interest. In that case, then only μ + a multiple of σ (the right tail), or μ – a multiple of σ (the left tail) is relevant. For example, VaR is concerned with downside (left-tail) risk. Suppose the stated distribution describes monthly returns on a portfolio. Then the point 7%

42 In the exhibit, "pdf" stands for probability distribution function.

43 More precisely, 1.96 standard deviations.

44 More precisely, 2.58 standard deviations.

– (2)(3%) = 1% would define 5%/2 = 2.5% monthly VaR or, stated another way, monthly VaR with 97.5% confidence. The interpretation is that there is a 2.5% chance that the portfolio will return 1% or less in a given month.

3 Regression

The following sections introduce regression analysis.

3.1 Linear Regression with One Independent Variable

Linear regression with one independent variable is a statistical modeling technique that can be used to estimate the relation between two variables. Specifically, it can be used to examine the extent to which one variable, the independent variable, can be used to predict the value of a second variable, the dependent variable. It is common to represent the dependent variable as the Y variable and the independent variable as the X variable. The linear regression equation takes the following general form:

$$Y = \alpha + \beta X + \varepsilon$$

where:

α = the intercept term and is an estimate of the value of the dependent variable when the value of the independent variable is zero

β = the slope or regression coefficient and indicates the amount by which the dependent variable changes for a one-unit change in the independent variable

ε = the error term and is the portion of the dependent variable that is not explained by the independent variable

Note that in practical terms the actual values of the parameters of the regression are unknown, the parameters are always estimated with some degree of error. This will be illustrated later in the appendix. The general form of the estimated regression is:

$$\hat{Y} = \hat{\alpha} + \hat{\beta} X$$

where $\hat{\alpha}$ and $\hat{\beta}$ are the estimated parameter values and $\hat{Y}$ is the predicted value of Y. For example, suppose we estimate that $\hat{Y} = 2.0 + 1.5X$. If $X = 3$ then the predicted value of Y is 2.0 + 1.5(3) = 6.5.

Regression analysis is used to calculate the beta of a stock, a widely known measure of the risk of a stock. Example 4 provides an example of the estimation of the beta of the stock of the UK corporation Marks and Spenser (MKS).

EXAMPLE 4

Estimating the beta of Marks and Spenser shares

The beta of MKS is estimated by regressing the stock's monthly returns on the monthly returns for the FTSE All Shares Index (FTAS). The regression equation is:

$$R_{MKS} = \alpha + \beta R_{FTAS} + \varepsilon$$

For the regression based on 36 months of return data from 1 July 2009 to 30 June 2012 the estimated regression equation is:

$$\hat{R}_{MKS} = -0.0049 + 1.0432\hat{R}_{FTAS}$$

The intercept term is –0.0049 or –0.49%. This indicates that even if the monthly return for the FTAS is zero, the monthly return on MKS is expected to be –0.49%. This equation also has a slope or beta coefficient of 1.0432 indicating that a 1% increase in FTAS returns will result in a 1.0432% increase in MKS returns.

Note that the estimated parameter values, $\hat{\alpha}$ and $\hat{\beta}$, are dependent on the values of the dependent and independent variables for the time period selected. To illustrate, consider the results of a similar regression run on data for the period 1 June 2006 to 1 May 2009:

$$\hat{R}_{MKS} = -0.0086 + 0.7566\hat{R}_{FTAS}$$

In this regression, the intercept term is –0.86% and the slope coefficient is 0.7566. That is, if the monthly return in FTAS is zero, the return on MKS is –0.86%, and a 1% change in the return on FTAS will result in a 0.7566% change in the return on MKS. Using data for different periods results in different estimates for the parameter values $\hat{\alpha}$ and $\hat{\beta}$. This is what we mean when we say that the parameter values are estimated with some degree of error.

3.2 Multiple Linear Regression with Two Independent Variables

When two or more independent variables are used to predict a dependent variable, the regression model is referred to as a multiple linear regression. A multiple linear regression with two independent variables takes the general form:

$$Y = \alpha + \beta_1 X_1 + \beta_2 X_2 + \varepsilon$$

The intercept term is α and β_1 and β_2 are slope coefficients or partial regression coefficients. The partial regression coefficient β_1 indicates the effect on the dependent variable Y of a one-unit change in the independent variable X_1 holding all other independent variables constant, in this case holding X_2 constant. Similarly, the partial regression coefficient β_2 indicates the effect on the dependent variable Y of a one-unit change in the independent variable X_2 holding X_1 constant. As the parameters must be estimated, the estimated regression equation is:

$$\hat{Y} = \hat{\alpha} + \hat{\beta}_1 X_1 + \hat{\beta}_2 X_2$$

EXAMPLE 5

Multiple Regression of Marks and Spenser on FTSE All Share and FTSE 350 Retail Indexes

The following regression is estimated using 36 months of return data for MKS, FTAS, and the FTSE 350 Retail Index (FTRT).

$$R_{MKS} = \alpha + \beta_{FTAS}R_{FTAS} + \beta_{FTRT}R_{FTRT} + \varepsilon$$

The estimated regression using data for the period 1 July 2009 to 30 June 2012 is:

$$R_{MKS} = -0.0049 + 1.0432R_{FTAS} + 0.9334R_{FTRT}$$

The value of the intercept is –0.0049 indicating that if the values of R_{FTAS} and R_{FTRT} were both zero, R_{MKS} would be –0.49%. The partial regression coefficient β_{FTAS} is 1.0432 indicating that if R_{FTAS} were to increase by 1%, R_{MKS} could be expected to increase by 1.0432%, holding the value of R_{FTRT} constant. The interpretation of partial regression coefficient β_{FTRT} is similar. If R_{FTRT} were to increase by 1%, R_{MKS} could be expected to increase by 0.9334%, holding the value of R_{FTAS} constant.

4 Equity Characteristics Related to Pricing

In this section we discuss and show calculations for the following ratios: price to earnings (P/E), earnings yield (E/P); price to book (P/B) and book to market (B/P); and price to dividend (P/D) and dividend yield (D/P). We also discuss the concept of equity market capitalization as well as the capital asset pricing model (CAPM) and the Fama–French three-factor model.

4.1 Price-to-Earnings Ratio and Earnings Yield

The price-to-earnings or P/E ratio is calculated by dividing a stock's current price per share by the previous year's earnings per share. It is common practice to adjust earnings per share by excluding nonrecurring earnings. The P/E ratio is a widely used valuation measure and indicates how much investors are willing to pay for a stock relative to its earnings.

EXAMPLE 6

The P/E Ratio

If a stock is currently priced at \$20 per share and had earnings per share of \$1.25 last year then the P/E ratio is \$20/\$1.25 = 16. That is, investors are willing to pay 16 times last year's earnings to purchase the stock. A stock's P/E ratio is generally compared to a benchmark such as an industry P/E ratio to determine whether a stock is considered expensive. In this example, if the industry P/E ratio is 20, then it may be reasonable to conclude that the stock is inexpensive relative to its industry peers.

A variant of the P/E ratio is the earnings yield, or E/P. The E/P ratio is the inverse of the P/E ratio and is calculated by dividing last year's earnings per share by the stock's current price per share. In our example the earnings yield is \$1.25/\$20 = 6.25%. Some investors compare a stock's earnings yield to Treasury bond yields to judge whether a stock is expensive. Generally, higher earnings yields may be interpreted as a sign that the stock is inexpensive.

4.2 Price-to-Book Ratio and Book-to-Market Value

The price-to-book ratio (P/B) is another well-known valuation measure and is calculated by dividing the current stock price per share by the company's current book value per share or shareholder equity per share. The book value per share (B) can be calculated by subtracting the firm's total liabilities from total assets and dividing the resulting value by the number of shares outstanding.

EXAMPLE 7

The P/B and B/P Ratios

The RMC Corporation has total assets of \$100 million and total liabilities of \$90 million. The company has 25 million shares outstanding and its shares sell for \$3.50 per share.

$$\text{Book value per share} = \frac{\$100{,}000{,}000 - \$90{,}000{,}000}{25{,}000{,}000} = \$0.40$$

P/B = \$3.50/\$0.40 = 8.75.

The stock currently sells at 8.75 times book value. In order to determine if the stock is undervalued or not, the company's P/B ratio can be compared to an industry average P/B ratio. If the company's P/B is less than the industry's P/B then this suggests that the stock is undervalued.

Another form of this valuation measure is book-to-market value (B/P) which is the inverse of the price-to-book ratio. For our example, the B/P ratio is $0.40/$3.50 = 0.11.

4.3 Price-to-Dividend Ratio and Dividend Yield

While the price to dividend ratio (P/B) may be used as a valuation metric, the more common approach to using this valuation measure is the dividend yield (D/P). The dividend yield is calculated by dividing last year's total dividends per share by the current stock price per share.

EXAMPLE 8

The P/D Ratio and Dividend Yield

Last year the MKC Corporation paid quarterly dividends of $0.35 per share. MKC shares currently sell for $65 per share.

The total dividends per share = 4 × $0.35 = $1.40

D/P = $1.40/$65 = 0.02154 or 2.15%

For MKC the price-to-dividend ratio is $65/$1.40 = 46.43. The stock trades at about 46 times last year's dividends per share.

4.4 Equity Market Capitalization

Market capitalization can be used to gauge the size or market value of a company. It is calculated as follows:

Market capitalization = Number of shares outstanding × Current share price

Thus, if a company has 50 million shares outstanding and has a current share price of $18.50, the market capitalization of the company is 50,000,000 × $18.50 = $925,000,000. Companies may be categorized by market capitalization, into groups such as large cap, mid cap and small cap. That is, companies with the highest market capitalization will fall in the large cap group, the next largest into mid cap and the smallest into the small cap group.

4.5 The Capital Asset Pricing Model (CAPM)

The CAPM is a predictive model based on a set of assumptions, which allows an investor to estimate equilibrium expected returns on risky assets. It provides a specific equation that describes the tradeoff between risk and return for a risky asset.

The assumptions of the CAPM are:

- Investors rely only on expected returns, variances, and covariances of asset returns to determine their optimal portfolio.
- Investors have homogenous expectations, that is, they all have identical views on the risk return characteristics of asset returns.
- All assets are publicly traded and investors can purchase or sell any quantity without impacting prices.

- Investors can borrow or lend any amount at the risk-free rate.
- Investors pay no taxes and incur no transaction costs.

One result of the CAPM is the capital market line or CML. The CML is the line tangential to the efficient frontier of all risky asset portfolios. It results when investors hold some combination of a risk-free asset (R_f) and the market portfolio (M) which is the optimal portfolio of all risky assets. The CML is shown in Exhibit 5.

Exhibit 5 The Capital Market Line or CML

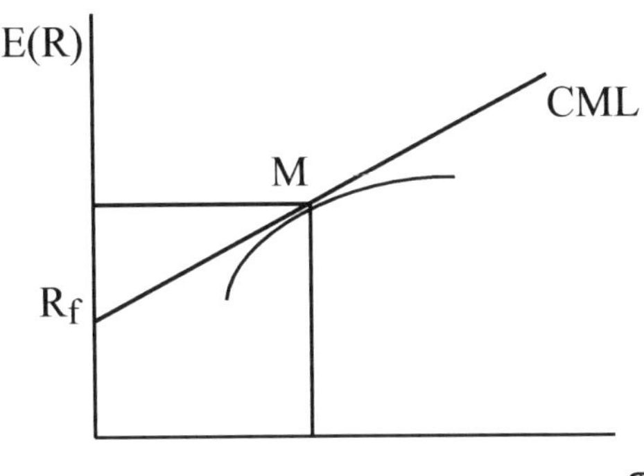

On the CML, points between R_f and M represent portfolios with allocations to the risk-free asset and the market portfolio. Points beyond M represent portfolios where all the investor's capital plus additional capital borrowed at the risk-free rate are invested in the market portfolio.

The security market line or SML is the graph of the CAPM. The SML postulates the relationship between expected return and beta for a risky asset. Beta is the slope coefficient in the SML. According to the SML, the expected return on a risky asset is:

$$E(R_i) = R_f + \beta_{iM}[E(R_M) - R_f]$$

where:

$E(R_i)$ = expected return on risky asset i
Rf = return on risk-free asset
β_{iM} = beta of the risky asset i relative to the market
$E(R_M)$ = expected return on the market portfolio.

EXAMPLE 9

Calculating Expected Return using the CAPM

The stock of the NPN Corporation has a beta of 1.2. The risk-free rate is 2.2% and the expected return on the market is 8.3%. According to the SML, the expected return on NPN stock is:

$$E(R_i) = 2.2\% + 1.2(8.3\% - 2.2\%) = 9.52\%$$

4.6 The Fama–French Model

In the CAPM, stock returns are explained by one factor, the market; the CAPM is a single-factor model. The Fama–French model is a three-factor model where, in addition to the market factor, two additional factors explain stock returns: firm size and the book-to-market ratio. The firm-size factor attempts to capture any systematic differences in mean return that result from different equity market capitalizations. The book-to-market factor attempts to capture any differences in mean return that result from different valuation levels as measured by the book-to-market ratio. As a three-factor model the Fama–French model attempts to offer a more accurate description of assets returns than the single-factor CAPM. The Fama–French model gives the expected return on an asset as:

$$E(R_i) = R_f + \beta_{iM}\text{E(RMRF)} + \beta_{iHML}\text{E(HML)} + \beta_{iSMB}\text{E(SMB)}$$

Where:

R_i = return on risky asset i
R_f = the risk-free rate of return
α_i = an intercept
β_{iM} = sensitivity of asset i's returns to
RMRF = the return on a market value weighted equity index minus the return on a risk-free asset, in this case one-month Treasury bills.
β_{iHML} = sensitivity of returns on asset i to the book-to-market factor
HML = High minus Low, the return of a high book-to-market portfolio minus the return of a low book-to-market portfolio
β_{iSMB} = sensitivity of returns on asset i to the size factor
SMB = Small minus Big, a size factor. It is the return of small-cap portfolio minus the return of a large-cap portfolio

The parameters of the Fama–French model are estimated by running the following multivariate regression model:

$$R_i - R_f = \alpha_i + \beta_{iM}\text{RMRF} + \beta_{iHML}\text{HML} + \beta_{iSMB}\text{SMB}$$

EXAMPLE 10

The Fama–French Model

A regression of annual stock returns for RKC Corporation on excess returns on the S&P500 stock index, returns on HML, and returns on SMB yields the following regression statistics:

$$\alpha_i = 0,\ \beta_{iM} = 1.32,\ \beta_{iHML} = -0.85, \text{ and } \beta_{iSMB} = -0.35$$

The risk free rate is 2.2%, the expected return on the market is 8.3%, the expected return on the book-to-market factor is 3.7% and the expected return on the size factor is 2.4%. The expected rate of return for RKC stock based on the Fama–French three-factor model is:

$$E(R_i) = 2.2\% + [1.32 \times (8.3\% - 2.2\%)] + (-0.85 \times 3.7\%) + (-0.35 \times 2.4\%)$$
$$= 6.267\%$$

5 Debt Characteristics Related to Pricing

The following sections review several measures of bond interest rate risk and other basic concepts.

5.1 Macaulay Duration and Modified Duration

Duration measures the sensitivity of a bond's price to interest rate changes and may be used to measure the interest rate risk of a bond. A bond with a higher duration is considered to have a higher level of interest rate risk.

Macaulay duration is the weighted average of the times until each coupon or principal payment is made. With CF_t = the cash flow at time t and y = the bond's yield to maturing, the weight, w_t, applied to CF_t is calculated as:

$$w_t = \frac{\dfrac{CF_t}{(1+y)^t}}{\text{Bond price}}$$

Macaulay duration is then calculated as:

$$D = \sum_{t=1}^{T} t \times w_t$$

Another common measure of duration is modified duration (MD), calculated as:

$$MD = \frac{D}{\left(1 + \dfrac{y}{n}\right)}$$

where y is the yield to maturity and n is the number of coupon payments per year.

Example 11 illustrates the calculation of Macaulay duration and modified duration.

EXAMPLE 11

Macaulay Duration and Modified Duration

A \$100 face value bond with a maturity of 3 years is priced at \$103.52. The bond pays semiannual coupon interest of 5.0% and has an annual yield to maturity of 3.75%. The calculation is shown in Exhibit 6.

Exhibit 6 Calculation of Macaulay Duration

Period t	Cash Flow CF	Weight w	$t \times w$
1	\$2.50	0.0237	0.0237
2	\$2.50	0.0233	0.0465
3	\$2.50	0.0228	0.0685
4	\$2.50	0.0224	0.0897
5	\$2.50	0.0220	0.1100
6	\$102.50	0.8857	5.3143
Total			5.6528

The Macaulay duration is 5.6528 six-month periods, or 2.8264 (= 5.6528/2) years. The modified duration of this bond is:

$$MD \approx \frac{5.6528}{\left(1 + \dfrac{0.0375}{2}\right)} = 5.5487$$

The modified duration is 5.5487 six-month periods, or 2.7743 years.

5.2 Estimating Bond Price Change using Duration

Modified duration can be used to estimate the change in the price of a bond for a given change in interest rates using the following equation:

Δ Price = −(Modified Duration × Δy × Price)

Alternatively, the percentage change in the price of the bond can be estimated as:

% Δ Price = −(Modified Duration)(Δy)

Note that, for reasons that will be discussed later, using these equations to estimate the price change or percentage price change is only appropriate for small changes in interest rates.

EXAMPLE 12

Bond Price Change

A bond is currently priced at $103.52 and has a modified duration of 2.77. If interest rates are expected to decline by 20 basis points the estimated change in the bond's price is:

Δ Price = −(2.77) × (−0.002 × $103.52) = $0.5735

The percentage price change is:

% Δ Price = −(2.77) × (−0.002) = 0.00554 or 0.55%

5.3 Convexity

A characteristic of bonds is that as interest rates increase bond prices decline and as interest rates fall bonds prices rise. The relationship between interest rates and bond price is inverse but non-linear as shown in Exhibit 7. The relationship is convex and the curvature is referred to as convexity.

Exhibit 7 Convexity

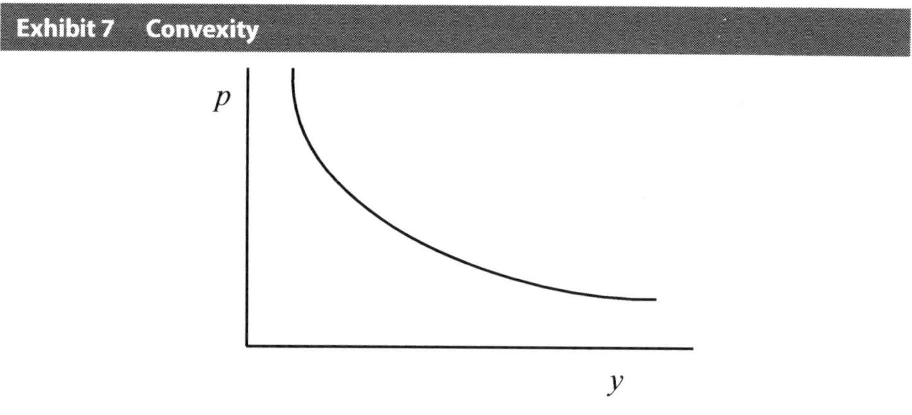

Using duration to estimate the percentage change in the price of a bond for a given change in interest rates does not take convexity into account. For relatively small changes in interest rates the duration approximation provides a reasonable estimate of the percentage bond price change. For larger changes in interest rates, a more accurate estimate can be obtained by incorporating convexity as follows:

% Δ Price = −(Modified Duration) × (Δy) + (1/2) × (Convexity) × $(\Delta y)^2$

EXAMPLE 13

Price Change Based on Duration and Convexity

Expanding on Example 12, assume that the bond has convexity of 141.6. If interest rates rise by 150 basis points the estimated percentage bond price change is:

$$\begin{aligned}\%\ \Delta\ \text{Price} &= -(2.77) \times (0.015) + (1/2) \times (141.6) \times (0.015) \\ &= -0.02562 \text{ or } -2.56\%\end{aligned}$$

5.4 Roll Down Return

An upward sloping yield curve implies that the required yield-to-maturity on shorter-term bonds is less than the required yield-to-maturity on longer-term bonds. Assuming stable interest rates, roll down return refers to the expected positive return earned with the passage of time when the yield curve is upward sloping.

EXAMPLE 14

Roll Down Return Illustration

On 30 April 2012, a US Treasury note paying a coupon of 2.875%, maturing in 5 years on 30 April 2017 sells for $100.227 with a yield of 2.826%. The bond pays interest semi-annually. A US Treasury bond with 3 years to maturity yields 2.382%.

Assume that an investor wishes to purchase and hold a bond for two years. The investor can purchase the 5 year bond with a view to "rolling-down" the yield curve for a period of two years. At the end of this two year period the 5 year bond will have a remaining maturity of 3 years. Assuming stable interest rates, this bond will now have a yield of 2.382% (the yield on a 3-year bond). During this two-year period the investor will have earned capital gains as well as coupons. The calculation of total return, assuming that coupons are reinvested at the risk-free rate of 2.22%, is shown below.

The price of the 5-year bond two years later on 30 April 2014 assuming a yield of 2.382% is:

$$\begin{aligned}\text{Price} &= \frac{1.4375}{(1.01191)^1} + \frac{1.4375}{(1.01191)^2} + \frac{1.4375}{(1.01191)^3} + \frac{1.4375}{(1.01191)^4} \\ &+ \frac{1.4375}{(1.01191)^5} + \frac{101.4375}{(1.01191)^6} = 101.4193\end{aligned}$$

From 30 April 2012 to 30 April 2014, the bond holder would have four semiannual coupon payments of $1.4375. The future value of these coupons reinvested at 2.22% annually or 1.11% semiannually is:

$$\begin{aligned}\text{FV} &= 1.4375(1.0111) + 1.4375(1.0111) + 1.4375(1.0111) + 1.4375 \\ &= \$5.8464\end{aligned}$$

The sum of the price of the bond plus the future value of the coupons is $101.4193 + $5.8464 = $107.2657. The holding period return (HPR) over the two year period is:

$$\text{HPR} = \frac{107.2657 - 100.227}{100.227} = 0.0702 \text{ or } 7.02\%$$

The annualized yield is:

$$\text{Yield} = (1.0702)^{0.5} - 1 = 0.0345 \text{ or } 3.45\%$$

END OPTIONAL SEGMENT

which exceeds the original 5-year bond's yield to maturity of 2.826%.

REFERENCES

Chance, D., K. Grant, and J. Marsland. 2007. "Risk Management." In *Managing Investment Portfolios: A Dynamic Process*. Edited by J.L. Maginn, D.L. Tuttle, J.E. Pinto, and D.W. McLeavey. 3rd ed. Hoboken, NJ: John Wiley & Sons.

Christopherson, J.A., D.R. Cariño, and W.E. Ferson. 2009. *Portfolio Performance Measurement and Benchmarking*. New York: McGraw-Hill.

DeFusco, R.A., D.W. McLeavey, J.E. Pinto, and D.E. Runkle. 2007. *Quantitative Investment Analysis*, 2nd ed. (Hoboken, NJ: John Wiley & Sons).

Degroot, G., and P. Greenwood. 2009/2010. "Equity Style Analysis: Beyond Performance Measurement." *Journal of Performance Measurement*, vol. 14, no. 2 (Winter).

Fama, E.F., and K.R. French. 1992. "The Cross-Section of Expected Stock Returns." *Journal of Finance*, vol. 47, no. 2 (June):427–465.

Fama, E.F., and K.R. French. 1993. "Common Risk Factors in the Returns on Stocks and Bonds." *Journal of Financial Economics*, vol. 33, no. 1:3–56.

Fama, E.F., and K.R. French. 1996. "Multifactor Explanations of Asset Pricing Anomalies." *Journal of Finance*, vol. 51, no. 1 (March):55–84.

Feibel, B.J. 2003. *Investment Performance Measurement*. Hoboken, NJ: John Wiley & Sons.

Grégoire, P. 2007. "Risk Attribution." In *Advanced Portfolio Attribution Analysis: New Approaches to Return and Risk*. Edited by C. Bacon. London: Risk Books.

Grégoire, P., and H. Van Oppens. 2006. "Risk Attribution." *Journal of Performance Measurement*, vol. 11, no. 1:67–77.

Grinold, R., and R. Kahn. 2000. *Active Portfolio Management*. 2nd ed. (New York: McGraw-Hill).

Hubert, L. 1972. "A Further Comment on N versus N − 1." *American Educational Research Journal*, vol. 9, no. 2 (Spring):323–325.

Jorion, P. 2009. *Financial Risk Manager Handbook*. 5th ed. Hoboken, NJ: Wiley & Sons.

Josephy, N.H., and A.D. Aczel. 1993. "A Statistically Optimal Estimator of Semivariance." *European Journal of Operational Research*, vol. 67, no. 2267–171.

Kahneman, D., and A. Tversky. 1979. "Prospect Theory: An Analysis of Decision under Risk." *Econometrica: Journal of the Econometric Society*, vol. 47, no. 2 (March):263–291.

Menchero, J., and J. Hu. 2006. "Portfolio Risk Attribution." *Journal of Performance Measurement*, vol. 10, no. 3 (Spring):22–33.

Rogers, D., and C. Van Dyke. 2006. "Measuring the Volatility of Hedge Fund Returns." *Journal of Wealth Management*, vol. 9, no. 1 (Summer):45–53.

von Hippel, P.T. 2005. "Mean, Median, and Skew: Correcting a Textbook Rule." *Journal of Statistics Education*, vol. 13, no. 2 (July): www.amstat.org/publications/jse/v13n2/vonhippel.html

PRACTICE PROBLEMS

1 Which of the following is *best* categorized as a financial risk?

A Credit risk

B Settlement risk

C Accounting risk

2 Which of the following is *best* categorized as a non-financial risk?

A Tax risk

B Funding risk

C Counterparty risk

3 Which of the following is *least* closely related to market risk?

A Changes in interest rates

B Changes in currency exchange rates

C Potential loss caused by a counterparty.

4 The sponsor of an endowment fund is concerned that the high return obtained by one of his portfolio managers in the most recent year resulted from the high level of risk taken by investing heavily outside the benchmark. The risk attribution process is *most likely* to address his concern by measuring the:

A probability that the return obtained outside of the benchmark was obtained by skill, rather than by luck.

B rate of return obtained outside of the benchmark in excess of the rate of return obtained by the benchmark.

C volatility of the returns obtained outside of the benchmark in comparison with the volatility of benchmark returns.

5 The investment policy of a pension plan specifies that some fixed-income assets must be earmarked to support payments to retired employees. The intent is that the value of the assets should move closely with the value of the liabilities (i.e. with the value of the payments to the retirees) irrespective of the changes in interest rate. The investment manager of the plan is responsible for choosing the portfolio manager of those fixed-income assets. In order to meet the requirements of the investment policy, which of the following risk measures shown in the portfolio managers' proposals would be *most* relevant?

A The duration of the fixed income fund proposed.

B The standard deviation of the fixed-income fund as shown in the GIPS compliant presentation.

C The difference between the standard deviation of the fixed-income fund and the standard deviation of the benchmark of that fund as shown in the GIPS compliant presentation.

6 A defined benefit pension fund sponsor should be *most* concerned with:

A active risk.

B surplus risk.

C absolute risk.

7 An index fund manager is *most likely* to be concerned with:

A surplus risk.

B tracking risk.

C absolute risk.

8 An investor who is concerned with the possibility of extreme losses will *most likely* want to measure:

A tail risk.

B downside risk.

C positive skewness.

9 Which of the following *best* characterizes the median as a measure of central tendency? The median:

A identifies the extent of tail risk.

B is slightly affected by the magnitude of extreme negative values.

C is referred to as the second quartile when dividing data into four sections.

10 Which of the following relationships is *most likely* to hold when negative skewness is observed in a data set?

A Median > Mean

B Median < Mean

C Median = Mean

11 The 5-year return history of a mutual fund is listed in the following table:

Year	Return
2006	5.0%
2007	8.0%
2008	−7.0%
2009	−13.0%
2010	10.0%

Its mean absolute deviation (MAD) over the period of 2006–2010 is *closest* to:

A 0.0%.

B 8.5%.

C 9.0%.

12 If the quarterly standard deviation of a series of returns is 5.0%, then the annualized standard deviation is *closest* to:

A 10.0%

B 20.0%

C 21.6%.

13 A portfolio and its benchmark had the following monthly returns:

	Portfolio	Benchmark
January	2.3%	1.9%
February	1.7%	1.6%
March	0.6%	0.4%
April	3.6%	2.3%

The tracking risk for the portfolio over the four-month period is *closest* to:

A 0.00%.

B 0.47%.

C 0.50%.

14 A portfolio had annual returns for the past three years of 13.0%, −7.0%, and 9.0%. The standard deviation of the portfolio returns is *closest* to:

A 0.8%.

B 8.0%.

C 8.7%.

15 Which of the following types of risk is *best* measured by beta?

A Portfolio

B Systematic

C Idiosyncratic

16 An asset with a beta less than one is added to a portfolio that tracks a broad market index. Relative to the broad market index, the new portfolio will have lower:

A systematic risk.

B idiosyncratic risk.

C idiosyncratic and systematic risk.

17 The stock of a corporation that has a 0.0025 covariance with the market index is added to a portfolio of domestic equity securities. The variance of the stock's returns is 0.0045 and the variance of the market index is 0.0014. The beta of the stock is *closest* to:

A 0.56.

B 1.79.

C 3.97.

18 The monthly returns of an equity portfolio and its benchmark are provided in the following table:

Portfolio and Benchmark Monthly Returns, 2015

Month	Portfolio Return (%)	Benchmark Return (%)
January	2.1	1.9
February	2.2	2.1
March	−1.4	−1.1
April	−2.1	−2.5
May	3.5	3.6
June	0.8	0.7
July	1.7	1.5
August	−0.1	0.1
September	3.1	2.8
October	3.3	3.4
November	1.1	0.9
December	4.4	4.0
Arithmetic mean	1.55	1.45

Based on the table, the semivariance of the portfolio is *closest* to:

A 0.021%.

B 0.036%.

C 1.458%.

19 The following are the monthly returns for a stock.

Month	Return
January	15%
February	−10%
March	12%
April	−18%
May	−8%
June	20%

The semi-variance of the monthly stock returns is *closest* to:

A 1.1%.

B 2.1%.

C 10.5%.

20 A portfolio has the following annual returns for the period 2005–2008:

Year	Return
2005	3.20%
2006	−1.60%
2007	1.10%
2008	−1.30%

The portfolio's semi-standard deviation over the four years is *closest* to:

A 0.0002.

B 0.0128.

C 0.0195.

21 Using semi-variance to measure portfolio risk would be preferred to using variance when:

A a portfolio return series is skewed.

B the return series is symmetrically distributed.

C the investor is concerned with variability on the upside.

22 Which of the following *best* describes a difference between semi-variance and target semi-variance?

A Only semi-variance is a measure of downside risk.

B Target semi-variance does not generally use the mean as a reference point.

C Target semi-variance is a better downside risk measure for a portfolio with tail risk.

23 Drawdown measures are *most frequently* used to analyze:

A hedge fund returns.

B short term government security fund returns.

C large capitalization diversified equity fund returns.

24 The following returns have been calculated for a fund:

Month	Unit Price at End of Month	Unit Return During Month
0	50	
1	49.4	−1.2%
2	46.9	−5.1%

Month	Unit Price at End of Month	Unit Return During Month
3	45.7	−2.6%
4	46.5	1.8%

Compared to the largest individual drawdown, the maximum drawdown for the fund is:

A smaller.

B equal.

C larger.

25 Which of the following measurement methods will *most likely* result in the greatest maximum drawdown?

A Daily returns over one year are used.

B Daily returns over two years are used.

C Weekly returns over one year are used.

26 The statement "The portfolio's daily 1% Value at Risk is €3,000,000" can *best* be interpreted as "There is a:

A 1% probability that over a day the portfolio will lose €3,000,000 or more."

B 1% probability that over a day the portfolio will lose €3,000,000 or less."

C 99% probability that over a day the portfolio will lose less than €30,000."

27 Which of the following *least* accurately describes Value at Risk?

A The maximum value that could be lost.

B A probability based measure of loss potential.

C A minimum value that would be expected to be lost with a given frequency.

28 Which of the following *best* represents a statement of stress tests?

A The average of the worst one percent of outcomes is a loss of $1.4 million.

B If interest rates were to increase by 4%, the portfolio would decrease in value by 15%.

C If the financial crisis of 2008 were to reoccur, the portfolio would decrease in value by 35%.

29 When the portfolio returns do not follow a normal distribution and the distribution of returns will likely change in the future, which of the following methods of estimating Value at Risk is *most* suitable?

A Historical

B Analytical

C Monte Carlo

30 A portfolio manager wants to analyze a fast-growing high technology company that has been operating for seven years. The company is not yet profitable and has significant intangible assets that are not recognized on the company's balance sheet. Which of the following measures is the *most appropriate* to use in this analysis given the characteristics of the company?

A Price-to-earnings ratio (P/E)

B Price-to-book ratio (P/B)

C Cash flow, five-year growth

31 Portfolio Manager A invests in growth stocks with only above average P/Es relative to peers. Portfolio Manager B invests in only low P/E value stocks. Portfolio Manager C invests in both growth stocks and value stocks with equal weights. Which manager is *most likely* to have the greater exposure to negative earnings surprise?

A Manager A

B Manager B

C Manager C

32 Which of the following investment characteristics could be aggregated to evaluate exposure across a bond asset class and a stock asset class?

A Convexity

B Free cash flow

C Economic sector

33 Which of the following risk measures would be *least* appropriate in analyzing a hedge fund invested in emerging market stocks?

A Duration

B Currency exposure

C Maximum drawdown

34 The risk measure that is *most* appropriate to evaluate a passive investment manager is:

A tracking risk.

B maximum drawdown.

C standard deviation of returns.

35 Which of the following risk measures would an insurance company *most likely* consider when measuring portfolio risk?

A Value at risk

B Maximum drawdown

C Risk relative to liability benchmark

36 A portfolio manager invests in four sectors. The investment weight and marginal contribution to risk of each sector are listed in the following table:

Sector	Weight	Marginal Contribution to Risk
Energy	30.0%	12.0%
Materials	40.0%	8.0%
Industrials	20.0%	13.0%
Utilities	10.0%	28.0%

Which of the following sectors contributes *most* to the total risk?

A Energy

B Utilities

C Materials

37 Relative to its benchmark, a portfolio is managed passively in asset allocation and actively in security selection. In a top-down risk attribution analysis, which of the following is *most likely* to be observed?

A The contribution of allocation effect to tracking risk will be negative.

B The tracking risk will be equal to the volatility of the selection effect.

C The correlation between allocation effect and active return will be equal to 1.

38 A portfolio manager has the mandate of beating the benchmark of a portfolio invested 50% in large-cap growth index and 50% in small-cap growth index without using stock picking. In the last year, he chose to invest constantly 35% in an ETF that replicates the large-cap index and 65% in an ETF that replicates the small-cap index. Preliminary risk calculations, based on twelve months of data, gave the following results:

- Tracking risk = 0.483%
- Standard deviation of the large cap ETF = 2.05%
- Correlation between the large-cap ETF and the portfolio active return = 0.40
- Contribution of small-cap ETF to tracking risk = 0.606%

Based on these results, the contribution of the large-cap ETF to tracking risk is *closest* to:

A −0.123%.

B 0.123%.

C 0.287%.

39 A portfolio manager constructs his portfolio by selecting under-valued stocks and compares his portfolio performance with the S&P 500. The *most appropriate* analysis model for risk attribution of his portfolio is:

A top-down risk attribution.

B marginal contribution to risk.

C marginal contribution to tracking risk.

40 A portfolio manager uses a top-down investment process to actively manage his portfolios. The results of return attribution and risk attribution are summarized in the following table:

	Return Attribution		Risk Attribution	
	Allocation	**Selection**	**Allocation**	**Selection**
Bond	1.5%	0.5%	0.3%	0.3%
Equity	−2.5%	5.5%	0.6%	8.1%
Real estate	3.0%	2.0%	0.9%	4.8%
Total active return	10.0%		15.0%	

From a risk return perspective, which of the following effects of active management made the *best* contribution to the portfolio?

A Bond selection

B Equity selection

C Real estate allocation

41 An equity portfolio is actively managed against the following benchmarks: 50% S&P mid-cap 400 and 50% S&P small-cap 600. Active management is used in asset allocation only, and active weights change each month. In the last year, the average monthly weight of the mid-cap ETF that the manager used was 40% and the average weight of the small-cap ETF 60%. Preliminary risk calculations, based on twelve months of data, gave the following results:

- Standard deviation of active contributions for mid-cap stocks = 0.106%
- Standard deviation of active contributions for small-cap stocks = 0.520%
- Correlation between active contributions for mid-cap stocks and active return = −0.641

- Correlation between active contributions for small-cap stocks and active return = 0.220

Based on these results, the tracking risk for the portfolio is *closest* to:

A 0.018%.

B 0.042%.

C 0.046%.

42 A portfolio's return and risk attribution results are provided in the following table (note that entries are contributions to allocation or selection):

Portfolio's Return and Risk Attribution Results

	Return Attribution (%)		Risk Attribution (%)	
	Allocation	**Selection**	**Allocation**	**Selection**
Bonds	1.23	2.56	0.22	3.79
Stocks	3.45	7.44	0.11	5.21
Total	14.68		9.33	

Which of the following investment decisions results in the highest ratio of return contribution to tracking risk?

A Bond selection

B Stock selection

C Stock allocation

43 Manager A has an active allocation policy but selects securities passively. Manager B passively follows the benchmark to allocate assets but overweights or underweights securities within each asset class. Manager C's strategy is to select stocks to capture risk premiums associated with small-cap stocks and value stocks. A factor-based model will be *most* appropriate for a risk attribution analysis of the portfolio of:

A Manager A.

B Manager B.

C Manager C.

44 A top-down return and risk attribution process applied to a portfolio that is not allowed to hold short positions produced the following results, when using the Brinson–Fachler model with selection and interaction combined:

	Returns			Contributions to Active Return		Contributions to Tracking Risk	
	Return of Portfolio	**Return of Benchmark**	**Active Return**	**Allocation**	**Selection**	**Allocation**	**Selection**
Bonds	4.67%	3.85%	0.82%	0.04%	0.42%	0.08%	1.23%
Equity	2.92%	2.65%	0.27%	0.61%	0.29%	0.60%	4.56%

Which of the following statements represents a valid interpretation of the results?

A Bond selection represents 12% of tracking risk.

B The total contribution of allocation to tracking risk was 0.68%.

C The total active return for the portfolio was between 0.27% and 0.82%.

45 Which of the following most likely indicates a non-financial risk of trading an over-the-counter swap?

A The swap broker quote has a wide bid–ask spread.

B The swap counterparties are located in different time zones.

C The credit rating of a counterparty has recently been lowered.

46 The decision to invest outside the portfolio benchmark is *best* evaluated by using:

A risk attribution only.

B return attribution only.

C both risk and return attribution.

47 A pension's investment policy specifies the maximum level of portfolio risk that may be contributed by different risk factors. Which type of analysis can be used to determine whether the pension performed within policy guidelines?

A *Ex ante* risk analysis

B Risk attribution analysis

C Standalone risk analysis

48 As the rate of asset turnover increases in a portfolio, the predictive power of an *ex post* risk measure will *most likely*:

A decline.

B remain the same.

C increase.

49 The risk of an unexpected change in GDP growth is an example of:

A systematic risk.

B asymmetric risk.

C idiosyncratic risk.

50 Which of the following risk measures is most suitable in the performance evaluation of a long-only equity mutual fund manager relative to its benchmark?

A Active risk

B Surplus risk

C Absolute risk

51 ABC Inc.'s return distribution for the last two years is as follows:

Frequency Distribution for ABC Inc. Monthly Stock Returns

Interval	Frequency of Observation
–15% to –10%	0
–10% to –5%	2
–5% to 0%	10
0% to 5%	6
5% to 10%	3
10% to 15%	2
15% to 20%	1
20% to 25%	0

Number of months: 24

(continued)

(Continued)

Interval	Frequency of Observation
Arithmetic mean return: 1.7%	
Median return: 0.0%	

ABC Inc.'s return distribution is *most likely*:

A symmetric.

B positively skewed.

C negatively skewed.

52 The correlation coefficient of a portfolio and its index is 0.92. The standard deviations are 3.8% for the portfolio and 4.4% for the index. The portfolio beta is *closest* to:

A 0.77.

B 0.80.

C 1.04.

53 The correlation of a portfolio and the market is 0.75. The standard deviation of the market returns is 2.7%. An increase in the stand-alone risk of the portfolio returns, all else being equal, will *most likely* cause the portfolio's beta to:

A decrease.

B stay the same.

C increase.

54 Based on the Exhibit below, using three drawdowns over a one-year period, the average drawdown (3) of the Portfolio is *closest* to:

Monthly Fund Returns

Month	Return (%)	Unit Value	Individual Drawdowns (in bold) (%)
0		1.000	
1	3.0	1.030	
2	−11.7	0.910	−11.7
3	−1.1	0.900	**−12.6**
4	6.7	0.960	
5	5.3	1.011	
6	3.4	1.045	
7	−2.1	1.023	**−2.1**
8	4.3	1.067	
9	−3.8	1.026	−3.8
10	−1.3	1.013	−5.1
11	−2.3	0.990	**−7.2**
12	11.1	1.100	

A −10.5%.

B –7.3%.

C –5.4%.

55 Which of the following methods of calculating value at risk relies on the assumption of a normal distribution of returns?

A Historical approach

B Analytical approach

C Monte Carlo simulation

56 In estimating value at risk, the Monte Carlo method:

A requires the use of proxy investments.

B relies on a past series of returns to generate estimates.

C uses a random number generator to estimate potential return outcomes.

57 A company sponsors a defined-benefit pension plan for its employees. The benefits paid to a participant on retirement are determined by a formula rather than by investment returns. Which of the following would be expected to have the *most* impact on the fund's ability to satisfy future payments to retirees?

A Variability of the pension plan's surplus

B Unexpected changes in individual tax rates

C The absolute variability of the pension plan's portfolio returns

58 An investment manager's allocation and selection contributions to tracking risk are provided in the following table.

	Allocation		**Selection**	
	Volatility	**Contribution**	**Volatility**	**Contribution**
Bonds	0.26%	0.11%	3.40%	0.17%
Equity	1.23%	0.26%	0.46%	0.38%

Which active decision added the most to the manager's tracking risk?

A Bond selection

B Equity selection

C Equity allocation

SOLUTIONS

1 A is correct. Credit risk refers to the risk of loss caused by a counterparty or debtor's failure to make payment and is thus due to an event in external financial markets.

B is incorrect. Settlement risk results from a breakdown in the settlement of a trade. C is incorrect. Accounting risk is related to the uncertainty about how a transaction should be recorded.

2 A is correct. Tax risk results from unexpected changes in tax rates or rulings and is thus categorized as a non-financial risk.

B is incorrect; funding risk (liquidity risk) results from events in external financial markets. C is incorrect; counterparty risk (credit risk) results from events in external financial markets.

3 C is correct. Potential loss related to a counterparty is categorized as credit risk rather than market risk. Market risk is risk that results from unexpected changes in share prices, interest rates, currency exchange rates, and commodity prices.

A and B are incorrect because they are both components of market risk.

4 C is correct. Risk attribution will measure the volatility of the overall portfolio returns and the sponsor will be in a position to judge the manager's active investment decision to invest outside of the benchmark better than if the sponsor relied on the return attribution process only.

A is incorrect because judging the skill of the investment manager is in the domain of performance appraisal and goes beyond risk attribution (although the results of the risk attribution and return attribution may be useful in performance appraisal). B is incorrect because analyzing the return by asset classes (which is return attribution), including the assets outside of the benchmark, will not explain the risk taken by the investment manager.

5 A is correct. The duration of the assets should be close to the duration of the liabilities if one wants the value of the assets to move with the value of the liabilities when interest rates change.

B is incorrect because although the standard deviation of the fund disclosed in the GIPS compliant presentation represents a measure of volatility, the asset value will move very differently than the liability value if the assets and liabilities do not have the same duration. C is incorrect because although the comparison of the standard deviation of the fund and of the benchmark may indicate a close correspondence between the fund and the benchmark, there is no assurance that the duration of the fund benchmark is the same as the duration of the pension plan liabilities.

6 B is correct. A pension fund must satisfy the payments owed to retirees. The potential difference between assets and liabilities is surplus risk.

A is incorrect. From the perspective of a defined-benefit plan sponsor, active risk is not as important as surplus risk. C is incorrect. Absolute risk measures the return volatility without comparison to a benchmark. Measuring absolute risk is not as important as the risk relative to the retiree liabilities.

7 B is correct. An index fund manager is expected to closely track the performance of an underlying index; tracking risk measures how well the manager does that.

A is incorrect because an index fund manager usually does not need to meet future liabilities and thus the potential difference between assets and liabilities (surplus) is not an issue. C is incorrect because absolute risk is measured without comparison to an index whereas an index fund is expected to track the performance of a specified index.

8 A is correct. Tail risk is the possibility of extreme losses. B is incorrect; downside risk is the potential for a loss (but not necessarily an extreme one). C is incorrect; positive skewness in a distribution occurs when there are extreme positive values, not extreme negative values.

9 C is correct. The median is referred to as the second quartile when dividing data into four sections.

A is incorrect because the median does not reflect the range of values and thus cannot measure tail risk. B is incorrect; a characteristic of the median is that it is not affected by extreme values.

10 A is correct. Negative skewness means that extreme negative values are present so that, in general, the middle observed value (median) is greater than the average of all values (mean).

B is incorrect as it describes the typical occurrence of positive skewness (extreme positive values). C is incorrect as it portrays a completely symmetrical distribution.

11 B is correct.

$$\overline{R} = \left(5\% + 8\% - 7\% - 13\% + 10\%\right) \div 5 = 0.6\%$$

$$\begin{aligned}\text{MAD} &= \left(\left|5\% - 0.6\%\right| + \left|8\% - 0.6\%\right| + \left|-7\% - 0.6\%\right| + \left|-13\% - 0.6\%\right| + \left|10\% - 0.6\%\right|\right) \div 5 \\ &= 8.48\%\end{aligned}$$

A is incorrect. In the formula above for MAD, it is adding numerical values instead of absolute values. C is incorrect. It is the standard deviation of the 5 yearly returns, using Equation 3.

12 A is correct:

$$\sigma_{annualized} = \sigma\sqrt{N} = 5\% \times \sqrt{4} = 10.0\%$$

B is incorrect because it is (5% × 4) = 20.0%. C is incorrect because it is $[(1 + 5\%)^4 - 1] = 21.6\%$.

13 B is correct. First, calculate the monthly differences between portfolio returns and benchmark returns and calculate the mean of those differences (fourth column in the table below). Next calculate the deviation of each monthly return difference from the mean of the monthly return differences (column 5 below) and square the deviations (column 6 below):

	Portfolio	Benchmark	Monthly Return Difference	Monthly Deviation from Mean Difference	Squared Monthly Deviation
January	2.3%	1.9%	0.4%	−0.1%	0.0001%
February	1.7%	1.6%	0.1%	−0.4%	0.0016%
March	0.6%	0.4%	0.2%	−0.3%	0.0009%
April	3.6%	2.3%	1.3%	0.8%	0.0064%
Mean			0.5%		
Total					0.0090%

Then, to get the tracking risk, sum the squared monthly deviations (column 6 above), divide by the number of observations, and take the square root:

$$[(0.000090)/4]^{0.5} = (0.000023)^{0.5} = 0.47\%$$

A is incorrect because 0.000023 rounded to 0.0000 or equivalently 0.00% is the variance, rather than the standard deviation, of the squared monthly deviations. C is incorrect because 0.50% is the mean of the monthly return differences.

14 C is correct. First calculate the average return: (13% −7% + 9%)/3 = 5%. Second, calculate the variance of the returns: $\sigma^2 = [(0.13 - 0.05)^2 + (-0.07 - 0.05)^2 + (0.09 - 0.05)^2]/3 = 0.0075$. Third, calculate the standard deviation: $\sigma = 0.0075^{0.5} = 8.64\%$ or 8.7%.

A is incorrect. It is the variance, calculated as 0.0075 rounded to 0.008 or 0.8%. B is incorrect. This is the mean absolute deviation (MAD) $= \left[|0.13 - 0.05| + |-0.07 - 0.05| + |0.09 - 0.05|\right] / 3 = 0.080$ or 8.0%.

15 B is correct. By measuring sensitivity to market movements, beta reflects systematic risk, i.e., that originating from broad financial markets conditions and the macro economy.

A is incorrect. Portfolio risk refers to the risk of a collection of assets, measured, for example, by the standard deviation of portfolio returns. C is incorrect. Idiosyncratic risk results from unexpected changes in firm-specific factors. Beta would not be a measure used to measure idiosyncratic risk.

16 A is correct. A portfolio that tracks a broad market index will have a beta equal to one and no idiosyncratic risk because it is well-diversified. An asset with a beta less than one has less systematic risk than the broad market index. Relative to the broad market index, the combined portfolio will have lower systematic risk but the same amount of idiosyncratic risk, which is zero.

B and C are incorrect because the combined portfolio will still have zero idiosyncratic risk.

17 B is correct.

$$\beta_A = \frac{\text{Cov}(R_A, R_M)}{\sigma_M^2} = 0.25 / 0.14 = 1.79$$

A is incorrect because it uses in the denominator the stock's variance instead of the market's variance. C is incorrect because it multiplies the two variances in the denominator calculation when it should just use the market variance.

18 A is correct. The semivariance of the portfolio is calculated by taking into account only those returns that are less than the arithmetic mean return (1.55% in the table) as follows:

$$\begin{aligned}\text{Semivariance} &= [(-1.4\% - 1.55\%)^2 + (-2.1\% - 1.55\%)^2 + (0.8\% - 1.55\%)^2 + \\ &\quad (-0.1\% - 1.55\%)^2 + (1.1\% - 1.55\%)^2]/12 \\ &= (0.00087025 + 0.00133225 + 0.00005625 + 0.00027225 + \\ &\quad 0.00002025)/12 \\ &= 0.255125\%/12 \\ &= 0.0212604\% \text{ or } 0.021\%.\end{aligned}$$

19 A is correct. The mean is (0.15 + −0.10 + 0.12 + −0.18 − 0.08 + 0.20)/6 = 0.018 or 1.8%. Only February, April, and May's returns are less than the mean of 1.8%. Since semi-variance measures downside risk, we calculate the underperformance for those months only:

February: −0.10 − 0.018 = −0.118

April: −0.18 − 0.018 = −0.198

May: $-0.08 - 0.018 = -0.098$

We then sum the squares of the underperformances and divide by (6) which is the total number of observations: $[(-0.118)^2 + (-0.198)^2 + (-0.098)^2]/6 = 0.011$ or 1.1%.

B is incorrect because it divides the sum of the squares by the underperforming periods (3) instead of all return periods (6). C is incorrect because it is the semi-standard deviation.

20 B is correct. First calculate the arithmetic mean return: (3.20% – 1.60% + 1.10% – 1.30%)/4 = 0.35%. Next determine which monthly returns are less than the mean return, then calculate their deviations from the mean, and then square the deviations:

	Portfolio	Mean	Underperformance from Mean	Square of Underperformance
2005	3.20%	0.35%		
2006	–1.60%	0.35%	–1.95%	0.000380
2007	1.10%	0.35%		
2008	–1.30%	0.35%	–1.65%	0.000272

Sum the squared deviations and divide by the total number of observations to obtain the semi-variance: (0.000380 + 0.000272)/4 = 0.000163. Finally, take the square root of the semi-variance to obtain the semi-standard deviation: $0.000163^{0.5} = 0.0128$ (i.e., 1.28%).

A is incorrect because 0.0002 is the approximate semi-variance. C is incorrect because 0.0195 is the standard deviation.

21 A is correct. The semi-variance calculation captures the effect of skewness, whereas the variance calculation does not.

B is incorrect. When the return series is symmetrical, calculation of the semi-variance would not provide any additional information about the return series. C is incorrect. Semi-variance as defined in the text addresses variability on the downside.

22 B is correct. The target semi-variance differs from the semi-variance by using a targeted return to calculate the negative return deviations. This benchmark can be zero, the risk-free rate, etc.

A is incorrect because target semi-variance also measures downside risk. C is incorrect because both forms of semi-variance account for tail risk, the possibility of extreme losses.

23 A is correct. Drawdown measures have frequently been used in analyzing hedge fund returns because (1) hedge fund return streams depart from the normal distribution, and (2) hedge funds generally have incentive fees that are related to surpassing a previous peak (high water mark). This means that any drawdown has to be made up for an incentive fee to be payable.

B is incorrect. Volatility-based risk measures are more useful in analyzing short term government security funds since their return streams tend to be much more normally distributed then those of hedge funds. C is incorrect. Volatility-based risk measures are more useful in analyzing large capitalization diversified equity funds since their return streams tend to be much more normally distributed then those of hedge funds.

24 B is correct. The maximum drawdown is the maximum peak to trough percentage loss experienced during the four-month period. Since the unique peak is 50 at the beginning of the four-month period, the maximum drawdown is calculated from time 0 until the end of the third month, when the unit price is at its lowest level.

The largest individual drawdown is the cumulative decline for a series of consecutive losses. Since the unique peak is 50 at the beginning of the four-month period, the largest decline in value is from time 0 until the end of the third month, when the unit price is at its lowest level. Thus, maximum drawdown = largest individual drawdown = (45.7/50) −1 = −8.6%.

25 B is correct. The measurement of maximum drawdown is based on a time-dependent data series. More data, in the form of more frequent returns or a longer track record, will usually generate a larger maximum drawdown because there are more observations. With more observations, there is a greater chance that extremely large and small values will be measured, resulting a larger maximum drawdown.

26 A is correct. VaR is defined as an estimate of the loss that we expect to be exceeded with a given level of probability over a specified time period. Here, the estimate of the loss is €3,000,000, the level of probability is 1%, and the time period is one day.

B and C are incorrect because they do not reflect the definition of VaR shown above.

27 A is correct. VaR is defined as an estimate of the loss that we expect to be exceeded with a given level of probability over a specified time period. It gives no indication as to the maximum loss. Thus, answer A is not a proper description of VaR.

Both B and C are incorrect because they provide accurate descriptions of VaR.

28 B is correct. Stress testing estimates the expected impact on the portfolio of changes in parameters such as equity markets, commodity prices or interest rates.

A is incorrect because it is a statement of tail value at risk (TVaR). C is incorrect because it is a statement of scenario analysis, which examines the expected portfolio impact of historic scenarios if they were to happen again.

29 C is correct. The Monte Carlo method uses a random generator to estimate potential return outcomes. Thus, it can display a return distribution significantly different from normal and historical distributions.

A is incorrect because the historical method assumes that historical returns are an appropriate representation of the likelihood of future returns and here future returns may be distributed much differently than in the past. B is incorrect because the analytical method assumes a normal distribution of returns.

30 C is correct. Cash flow, five-year growth is a useful measure of growth for companies that do not have earnings, have weak earnings, or whose book values do not reflect intangible assets.

The P/E is not calculated based on negative earnings per share. Because the company's book value is stated not to reflect significant intangible assets, the P/B is less relevant.

31 A is correct. The higher a portfolio's valuation levels (P/E, price-to-book ratio, ratio of price to cash flow, etc.), the higher the earnings expectations and the greater the risk of having a significant amount of negative earnings surprise.

32 C is correct. Economic sector associates the company that issued the equity or debt with the economic sector in which this company operates, and the economic sector exposure will affect both the bonds and stocks.

A is incorrect because the convexity characteristic applies only to bonds. B is incorrect because the free cash flow characteristic applies only to equity.

33 A is correct. Duration is a risk measure related to fixed income investment. Therefore it is not appropriate for hedge funds invested in emerging market stocks.

B is incorrect because emerging market portfolios are exposed to currency risk. C is incorrect because drawdown measures can reveal the business risks of a hedge fund due to compensation structure.

34 A is correct. The client would wish the manager's performance to closely track that of the benchmark index. The tracking risk (or tracking error) measures the volatility of differences between the portfolio and benchmark returns.

B is incorrect because the maximum drawdown will show the maximum peak to trough experienced by the fund but will provide no indication as to the deviations from the passive investment strategy. C is incorrect because the standard deviation of returns will provide the volatility of the portfolio but will not provide the deviations from the passive investment strategy.

35 C is correct. Because insurance companies manage assets relative to liabilities, using a liability based benchmark would be an appropriate benchmark. A liability benchmark may not be appropriate to measure manager skill but it would be appropriate to represent the investment goals of the insurance company.

A is incorrect. Absolute risk measures such as VaR are likely to be more appropriate than benchmark relative measures for hedge fund investor's but not for insurance companies. Hedge funds often use VaR measures to manage their strategies dynamically, without reference to benchmarks or client reporting. B is incorrect. Drawdown analysis is more appropriate for hedge funds than for insurance companies.

36 A is correct. The risk contribution of the energy sector =12% × 30% = 3.6%, which is larger than utilities (answer B) or material (answer C).

B is incorrect because the utilities sector risk contribution is 2.8% (= 10% × 28%). Although its marginal contribution to risk is the highest, its small investment weight makes the risk contribution low. C is incorrect because the materials sector risk contribution is 3.2% (= 40% × 8%). Although its investment weight is the largest, its small marginal contribution to risk makes the risk contribution low.

37 B is correct. The selection effect will explain the active return (reflected in the tracking risk) completely. This is because only the selection effect is managed actively.

A is incorrect because the contribution of allocation to tracking risk will be zero, not negative. C is incorrect because allocation effect has no correlation with active return due to passively following the benchmark allocation.

38 A is correct. The tracking risk is equal to the sum of the contributions of small-cap ETF and large-cap ETF to tracking risk. Since we are given that the portfolio tracking risk is 0.483% and that the contribution of small-cap ETF to tracking risk is 0.606%, it follows that the contribution of large-cap ETF to tracking risk is −0.123%. Alternatively, the contribution of large-cap ETF can be calculated as:

Active weight × marginal contribution to tracking risk

= active weight × correlation × standard deviation

= −15% × 0.40 × 2.05%

= −0.123%

B is incorrect because in the formula shown in the justification for A above, it uses an active weight of 15% rather than −15%. C is incorrect because in the formula shown in the justification for A above, it uses the actual weight of 35% rather than active weight of −15%.

39 C is correct. The manager selects stocks and then compares his performance against the S&P 500. Thus the manager is using a bottom-up investment decision process and relative performance analysis. The marginal contribution to tracking risk is appropriate for the relative risk attribution of a bottom-up investment decision process.

A is incorrect because top-down risk attribution is appropriate for a top-down investment decision process, which decides allocation first and then security selection. B is incorrect because the marginal contribution to risk is used for absolute risk attribution.

40 C is correct. The allocation effect of real estate contributed 3.0% ÷ 10.0% = 30% of total active return, but only contributed 0.9% ÷ 15% = 6% of tracking risk.

A is incorrect because the selection effect of bond contributed 0.5% ÷ 10.0% = 5% of total active return and contributed 0.3% ÷ 15% = 2% of tracking risk. Compared to the real estate allocation effect, the return per unit of risk for bond selection is not as favorable. B is incorrect because the selection effect of equity contributed 5.5% ÷ 10.0% = 55% of total active return and contributed 8.1% ÷ 15% = 54% of tracking risk. Compared to the real estate allocation effect, the return per unit of risk for equity selection is not as favorable.

41 C is correct. Tracking risk for the portfolio is the sum of the two contributions to risk and the contributions to risk are equal to the standard deviation times the correlation. So, tracking risk = (0.106% × −0.641) + (0.520% × 0.220) = 0.046%.

A is incorrect because in each of the terms of the above formula, it introduces the average deviation of the weights of each asset class (−10% for mid-caps and + 10% for small-caps). This would be applicable only if the manager had maintained the weights constant in each month: (−10%) × (0.106% × −0.641) + 10% × (0.520% × 0.220) = 0.018%. In this particular example, standard deviation and correlation are already measured with respect to active contributions.

B is incorrect because in each of the terms of the above formula, the actual weights of each asset class (40% for mid-caps and 60% for small-caps) are introduced: 40% × (0.106% × −0.641) + 60% × (0.520% × 0.220) = 0.042%.

42 C is correct. The stock selection decision results in the highest ratio of return contribution to tracking risk.

Bond selection represents 40.62% (= 3.79%/9.33%) of tracking risk for 17.44% (= 2.56%/14.68%) of total active return, so the return contribution per unit of tracking risk is 17.44%/40.62% = 0.429.

Stock selection represents 55.84% (= 5.21%/9.33%) of tracking risk for 50.68% (= 7.44%/14.68%) of total active return, so the return contribution per unit of tracking risk is 50.68%/55.84% = 0.908.

Stock allocation represents 1.18% (= 0.11%/9.33%) of tracking risk for 23.50% (= 3.45%/14.68%) of total active return, so the return contribution per unit of tracking risk is 23.50%/1.18% = 19.915.

43 C is correct. Manager C focuses on only stock selection and takes different-from-benchmark exposures to such risk factors as size (small-cap) and style (value). Such a strategy is a factor-based investment and a factor-based attribution model would be most suitable to analyze its results.

44 B is correct. The total contribution of allocation to tracking risk is equal to the sum of the bond contribution and the equity contribution = 0.08% + 0.60% = 0.68%.

A is incorrect because bond selection represents 19% of tracking risk i.e., (1.23%)/(0.08% + 0.60% + 1.23% + 4.56%). C is incorrect because the total active return is equal to the sum of the allocation and selection (including interaction) contributions for bonds and equity = 0.04% + 0.42% + 0.61% + 0.29% = 1.36%.

45 B is correct. Non-financial risks include operational, model, and settlement risk. Settlement risk is the risk of a breakdown in the settlement of a trade and can increase when the counterparties are in different time zones.

46 C is correct. Risk attribution in combination with return attribution enables a more comprehensive analysis of the effects of management decisions on the portfolio. If return attribution revealed, for example, that a manager outperformed as a result of investing outside the portfolio's benchmark, then risk attribution could be used to show how the active decision increased or reduced overall portfolio volatility.

47 B is correct. Risk attribution analysis can help a portfolio manager determine the level of portfolio risk contributed by different factors.

48 A is correct. The predictive power of *ex post* risk measurements for *ex ante* risk declines as changes to an investor's portfolio composition increase.

49 A is correct. Systematic risk originates from broad financial market conditions and the macroeconomy. Examples include changes in economic growth forecasts, changes in consumer confidence, and any other factor that affects the majority of securities.

50 A is correct. Active risk is a relative risk measure and refers to the variability of the deviations when manager returns deviate from those of the benchmark.

51 B is correct. The data appear to be skewed: The peak of the distribution is to the left of the arithmetic mean, and the arithmetic mean is greater than the median. If the arithmetic mean is greater than the median, it is usually the case that there are extreme positive values pulling the arithmetic mean up. This scenario generally results in positive skewness.

52 A is correct. The beta of the portfolio can be calculated in the following way:

$$\begin{aligned} \text{cov}(R_A,R_I) &= \rho_{A,I} \times \sigma_A \times \sigma_I \\ &= 0.92 \times 0.038 \times 0.044 \\ &= 0.0015 \end{aligned}$$

$$\beta_{\text{portfolio}} = \frac{\text{cov}(R_A,R_I)}{\sigma_I^2} = \frac{0.0015}{(0.044)^2} = 0.7748$$

53 C is correct. The standard deviation is the root of the variance. Both the variance and the standard deviation can be used to quantify stand-alone risk. One way to calculate beta uses the correlation in the formula for beta.:

$$\text{cov}(R_p,R_m) = \rho_{p,m} \times \sigma_p \times \sigma_m$$

$$\beta = \frac{\text{cov}(R_p,R_m)}{\sigma_m^2}$$

$$= \frac{\rho_{p,m} \times \sigma_p \times \sigma_m}{\sigma_m^2}$$

$$= \rho_{p,m} \times [(\sigma_p)/(\sigma_m)]$$
$$= 0.75 \times [(\sigma_p)/(2.7\%)]$$

A change in stand-alone risk will not change the correlation. Thus, as σ_p increases, with σ_m and $\rho_{p,m}$ unchanged, beta will increase.

54 B is correct. The average drawdown is the average of a specified number (3) of the largest drawdowns over a given period. The average drawdown in this case would be:

$$\text{Average drawdown} = \frac{[(-12.6\%) + (-2.1\%) + (-7.2\%)]}{3} = -7.3\%$$

55 B is correct. The analytical approach relies on the assumption of a normal distribution of returns.

56 C is correct. The Monte Carlo method uses a random number generator to estimate potential return outcomes. The random number method may be more appropriate for estimating the VaR of a portfolio that displays a return distribution that is significantly different from a normal distribution.

57 A is correct. The goal of a company's pension plan is to pay current and future retiree benefits with a high degree of confidence. The sponsor faces the risk of not being able to meet those pension liabilities if there is a large degree of variability in a plan's surplus.

58 B is correct. Equity selection made a positive contribution of 0.38% to tracking risk.

READING

8

Equity Portfolio Characteristics in Performance Analysis

by Stephen C. Gaudette, CFA, and Philip Lawton, PhD, CFA, CIPM

Stephen C. Gaudette, CFA, is at Northfield Information Services, Inc. (USA). Philip Lawton, PhD, CFA, CIPM (USA).

LEARNING OUTCOMES

Mastery	The candidate should be able to:
☐	**a.** identify and explain the uses of portfolio characteristics analysis in performance evaluation;
☐	**b.** calculate the mean of a distribution that includes outliers and evaluate the various methods in doing so;
☐	**c.** calculate the weighted arithmetic mean and the weighted harmonic mean of a portfolio using security-level characteristic values;
☐	**d.** classify characteristics as macroeconomic, company fundamental, or company share-related;
☐	**e.** calculate and interpret the following equity characteristics: economic sector and industry membership; beta; debt-to-equity (D/E) ratio; return on equity (ROE); market capitalization; price-to-book (P/B) ratio; price-to-earnings (P/E) ratio; dividend yield (D/P); price-to-sales (P/S) ratio; price-to-cash flow (P/CF) ratio; relative strength; liquidity; and volatility;
☐	**f.** determine the investment style of a portfolio, given pertinent data such as the market capitalization, price-to-earnings (P/E) and price-to-book (P/B) ratios, dividend yield (D/P), and growth characteristics of the portfolio and one or more style indexes;
☐	**g.** compare holdings-based and returns-based style analysis;
☐	**h.** compare single-factor and fundamental multifactor attribution models.

"... when you can measure what you are speaking about, and express it in numbers, you know something about it; but when you cannot measure it, when you cannot express it in numbers, your knowledge is of a meagre and unsatisfactory kind...."

Lord Kelvin, PLA, vol. 1, "Electrical Units of Measurement", 1883-05-03

1 INTRODUCTION

The investment management process is composed of integrated activities that combine the client's objectives, constraints, and preferences with the portfolio manager's capital market expectations. (See Exhibit 1.) Portfolio managers make investment decisions under conditions of uncertainty; performance analysts quantify the results of those decisions, providing feedback on the execution of investment strategies in the light of actual outcomes. Portfolio managers can use this information to evaluate their security selection and portfolio construction processes, and their clients can use it as one element in an ongoing endeavor to monitor the manager's organization and to appraise the manager's performance.

Managers look at the capital markets and individual securities in different ways reflecting their distinctive competence, portfolio construction process, and investment strategy. Some organizations with forecasting expertise adopt a top-down approach to portfolio construction, selecting securities in line with their expectations for the overall economy and their judgment about the relative attractiveness of specific sectors and industries. Other organizations may stress their stock-picking skills and employ a bottom-up process, selecting the most undervalued securities across all sectors and industries within the client's or the firm's exposure limits. Managers' strategies and clients' guidelines also govern investment decisions. For example, a manager investing on behalf of a risk-averse client may purchase defensive stocks with high dividend yields, while a manager whose client is willing and able to accept market risk may purchase stocks with greater upside price potential. These factors lead to discernible differences among portfolios.

Equity analysts employed by investment management firms that adopt a fundamental approach to valuation often calculate and evaluate the characteristics of their assigned companies and stocks. In this context, characteristics derived from market data and the issuer's financial statements are one kind of input in a comprehensive process whose essential objective is to identify misvalued securities. Consistent with the portfolio's investment strategy and constraints, portfolio managers may act on the equity analysts' recommendations by purchasing undervalued stocks and selling overvalued stocks.

Unlike equity analysts, investment performance practitioners are rarely if ever called upon to examine issuers' financial statements or to calculate security-level characteristics. Rather, their role is typically to evaluate system-generated portfolio characteristics in comparison with benchmark characteristics. As explained below, portfolio characteristics are the weighted averages of the characteristics of the securities held in the portfolio. Holdings data are provided by the portfolio accounting system, and calculated security-level characteristics are typically received electronically from external capital market data service providers. Performance analysts then analyze and interpret these data to address specific issues. In order to interpret the data, however, performance analysts must understand how they are prepared.

Exhibit 1 The Portfolio Construction, Monitoring, and Revision Process

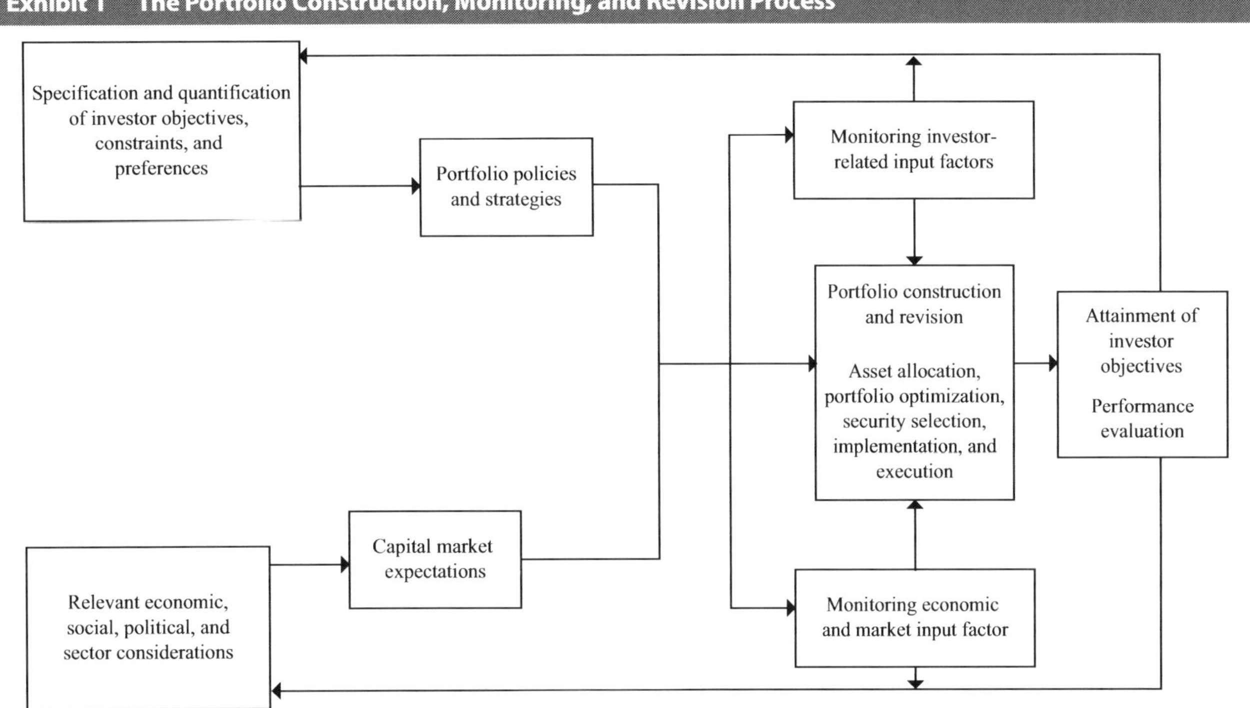

Source: John L. Maginn, Donald L. Tuttle, Dennis W. McLeavey, and Jerald E. Pinto, "The Portfolio Management Process and the Investment Policy Statement," Chapter 1 in John L. Maginn, Donald L. Tuttle, Dennis W. McLeavey, and Jerald E. Pinto, eds., *Managing Investment Portfolios; A Dynamic Approach* (CFA Institute, 2007), p. 6.

The following sections will summarize some useful techniques for examining an equity portfolio's composition and relating the portfolio's characteristics to its performance. In the next section, we introduce three principal uses of portfolio characteristics analysis—identifying possible shifts in investment strategy, conducting holdings-based style analysis, and determining the sources of portfolio returns.[1] We then address input data and portfolio-level characteristic calculation issues, survey and illustrate the types of characteristics, and present portfolio monitoring, style analysis, and characteristic- or factor-based attribution in more detail. We close with remarks on the limitations of portfolio characteristics analysis.

USES OF PORTFOLIO CHARACTERISTICS

2

Macroeconomic, social, political and other external influences can be expected to alter the revenues and expenses of companies and therefore their profitability. In many cases, companies with similar exposures to external factors will respond similarly to changes in their operating environment. For example, unrest in oil-producing regions may raise the political risk premium by influencing the outlook for future supplies of petroleum products. The impact on current fuel prices may be favorable for oil

1 In addition, portfolio characteristics analysis may be used by investment management firms in the construction and maintenance of custom security-based benchmarks, also known as strategy benchmarks. See Jeffery V. Bailey, Thomas M. Richards, and David E. Tierney, "Evaluating Portfolio Performance," Chapter 12 in John L. Maginn, Donald L. Tuttle, Dennis W. McLeavey, and Jerald E. Pinto, eds., *Managing Investment Portfolios: A Dynamic Process*, Third Edition (CFA Institute, 2007), pp. 737–738; and David E. Kuenzi, "Strategy Benchmarks," *Journal of Portfolio Management* (Winter 2003), pp. 46–56.

companies, which benefit from rising revenues, and unfavorable for airlines, which suffer from rising expenses. Investors' expectations of profit changes in the oil and airline industries will result in new security valuations, directly affecting returns. Similarly, an increase in interest rates may be auspicious for lending companies and detrimental to borrowers. Investors' revised estimates of the future earnings of banks, insurance companies, utilities, and other companies with significant interest rate exposures will trigger market adjustments affecting security returns.

Like many athletes, many investment managers believe that their competitive performance improves when they focus on their strengths. Consequently, some investment organizations and most equity portfolio managers adopt strategies centered on particular types of stocks. Since common external influences—including, of course, other investors' expectations—can have a large impact on the performance of groups of securities, it is informative to identify and monitor security characteristics that may affect valuations.

From the client's or the consultant's perspective, periodic comparisons between portfolio and benchmark characteristics may disclose possible deviations from the manager's stated investment strategy or discipline. For example, a sector rotator would not be expected to have a large positive active position in financials when the firm anticipates accelerating inflation. Investors who are attentive to portfolio characteristics are well-positioned to engage their managers in informative dialogue; it may turn out, after all, that the manager has valid reasons for overweighting financial stocks.

Beyond economic sector and industry classifications, other factors commonly used to characterize a domestic equity portfolio are the size of the stocks in which the manager invests and the issuing companies' growth or value traits. As explained below, comparing the market capitalization and value–growth characteristics of an investment portfolio to those of a valid benchmark at a point in time may help identify how the active manager has attempted to outperform the benchmark or how the manager is positioning the portfolio for expected market conditions. Moreover, periodic comparisons over time may help identify style drift or, alternately, confirm that the manager is adhering to the agreed-upon style or strategy mandate.

Finally, in addition to using portfolio characteristics for the purposes of manager monitoring and style analysis, performance analysts can view them as sources of return or, more rigorously, as risk factors with which security returns are correlated. Attribution analysis based upon portfolio characteristics or fundamental factor exposures can illuminate investment results and lead to constructive dialogue about the intended and unintended consequences of the manager's security selection and portfolio construction processes.

3 DATA AND CALCULATION ISSUES

Portfolio characteristics—the market value-weighted characteristics of the individual non-cash securities held in the portfolio at a point in time—can be meaningfully presented only if reasonably complete and consistent security-level data are available.

Despite the tremendous growth in capital market data services, the performance analyst cannot be assured of complete coverage for all portfolios. Data may be missing for numerous securities, especially if the portfolio is invested in relatively illiquid issues such as micro-cap or emerging market stocks. In practice, the simplest solution for missing data points is to report the weighted average characteristic values of the securities for which data are available along with the percentage of the portfolio's total market value captured by each characteristic. For instance, if a portfolio is valued at

£12,548,960 but dividend yields are available only for portfolio holdings that add up to £8,068,981, then the best practice is to indicate that the average dividend yield is based upon 64.3 percent of the portfolio's total market value.

Organizations that attempt to improve security-level coverage by subscribing to several market data services should be alert to potential methodological differences among their providers. For example, the earnings of companies that issue common stock are used in calculating certain characteristics such as price-to-earnings ratios and the growth in earnings per share. One market data service provider may report earnings as shown in the issuer's income statement, while another may make adjustments to eliminate extraordinary, non-recurring, and/or non-cash items. The performance analyst should be aware of such differences; although they generally will not invalidate portfolio characteristics analyses, they may reduce their reliability.

Another issue that arises when calculating portfolio characteristics is the validity of calculated means if potential outliers are observed among the constituent stocks. For example, a portfolio containing 40 stocks is found to have an average five-year earnings per share growth rate of 34.5 percent. However, one of the holdings has a reported historical growth rate of 500 percent; the other 39 have historical growth rates ranging from 12.4 to 38.7. There are several possible reasons for the exceptionally high five-year EPS growth rate reported for the one stock. The company may have had a small positive starting value such as $0.01, or the growth rate as given by the characteristic provider may simply be erroneous. In a production environment, the performance analyst typically does not have the time to examine the company's financial statements and independently validate the data. How should the apparent outlier be handled?

One approach, of course, is to include all the data points, reporting the mean of 34.5 percent. Another approach is to exclude data points that fall outside a tolerance range. For instance, in a normal distribution the range defined as ± 2.33 standard deviations around the mean excludes approximately the largest one percent and smallest one percent of observations. In the example shown the standard deviation is 75.9 percent, so including only the observations falling within 2.33 standard deviations of the mean excludes the 500-percent observation. A third approach is to calculate a trimmed mean that excludes a certain percentage of the largest and smallest data points. In this example, excluding the top and bottom data points in an ordered list results in a trimmed mean of 22.8 percent. A fourth approach is to calculate a winsorized mean, which involves a reassignment of the values of extreme observations. For example, for a 99 percent winsorized mean, the top 0.5 percent of values would be set equal to the value of the observation at the cut-off point for the top 0.5 percent group; similarly, the lowest 0.5 percent of values would assume the value of the observation at their cut-off point. For simplicity, in the case of the 40-stock portfolio described above, Exhibit 2 shows the winsorized mean growth rate is 23.0 based on re-assigning the values of the largest observation and the smallest observation in the sample. This exhibit also illustrates the other methods discussed above.

Exhibit 2 Five-Year EPS Growth Percent

Rank	Arithmetic	Tolerance Range	Trimmed	Winsorized
1	500.0	—	—	38.7
2	38.7	38.7	38.7	38.7
3	38.1	38.1	38.1	38.1
...	...	...	...	...
38	13.6	13.6	13.6	13.6
39	12.9	12.9	12.9	12.9

(continued)

Exhibit 2 (Continued)

Rank	Arithmetic	Tolerance Range	Trimmed	Winsorized
40	12.4	12.4	—	12.9
Sum	1380.3	880.3	867.9	919.5
N	40	39	38	40
Mean	34.5	22.6	22.8	23.0

Portfolio characteristics are usually calculated as the weighted mean of the observations where the weight applied to each observation is the fraction of the portfolio's value invested in the holding associated with that observation. However, the weighted harmonic mean may be the most appropriate representation of an average rate or ratio. If the ratio of an individual holding is represented by X_i, the expression for the weighted harmonic mean of the ratio is

$$X_{WH} = \frac{1}{\sum_{i=1}^{n}\left(\frac{w_i}{X_i}\right)} \quad (1)$$

where the w_i are portfolio value weights (summing to 1) and $X_i > 0$ for $i = 1, 2, \ldots, n$.

The superiority of weighted harmonic mean estimates over weighted arithmetic mean estimates in this context may be conveyed by an example. Consider a hypothetical portfolio that contains two stocks. One stock has a market capitalization of €700 million and earnings of €70 million, giving it a P/E ratio of 10. The other stock has a market capitalization of €600 million and earnings of €3 million, for a P/E ratio of 200. Exhibit 3 displays the calculation of the hypothetical portfolio's weighted arithmetic mean P/E and its weighted harmonic mean P/E.

Exhibit 3 P/E Ratio—Weighted Arithmetic and Harmonic Means

	Market Capitalization						
	€ Million	% of Total	Earnings € Million	P/E	Weighted P/E	E/P	Weighted E/P
Stock 1	700	53.85%	70	10	5.38	0.10	0.0538
Stock 2	600	46.15%	3	200	92.31	0.005	0.0023
	1300	100.00%			97.69		0.0562
Weighted Harmonic Mean							17.81

In this example, the weighted harmonic mean of 17.81 is much lower than the weighted arithmetic mean of 97.69. (Note that the harmonic mean inherently gives less weight to higher P/E ratios and more weight to lower P/Es. In general, unless all the observations in a data set have the same value, the harmonic mean is less than the arithmetic mean.) Which is the more accurate value? In fact, the weighted harmonic mean precisely corresponds with the P/E calculated directly by aggregating the companies' market capitalization and earnings: (700 + 600)/(70 + 3) = 17.81.

Finally, investment professionals have differences of opinion on the proper treatment of negative ratios. For example, stocks with negative earnings (losses) will have negative P/E ratios.[2] Many consider negative P/Es meaningless and omit them when calculating portfolio averages, while others contend that averaging only the positive P/E ratios falsely overstates the portfolio-level ratio. Whether negative ratios are included in or excluded from the portfolio mean, it is important to treat the benchmark the same way.

Another consideration that a performance analyst must take into account when calculating weighted averages is how to handle short positions. It is inappropriate simply to exclude short positions from the calculation of portfolio-level characteristics, since they are integral to the execution of a long-short strategy. The remaining alternatives are to show net characteristic exposures or to present the components of the net exposure by separately displaying the characteristics of the long and the short portions of the portfolio. Although it may require additional work, the latter method is the more informative because portfolios whose net value is near zero can have distorted weighted average characteristics.

4 TYPES OF CHARACTERISTICS

Characteristics may generally be classified as belonging to three major groups: macroeconomic characteristics, company fundamental characteristics, and company share-related characteristics.

A company's economic sector and industry membership, already mentioned, is a macroeconomic characteristic. The Global Industry Classification System (GICS®) developed by Standard & Poor's and MSCI Barra is widely used in equity investing and performance measurement. GICS is a four-tier system composed of ten sectors that are composed, in turn, of 24 industry groups, 67 industries, and 147 sub-industries. For example, the Asset Management & Custody Banks sub-industry belongs to the Capital Markets industry, which belongs to the Diversified Financials industry group, which belongs to the Financials sector. Standard & Poor's and MSCI Barra jointly assign a company to a single GICS sub-industry in accordance with the company's principal business activity.[3] Similar breakdowns are done by other data service providers using the companies' Standard Industry Classification code or the providers' internal classification schemes.

Another macroeconomic characteristic is beta, a linear measure of the sensitivity of a given stock to movements in the overall market under the capital asset pricing model (CAPM). A stock's historical beta may be estimated by taking the ratio of the covariance between the stock's return and the market return to the variance of the market return:

$$\beta_i = \frac{\text{Cov}(R_i, R_M)}{\text{Var}(R_M)} \tag{2}$$

2 Faced with the task of ranking stocks, equity analysts have several alternatives for handling negative P/E ratios that are not usually available to performance practitioners. In some cases, replacing trailing earnings with normalized earnings or with estimated prospective earnings may produce positive price-to-earnings ratios. In addition, using the earnings yield ratio (E/P) will result in the correct ordering of positive- and negative-P/E stocks by what may be deemed the cost of earnings. See John D. Stowe, Thomas R. Robinson, Jerald E. Pinto, and Dennis W. McLeavey, *Analysis of Equity Investments: Valuation* (CFA Institute, 2002), pp. 188–189.

3 "Global Industry Classification Standard Methodology" (Standard & Poor's, 2006), pp. 5–6.

where

β_i = the beta of stock i
R_i = the return on stock i
R_M = the return on the market portfolio

A beta greater than 1 indicates greater than average market risk and, according to the CAPM, is expected to earn a higher-than-market return above the risk-free rate. In other words, a stock with a beta greater than 1 has above-average exposure to systematic risk. Its price may be expected to rise more than the market rises and to fall more than the market falls. Conversely, a beta less than 1 indicates less than average market risk and earns a smaller expected excess return.

Company fundamental characteristics include activity, liquidity, solvency, and profitability measures. For example, the ratio of sales to assets is an activity measure. The current ratio, a liquidity measure, compares the obligations that will become payable during the current operating cycle (current liabilities) with the cash that is or will become available to pay them (current assets). The debt-to-equity (D/E) ratio, an indicator of the company's solvency, is the ratio of total debt to total shareholders' equity. Return on equity (ROE) is a critically important profitability measure frequently encountered in portfolio characteristics analyses. It is calculated by dividing average common shareholders' equity into the difference between net income and preferred dividends:

$$\text{ROE} = \frac{\text{Net Income} - \text{Preferred Dividends}}{\text{Average Common Shareholders' Equity}} \tag{3}$$

Of particular interest to performance analysts are company share-related characteristics. For example, market capitalization, broadly defined as the number of common stock shares outstanding multiplied by the price of a single share, is a key measure of the company's size that is used in holdings-based style analysis, as explained below.

The price-to-book (P/B) ratio is another valuation measure frequently used to indicate the style of a portfolio. It is calculated by dividing the stock's current market price by the book value per share, where the book value per share is defined as the total common shareholders' equity on the business's balance sheet divided by the number of common stock shares outstanding.

Other ratios that are frequently used to describe the style of the portfolio include the price-to-earnings (P/E) ratio, dividend yield (D/P), and the dividend payout ratio. The trailing P/E ratio, sometimes referred to as the current P/E, is calculated by dividing the current market price of a stock by the most recent four quarters' earnings per share (EPS). The leading P/E ratio, also called the forward P/E or the prospective P/E, is the stock's current price divided by next year's expected earnings; in performance analysis, expected earnings may reflect consensus estimates compiled by market data service providers. For both historical and forward P/E ratios, data providers may have different policies regarding what earnings figures should be used when extraordinary items appear on the income statement. As the next section shows, comparatively high P/B and P/E ratios generally characterize growth stocks, whereas relatively low P/B and P/E ratios typify value stocks.

Dividend yield (D/P) expresses the relationship between a company's distributions to shareholders and the price of its stock, or, from the investor's point of view, between the investment income produced by an asset and the asset's market value. Trailing dividend yield is generally calculated as four times the most recent quarterly per-share dividend divided by the current market price per share. (Note that, unlike the trailing P/E ratio, trailing dividend yield does not look to the historical record for the last four quarters.) The leading dividend yield is calculated as forecasted dividends per share over the next year divided by the current market price per share. The dividend payout ratio equals the percentage of earnings paid out as dividends, that is, dividends divided by net income. Relatively high dividend yields are generally indicators of value stocks, while comparatively low dividend yields are characteristic of growth stocks.

The price-to-sales (P/S) and price-to-cash-flow (P/CF) ratios are also often used by equity analysts in valuation and by performance analysts in portfolio characteristics analysis. The P/S ratio is calculated as price per share divided by annual net sales per share, where net sales is defined as total sales less returns and customer discounts. Annual sales from the company's most recent fiscal year are usually used in the calculation. The P/CF ratio is most frequently calculated using the current price divided by the most recent four quarters' cash flow. Although there are other, more accurate cash flow concepts, in practice data vendors often estimate cash flow by adding non-cash charges back to income. A typical approximation of cash flow per share is EPS plus per-share depreciation, amortization, and, in the case of natural resource companies, depletion.

Other company share-related characteristics include relative strength, typically defined as the ratio of a stock's performance to the performance of an index, liquidity, which is a measure of the number of shares traded relative to the total number of shares outstanding, and volatility, which may be calculated as the annualized standard deviation of an asset's continuously compounded daily returns. Clients and consultants would expect a portfolio containing high-volatility stocks to be adequately diversified and might wish to afford the manager a longer-than-usual evaluation period.

There are many other characteristics in addition to those mentioned here. Given the wide range of characteristics available, how should the performance analyst select the most meaningful measures?

The answer depends upon the intended use of the portfolio characteristics analysis. When designing standard reports, a mix of macroeconomic, company fundamental, and company share-related characteristics may be most useful to clients. When preparing custom reports, on the other hand, it is sensible to include characteristics that are likely to corroborate or disconfirm that the manager is adhering to the investment strategy. For example, if a manager states that companies' spending on research and development (R & D) is a critical factor in security selection, it is reassuring to see that average R & D spending (for instance, as a percentage of revenues) is higher in the portfolio than in the benchmark. Managers' explanations of their investment philosophy and strategy may indicate which characteristics are most promising. In addition, performance analysis fosters dialogue between clients and managers; in this context, the managers themselves may have helpful suggestions about pertinent characteristics based upon their security selection and portfolio construction processes.

MANAGER MONITORING AND STYLE ANALYSIS 5

Examining portfolio composition, and tracking changes over time, is an essential element in a sound manager monitoring process.[4] In combination with performance attribution, portfolio characteristics analysis can provide valuable insights into the manager's thinking. Comparing the portfolio's sector weights and other pertinent characteristics with those of a valid benchmark at the same point in time enables the client or consultant to see what bets the manager has made. In addition, while tactical adjustments are normal, an apparent trend in portfolio characteristics relative to the benchmark may alert the client or consultant to possible departures from the manager's investment mandate.

4 See Russell L. Olson, *The Independent Fiduciary; Investing for Pension Funds and Endowment Funds* (John Wiley & Sons, 1999), pp. 124–125.

Style analysis is a specific type of manager monitoring based upon the characterization of investment strategies in two dimensions: size (small cap, mid-cap, and large cap) and valuation (value, neutral or core, and growth). In a given measurement period, one style may be in favor, generating highly positive returns, while another is out of favor, producing disappointing results. For example, the returns of small cap growth portfolios, taken as a group, may differ systematically from those of large cap value portfolios in the same period. Style analysis has two major variations: returns-based and holdings-based.

Returns-based style analysis[5] determines the combination of indexes that best explains the style in which a portfolio is managed. For example, a portfolio might be described as 53.2% large growth, 32.7% small growth, and 14.1% small value. Given the ease with which commercially available returns-based style models can be used, this approach has great practical appeal; the only data the performance analyst need compile is the portfolio's historical return series and those of appropriate indexes. In comparison, holdings-based style analysis requires extensive security-level data. In addition, returns-based style analysis graphically displays how the manager's profile has changed over time. It is more effortful to interpret period-to-period comparisons of holdings-based characteristics. However, beyond observing that the manager's effective mix of style-based benchmarks has evolved, the holdings-based approach described below may enable astute clients and consultants to ask the manager appreciably more pointed questions about potentially significant changes in portfolio structure.

In holdings-based style analysis, an equity portfolio's investment strategy may be profiled by observing its size and value–growth characteristics. Rather than merely tracking changes in the portfolio, however, it is essential to compare the portfolio to a valid benchmark in each period, because the general level of market valuations changes over the course of the business cycle (and over longer periods as well). For example, price-to-earnings (P/E) ratios tend to be high and rising when the outlook for earnings improves, as in the early stages of an economic recovery, and low and falling when the outlook worsens.[6]

Size is measured by the stock's market capitalization. Some capital market index providers adjust market cap weights for each issue's floating supply of shares or "free float," the number of shares outstanding that are actually available to investors after excluding such categories as corporate cross-holdings in the same index, large corporate and private holdings, and government positions in partially privatized companies.

A stock's position on the value–growth spectrum may be indicated by its price-to-earnings (P/E) ratio and/or its price-to-book (P/B) ratio, among other factors. Because the market pays a premium for projected earnings increases, growing companies generally have higher P/E and P/B ratios than companies that are considered to have more limited prospects for expansion.

A stock's dividend yield (D/P) and its issuer's dividend payout ratio provide further information. Generally, growth companies have low dividend yields and dividend payout ratios because they retain most of their income to finance future expansion. Mature companies which do not have attractive reinvestment opportunities distribute a greater portion of their earnings to shareholders. Other measures of a company's relative position are its trailing and forecasted growth in per-share earnings.

Index providers typically use multiple factors when assigning companies to value and growth style categories. For example, the methodology employed in the construction of Standard & Poor's US Style indexes and the S&P/Citigroup style benchmark series uses three factors to measure growth and four factors to measure value. The

5 For an account of the development and interpretation of returns-based style analysis, see Laurence B. Siegel, *Benchmarks and Investment Management* (The Research Foundation of CFA Institute, 2003), pp. 66–73.

6 John P. Calverley, Alan M. Meder, Brian D. Singer, and Renato Staub, "Capital Market Expectations," Chapter 4 in John L. Maginn, Donald L. Tuttle, Dennis W. McLeavey, and Jerald E. Pinto, eds., *Managing Investment Portfolios; A Dynamic Process*, Third Edition (CFA Institute, 2007), pp. 219–220.

growth factors are the five-year EPS growth rate, the five-year sales per share growth rate, and the five-year internal growth rate, defined as the product of ROE and the earnings retention rate. The value factors are B/P, the cash flow-to-price ratio, the sales-to-price ratio, and dividend yield. Standard & Poor's classifies stocks after ranking them according to their scores on the growth and value dimensions.[7] Russell uses a probability algorithm to assign stocks to the growth and value style indexes on the basis of their relative B/P ratios and I/B/E/S forecast long-term growth mean.[8] Complete descriptions of these providers' style index construction methodologies are available on their websites.

Exhibit 4 displays comparative values of four Russell style indexes. The Russell 1000® indexes are large-cap indexes and the Russell 2000® indexes are small-cap indexes. As expected, the large-cap and small-cap value indexes have lower P/B and P/E ratios, higher dividend yields, and lower earnings growth statistics than the corresponding growth indexes. Similar comparisons may be done within other index families.

Exhibit 4 Comparative Index Characteristics

	Monthly Data From 31 May 2006 Through 31 May 2007			
Characteristic	**Russell 1000® Value Index**	**Russell 1000® Growth Index**	**Russell 2000® Value Index**	**Russell 2000® Growth Index**
Average Market Cap in Billions ($-WTD)	115.939	73.622	1.347	1.420
Median Market Cap in Billions	6.033	6.223	0.686	0.677
Price/Book	2.29	4.30	1.94	3.67
Dividend Yield	2.35	1.11	1.75	0.43
P/E Ex-Neg Earnings	14.88	21.44	19.25	23.93
LT Growth Forecast-IBES	9.48%	14.51%	11.22%	18.77%
EPS Growth 5 years	19.42	22.15	12.64	21.95

Russell Investment Group is the source and owner of the trademarks, service marks and copyrights related to the Russell Indexes. Russell® is a trademark of Russell Investment Group.

When conducting holdings-based style analysis, it is helpful to be familiar with the methodologies employed by the market data service provider who supplies security-level characteristics for the portfolio as well as by the index provider who assigns individual stocks to style categories according to its own index construction rules. By observing the different characteristics of the portfolio and those of the benchmark, it is possible to go beyond a simple classification of the manager's style and gain a deeper understanding of some of the factors that the manager emphasizes in his security selection process.

7 "S&P US Style Indices: Index Methodology" (Standard & Poor's, 2006), pp. 7–9.
8 "Russell US Equity Indexes: Construction and Methodology" (Russell, 2007), pp. 13–14.

6 ATTRIBUTION ANALYSIS

Viewed as sources of return, portfolio characteristics are also serviceable in performance attribution analysis. Indeed, the classic sector weighting/stock selection attribution model exemplifies characteristic-based attribution analysis.[9] This single-factor model can be used with characteristics in addition to economic sectors. For example, a portfolio's holdings can be sorted by their P/E ratios and grouped into ranges such as "stocks with P/E ratios equal to or less than 5," "stocks with P/E ratios greater than 5 but less than 10," and so forth. It is then a trivial matter to determine the market value weights of each range and to calculate their contributions to absolute return. If stock-level characteristics and capitalization weights are available for the benchmark, the contribution of each P/E range to the portfolio's value-added return—the return in excess of the benchmark—can also be determined.

While the single-factor approach outlined in the preceding paragraph may offer some insight into the manager's performance, its usefulness is limited at best. In a single-factor model, each view of the portfolio excludes, by definition, all other views. For instance, a single-factor attribution analysis using P/E ranges "explains" all, or almost all, of the portfolio's value-added returns—but so does a single-factor attribution analysis by price-to-book (P/B) ratios or by any other characteristic. There is no perspective in which the analyst can simultaneously evaluate the relative return contributions of multiple portfolio characteristics. A single-factor model may also confound the effects on performance of distinct but correlated risk factors. This can lead the analyst to draw a conclusion for the wrong reason. Consider a situation where tax laws are changed to make dividends more attractive to investors. If an attribution is done based on industry, utilities and REITs might appear to have added to performance when in reality it was their propensity to pay high dividends, rather than their industry membership, that contributed to performance.

In addition, a single-factor model is likely to have less explanatory power than a well-specified multifactor model. Indeed, without conducting tests of statistical significance the analyst cannot be assured that the results of a single-factor attribution analysis are valid. A single-factor attribution analysis using the ratio of blue-eyed to brown-eyed employees of portfolio companies will produce economically meaningless results. At a minimum, attribution analyses must be based upon factors that make sense in light of the manager's investment strategy.

Research has shown that multiple factor affect securities' returns. In contrast with single-factor models, multivariate analysis permits examination of individual characteristics' incremental effects and provides a more nuanced picture of risk. Multifactor models for performance attribution can be built using a variety of factors ranging from fundamental factors to macroeconomic to a combination of the two.

In performance applications, for example, fundamental multifactor models use techniques of statistical analysis to unpack a stock's return, breaking out the contributions from the stock's exposure to underlying elements found to have systematic effects—for example, membership in an economic sector or industry, forecasted beta, market capitalization, the P/E ratio, the P/B ratio, and the issuing company's financial leverage. At the level of individual securities, the general form of a multifactor model can be expressed by a standard regression equation:

$$R_i = a_i + b_{i1}F_1 + b_{i2}F_2 + \ldots + b_{iK}F_K + \varepsilon_I \quad (4)$$

9 Sector weighting/stock selection attribution analysis is presented and explained in Jeffery V. Bailey, Thomas M. Richards, and David E. Tierney, *op. cit.*, pp. 755–759.

where

R_i = the return to stock i over the regression period
a_i = the intercept of the regression equation
b_{i1} = the sensitivity of the return to stock i to factor 1
F_1 = the average value of factor 1 across all stocks
K = the number of factors in the model
ε_i = an error term that represents the portion of the return to stock i not explained by the factor model

By looking at a broad universe of stocks over an extended period, one can estimate the return associated with the average exposure to each factor. The empirically determined factor returns can then be combined with a specific stock's relative factor exposures to account for the stock's return. The market value-weighted factor exposures of all holdings can be summed to determine the portfolio's aggregate exposure to each factor and, by extension, the portion of the portfolio's return that is attributable to each exposure. Applying the same procedures to the benchmark constituents enables the performance analyst to establish the portfolio's active factor exposures and to quantify their contributions to the manager's value-added return.

A significant advantage of fundamental multifactor attribution analysis over the single factor approach is that the analyst can see the impact of all of the factors in the model simultaneously. This reduces the likelihood of misconstruing one effect for another. For instance, in a single-factor model, because integrated oil stocks have large market capitalizations, an exposure to integrated oil stocks in an industry view might look very much like the exposure to large capitalization stocks in a size view. By contrast, a fundamental multifactor model that includes industry and size factors distinguishes between the two effects. The most significant disadvantage is that there is an assumption of linearity in the multifactor approach. For example, if large cap and small cap stocks perform poorly but mid cap stocks perform well, the multifactor approach will not properly identify their contributions. As a result, looking at both single and multifactor analyses may give the most meaningful results.

LIMITATIONS OF PORTFOLIO CHARACTERISTICS ANALYSIS 7

Portfolio characteristics analysis may not be appropriate in all situations, and common sense must determine whether it is suitable. Some investment strategies do not consider fundamental characteristics either explicitly or implicitly. For example, when monitoring a merger arbitrage strategy it makes more sense to evaluate the manager's ability to anticipate and analyze deals than to examine the characteristics of the stocks held in the portfolio. Similarly, evaluating a portfolio's leverage and dividend yield is unlikely to provide meaningful information about a manager who picks stocks on the basis of technical analysis. Market data and the analyst's time are expensive. Portfolio characteristics analysis should be employed only where it adds value, for instance, by raising questions about the manager's execution of an investment strategy. In employing portfolio characteristics analysis, it is most important to ensure that the evaluation reflects the different steps in the manager's investment process.

PRACTICE PROBLEMS

1 An investment consultant is analyzing the market capitalization and the P/E of stocks in a portfolio managed by an active equity investment manager to determine whether the manager's agreed on strategy has been implemented. By doing so, the investment consultant performs:

A style analysis only.

B attribution analysis based on only fundamental factors.

C both style analysis and attribution analysis based on fundamental factors.

2 A hypothetical portfolio contains three stocks as shown in the following exhibit:

Stock	Market Value %	P/E Ratio
Boeing	17.5	21.3
Lincoln National	36.2	12.1
Motorola	46.3	44.2
Total Portfolio	100.0	

A What is the portfolio's weighted arithmetic mean P/E ratio?

B What is the portfolio's weighted harmonic mean P/E ratio?

3 Characteristics analysis is *least likely* to provide evidence whether:

A portfolios' benchmarks are appropriate.

B managers have adhered to their investment mandate.

C investments are suitable to the client's financial situation.

4 When preparing investment performance reports for its custody clients, Saybrook Bank and Trust Company calculates trimmed means to represent average portfolio characteristics. Compared to using tolerance ranges, Saybrook's method is *more likely* to:

A misrepresent the average value.

B include data points that are outliers.

C exclude data points that are not outliers.

5 A portfolio holds the four stocks described in the following table:

Stock	Market Value %	P/E Ratio
Stock #1	17.3	18.7
Stock #2	29.8	24.8
Stock #3	24.7	33.3
Stock #4	28.2	12.4
Total Portfolio	100.0	

As a percentage of the weighted harmonic mean, the portfolio's weighted arithmetic mean P/E ratio is *closest* to:

A 87.0%.

B 114.9%.

C 126.3%.

6 A CAPM beta of 0.90 implies that the portfolio will *most likely*:

A outperform in a rising market.

B outperform in a falling market.

C underperform in a falling market.

7 Which of the following is a fundamental characteristic of a company?

A Return on equity

B Price-to-book ratio

C Sector under the Global Industry Classification System

8 Stormfield Corporation and its competitor, Hadleyburg Company, reported the following information as of year-end:

	Stormfield	Hadleyburg
Stock price ($)	12	17
Total common shareholders' equity ($ millions)	112.5	142.8
Total assets ($ millions)	297.3	253.6
Number of common shares outstanding (millions)	45.7	37.2

Compared to Hadleyburg Company, Stormfield Corporation has a:

A lower market capitalization and a higher P/B ratio.

B higher market capitalization and a lower P/B ratio.

C higher market capitalization and a higher P/B ratio.

9 A large cap equity portfolio's weighted harmonic mean P/E ratio falls significantly from one period to the next. In evaluating the change, it is *most* important for a performance analyst to consider the:

A portfolio's cash position in both periods.

B general level of market valuations in both periods.

C change in average price compared to the change in average earnings.

10 Growth portfolios typically have lower dividend yields than value portfolios because:

A growth companies reinvest their earnings.

B the market prices of growth stocks are higher.

C growth-oriented investors are usually tax-averse.

11 Which statement is *least* accurate? Fundamental multifactor attribution analysis assumes that:

A factor exposures are non-linear.

B systematic risks explain stock returns.

C market timing affects portfolio returns.

SOLUTIONS

1 A is correct. Style analysis is a specific type of manager monitoring based on the characterization of an investment strategy in two dimensions: size (small-cap, large-cap, and mid-cap) and valuation (value, neutral or core, and growth). In style analysis, market capitalization is a characteristic that is commonly used to measure size, whereas the P/E is a characteristic that that is commonly used to assess a stock's position on the value–growth spectrum. In this scenario, the investment consultant's use of market capitalization and the P/E is consistent with their typical use in style analysis. In attribution analysis based on fundamental factors, portfolio characteristics are used with the goal of determining sources of returns and risk factors with which security returns are correlated, which is not the case in this example. Company fundamental characteristics include activity, liquidity, solvency, and profitability measures

2 **A** Weighted arithmetic mean P/E:

$$(0.175 \times 21.3) + (0.362 \times 12.1) + (0.463 \times 44.2) = 28.6$$

B Weighted harmonic mean P/E:

First, inverting the P/E ratios to determine the corresponding E/P ratios, sum the weighted E/P ratios:

$$[0.175 \times (1/21.3)] + [0.362 \times (1/12.1)] + [0.463 \times (1/44.2)]$$

$$= (0.175 \times 0.0469) + (0.362 \times 0.0826) + (0.463 \times 0.0226)$$

$$= 0.0486$$

Then invert the sum: $1/0.0486 = 20.6$

3 C is correct. Although portfolio characteristics analysis helps determine whether an investment strategy is being followed as expected, it does not shed light on whether the strategy is suitable in the first place. A is incorrect because significant, persistent differences between portfolio and benchmark characteristics may raise questions about the appropriateness of the benchmark. B is incorrect because characteristics analysis may corroborate or challenge the manager's adherence to the agreed-upon investment strategy.

4 C is correct. Trimmed means are calculated after excluding a certain percentage of the largest and smallest data points without regard to the dispersion of values. Therefore, trimmed means may arbitrarily exclude data points which do not lie outside the overall pattern of a distribution. There is no basis for presuming that trimmed means are more likely than tolerance ranges to misrepresent average values.

5 B is correct, calculated as follows:

The weighted arithmetic mean P/E ratio = $(0.173 \times 18.7) + (0.298 \times 24.8) + (0.247 \times 33.3) + (0.282 \times 12.4) = 22.3$.

The weighted harmonic mean P/E ratio = $1/[0.173 \times (1/18.7)] + [0.298 \times (1/24.8)] + [0.247 \times (1/33.3)] + [0.282 \times (1/12.4)] = 19.4$.

The weighted arithmetic mean as a percentage of the weighted harmonic mean = $22.3/19.4 = 1.149 = 114.9\%$.

6 B is correct. A CAPM beta of 0.90 indicates that the portfolio has less-than-average market risk, or systematic risk, and thus would be expected to outperform the market when the market falls.

7 A is correct. Return on equity measures the profitability of a company. Fundamental characteristics of a company include activity, liquidity, solvency, and profitability measures.

8 A is correct. Stormfield's market capitalization is 12 × 45.7 = \$548.4 million, whereas Hadleyburg's is 17 × 37.2 = \$632.4 million.

Stormfield's price-to-book (P/B) ratio is 12/(112.5/45.7) = 4.87, whereas Hadleyburg's is 17/(142.8/37.2) = 4.43.

9 B is correct. The performance analyst should compare the portfolio to a valid benchmark in each period because the general level of market valuations may have changed.

10 A is correct. Generally, growth companies have relatively low dividend yields and dividend payout ratios because they retain most of their income to finance future expansion.

11 A is correct. There is an assumption of linearity in the multifactor approach. B and C are incorrect because, as illustrated in the reading, fundamental multifactor attribution analysis does assume that systematic risk exposures explain stock returns and market timing affects portfolio returns.

PERFORMANCE EVALUATION

STUDY SESSION 5

Performance Appraisal

Fund sponsors are concerned with whether an investment manager has generated sufficient returns to compensate for the risk taken, how the manager's performance compares versus peers, and whether the manager's performance displays investment skill, as opposed to luck, that can be sustained over time.

The reading in this study session introduces several appraisal measures that capture risk in a single number: the Sharpe ratio, M^2, the Treynor ratio, Jensen's alpha, alpha, the information ratio, the Sortino ratio, and the Calmar ratio.

It should be noted that this list of appraisal methods is not exhaustive, but illustrates those commonly used in practice. Given that risk is typically multidimensional, the study session discusses multifactor models that build upon these measures and provide a more complete view of performance appraisal.

READING ASSIGNMENT

9 Investment Performance Appraisal

by Stephen E. Wilcox, PhD, CFA, Edward W. Aw, CFA, Yusif Simaan, PhD, and Gregory Y. Sivin, CFA

READING

9

Investment Performance Appraisal

by Stephen E. Wilcox, PhD, CFA, Edward W. Aw, CFA, Yusif Simaan, PhD, and Gregory Y. Sivin, CFA

Stephen E. Wilcox, PhD, CFA, is at Minnesota State University, Mankato (USA). Edward W. Aw, CFA, is at Bessemer Trust (USA). Yusif Simaan, PhD, is at Fordham University (USA). Gregory Y. Sivin, CFA, is at Bessemer Trust (USA).

LEARNING OUTCOMES

Mastery	*The candidate should be able to:*
☐	**a.** define active investment management skill;
☐	**b.** contrast the use in performance appraisal of gross returns and returns net of fees and expenses;
☐	**c.** describe the problem of distinguishing skill from luck;
☐	**d.** describe the need to take risk into account in investment performance appraisal;
☐	**e.** describe types of risk adjustment and identify contexts in which each type might be appropriate;
☐	**f.** calculate, interpret, and compare the Sharpe ratio, M^2, the Treynor ratio, Jensen's alpha, alpha, the information ratio (Treynor–Black appraisal ratio), and the information ratio–active return definition;
☐	**g.** identify and justify appropriate uses of performance appraisal measures;
☐	**h.** describe limitations of the Sharpe ratio, M^2, the Treynor ratio, Jensen's alpha, alpha, the information ratio (Treynor–Black appraisal ratio), and the information ratio–active return definition;
☐	**i.** describe how non-symmetrical return distributions affect various appraisal measures;
☐	**j.** describe challenges in determining Jensen's alpha;
☐	**k.** analyze the determinants of the information ratio according to the fundamental law of active management;
☐	**l.** calculate, interpret, and contrast the Sortino and Calmar ratios;
☐	**m.** describe uses of multifactor models in performance appraisal;
☐	**n.** compare returns-based and holdings-based performance appraisal, including the potential advantages and disadvantages of each.

1 INTRODUCTION

Active portfolio management embodies the hope that investing skill can transform a portfolio into one that consistently earns superior risk-adjusted returns. Is such a transformation truly possible? Three questions naturally arise in appraising the performance of a managed investment fund:

1 Do the portfolio's returns sufficiently compensate investors for the risks taken?
2 How does a portfolio manager compare to her or his peers?
3 Is a manager's performance attributable to luck, or to a skill that can be repeatedly relied on in the future?

This reading examines how experts have proposed that investment skill be identified and measured, including the appropriate uses and limitations of alternative approaches. The reading will focus on evaluating an active manager's past record of investment results but will also address forward-looking performance appraisal. A major focus will be performance appraisal measures that have been developed in relation to three ways of viewing risk: volatility of returns, systematic risk, and downside risk.

The reading is organized as follows. Section 2 provides context for the study of performance appraisal by addressing the definition of investment skill, the treatment of expenses, the need for proper risk adjustment, and the challenge of distinguishing skill from luck. Section 3 addresses measures that attempt to summarize investment skill in a single number, explaining their calculation, interpretation, and appropriate uses and limitations. Section 4 presents multifactor approaches to performance appraisal. Section 5 addresses how investors can use information about portfolio holdings in performance appraisal. Section 6 provides a summary of the reading.

2 OVERVIEW OF PERFORMANCE APPRAISAL

Investment performance appraisal is concerned with identifying and measuring investment skill. Performance appraisal can be viewed as the quality control element of the investment decision process. Consisting of a set of concepts and related measurement tools, performance appraisal provides the necessary information for investors to assess how effectively their money has been invested given the risks that were taken. But risk-adjusted past performance should be just one of many considerations when choosing investment managers. Qualitative considerations, such as the alignment of the manager's investment discipline with a client's investment objectives and constraints, trust in the manager, and the manager's financial and operating stability, are also very important.

Performance appraisal is also related to, but distinct from, **return attribution**. Return attribution generally depends on access to information on holdings and provides information as to *why* the portfolio's performance differed from that of the benchmark. It can provide detail on the type or types of investment decision making—for example, market timing, sector selection, or individual security selection—in which the manager appears to be skillful.

Performance appraisal is more simply concerned with overall skill assessment. As will be discussed in Section 3.5, this overall return difference from the benchmark return is an approximation to a measure of investment skill known as alpha. Many well-known performance appraisal techniques have been based on only having access to information about returns.[1] More recently, performance appraisal techniques have been developed to take advantage of information on holdings as discussed in Section 5.

To summarize, performance appraisal is most often concerned with ranking investment managers following similar investment disciplines. Return attribution provides information that can complement a performance appraisal analysis by providing more details about the consequences of managerial decisions. In essence, performance attribution identifies and quantifies the sources of value added, whereas performance appraisal seeks to ascertain whether value added was a result of managerial skill.

In the following sections, we address three topics that complete an essential background for the study of performance appraisal:

- What is investment skill?
- What return series should an analyst use in performance appraisal: gross-of-expenses or net of expenses?
- How does the riskiness of asset returns complicate the evaluation of investment skill?

2.1 Investment Skill

Skill in any profession can be thought of as the ability to influence outcomes in desired directions. A working definition of **active investment management skill** is the ability of a portfolio manager to add value on a risk-adjusted basis through investment analysis and insights. In everyday language, active investment skill is typically viewed as the ability to "beat the market" or an assigned benchmark with some consistency. The evaluation of active management skill is the focus of performance appraisal and this reading.

Passive investment management skill represents skill in portfolio construction. For this discussion, we can identify passive investing with indexing. An indexed portfolio has the objective of closely tracking the returns of a specified benchmark index. For example, an index portfolio manager might be tasked with constructing a portfolio whose returns closely track the returns of MSCI World Index.[2] The index portfolio manager would be considered skillful if actual performance closely tracks the designated index on a consistent basis.

Among other things, tracking a benchmark requires expertise in available tracking methodologies and effective trade execution. Yet an indexer does not need, or make any use of, investment insights into any individual sector or component security of the benchmark index. Without the need to research and formulate viewpoints about sectors or individual securities, specialists in indexing can provide their services at much lower cost.

In general, active portfolio managers strive to have sector- and/or security-specific insights and will hold individual investments in different-than-benchmark weights as a result of their beliefs. One kind of active manager, however, known as tactical asset allocators, actively shifts assets among distinct markets and/or asset classes to reflect their perceptions of the relative attractiveness of these markets/asset classes.

1 These measures were first developed to study public investment funds, in particular US mutual funds.

2 An example is the iShares MSCI World exchange-traded fund (ETF), which has the objective of tracking the MSCI World Index; this ETF earned a return within 6 bps of the MSCI World in 2013.

The Performance Threshold for Active Management

When there is a passive alternative to an active strategy, an investor can expect reliable exposure to a desired set of risk factors, frequently an assured level of diversification, with low trading costs and very low investment management fees. Furthermore, active managers in most investment disciplines face a high level of competition from other active investors for available opportunities to earn superior returns. In total, the hurdle to covering the expenses in active management by superior performance is, depending on the underlying asset class and investment discipline, sometimes quite high.

The existence of a low cost passive investment strategy also provides a reasonable comparison point to assess the performance of a fund manager, provided that the risk profile and investment objectives of that strategy are a close match. If the manager has skill, his performance should, on average and over a long evaluation period, be superior to the passive strategy, at least on a gross-of-expenses basis. If such performance is not superior on a net-of-expenses basis, the level of skill does not justify active management. A simple approach to performance appraisal is to compare—after confirming that the manager's benchmark is appropriate—the manager's returns to those of his benchmark. If the manager's active investment discipline is logical and the manager has performed well on the relative basis just described, the analyst has a practical basis to believe the manager exhibited skill during the time period under review.

2.2 Expenses in Investment Performance Apppraisal

To understand the treatment of expenses in investment performance appraisal we need to discuss very briefly the theory of market information efficiency (for short, market efficiency). The traditional perspective on market efficiency asserts that an asset's market price is the best available estimate of its true or intrinsic value. An advanced and more modern formulation—the **rational efficient markets hypothesis** or **costly information efficient market hypothesis** (Grossman and Stiglitz 1980)—is based on these observations:

- Investors could, without any cost, accept the market price of an asset as an estimate of its intrinsic value,
- Active investing involves gathering and analyzing information to attempt to improve on market prices as indicators of value, and
- Information gathering and its analysis can be expensive.

According to this theory, rational active investors would not incur the costs of information gathering and analysis if they did not expect to be rewarded by earning higher returns gross of expenses compared with the free alternative of accepting market prices as correct indications of value. In equilibrium, the returns to information gathering and analysis should just cover the associated costs. Although gross returns (short for returns gross of expenses) have typically been used in research on efficient markets, performance appraisal should be conducted using net returns (short for returns net of expenses). This preference reflects that a change in the value of a portfolio is a function of net returns. For performance appraisal, the client benefits only if an active manager earns positive incremental returns net of expenses relative to that of a passive alternative.

As an example of the importance of fees, consider two portfolio managers who follow an identical strategy that earns 10% per year gross of fees. One manager has annual expenses of 1.50% (150 bps), the other has annual expenses of 0.50% (50 bps.).

After 10 years, the impact of lower fees, based on an initial €10,000 investment, results in €24,669 − €22,299 = €2,370 more for the investor as compared with the higher-fee manager. Exhibit 1 shows the effects of fees on investment results at various time intervals for a range of fee ratios.[3]

Exhibit 1 Impact of Expense on Portfolio Performance

	Year											
Fee	0	1	2	3	4	5	6	7	8	9	10	Net Return
0.25%	10,000	10,973	12,040	13,210	14,495	15,905	17,452	19,149	21,011	23,054	25,296	9.73%
0.50%	10,000	10,945	11,979	13,111	14,350	15,706	17,191	18,815	20,593	22,539	24,669	9.45%
0.75%	10,000	10,918	11,919	13,013	14,207	15,510	16,933	18,487	20,183	22,035	24,056	9.18%
1.00%	10,000	10,890	11,859	12,915	14,064	15,316	16,679	18,163	19,780	21,540	23,457	8.90%
1.25%	10,000	10,863	11,799	12,817	13,923	15,123	16,428	17,845	19,384	21,056	22,872	8.63%
1.50%	10,000	10,835	11,740	12,720	13,782	14,933	16,180	17,531	18,995	20,581	22,299	8.35%

Note: Ending value is net of expenses assuming a gross return of 10%.

Fees may differ among active managers for several reasons. First, one manager may be less efficient in gathering information and passes on higher costs to investors. Second, some management fees are relatively fixed and expense ratios often vary inversely with assets under management. Third, a manager may charge a premium for some unique investment approach not offered by competitors. Finally, a manager may provide superior services for investors, such as allowing investors to liquidate or invest on a daily basis, and may charge more for such services. The investor, therefore, must balance the possible benefits against the level of fees charged to determine whether the skills and services offered are worth the cost.

Another important point concerns the risks associated with the expenses paid for active management: The expenses of an active strategy have to be paid for *certain*, whereas the value added of the active strategy over the passive one is *uncertain*. For example, suppose a passive strategy provides an expected return of 10%, the active strategy provides an expected return of 12%, and the cost of the active strategy is an additional 2%. Many risk averse investors would prefer the passive alternative even though the expected net return of the active strategy is equal to the passive one. This preference results from the fact that the gross performance advantage of the active strategy is uncertain (12% and 10% are the *expected* returns from two probability distributions of possible returns), whereas the additional cost is certain to be 2%.

EXAMPLE 1

Treatment of Returns: Expenses

1 Fund A has an expected gross return of 11.0% and an expense ratio of 0.5%. Fund B has an expected gross return of 12.0% and an expense ratio of 1.5%. The standard deviation of possible gross returns is 22.0% for Fund A and 24% for Fund B. Which fund would a risk-averse investor *most likely* prefer?

A Fund A

3 The calculations assume the management fee is a percentage of gross ending value and are deducted at the end of the year.

B Fund B

C The investor would be indifferent; he or she would view the two funds as equivalent investments.

2 In an efficient market, on a gross returns basis, rational active investors would *most likely* be expected to:

A underperform a risk-matched benchmark.

B earn the same returns as a risk-matched benchmark.

C outperform a risk-matched benchmark.

3 Performance appraisal analysis should focus on:

A after-tax returns.

B net returns.

C gross returns.

Solution to 1:

A is correct. The net-of-expenses expected return is 10.5% for both funds (11.0% – 0.5% = 12.0% – 1.5% = 10.5%). But this return is an expected return and the actual net-of-expenses return is unknown. For example, if actual gross returns were one standard deviation lower than the expected return, then the net-of-expenses return favors Fund A (11.0% – 22.0% – 0.5% = –10.5%) over Fund B (12.0% – 24.0% –1.5% = –13.5%). Although actual returns one standard deviation higher than the expected return would favor Fund B (a net-of-expenses return of 34.5% versus 32.5% for Fund A), a risk-averse investor is more likely to be concerned with possible losses and would choose Fund A.

Solution to 2:

C is correct. According to the rational efficient market hypothesis, investors will continue to gather and analyze securities data until the higher returns from active trading are exactly offset by higher information processing costs. At this equilibrium, net active returns would be equal to net passive returns, but gross active returns would exceed gross passive returns.

Solution to 3:

B is correct. Net returns are gross returns minus investment management fees. Obviously investors incur other costs and a rate of return net of all expenses could include the effect of commissions or sales charges, bid–ask spreads, and taxes, as well as investment management fees. But the relevant measure of net return depends on what needs to be measured. If the goal is to measure the ability of an investment manager to add value through investment insights, then the return net of all management expenses, but gross of all other fees, expenses, and taxes, is an appropriate performance measure because these other costs do not relate to information acquisition and analysis.

The Success of Actively Managed Investment Funds

Exhibit 2 shows the performance of US actively managed funds relative to Standard & Poor's comparison indexes as published by S&P Dow Jones Indices in their annual S&P Indices Versus Active (SPIVA) report. The report reflects performance as of 31 December 2013. Index returns are total returns assuming full dividend reinvestment with no deductions to account for fund investment expenses. Active fund returns are after expenses, but do not include loads and entry fees.

Exhibit 2 The S&P SPIVA Report

Report 1. Percentage of US Equity Funds Outperformed by Benchmarks

Fund Category	Comparison Index	One Year (%)	Three Years (%)	Five Years (%)
All domestic equity funds	S&P Composite 1500	46.05	77.53	60.93
All large-cap funds	S&P 500	55.80	79.95	72.72
All mid-cap funds	S&P MidCap 400	38.97	74.00	77.71
All small-cap funds	S&P SmallCap 600	68.09	87.32	66.77
All multi-cap funds	S&P Composite 1500	52.84	80.38	71.74
Large-cap growth funds	S&P 500 Growth	42.63	79.78	66.67
Large-cap core funds	S&P 500	57.74	80.56	79.39
Large-cap value funds	S&P Value	66.56	76.75	70.26
Mid-cap growth funds	S&P MidCap 400 Growth	36.72	79.37	86.19
Mid-cap core funds	S&P MidCap 400	43.48	67.27	83.94
Mid-cap value funds	S&P MidCap 400 Value	45.33	73.97	67.14
Small-cap growth funds	S&P SmallCap 600 Growth	55.61	86.10	69.60
Small-cap core funds	S&P SmallCap 600	77.70	91.10	74.73
Small-cap value funds	S&P SmallCap 600 Value	78.99	88.00	60.74
Multi-cap growth funds	S&P Composite 1500 Growth	38.14	86.54	68.56
Multi-cap core funds	S&P Composite 1500	62.74	84.51	77.15
Multi-cap value funds	S&P Composite 1500 Value	49.21	70.68	67.98
Real estate funds	S&P US Real Estate Investment Trust	50.00	86.71	80.28

Notes: For periods ended 31 December 2013. Outperformance is based on equal-weighted fund counts. All index returns used are total returns. Past performance is not a guarantee of future results.
Source: Based on data from S&P Dow Jones Indices and CRSP.

Exhibit 2 shows that over the most recent five-year time period, the majority of investment funds failed to match the performance of their comparison index. In the most recent year, however, a majority of mid-cap managers were able to exceed the performance of the comparison index. The best performance was by mid-cap growth funds, as only 36.72% of those funds failed to outperform the comparison index.

The case can certainly be made that Exhibit 2 provides "apples to oranges" comparisons because the index returns are essentially gross whereas the fund returns are net of some expenses. But at the very least, the results do provide evidence that suggests investment management fees and expenses should be considered important given their adverse effect on long-term net-of-expenses returns.

2.3 Distinguishing Investment Skill from Luck

An investment manager's record for any specific time period will reflect good luck (unanticipated good developments) and/or bad luck (unanticipated bad developments). One reason that luck should be considered important when appraising investment performance is the paradox of skill. As people become more knowledgeable about an activity, the difference between the worst and the best performers becomes narrower. Thus, the ever increasing aggregate skill level of investment managers, supplemented by massive computing power and access to "big" data, may lead to narrower investment performance differentials and a greater likelihood that these differentials can be explained by luck.

Deciding whether a portfolio manager has or lacks active investment skill based on past returns is difficult and always subject to error. Financial market returns have a large element of randomness. Some of this randomness reflects the impact of news and information that relate directly or indirectly to asset values. Trading motivated by liquidity needs (i.e., to raise money rather than motivated by analysis) and by the sentiments and emotions of investors adds to return volatility.

When the historical performance of an investment portfolio is observed, the record we see is only one out of a potentially unlimited number that the investment manager might have achieved applying the same investment discipline but with different luck. Additional insight into skill can sometimes be gained by examining consistency of performance. But the hypothesis that the manager's underlying mean return exceeds the benchmark's mean return may require many years of observations to confirm with a reasonably high degree of confidence.[4]

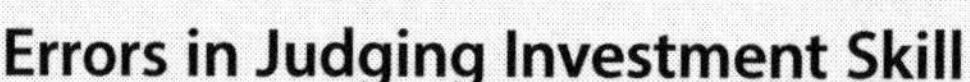

Errors in Judging Investment Skill

Any conclusion about the skill of an active manager is subject to two types of errors. Suppose that the null hypothesis is that an investment manager is unskilled. On the one hand, one may conclude that the manager is skillful when he or she has mediocre abilities and superior performance was a result of luck. In other words, the null hypothesis was rejected, when it should not have been. This is known as a Type I error. On the other hand, one may accept the null hypothesis of no skill when, in fact, the manager actually is skilled. This is known as a Type II error. A Type I error risks incurring the extra expenses of active management without any advantage over indexing. A Type II error runs the risk of missing the opportunity to invest with a skilled manager. The availability of more observations on past investment performance reduces both errors. But for

4 Can you be lucky once and correctly pick the flip of a fair coin? Of course! How about four times in a row? Yes, although much less likely. Can a portfolio manager be lucky enough to generate 15 continuous years of superior investment performance? Very unlikely, but with hundreds or even thousands of portfolio managers trying, a few might succeed solely because of luck. One problem faced in investment performance appraisal is that many investment management performance records are short, making it difficult to separate luck from skill.

a given number of observations, the investor always faces a trade-off between these two types of errors—the probability of one cannot be decreased without the probability of the other increasing.[5]

Randomness in Returns and Evaluation Periods: 1 of 2

To illustrate the difficulty of discerning skill, consider an analyst presented with a three-year record for an investment manager, as shown in Exhibit 3A.

Exhibit 3A An Investment Manager's Record Most Recent Performance

	Annualized Returns	
	Previous One Year	**Previous Three Years**
Portfolio	-38.9%	0.5%
Benchmark	-28.2%	1.9%
Excess	-10.7%	-1.4%

The manager has underperformed the benchmark by 10.7% in the most recent year and 1.4% over the last three years. These results are consistent with a hypothesis that the manager lacks skill.

Exhibits 3A, 3B, and 3C have been constructed to be mutually consistent with each other. As reported in Exhibit 3B, the manager delivered a small positive excess return of 0.5% over the benchmark over the previous five years. This result suggests that the most recent year's record depressed a five-year record that might otherwise look somewhat favorable. These results are more consistent with a hypothesis that the manager possesses some skill.

Exhibit 3B Performance To Five Years

	Annualized Returns		
	Previous One Year	**Previous Three Years**	**Previous Five Years**
Portfolio	-38.9%	0.5%	3.6%
Benchmark	-28.2%	1.9%	3.1%
Excess	-10.7%	-1.4%	0.5%

Next, the manager might examine the manager's investment record year by year. Exhibit 3C shows one-year performance over the previous five years.

5 This is explored in detail in the reading "Investment Manager Selection: An Introduction" by Jeffrey Heisler and Donald W. Lindsey in the CIPM Level I curriculum.

Exhibit 3C Trailing 1 Year Performance

	Last Year	Two Years Ago	Three Years Ago	Four Years Ago	Five Years Ago
Portfolio	−38.9%	13.73%	45.77%	−0.90%	18.82%
Benchmark	−28.2%	12.61%	30.69%	−6.05%	17.20%
Excess	−10.7%	1.11%	15.08%	5.15%	1.62%

Exhibit 3C shows four years of positive excess returns in relation to the benchmark. This result tends to support a quite different and much more positive conclusion compared with Exhibit 3A. The analyst would need to explore the data and manager further, but one possibility is that the manager is skillful but was unlucky in the most recent year.

Randomness in Returns and Evaluation Periods: 2 of 2

Assume the analyst who evaluated the investment manager based on Exhibit 3 data advises against hiring the manager. Is the client taking a risk by following the analyst's advice?

The answer is, Yes. A manager who beats the benchmark with a probability exceeding 0.5 might be considered skillful. Given that the manager beat the benchmark in four out of five years, assume that the manager's actual probability of beating the benchmark is 0.8. Assuming the changes in the manager's performance from year-to-year are uncorrelated, his or her probability of beating the benchmark five times in five years is 0.328 ($0.8^5 = 0.328$). The probability that the manager does not beat the benchmark five times in five years is 1 − 0.328 = 0.672. Even a high probability of 0.95 of outperforming the benchmark in any given year would leave a 0.226 probability of underperforming the benchmark in one or more of the five years.[6]

2.4 The Need to Take Risk into Account in Performance Appraisal

Risk is most simply defined as exposure to uncertainty (Grégoire 2007). The financial media often reports rankings of investment funds based on average returns over various time horizons, frequently one, three, and five years. Evaluating performance by average return alone, however, is not adequate because the majority of investors are risk averse.

Consider investing $1,000 in one of two choices. Choice A returns $1,050 with certainty. Choice B returns $950 half the time and $1,150 half the time, so it has an expected value of $1,050. By definition, a risk-neutral investor would be indifferent between Choice A and Choice B, whereas a risk-seeking investor would choose B because he or she is attracted by the chance of getting $1,150. A risk-averse investor would choose A, the investment with the certain return. Because investors are risk-averse in the aggregate, risk must be taken into account in performance appraisal.

6 $1 - (0.95)^5 = 1 - 0.774 = 0.226 = 22.6\%$.

Various perspectives on risk are relevant to performance appraisal. According to capital market theory, in equilibrium, all assets and securities are correctly priced according to their exposure to risks that affect broad cross-sections of investors. Such risks are called **priced risks** and bear risk premiums (expected returns in excess of a risk-free interest rate).

For example, the business cycle leads to fluctuations in revenues and incomes and an asset's exposure to the effects of the business cycle would be expected to affect its value. Because such risk is "system wide," priced risk can be called **systematic risk**. Systematic risk can also be called **non-diversifiable risk** because an asset's exposure to such risks cannot be reduced by holding it in a portfolio. Sometimes systematic risk is identified in relation to a sensitivity factor or **beta** to the movement of a market portfolio. This reasoning follows a theoretical pricing model called the capital asset pricing model (CAPM), but that risk is most precisely called **market risk**. Appraisal measures based on the CAPM are covered in Section 3.

The preponderance of evidence points to multiple factors affecting asset returns, so systematic risk need not be limited to market risk. Capital market theory implies that investors who bear greater systematic risk expect to be rewarded with higher average returns and directs performance appraisal to focus on the systematic risk that active managers bear to earn their returns. Because such risk exposures can be taken more cheaply through passive investment, active managers should be able to earn superior risk-adjusted returns after adjustments for higher fees. Adjustment for systematic risk is most appropriate when the manager is being evaluated in relation to other managers, or the potential valued added is being assessed relative to other portfolios constituting the investor's wealth.

Capital market theory also contends that investors focus on the volatility, or return standard deviation, of their total portfolios rather than that of individual securities. Return volatility is often referred to as **total risk** or **stand-alone risk**. Total risk is the sum of systematic risk and non-systematic risk. Thus, a portfolio's total risk exceeds its systematic risk whenever a portfolio has any non-systematic risk (i.e., is less than perfectly well diversified).

Some risk-averse investors prefer to focus only on the risk of losses, or **downside risk**. Capital preservation is a major objective of such investors. In addition, some investment strategies have built in asymmetrical return patterns. Consideration of downside risk is appropriate in either case.

This reading will focus on total risk, systematic risk, and downside risk adjustments in performance appraisal. But this is not an exhaustive list of possible risk adjustments. For instance, some fund managers may provide positively skewed returns, which are attractive to investors. Approaches to measuring the value of such non-normal returns, however, are quite complicated and are outside the scope of this reading.

PERFORMANCE APPRAISAL MEASURES 3

The academic and the professional investment literatures have developed several returns-based measures to assess the value of active management. The measures in this section were developed on the assumption that risk could be captured by a single factor, such as the portfolio's standard deviation or its beta. With the exception of M^2, these measures were developed in the 1960s. For these measures, the selection of which are appropriate for a client's specific needs involves evaluating which aspect of risk is most important given the role of the investment in the client's total portfolio, the plausibility of the assumptions a measure makes about the probability distribution of possible returns, the assumed theoretical pricing model, and possibly other considerations.

In this section, the order of presentation reflects a grouping by the risk measure or model underlying the performance appraisal measure.[7] In Section 4, we show how the CAPM-based measure called Jensen's alpha (described in Section 3.4) can be adapted to make use of more recently developed, multifactor risk models.

3.1 The Sharpe Ratio

The **Sharpe ratio** measures the additional return for bearing risk above the risk-free rate, stated per unit of return volatility. In performance appraisal, this additional return is often referred to as **excess return**. This use contrasts with how "excess return" is used in return performance attribution—that is, as a return in excess of a benchmark's return. Nobel laureate William F. Sharpe introduced the measure in 1966 and used the term **reward-to-variability ratio** to describe that measure. The measure quickly became known as the Sharpe ratio (and sometimes as the Sharpe measure).

The Sharpe ratio (SR) stems from the mean–variance portfolio theory developed by Markowitz (1952) in which risk-averse investors make portfolio decisions based only on mean return (expected return) and the variance or standard deviation of returns. Such an investor (a so-called "mean–variance investor") prefers a higher Sharpe ratio and will seek to maximize the Sharpe ratio of his or her total portfolio. According to the CAPM developed by Sharpe (1964), the market portfolio is the portfolio with the highest Sharpe ratio and it is mean–variance efficient in the sense of offering the highest mean return per unit of return volatility.

An appealing feature of the Sharpe ratio is that its use can be justified on a theoretical *ex ante* basis and *ex post* values can easily be determined by using readily available market data. The Sharpe ratio is also easy to interpret, essentially being an efficiency ratio relating reward to risks taken. It is the most widely recognized and used appraisal measure.

Equation 1 defines the *ex ante* Sharpe ratio in terms of three inputs: (1) the portfolio's expected return, $E[rp]$; (2) the risk-free rate of interest, r_F; and (3) the portfolio's standard deviation of returns (return volatility), σ_p, a quantitative measure of total risk.

$$\mathrm{SR} = \frac{E\left[r_p\right] - r_F}{\sigma_p} \tag{1}$$

As shown in Equation 1, the numerator of the Sharpe ratio is the portfolio's excess return: it is expected return less the risk-free rate. Dividing this quantity by the return volatility produces an appraisal measure that reflects expected excess return per unit of total risk. Thus, if expected return on a portfolio is 8%, the risk-free rate is 2%, and return volatility is 12%, the portfolio's Sharpe ratio is (8% − 2%)/12% = 6%/12% = 0.5.

All else being equal, a higher Sharpe ratio is preferable to a lower Sharpe ratio—0.5 is preferable to 0.2—because it implies greater reward per unit of total risk. In short, the higher the Sharpe ratio, the better a portfolio's expected risk-adjusted performance. What constitutes a "good" Sharpe ratio, however, needs to be judged in relation to the portfolio's benchmark or some other accepted point of comparison.[8] Thus, for example, a Sharpe ratio of 0.40 for the portfolio's benchmark would provide some evidence in favor of believing that the manager in the earlier example was skillful.

---

7 Risk measures, including their calculation, are described in the CIPM reading on "Risk Measurement and Risk Attribution" (CFA Institute 2012) by Frances Barney, C. Mitchell Conover, and Philippe Grégoire.

8 According to the CAPM, the market portfolio provides the highest Sharpe ratio of all available investments. Thus, in the absence of a specified benchmark, a comparison is sometimes made to a very well-diversified portfolio taken to represent the market portfolio.

The Sharpe ratio can also be used on an *ex post* basis to evaluate historical risk-adjusted returns. Assume we have a sample of historical data that can be used to determine the sample mean portfolio return, $\bar{r}_p$; the standard deviation of the sample returns, $\hat{\sigma}_p$; and the sample mean risk-free rate, $\bar{r}_F$. The *ex post* (or realized or historical) Sharpe ratio can then be determined by using Equation 2.

$$\widehat{SR} = \frac{\bar{r}_p - \bar{r}_F}{\hat{\sigma}_p} \tag{2}$$

The numerator of the Sharpe ratio is the portfolio's mean return less the mean return on the risk-free asset over the sample period. It measures the extra reward that investors actually received over the evaluation period for bearing risk. We call this difference the mean excess return. The denominator is the standard deviation of the portfolio's returns over the evaluation period.[9]

For example, if we assume that the mean annual return of a portfolio is 12%, the annual standard deviation of those returns is 20%, and the mean annual risk-free rate is 4%, then the Sharpe ratio is 0.4 $\left(\widehat{SR} = \frac{0.12 - 0.04}{0.2} = 0.4\right)$. This result means that the portfolio had an excess return of 0.40% for every 1% of standard deviation risk taken by its investors. Comparing this ratio with the Sharpe ratio for other funds over this same time period allows us to evaluate the risk-adjusted performance of the portfolio. For example, if we assume that during the sample period the Sharpe ratio for the S&P 500 Index was 0.375, we could conclude that our portfolio delivered a higher excess return per unit of total risk than the S&P 500.[10]

Exhibit 4 provides an illustration of this last point. Assume two portfolios, X and Y, whose mean excess return standard deviation combinations are shown in Exhibit 4. The Sharpe ratio for each portfolio is the slope of the ray that emanates from the risk-free rate through the point plotted for the portfolio. Based on Exhibit 4, Portfolio X is preferred to Portfolio Y because it delivers a higher excess return per unit of total risk.

Exhibit 4 The Sharpe Ratio for Two Portfolios

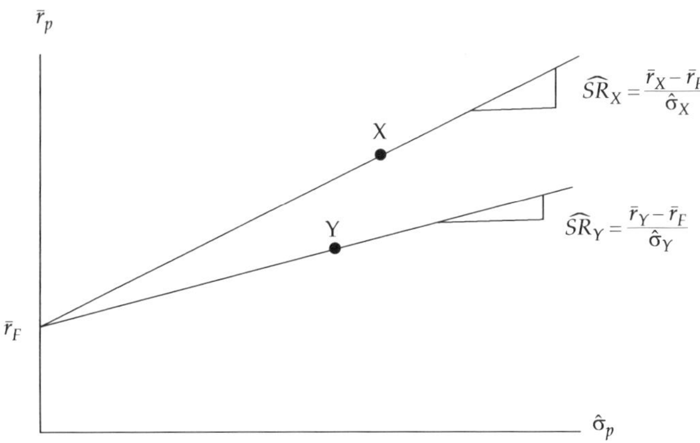

9 Sharpe (1994) defines the denominator of the *ex post* Sharpe ratio as the standard deviation of a portfolio's excess returns.

10 The example assumes that returns are determined net of investment management fees. If the fund did have management fees that were not reflected in its returns, one would need to examine whether its superior performance relative to the S&P 500 justified paying the extra fees.

A complexity arises when a calculated Sharpe ratio is negative. Clearly, a positive Sharpe ratio is preferred to a negative Sharpe ratio. Opinions differ concerning the comparison of negative Sharpe ratios. If return volatilities are equal, it is logical to conclude that the portfolio with the Sharpe ratio closer to zero is superior. The analysis of cases involving the comparison of negative Sharpe ratios is beyond the scope of this introduction.[11] Practically, the analyst may consider extending the evaluation period such that the comparison then includes positive Sharpe ratios.

What Is the "Risk-free Rate"?

In financial theory, the risk-free rate is the rate of return on an asset that produces the same known rate of return in all future economic states. Thus, for a risk-free asset, expected return and actual return are equal. In investment practice, "risk-free rate" typically refers to a rate of return on an investment with assured (or nearly assured) payments. This risk-free rate then serves as a reference rate for practical purposes, such as pricing other investments. In a given market, the yield on a sovereign debt instrument (e.g., US Treasury bonds for US dollar–denominated investments, UK gilts for British pound–denominated investments, or German bunds in the Eurozone) is typically used by practitioners to represent the risk-free rate.

In the view of many practitioners, the most appropriate risk-free rate to use to measure an asset's expected excess return should be default-free, zero-coupon, spot rate that is matched to the currency, and to the extent feasible, to the maturity of the asset's expected cash flows. Obviously, problems arise if these currency and maturity matches do not exist or are difficult to find.

Because of its reliance on standard deviation, the Sharpe ratio is traditionally viewed as most useful when applied to an investor's *entire portfolio* as opposed to any single security or subset of securities or even an individual fund manager. For instance, a technology fund manager, such as the Janus Twenty fund in the 1990s, may provide superior returns to a benchmark, but have huge return volatility. Yet, investors may highly value the Janus Twenty fund as part of their entire portfolio because they realize that they can add other managers to diversify away much of the unique risk of that fund.

An arguably more appropriate measure of risk for a component holding of a diversified portfolio is beta. Beta is a measure of market risk that reflects the correlation of a security's returns with a well-diversified portfolio. Standard deviation does not reflect co-movement, which is the reason it is frequently referred to as stand-alone risk.

One weakness of the Sharpe ratio is that the use of standard deviation as a measure of risk assumes a similar treatment of upside and downside volatility. For example, for an investor looking for a potentially high-rewarding investment, volatility to the upside is not necessarily a negative. Similarly, risk-averse investors concerned about the preservation of capital are clearly most concerned with downside risk.

Finally, one other problem with using the Sharpe ratio occurs when returns are not symmetrically distributed—that is, returns that are a given amount above or below the mean are not equally likely. For example, many hedge funds follow option-like strategies that produce asymmetrical returns. As an example, a trading strategy

11 Note that if excess return is negative, a higher standard deviation would result in a less negative Sharpe ratio, which suggests that volatility is beneficial. Bacon (2008) argues that this might actually be the case because greater variability may allow an investor to more quickly recoup losses.

might generate steady income and small positive returns most of the time but may also incur an occasional extremely large negative return (a negatively skewed return distribution). If the negative return events are infrequent, they may not occur during a given evaluation period. Thus, the measured return volatility would be very small and the Sharpe ratio would be high.[12]

The Sharpe Ratio and Return Frequency

In general, the calculated value of the Sharpe ratio depends on the time period over which it is measured. Exhibit 5 provides the average of the T-bill yield, $\bar{r}_F$; the average return on SPY (an ETF tracking the S&P500), $\bar{r}_{SPY}$; the excess return, $\bar{r}_{SPY} - \bar{r}_F$; and the standard deviation of returns, $\hat{\sigma}_{SPY}$, for monthly, quarterly, and annual return windows for 1 February 1993 through 1 December 2013.

Exhibit 5 Sharpe Ratio Results for SPY, 1 February 1993 to 1 December 2013

Return period	$\bar{r}_F$	$\bar{r}_{SPY}$	$\bar{r}_{SPY} - \bar{r}_F$	$\hat{\sigma}_{SPY}$	$\widehat{SR}$	$\widehat{SR}\sqrt{t}$
Monthly	0.002368	0.008217	0.005849	0.043716	0.133791	0.463466
Quarterly	0.007104	0.020507	0.013403	0.062719	0.213699	0.427398
Annual	0.028417	0.109148	0.080732	0.200134	0.403387	0.403387

Note: Returns in decimal format.

Note that the Sharpe ratio is very sensitive to the return period over which it is measured. The monthly return Sharpe ratio is (approximately) 0.13, the quarterly return Sharpe ratio is 0.21, and the annual return Sharpe ratio is 0.4. The reason for this disparity is that although both the mean return of a security and the standard deviation of those returns increase with increases in the return window, the standard deviation increases at a much slower rate. This characteristic means a serious error could be committed if we compare the Sharpe ratio of one fund based on monthly returns with a Sharpe ratio of another fund that is based on quarterly returns.

To correct for this problem, an adjustment that is frequently made in practice is to assume that the Sharpe ratio increases linearly with the square root of time. The last column of Exhibit 5 multiplies the monthly Sharpe ratio by the square root of twelve, because there are twelve months in a year, and the quarterly Sharpe ratio by the square root of four, because there are four quarters in a year. Note that the adjustment is not perfect, because the square root adjustment is a linear adjustment for returns that have differing compounding effects.

12 Rollinger and Hoffman (2013) show that for positively skewed return distributions, performance is actually achieved with less risk than the Sharpe ratio suggests. Conversely, the Sharpe ratio understates risk for negatively skewed return distributions. The authors argue that comparing rankings by the Sharpe ratio and the Sortino ratio can be useful when an analyst is concerned about skewed return distributions. See Goetzmann, Ingersoll, Spiegel, and Welch (2002) for more information about how the Sharpe ratio can be "tricked." Extensions of the Sharpe ratio have been proposed to account for skewness, but such measures are outside the scope of this reading.

Whenever an analyst conducts ex post analysis of investment skill, consideration must be given to the question of whether the analyst is sampling from more than one return distribution. If so, the risk of incorrect inferences increase, as the following box on calculating Sharpe ratios indicates.

Calculating Sharpe Ratios: One or Two Years of Quarterly Data?[13]

To compute the Sharpe ratio, suppose that an analyst collects eight quarterly excess returns (i.e., total return in excess of the risk-free rate). During the first year, the investment manager of the portfolio followed a low-risk strategy, and during the second year, the manager followed a high-risk strategy. For each of these years, the analyst also tracks the quarterly excess returns of some benchmark against which the manager will be evaluated. For each of the two years, the Sharpe ratio for the benchmark is 0.21. Exhibit 6 gives the calculation of the Sharpe ratio of the portfolio.

Exhibit 6 Calculation of Sharpe Ratios—Low-Risk and High-Risk Strategies

Quarter/Measure	Year 1 Excess Returns	Year 2 Excess Returns
Quarter 1	−3%	−12%
Quarter 2	5	20
Quarter 3	−3	−12
Quarter 4	5	20
Quarterly average	1%	4%
Quarterly standard deviation*	4.62%	18.48%
Sharpe ratio = 0.22 = 1/4.62 = 4/18.48		

* The quarterly standard deviation is a "sample" rather than "population" standard deviation. The population standard deviation is used if: (1) you have the entire population (all possible observations); or, (2) you have a sample of a population, but you are only interested in the sample and do not wish to generalize your findings to the population. Neither is typically the case with investment performance appraisal and it relies on the sample standard deviation as an unbiased estimator of the population standard deviation.

For the first year, during which the manager followed a low-risk strategy, the average quarterly return in excess of the risk-free rate was 1% with a standard deviation of 4.62%. The Sharpe ratio is thus 1/4.62 = 0.216 (0.433 annualized). The second year's results mirror the first year except for the higher average return and volatility. The Sharpe ratio for the second year is 4/18.48 = 0.216 (0.433 annualized). The Sharpe ratio for the benchmark is 0.21 during the first and second years (0.420 annualized). Because larger Sharpe ratios are better than smaller ones (providing more return per unit of risk), the manager appears to have outperformed the benchmark.

13 Excerpted from Example 6-2 in DeFusco, McLeavey, Pinto, and Runkle (2007).

Now, suppose the analyst believes a larger sample to be superior to a small one. She thus decides to pool the two years together and calculate a Sharpe ratio based on eight quarterly observations. The average quarterly excess return for the two years is the average of each year's average excess return. For the two-year period, the average excess return is (1 + 4)/2 = 2.5% per quarter. The standard deviation for all eight quarters measured from the sample mean of 2.5% is 12.57%. The portfolio's Sharpe ratio for the two-year period is now 2.5/12.57 = 0.199; (0.398 annualized) the Sharpe ratio for the benchmark remains 0.21 (0.420 annualized). Thus, when returns for the two-year period are pooled, the manager appears to have provided less return per unit of risk than the benchmark and less when compared with the separate yearly results.

The problem with using eight quarters of return data is that the analyst has violated the assumption that the sampled returns come from the same population. As a result of the change in the manager's investment strategy, returns in Year 2 followed a different distribution than returns in Year 1. Clearly, during Year 1, returns were generated by an underlying population with lower mean and variance than the population of the second year. Combining the results for the first and second years yielded a sample that was not representative of any population. Because the larger sample did not satisfy model assumptions, any conclusions the analyst reached based on the larger sample are incorrect. For this example, she was better off using one year samples than a two year sample because the smaller samples represented a more homogeneous distribution of returns.

EXAMPLE 2

Sharpe Ratio

1 Portfolio A delivered 10.0% annualized returns on average over the past 60 months. Its volatility as measured by annualized standard deviation over the past 60 months is 14.0%. Assuming the risk-free rate over the past 60 months averaged 3.0% per year, the Sharpe ratio of Portfolio A is *closest* to:

   A 0.50.

   B 0.71.

   C 2.00.

2 The following Sharpe ratios are available for the three funds: Portfolio M's Sharpe ratio is 0.125, based on weekly returns over the last five years. Portfolio N's Sharpe ratio is 0.175, based on monthly returns over the last five years. Portfolio O's Sharpe ratio is 0.500 over the last five years based on annual returns. Based on the Sharpe ratios, which of the three funds has been the *best* performer over the last five years?

   A Portfolio M

   B Portfolio N

   C Portfolio O

3 Guy LaFleur has invested in Portfolio Z. Which of the following is *most likely* to lead him to the conclusion that the Sharpe ratio is an appropriate measure for his portfolio's performance?

   A Portfolio Z's returns are symmetrically distributed.

B LaFleur has much of his wealth invested in assets other than Portfolio Z.

C One of Portfolio Z's goals is capital preservation and LaFleur is most concerned with downside risk.

Solution to 1:

A is correct. The Sharpe ratio is determined as excess return divided by the standard deviation of returns, $\widehat{\text{SR}} = \frac{10\% - 3\%}{14\%} = 0.50$.

Solution to 2:

A is correct. The Sharpe ratio is not independent of the time period over which it is measured. Because their return windows differ, the Sharpe ratios for Portfolio M and Portfolio N must be adjusted to make them comparable to Portfolio O. The adjusted Sharpe ratio for Portfolio M is $0.125 \times \sqrt{52} = 0.901$ and the adjusted Sharpe ratio for Portfolio N is $0.175 \times \sqrt{12} = 0.606$.

Solution to 3:

A is correct. The Sharpe ratio is based on capital market theory, which assumes returns are drawn from a symmetrical distribution, the normal distribution. B is incorrect because if Portfolio Z is only a small portion of LaFleur's wealth, then beta is arguably a more appropriate measure of risk. C is incorrect because the Sharpe ratio's use of standard deviation as a risk adjustment assumes a similar treatment of upside and downside volatility.

3.2 M²: Risk-Adjusted Performance (RAP)

M² provides a measure of portfolio return that is adjusted for the total risk of the portfolio relative to that of some benchmark. In 1997, Nobel Prize winner Franco Modigliani and his granddaughter, Leah Modigliani, developed what they called a risk-adjusted performance measure, or RAP. The RAP measure has since become more commonly known as M^2 reflecting the Modigliani names. It is related to the Sharpe ratio and ranks portfolios identically, but it has the useful advantage of being denominated in familiar terms of percentage return advantage assuming the same level of total risk as the benchmark.[14]

M^2 borrows from capital market theory by assuming a portfolio is leveraged or de-leveraged until its volatility (as measured by standard deviation) matches that of its benchmark. This adjustment produces a portfolio-specific leverage ratio that equates the portfolio's risk to that of its benchmark. The portfolio's excess return times the leverage ratio plus the risk-free rate is then compared with the benchmark's actual return to determine whether the portfolio has outperformed or underperformed the benchmark on a risk-adjusted basis.

Equation 3 provides a formula for M^2, where σ_B is the standard deviation of the benchmark portfolio and σ_B/σ_p is the portfolio-specific leverage ratio. Because the Sharpe ratio is defined as $\frac{E[r_p] - r_F}{\sigma_p}$, Equation 3 also shows that M^2 can be thought of as a rescaling of the Sharpe ratio that allows for easier comparisons among different

14 Scholz and Wilkens (2005) note that because M^2 uses standard deviation as the risk measure, it is relevant only to investors with diversified portfolios. They propose a measure called market risk-adjusted performance (MRAP), following the same principle as Modigliani and Modigliani's measure, but measuring returns relative to market risk instead of total risk. As a result, MRAP is more suitable for investors who invest in a broad range of securities.

funds and benchmarks. The reason that M^2 and Sharpe ratios rank portfolios identically is because, in a given time period—and for any given comparison benchmark *B*—both the risk-free rate and the benchmark volatility are constant across all comparisons. Only the Sharpe ratio differs, so it determines all rankings. Based on sample estimates, Equation 3 can be expressed as Equation 4.

$$M^2 = \left(E\left[r_p\right] - r_F\right)\frac{\sigma_B}{\sigma_p} + r_F = \text{SR} \times \sigma_B + r_F \quad (3)$$

$$\widehat{M^2} = \left(\bar{r}_p - \bar{r}_F\right)\frac{\hat{\sigma}_B}{\hat{\sigma}_p} + r_F = \widehat{\text{SR}} \times \hat{\sigma}_B + r_F \quad (4)$$

For example, assume that $\bar{r}_F = 4.0\%$, $\bar{r}_p = 14.0\%$, $\sigma_p = 25.0\%$ and $\sigma_B = 20.0\%$. The Sharpe ratio is 0.4, $\widehat{SR} = \dfrac{0.14 - 0.04}{0.25} = 0.4$, and $\widehat{M^2}$ is 12.0%, $\widehat{M^2} = 0.4(0.2) + 0.04 = 0.12 = 12.0\%$. If the return on the benchmark was 10%, then the fund outperformed the benchmark on a risk-adjusted basis by 12.0% − 10.0% = 2.0%. This difference between the risk-adjusted performance of the portfolio and the performance of the benchmark is frequently referred to as **M^2 alpha**.

The Sharpe ratio of the benchmark is $\widehat{\text{SR}} = \dfrac{0.10 - 0.04}{0.20} = 0.3$. Comparing the Sharpe ratio of the portfolio with the Sharpe ratio of the benchmark shows that the fund outperformed the benchmark. But the 2.0% difference between M^2 and the benchmark's return tells us the risk-adjusted outperformance as a percentage return.

Exhibit 7 provides an illustration of the M^2 performance measure and compares Portfolio Z to its benchmark, Portfolio B. The slope of the ray that emanates from the risk-free rate through the point for the portfolio is the portfolio's Sharpe ratio. Multiplying Portfolio Z's Sharpe ratio by the standard deviation of Portfolio B provides a leverage adjustment that equates Portfolio Z's risk to that of its benchmark portfolio. Adding the risk-free rate to the product of Portfolio Z's Sharpe ratio and the standard deviation of Portfolio B produces M^2, which is the theoretical rate of return Portfolio Z would have earned if it had the same total risk as the benchmark. The difference between this rate of return and that earned by Portfolio B is the M^2 alpha for Portfolio Z, represented by α_Z in Exhibit 7.

Exhibit 7 M^2 and M^2 Alpha for Portfolio Z

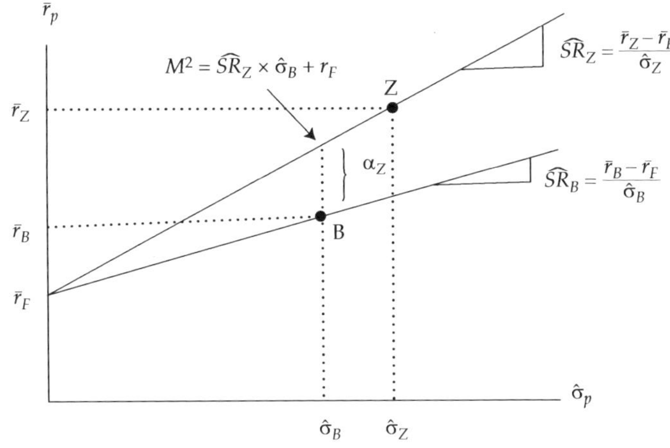

EXAMPLE 3

M^2

1 M^2 adjusts for:

A systematic risk as measured by beta.

B total risk as measured by standard deviation.

C non-systematic risk as measured by 1 – R^2 in a market model regression.

2 Portfolio Y delivered 10.0% annualized returns on average over the past 60 months. Annualized volatility, reflecting sample standard deviation over the past 60 months, was 14.0%. The benchmark portfolio returned 8.0% on average over the same time period with a standard deviation of 12.0%. Assuming the risk-free rate is 3.0%, M^2 of Portfolio Y is *closest* to:

A 6.0%.

B 9.0%.

C 11.2%.

3 Portfolio X delivered 10.0% annualized returns on average over the past 60 months. Annualized volatility, reflecting sample standard deviation over the past 60 months, was 16.80%. The benchmark portfolio returned 8.0% on average over the same time period with a standard deviation of 12.0%. The risk-free rate is 3.0%. The M^2 alpha for Portfolio X is *closest* to:

A 0.0%.

B 2.0%.

C 4.8%.

Solution to 1:

B is correct. M^2 is derived from the Sharpe ratio and both measures adjust for total risk as measured by portfolio standard deviation.

Solution to 2:

B is correct. $\widehat{M^2} = (10.0\% - 3.0\%)\dfrac{12.0\%}{14.0\%} + 3.0\% = 9.0\%$

Solution to 3:

A is correct. $\widehat{M^2} = (10.0\% - 3.0\%)\dfrac{12.0\%}{16.8\%} + 3.0\% = 8.0\%$; M^2 alpha $= \widehat{M^2}$ – Benchmark return = 8.0% – 8.0% = 0.0%.

3.3 The Treynor Ratio

The **Treynor ratio** (Treynor 1965) measures the excess return per unit of systematic risk. With the Treynor ratio (TR), and the systematic-risk-based appraisal measures to follow, we must carefully choose an efficient market benchmark against which to measure the systematic risk of the manager's fund. By contrast, the Sharpe ratio can be compared among different funds without the explicit choice of a market benchmark. Similarly, the M^2 measure can, in principle, be computed for a fund with respect to a benchmark of the user's choice.

In the following, we assume that β_p is the beta of the fund relative to a broad-based, market value-weighted index, such as the FTSE All Share Index for UK equities. (Such a market benchmark choice is common in practice.) The Treynor ratio is given by Equation 5 and its sample estimate is given by Equation 6.

$$\text{TR} = \frac{E\left[r_p\right] - r_F}{\beta_p} \quad (5)$$

$$\widehat{\text{TR}} = \frac{\overline{r}_p - \overline{r}_F}{\hat{\beta}_p} \quad (6)$$

Thus, if expected return on a portfolio is 8%, the risk-free rate is 2%, and the portfolio's beta with respect to an accepted market index is 1.2, the portfolio's Treynor ratio is (8% − 2%)/1.2 = 6%/1.2 = 5%, which would be more commonly stated as 5. In contrast to the Sharpe ratio, the Treynor ratio is expressed in units of percentage return. However, most analysts suppress the percentage sign.

The Treynor ratio is similar to the Sharpe ratio in that it measures reward per unit of risk. In their numerators, both ratios measure excess return above the risk-free rate. The two measures differ in that the Sharpe ratio considers total risk as measured by the standard deviation of the portfolio whereas the Treynor ratio considers systematic risk as measured by beta. Similar to the Sharpe ratio, the Treynor ratio does not quantify the value added; it is simply a ranking mechanism.

The usefulness of the Treynor ratio is dependent on whether systematic risk or total risk is most appropriate in evaluating performance. Because of its reliance on beta, the Treynor ratio shows how a fund has performed not in relation to its own volatility, but the volatility it would bring to a well-diversified portfolio. Thus, a ranking of portfolios based on the Treynor ratio is most useful if the portfolios whose performances are being evaluated are being combined in a broader, fully diversified portfolio. The ratio is most informative when the portfolios being evaluated are compared with the same benchmark index.

Conversely, the Treynor ratio has limited utility when the investor's intent is to place most of their wealth in a single portfolio. Holding excess return constant, portfolios with identical systematic risk would have the same Treynor ratio. But these portfolios could vary in terms of their non-systematic risk, meaning such performance measures as the Sharpe ratio and M^2, which compensate for a portfolio's total risk as measured by standard deviation, are more appropriate for single-portfolio investors.

Exhibit 8 illustrates the Treynor ratio. Assume two portfolios, U and V, whose mean excess return–beta combinations are shown in Exhibit 8. The Treynor ratio for each portfolio is the slope of the ray that emanates from the risk-free rate through the point plotted for the portfolio. Based on Exhibit 8, Portfolio U is preferred to Portfolio V because it delivers a higher excess return per unit of systematic risk as measured by beta.

Exhibit 8 The Treynor Ratio

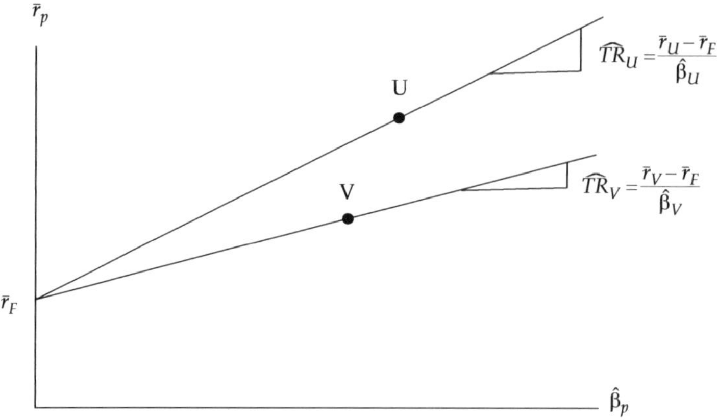

EXAMPLE 4

Treynor Ratio

1 A portfolio generated an average return of 10% per year over the past five years. The standard deviation of the portfolio's returns over this period was 14% per year, and the portfolio had an estimated beta of 0.8 versus its benchmark market index over the same period. Assuming the risk-free rate is 3.0%, the Treynor ratio of the portfolio is:

A 0.0875.

B 0.1250.

C 0.5000.

2 Portfolio X has a Treynor ratio of 0.08, determined as an excess return of 8% divided by a beta of 1.0. Portfolio Y has a Treynor ratio of 0.075, determined as an excess return of 9% divided by a beta of 1.2. Which scenario might lead to the conclusion that Portfolio Y's risk-adjusted performance is superior to Portfolio X's?

A The same benchmark portfolio is used to evaluate Portfolio X and Portfolio Y.

B The benchmark portfolio for Portfolio X is more volatile than the benchmark portfolio for Portfolio Y.

C The benchmark portfolio for Portfolio X is less volatile than the benchmark portfolio for Portfolio Y.

Solution to 1:

A is correct. The Treynor ratio equals the ratio of (i) the portfolio return less the risk free rate divided by (ii) the beta. In this case (0.1 − 0.03)/0.8 = 0.07/0.8 = 0.0875.

Solution to 2:

B is correct. Portfolio X has a higher Treynor ratio than Portfolio Y. The only way Portfolio Y's risk-adjusted performance could be considered better is if the benchmark portfolios used to determine beta differed. If the benchmark for Portfolio X is much more volatile than the benchmark for Portfolio Y, then the risk-adjusted performance for Portfolio Y might actually be superior. Under this scenario, the beta for Portfolio X would reflect average sensitivity to a high-volatility benchmark whereas the beta for Portfolio Y would reflect above average sensitivity to a low-volatility benchmark.

3.4 Jensen's Alpha

In this reading, we distinguish two definitions of "alpha," one based on the CAPM—Jensen's alpha—the other not specifying the model for priced risk. Jensen (1968) did not give his measure a name but referred to it using α, the Greek letter alpha. Subsequently, the measure he described was called **Jensen's alpha** (or just alpha) or the **Jensen measure**. This reading uses Jensen's alpha for the measure as exactly described by Jensen, and alpha for a more general concept allowing for other asset pricing models. One authority captures this well by treating alpha as we do and labeling Jensen's alpha as "single-factor alpha" (Fischer and Wermers 2013).

Jensen's alpha measures the return of a portfolio in excess of the theoretical required return given the equilibrium model for asset returns known as the CAPM. According to the CAPM, the theoretical expected value of a portfolio's return is given by Equation 7, where β_p is the beta of the portfolio.

$$E(r_p) = r_F + \beta_p\left[E(r_m) - r_F\right] \tag{7}$$

Based on a particular outcome of market return in month t, $r_m(t)$, and the risk-free rate of month t, $r_F(t)$, the expected return for the portfolio is given by Equation 8.

$$E(r_p) = r_F(t) + \beta_p\left[r_m(t) - r_F(t)\right] \tag{8}$$

Consider a sample of monthly returns of a portfolio and the market. Let the fund's return in month t be $r_p(t)$. Then Jensen's alpha, $\alpha_p(t)$, is given by Equation 9 and is the difference between the fund's actual return and that which is predicted by the CAPM. As Equation 9 also shows, Jensen's alpha is equivalent to the fund's actual risk premium less the risk premium predicted by the CAPM.

$$\begin{aligned}\alpha_p(t) &= r_p(t) - \left\{r_F(t) + \beta_p\left[r_m(t) - r_F(t)\right]\right\} \\ &= \left[r_p(t) - r_F(t)\right] - \left\{\beta_p\left[r_m(t) - r_F(t)\right]\right\}\end{aligned} \tag{9}$$

If we assume that the portfolio's beta is 1.25, the portfolio's excess return is 12%, and the market's excess return is 8%, then Jensen's alpha is 2%: $\alpha_p(t)$ = 12% – 1.25(8%) = 2%. The graphical representation of the CAPM formula, showing the relationship between expected return and beta, is called the **security market line** (SML). Jensen's alpha represents vertical deviation from the equilibrium expected return predicted by the SML and thus a return greater or less than the CAPM required rate of return.

Exhibit 9 illustrates Jensen's alpha. The formula for the SML is the CAPM. The risk-free rate, $\overline{r}_F$, is the intercept of the SML and the market risk premium, $\overline{r}_m - \overline{r}_F$, is the slope term. The mean return-beta combinations for Portfolio A and Portfolio B are shown. Given its beta, Portfolio A's mean return is higher than that predicted by the CAPM and it has a positive Jensen's alpha. Given its beta, Portfolio B's mean return is lower than predicted by the CAPM and it has a negative Jensen's alpha.

Exhibit 9 Jensen's Alpha

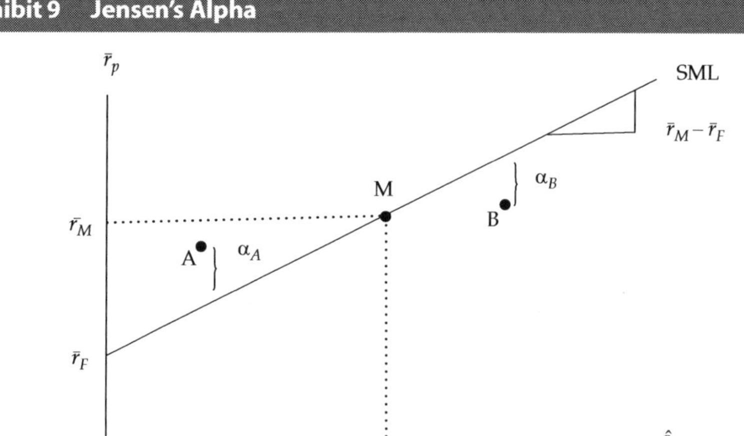

In practice, Jensen's alpha is frequently determined by the coefficient estimate of the intercept in a **market model** regression as given by Equation 10, where $\varepsilon_p(t)$ is the error term of the regression.

$$r_p(t) - r_F(t) = \alpha_p + \beta_p\left[r_m(t) - r_F(t)\right] + \varepsilon_p(t) \quad (10)$$

Common practice is to assemble 60 months of return data for both the fund and a proxy for the market portfolio, such as the S&P 500, as well as (the same) 60 months of monthly returns on T-bills as a proxy for the risk-free rate. Note that the market model provides an estimate of both the portfolio's beta and Jensen's alpha.

Exhibit 10 presents the results of a market model regression for Invesco's Power Shares Dynamic Market ETF using monthly data from January 2009 to December 2013. Beta was estimated to be 0.9996 and Jensen's alpha was estimated to be −0.01%. Over this time period, PWC's empirical beta was virtually equal to that of the market (1.0) and its Jensen's alpha was estimated to be very close to zero, and that estimate was statistically insignificant. The R^2 indicates that variation in the market's excess return explained roughly 89% of the variation in PWC's excess return.

Exhibit 10 Market Model Results for PWC, January 2009 to December 2013

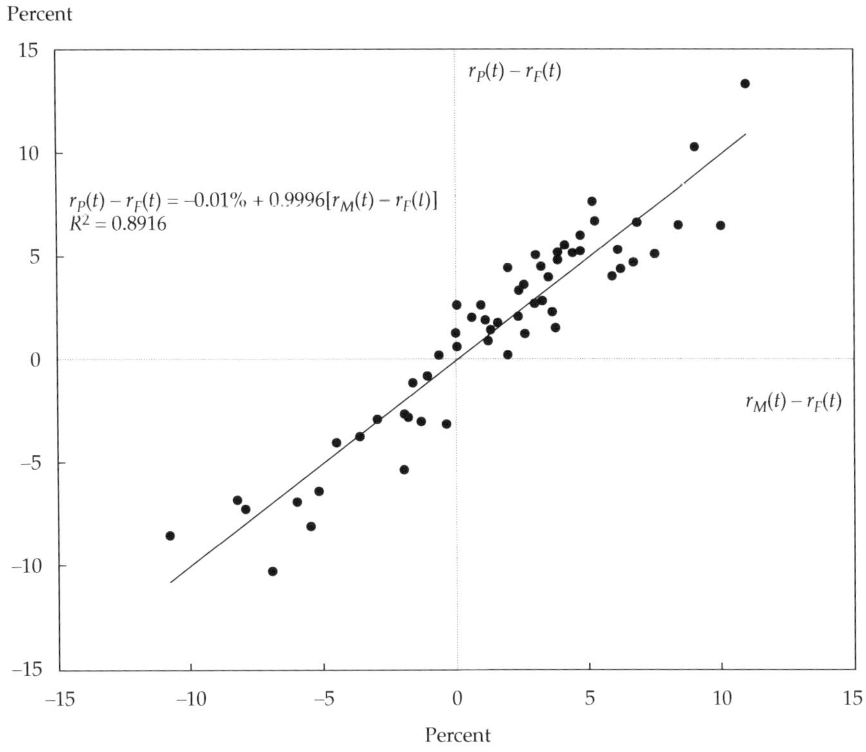

Note: The results are based on monthly data.

In the case of index replication, a performance appraisal could conclude that PWC tracked changes in the underlying index essentially one-for-one (technically, 0.9996-to-1) while only slightly underperforming the index (−0.01% Jensen alpha per month or −0.12% per year)—most likely a result of modest operating expenses. Furthermore, most of the variation in monthly returns, 89%+, can be attributed to the underlying benchmark portfolio returns. This high level of explanatory power of a single broad market factor is typical for a diversified equity fund, and it indicates that the model results for alpha and beta, at least as a first pass, contain useful information about the fund.

Jensen's alpha can be calculated relative to any benchmark by replacing the S&P 500 return with the return on the benchmark portfolio. Positive and statistically significant coefficient estimates for Jensen's alpha indicates the presence of excess return that can be attributed to non-benchmark factors. Typically, one of the factors is assumed to be the security selection ability of the fund's manager. This conclusion is most valid when the systematic risk of the fund matches that of the benchmark—that is, the fund's beta is approximately 1.0. A negative and statistically significant coefficient estimate for Jensen's alpha indicates underperformance.

Versions of Jensen's alpha, until about 1997, were the most popular performance measures in academic studies. Since about 1997, multifactor versions of performance measurement and holdings-based versions have become more popular, but Jensen's alpha is usually also presented in academic studies as a baseline measure. (Multifactor versions are presented in a later section).

Jensen's alpha has been widely used to evaluate a portfolio manager's ability to "beat the market." Intuitively, Jensen's alpha computes risk-adjusted performance by adjusting for the systematic risk of the fund as measured by beta. Implicit in this approach is that there are two determinants of a fund's return: (1) its exposure to the market, and

(2) the security selection ability of its manager. Thus, the major advantage of Jensen's alpha over simply comparing a fund's return to the benchmark is that it controls for systematic risk differences between the fund and the benchmark.[15]

Another advantage of Jensen's alpha is it is easy to interpret because it is measured as an excess return rather than being a ratio, as is the case for the Treynor ratio. For example, the implications of a Jensen's alpha of 2.0% versus a Jensen's alpha of –0.5% are much easier to understand than are Treynor indexes of 0.90 and 0.72. The market model approach also provides an easy way to test the statistical significance of the Jensen's alpha estimate.

There are several limitations and concerns in using Jensen's alpha. First, like the Treynor ratio, it may not well serve an investor dedicated to a single fund. Although adjusting for systematic risk makes sense for an investor holding the market portfolio, it may not be adequate when the fund under evaluation is not fully diversified and is the investor's only investment.

Second, Dybvig and Ross (1985) have argued that Jensen's alpha can be misleading if the fund manager attempts to time the market. With a market-timing strategy, portfolio beta will frequently change. Yet estimating beta via a market model regression assumes beta is constant over the time period of the study.

Finally, using Jensen's alpha as a performance measure is only as accurate as the predictions of the pricing model used to estimate the expected return. For example, if the CAPM is not an adequate approach for pricing securities, then determining Jensen's alpha by assuming the CAPM is the correct pricing model is a flawed approach. In this regard, Fama and French (1992, 1993) provided evidence that in US capital markets and over a very long term, small-cap stocks have outperformed large-cap stocks and value stocks have outperformed growth stocks. These capitalization and value effects are not captured by the CAPM. Using multiple risk factors to incorporate these additional risk premiums is common practice and will be addressed in Section 4.

EXAMPLE 5

Jensen's Alpha

1 Bob O'Reilly, a portfolio manager at Overture Asset Management, manages a portfolio consisting of large-cap US equities. He wants to determine how well his portfolio performed relative to the S&P 500 last year. During the prior year, the S&P 500 had a total return of 15%, the beta of his portfolio relative to the S&P 500 was 0.90, and the risk-free rate is 3%. Using the CAPM, if O'Reilly's portfolio generated a total return of 16% in the prior year, his realized Jensen's alpha was:

   A 1.0%.

   B 2.2%.

   C 5.2%.

2 Which of these risk-adjusted performance indicators is **not** measured in units of percent?

   A Sharpe ratio

   B Treynor ratio

15 For example, assume a fund's return is 12% and the benchmark's return is 10%. Also assume that the systematic risk of the fund greatly exceeds that of the benchmark and the fund's beta is 1.5. The fund outperformed the benchmark by 12% – 10% = 2% if differences in systematic risk are ignored. But assuming a risk-free rate of 3%, Jensen's alpha is 12% – [3% + 1.5(10% – 3%)] = –1.5%. Based on Jensen's alpha, the fund underperformed the benchmark on a risk-adjusted basis.

C Jensen's alpha

3 In which of the following applications is Jensen's alpha *most* appropriate as a measure of risk-adjusted performance? Evaluating a fund manager who attempts to outperform his or her benchmark by:

A timing the market.

B superior security selection.

C timing the market and superior security selection.

4 Assume the manager of a small-cap value fund chooses the S&P 500 as her fund's benchmark and estimates Jensen's alpha using the market model with the CAPM as the assumed pricing model. Which result is *most likely* to occur?

A Her estimate of Jensen's alpha is unbiased.

B Her estimate of Jensen's alpha is upwardly biased.

C Her estimate of Jensen's alpha is downwardly biased.

Solution to 1:

B is correct. Required return according to the CAPM = $r_P = r_F + \beta_p[r_M - r_F]$ = 3% + (0.90)(15% – 3%) = 13.8%. *Ex post* alpha = 16% – 13.8% = 2.2%.

Solution to 2:

A is correct. Jensen's alpha and the Treynor ratio, but not the Sharpe ratio, are stated in units of percent.

Solution to 3:

B is correct. A market model regression is the typical approach for estimating Jensen's alpha. Implicit to that approach is that a fund's beta is constant over the time period of the study. A fund manager who moves in and out of equities in an effort to time the market is constantly changing the beta of his or her portfolio.

Solution to 4:

B is correct. The manager's estimate of Jensen's alpha would likely reflect risk premiums not captured in the performance of the S&P 500 because it is a large-cap index consisting of both value and growth stocks. The estimate would most likely be upwardly biased because small-cap stocks have historically outperformed large-cap stocks.

The term "alpha," which once made clear reference to the CAPM, has for a long time become generic in the investment industry as a reference to incremental risk-adjusted performance. In the most precise current writing, alpha can be interpreted as an excess risk-adjusted return based on any model assumed to explain differences in expected returns across assets. The next section describes this more expansive usage.

3.5 Alpha

Alpha measures the difference between a portfolio's or security's return and the return required in the marketplace given that portfolio's or security's risk.[16] Alpha is sometimes referred to as an **abnormal return**. It can be estimated on both an expected or *ex ante* basis and an actual or *ex post* basis.

16 Models, such as the Fama-French three-factor model (1992, 1993) or the Carhart four-factor model (1997), that could be used for estimating required return will be covered in Section 4. But alpha, as used in this reading, includes Jensen's alpha because the CAPM is one possible model for required return.

The difference between the expected return and the required rate of return on an asset is the asset's **expected alpha** or ***ex ante* alpha**, as shown in Equation 11.

$$\text{Expected alpha} = \text{Expected return} - \text{Required return} \quad (11)$$

A fundamental issue in finance is the *ex ante* determination of the required return for a risky portfolio or security. A typical and conceptually appealing approach is to assume an asset pricing model, such as the CAPM (developed in the 1960s), Fama–French three-factor model (published in 1993), or the Carhart four-factor model (an extension of Fama–French model published in 1997). Unfortunately, although many of these models are theoretically and intuitively attractive, empirical testing suggests that none of them truly offers a complete explanation of security returns. Thus, although portfolio managers ordinarily choose among alternative securities based on their expected alphas, it is very difficult to even attempt to judge decision-making skills until actual returns are revealed.

To evaluate the actual results of an investment strategy, an analyst would examine **realized alpha** or ***ex post* alpha** over a given holding period, as shown in Equation 12. Contemporaneous required return is what assets of similar risk actually earned during the holding period.

$$\text{Realized alpha} = \text{Actual holding-period return} - \text{Contemporaneous required return} \quad (12)$$

It is practically important to be aware that the term "alpha" is commonly but imprecisely used by practitioners to refer to what is more precisely called "active return." **Active return** is return in excess of the benchmark return. In this view, the return on the benchmark portfolio is considered to be the contemporaneous required return in Equation 12.

Assuming that the benchmark represents a "passive" investment alternative to active management, the benchmark return is a plausible measuring rod to compare the performance of a portfolio that is actively managed. Unfortunately, active return generally provides only an approximation of alpha. The two quantities are technically equivalent only if we assume that the manager's portfolio is exactly risk-matched with the benchmark (equivalently, the portfolio's beta or sensitivity to the benchmark equals 1.0). If this assumption is incorrect and there is continued long-term reward for bearing systematic risk, outperformance or underperformance might be more closely linked to a systematic bias in tracking the benchmark. For example, during a time period of increasing security prices, outperformance could be the result of the manager tilting a portfolio to having greater systematic risk than the benchmark. During a time period of increasing security prices, underperformance might be explained by a manager who tilts the portfolio to having less systematic risk than the benchmark.

However, altering the systematic risk of a portfolio away from the benchmark need not be an indictment of the manager. Market-timing funds do frequently alter their systematic risk exposure as market expectations change, and a manager's skill would clearly be associated with doing this successfully. Thus, active return is best used to evaluate managers whose supposed skill is in security selection and their portfolio remains risk-matched with the benchmark.

EXAMPLE 6

Alpha

1 Using a three factor model describing asset required returns, an analyst forecasts a return for Stock Y of 15%, whereas the required return is 12%. The analyst's excess return forecast of 15% - 12% = 3% for Stock Y can *best* be described as:

A realized alpha.
B Jensen's alpha.
C expected alpha.

2 Active return is *most* appropriately described as:
A realized alpha.
B expected alpha.
C a return in excess of the benchmark return.

Solution to 1:

C is correct, given that the analyst is forecasting an excess return. A is incorrect because realized alpha is based on past data. B is incorrect because the analyst is making use of a three-factor model and Jensen's alpha assumes the CAPM predicts returns.

Solution to 2:

C is correct. Active return is an approximation of alpha, so neither choice A nor choice B is the most appropriate description.

3.6 Information Ratio (Treynor–Black Appraisal Ratio)

An important metric of active investment skill is the ratio of Jensen's alpha to the standard deviation of the portfolio's residual or non-systematic risk. Treynor and Black (1973) first described this measure and argued that security selection ability implies that deviations from benchmark portfolio weights can be profitable. They showed that the optimal deviations from the benchmark holdings for securities depend on what they called an "appraisal ratio." The **appraisal ratio** is also referred to as the **Treynor–Black ratio**, the **Treynor–Black appraisal ratio**, and by modern authorities, such as Grinold and Kahn (2000) and Fischer and Wermers (2013), as the **information ratio**.[17] In using the term "information ratio" for the measure described in this section, these cautions should be shared:

- In a particular case, the analyst might be using a multifactor model, such as those discussed in Section 4, not the CAPM, and the residual risk would be with respect to that multifactor model.
- There is a somewhat different, simpler definition of the information ratio that will also be frequently encountered, presented in Section 3.7.

It is unfortunate that there is so much variety in labels and in the definitions of basic terms, but that variety is a fact that cannot be escaped if one works in investments.

Recall that Jensen's alpha is frequently determined by the coefficient estimate of the intercept in a market model regression as given previously as Equation 10 and repeated below.

$$r_p(t) - r_F(t) = \alpha_p + \beta_p\left[r_m(t) - r_F(t)\right] + \varepsilon_p(t)$$

In this description, $\beta_p[r_m(t) - r_F(t)]$ reflects the contribution of the benchmark to the excess return of the portfolio. As before, Jensen's alpha, α_p, reflects the reward for active management in that it is the average return in excess of what is expected given the portfolio's systematic risk or sensitivity to benchmark excess returns. The error term $\varepsilon_p(t)$ is a random variable whose mean is zero, and the excess return that cannot be attributed to the benchmark for a given time period t is $\alpha_p + \varepsilon_p(t)$. The larger the

17 See Fischer and Wermers (2013), pages 75–80 for a clear treatment of theory and practice.

variance of $\varepsilon_p(t)$, denoted by $\sigma^2_{\varepsilon_p}$, the higher the unsystematic risk (sometimes called non-systematic or residual risk) of the portfolio and the higher the risk associated with active management.

Given the standard linear regression assumptions, $\sigma^2_{\varepsilon_p}$ can also be estimated using Equation 13. The variance of the portfolio, σ^2_p, is a measure of total risk that consists of two components: (1) systematic or market risk, and (2) non-systematic or company-specific risk. The systematic component is $\beta^2_p\sigma^2_m$, and the non-systematic component is $\sigma^2_{\varepsilon_p}$. Thus, non-systematic risk can be determined if the variance and beta of the portfolio and the variance of the market portfolio are known.

$$\sigma^2_p = \beta^2_p\sigma^2_m + \sigma^2_{\varepsilon_p} \tag{13}$$

The **coefficient of determination** or R^2 of a regression is a measure of how well data points fit a linear statistical model. In the case of the market model, it is the ratio of the explained variance or systematic risk to the total variance and can be determined using Equation 14. It follows that the proportion of unexplained variance or non-systematic risk of the portfolio's return to the total variance is one minus R^2, as shown in Equation 15. Thus, non-systematic risk can be determined if the variance of the portfolio and the R^2 of the market model regression are known.

$$R^2 = \frac{\text{Systematic risk}}{\text{Total risk}} = \frac{\beta^2_p\sigma^2_m}{\beta^2_p\sigma^2_m + \sigma^2_{\varepsilon_p}} \tag{14}$$

$$1 - R^2 = \frac{\text{Unsystematic risk}}{\text{Total risk}} = 1 - \frac{\beta^2_p\sigma^2_m}{\beta^2_p\sigma^2_m + \sigma^2_{\varepsilon_p}} = \frac{\sigma^2_{\varepsilon_p}}{\beta^2_p\sigma^2_m + \sigma^2_{\varepsilon_p}} \tag{15}$$

The information ratio (IR) measures the reward of active management relative to the risk of active management, as noted in Equation 16. Based on sample estimates, Equation 16 can be expressed as Equation 17. Recall that $\sigma_{\varepsilon_p} = \sqrt{\sigma^2_{\varepsilon_p}}$ and $\hat{\sigma}_{\varepsilon_p} = \sqrt{\hat{\sigma}^2_{\varepsilon_p}}$.

$$\text{IR} = \frac{\alpha_p}{\sigma_{\varepsilon_p}} \tag{16}$$

$$\widehat{\text{IR}} = \frac{\hat{\alpha}_p}{\hat{\sigma}_{\varepsilon_p}} \tag{17}$$

For example, assume Portfolio J delivered 10.0% returns with volatility as measured by standard deviation of 16.8%. The market index returned 8.0% over the same time period with a standard deviation of 12.0%. Portfolio J has an estimated beta of 1.20 and the risk-free rate is 3.0%. Jensen's alpha is 1.0%, $\alpha_p = 10.0\% - [3.0\% + 1.20(8.0\% - 3.0)] = 1.0\% = 0.01$. Non-systematic risk is 0.007488, $\sigma^2_{\varepsilon_p} = 0.168^2 - 1.20^2(0.12^2) = 0.007488$. The information ratio is approximately 0.1156, $\widehat{\text{IR}} = \frac{0.01}{\sqrt{0.007488}} = 0.1156$.

As another example, assume Portfolio K delivered 9.0% returns with volatility as measured by standard deviation of 12.0%. The market index returned 12.0% over the same time period with a standard deviation of 15.0%. A market model regression estimates beta of 0.80 for Portfolio K with an R^2 of 0.81. The risk-free rate is 3.0%.

Jensen's alpha is −1.2%, $\alpha_p = 9.0\% - [3.0\% + 0.80(12.0\% - 3.0\%)] = -1.2\% = -0.012$. Non-systematic risk is 0.002736, $\sigma^2_{\varepsilon_p} = (1 - 0.81)0.12^2 = 0.002736$. The information ratio is approximately −0.2294, $\widehat{\text{IR}} = \dfrac{-0.012}{\sqrt{0.002736}} = -0.2294$.

Exhibit 11 provides an illustration of the appraisal ratio. Assume three portfolios, D, E, and F, whose Jensen's alpha–residual risk combinations are shown in Exhibit 11. The information ratio for each portfolio is the slope of the ray that emanates from the (0, 0) intersection of the axes through the point plotted for each portfolio. Based on Exhibit 11, Portfolio D has the highest information ratio. The result is that, for a given level of non-systematic risk, Portfolio D has the highest return and for a given level of return, Portfolio D has the lowest non-systematic risk. Although Portfolio E has a positive Jensen's alpha, it is lower than that of Portfolio D and its higher non-systematic risk results in an information ratio lower than Portfolio D. Although Portfolio F has less non-systematic risk than both Portfolio D and Portfolio E, its negative Jensen's alpha results in an information ratio that is lower than both of these other two portfolios.

Exhibit 11 The Information Ratio (Treynor–Black Appraisal Ratio)

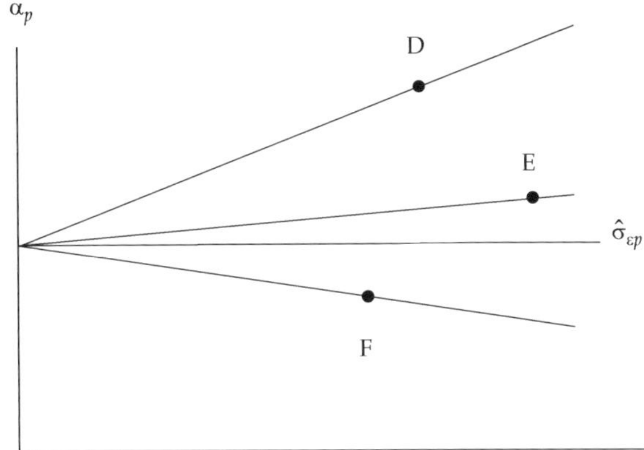

The information ratio compares a portfolio's Jensen's alpha with its residual risk. Jensen's alpha corresponds to the return that is not explained by the benchmark's return. It results from choices made by the manager in an effort to outperform the benchmark. Residual risk reflects deviations in the difference between portfolio and benchmark returns. Thus, the information ratio allows analysts to check whether the risk taken by a manager in deviating from the benchmark is sufficiently rewarded by the portfolio's returns.

A portfolio's information ratio, unlike Jensen's alpha, is invariant to both the amount of benchmark risk and the amount of leverage used in the portfolio.[18] These are important advantages. It can be thought of as the Sharpe ratio of abnormal returns: Jensen's alpha measures abnormal returns, whereas the information ratio measures abnormal return per unit of active management risk. There is general agreement in the active portfolio management literature that the best measure of this benefit is the ratio of the portfolio's alpha to the portfolio's residual risk.

As presented here, one disadvantage of the information ratio is that the benchmark portfolio may not correctly capture the portfolio's systematic risk; a multifactor model might be more appropriate than a single-factor model.

18 The information ratio is invariant to benchmark risk because the measure controls for unsystematic rather than systematic risk. It is also invariant to leverage because the excess return and the measure of risk are proportionate to the fraction of investment financed by borrowing.

EXAMPLE 7

Information Ratio (Treynor–Black Appraisal Ratio)

1 Portfolio Y delivered an average annualized return of 9.0% over the past 60 months. The annualized standard deviation over this same time period was 20.0%. The market index returned 8.0% per year on average over the same time period with an annualized standard deviation of 12.0%. Portfolio Y has an estimated beta of 1.40 versus the market index. Assuming the risk-free rate is 3.0% per year, the information ratio is *closest* to:

A -0.8492.

B -0.0922.

C -0.0481.

2 The information ratio is the ratio of Jensen's alpha to the standard deviation of the portfolio's:

A total risk.

B systematic risk.

C non-systematic risk.

3 Portfolio C delivered an average annualized return of 11.0% with an annualized standard deviation of 14.0% based on the past 60 months of data. The market index returned 12.0% per year over the same time period with annualized standard deviation of 16.0%. A market model regression estimates beta of 0.90 for Portfolio C with an R^2 of 0.64. Assuming the risk-free rate is 3.0% per year, the information ratio is *closest* to:

A -0.1701.

B -0.1304.

C -0.0119.

Solution to 1:

B is correct. Jensen's alpha is –1.0%, α_p = 9.0% – [3.0% + 1.40(8.0% – 3.0%)] = –1.0% = –0.01. Non-systematic risk is 0.011776, $\sigma^2_{\varepsilon_p} = 0.20^2 - 1.40^2(0.12^2) =$ 0.011776. The information ratio is approximately –0.0922, $\widehat{\text{IR}} = \frac{-0.01}{\sqrt{0.011776}} =$ –0.0922.

Solution to 2:

C is correct. The information ratio is the ratio of Jensen's alpha to the standard deviation of the portfolio's non-systematic risk. Essentially, the ratio allows an investor to evaluate whether excess returns warrant the additional non-systematic risk that is found in actively managed portfolios.

Solution to 3:

C is correct. Jensen's alpha is –0.10%, α_p = 11.0% – [3.0% + 0.90(12.0% – 3.0%)] = –0.10% = –0.001. Non-systematic risk is 0.007056, $\sigma^2_{\varepsilon_p} = (1 - 0.64)0.14^2 =$ 0.007056. The information ratio is approximately –0.0119, $\widehat{\text{IR}} = \frac{-0.001}{\sqrt{0.007056}} =$ –0.0119.

3.7 Information Ratio–Active Return Definition

Practitioners often use a definition of the information ratio that differs from the information ratio understood as the Treynor–Black appraisal ratio. This second definition uses active return rather than alpha as a measure of value added. There is no accepted terminology to distinguish the two definitions. Defined either way, the information ratio tries to accomplish the objective of scaling a measure of value added by non-systematic risk. The Treynor–Black definition reduces to this active-return definition if the sensitivity (beta) of the portfolio to the benchmark is one. So, the definition in Section 3.6 is more robust in the sense that it is less likely to lead to incorrect conclusions. In contrast, the active return variation is simpler to calculate and simple benchmark relative performance is a major focus in practice. The context of a description or question usually makes it clear which definition is being referred to.

The version of the information ratio (IR_a) presented in this section tells an investor how much excess return is generated from the amount of excess risk taken relative to the benchmark. It is calculated by dividing the portfolio's mean excess return relative to its benchmark by the variability of that excess return, as shown by Equation 18. The denominator of the information ratio, $\sigma(r_p - r_B)$ is the portfolio's **tracking risk**, a measure of how closely a portfolio follows the index to which it is benchmarked. (Many writers use "tracking error" in the sense of "tracking risk," although, confusingly, tracking error is sometimes used to refer to just the return difference between the portfolio and its benchmark.) Equation 19 is the version of Equation 18 based on sample estimates of parameters.

$$IR_a = \frac{E(r_p) - E(r_B)}{\sigma(r_p - r_B)} \qquad (18)$$

$$\widehat{IR}_a = \frac{\bar{r}_p - \bar{r}_B}{\hat{\sigma}(r_p - r_B)} \qquad (19)$$

For example, Portfolio L delivered a 10.0% return over a time period when the benchmark portfolio returned 8.0%. The tracking risk was 4.5%. The information ratio is equal to approximately 0.44, $\widehat{IR}_a = \frac{0.10 - 0.08}{0.045} = 0.44$. Note the numerator of the information ratio is an excess return and is not risk-adjusted or a Jensen's alpha determined by a market model regression.

Exhibit 12 presents hypothetical monthly returns for a fund and its benchmark, expressed as percentages rather than decimals. Exhibit 13 shows a plot of monthly excess returns for the fund. Based on monthly data, the information ratio is 0.5508 using full precision $\left(\widehat{IR}_a = \frac{2.1083 - 2.050}{0.1059} = 0.5508\right)$ or 0.5505 using the truncated values shown in the spreadsheet.

Exhibit 12 Hypothetical Monthly Returns and Excess Returns

Month	Portfolio Return (%) r_p	Benchmark Return (%) r_B	Excess Return (%) $r_p - r_B$
1	4.15	4.12	0.03
2	7.26	7.19	0.07
3	1.55	1.58	-0.03
4	-0.13	-0.16	0.03
5	4.62	4.38	0.24

(continued)

Exhibit 12 (Continued)

Month	Portfolio Return (%) r_P	Benchmark Return (%) r_B	Excess Return (%) $r_P - r_B$
6	−4.75	−4.74	−0.01
7	3.81	3.79	0.02
8	−0.72	−0.88	0.16
9	2.05	2.13	−0.08
10	1.76	1.81	−0.05
11	−4.32	−4.4	0.08
12	10.02	9.78	0.24
Mean (%)	2.1083	2.0500	0.0583
Standard deviation (%)	4.3097	4.2680	0.1059
Information ratio			0.5508

Exhibit 13 Hypothetical Excess Returns

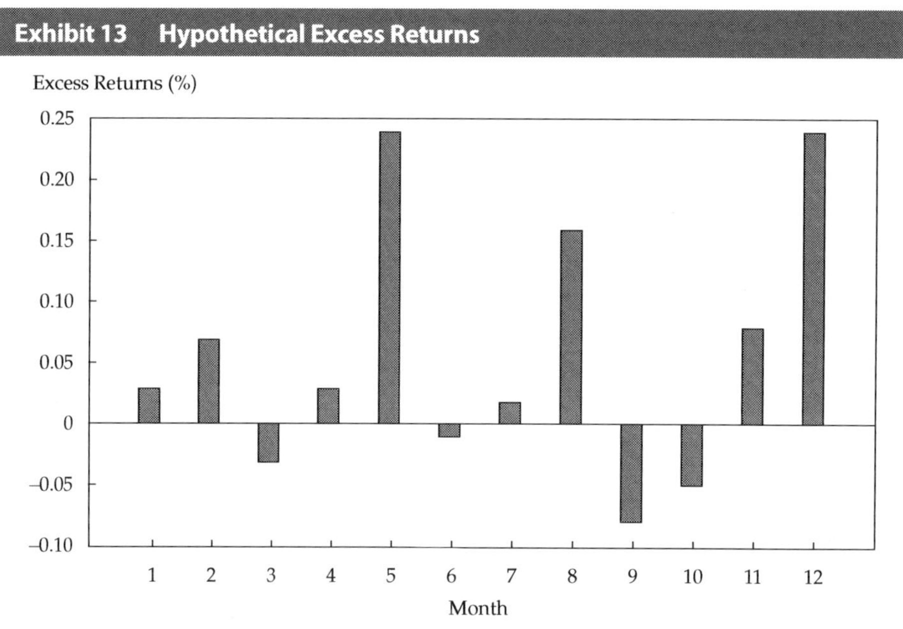

Exhibit 14 provides an illustration of the information ratio. Assume three portfolios, N, O, and P, whose excess return versus the benchmark and tracking risk combinations are shown in Exhibit 14. The information ratio for each portfolio is the slope of the ray that emanates from the (0, 0) intersection of the axes through the point plotted for each portfolio. Based on Exhibit 14, Portfolio N has the highest information ratio. Although Portfolio O has a positive excess return versus the benchmark, it is lower than that of Portfolio N and its larger tracking risk results in an information ratio lower than Portfolio N. Although Portfolio P has lower tracking risk than both Portfolio N and Portfolio O, its negative excess return versus the benchmark results in an information ratio that is lower than both of the other two portfolios.

Exhibit 14 Information Ratio

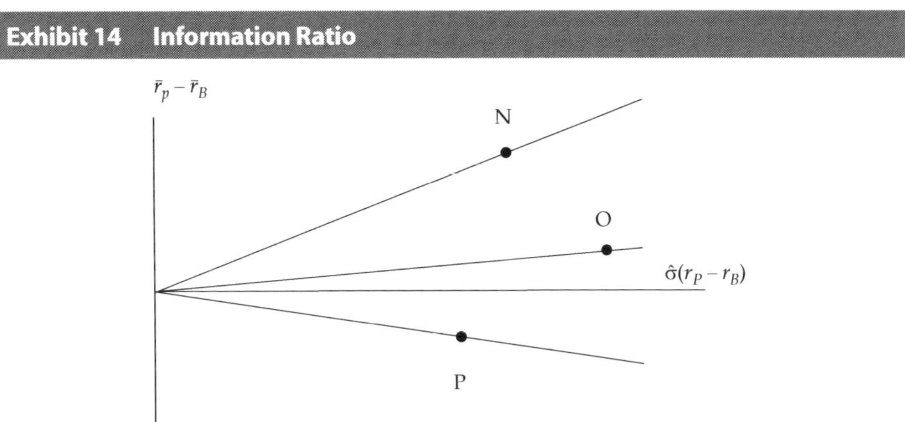

Fundamental Law of Active Management:

The **fundamental law of active management** (fundamental law) was first proposed by Grinold (1989). According to Grinold, the information ratio is equal to the information coefficient (IC) multiplied by the square root of market breadth, $\sqrt{n}$, as shown by Equation 20. Conceptually, the information coefficient is the correlation between the manager's forecasted returns and actual returns. Breadth is the number of independent "bets" or positions the manager takes with the portfolio. Thus, the information ratio is a measure of value added: It is a product of managerial skill and the number of times the manager uses that skill.

$$\text{IR} = \text{IC}\sqrt{n} \quad (20)$$

As a qualitative example, a portfolio manager could have a thorough understanding of a specific industry, such as social media. Within that specific sector, it is reasonable to assume that the manager's information coefficient would be relatively large. But the number of independent bets the manager could make might be limited by his or her lack of expertise in other industries, so breadth would be small. Conversely, another manager might follow several industries in an effort to improve portfolio breadth. But the trade-off is that his or her information coefficients might be smaller because he or she is trying to extract an informational advantage over a larger pool of possible investments.

The fundamental law was later expanded by Clarke, de Silva, and Thorley (2002) to include a transfer coefficient (TC), as shown by Equation 21, where $0 \leq \text{TC} \leq 1.0$. The transfer coefficient measures the degree to which an investor's forecasts are translated into active (i.e., different-than-benchmark) weights. Portfolio constraints, trading costs, market impact, and other market constraints ensure that the transfer coefficient will be less than one. According to Clarke, de Silva, and Thorley, a long-only portfolio constraint can reduce the transfer coefficient by up to 40%.

$$\text{IR} = \text{IC} \times \sqrt{n} \times \text{TC} \quad (21)$$

Exhibit 15 provides a visual summary of the decomposition of the information ratio that is provided by the fundamental law. The information ratio is a benchmark-relative, excess return metric versus a risk metric. The measure of risk is tracking risk, which reflects how closely the portfolio's performance mirrors that of the benchmark. According to the fundamental law, the expected value added to an actively managed portfolio is dependent on (1) the manager's forecasting skill, (2) the number of assets in the forecasting pool (or breadth of the forecasting pool), and (3) portfolio constraints that reduce the expected value of the manager's forecasting ability.

Exhibit 15 The Fundamental Law of Active Management

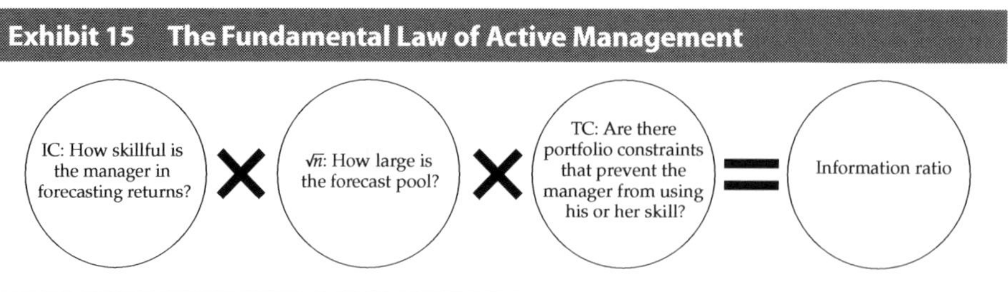

As an example, many portfolio managers would view a "good" information coefficient as 0.05 and a "very good" information coefficient as 0.10 (see Gleiser and McKenna 2010). Exhibit 16 shows information ratios for information coefficients of 0.05 and 0.10, assuming breadth is either 100 or 200 securities[19] and the transfer coefficient is either 0.60 or 0.70.

Exhibit 16 Fundamental Law of Active Management

Information Coefficient	Breadth	Transfer Coefficient	Information Ratio
IC	n	TC	$\text{IR} = \text{IC} \times \sqrt{n} \times \text{TC}$
0.05	100	0.60	0.30
0.05	100	0.70	0.35
0.05	200	0.60	0.42
0.05	200	0.70	0.49
0.10	100	0.60	0.60
0.10	100	0.70	0.70
0.10	200	0.60	0.85
0.10	200	0.70	0.99

EXAMPLE 8

Active Return Information Ratio

1 Portfolio D delivered 11.0% annualized returns on average over the past 60 months whereas its benchmark returned 9.0% per year on average over the same time period. Portfolio D's beta is 0.8 and the risk-free rate is 3.0%. Assuming an annualized tracking risk of 5.0%, the active return information ratio of Portfolio D is *closest* to:

A 0.40.

B 0.64.

19 What constitutes breadth is often a contentious issue. Analysts frequently use the number of stocks in the investment universe as a proxy for breadth. But Grinold (1989) emphasized the importance of counting only "independent" bets in the determination of breadth.

C 0.76.

2 Over the past 20 years, the managers of Portfolio R produced an active return information ratio of 0.30. Portfolio R's tracking risk averaged 3.50% annually. On an annual basis, by how much did Portfolio R outperform its benchmark over the 20-year period?

A 1.00%

B 1.05%

C 1.10%

Solution to 1:

A is correct. $\widehat{\text{IR}}_a = \dfrac{0.11 - 0.09}{0.05} = 0.40.$

Solution to 2:

B is correct. The information ratio is determined as $\widehat{\text{IR}}_a = \dfrac{\bar{r}_p - \bar{r}_B}{\hat{\sigma}(r_p - r_B)}$. Using the data from the question, $0.30 = \dfrac{\bar{r}_p - \bar{r}_B}{0.035}$, $\therefore \bar{r}_p - \bar{r}_B = 0.30 \times 0.0305 = 0.0105 =$ 1.05%.

3.8 Appraisal Measures Based on Downside Risk: Sortino Ratio

The Sortino ratio was created by Brian Rom in 1986 and named for Dr. Frank A. Sortino, an expert in downside risk optimization (see Sortino and van der Meer 1991). It is a modification of the Sharpe ratio, but penalizes only those returns that are less than a user-specified return. The Sharpe ratio penalizes both upside and downside volatility equally.

Equation 22 presents the *ex ante* Sortino ratio, where r_T is the minimum acceptable return (MAR), which is sometimes referred to as a target rate of return.[20] Based on sample estimates, Equation 22 can be expressed as Equation 23. Instead of using standard deviation in the denominator, the Sortino ratio uses a measure of downside risk, known as **target semi-standard deviation** or **target semideviation**, σ_D, as shown in Equation 24. By using this value, the Sortino ratio penalizes managers for only "harmful" volatility and is a measure of return per unit of downside risk.

$$\text{SR}_D = \frac{E\left[r_p\right] - r_T}{\sigma_D} \quad (22)$$

$$\widehat{\text{SR}}_D = \frac{\bar{r}_p - \bar{r}_T}{\hat{\sigma}_D} \quad (23)$$

$$\sigma_D = \left[\frac{\sum_{t=1}^{N} \min\left(r_t - r_T, 0\right)^2}{n}\right]^{1/2} \quad (24)$$

20 The MAR is the lowest rate of return at which an investor will consider investing. For example, a MAR set equal to the expected rate of inflation would be associated with capital preservation in real terms. The MAR is not used to determine intrinsic value. Rather, it is a constraint or decision criterion that applies to all investment considerations.

Assume a portfolio has a MAR of 4.0%. The portfolio's returns over a 10-year period are given in Exhibit 17. The numerator of the Sortino ratio is the average portfolio return minus the target return or 2.0%, $\bar{r}_p - r_T = 6.0\% - 4.0\% = 2.0\%$. The calculation of target semi-standard deviation is reported in Exhibit 17. Based on the information in the table, the Sortino ratio is approximately 0.65, $\widehat{\text{SR}}_D = \frac{0.06 - 0.04}{0.0307} \approx 0.65$

Exhibit 17 Sortino Ratio Using Target Semi-Standard Deviation

Year	Rate of Return: r_t	Target return: $r_T = 4\%$ $\min(r_t - r_T, 0)^2$
1	6.0%	0
2	8.0%	0
3	−1.0%	0.0025
4	18.0%	0
5	12.0%	0
6	3.0%	0.0001
7	−4.0%	0.0064
8	5.0%	0
9	2.0%	0.0004
10	11.0%	0
	$\sum_{t=1}^{n} \min(r_t - r_T, 0)^2 =$	0.0094

$$\sigma_D = \left[\frac{\sum_{t=1}^{n} \min(r_t - r_T, 0)^2}{n}\right]^{1/2} = \left(\frac{0.0094}{10}\right)^{1/2} \approx 0.0307 = 3.07\%$$

Exhibit 18 provides an illustration of the Sortino ratio. Assume two portfolios, G and H, whose mean return in excess of the target return and target semi-standard deviation combinations are shown in Exhibit 18. The Sortino ratio for each portfolio is the slope of the ray that emanates from the target return through the point plotted for the portfolio. Based on Exhibit 18, Portfolio G is preferred to Portfolio H because it delivers a higher mean return in excess of the target return per unit of downside risk.

Exhibit 18 Sortino Ratio

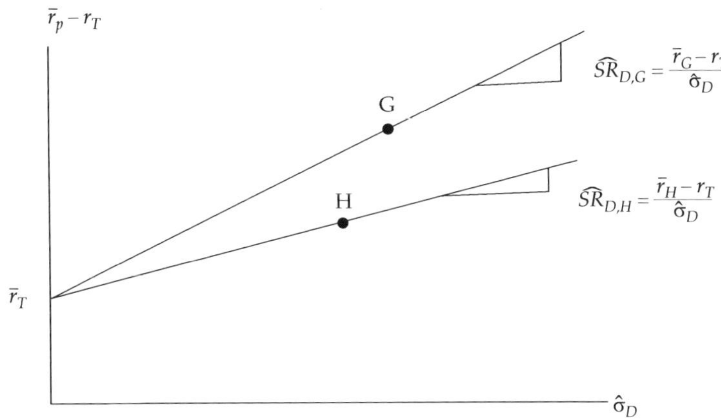

One benefit the Sortino ratio offers over traditional performance measures is the ability to more accurately assess performance when return distributions are not symmetrical. For example, because of its underlying assumption of normally distributed returns, the Sharpe ratio would suffer when comparing positively skewed strategies, such as trend-following, with negatively skewed strategies, such as option writing. Thus, the Sortino ratio is arguably a better performance metric for such assets as hedge funds or commodity trading funds whose return distributions are purposefully skewed away from the normal.

Another benefit is the numerator in the Sortino ratio formula is not a risk premium. It is the return a portfolio manager is able to generate that is greater than what is minimally acceptable to the investor. Essentially, the Sortino ratio penalizes a manager when portfolio return is less than the MAR, and it is most relevant when one of the investor's primary objectives is capital preservation.

Although there are arguments in favor of both the Sharpe ratio and the Sortino ratio, the Sharpe ratio has been much more widely used. In some cases, this preference may reflect a certain comfort level associated with the use of standard deviation, which is a more traditional measurement of volatility. Another issue is the difficulty in making cross-sectional comparisons of Sortino ratios that are applicable to every investor because the MAR is investor specific.

EXAMPLE 9

Sortino Ratio

1 Portfolio B delivered 10.0% annual returns on average over the past 60 months. Its average annual volatility as measured by standard deviation was 14.0% and its downside volatility as measured by target semi-standard deviation was 8.0%. Assuming the target rate of return is 3.0% per year, the Sortino ratio of portfolio B is *closest* to:

A 0.66.

B 0.77.

C 0.88.

2 Assume a target return of 3.0%. Annual returns over the past four years have been 6.0%, −3.0%, 7.0%, and 1.0%. The target semi-standard deviation is *closest* to:

A 1.33%.

B 3.16%.

C 4.65%.

Solution to 1:

C is correct. $\widehat{SR}_D = \frac{0.10 - 0.03}{0.08} = 0.88$.

Solution to 2:

B is correct.

Year	Rate of Return: r_t	Target return: $r_T = 3\%$ $\min(r_t - r_T, 0)^2$
1	6.0%	0
2	−3.0%	0.0036
3	7.0%	0
4	1.0%	0.0004

$$\sum_{t=1}^{n}\min(r_t - r_T, 0)^2 = \quad 0.004$$

$$\sigma_D = \left[\frac{\sum_{t=1}^{n}\min(r_t - r_T, 0)^2}{n}\right]^{1/2} = \left(\frac{0.004}{4}\right)^{1/2} \approx 0.0316 = 3.16\%$$

3.9 Appraisal Measures Based on Downside Risk: Calmar Ratio

The Calmar ratio (or drawdown ratio) is a performance measurement first used to evaluate commodity trading advisers and, subsequently, hedge funds. It was created by Terry W. Young and initially published in 1991 in the trade journal *Futures*. At the time, Young owned California Managed Accounts, which managed client funds and published the newsletter *CMA Reports*. Calmar is an acronym based on the company's name and its newsletter.

The Calmar ratio (CR) is used to measure return versus the fund's maximum drawdown. **Drawdown** is the percentage decline peak-to-trough from the most recent high. The Calmar ratio is typically estimated over a 36-month period. It is calculated by taking a fund's compound annualized rate of return divided by the fund's maximum drawdown, as shown by Equation 25, where R_t is the monthly return. Maximum drawdown (MD) represents the maximum loss an investor would have suffered if he or she had bought the fund at a high and sold it at a low during the evaluation period. The negative sign of the drawdown is a convention such that the denominator becomes positive and, as a result, high values of the denominator stand for greater risk.

$$\mathrm{CR} = \frac{\left[\prod_{1}^{T}(1 + R_t)\right]^{12/T} - 1}{-\mathrm{MD}} \tag{25}$$

One reason the Calmar ratio is frequently used to evaluate hedge fund performance relates to the manner in which managers are compensated. The typical arrangement includes a fixed fee plus an incentive fee that is subject to a high-water-mark clause. Both fees are a percentage of assets under management with the incentive fee being significantly higher than the fixed fee thereby making the collection of incentive fees the main goal of the hedge fund manager.

However, the high-water-mark clause only allows the manager to collect incentive fees when the net asset value of the fund at the end of its evaluation period is above its high point during the evaluation periods since the investor began investing in the fund. Thus, hedge funds currently operating at their high-water mark are expected to generate larger incentive fees because doing so only requires positive future returns. Conversely, hedge funds currently facing a large drawdown will not collect incentive fees from those investors who entered the fund prior to the drawdown. These funds are also likely to lose new business because potential investors view the large drawdown as a signal of poor management.

The result is that hedge fund managers will strive to keep drawdowns to a minimum. Thus, drawdown status can be linked to managerial skill, so it follows that the Calmar ratio is a performance metric that can be used to identify skilled hedge fund managers.

Exhibit 19 presents a Calmar ratio example for a hypothetical fund with a beginning size of €113,250,000. Data are for 36 months. The drawdown reflects how far the fund has fallen in value in percentage terms from its previous high.

Exhibit 19 Calmar Ratio Calculations

Month	Portfolio Value (€ thousands)	1 + Return	Highest Close	Drawdown
0	113,250		113,250	
1	114,340	1.009625	114,340	0
2	112,400	0.983033	114,340	-0.016967
3	113,310	1.008096	114,340	-0.009008
4	110,280	0.973259	114,340	-0.035508
5	113,280	1.027203	114,340	-0.009271
6	110,590	0.976254	114,340	-0.032797
7	108,890	0.984628	114,340	-0.047665
8	111,770	1.026449	114,340	-0.022477
9	111,810	1.000358	114,340	-0.022127
10	116,900	1.045524	116,900	0
⋮	⋮	⋮	⋮	⋮
30	126,020	1.005666	130,220	-0.032253
31	128,720	1.021425	130,220	-0.011519
32	131,780	1.023773	131,780	0
33	136,340	1.034603	136,340	0
34	138,860	1.018483	138,860	0
35	141,640	1.02002	141,640	0
36	141,240	0.997176	141,640	-0.002824

Annualized geometric mean return	7.64%
Maximum drawdown	-4.77%
Calmar ratio	1.60

Exhibit 20 provides an illustration of the Calmar ratio. Assume three portfolios, Q, R, and S, whose mean return and maximum drawdown (–MD) combinations are shown in Exhibit 20. The Calmar ratio for each portfolio is the slope of the ray that emanates from the (0, 0) intersection of the axes through the point plotted for each portfolio. Based on Exhibit 20, Portfolio Q has the highest Calmar ratio. Although Portfolio R has a positive mean return, it is lower than that of Portfolio Q and its larger maximum drawdown results in a Calmar ratio lower than Portfolio Q. Although Portfolio S has a smaller maximum drawdown than both Portfolio Q and Portfolio R, its negative mean return results in a Calmar ratio that is lower than both of the other two portfolios.

Exhibit 20 Calmar Ratio

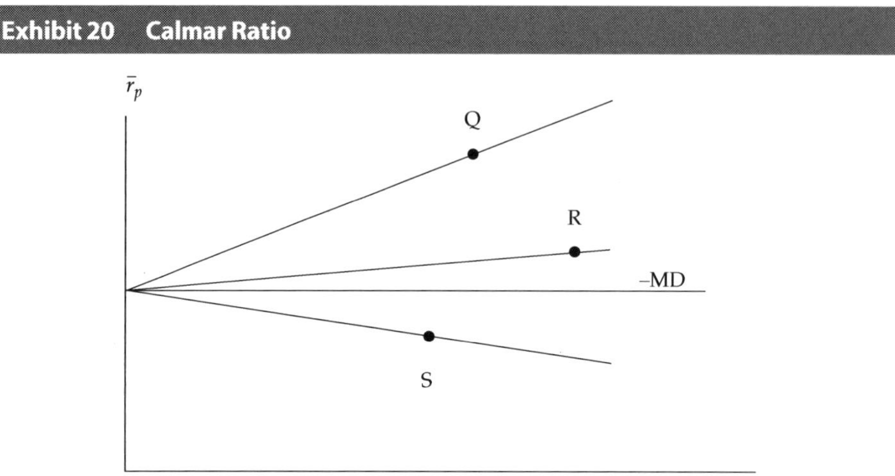

A frequent criticism of the Calmar ratio is that it is sensitive to outliers because of its use of the maximum drawdown. Critics also argue that maximum drawdown is only relevant if one expects to sell or be forced to sell at the worst possible time. Instead of the maximum drawdown, the Sterling ratio[21] uses the average of a specified number of drawdowns of an asset within the time period under consideration. For example, if a 36-month period is used, a typical Sterling ratio approach would be to average the maximum drawdown for each of the three consecutive 12-month time periods during the 36-month evaluation period. The third ratio based on drawdown, which has found widespread use in the literature, is the Burke ratio (Burke 1994). In this measure, risk is described by the square root of the sum of the squares of a specified number of drawdowns within the time period under consideration. The effect of squaring the drawdowns is to put greater weight on the larger drawdowns.

EXAMPLE 10

The Calmar Ratio

1 How is risk measured with the Calmar ratio?

 A The maximum drawdown over the measurement period

 B An average of the maximum drawdowns over the measurement period

 C The square root of the sum of the squares of the maximum drawdowns over the measurement period

2 The Calmar ratio for Fund H was 1.5 and it had an annualized return of 6%. What was the maximum drawdown?

 A 4.0%

21 The original Sterling ratio was developed by Deane Sterling Jones, a company that is no longer in existence.

B 4.5%

C 7.5%

Solution to 1:

A is correct. A frequent criticism of the Calmar ratio is its use of maximum drawdown as a measure of risk.

Solution to 2:

A is correct. The Calmar ratio is average annualized return divided by maximum drawdown. Thus, maximum drawdown is the average annualized return divided by the Calmar ratio, 6%/1.5 = 4.0%.

3.10 Performance Appraisal: An Analysis of Three Funds

In this section, we examine the historical performance of three equity funds invested primarily in the United Kingdom. All three funds are authorized unit trusts and categorized as UCITS (Undertakings for Collective Investment in Transferable Securities). UCITS follow a set of European Union directives that allow collective investment schemes to operate freely throughout the EU on the basis of a single authorization from one member state. The three funds are

- **Fidelity Investment Funds–UK Select.** The fund aims to provide long-term capital growth. It is likely to have a bias toward medium- and smaller-sized companies, and it has the freedom to invest outside the fund's principal geographies, market sectors, industries, or asset classes. It can use derivatives for risk or cost reduction or to generate additional capital or income in line with the fund's risk profile.
- **GAM UK Diversified.** The fund seeks to exploit areas with excessively negative sentiment and a catalyst for change. Stocks are selected on the basis of fundamental and technical analysis. Currency hedging may be used to protect against exchange rate risk.
- **Liontrust UK Growth Fund.** The fund invests primarily in large and mid-capitalization stocks, with smaller companies limited to a maximum 10% total weight. The fund's investment philosophy is to invest in companies that have a durable economic advantage that allows them to sustain a higher-than-average level of profitability. The fund is permitted to use derivatives for the purpose of efficient portfolio management and for investment purposes.

The market and benchmark portfolio that is used to evaluate the performance of these funds is the FTSE All-Share Index. It represents the performance of all eligible companies listed on the London Stock Exchange's (LSE) main market that pass screening for size and liquidity. The index captures 98% of the UK's market capitalization. The FTSE All-Share is the aggregation of the FTSE 100, FTSE 250, and FTSE Small Cap Indices.

The proxy chosen for the risk-free rate is the one-month constant maturity British pound London Interbank Offered Rate (Libor) interest rate from Bank of America Merrill Lynch (BAML). It is the average interest rate at which a selection of banks in London are prepared to lend to one another in British pounds with a maturity of one month. The Libor interest rates are frequently used by banks as the base rate in setting the level of their savings, mortgage, and loan interest rates.

Monthly data for the five-year period of April 2009 through March 2014 were used in this analysis. Exhibit 21 presents summary statistics for the evaluation period and also the results of a market model regression for all three funds. Exhibit 22 presents the performance measures for all three funds whose computations are based on the data presented in Exhibit 21.

Exhibit 21 Summary Statistics and Market Model Regression Results, April 2009–March 2014

Summary Statistics

Variable	FTSE All-Share	BAML British Pound Libor (one month constant maturity)	Fidelity Investment Funds–UK Select Fund	GAM Funds–GAM UK Diversified Class A	Liontrust UK Growth Fund
Annualized return	12.37%	—	15.98%	18.45%	17.98%
$\bar{r}_p$	—	—	1.33%	1.50%	1.44%
$\hat{\sigma}_p$	—	—	4.27%	3.93%	3.40%
$\hat{\sigma}_D$	—	—	2.23%	1.88%	1.70%
-MD	—	—	8.49%	8.11%	6.71%
$\bar{r}_F$	—	0.05%	—	—	—
$\bar{r}_m$	1.06%	—	—	—	—
$\hat{\sigma}_m$	4.04%	—	—	—	—
$\bar{r}_p - \bar{r}_F$	—	—	1.28%	1.45%	1.39%
$\bar{r}_m - \bar{r}_F$	1.01%	—	—	—	—
$\bar{r}_p - \bar{r}_m$	—	—	0.27%	0.44%	0.39%
$\hat{\sigma}(r_p - r_m)$	—	—	1.30%	1.84%	1.85%

Market Model Regression Results

Variable	Fidelity Investment Funds–UK Select Fund	GAM Funds–GAM UK Diversified Class A	Liontrust UK Growth Fund
$\hat{\alpha}_p$	0.27%	0.57%[a]	0.64%[b]
$\hat{\beta}_p$	1.01[b]	0.87[b]	0.75[b]

Exhibit 21 (Continued)

Market Model Regression Results

Variable	Fidelity Investment Funds–UK Select Fund	GAM Funds–GAM UK Diversified Class A	Liontrust UK Growth Fund
$\hat{\sigma}_{\varepsilon_p}$	1.30%	1.76%	1.55%
R^2	0.9077	0.7984	0.7930

[a] Statistically significant at the 5% significance level.
[b] Statistically significant at the 1% significance level.
Note: The target semi-standard deviation and Sortino ratio are based on an assumed target return of 0%.

Exhibit 22 Performance Appraisal Measures, April 2009–March 2014

Performance Appraisal Measure	Formula or Variable	Fidelity Investment Funds–UK Select Fund	GAM Funds–GAM UK Diversified Class A	Liontrust UK Growth Fund
Sharpe ratio	$\widehat{SR} = \dfrac{\bar{r}_p - \bar{r}_F}{\hat{\sigma}_p}$	0.30	0.37	0.41
M²	$\widehat{M^2} = \widehat{SR} \times \hat{\sigma}_m + r_F$	1.26%	1.54%	1.71%
Treynor ratio	$\widehat{TR} = \dfrac{\bar{r}_p - \bar{r}_F}{\hat{\beta}_p}$	0.0127	0.0166	0.0186
Jensen's alpha	$\hat{\alpha}_p$	0.27%	0.57%	0.64%
Active return	$\bar{r}_p - \bar{r}_m$	0.27%	0.44%	0.39%
Information ratio/ Treynor–Black appraisal ratio	$\widehat{IR} = \dfrac{\hat{\alpha}_p}{\hat{\sigma}_{\varepsilon_p}}$	0.21	0.32	0.41
Information ratio– active return definition	$\widehat{IR}_a = \dfrac{\bar{r}_p - \bar{r}_m}{\hat{\sigma}(r_p - r_m)}$	0.21	0.24	0.21
Sortino ratio	$\widehat{SR}_D = \dfrac{\bar{r}_p - \bar{r}_T}{\hat{\sigma}_D}$	0.60	0.79	0.85
Calmar ratio	$CR = \dfrac{\left[\prod_{1}^{T}(1 + R_t)\right]^{12/T} - 1}{-MD}$	1.88	2.28	2.68

A review of Exhibit 21 shows that all three funds earned higher returns than the FTSE All-Share during the evaluation period. The highest return was earned by the GAM UK Diversified fund, with an annualized return of 18.45% compared with 12.37% for the FTSE All-Share. The annualized returns for the Liontrust UK Growth Fund and the Fidelity Investment Funds–UK Select Fund were 17.98% and 15.98%, respectively. All but the UK Select Fund earned those return with lower return volatility than the FTSE All-Share Index.

If investors could foresee the future—knew what returns were going to be—everyone would have selected the GAM fund. However, because returns are risky it is appropriate to consider not only the magnitude of gains, but also the risks taken.

Investment performance appraisal measures matter most when analysts are trying to assess what might happen to fund returns in the future. Essentially, interpreting these performance appraisal measures reduces to whether the risk assumed from investing in a fund is "worth it" given the potential for returns to exceed those of the benchmark portfolio. Thus, they are best viewed as *ex ante* selection tools that allow investors to make informed decisions.

Exhibit 21 shows that the volatility measures for the Liontrust fund are the lowest of the three funds. The standard deviation of monthly returns $\left(\hat{\sigma}_P\right)$, the target semi-standard deviation $\left(\hat{\sigma}_D\right)$, and the maximum drawdown (–MD) are all significantly lower for the Liontrust fund. Thus, it was the least risky of the three funds during the evaluation period.

The performance of the Fidelity fund most closely tracked that of the FTSE All-Share benchmark. As Exhibit 21 shows, the tracking risk $\left[\hat{\sigma}\left(r_p - r_m\right)\right]$ and the standard deviation of the residual error terms from the market model regression $\left(\hat{\sigma}_{\varepsilon_p}\right)$ are the lowest for the Fidelity fund. The market model R^2 of 0.9077 indicates that more than 90% of the changes in the Fidelity fund's excess returns are explained by changes in the excess returns for the FTSE All-Share. This result compares with an R^2 of less than 80% for the other two funds.

Exhibit 22 shows that most of the risk-adjusted performance measures favor the Liontrust fund. Of the three funds, it has the highest Sharpe ratio and the highest M^2. Both of these measures use standard deviation to adjust for risk and thus control for the total risk of the portfolio. Using the Sharpe ratio and M^2 to appraise performance is most appropriate if they are applied to an investor's entire portfolio.

Adjusting fund performance for market risk is considered a preferred approach to performance appraisal if the funds under consideration are a small part of the investor's total portfolio. As Exhibit 22 shows, the Liontrust fund also had the highest Treynor ratio, Jensen's alpha, and information ratio. Note from Exhibit 21 that the Jensen alpha coefficient estimate is statistically significant at the 1% significance level. All of these performance measures assume the CAPM is the theoretically correct pricing model and that a fund's market risk is correctly reflected by its beta.

Exhibit 22 also shows that the Liontrust fund had the highest Sortino ratio and Calmar ratio. Both of these performance measures adjust for downside risk. Their use is considered to be most appropriate when returns are believed to be asymmetrical or if a primary concern of the investor is capital preservation.

There are two performance measures that favor the GAM fund in Exhibit 22. The first, active return, is not a risk-adjusted measure and simply reiterates that the GAM fund outperformed the FTSE All-Share by more than the other two funds. The information ratio–active return, which is a risk-adjusted measure, favors the GAM fund because it has the highest active return and a tracking risk that is approximately equivalent to that of the Liontrust fund.

In summary, the majority of the risk-adjusted performance measures presented in Exhibit 22 favor the Liontrust fund as the top performer. These results support the hypothesis that Liontrust management demonstrated superior investment skill during this evaluation period. "Skill," in this sense, means investors were compensated well for the risks taken.

MULTIFACTOR MODELS IN PERFORMANCE APPRAISAL

4

One of the goals of performance appraisal is to determine the factors that explain the difference between the portfolio return and its investors' required return. Most of the measures discussed in Section 3 of this reading are based on a single risk factor, either the total risk of the fund (Sharpe ratio) or the market or benchmark risk of the fund (Treynor index). But there are both theoretical and practical reasons that argue for risk to be considered multi-dimensional.

A general multifactor approach to asset pricing holds that the expected return of a financial asset can be modeled as a linear function of various risk factors, where sensitivity to changes in each factor is represented by a factor-specific sensitivity or "beta" coefficient. The formula for such a linear factor model is given by Equation 26. According to Equation 26, a total of K risk factors, F_k, and a portfolio's sensitivity to each of those factors, b_k, determine expected return.

$$E\left(R_p\right) = r_F + \sum_{k=1}^{K} b_k F_k \tag{26}$$

Multifactor models enable portfolio returns to be explained by a set of risk factors, rather than simple exposure to a market or benchmark portfolio. Thus, they can provide much more detailed information on risk analysis and the evaluation of managerial performance.

Empirically, performance attribution essentially follows a generalized Jensen's alpha approach. The formulation for these approaches is given by Equation 27.

$$r_{p,t} - r_{F,t} = \alpha_p + \sum_{k=1}^{K} b_{p,k} F_{k,t} + \varepsilon_{p,t} \tag{27}$$

Equation 27 defines what may be called multifactor alpha (α_p). The Carhart (1997) four-factor model, a widely used multifactor model in performance appraisal, models systematic risk as a portfolio's sensitivities to market, value, size, and momentum risk factors. Thus, a fund's performance is a function of its sensitivities to these four factors and its alpha. Possible explanations for a positive alpha include (1) exposure to risk factors not incorporated in the model, (2) a successful market timing strategy for exposure to factors included in the model, and (3) superior skill in security selection.

The Carhart four-factor model is an extension of the Fama–French (1992, 1993, and 1996) three-factor model to incorporate the momentum factor documented by Jegadeesh and Titman (1993). The basis for the Fama–French model started with the observation that two types of stocks tended to perform better than what was predicted by the CAPM: (1) stocks with high ratios of book value to price (customarily called "value" stocks; their opposites are called "growth" stocks) and (2) small stocks (as measured by their market capitalization). The Carhart model also includes a momentum factor that reflects the tendency for a stock's price to continue rising if it has been rising or to continue declining if it has been declining, as per Jegadeesh and Titman.

The regression model used to estimate Carhart model sensitivities and portfolio alpha is presented in Equation 28. Most professionals gather freely available data for the risk-free rate and the four risk factors from Professor Kenneth French's website.[22] Downloadable files are available in default monthly, annual, weekly or daily format.

$$r_{p,t} \quad r_{F,t} = a_p + b_{p,MKT}F_{MKT,t} + b_{p,SMB}F_{SMB,t} + b_{p,HML}F_{HML,t} + b_{p,MOM}F_{MOM},t + e_{p,t} \quad (28)$$

The factors are defined as follows:[23]

F_{MKT}: (market risk premium) the market rate of return minus the return on one-month Treasury bills. For the United States, the market return is a value-weighted return of all CRSP companies incorporated in the United States and listed on the NYSE, Amex, or NASDAQ.

F_{SMB}: (small minus big) the average return on the three smallest capitalization portfolios minus the average return on the three largest capitalization portfolios.

F_{HML}: (high minus low) the average return on the two highest book-to-market (value) portfolios minus the average return on the two lowest book-to-market (growth) portfolios.

F_{MOM}: (momentum) the average return on the two highest prior return portfolios minus the average return on the two lowest prior return portfolios.

There are two well-known approaches for estimating factor sensitivities for a portfolio: one is returns-based and the other holdings-based. The returns-based approach estimates factor sensitivities by regressing portfolio excess returns on the factor returns. In the holdings-based approach, factor sensitivities for a portfolio are obtained by first estimating the factor sensitivities of the constituent stocks and then taking the value-weighted average factor sensitivities of the stocks as the factor sensitivities of the portfolio or, more commonly, by using a matching portfolio technique (as described in the Grinblatt and Titman approach in Section 5).

In the following analysis, the factor sensitivities are returns-based estimates. Specifically, they were estimated by regressing monthly portfolio excess returns on monthly factor returns over a 60-month period from January 2009 through December 2013.

The fund that is evaluated is the Class A shares of the American Mutual Fund (AMRMX), which is one of a family of funds issued by American Funds. The fund is considered a large-cap value fund by Morningstar. The fund strives for the balanced accomplishment of three objectives: current income, growth of capital, and conservation of principal. As of 31 October 2013, 90.79% of the fund was invested in common stock, 7.25% in short-term debt securities, and the remainder in preferred stock, bonds, notes, and other debt instruments. As reported in the prospectus, the fund has an expense ratio of 0.61%. The maximum sales charge is 5.75%. Thus, investors would additionally need to account for the impact of sales charges when evaluating this fund as an investment.

Data for the regression appears in Exhibit 23. Price data for AMRMX are from Yahoo Finance and are adjusted for dividends and splits. Data for the risk-free return and the risk premiums are from Professor French's website. Returns are expressed as whole numbers rather than decimals. For example, the January 2009 excess return, $r_{p,t} - r_{F,t}$, for AMRMX is approximately −6.27% and is computed as $\left(\frac{15.39 - 16.42}{16.42}\right) \times 100 - 0.00 = -6.27$.

22 http://mba.tuck.dartmouth.edu/pages/faculty/ken.french/data_library/f-f_factors.html

23 See Professor French's website for a complete description of the factors.

Exhibit 23 Carhart Four-Factor Model

Observations	Date	AMRMX	$r_{F,t}$	$r_{p,t} - r_{F,t}$	$F_{MKT,t}$	$F_{SMB,t}$	$F_{HML,t}$	$F_{MOM,t}$
0	12/2008	16.42						
1	1/2009	15.39	0.00	-6.27	-8.12	-0.98	-9.86	-1.88
2	2/2009	14.00	0.01	-9.04	-10.10	-0.35	-6.90	4.23
3	3/2009	15.03	0.02	7.34	8.95	0.73	2.60	-11.35
4	4/2009	16.12	0.01	7.24	10.19	5.40	5.42	-34.72
5	5/2009	16.91	0.00	4.90	5.21	-2.66	0.56	-12.47
6	6/2009	17.05	0.01	0.82	0.43	2.67	-2.44	5.31
7	7/2009	18.15	0.01	6.44	7.72	2.50	4.73	-5.47
8	8/2009	18.69	0.01	2.97	3.32	-0.51	7.59	-8.87
9	9/2009	19.21	0.01	2.77	4.08	2.47	1.40	-5.02
10	10/2009	19.00	0.00	-1.09	-2.59	-4.22	-4.37	2.67
11	11/2009	20.14	0.00	6.00	5.56	-2.65	0.17	0.37
12	12/2009	20.60	0.01	2.27	2.75	5.79	0.73	2.89
⋮	⋮	⋮	⋮	⋮	⋮	⋮	⋮	⋮
49	1/2013	28.36	0.00	4.23	5.58	0.49	1.35	-1.87
50	2/2013	28.92	0.00	1.97	1.28	-0.38	0.31	1.47
51	3/2013	30.10	0.00	4.08	4.03	0.84	-0.06	2.08
52	4/2013	30.89	0.00	2.62	1.56	-2.43	0.36	0.34
53	5/2013	30.89	0.00	0.00	2.81	1.93	1.31	-1.89
54	6/2013	30.61	0.00	-0.91	-1.21	1.23	-0.45	0.65
55	7/2013	31.92	0.00	4.28	5.66	1.85	0.79	1.69
56	8/2013	31.16	0.00	-2.38	-2.69	0.28	-2.46	0.05
57	9/2013	32.05	0.00	2.86	3.76	2.85	-1.52	3.02
58	10/2013	33.40	0.00	4.21	4.17	-1.53	1.39	0.16
59	11/2013	34.09	0.00	2.07	3.12	1.31	-0.38	0.37
60	12/2013	34.81	0.00	2.11	2.81	-0.44	-0.17	0.05

Results of the regression appear in Exhibit 24. In a multiple regression with an intercept, R^2 represents the square of the multiple correlation coefficient, and an R^2 of 1.0 means that the model's predicted values perfectly fit the data. **Adjusted R^2** adjusts for R^2 increasing when explanatory variables are added to the model; it controls for the number of predictors in a model relative to the number of data points. Adjusted R^2 increases only if a new explanatory variable improves the model more than would be expected by chance and decreases when a predictor improves the model by less than expected by chance. The adjusted R^2 can be negative and is always lower than R^2. The adjusted R^2 for the AMRMX regression is 96.57%, and it is not unusual for a Carhart multifactor alpha regression model to have an R^2 greater than 90.00% (Fischer and Wermers 2013).

Exhibit 24 Regression Results

Summary Output

Regression Statistics

R^2	0.9680
Adjusted R^2	0.9657
Standard error	0.6807
Observations	60

Analysis of Variance

	df	SS	MS	F-test	Significance F
Regression	4	770.5289	192.6322	415.7859	0.0000
Residual	55	25.4813	0.4633		
Total	59	796.0102			

Variable	Coefficient Estimate	Standard Error	*t*-statistic	P-value	Lower 95%	Upper 95%
α_p	0.1545	0.0951	1.62	0.1101	−0.0362	0.3451
$b_{p,MKT}$	0.8116	0.0254	31.96	0.0000	0.7607	0.8625
$b_{p,SMB}$	−0.2047	0.0462	−4.43	0.0000	−0.2973	−0.1122
$b_{p,HML}$	0.0520	0.0397	1.31	0.1960	−0.0276	0.1315
$b_{p,MOM}$	0.0287	0.0167	1.72	0.0913	−0.0048	0.0622

The **F-test** for a multiple regression with an intercept tests the null hypothesis that all of the coefficient estimates are zero versus the alternative hypothesis that one or more of the coefficient estimates is not equal to zero. The exceptionally high F-test value and its corresponding statistical significance being very close to zero (rounded to 0.0000 in Exhibit 24) provides strong evidence that the null hypothesis can be rejected. Thus, it is reasonable to assume that at least one or more of the coefficient estimates (factor sensitivities) differs significantly from zero.

The ***t*-statistic**, the ratio of the coefficient estimate to the standard error, is used to check the statistical significance of an individual estimated regression coefficient. It tests the null hypothesis that the estimated coefficient is zero versus the alternative hypothesis that the estimated coefficient differs from zero. The **P-value** is the probability of obtaining a *t*-statistic at least as extreme as the one that was actually observed, assuming that the null hypothesis is true. A researcher will reject the null hypothesis when the P-value turns out to be less than a certain significance level, often 0.10, 0.05, or 0.01 (10%, 5%, 1%).

A **confidence interval** provides an estimate of the reliability of the estimated coefficient. Consistent with common practice, Exhibit 24 presents 95% confidence intervals. The interpretation is that there is a 95% probability that the "true" coefficient (factor sensitivity) lies within the interval. For example, Exhibit 24 indicates that the 95% confidence band for the true value of $b_{p,MKT}$ is the interval 0.7607 to 0.8625.

Exhibit 24 shows that AMRMX's excess returns are most sensitive to changes in the market risk premium, $F_{MKT,t}$. The extremely high *t*-statistic of 31.96 indicates the standard error is quite low relative to the estimate of $b_{p,MKT}$, which results in a relatively narrow 95% confidence interval. The coefficient estimate of 0.8116 is less than the beta of 1 for the market portfolio, which is consistent with the fund's goals of growth in the context of capital preservation.

AMRMX's excess returns also have a statistically significant sensitivity to the size factor, F_{SMB}. The estimate of $b_{p,SMB}$ is negative, a result that is consistent with Morningstar categorizing AMRMX as a large-cap fund. A positive $b_{p,SMB}$ would indicate the fund had a small-cap tilt.

The estimate of $b_{p,HML}$ is positive and thus consistent with Morningstar categorizing AMRMX as a value fund. But the p-value for this coefficient estimate is 0.1960, higher than the 0.10 significance level considered minimally acceptable by most analysts. The 95% confidence interval includes both negative and positive values, casting further doubt on whether the true factor sensitivity differs from zero. A significantly negative estimate of $b_{p,\text{HML}}$ would indicate the fund had a growth tilt.

The estimate of $b_{p,MOM}$ is positive and the *t*-statistic has a P-value of 0.0913, which indicates the estimate is statistically significant at the 0.10 level, but not the 0.05 or 0.01 levels. This result suggests that the fund had exposure to stocks that have recently performed well and this exposure positively contributed to its excess returns. However, the statistical significance of that contribution is debatable because the 95% confidence interval includes both negative and positive values.

The Carhart four-factor model estimate of alpha (α_p) for AMRMX is 0.1545 (0.15%) based on monthly data, or approximately 1.85% annually. But the *t*-statistic has a P-value of 0.1101, which indicates that the estimate is not statistically significant at the 0.10 confidence level. The 95% confidence interval includes both negative and positive values. The prices used to determine AMRMX's excess returns also did not reflect the effects of the maximum sales charge of 5.75%. This information would be highly relevant in a performance appraisal, especially because the impact varies as a function of the holding period.

The major purpose of a factor model is to describe the return generation process. The Carhart four-factor model used to evaluate AMRMX's performance could certainly be expanded to include other factors. It should be expected that researchers will continue to find new style factors that correlate significantly with returns and that, in turn, will lead to an evolution in factor models used to appraise performance.

As an example, quality, like size, value, and momentum, has been identified as a popular style factor tilt that is used by many portfolio managers. Recent research (see, for example, Novy-Marx 2013 and Asness, Frazzini, and Pederson 2014) connects quality investing to gross profitability, which is the difference between revenue and cost of goods divided by company assets. Using a model that includes a quality factor would provide an alternative and possibly superior approach to evaluating AMRMX's performance.

HOLDINGS-BASED PERFORMANCE APPRAISAL

5

The availability of data on investment fund holdings has been an important driver of the boom in performance measurement research. Some of this availability has been the result of regulatory changes. For example, the US SEC has required registered investment management companies to report their holdings semi-annually since 1985 and quarterly since 2004. This data on the holdings of institutional investors are available to researchers at low cost via the SEC's EDGAR database.

In addition, since the early 1990s, many funds have voluntarily reported their investment holdings to Morningstar on a monthly basis. The Lipper TASS Research database has included data on hedge fund holdings since the early 1990s. Non-US data on institutional investors' portfolio holdings have been more recently made available to academics through data vendors, such as Abel Noser.

As a result of technological advancements, the cost of producing investment performance research has declined significantly. The combination of greater data availability and lower analysis costs has allowed for a new range of analyses that will undoubtedly continue to grow in the future. This section provides a brief introduction to holdings-based performance appraisal through a discussion of the Grinblatt–Titman performance measure.

In a pioneering study, Grinblatt and Titman (1989) derived holdings-based measures in a single-period model assuming a fund manager makes portfolio decisions to maximize the expected utility of the terminal wealth. They show that the covariance between previous period portfolio weights and current period returns for a skilled manager will be positive, as shown by Equation 29:[24]

$$\mathrm{cov}(w_{t-1}, r_t) > 0 \quad (29)$$

Equation 29 essentially says that a manager who increases the portfolio weight of a security or asset class before it performs well has investment ability. Thus, the services provided by money managers can be evaluated by looking at their portfolio weight adjustments. Assuming that the investor knows the exact investment proportions of each security position in the portfolio on two consecutive reporting dates, the manager's security selection ability can be established by how he or she adjusted these weights.

The Grinblatt–Titman (GT) performance measure is shown in Equation 30, where k is the lag in reporting dates.

$$\mathrm{GT}_t = \sum_{i=1}^{n}\left(w_{i,t-1} - w_{i,t-k-1}\right)r_{i,t} \quad (30)$$

Note that current period performance is $\sum_{i=1}^{n} w_{i,t-1} r_{i,t}$. It is determined using beginning of period weights, $w_{i,t-1}$, and current period returns, $r_{i,t}$, for each security, i, and is evaluated using a benchmark that is based on current period returns and portfolio weights from k periods ago, $\sum_{i=1}^{n} w_{i,t-k-1} r_{i,t}$.

For example, assume t is denominated in months and the lag is $k = 3$ months. If data availability begins in January, the first month t that performance could be evaluated would be May because month $t - k - 1$ is initially January. In May, the manager's current period performance would be based on portfolio weights from the end of April and security returns for the month of May. The benchmark performance would be based on portfolio weights from the end of January and security returns for the month of May. The GT performance measure for May is the difference between current period and benchmark performance.

In June, the manager's current period performance would be based on portfolio weights from the end of May and security returns for the month of June. The benchmark would be based on portfolio weights from the end of February and security returns for the month of June. The GT performance measure for June is again the difference between current period and benchmark performance. Given data availability that begins in January, the GT performance measure data series, GT_t, would begin in May and "roll forward" one month at a time until performance measurement is changed or no longer needed.

24 See Fischer and Wermers (2013) for a more detailed discussion, including a statement of the assumptions being made.

Essentially, GT_t represents the return on a zero-investment portfolio that is long the manager's current portfolio and short the manager's historical portfolio. Grinblatt and Titman also recommended that performance be averaged over several time periods to provide a better indication of on-going decision making, as shown in Equation 31.

$$\overline{GT} = \frac{\sum_{t=1}^{T} GT_t}{T} \quad (31)$$

Applying $\overline{GT}$ to 155 US domestic equity mutual funds, Grinblatt and Titman (1993) found evidence that differences in performance between funds persist over time and that this persistence is consistent with the ability of fund managers to earn abnormal returns. The authors found that fund performance appears to improve with increases in k, although beyond a certain point, increased k has much less of a positive impact on fund performance. They recommended a lag of k = 12 months when evaluating US domestic equity mutual funds.

Wermers (1997) updated the Grinblatt and Titman (1993) study to include all funds existing between 1975 and 1994, inclusive. Wermers found $\overline{GT}$ for US domestic equity funds, equally weighted over all survivors and non-survivors with rebalancing at the beginning of each year to be 1.7% per year using k = 12 months.

Grinblatt–Titman Performance Measure

Assume that the entire investable universe consists of five stocks. Portfolio weights, stock returns, and the calculation of the GT performance measure is shown in Exhibit 25 below. The assumed lag is one quarter (i.e., k = 1).

Exhibit 25 GT Performance Measure

Portfolio Weights

	Quarter				
Stock	**0**	**1**	**2**	**3**	**4**
1	0.200	0.000	0.250	0.300	0.200
2	0.200	0.250	0.125	0.100	0.100
3	0.200	0.250	0.125	0.100	0.100
4	0.200	0.250	0.250	0.250	0.400
5	0.200	0.250	0.250	0.250	0.200

Stock Returns

	Quarter				
Stock	**0**	**1**	**2**	**3**	**4**
1		8.00%	8.00%	−1.00%	−2.00%
2		−3.00%	6.00%	10.00%	5.00%
3		6.00%	4.00%	−2.00%	4.00%
4		7.00%	4.00%	7.00%	6.00%
5		2.00%	9.00%	7.00%	1.00%

(continued)

Exhibit 25 (Continued)

Calculation of GT

	Quarter				
Stock	**0**	**1**	**2**	**3**	**4**
1		−1.60%	2.00%	−0.05%	0.20%
2		−0.15%	−0.75%	−0.25%	0.00%
3		0.30%	−0.50%	0.05%	0.00%
4		0.35%	0.00%	0.00%	0.90%
5		0.10%	0.00%	0.00%	−0.05%
GT		−1.00%	0.75%	−0.25%	1.05%

For Quarter 1:

GT_1 = (0.00 − 0.20)8.0% + (0.25 − 0.20)(−3.0%) + (0.25 − 0.20)6.0% + (0.25 − 0.20)7.0% + (0.25 − 0.20)2.0% = −1.6% − 0.15% + 0.3% + 0.35% + 0.1% = −1.0%. The manager's performance suffered from eliminating Stock 1 from the portfolio, which had a positive return, and increasing the weight of Stock 2, which had a negative return. The manager's performance benefited from increasing the weights in Stocks 3, 4 and 5, which had positive returns.

For Quarter 2:

GT_2 = (0.25 − 0.00)8.0% + (0.125 − 0.25)6.0% + (0.125 − 0.25)4.0% + (0.25 − 0.25)4.0% + (0.25 − 0.25)9.0% = 2.0% − 0.75% − 0.5% + 0.0% + 0.0% = 0.75%. The manager's performance benefited from increasing the weight invested in Stock 1, which had a positive return, but suffered from reducing the weight invested in Stock 2 and Stock 3, both of which had positive returns.

For Quarter 3:

GT_3 = (0.30 − 0.25)(−1.0%) + (0.10 − 0.125)10.0% + (0.10 − 0.125)(−2.0%) + (0.25 − 0.25)7.0% + (0.25 − 0.25)7.0% = −0.05% − 0.25% + 0.05% + 0.0% + 0.0% = −0.25%. The manager's performance suffered from increasing the weight invested in Stock 1, which had a negative return, and by reducing the weight invested in Stock 2, which had a positive return. The manager's performance benefited from reducing the weight invested in Stock 3, which had a negative return.

For Quarter 4:

GT_4 = (0.20 − 0.30)(−2.0%) + (0.10 − 0.10)5.0% + (0.10 − 0.10)4.0% + (0.40 − 0.25)6.0% + (0.20 − 0.25)1.0% = 0.2% + 0.0% + 0.0% + 0.9% − 0.05% = 1.05%. The manager's performance benefited by reducing the weight invested in Stock 1, which had a negative return, and by increasing the weight invested in Stock 4, which had a positive return. The manager's performance suffered from reducing the weight invested in Stock 5, which had a positive return.

The four quarter average for the Grinblatt–Titman performance measure is approximately 0.14%, $\overline{GT} = \dfrac{-1.0\% + 0.75\% - 0.25\% + 1.05\%}{4} = 0.14\%$.

One limitation of the GT performance measure is that portfolio holdings for the first *k* periods must be set aside as benchmarks. Therefore, managerial performance cannot be evaluated during that time period, which makes the choice of *k* important. The choice of *k* can also create other problems: (1) A short *k* can be problematic because it eliminates an appraisal of performance that occurs after the first k periods that a manager holds a stock, and (2) a long k makes it more likely that changes in portfolio risk will emerge.

In regard to the latter problem, Fischer and Wermers (2013) argue that $\overline{\text{GT}}$ will be biased if a portfolio tilts toward stocks with temporarily high factor sensitivities. In such a case, the current portfolio would have a higher risk exposure than the historical portfolio and $\overline{\text{GT}}$ would thus provide a biased estimate of managerial performance. They suggest correcting for this bias by regressing the performance measure on standard benchmarks, one approach being the use of the Carhart four-factor model, as shown in Equation 32.

$$GT_t = a_p + b_{p,MKT}F_{MKT,t} + b_{p,SMB}F_{SMB,t} + b_{p,HML}F_{HML,t} + b_{p,MOM}F_{MOM,t} + e_{p,t} \quad (32)$$

The coefficient estimate for α_p is a "benchmark-adjusted $\overline{\text{GT}}$" and reflects managerial skill, adjusted for any strategy or chance activity that tilts toward stocks with high factor sensitivities. As an example, if a manager, by choice or by chance, adds stocks that have performed well recently, the current portfolio would be more sensitive to the momentum factor, F_{MOM}. The regression model would control for this sensitivity via a higher coefficient estimate for $b_{p,MOM}$.

SUMMARY

This reading has introduced performance appraisal, focusing on the appraisal of active managers. The following are key points that were made:

- A working definition of active investment management skill is the ability of an active manager to add value on a risk-adjusted basis as a result of investment analysis and insights.
- Performance appraisal of passive managers largely addresses an indexer's ability to track a specified benchmark closely. The focus of appraisal is much narrower when the analysis concerns passive managers.
- The focus of performance appraisal is primarily on evaluating active investment managers.
- Performance appraisal is generally conducted using net-of-expenses returns. Relevant expenses include trading costs and investment management fees.
- Because financial market returns reflect a high degree of randomness, it is frequently difficult to distinguish investment skill from luck.
- A very long evaluation period is typically needed to be confident about an appraisal of skill. Evaluations can be sensitive to the starting and ending dates selected for an evaluation period. The drawback to long evaluation periods, however, is that the investment strategy processes, or the individuals implementing them, are more likely to change, thus complicating both inter-temporal comparisons and prospective inferences.
- The ability to repeat superior performance in successive time periods provides evidence in favor of a manager's skill.
- Analysis of skill needs to take risk into account because investors are, in the aggregate, risk averse.

- Quantitative adjustment for risk can involve accounting for total risk as measured by standard deviation, market risk as measured by beta with respect to a market index or the sensitivity to other risk factors, or by various measures of downside risk.
- The Sharpe ratio, M^2, the Treynor ratio, Jensen's alpha, alpha, information ratio (Treynor–Black appraisal ratio), information ratio–active return, the Sortino ratio, and the Calmar ratio are all examples of appraisal measures that summarize performance in terms of a single number.
- Performance appraisal measures vary by the measure of risk used. The Sharpe ratio and M^2 are based on total risk; the Treynor ratio and Jensen's alpha are based on market risk; the information ratio (Treynor–Black appraisal ratio) is based on unsystematic risk, and the information ratio–active return is based on tracking error.
- Measures that adjust for downside risk, such as the Sortino ratio and the Calmar ratio, may be better choices for investment performance appraisal if the return distribution is believed to be asymmetrical.
- According to the fundamental law of active management, the information ratio is determined by the information coefficient, the number of independent insights, and the ability to implement such insights on a timely basis without undue constraints.
- A multifactor alpha may be calculated on the basis of a model that incorporates several risk factors, such as the Fama–French and Carhart models.
- Holdings-based performance appraisal is based on the idea that if an active manager is skilled, changes in portfolio weights should be positively correlated with subsequent returns.
- The Grinblatt–Titman model uses as its inputs the portfolio weight differentials between the portfolio and its benchmark and subsequent period portfolio returns.

REFERENCES

Asness, C., A. Frazzini, and L. Pederson. 2014. "Quality Minus Junk." Working paper (June).

Bacon, C. 2008. *Practical Portfolio Performance Measurement and Attribution*. Hoboken, New Jersey: John Wiley & Sons.

Burke, G. 1994. "A Sharper Sharpe Ratio." *Futures* magazine (March):56.

Carhart, M. 1997. "On Persistence in Mutual Fund Performance." *Journal of Finance*, vol. 52, no. 1 (March):57–82.

Clarke, R., H. de Silva, and S. Thorley. 2002. "Portfolio Constraints and the Fundamental Law of Active Management." *Financial Analysts Journal*, vol. 58, no. 2 (September/October):48–66.

DeFusco, Richard A., Dennis W. McLeavey, Jerald E. Pinto, and David E. Runkle. 2007. *Quantitative Investment Analysis*. 2nd Edition. Hoboken, NJ: John Wiley & Sons.

Fama, E., and K. French. 1992. "The Cross-Section of Expected Stock Returns." *Journal of Finance*, vol. 47, no. 2 (June):427–465.

Fama, E., and K. French. 1993. "Common Risk Factors in the Returns on Stocks and Bonds." *Journal of Financial Economics*, vol. 33, no. 1 (February):3–56.

Fama, E., and K. French. 1996. "Multifactor Explanations of Asset Pricing Anomalies." *Journal of Finance*, vol. 51, no. 1 (March):55–84.

Fischer, B., and R. Wermers. 2013. *Performance Evaluation and Attribution of Security Portfolios*. Oxford, UK: Elsevier.

Gleiser, I., and D. McKenna. 2010. "Converting Scores into Alphas." *MSCI/Barra Insights* (May):1–13.

Goetzmann, W., J. Ingersoll, M. Spiegel, and I. Welch. 2002. "Sharpening Sharpe Ratios." NBER Working Paper 9116 (August).

Grégoire, P. 2007. "Risk Attribution." In *Advanced Portfolio Attribution Analysis: New Approaches to Return and Risk*. Edited by C. Bacon. London: Risk Books.

Grinblatt, M., and S. Titman. 1989. "Mutual Fund Performance: An Analysis of Quarterly Portfolio Holdings." *Journal of Business*, vol. 62, no. 3 (July):393–416.

Grinblatt, M., and S. Titman. 1993. "Performance Measurement without Benchmarks: An Examination of Mutual Fund Returns." *Journal of Business*, vol. 66, no. 1 (January):47–68.

Grinold, R. 1989. "The Fundamental Law of Active Management." *Journal of Portfolio Management*, vol. 15, no. 3 (Spring):30–37.

Grinold, R., and R. Kahn. 2000. *Active Portfolio Management*. 2nd ed. New York: McGraw-Hill.

Grossman, S., and J. Stiglitz. 1980. "On the Impossibility of Informationally Efficient Markets." *American Economic Review*, vol. 70, no. 3 (June):393–408.

Jegadeesh, N., and S. Titman. 1993. "Returns to Buying Winners and Selling Losers: Implications for Stock Market Efficiency." *Journal of Finance*, vol. 48, no. 1 (March):65–91.

Markowitz, H. 1952. "Portfolio Selection." *Journal of Finance*, vol. 7, no. 1 (March):77–91.

Modigliani, F., and L. Modigliani. 1997. "Risk Adjusted Performance." *Journal of Portfolio Management*, vol. 23, no. 2 (Winter):45–54.

Novy–Marx, R. 2013. "The Other Side of Value: The Gross Profitability Premium." *Journal of Financial Economics*, vol. 108, no. 1 (April):1–28.

Rollinger, Thomas N., and Scott T. Hoffman. 2013 "Sortino: A 'Sharper' Ratio." White Paper, Red Rock Capital (June).

Scholz, H., and M. Wilkens. 2005. "A Jigsaw Puzzle of Basic Risk-Adjusted Performance Measures." *Journal of Performance Measurement*, vol. 9, no. 3 (Spring):57–64.

Sharpe, W. 1964. "Capital Asset Prices: A Theory of Market Equilibrium under Conditions of Risk." *Journal of Finance*, vol. 19, no. 3 (September):425–442.

Sharpe, W. 1966. "Mutual Fund Performance." *Journal of Business*, vol. 39, no. 1 (January):119–138.

Sharpe, W. F. 1994. "The Sharpe Ratio." *Journal of Portfolio Management*, vol. 21, no. 1 (Fall):49–58.

Sortino, F. A., and R. van der Meer. 1991. "Downside Risk." *Journal of Portfolio Management*, vol. 17, no. 4 (Summer):27–31.

Treynor, J. 1965. "How to Rate Management Investment Funds." *Harvard Business Review*, vol. 43, no. 1:63–75.

Treynor, J., and F. Black. 1973. "How to Use Security Analysis to Improve Portfolio Selection." *Journal of Business*, vol. 46, no. 1 (January):66–86.

Wermers, R. 1997. "Momentum Investing Strategies of Mutual Funds, Performance Persistence, and Survivorship Bias." Working paper (March).

Young, T. 1991. "Calmar Ratio: A Smoother Tool." *Futures* magazine (October):40.

PRACTICE PROBLEMS

1 A manager with active investment management skill would *most likely* have:

A tracking risk equal to zero.

B an M^2 alpha greater than zero.

C a Treynor ratio greater than the Sharpe ratio.

2 Skilled passive managers have:

A effective trade execution.

B insights on market sectors.

C portfolios with less volatility than the benchmark's.

3 Which of the following statements *best* describes an assumption of the rational efficient markets hypothesis?

A Information gathering is costly.

B Investor irrationality results in bubbles.

C Market efficiency is bounded by the marginal investor.

4 An active manager has annual expenses of 1.00% and the return on a risk-matched benchmark is 6.00%. Which of the following scenarios is *most likely* consistent with the rational efficient markets hypothesis? The manager has:

A net returns of 5.00%.

B gross returns of 6.00%.

C gross returns of 7.00%.

5 If a manager has a 99% chance of beating the benchmark in any one year, the probability of underperformance in one or more years during a five-year period is *closest* to:

A 0%.

B 1%.

C 5%.

6 Risk should be considered in investment performance appraisal because most investors are:

A risk averse.

B risk neutral.

C risk seeking.

7 A highly diversified portfolio will *most likely* have:

A zero systematic risk.

B systematic risk less than non-systematic risk.

C total risk consisting almost entirely of systematic risk.

8 In which of the following situations are downside risk measures *most likely* applicable?

A Systematic risk is high.

B An asset has asymmetric returns.

C An investor seeks capital growth.

9 The Sharpe ratio is positively related to the:

A risk-free rate.

B portfolio's risk.

C portfolio's return.

10 The risk-free rate is 2%. Given the following returns and risk, which portfolio has the *most* attractive risk-adjusted performance using the Sharpe ratio?

Portfolio	A	B	C
Expected return	32.0%	16.0%	8.0%
Standard deviation	16.0%	8.0%	4.0%

A Portfolio A

B Portfolio B

C Portfolio C

11 If returns are plotted on the y-axis and risk on the x-axis, the Sharpe ratio is the:

A distance from the x-axis.

B distance from the y-axis.

C slope of a line emanating from the y-axis.

12 In which of the following cases would the Sharpe ratio be *least* appropriate? The portfolio:

A has negative skewed returns.

B uses leverage to magnify returns.

C includes both long and short positions.

13 Which of the following applications would be the *most* appropriate use of the Sharpe ratio?

A An equity fund is evaluated for addition to an all equity portfolio.

B An equity portfolio that represents an investor's entire wealth is evaluated.

C The US Treasury bill is used as the risk-free rate for a British investor's portfolio.

14 Portfolio A has an annual Sharpe ratio three times greater than Portfolio B's quarterly Sharpe ratio. Portfolio C's monthly Sharpe ratio is one-fifth of Portfolio A's. Based on this information, which portfolio has the most attractive risk-adjusted performance?

A Portfolio A

B Portfolio B

C Portfolio C

15 Which of the following statements *best* describes the M^2 performance measurement? It:

A will rank portfolios the same as the Sharpe ratio.

B uses systematic risk as the measure of portfolio risk.

C leverages the portfolio's Sharpe ratio by the benchmark's return.

16 Portfolio X has a higher Treynor ratio but a lower Sharpe ratio than Portfolio Y. If the portfolios' excess returns are equal, Portfolio X has more:

A market risk.

B systematic risk.

C non-systematic risk.

17 Which of the following statements is *least* accurate regarding the Treynor ratio? The Treynor ratio will be:

A overstated if a low-volatility benchmark is used.

B equal to one if the excess return is equal to the beta.

C most useful when a fund is added to a well-diversified portfolio.

18 Jensen's alpha assumes that returns are a function of the:

A market risk premium.

B market and small-firm risk premiums.

C market, small-firm, and value risk premiums.

19 The risk-free rate is 4%. Given the following information, what is the portfolio's Jensen's alpha?

	Portfolio	Market Index
Expected return	12.0%	9.0%
Beta	1.4	1.0

A −3.2%

B 1.0%

C 5.0%

20 Which of the following statements *best* describes Jensen's alpha? It:

A assumes the portfolio beta is variable.

B is assumed to reflect market timing ability.

C is more easily interpreted than the Treynor ratio.

21 A portfolio's active return always equals its Jensen's alpha. If the market index increases in value, the portfolio return should:

A lag that of the market index.

B equal that of the market index.

C exceed that of the market index.

22 The risk-free rate is 2%. Given the following information, what is the portfolio's Treynor–Black appraisal ratio?

	Portfolio	Market Index
Expected return	12.0%	11.0%
Standard deviation	20.0%	17.0%
Beta	0.80	1.0

A 0.1107

B 0.1909

C 0.2155

23 The risk-free rate is 4% and the market index return is 10%. Given the following information, what is the portfolio's Treynor–Black appraisal ratio?

	Portfolio
Expected return	15.0%
Standard deviation	22.0%
Beta to market index	1.20
R-squared to market index	0.40

A 0.1046

B 0.2230

C 0.2731

24 In the calculation of the Treynor–Black appraisal ratio for a manager who closely tracks the index, the non-systematic risk will approach zero because:

A beta will approach zero.

B the portfolio's volatility will approach the index's volatility.

C the R-squared between the portfolio and index will approach zero.

25 Given the following information, what is the portfolio's quarterly active return information ratio?

Quarter	Portfolio Return (%)	Benchmark Return (%)	Excess Return (%)
1	1.6	1.4	0.2
2	−1.2	−0.5	−0.7
3	2.8	2.0	0.8
4	1.6	0.8	0.8
Mean	1.2000	0.9250	0.2750
Standard deviation	1.6971	1.0689	0.7089

A 0.2750

B 0.3879

C 0.4378

26 The Fundamental Law states that the information ratio is inversely related to the investor's:

A breadth.

B trading costs.

C information coefficient.

27 Which of the following statements *best* describes the Sortino ratio? The Sortino ratio:

A does not easily allow for cross-sectional comparisons.

B is an excess market return divided by the downside deviation.

C uses the deviations of returns below zero in the denominator.

28 Given the following information, what is the portfolio's Calmar ratio?

Month	Portfolio Value	1 + Return	Highest Close	Drawdown
0	100,000		100,000	
1	101,097	1.010970	101,097	0.0000
2	102,172	1.010630	102,172	0.0000
3	102,856	1.006694	102,856	0.0000
4	104,203	1.013095	104,203	0.0000
5	103,934	0.997425	104,203	−0.0026
6	104,283	1.003354	104,283	0.0000
7	103,160	0.989236	104,283	−0.0108
8	102,885	0.997331	104,283	−0.0134
9	102,372	0.995016	104,283	−0.0183
10	103,619	1.012179	104,283	−0.0064
11	103,977	1.003450	104,283	−0.0029

(continued)

Month	Portfolio Value	1 + Return	Highest Close	Drawdown
12	103,672	0.997067	104,283	−0.0059
		Annualized geometric mean		3.67%

A 0.50

B 2.00

C 4.27

29 In a multifactor model, factors thought to *best* explain portfolio returns have:

A large, positive p-values.

B large confidence intervals.

C coefficient estimates larger than the standard errors.

30 Which of the following appraisal techniques does **not** require knowledge of the individual securities and their weightings in a portfolio?

A Returns-based analysis

B Holdings-based analysis

C Grinblatt–Titman performance analysis

31 Suppose stocks in a portfolio change in risk frequently. The Grinblatt–Titman performance analysis for a skillful manager should show weight changes and returns that are:

A opposite in sign and the analysis would use a long k-lag.

B the same in sign and the analysis would use a long k-lag.

C the same in sign and the analysis would use a short k-lag.

32 An investor's main requirement is that she earns at least 5% over a given year. Which of the following appraisal measures would be *most* appropriate?

A Sharpe ratio

B Sortino ratio

C Jensen's alpha

33 A manager employs an indexing strategy in which the portfolio attempts to mimic the return on an index by buying a subset of the index. Which of the following appraisal measures would be *most* appropriate?

A M^2 ratio

B Treynor ratio

C Information ratio

34 An investor has all his wealth in a single fund. Which of the following appraisal measures would be *most* appropriate?

A M^2 ratio

B Treynor ratio

C Jensen's alpha

35 An investor is evaluating an asset that has positively skewed returns. Which of the following appraisal measures would be *most* appropriate?

A M^2 ratio

B Sharpe ratio

C Sortino ratio

Use the following information for Questions 36–44

An investor has a minimum acceptable return of 4% and the risk-free rate is 3%. The benchmark is expected to generate a return of 4.92% with a standard deviation of 13.90%. Data for two hedge funds under consideration follow:

	Fund A	Fund B
Expected annual return	8.82%	8.96%
Standard deviation	23.87%	21.56%
Beta	0.67	0.81
Target semi-standard deviation	13.24%	14.22%
Maximum drawdown	−36.40%	−42.71%

36 Using the Sharpe ratio, compared with Fund B:

A Fund A is less attractive.

B Fund A is equally attractive.

C Fund A is more attractive.

37 Using the M^2 ratio, compared with Fund B:

A Fund A is less attractive.

B Fund A is equally attractive.

C Fund A is more attractive.

38 Using the Treynor ratio, compared with Fund B:

A Fund A is less attractive.

B Fund A is equally attractive.

C Fund A is more attractive.

39 Using Jensen's alpha, compared with Fund B:

A Fund A is less attractive.

B Fund A is equally attractive.

C Fund A is more attractive.

40 Assuming the investor will choose either fund to add to his current portfolio, based on the previous analyses:

A the investor would invest in Fund A.

B both funds are equally attractive.

C the investor would invest in Fund B.

41 The data indicate that, compared with Fund B:

A Fund A is less diversified.

B Fund A is as diversified.

C Fund A is more diversified.

42 Using the Treynor–Black appraisal ratio, compared with Fund B:

A Fund A is less attractive.

B Fund A is equally attractive.

C Fund A is more attractive.

43 Using the Sortino ratio, compared with Fund B:

A Fund A is less attractive.

B Fund A is equally attractive.

C Fund A is more attractive.

44 Using the Calmar ratio, compared with Fund B:

A Fund A is less attractive.

B Fund A is equally attractive.

C Fund A is more attractive.

---

45 In performance appraisal, benchmarks are used in assessing the investment management skill of:

A active investment managers only.

B passive investment managers only.

C both active investment managers and passive investment managers.

46 According to the rational efficient market hypothesis, on a net return basis, rational active investors would:

A underperform a risk-matched benchmark.

B earn the same return as a risk-matched benchmark.

C outperform a risk-matched benchmark.

47 A pension fund has traditionally set a standard of hiring managers who are expected to outperform their benchmarks at least 55% of the time. The pension fund's management has decided to raise the standard to 60%. The decision will *most likely* increase the probability of:

A a Type I error only.

B a Type II error only.

C both a Type I and a Type II error.

48 An asset's exposure to the effects of the business cycle is an example of:

A priced risk.

B stand-alone risk.

C diversifiable risk.

49 Active return is equivalent to alpha when:

A the market portfolio is used as the benchmark.

B realized alpha and expected alpha are the same.

C the portfolio's sensitivity to the benchmark is 1.0.

50 The M^2 measure equates the risk of a portfolio to that of its benchmark by:

A adjusting for the systematic risk of the portfolio as measured by beta.

B adjusting for the unsystematic risk of the portfolio as measured by $1 - R^2$.

C leveraging or de-leveraging the portfolio until its volatility matches that of its benchmark.

51 Which one of the following performance appraisal measures adjusts for total risk?

A M^2

B Sortino ratio

C Jensen's alpha

52 A fund had a Jensen's alpha of 0.30%. The fund had a beta of 0.7 against the market index. The market index returned 1.20% over the period, and the risk-free rate of return averaged 0.20%. The fund's return for the period was *closest* to:

A 1.20%.

B 1.34%.

C 1.50%.

53 The information ratio–active return is the ratio of a portfolio's excess return to the:

A standard deviation of the portfolio's return.

B square root of the portfolio's systematic risk.

C standard deviation of the portfolio's excess return.

54 Which of the following statements is accurate? The information ratio (Treynor–Black appraisal ratio):

A considers a portfolio's Jensen's alpha in relation to its systematic risk.

B measures the reward of active management relative to the risk of active management.

C changes relative to both the amount of benchmark risk and the amount of leverage used in the portfolio.

55 Drawdown is used in which of the following appraisal measures?

A Sharpe ratio

B Calmar ratio

C Sortino ratio

56 An undiversified fund is under consideration for addition to a broadly diversified investment portfolio. Which of the following appraisal measures would be *most appropriate*?

A M^2

B Sharpe ratio

C Treynor ratio

Use the following information for Questions 57 and 58

The returns and portfolio values calculated for Portfolio A are presented in Exhibit 1.

Exhibit 1

Month	Return	Portfolio A Value
		1.00000
1	–1%	0.99000
2	2%	1.00980
3	3%	1.04009
4	1%	1.05049
5	–2%	1.02949
6	–4%	0.98831
7	3%	1.01795
8	4%	1.05867
9	2%	1.07985
10	–1%	1.06905

(continued)

Exhibit 1 (Continued)

Month	Return	Portfolio A Value
11	0%	1.06905
12	2%	1.09043
Arithmetic Average	0.75%	

57 Using the data in Exhibit 1, the Calmar ratio for Portfolio A is *closest* to:

A 0.127.

B 1.527.

C 2.261.

58 Assuming that the population standard deviation is 2.278% and that the minimum acceptable return is 0.0%, the monthly Sortino ratio for Portfolio A is *closest* to:

A 0.320.

B 0.329.

C 0.554.

Use the following information for Questions 59–61

A fund manager has run the Carhart four-factor model for sixty months of returns. The following output was generated from the regression model:

Carhart Four-Factor Model Regression Results: Summary Output

Regression Statistics	
Multiple R	0.8831
R^2	0.7798
Adjusted R^2	0.7638
Standard Error	2.6787
Observations	60

ANOVA

	df	SS	MS	F-test	Significance F
Regression	4	1397.5916	349.3979	48.6938	0.0000
Residual	55	394.6473	7.1754		
Total	59	1792.2389			

(Continued)

	Coefficient Estimate	Standard Error	t Stat	P-value	Lower 95%	Upper 95%
α_p	0.6298	0.3504	1.80	0.0778	−0.0725	1.3320
$b_{p,MKT}$	0.8450	0.0842	10.03	0.0000	0.6762	1.0139
$b_{p,SMB}$	0.1020	0.1532	0.67	0.5083	−0.2051	0.4091
$b_{p,HML}$	−0.3294	0.1079	−3.05	0.0035	−0.5456	−0.1132
$b_{p,MOM}$	−0.1991	0.0618	−3.22	0.0021	−0.3229	−0.0753

59 Which information in the regression output *best* indicates that the fund had a growth tilt over the time frame of the analysis?

A A positive coefficient and a p-value smaller than 10% for α_p.

B A positive coefficient and a p-value larger than 10% for $b_{p,SMB}$.

C A negative coefficient and a p-value smaller than 10% for $b_{p,HML}$.

60 Evidence supporting the assertion that this manager exhibited skill is *best* provided by the value of the:

A regression R^2.

B coefficient estimate of $b_{p,MOM}$.

C coefficient estimate of the intercept.

61 The annualized value-added from managerial skill is *closest* to:

A 0.6298%.

B 0.8450%.

C 7.5576%.

---

62 The results of the regression indicate that the fund had:

A a statistically significant tilt toward high momentum stocks.

B a statistically significant tilt toward high book-to-market ratio stocks.

C no statistically significant tilt on differential movements in small and large stocks.

63 Which of the following is a correct statement regarding the Grinblatt–Titman (GT) performance measure? It:

A does not use a benchmark return.

B uses a benchmark return that is adjusted for market risk.

C uses a benchmark return based on a portfolio's own past holdings.

SOLUTIONS

1 B is correct. An M^2 alpha greater than zero would indicate that, on a risk-adjusted basis, the manager outperformed the benchmark. A is incorrect because a tracking risk equal to zero would simply indicate how closely a portfolio follows its benchmark. This would be the objective of a passive manager, not an active manager. C is incorrect because a Treynor ratio greater than the Sharpe ratio would not indicate active investment management skill. To be evaluated for active management skill, the Treynor ratio and/or the Sharpe ratio would be compared to a benchmark, not to each other.

2 A is correct. A skilled passive manager will have effective trade execution so performance does not differ much from an index. B is incorrect because passive managers do not utilize insights on sectors or securities but rather invest using the same weights as the benchmark. C is incorrect because passive managers invest to have the same volatility as their benchmarks, not less.

3 A is correct. Because information gathering is costly, investors will gather information until the costs of doing so are equal to its benefits, i.e., until the net returns from active investing are equal to that of passive investing. B and C are incorrect because, as described in the reading, the rational efficient markets hypothesis does not focus on the existence of bubbles or its bounding by the marginal investor.

4 C is correct. If the return on a risk-matched benchmark is 6.00%, then the rational efficient markets hypothesis states that the manager will gather information until his net return is 6.00%. If his annual expenses are 1.00%, then the manager will gather information until his gross return is 7.00% (net return equals 7.00% – 1.00% = 6.00%). A is incorrect because the manager will not gather information if net returns are 5.00%. B is incorrect because the manager will not gather information if net returns are 5.00% (gross returns of 6.00% minus annual expenses of 1.00%).

5 C is correct. If the manager's probability of beating the benchmark in a year is 0.99, the probability of beating the benchmark five times in five years is $0.99^5 = 0.9510$. Thus, the probability of under-performing the benchmark in one or more of the five years is closest to 5% ($\approx 1 - 0.9510$).

6 A is correct. Given two investments with the same expected returns, most investors will choose the one with less risk. Because most investors are risk averse, risk should be considered in investment appraisal.

7 C is correct. Total risk is equal to systematic plus unsystematic risk. A highly diversified portfolio will most likely have total risk equal to systematic risk because unsystematic risk will have been diversified away. A is incorrect because only a risk-free asset will have zero systematic risk. Risky securities will possess some degree of systematic risk. B is incorrect because in a diversified portfolio, unsystematic risk will be negligible and less than systematic risk.

8 B is correct. If an asset has asymmetric return patterns, downside risk measures that focus on the risk of losses will be appropriate. A is incorrect because a high degree of systematic risk does not necessitate the use of downside risk measures. C is incorrect because investors concerned with capital preservation, not growth, would utilize downside risk measures.

9 C is correct. Using the portfolio's expected return $E[r_p]$, the risk-free rate, r_F, and the portfolio's standard deviation of returns (risk) σ_p, the ex-ante Sharpe ratio is $SR = \frac{E[r_p] - r_F}{\sigma_p}$. Thus the Sharpe ratio is positively related to the portfolio's expected return and inversely related to the risk-free rate and the portfolio's risk.

10 A is correct. The ex-ante Sharpe ratio for Portfolio A is $SR = \frac{E[r_p] - r_F}{\sigma_p} =$ (32% – 2%)/16% = 1.88. For Portfolio B, it is (16% – 2%)/8% = 1.75. For Portfolio C, it is (8% – 2%)/4% = 1.50. Thus, Portfolio A has the most attractive risk-adjusted performance using the Sharpe ratio.

11 C is correct. The Sharpe ratio is the slope of the ray that emanates from the risk-free rate through the point plotted for the portfolio.

12 A is correct. If the portfolio has a negatively skewed return distribution, then the standard deviation will misstate risk and the Sharpe ratio will be overstated. B and C are appropriate uses of the Sharpe ratio because the Sharpe ratio can be used to compare different investment alternatives including levered and long and short strategies.

13 B is correct. The Sharpe ratio is most useful when applied to an investor's entire portfolio. A is incorrect because the Sharpe ratio is less useful when applied to a single asset within a portfolio. C is incorrect because the risk-free rate should be currency-matched and maturity-matched with the asset's expected cash flows. The US Treasury bill is dollar denominated and the British investor's portfolio is likely pound denominated.

14 A is correct. The Sharpe ratio is assumed to increase linearly with the square root of time. To convert Portfolio B's quarterly Sharpe ratio to an annual Sharpe ratio, we would multiply it by the square root of 4, which is 2. Thus Portfolio B's annual Sharpe ratio is less than Portfolio A's annual Sharpe ratio. To convert Portfolio C's monthly Sharpe ratio to an annual Sharpe ratio, we would multiply it by the square root of 12, which is 3.46. Thus Portfolio C's annual Sharpe ratio is less than Portfolio A's annual Sharpe ratio.

15 A is correct. M^2 and the Sharpe ratio will rank portfolios identically if the risk-free rate and benchmark volatility are constant across all comparisons. B is incorrect because M^2, based on the Sharpe ratio, uses total risk as the measure of portfolio risk. C is incorrect because M^2 levers the portfolio's Sharpe ratio by the benchmark's standard deviation, not return.

16 C is correct. The Sharpe ratio uses total risk whereas the Treynor ratio uses systematic risk. Given equal excess returns, if Portfolio X has a higher Treynor ratio but a lower Sharpe ratio than Portfolio Y, it must be the case that Portfolio X has a greater degree of non-systematic and hence total risk. A and B are incorrect because Portfolio X must have lower systematic or market risk (as reflected in the higher Treynor ratio).

17 A is correct. If a low-volatility benchmark is used, the portfolio beta will be inflated, resulting in an understated Treynor ratio. B is accurate because the Treynor ratio, the excess return divided by beta, will equal one if they are equal. C is accurate because the Treynor ratio is most useful when a fund is added to a well-diversified portfolio because systematic risk will be the relevant measure of risk.

18 A is correct. Jensen's alpha is a single factor model and assumes security returns are a function of the security's systematic risk and market risk premium. B and C are incorrect because Jensen's alpha and the CAPM on which it is based do not incorporate risk factors besides the market.

19 B is correct. Using the formula for Jensen's alpha, $\alpha_p(t) = r_p(t) - \{r_F(t) + \beta_p[r_m(t) - r_F(t)]\} = 12\% - \{4\% + 1.4[9\% - 4\%]\} = 1\%$. A is incorrect because the portfolio return was used instead of the market return in the calculation of the risk premium. C is incorrect because the risk- free return was omitted in the calculation of the expected return.

20 C is correct. Jensen's alpha is more easily interpreted than the Treynor ratio because it is an excess return rather than a ratio. A is incorrect because Jensen's alpha assumes the portfolio beta is constant. If the manager uses a market-timing strategy where beta varies through time, then Jensen's alpha can be misleading. B is incorrect because Jensen's alpha is assumed to reflect the security selection ability of its manager.

21 B is correct. If a portfolio's active return always equals its Jensen's alpha, then the portfolio is exactly risk-matched to the benchmark market index, i.e., the portfolio's beta to the market index equals 1.0. Therefore, the portfolio return should equal that of the market index.

22 B is correct. Jensen's alpha, $\alpha_p = 12.0\% - [2.0\% + 0.80(11.0\% - 2.0\%)] = 2.80\%$. Non-systematic risk is $\sigma^2_{\varepsilon_p} = \sigma^2_p - \beta^2_p\sigma^2_m = 0.20^2 - 0.80^2(0.17^2) = 0.021504$. The Treynor–Black appraisal ratio (information ratio) is $\widehat{\text{IR}} = \dfrac{\alpha_p}{\sigma_{\varepsilon_p}} = \dfrac{0.028}{\sqrt{0.021504}} = 0.1909$. A is incorrect because the terms in the calculation of non-systematic risk are not squared. C is incorrect because the beta term in the calculation of non-systematic risk is not squared.

23 B is correct. Jensen's alpha $\alpha_p = 15.0\% - [4.0\% + 1.20(10.0\% - 4.0\%)] = 3.80\%$. Non-systematic risk, $\sigma^2_{\varepsilon_p} = \left(1 - R^2\right)\sigma^2_p = (1 - 0.40)0.22^2 = 0.029040$. The Treynor–Black appraisal ratio (information ratio) is $\widehat{\text{IR}} = \dfrac{\alpha_p}{\sigma_{\varepsilon_p}} = \dfrac{0.0380}{\sqrt{0.029040}} = 0.2230$. A is incorrect because the portfolio standard deviation term in the calculation of non-systematic risk is not squared. C is incorrect because R-squared is used instead of one minus R-squared in the calculation of non-systematic risk.

24 B is correct. A tracking portfolio should have volatility similar to the index, a beta close to one, and an R-squared close to one, resulting in a non-systematic risk that approaches zero.

25 B is correct. The information ratio is $\widehat{\text{IR}}_a = \dfrac{1.200 - 0.9250}{0.7089} = 0.3879$. A is incorrect because it is simply the return difference. C is incorrect because it uses the difference in portfolio and benchmark standard deviations, not the provided standard deviation of the return differences.

26 B is correct. The Fundamental Law states that the information ratio is positively related to the transfer coefficient, which is reduced by portfolio constraints, trading costs, market impact, and other market constraints. Thus the information ratio is inversely related to trading costs. A and C are incorrect because the information ratio is positively related to the investor's breadth (number of independent "bets") and the information coefficient (forecasting skill).

27 A is correct. The Sortino ratio does not easily allow for cross-sectional comparisons because the MAR is investor-specific. B is incorrect because the numerator in the Sortino ratio formula is the manager's return above the MAR. C is incorrect because the denominator in the Sortino ratio formula uses the returns below the MAR.

28 B is correct. The maximum drawdown for this series is in the 9th month at −1.83%. The Calmar ratio is the annualized return divided by the negative of the maximum drawdown, 3.67/1.83 = 2.00. A is incorrect because it is the inverse of the Calmar ratio. C is incorrect because it uses the average of the drawdowns instead of the maximum drawdown.

29 C is correct. In a multifactor model, factors that explain portfolio returns will have coefficient estimates larger than the standard errors, resulting in high t-statistics and low p-values. A is incorrect because factors thought to explain portfolio returns should have low p-values, e.g., 5%. B is incorrect because a large confidence interval would imply less reliability in the coefficient estimate.

30 A is correct. Returns-based analysis estimates factor sensitivities using a regression of portfolio excess returns on factor returns, so it does not require knowledge of the individual securities and their weightings. B and C are incorrect because both holdings-based analysis and the Grinblatt–Titman measure require the individual securities and their weightings in the analysis.

31 C is correct. In Grinblatt–Titman performance analysis, a skillful manager will have weight changes and returns that will be the same in sign, i.e., allocation reductions should precede negative returns and allocation increases should precede positive returns. A short k-lag would be favored if stocks in the portfolio change in risk frequently.

32 B is correct. The Sortino ratio allows the specification of a minimum acceptable return, in this case 5%. A is incorrect because the risk-free rate is essentially pre-specified as the minimum acceptable return in the Sharpe ratio. C is incorrect because Jensen's alpha is not as well-suited to this investor's requirements as the Sortino ratio.

33 C is correct. The information ratio only adjusts for a single risk factor, market risk, which is the risk factor important to this manager. The information ratio measures the manager's deviations from the index's returns, which in this case the manager is attempting to minimize. A and B are incorrect because the M^2 and Treynor ratios do not measure deviations from an index as specifically as the information ratio.

34 A is correct. The M^2 ratio is the most appropriate of these measures if an investor's wealth is in a single fund because it measures total risk (using the standard deviation) and the fund may have a significant amount of unsystematic risk. B and C are incorrect because the Treynor ratio and Jensen's alpha only account for systematic risk.

35 C is correct. The Sortino ratio does not penalize managers for upside volatility because it only measures downside risk in its denominator. A and B are incorrect because the Sharpe and M^2 ratios are based on the standard deviation which assumes a symmetric distribution of returns.

36 A is correct. The ex-ante Sharpe ratio for Fund A is $SR = \frac{E\left[r_p\right] - r_F}{\sigma_p}$ = (8.82% − 3%)/23.87% = 0.24. For Fund B, it is (8.96% − 3%)/21.56% = 0.28. Thus, Fund A has less attractive risk-adjusted performance using the Sharpe ratio.

37 A is correct. The M^2 for Fund A is $\left(E\left[r_p\right] - r_F\right)\frac{\sigma_B}{\sigma_p} + r_F$

$= (0.0882 - 0.03)\frac{0.1390}{0.2387} + 0.03 = 0.0639$. The M^2 alpha subtracts the benchmark return: 0.0639 – 0.0492 = 1.47%. The M^2 for Fund B is $(0.0896 - 0.03)\frac{0.1390}{0.2156} + 0.03 = 0.0684$. The M^2 alpha is: 0.0684 – 0.0492 = 1.92%. Thus Fund A has less attractive risk-adjusted performance using the M^2 ratio.

38 C is correct. The ex-ante Treynor ratio for Fund A is $TR = \frac{E\left[r_p\right] - r_F}{\beta_p}$ = (8.82% – 3%)/0.67 = 8.7. The ex-ante Treynor ratio for Fund B is (8.96% – 3%)/0.81 = 7.4. Thus, Fund A has the more attractive risk-adjusted performance using the Treynor ratio.

39 C is correct. The ex-ante CAPM expected return for Fund A is $E(r_p) = r_F + \beta_p[E(r_m) - r_F]$ = 3% + 0.67[4.92% – 3%] = 4.29%. Subtracting the expected return from the fund return provides Jensen's alpha, 8.82% – 4.29% = 4.5%. For Fund B, the CAPM expected return is 3% + 0.81[4.92% – 3%] = 4.56%. Subtracting the expected return from the fund return provides Jensen's alpha, 8.96% – 4.56% = 4.4%. Thus, Fund A has the more attractive risk-adjusted performance using Jensen's alpha.

40 A is correct. If the fund is to be added to the investor's current portfolio, systematic risk is the relevant measure of portfolio risk. The Sharpe and M^2 ratios use total risk, whereas Treynor ratio and Jensen's alpha measure systematic risk. Fund A has the more attractive risk-adjusted performance using the Treynor ratio and Jensen's alpha, so the investor would choose Fund A.

41 A is correct. The standard deviation, which measures total risk, is higher for Fund A. The beta, which measures only systematic risk, is lower for Fund A. This implies that Fund A has a larger amount of unsystematic risk than Fund B and thus Fund B is more diversified.

42 A is correct. From above, Jensen's alpha for Fund A is 4.5%. Non-systematic risk for Fund A is $\sigma^2_{\varepsilon_p} = \sigma^2_p - \beta^2_p\sigma^2_m = 0.2387^2 - 0.67^2(0.1390^2) = 0.0483$. The Treynor–Black appraisal ratio (information ratio) for Fund A is $\widehat{IR} = \frac{\alpha_p}{\sigma_{\varepsilon_p}} = \frac{0.045}{\sqrt{0.0483}} = 0.20$.

From the above, Jensen's alpha for Fund B is 4.4%. Non-systematic risk for Fund B is $\sigma^2_{\varepsilon_p} = \sigma^2_p - \beta^2_p\sigma^2_m = 0.2156^2 - 0.81^2(0.1390^2) = 0.0338$. The Treynor–Black appraisal ratio (information ratio) for Fund B is $\widehat{IR} = \frac{\alpha_p}{\sigma_{\varepsilon_p}} = \frac{0.044}{\sqrt{0.0338}} = 0.24$.

Thus, Fund B has the more attractive risk-adjusted performance using the Treynor–Black appraisal ratio.

Notice that the measured higher non-systematic risk for Fund A confirms the analysis in the previous question that Fund A has a larger amount of unsystematic risk and that Fund B is more diversified.

43 C is correct. The Sortino ratio for Fund A is $SR_D = \frac{E[r_p] - r_T}{\sigma_D} = \frac{8.82\% - 4\%}{13.24\%}$ $= 0.36$. The Sortino ratio for Fund B is $SR_D = \frac{E[r_p] - r_T}{\sigma_D} = \frac{8.96\% - 4\%}{14.22\%} =$ 0.35. Thus, Fund A has the more attractive risk-adjusted performance using the Sortino ratio.

44 C is correct. The Calmar ratio for Fund A is the annualized return divided by the negative of the maximum drawdown, 8.82/36.40 = 0.24. The Calmar ratio for Fund B is 8.96/42.71 = 0.21. Thus, Fund A has the more attractive risk-adjusted performance using the Calmar ratio.

45 C is correct. Active investment management skill can be viewed as the ability to "beat the market" or an assigned benchmark. Passive investment management skill represents skill in tracking the returns of a specified benchmark index. Benchmarks are used in assessing the investment management skills of both active and passive managers.

46 B is correct. According to the rational efficient market hypothesis, rational active investors would not incur the costs of information gathering and analysis if they did not expect to be rewarded by earning higher gross returns compared with the free alternative of accepting market prices as correct indications of value. According to the theory, the returns to information gathering and analysis should just cover the associated costs and, in equilibrium, an investor's net returns would be equal to that of a risk-matched benchmark.

47 B is correct. The raised standard will lead to rejecting more managers who are actually skillful. This is a Type II error, whereby the null hypothesis (manager is unskilled) is accepted, but it is not true (the manager is actually skillful).

48 A is correct. According to capital market theory, assets are priced according to the risks that affect broad cross sections of investors. Therefore, an asset's sensitivity to the business cycle will be a priced risk factor. Priced risk is also referred to as systematic risk.

49 C is correct. Active return is the return in excess of the benchmark return, which generally provides only an approximation of alpha. The two are technically equivalent only if the portfolio's beta or sensitivity to the benchmark is 1.0.

50 C is correct. M^2 assumes a portfolio is leveraged or de-leveraged until its volatility (as measured by standard deviation) matches that of its benchmark.

51 A is correct. M^2 is derived from the Sharpe ratio, and both measures adjust for total risk as measured by portfolio standard deviation.

52 A is correct. The formula for Jensen's alpha is given in Equation 9 in the reading as:

$$\alpha_p(t) = r_p(t) - \{r_F(t) + \beta_p[r_m(t) - r_F(t)]\}$$
$$0.30\% = r_p(t) - \{0.20\% + 0.7[1.20\% - 0.20\%]\}$$
$$0.30\% = r_p(t) - \{0.90\%\}$$
$$r_p(t) = 1.20\%$$

53 C is correct. The information ratio–active return is defined as: $IR_a = \frac{E(r_p) - E(r_B)}{\sigma(r_p - r_B)}$, the portfolio's active return divided by the standard deviation of the portfolio's excess return.

54 B is correct. The information ratio measures the reward of active management relative to the risk of active management (measured by residual risk). The reward of active management is measured by Jensen's alpha.

55 B is correct. The Calmar ratio is used to measure return versus the fund's maximum drawdown. It is calculated by taking a fund's compound annualized rate of return divided by the fund's maximum drawdown.

56 C is correct. The Treynor ratio, which uses market risk to represent the relevant risk, is the correct measure because it considers the contribution of a new asset to the risk of an investor's entire portfolio.

57 B is correct. The annual rate of return is 1.0904 – 1 = 0.0904 or 9.04%, and the maximum drawdown (calculated below) is 0.0592, resulting in a Calmar ratio of:

$$\frac{\left[\prod_{1}^{T}(1+R_t)\right]^{12/T} - 1}{-\text{MD}} = 0.0904/0.0592 = 1.527 \text{ (Equation 25).}$$

The maximum drawdown is calculated as follows: drawdowns only happen in periods 1, 5, 6, 10, and 11. For periods 1, 5, and 10, the drawdown is the loss for the single period: 1%, 2%, and 1%, respectively. For period 11, the drawdown is still at 1%, with no additional movement from period 10. All that remains is the drawdown in period 6, which is found by taking the portfolio value in period 6, dividing by the value in period 4, and subtracting 1: 0.98831/1.05049 – 1 = –0.0592, so the maximum drawdown is 5.92%.

Month	Return	Portfolio Value	Drawdown
		1.00000	
1	–1%	0.99000	–0.0100
2	2%	1.00980	0.0000
3	3%	1.04009	0.0000
4	1%	1.05049	0.0000
5	–2%	1.02949	–0.0200
6	–4%	0.98831	–0.0592
7	3%	1.01795	0.0000
8	4%	1.05867	0.0000
9	2%	1.07985	0.0000
10	–1%	1.06905	–0.0100
11	0%	1.06905	–0.0100
12	2%	1.09043	0.0000
Arithmetic average	0.75%		

58 C is correct. The average monthly return is 0.75%. The semi-standard deviation is calculated using Equation 24 as follows:

$$\{[(-1)^2 + 0 + 0 + 0 + (-2)^2 + (-4)^2 + 0 + 0 + 0 + (-1)^2 + 0 + 0]/12\}^{1/2}$$

$$= [(1 + 4 + 16 + 1)/12]^{1/2} = (22/12)^{1/2} = 1.833^{1/2} = 1.354\%$$

So, the Sortino ratio using Equation 22 is (0.75% – 0%)/1.354% = 0.554.

59 C is correct. The HML factor, the difference in return on a selection of high book-to-market firms and a selection of low book-to-market firms, is referenced as the "value" factor. This is because high book-to-market stocks are often called value stocks, whereas low book-to market stocks are called growth stocks. A negative, statistically significant (p-value below 10%) coefficient thus indicates a growth factor tilt.

60 C is correct. The intercept coefficient α_p (0.6298) may be called a multifactor alpha, and possible explanations for a positive alpha include a successful market timing strategy or superior skill in security selection.

61 C is correct. The monthly alpha is 0.6298%, and the annualized alpha is 0.6298% × 12 = 7.5576%.

62 C is correct. The coefficient on SMB, $b_{p,SMB}$, is not statistically significant [with a p-value bigger than 10% (0.5083)]. A statistically significant coefficient would indicate that the manager had made investing tilts toward small (for a positive coefficient) or large (for a negative coefficient) cap stocks.

63 C is correct. Current period performance for the Grinblatt–Titman performance measure is determined using beginning of period weights and current returns and is evaluated using a benchmark that is based on current period returns and portfolio weights from *k* periods ago.

PERFORMANCE EVALUATION

STUDY SESSION

6

Manager Selection

Manager selection is closely related to performance appraisal, as both are concerned with the identification of investment skill. Manager selection involves a broad set of qualitative and quantitative considerations to determine whether a manager displays skill and the likelihood that the manager will continue to display skill in the future. Evaluating an investment manager is part science and part art.

The purpose of this reading is to provide a framework that introduces and describes the important elements of the manager selection process. Although it is important to have a well-defined methodology, this reading is not intended to be a rigid checklist, a step-by-step guide, or in-depth analysis, but rather to present a structure from which the reader can develop their own approach.

READING ASSIGNMENTS

10 Investment Manager Selection: An Introduction
by Jeffrey C. Heisler, PhD, CFA, and Donald W. Lindsey, CFA

11 The Role of Investment Philosophy in Evaluating Investment Managers: A Consultant's Perspective on Distinguishing Alpha from Noise
by John R. Minahan, PhD, CFA

READING

10

Investment Manager Selection: An Introduction

by Jeffrey C. Heisler, PhD, CFA, and Donald W. Lindsey, CFA

Jeffrey C. Heisler, PhD, CFA, is at TwinFocus Capital Partners (USA). Donald W. Lindsey, CFA (USA).

LEARNING OUTCOMES

Mastery	The candidate should be able to:
☐	**a.** contrast investment manager selection to performance appraisal;
☐	**b.** describe how investment manager selection takes place in the context of the client's investment policy statement;
☐	**c.** describe qualitative considerations in evaluating investment managers;
☐	**d.** compare the selection of active and passive investment managers;
☐	**e.** describe the components of a manager selection process, including due diligence;
☐	**f.** contrast Type I and Type II errors in manager hiring and continuation decisions;
☐	**g.** describe uses of style analysis in investment manager selection;
☐	**h.** compare returns-based and holdings-based style analysis, including the advantages and disadvantages of each;
☐	**i.** describe uses of the upside capture ratio, downside capture ratio, maximum drawdown, drawdown duration, and up/down capture in evaluating managers;
☐	**j.** describe uses of the "batting average" in evaluating managers;
☐	**k.** evaluate a manager's investment philosophy and investment decision-making process;
☐	**l.** evaluate the costs and benefits of pooled investment vehicles and separate accounts;
☐	**m.** compare types of investment manager contracts, including their major provisions and advantages and disadvantages;
☐	**n.** evaluate a manager's adherence to a stated investment philosophy and investment decision-making process;

(continued)

LEARNING OUTCOMES

Mastery	The candidate should be able to:
□	o. define style drift and judge whether style drift has occurred;
□	p. describe considerations in investment manager continuance;
□	q. describe criteria for evaluating passive managers.

1 INTRODUCTION

Most investors do not hold securities directly but rather invest using intermediaries. Whether the intermediary is a separately managed account or a pooled investment vehicle, such as mutual funds in the United States, unit trusts in the United Kingdom, Undertakings for the Collective Investment of Transferable Securities (UCITS) in the European Union, hedge funds, private equity funds, or exchange-traded funds (ETFs), a professional investment manager is being entrusted with helping investors achieve their investment objectives. In all of these cases, the selection of appropriate investment managers is a challenge with important financial consequences. Even when investors are not making the final decision on which manager(s) to select, they still should understand the manager selection process. Such knowledge should help investors judge whether a sound manager selection process is being used and, more broadly, facilitate communication about how their investments are being managed.

Evaluating an investment manager is a complex and detailed process that encompasses a great deal more than analyzing investment returns. A manager's investment results are historical and, as we know, past performance does not guarantee future performance, for several reasons, including the large random element in asset returns. In conducting investment manager due diligence, the focus is on understanding how the investment results were achieved and on assessing the likelihood that the investment process that generated these returns will produce superior or at least satisfactory investment results going forward. Due diligence also entails an evaluation of a firm's integrity, operations, and personnel. As such, due diligence involves both quantitative and qualitative analysis.

The purpose of this reading is to provide a framework that introduces and describes the important elements of the manager selection process. The evaluation of an investment manager is part science and part art. Although it is important to have a well-defined methodology, this reading is not intended to be a rigid checklist, a step-by-step guide, or an in-depth analysis but rather to present a structure from which the reader can develop their own approach.

The reading assumes that the investment policy statement (IPS) has been drafted, the asset allocation determined, and the decision to use an outside adviser has been made. As a result, the focus is on determining which manager offers the "best" means to implement or express those decisions. The discussion has four broad topics:

- Placing investment manager selection in the context of performance appraisal, investor needs, and the decision of whether to use active or passive managers (Section 2).
- Outlining a framework for identifying, evaluating, and ultimately selecting investment managers (Section 3).

- Outlining a framework for monitoring existing managers and the considerations used to assess whether a manager should be retained or replaced (Section 4).
- Reviewing the criteria for selecting passive managers (Section 5, which adapts the earlier framework to the task of selecting passive managers).

Section 6 summarizes selected important points.

THE CONTEXT OF INVESTMENT MANAGER SELECTION

2

Prior to laying out a framework for manager selection, it is important to place the manager selection process in context. In selecting a manager, an investor is attempting to find the "best" manager for expressing a particular portfolio need. This entails a broader set of considerations than whether the manager appears to display skill. The manager must also be suitable for the investor's needs, as expressed by the IPS, as well as the investor's views on active and passive management.

2.1 Manager Selection Contrasted to Performance Appraisal

It is important to bear in mind throughout the manager selection process that past performance does not necessarily indicate how well a manager will perform in the future or even whether or not a particular manager exhibits skill. Whereas performance appraisals provide insights into how well the manager performed relative to the assigned mandate during past periods, manager selection, although taking account of such information, involves evaluating the investment process and personnel that delivered the performance. Such information is critical in understanding the investment manager and judging how likely it is that investor needs and objectives will be satisfied going forward if assets are invested with that manager. As a result, the manager selection process involves both quantitative as well as qualitative analysis. Although performance appraisal is necessary, it is insufficient by itself for manager selection.

Performance appraisal is the systematic evaluation of the investment performance of a fund or strategy in order to understand and assess the past decisions and abilities of a portfolio manager. The evaluation includes a formal, structured, and largely quantitative process that evaluates the strengths and weaknesses of a manager as measured by their ability to add value to a stated benchmark. As such, performance appraisal is a necessary component of the manager selection process.

Manager selection involves a broad set of qualitative and quantitative considerations to determine whether a manager displays skill and the likelihood that the manager will continue to display skill in the future.

Qualitative aspects of manager selection are part of **due diligence**, which seeks to understand the manager's philosophy and portfolio construction process as a means for gaining confidence that historical performance is a reasonable guide to future performance. It is important to keep in mind that apparently skillful managers with attractive performance records may not actually have skill and may have exhibited attractive performance solely because of good luck rather than a repeatable investment process. The following are important qualitative considerations in evaluating investment managers:

- **Suitability:** The manager must be suitable for the portfolio based on the IPS. Even a skillful manager with a repeatable process may not be a good fit based on the client's particular needs.

- **Complementarity:** Selected managers should, in general, complement each other in terms of perceived value added and roles in the overall portfolio.
- **Firm:** The investment organization provides the foundation for attracting investment talent and sets the tone for its investment professionals' motivation. It is essential that the firm is likely to be an ongoing entity with continued employment of key personnel. It is difficult to be confident in the future performance of an unstable firm.
- **People:** The investment management industry is highly competitive, so attracting and retaining talented investment professionals is important for success. Successful teams are more likely to be stable, experienced, and have the courage to take a different view than that of the market consensus.
- **Investment process:** A critical element of manager selection is to assess whether the investment process is superior, is repeatable, and can be consistently applied, suggesting that the manager will continue to display skill in the future. The goal is to understand the philosophy and portfolio construction process in order to judge whether the manager has a sustainable competitive advantage such that history will be a guide to future performance. Additionally, one needs to assess whether the manager's process can be skillfully applied to the current assets under management (AUM) in the investment strategy. For example, an investment manager specializing in so-called frontier markets may have capacity limits in terms of AUM that they can effectively invest according to their investment discipline.
- **Operational process:** Manager selection involves operational due diligence, which entails verifying that adequate controls, policies, and procedures are in place to ensure accurate performance reporting with independent verification. In addition, proper risk management entails verifying that the procedures are actually being adhered to regularly. The investment manager must provide detailed documentation of how it tracks operational and market risk exposures. Performance appraisal assumes that the returns analyzed are an accurate record of the manager's performance. When performance records have inaccuracies, incorrect inferences about manager performance become more likely.
- **Transparency:** The manager must be willing to provide the information required for initial and ongoing due diligence. Although returns are typically available through third-party sources, access to key personnel, portfolio holdings, risk statistics, and third-party service provider data is necessary to properly evaluate and monitor a manager. Managers unwilling to provide the necessary transparency, even if apparently skillful, make it difficult to fulfill one's fiduciary duty.
- **Costs:** No assessment is complete without considering costs, which are the only certainty and a crucial element of manager evaluation. Fees affect not only the level of net return realized by the investor (as discussed later in the reading) but also affect portfolio volatility. In addition to the management fee, it should be determined whether the manager offers the option of a performance-based fee in addition to a market value-based fee and how the two types of structures have compared in the past. This comparison is particularly important if the manager has a soft dollar agreement in place. It should be determined whether or not all investors receive the same fee structure. If not, the application and rationale for such arrangements needs to be understood to ensure that the incentives of the manager and all investors remain aligned.

In addition to the qualitative considerations, various quantitative considerations are important in manager selection. These considerations include the assessment of the amount of risk assumed by the manager to generate its results and the analysis of the manager's performance in relation to stated investment objectives. Quantitative analysis includes calculating and analyzing risk metrics, such as standard deviation, upside/downside capture, and drawdown, as well as conducting a returns-based or holding-based style analysis.

EXAMPLE 1

Investment Manager Selection and Performance Appraisal

1 Which statement *best* describes considerations involved in manager selection?
   A The quantitative evaluation of investment performance to identify the manager with the highest risk-adjusted return.
   B The systematic evaluation of the investment performance of a fund or strategy to understand and assess the abilities of a fund manager.
   C The evaluation of a broad set of qualitative and quantitative factors to determine whether a manager displays skill and the likelihood that the manager will continue to display skill in the future.
2 Which is of the following is **not** an important qualitative consideration in manager selection?
   A Suitability
   B Transparency
   C Manager's past returns

Solution to 1:

C is correct. Manager selection involves analyzing the investment process that delivered the investment performance and includes both quantitative and qualitative analysis.

Solution to 2:

C is correct. The manager's past returns are a quantitative, not qualitative, consideration in manager selections.

2.2 Manager Selection and the Investment Policy Statement

Each investor has particular assumptions about, expectations for, and biases surrounding their investments. The **investment policy statement** frames the manager selection process by capturing all of this information in addition to investor constraints (liquidity, time horizon, tax concerns, legal and regulatory factors, and unique circumstances).

The IPS's sections concerning objectives and constraints will determine the universe of managers that is suitable for the investor and which therefore should be considered. It is important to identify the appropriate universe from which to search and select managers: Managers that display skill but are not suited for the role the investor seeks to fill will not be a good fit.

The first consideration in screening managers is to determine the appropriate benchmark for the allocation (e.g., to equities or fixed income) being considered. This process naturally incorporates the return requirements and some aspects of the risk tolerance specified in the IPS.

The following investment objectives and constraints are generally specified in the IPS:

- **Risk tolerance:** What is the investor's willingness and ability to bear risk? The IPS may place limitations, stated in absolute or relative terms, on risk.
- **Investment objectives:** Absolute and/or benchmark relative return objectives may be stated. For some investors, an important goal is to fund the payment of a set of long-term liabilities. The objective in such cases may be stated relation to the liabilities.
- **Investment disciplines (investment philosophy):** The IPS often provides guidance on how the investor's assets are to be managed. It may indicate a preference for, or place a constraint on, the use of active and/or passive managers. This preference or constraint can be based on investor or asset allocator assumptions about market efficiency in general or for particular segments of the market. A liability-relative investment approach may be relevant if funding the payment of liabilities is an investment objective.
- **Liquidity:** The portfolio's liquidity must be fitting with the investor's demands. An investor with shorter-term liquidity needs typically does not hold long-term assets, such as private equity or real estate.
- **Time horizon:** In addition to liquidity needs, the investment horizon relates to the tolerance for risk. An investor closer to retirement has less time to recover from losses, which places more emphasis on absolute measures of risk, such as capture ratio and drawdown. It is appropriate for investors with a long-term horizon to take on more risk to ensure that the purchasing power of the portfolio is maintained.
- **Taxes:** Taxes may be an important consideration for some investors, in which case lower-turnover, more tax efficient strategies are preferred. In addition, separately managed accounts may be preferable to pooled investment vehicles to customize the strategy in a way that minimizes tax liabilities.
- **Regulatory:** Individual investors may have trust and estate considerations, and institutional investors may face legal and regulatory issues.
- **Unique circumstances (investment preferences):** The IPS may state any unique considerations or concerns that need to be observed. Examples include restrictions on allowable investments dictated by religious or other beliefs, or a requirement to maintain voting control of a family-owned portfolio investment. Such considerations might make a separately managed account preferable.

Exhibit 1 lists some of the key features of an IPS that are particularly important to the manager selection process as well as their potential implications for the process. Although the specifics may vary significantly across investors based on their views, investment horizons, size of assets, and past investment experience, every IPS should include these key features regardless of the investor's individual circumstances and characteristics.

Exhibit 1 Various IPS Features and Their Implications for Manager Selection

IPS Feature	Potential Implications for Manager Selection
Objectives	
Philosophy	Compatibility of investment philosophy and process.
Asset size considerations	Investment vehicle compatibility; capacity of market to support execution of the strategy for given asset amount.

Exhibit 1 (Continued)

IPS Feature	Potential Implications for Manager Selection
Return objectives	
■ Total vs. relative	Manager ability to generate a specific absolute return, or return in excess of a specified benchmark.
■ Real vs. nominal	Level and type of net risk exposures; inflation hedging characteristics of the portfolio.
■ Net vs. gross	Level and structure of fees and expenses, portfolio turnover.
Risk tolerance	Level and type of net risk exposures. Acceptable level of portfolio volatility, either in absolute terms or relative to a benchmark. Level of downside risk.
Constraints	
Liquidity	Fund terms regarding withdrawals and redemptions. Investor types and concentrations.
Horizon	Drawdown risk over investor's horizon.
Taxes	Tax management ability.
Legal and regulatory	Allowable investments, manager diversification, short sales.
Unique circumstances	Allowable investments, level, and type of net risk exposures
Other considerations	
Asset class selection	Level and type of net risk exposures, manager investment style.
Rebalancing frequency	Portfolio and market liquidity.
Review and reporting frequency	Transparency.

Source: Based on Stewart 2013.

EXAMPLE 2

Investment Manager Selection and the IPS

1 Which of the following sections of an IPS *most likely* relates to the feasibility of adding a distressed debt investment manager as part of an institution's diversified investment portfolio?

A Risk tolerance

B Return objectives

C Legal and regulatory constraints

2 Which of the following IPS constraints might suggest the use of a separately managed account rather than a pooled vehicle?

A Taxes and preferences

B Liquidity and transparency

C Regulatory and time horizon

Solution to 1:

C is correct. Within a diversified portfolio, distressed debt may have a role for various levels of risk tolerance and investment objectives. Regulatory and legal constraints, however, may rule out distressed debt investment.

Solution to 2:

A is correct. Separately managed accounts allow for customization, which may be preferable to pooled investment vehicles if minimizing tax liabilities or if the IPS includes any special considerations or concerns that need to be expressed.

2.3 Active and Passive Manager Selection

A fundamental decision in the manager selection process is whether to use active or passive managers. Regardless of the choice, the objective is the same: selection of the "best" manager to fill a particular portfolio need. Although the manager selection framework will be the same, the importance of the components examined and their interpretation will differ for active versus passive managers. The choice between active and passive managers is a function of the investor's assumptions about market efficiency, confidence in the ability to identify skilled managers, and the expectation that the manager can add value relative to the benchmark after fees and taxes in taxable portfolios.

Investor beliefs regarding the degree of market efficiency may vary across asset classes, capitalization ranges, and other investment characteristics. When an investor believes that a particular market is highly efficient, the investor would expect no net advantage to attempting to identify mispriced securities. Thus, that investor would likely prefer passive management in that market. Passive managers seek to closely match the risk and return characteristics of the benchmark rather than to outperform the benchmark. For passive managers, the portfolio construction process can be either full replication of benchmark holdings or sampling of them (which has the goal of holding risk factor exposures that closely align with those of the benchmark). The selection process seeks to determine whether the manager's investment process is effective and cost efficient in achieving the objectives of passive management. Passive managers typically charge lower fees than active managers within the same investment universe. It is important to recognize that even low fees constitute a drag on performance compared with an unmanaged index (e.g., the FTSE 100 or Russell 1000 indexes). Effective passive managers are expected to have relatively low tracking risk, which indicates that the portfolio's returns closely approximate the returns on the benchmark. **Tracking risk**, also known as tracking error, is calculated as the standard deviation of the return difference between the manager and the benchmark.

A limit on tracking risk is often specified as a constraint for active managers. That is, the manager is expected to deliver positive alpha while still providing sensitivity to systematic risk factors similar to the benchmark. In general, as the constraints on tracking risk become tighter, the manager has less opportunity to add alpha. If the investor wants to track the benchmark very closely, a passive manager is more suitable than an active manager. This choice is more consistent with the mandate of low tracking risk, which implies a bias toward an assumption of market efficiency, and it makes little sense to pay higher active fees to closely track a passive benchmark.

EXAMPLE 3

Active and Passive Investment Managers

1 The choice between active and passive managers is a function of assumptions about:

   A liquidity needs of the investor.

   B market efficiency and manager skill.

   C manager skill and the investor's investment horizon.

2 If low tracking risk of the benchmark is desired:

   A a passive manager is more suitable than an active manager.

   B an active manager is more suitable than a passive manager.

   C either a passive manager or an active manager is equally suitable.

Solution to 1:

B is correct. Passive managers assume that markets are sufficiently efficient that there is no net advantage in attempting to identify mispriced securities. As such, they seek to replicate, not outperform, the benchmark. Tracking the benchmark is often specified as a constraint for active managers. That is, the manager is expected to deliver positive alpha while still providing systematic risk exposures similar to the benchmark.

Solution to 2:

A is correct. Close tracking of the benchmark is consistent with the assumption of market efficiency, making a passive manager more suitable than an active manager because it makes little sense to pay active fees to closely track a passive benchmark.

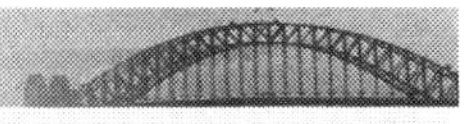

Rules-Based Active Investing

The discussion so far has focused on passive and traditional active management, but there is a third approach. Rules-based active investing is an active approach that embeds elements of passive management. It uses a rules-based system to weight each stock in an index. This approach grew out of the anomalies literature, in which early tests of the capital asset pricing model (CAPM) showed the model was insufficient and additional risk factors, such as size and style, also explained returns.

One approach is to equal-weight the securities in a capitalization-weighted index. This strategy avoids buying more of the stocks that have increased the most in price after the index has risen. Another approach is to assign a greater weight to low-volatility stocks or to weight by financial characteristics, such as sales, dividends, or cash flow.

Rules-based active investing takes on risk exposures that are not present in the index, and thus using this strategy inherently means greater tracking risk and underperformance in times when the risk exposures are not being rewarded. Because such approaches to investing seek to capture risk premiums as a method to outperform rather than traditional stock picking, the evaluation of managers in this area follows similar lines as the evaluation of passive managers. The focus is on operational efficiency and the manager's ability to capture the desired risk premiums, in addition to an assessment of the construction of the particular factor.

3 INVESTMENT MANAGER SEARCH AND SELECTION

Past performance is no guarantee of future performance. The investor, however, may anticipate that a consistent, robust process will generate a similar return distribution relative to risk factors through time, assuming the underlying dynamics of the market have not dramatically changed. One important goal in studying an investment manager is to understand whether the manager's investment process, people, and portfolio construction satisfy this assumption—that is, will the investment process generate the expected return from the expected sources? The manager search and selection process has three broad components: the universe, a quantitative analysis of the manager's performance track record, and a qualitative analysis of the manager's investment process. The qualitative analysis consists of investment due diligence, which evaluates the manager's investment process, and operational due diligence, which evaluates the manager's infrastructure and firm. Exhibit 2 details these components.

Exhibit 2 Manager Selection Process Overview

Key aspects	Key Question
Universe	
Defining the universe	What is the feasible set of managers that fit the portfolio need?
■ Suitability	Which managers are suitable for the IPS?
■ Style	Which have the appropriate style?
■ Active vs. passive	Which fit the active versus passive decision?
Quantitative Analysis	
Investment due diligence	Which manager "best" fits the portfolio need?
Quantitative	What has been the manager's return distribution?
■ Attribution	Has the manager displayed skill?
■ Capture ratio	How does the manager perform in "up" markets versus "down" markets?
■ Drawdown	Does the return distribution exhibit large drawdowns?
Qualitative Analysis	
Investment due diligence	Which manager "best" fits the portfolio need?
Qualitative	Is the manager expected to continue to generate this return distribution?
■ Philosophy	What market inefficiency does the manager seek to exploit?
■ Process	Is the investment process capable of exploiting this inefficiency?
■ People	Do the investment personnel possess the expertise and experience necessary to effectively implement the investment process?

Exhibit 2 (Continued)

Key aspects	Key Question
■ Portfolio	Is portfolio construction consistent with the stated investment philosophy and process?
Operational due diligence	Is the manager's track record accurate, and does it fully reflect risks?
■ Process and procedure	Is the back office strong, safeguarding assets and able to issue accurate reports in a timely manner?
■ Firm	Is the firm profitable, with a healthy culture, and likely to remain in business? Is the firm committed to delivering performance over gathering assets?
■ Investment vehicle	Is the vehicle suitable for the portfolio need?
■ Terms	Are the terms acceptable and appropriate for the strategy and vehicle?
Monitoring	Does the manager continue to be the "best" fit for the portfolio need?

EXAMPLE 4

Components of the Manager Selection Process

1 Qualitative analysis of the manager selection process includes:
   - **A** attribution.
   - **B** defining the universe.
   - **C** investment and operational due diligence.

2 Which of the following is considered a key aspect of operational due diligence?
   - **A** People
   - **B** Philosophy
   - **C** Procedures

Solution to 1:

C is correct. Qualitative analysis consists of investment due diligence, which evaluates the manager's investment process, and operational due diligence, which evaluates the manager's infrastructure and firm.

Solution to 2:

C is correct. Process and procedures are key aspects of operational due diligence, whereas people and philosophy are key aspects of investment due diligence.

3.1 Defining the Manager Universe

The manager selection process begins by defining the universe of feasible managers, those managers that potentially satisfy the identified portfolio need. The objective is to reduce the manager universe to a manageable size relative to the resources and time available to evaluate it. This process also involves balancing the risks of too narrow a search, which potentially excludes interesting managers, and too broad a search, which leads to little gain in reducing the list of potential managers. Like many interesting problems, this step is a combination of art and science. In the initial screening process, the search parameters can be narrowed and widened to determine which managers enter and exit and to evaluate whether these additions or deletions improve the universe.

The IPS and the reason for the manager search largely determine the universe of managers considered and the benchmark against which they are compared. A new search based on a strategic or tactical view, such as adding a new strategy or risk exposure, will examine a broad universe of comparable managers and look to select the best within the universe. Adding a manager to increase capacity or diversification within a strategy already held will look for a complement to current holdings. Replacing a single manager in a particular strategy will look for the best manager within the strategy universe. The IPS in part determines what the relative terms "best," "complement," and "cost/benefit" mean.

Typically a search starts with a benchmark that represents the manager's role within the portfolio. The benchmark also provides a reference for performance attribution and appraisal. There are several approaches to assigning a manager to a benchmark:

- **Third-party categorization:** Database or software providers and consultants typically assign managers to a strategy sector. This categorization provides an easy and efficient way to define the universe. The risk is that the provider's definition may differ from the desired portfolio role. As such, it is important to understand the criteria used by the provider.
- **Returns-based style analysis:** The risk exposures derived from the manager's actual return series has the advantage of being objective. The disadvantage is additional computational effort and the limitations of returns-based analysis (see Section 3.2.2).
- **Holdings-based style analysis:** This approach allows for the estimation of current factor exposures but adds to computational effort and depends on timing and amount of transparency (see Section 3.2.2).
- **Manager experience:** The assignment can be based on an evaluation of the manager and observations of portfolios and returns over time.

Not surprisingly, a hybrid strategy that combines elements of each approach is recommended. Using third-party categorizations is an efficient way to build the initial universe that can be complemented and refined with quantitative methods and experience. Most importantly, the screening should avoid using performance at this point. Notice that all the approaches listed attempt to understand the manager's risk profile and identify candidates to fill the desired role in the portfolio. The focus is not on historical performance. Lastly, the universe is not static. The universe will evolve through time not only as manager strategies evolve but also as a result of the entry and exit of managers.

The Concept of Active Share

Active share measures the difference in portfolio holdings relative to the benchmark. A manager that precisely replicates the benchmark will have an active share of zero; a manager with no holdings in common with the benchmark will have an active share of one.

Given a strategy with N securities (i = 1, 2, …, N), active share is calculated as

$$\text{Active Share} = \frac{1}{2}\sum_{i=1}^{N}\left|\text{Strategy Weight}_i - \text{BenchmarkWeight}_i\right|$$

Typically, managers are somewhere along the spectrum. The categorization of active share and tracking risk in Exhibit 3 has been suggested for active managers. It is clear that full replication will appear as a closet indexer. A manager that uses sampling techniques to build the portfolio may, however, appear as a diversified stock picker depending on the universe under consideration and the dispersion of active share of the constituents. Tracking risk will be low, but active share might not be because only a subset of constituents is held. One reason is that high and low are relative to the universe being examined and the category definitions used. As such, it is important to examine risk factors and portfolio construction techniques of both active and passive managers.

Exhibit 3 Active Share vs. Tracking Risk

		Active Share	
		Low	High
Tracking risk	High	Sector rotation	Concentrated stock pickers
	Low	Closet indexer	Diversified stock pickers

3.2 Quantitative Considerations in Manager Selection

Performance appraisal captures most aspects of quantitative analysis, evaluating a manager's strengths and weaknesses as measured by that manager's ability to add value to a stated benchmark. Although the determination of whether the manager possesses skill is important, it is equally important to understand the manager's risk profile. As noted, the manager has likely been selected to fill a particular role in the portfolio. As such, although it is important to select a skillful manager, the "best" manager may be one that delivers the desired exposures and is suitable for the investor's assumptions, expectations, and biases.

3.2.1 *Type I and Type II Errors*

Certain concepts from the area of inferential statistics known as hypothesis testing can be relevant to the decision to hire an investment manager or to retain or dismiss a manager previously hired.

The determination of whether a manager is skillful typically starts with the null hypothesis (the hypothesis assumed to be true until demonstrated otherwise) that the manager is not skillful. As a result, there are two types of potential error, also shown in Exhibit 4:

- Type I: Hiring or retaining a manager who subsequently underperforms expectations. Rejecting the null hypothesis of no skill when it is correct.
- Type II: Not hiring or firing a manager who subsequently outperforms, or performs in line with, expectations. Not rejecting the null hypothesis when it is incorrect.

Exhibit 4 Type I and Type II Errors

	Realization	
	Below expectations (no skill)	At or above expectations (skill)

(continued)

Exhibit 4 (Continued)

Decision	Hire/Retain	Type I	Correct
	Not Hire/Fire	Correct	Type II

Type I and Type II errors can occur anytime a decision is made regarding the hiring or firing of a manager. Type I compares the manager with the broader universe of potential managers (those managers not hired) and potentially the specific manager replaced. Type II compares the manager with the broader universe (possible managers that could have replaced the manager), but specifically to the manager hired to replace the fired manager. The decision maker must determine which error is preferred based on the expected benefits and costs of changing managers. Expectations are based on the role the manager plays within the portfolio. Ideally, the goal is to hire and retain the "best" manager for the intended role within the portfolio. So, the parameters for evaluation are as follows:

- **Relative performance to peers and benchmark:** A focus on absolute return, or the manager with the highest return, although attractive, may be misleading. Even risk-adjusted return, outperforming the benchmark for active managers and tracking the benchmark for passive managers, needs to account for the risk profile of the manager. If the fund has an attractive risk bias relative to the benchmark (and that was one reason the manager was selected), it may skew the results. For instance, international stock and bond funds with above-average emerging market (EM) exposure may be desirable because they capture the desired level of EM exposure, on a look-through basis, without the need for a dedicated EM fund, thus reducing the total number of funds held. Compared with the universe of international peers, however, holding these funds may result in over/under-performance through time. A simple comparison or performance metrics might not account for this (preferred) risk profile.
- **Style drift:** Even if performance is not an issue, a manager that deviates from its style may be problematic for portfolio construction and could represent an error.
- **Operational issues:** These issues include any sign of potential operational costs that may affect performance or signal a deeper problem.

Qualitative considerations in Type I and Type II errors Decision makers appear predisposed to worry more about Type I errors than Type II errors. Potential reasons for this focus on Type I errors are as follows:

- Psychologically, people seek to avoid feelings of regret. Type I errors are errors of commission, an active decision that turned out to be incorrect, whereas Type II errors are errors of omission, or inaction. As a result, Type I errors create explicit costs, whereas Type II errors create opportunity costs. Because individuals appear to put less weight on opportunity costs, Type I errors are psychologically more painful than Type II errors.
- Type I errors are relatively straightforward to measure and are often directly linked to the decision maker's compensation. Portfolio holdings are regularly monitored, and managers' out- and underperformance expectations are clearly

identified. Type II errors are less likely to be measured—what is the performance impact of not having selected a particular manager? As such, the link between compensation and Type II errors is less clear.

- Similarly, Type I errors are more transparent to investors, so they entail not only the regret of an incorrect decision but the pain of having to explain this decision to the investor. Type II errors, not hiring or firing a manager with skill, are less transparent to investors, unless the investor tracks fired managers or evaluates the universe themselves.

Although Type I errors are likely more familiar and more of a concern to most decision makers, a consistent pattern of Type II errors can highlight weaknesses in the manager selection process. One approach to examine this issue is to monitor not only managers currently held but also managers that were evaluated and not hired as well as managers that were fired. The goal of monitoring is to determine the following:

- Are there identifiable factors that differentiate managers hired and managers not hired?
- Are these factors consistent with the investment philosophy and process of the decision maker?
- Are there identifiable factors driving the decision to retain or fire managers?
- Are these factors consistent with the investment philosophy and process of the decision maker?
- What is the added value of the decision to retain or fire managers?

The objective is to avoid making decisions based on short-term performance (trend following) and to identify any evidence of behavioral biases (regret, loss aversion) in the evaluation of managers during the selection process.

Performance implications The performance costs of Type I and Type II errors are different aspects of the same issue: Do the managers in the portfolio possess skill? The cost of Type I errors is holding those without skill, as opposed to the cost of Type II errors, which is not holding those with skill. The difference in cost appears to be driven by the size, shape, mean, and dispersion of the respective return distributions of skilled and unskilled managers within the universe. The smaller the difference in sample size and distribution mean and the wider the dispersion of the distributions, the smaller the difference in expected cost. In addition, the degree of skewness and thickness of the tails also matter. The less distinct the distribution of skilled managers from unskilled managers, the lower the opportunity cost of retaining and the lower the cost of hiring an unskilled manager. That is, the smaller the perceived difference between the distribution of skilled and unskilled managers, the lower the cost and lower the incentive to fire a manager. As Exhibit 5 illustrates, the cost of Type I and Type II errors is higher for the solid line distributions than the dotted line distribution. Although these distributions cannot be directly observed, one can form an opinion based on the degree of market efficiency, performance measurement, attribution, and appraisal for manager universe. More-efficient markets are likely to exhibit smaller differences between skilled and unskilled managers.

Exhibit 5 Return Distributions of Skilled and Unskilled Managers

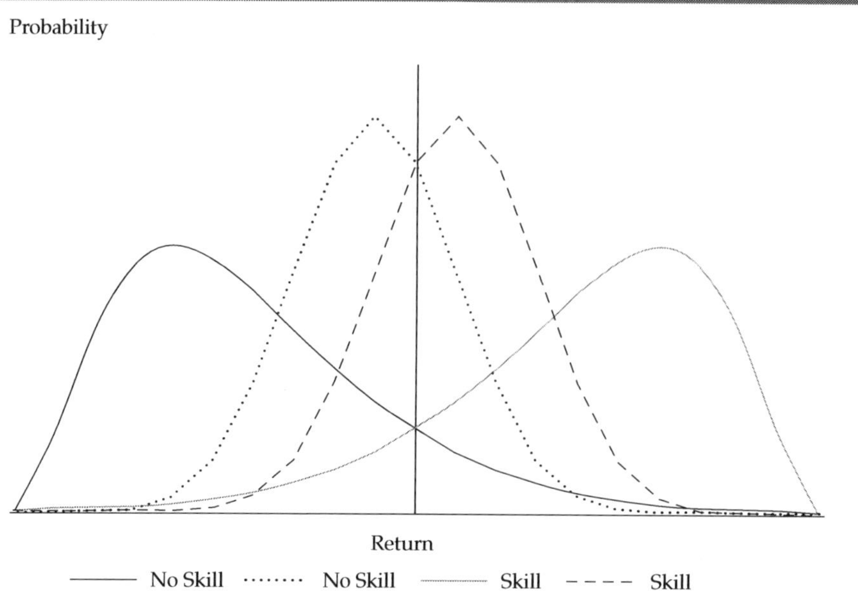

A related aspect is mean reversion and the cost of performance chasing. If performance is mean reverting, a Type I error would be hiring a strong performer or firing a poor performer only to see a reversion in performance. A Type II error would be not trimming strong performers and avoiding hiring managers with weaker short-term track records, which can be costly. One study found that individual investors significantly underperformed the average mutual fund because of poor timing and fund selection decisions (DALBAR 2005). A study of institutional plan sponsor allocation decisions found that investment products receiving contributions subsequently underperformed products experiencing withdrawals. The study estimated that more than $170 billion was lost during the period examined (Stewart, Neumann, Knittel, and Heisler 2009).

Lastly, there are the potential effects of switching managers on the portfolio and its risk exposures. The greater the ability to identify and gain access to managers with similar risk profiles to a current manager, the lower the impact on the portfolio's risk exposures, and the lower the transition costs to manager replacement.

Non-performance implications of replacing a manager Beyond the performance implications outlined, there are additional costs that require consideration when assessing whether to retain or fire a manager. Often, the costs of replacing a manager may be greater than the expected performance benefits. One reason is that many of these costs are certain and realized in the near term, whereas the performance benefits are less certain and may be fully realized only after a longer period. As such, in some cases, it may be optimal to retain an apparently less skillful manager.

- **Transaction costs:** An explicit trading fee may be required to sell the fund. The lower the fee, the lower the cost of replacing the manager.
- **Redemption fees:** Many funds charge a fee for exiting a fund within a fixed period after investing. Many mutual funds charge redemption fees to discourage "market timing" strategies, which is the active trading of mutual funds. A typical redemption fee is 2%–3% if the fund is sold within three months of purchase. Hedge funds often impose lockups, particularly strategies that hold less liquid securities, to discourage active trading that may result in having to sell securities at unfavorable times to the detriment of other investors. Typically,

lockups either prevent redemption or charge a 2%–3% fee (that is paid to the other investors in the fund) for redeeming the fund within the first year. The lower the redemption fee, the lower the cost of replacing a manager.

- **Holdbacks:** For a full redemption, some hedge funds will retain a portion of assets, typically 5%–10%, until a year-end audit has been completed. This retention provides leeway should the net asset value (NAV) of the portfolio be revised. Depending on when the redemption is placed, the holdback can last more than a year, and the assets do not share in the gains and losses of the strategy and often do not earn interest. The lower the holdback, the lower the cost to replacing the manager.
- **Tax liabilities:** The longer a manager, particularly one that has performed well previously, has been held, the greater the likely tax implication of replacing the manager. The lower the tax liability, the better the investor is able to offset any gains with losses, or the greater the degree of long-term gains, the lower the cost of replacing the manager.
- **Portfolio implications:** The manager under consideration for replacement was held to satisfy a particular need in the portfolio. The easier it is to identify a comparable manager, one that also satisfies this need, the lower the cost of replacing the manager.

As a result, the decision of whether and when to replace a manager depends on whether the expected benefits are sufficient to account for the explicit and implicit costs.

EXAMPLE 5

Type I and Type II Errors

1 A Type I error is:

A hiring or retaining a manager that subsequently underperforms expectations.

B hiring or retaining a manager that subsequently outperforms, or performs in line with, expectations.

C not hiring or firing a manager who subsequently outperforms, or performs in line with, expectations.

2 A Type II error is:

A hiring or retaining a manager that subsequently underperforms expectations.

B hiring or retaining a manager that subsequently outperforms, or performs in line with, expectations.

C not hiring or firing a manager who subsequently outperforms, or performs in line with, expectations.

3 The difference in expected cost between Type I and Type II errors is *most likely*:

A higher the smaller the perceived difference between the distribution of skilled and unskilled managers.

B lower the smaller the perceived difference between the distribution of skilled and unskilled managers.

C the expected cost difference of Type I and Type II error is zero, because they reflect different aspects of the same issue.

Solution to 1:

A is correct. The error consists of rejecting the null hypothesis (no skill) when it is correct.

Solution to 2:

C is correct. The error consists of not rejecting the null hypothesis (no skill) when it is incorrect.

Solution to 3:

B is correct. The less distinct the distribution of skilled managers from unskilled managers, the lower the opportunity cost of retaining and cost of hiring an unskilled manager. That is, the smaller the perceived difference between the distribution of skilled and unskilled managers, the lower the cost and incentive to fire a manager.

3.2.2 *Style Analysis*

An important component of performance appraisal and manager selection is understanding the manager's risk exposures relative to the benchmark and how they evolve over time. This understanding helps define the universe of potential managers and the monitoring of selected managers. The process is referred to as style analysis.

A manager's self-reported risk exposures, such as portfolio concentration, industry exposure, capitalization exposure, and other quantitative measures, are the starting point in style analysis. They provide a means to classify managers by style for defining the selection process, a point of reference for evaluating the returns-based and holdings-based style analysis, and an interesting operational check on the manager.

The results of the returns-based style analysis (RBSA) and the holdings-based style analysis (HBSA) should be consistent with the manager's philosophy and the investment process. If not, the process might not be repeatable or might be implemented inconsistently. It is essential to look at all portfolio construction and risk management issues.

The results of the returns-based style analysis and the holdings-based style analysis should be tracked over time in order to ascertain if the risk trends or exposures are out of line with expectations or the manager's stated style. Deviations may signal that issues, such as style drift, are developing.

3.2.3 *Returns-Based Style Analysis and Holdings-Based Style Analysis*

Returns-based and holdings-based style analyses provide a means to determine the risks and sources of return for a particular strategy. To highlight the use of style analysis, compare and contrast by using the four attributes of effective risk reporting: meaningful, accurate, consistent, and timely.

- **Meaningful:** The risks reported represent the important sources of performance return and risk.
- **Accurate:** The reported values reflect the manager's actual risk exposures.
- **Consistent:** The methodology used allows for comparison over time and across multiple managers.
- **Timely:** The report is available in a timely manner so that it is useful for making informed investment decisions.

Returns-based style analysis (RBSA) is a top-down approach that involves estimating a portfolio's sensitivities to security market indexes representing a range of distinct factors. Although RBSA adds the additional analytical step of estimating the risk factors, as opposed to using a third-party or self-reported style categorization, the analysis is straightforward and typically does not require a large amount of additional, or difficult to acquire, data. RBSA should identify the important drivers of return and risk factors for the period analyzed and can be estimated even for complicated strategies. In addition, the process is comparable across managers and through time, and the use of returns data provides an objective style check that is not subject to window dressing. The analysis can be run immediately after the data is available, particularly in the case of publicly traded securities. As such, RBSA has many of the attributes of effective risk reporting.

The disadvantage is that RBSA is an imprecise tool. Although the additional computational effort required is not onerous, accuracy may be compromised, because RBSA effectively attributes performance to an unchanging average portfolio during the period. This attribution limits the ability to identify the impact of dynamic investment decisions and may distort the decomposition across sources of added value. Furthermore, the portfolio being analyzed might not reflect the current or future portfolio exposures. If the portfolio contains illiquid securities, stale prices may understate the risk exposure of the strategy. This is a particular problem for private equity (PE) and venture capital (VC) managers that hold illiquid or non-traded securities. VC and PE firms report performance based on the internal rate of return of cash distributions and appraisals of ongoing projects. As a result, reported performance can understate the volatility of return for shorter horizons or time periods with limited liquidity events. Longer periods generally provide more-accurate estimates of the manager's underlying standard deviation of return. The timeliness of any analysis depends on the securities that take the longest to price, which can be challenging for illiquid or non-traded securities.

Holdings-based style analysis (HBSA) is a bottom-up approach that estimates the risk exposures from the actual securities held in the portfolio at a point in time. This approach allows for estimation of current risk factors and offers several advantages. Similar to RBSA, HBSA should identify all important drivers of return and risk factors; be comparable across managers and through time; provide an accurate view of the manager's risk exposures, although potentially subject to window dressing; and be estimated immediately after the data become available.

Exhibit 6 presents a typical holdings-based style map. The manager being evaluated, along with the other managers in the universe, is placed along the size (y-axis) and style (x-axis) dimensions. The portfolio holdings of the manager being evaluated exhibit a large-cap value bias in what is otherwise a rather diverse universe.

Exhibit 6 Example of Holdings-Based Style Analysis

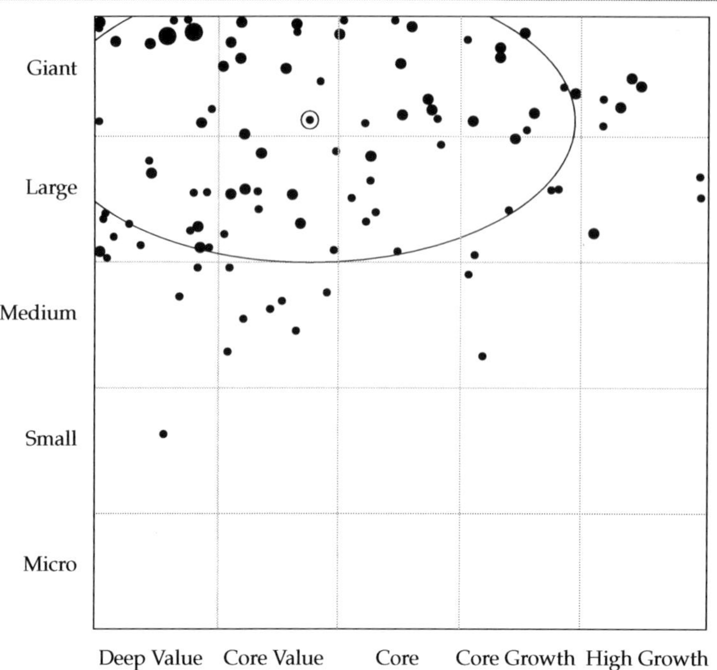

Source: Morningstar Direct, The Mutual Fund Research Center.

As with RBSA, HBSA has some disadvantages. The additional computational effort increases with the complexity of the strategy and depends on the timing and degree of the transparency provided by the manager. This extra effort can be challenging for hedge fund, private equity, and venture capital managers that may be averse to or unable to provide position-level pricing. Even with mutual funds, the necessary transparency may come with a time lag. The usefulness of the analysis may be compromised, because the portfolio reflects a snapshot in time and might not reflect the portfolio going forward, particularly for high-turnover strategies. Some factors may be difficult to estimate if the strategy is complex because HBSA requires an understanding of the underlying strategy. In general, HBSA is typically easier with equity strategies. If the portfolio has illiquid securities, stale pricing may underestimate the risk exposure of the strategy. The report's timeliness depends on the securities that take the longest to price, which can be challenging for illiquid or non-traded securities.

EXAMPLE 6

Style Analysis

1 Which of the following is an advantage of RBSA?

   A It is a more precise tool than HBSA.

   B It does not require potentially difficult to acquire data.

   C It is more accurate than HBSA when the portfolio contains illiquid securities.

2 Which of the following is an advantage of HBSA?

   A It works well for high-turnover strategies.

B It can identify important drivers of return and risk factors and is comparable across managers and through time.

C It effectively attributes performance to a snapshot of the portfolio at a particular time and thus is not subject to window dressing.

Solution to 1:

B is correct. The data needed for RBSA are usually easier to obtain than the data required for HBSA. RBSA is not a precise tool, and it is not more accurate than HBSA when the portfolio holds illiquid securities.

Solution to 2:

B is correct. Although HBSA allows for estimation of current risk factors and is comparable across managers and through time, the necessary computational effort increases with the strategy's complexity and depends on the timing and degree of the transparency provided by the manager. Some factors may be difficult to estimate if the strategy is complex because this approach requires an understanding of the underlying strategy. In general, HBSA is typically easier for equity strategies. If the portfolio has illiquid securities, stale pricing may underestimate the risk exposure of the strategy. Window dressing and high turnover can compromise the results because the results are attributed to a snapshot of the portfolio.

3.2.4 *Capture Ratios and Drawdowns*

One well-known aspect of investment performance is that large losses require proportionally greater gains to reverse or offset. As a result, drawdowns and capture ratios can be important factors in investment manager selection and an important signal in the monitoring of managers. Capture ratios have several variations that reflect various aspects of the manager's gain or loss relative to the gain or loss of the benchmark. Capture ratios also help assess manager suitability relative to the investor's IPS, especially in relation to the investor's time horizon and risk tolerance. **Drawdown** is the loss in value incurred in any continuous period of negative returns. A manager that experiences larger drawdowns may be less suitable for an investor closer to the end of their investment horizon. This section reviews capture ratios and drawdowns, their implications for performance, and their use in evaluating manager performance and suitability.

3.2.4.1 Capture Ratios Capture ratios measure the manager's participation in up and down markets—that is, the manager's percentage return relative to that of the benchmark. The **upside capture ratio**, or upside capture (UC) for short, measures capture when the benchmark return is positive. The **downside capture ratio**, or downside capture (DC), measures capture when the benchmark return is negative. Upside capture greater (less) than 100% generally suggests out- (under-) performance relative to the benchmark, and downside capture less (greater) than 100% generally suggests out- (under-) performance relative to the benchmark. One problem is that when the manager and benchmark returns are of the opposite sign, the ratio will be negative—for example, a manager with a 1% return when the market is down 1% will have a downside capture ratio of –100%. The expressions for upside capture and downside capture are

$$\mathrm{UC}(m,B,t) = \mathrm{R}(m,t)/\mathrm{R}(B,t) \text{ if } \mathrm{R}(B,t) \geq 0, \text{ and}$$

$$\mathrm{DC}(m,B,t) = \mathrm{R}(m,t)/\mathrm{R}(B,t) \text{ if } \mathrm{R}(B,t) < 0$$

where

$UC(m,B,t)$ = up capture for manager m relative to benchmark B for time t
$DC(m,B,t)$ = down capture for manager m relative to benchmark B for time t
$R(m,t)$ = return of manager m for time t
$R(B,t)$ = return of benchmark B for time t

The up/down capture, or simply the **capture ratio** (CR), is the upside capture divided by downside capture. It measures the asymmetry of return and, as such, is similar to bond convexity and option gamma. A capture ratio greater than 1 indicates positive asymmetry, or a convex return profile, whereas a capture ratio less than 1 indicates negative asymmetry, or a concave return profile. Exhibit 7 illustrates what is meant by concave and convex return profiles. The dotted-line curve for a concave return profile resembles a downward-facing bowl, and the black-line curve for convex return profile resembles an upward-facing bowl. The horizontal and vertical axes are, respectively, benchmark returns [R(B)] and portfolio returns [R(m)]. As benchmark returns increase (i.e., moving to the right on the horizontal axis), portfolio returns increase—but at a *decreasing* rate for a concave return profile and at an *increasing* rate for a convex return profile. The expression for the capture ratio is

$$CR(mB,t) = UC(m,B,t)/DC(m,B,t)$$

where

$CR(m,B,t)$ = capture ratio for manager m relative to benchmark B for time t

Exhibit 7 Convex and Concave Return Profiles

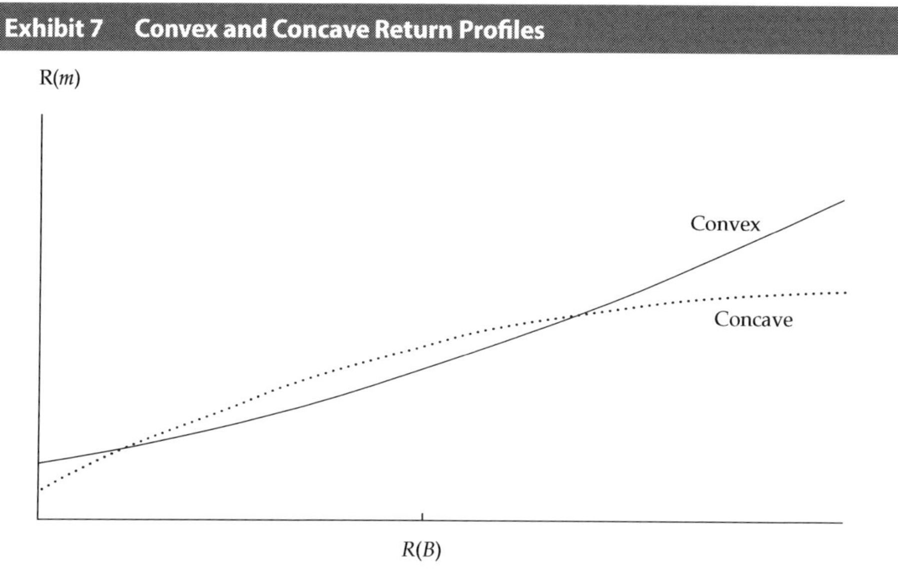

Consider the following return series for the manager, R(m), and the benchmark, R(B), shown in Exhibit 8. The upside columns calculate the cumulative return for the manager, Cum R(m), and the benchmark, Cum R(B), for those periods when the benchmark return is positive. The downside columns calculate the cumulative returns when the benchmark return is negative.

Exhibit 8 Capture Ratio

			Upside Return				Downside Return			
t	R(*m*)	R(*B*)	R(*m*)	R(*B*)	Cum R(*m*)	Cum R(*B*)	R(*m*)	R(*B*)	Cum R(*m*)	Cum R(*B*)
1	0.6%	1.0%	0.6%	1.0%	0.60%	1.00%			0.00%	0.00%
2	−0.3%	−0.5%			0.60%	1.00%	−0.3%	−0.5%	−0.30%	−0.50%
3	1.0%	1.5%	1.0%	1.5%	1.61%	2.52%			−0.30%	−0.50%
4	0.1%	0.2%	0.1%	0.2%	1.71%	2.72%			−0.30%	−0.50%
5	−1.0%	−2.0%			1.71%	2.72%	−1.0%	−2.0%	−1.30%	−2.49%
6	0.5%	0.6%	0.5%	0.6%	2.22%	3.34%			−1.30%	−2.49%
7	0.2%	0.1%	0.2%	0.1%	2.42%	3.44%			−1.30%	−2.49%
8	−0.8%	−1.0%			2.42%	3.44%	−0.8%	−1.0%	−2.09%	−3.47%
9	0.8%	1.0%	0.8%	1.0%	3.24%	4.47%			−2.09%	−3.47%
10	0.4%	0.5%	0.4%	0.5%	3.65%	5.00%			−2.09%	−3.47%
Geometric average			0.51%	0.70%			−0.70%	−1.17%		
Upside capture			0.51%/0.70% = 72.8%			Downside capture		−0.70%/−1.17% = 59.8%		
Capture ratio			72.8%/59.8% = 121.7%							

During up markets, the geometric average return is 0.51% for the manager and 0.70% for the benchmark, giving an upside capture of 72.8%. During down markets, the geometric average return is −0.70% for the manager and −1.17% for the benchmark, giving a downside capture of 59.8%. The manager's capture ratio is 1.217, or 121.7%. Exhibit 9 shows a graph the cumulative upside and downside returns.

Exhibit 9 Cumulative Upside and Downside Returns

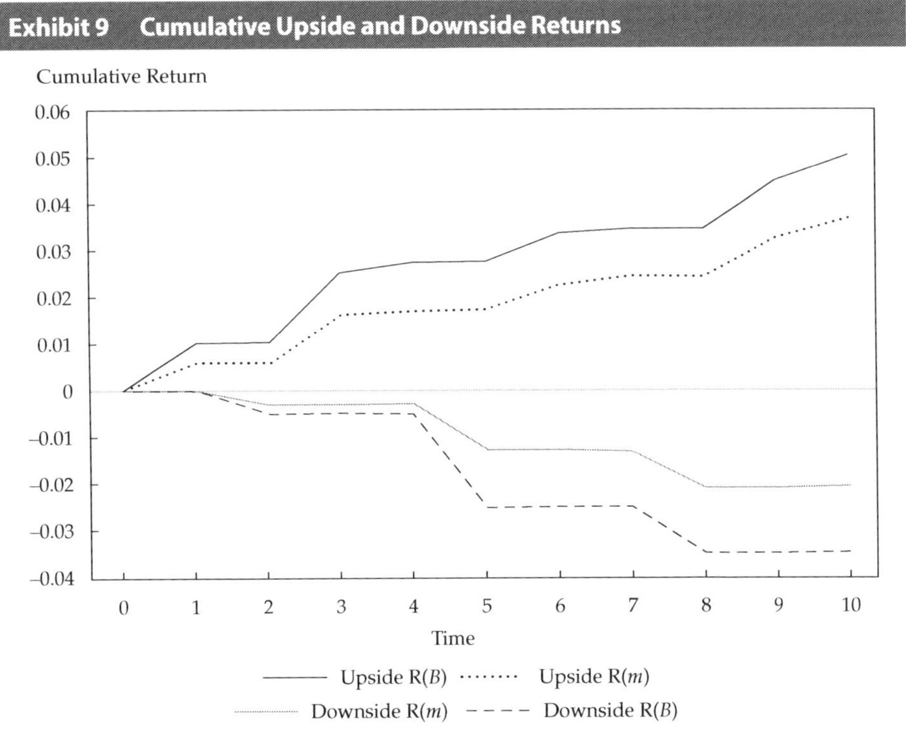

3.2.4.2 Drawdown Drawdown is measured as the cumulative peak-to-trough loss during a particular continuous period. Drawdown duration is the total time from the start of the drawdown until the cumulative drawdown recovers to zero, which can be segmented into the drawdown phase (start to trough) and recovery phase (trough-to-zero cumulative return).

$$\text{Maximum DD}(m,t) = \text{Min}([V(m,t) - V(m,t^*)/V(m,t^*)], 0)$$

where

$V(m,t)$ = portfolio value of manager m at time t
$V(m,t^*)$ = peak portfolio value of manager m
$t > t^*$

Consider the return on the S&P 500 Index from January 2011 to February 2012, shown in Exhibit 10A and 10B. The drawdown is 0% until May 2011, when the return is −1.13% and the drawdown continues to grow, reaching a maximum of −16.26% in September 2011. The strong returns from October 2011 to February 2012 reverse the drawdown. The total duration of the drawdown was 10 months, with a 5-month recovery period.

Exhibit 10A Drawdown

Month	R(*m*)	Cumulative R(*m*)	Drawdown	Cumulative Drawdown	
January 2011	2.37%	2.37%		0.00%	
February 2011	3.43%	5.88%		0.00%	
March 2011	0.04%	5.92%		0.00%	
April 2011	2.96%	9.06%		0.00%	
May 2011	−1.13%	7.83%	−1.13%	−1.13%	Drawdown begins
June 2011	−1.67%	6.03%	−1.67%	−2.78%	
July 2011	−2.03%	3.87%	−2.03%	−4.75%	
August 2011	−5.43%	−1.77%	−5.43%	−9.93%	
September 2011	−7.03%	−8.67%	−7.03%	−16.26%	Maximum drawdown
October 2011	10.93%	1.31%		−7.11%	Recovery begins
November 2011	−0.22%	1.09%	−0.22%	−7.31%	
December 2011	1.02%	2.12%		−6.36%	
January 2012	4.48%	6.69%		−2.17%	
February 2012	4.32%	11.30%		0.00%	Drawdown recovered

Exhibit 10B Drawdown

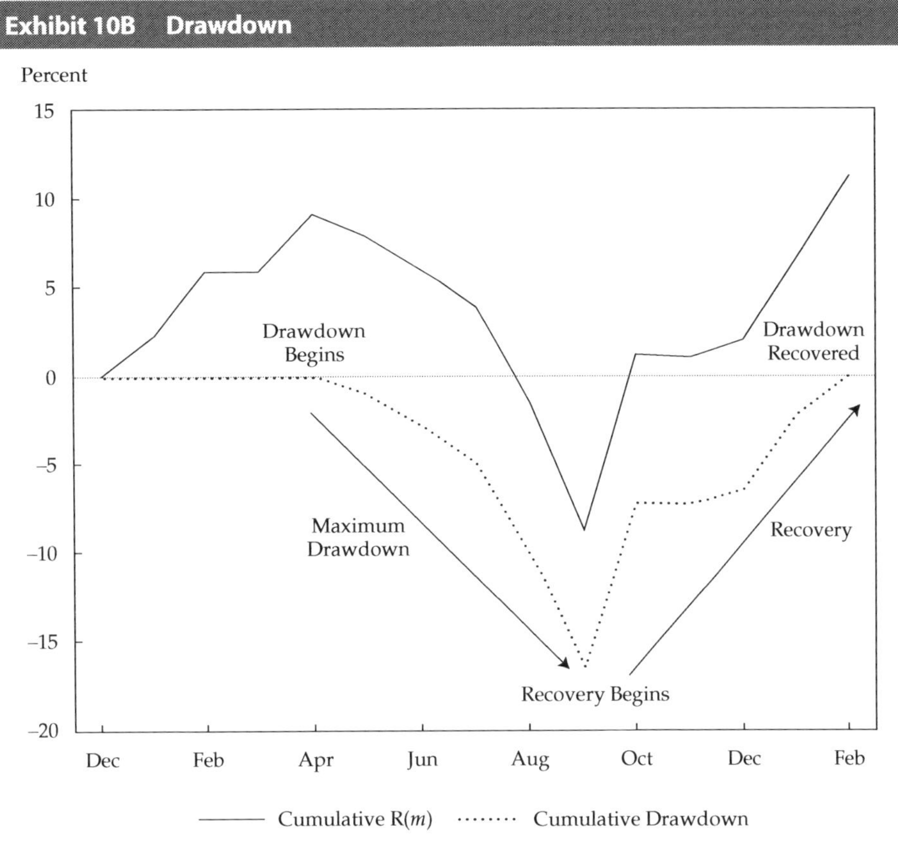

An asymmetrical return profile or avoiding large drawdowns, particularly during periods when the market is not trending strongly upward, can result in higher risk-adjusted returns. The reason is the all too familiar reality for investors that it takes proportionally larger gains to recover from increasingly large losses. This asymmetry arises from basis drift, from the change in the denominator when calculating returns, or from the practical problem of recovering from a smaller asset base after a large loss. For example, a portfolio decline of 50% must be followed by a gain of 100% to return to its previous value. Exhibit 11 illustrates this relationship.

Exhibit 11 Percentage Gain Necessary to Offset a Given Loss

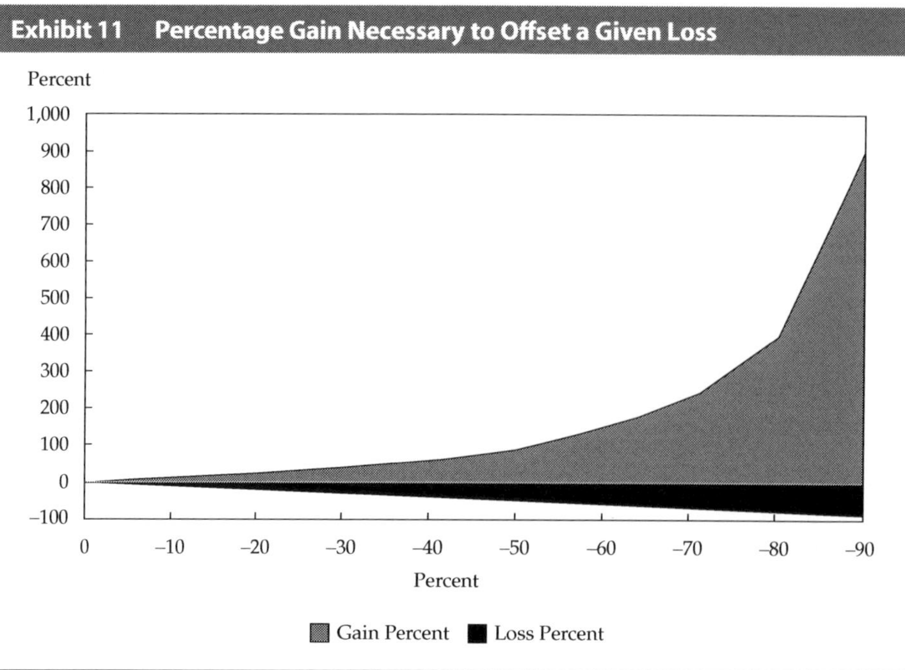

To further illustrate, consider the four return profiles with different upside and downside capture ratios shown in Exhibit 12.

Exhibit 12 Return Profile Summary

Profile	Upside Capture	Downside Capture	Ratio
Long only	100%	100%	1.0
Positive asymmetry	75%	25%	3.0
Low beta	50%	50%	1.0
Negative asymmetry	25%	75%	0.3

The profiles are implemented by varying the allocation to the S&P 500 Total Return (TR) Index and to 90-day T-bills (assuming monthly rebalancing to simplify the calculations) based on the realized monthly return from January 2000 to December 2013. The long-only profile is 100% allocated to the S&P 500 throughout the period. The low-beta profile is allocated 50% to the S&P 500 throughout the period. The positive asymmetry profile is allocated 75% to the S&P 500 for months when the S&P 500 return is positive and 25% when the S&P 500 return is negative. The negative asymmetry profile is allocated 25% to the S&P 500 for months when the S&P 500 return is positive and 75% when the S&P 500 return is negative. The remainder for all profiles is allocated to the 90-day T-bill. Exhibit 13 shows each profile's cumulative monthly return for the time period.

Obviously, these trading strategies are not realistic. Rather, they are stylized return profiles to illustrate the potential effects of the capture ratio and drawdown on return performance and to highlight why understanding the capture ratio and drawdown is important for manager selection.[1]

1 If market return were known beforehand, the correct strategy would be 100% allocated to the S&P 500 TR Index in up months and 100% allocated to 90-day T-bills in down months (or –100% to the S&P if shorting were allowed).

Exhibit 13 Each Profile's Cumulative Monthly Return, January 2000–December 2013

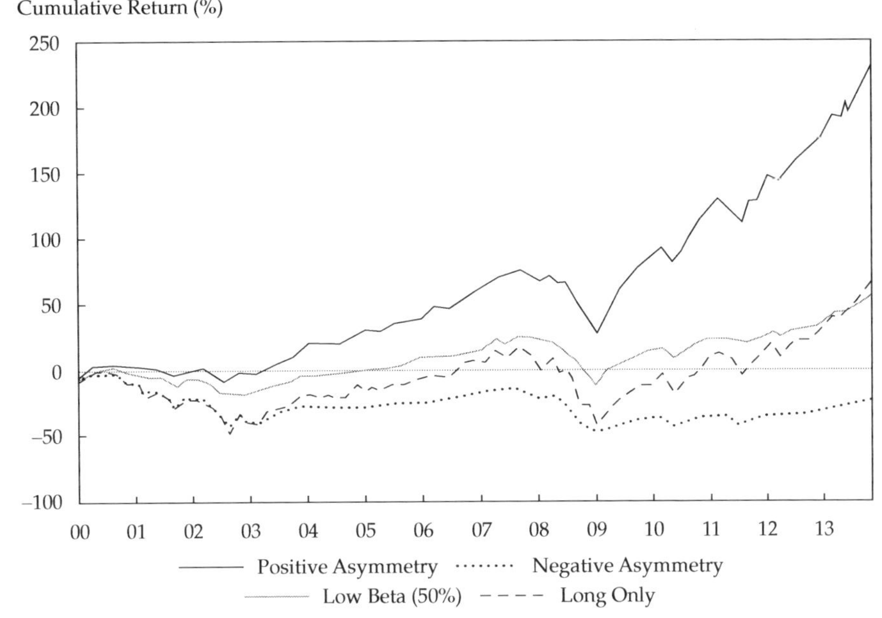

Exhibit 14 provides summary statistics for each profile based on monthly returns from January 2000 to December 2013. Although the long-only profile outperformed the low-beta profile, this outperformance resulted from the strong up market of 2013. The low-beta profile actually outperformed the long-only profile for most of the period, with lower realized volatility and higher risk-adjusted returns during the entire period. The low-beta profile declined only 18.8%, compared with the long-only decline of 42.5%, from January 2000 to September 2002. As a result, the low-beta profile had higher cumulative performance from January 2000 to October 2007 despite markedly lagging the long-only profile (56.0% to 108.4%) from October 2002 to October 2007. Although a low-beta approach may sacrifice performance, it shows that limiting drawdowns can result in better absolute and risk-adjusted return in certain markets.

Not surprisingly, positive asymmetry results in better performance relative to long only, low beta, and negative asymmetry. Although the positive asymmetry profile lags in up markets, this lag is more than offset by the lower participation in down markets. Not surprisingly, the negative asymmetry profile lags, with lower participation in up markets insufficient to offset the greater participation in down markets.

Exhibit 14 Summary Statistics for Each Profile, January 2000–December 2013

Strategy	Long Only	Low Beta	Positive Asymmetry	Negative Asymmetry
Cumulative return	64.0%	54.2%	228.1%	–24.4%
Annualized return	3.60%	3.14%	8.86%	–1.98%
Annualized standard deviation	15.64%	7.79%	9.61%	10.01%
Sharpe ratio	0.10	0.14	0.71	–0.40

(continued)

Exhibit 14 (Continued)

Strategy	Long Only	Low Beta	Positive Asymmetry	Negative Asymmetry
Beta	1.00	0.50	0.61	0.64
Drawdown (maximum)	–50.9%	–28.3%	–26.9%	–48.9%

Although positive asymmetry is a desirable trait, only some strategies are convex. It is important to understand the strategy and how the return profile is created. An important consideration is whether the strategy is inherently convex or whether the convexity relies on the manager's skill. For example, a hedging strategy that is implemented by rolling forward out-of-the-money put options will typically return many small losses because more options expire worthless than are compensated for by the occasional large gain during a large market downturn. This strategy will likely exhibit consistent positive asymmetry because it depends more on the nature of the strategy than on investment skill. Alternatively, a long-only equity strategy that requires the active trading of positions to limit losses while participating in large gains requires a skillful manager and may exhibit less-consistent asymmetry.

It is important to evaluate the consistency between the stated investment process and reported investment performance. An inconsistency could indicate issues with the strategy's repeatability and implementation or more serious reporting and compliance concerns. Capture ratios can be useful in evaluating consistency issues. It is also important to understand the strategy's robustness and potential risks. For example, the expected benefits of diversification—in particular, mitigating downside capture—might not be realized in a crisis as correlations converge to one. The analysis of downside capture and drawdowns are relevant in that regard.

How a manager responds to a large drawdown, at the time, and what lessons are learned, provide evidence of the robustness and repeatability of the investment, portfolio construction, and risk management processes, as well as insight into the people implementing the processes. This information requires an understanding of the source of the drawdown and the potential principal–agent risk, operational risk, and business risk that it entails. As G. Gordon Liddy once said, "That which does not kill us makes us stronger."[2]

Investment strategies need to be adaptive, and managers should strive to improve on the strategy and its implementation. Drawdowns are stress-tests of the investment process and provide a natural point to evaluate and improve processes, which is particularly true of firm-specific drawdowns; they can indicate potentially flawed or inconsistently implemented investment processes, inadequate risk controls, or operational issues. On the one hand, the allocator must determine whether any subsequent changes are consistent with the investment philosophy and correctly and completely address the weakness in the process. On the other hand, the allocator must also judge whether the number of adjustments is excessive and indicates more-fundamental problems with the process. To quote Robert Freeman, "Character is not made in a crisis, it is only exhibited."

During a large or long drawdown, a manager could start to worry more about business risk than investment risk and act in their own best interest rather than that of their investors. Such principal–agent conflicts are a key reason why large drawdowns should be examined and understood.

2 The quote is a paraphrase of a quote by Friedrich Nietzche: "From life's school of war: what does not kill me makes me stronger."

Events of August 2007

Starting on 7 August 2007, many quantitative equity long–short strategies began to experience large drawdowns. Many managers had never experienced such losses or market conditions and started to sell positions as stop-loss and risk management policies were triggered (Khandani and Lo 2011). This activity added to additional selling pressure, and the S&P 500 declined 13.4% by 8 August. Those managers that sold ended up locking in large losses because the underperforming stocks and market subsequently recovered, with the S&P 500 down only 5.7% for the month. In many cases, those funds that sold experienced redemptions or ended up closing.

As August 2007 demonstrated, distinguishing prudent risk management from a misalignment of interests is not always straightforward. Should a manager continue to actively trade a portfolio if the market environment no longer reflects their investment philosophy? In addition, traders will claim that it is better to cut losses because losses can signal that something has changed or that the timing of the trade is not right. Conversely, selling into a down market raises the risk of crystallizing losses and missing any subsequent reversal. The decision maker must assess whether the manager's behavior was a disciplined application of the investment process, reflected a misalignment of interests, or simply resulted from panic or overreaction by the manager.

As noted, one aspect of suitability for the IPS is the investment horizon and its relationship to risk capacity. An investor closer to retirement, with less time to recover from losses, places more emphasis on absolute measures of risk. In addition, even if the manager maintains their discipline during a large drawdown, the investor may not. This dynamic happens if the investor's perception of risk is path dependent or the drawdown changes risk tolerance. If there has been no change to investment policy and no change in the view that the manager remains suitable, the temptation to exit should be resisted to avoid exiting at an inauspicious time. Investors with shorter horizons, with lower risk capacity, or prone to overreact to losses may bias selection toward managers with shallower and shorter expected drawdowns.

EXAMPLE 7

Capture Ratios

t	R(*m*)	R(*B*)
1	−3.06%	−3.60%
2	6.32%	3.10%
3	6.00%	6.03%
4	3.21%	1.58%
5	−9.05%	−7.99%
6	−4.09%	−5.23%
7	4.34%	7.01%
8	−5.72%	−4.51%
9	12.76%	8.92%
10	5.38%	3.81%
11	0.33%	0.01%
12	5.68%	6.68%

Using the return information in the table, what is the manager's downside capture ratio?

A 103%

B 115%

C 118%

Solution:

A is correct.

			Upside Return				Downside Return			
t	**R(*m*)**	**R(*B*)**	**R(*m*)**	**R(*B*)**	**Cum R(*m*)**	**Cum R(*B*)**	**R(*m*)**	**R(*B*)**	**Cum R(*m*)**	**Cum R(*B*)**
1	-3.06%	-3.60%			0.00%	0.00%	-3.06%	-3.60%	-3.06%	-3.60%
2	6.32%	3.10%	6.32%	3.10%	6.32%	3.10%			-3.06%	-3.60%
3	6.00%	6.03%	6.00%	6.03%	12.70%	9.32%			-3.06%	-3.60%
4	3.21%	1.58%	3.21%	1.58%	16.32%	11.04%			-3.06%	-3.60%
5	-9.05%	-7.99%			16.32%	11.04%	-9.05%	-7.99%	-11.83%	-11.30%
6	-4.09%	-5.23%			16.32%	11.04%	-4.09%	-5.23%	-15.44%	-15.94%
7	4.34%	7.01%	4.34%	7.01%	21.36%	18.83%			-15.44%	-15.94%
8	-5.72%	-4.51%			21.36%	18.83%	-5.72%	-4.51%	-20.28%	-19.73
9	12.76%	8.92%	12.76%	8.92%	36.85%	29.43%			-20.28%	-19.73%
10	5.38%	3.81%	5.38%	3.81%	44.21%	34.36%			-20.28%	-19.73%
11	0.33%	0.01%	0.33%	0.01%	44.69%	34.37%			-20.28%	-19.73%
12	5.68%	6.68%	5.68%	6.68%	52.91%	43.35%			-20.28%	-19.73%
Geometric average			5.45%	4.60%			-5.51%	-5.35%		
Upside capture			5.45%/4.60% = 118%			**Downside capture**		**−5.51%/−5.35% = 103%**		
Capture ratio			118%/103% = 115%							

3.2.5 *Batting Average*

Consistent performance is important. Sustained underperformance can lead to increased funding requirements for individual and institutional portfolios, negatively affecting earnings and cash flow. For the advisers or investment officer, inconsistent results can make reporting to the investor or investment committee uncomfortable and time consuming, and it might test the investor's or committee's investment discipline. Lastly, inconsistent performance can signal a lack of skill. As we have noted, one goal of manager selection is to determine whether the investment process is repeatable and consistently implemented to provide some sense that past performance provides guidance for expected future performance. That is, consistency is an important aspect of skill. One measure of performance consistency is batting average. **Batting average** measures the frequency of positive outcomes that can alternatively be defined as

- the number of investment decisions that result in a profit divided by the total number of investment decisions, or
- the number of positive return periods relative to the benchmark or peers divided by the total number of return periods.

The first definition, which we can call "absolute" batting average, highlights the importance of trade frequency in performance appraisal and allows different strategies to be distinguished by the frequency of trades. The number of investment decisions can be used as a measure for the frequency with which the manager creates implementable investment ideas (Constable and Armitage 2006). Higher trade frequency can be desirable because less frequent trading requires higher batting averages to produce the same level of risk-adjusted return. This effect is accentuated if the returns from negative trades are larger than those from positive trades. As Stewart found, the greater the number of independent positive value-added trades, the higher the probability that the portfolio will outperform during a given period (Stewart 1998).

The second definition, which we can call "relative" batting average, captures the intuition that a higher batting average might improve performance by limiting losses. What better way to limit drawdowns than consistent positive returns as reflected by a high batting average? The problem is that batting average does not measure the magnitude of returns. Consider a strategy characterized by many small gains with the occasional large loss—that is, the approach of "picking up nickels in front of a steam-roller" implemented by "arbitrage" strategies, such as Long Term Capital Management. Such a strategy has a high batting average, but the distribution of returns is negatively skewed. This return distribution is in fact less attractive to investors looking to limit large drawdowns. Alternatively, a strategy with many small losses that are compensated for by the occasional large gain, such as long volatility strategies, exhibits positive skew and provides a useful hedge but has a lower batting average. As such, although batting average does provide a measure of consistency, it is best used in combination with other measures.

EXAMPLE 8

Batting Average

t	R(*m*)	R(*B*)
1	−3.06%	−3.59%
2	6.31%	3.09%
3	6.00%	6.03%
4	3.20%	1.57%
5	−9.05%	−7.98%
6	−4.08%	−5.23%
7	4.33%	7.00%
8	−5.71%	−4.51%
9	12.75%	8.92%
10	5.37%	3.80%
11	0.33%	0.01%
12	5.68%	6.68%

1 Using the return information in the table, what is the manager's batting average relative to the benchmark?

A 42%

B 58%

C 67%

2 A limitation of batting average is that it does **not**:

A measure the magnitude of returns.

B measure the frequency of positive outcomes.

C allow different strategies to be distinguished by the frequency of trades.

Solution to 1:

B is correct. The manager outperformed the benchmark in 7 out of the 12 periods (t = 1, 2, 4, 6, 9, 10, and 11).

Solution to 2:

A is correct. The batting average does not measure the magnitude of returns. Strategies characterized by many small gains with the occasional large loss will have high batting averages, but the distribution of returns will be negatively skewed. This return distribution is in fact less attractive to investors that want to limit large drawdowns.

3.3 Qualitative Considerations in Manager Due Diligence

The goal of manager due diligence is to weigh the potential risks that may arise from entering into an investment management relationship and entrusting assets to a firm. Although it is impossible to eliminate all potential risks, the allocator must assess how the firm will manage the broad range of risks it is likely to face in the future. This section outlines the general aspects of manager due diligence and the particular questions the investor needs to answer.

Investment due diligence examines and evaluates the qualitative considerations that illustrate that the manager's investment process is repeatable and consistently implemented. The objective is to understand whether the investment philosophy, process, people, and portfolio construction satisfy the assumption that past performance provides some guidance for expected future performance. That is, performance measurement, attribution, and appraisal are reliable selection criteria. In addition, it is important to remember that investment managers are businesses. Regardless of the strength of the investment process or historical performance, investment management firms must be operated as successful businesses to ensure sustainability. Operational due diligence examines and evaluates the firm's policies and procedures, to identify potential risks that might not be captured in historical performance and to assess the firm's sustainability.

3.3.1 *Investment Philosophy*

The investment philosophy is the foundation of the investment process. Every investment strategy is based on a set of assumptions about the factors that drive performance and the manager's beliefs about their ability to successfully exploit these sources of return. The investment manager should have a clear and concise investment philosophy.

First, every manager makes assumptions about market efficiency, including the degree and the time frame. Passive strategies assume markets are sufficiently efficient and that active management adds only negative value after transaction costs and fees. As a result, passive strategies seek to earn risk premiums. A **risk premium** is the expected return in excess of a minimal-risk ("risk-free") rate of return that accrues to bearing a risk that is not easily diversified away—so-called systematic risk. In contrast, active strategies assume markets are sufficiently inefficient for a long enough period that mispriced securities can be identified and exploited.

Strategies also typically make assumptions about the dynamics and structures of the market, such as the following: The correlation structure of the market is sufficiently stable over the investment horizon to make diversification useful for risk management; prices eventually converge to intrinsic value, which can be estimated by using a discounted cash flow model; or market prices are driven by predictable macroeconomic trends.

Passive strategies seek to capture return through exposure to systematic risk premiums, such as equity risk, duration risk, or credit risk. These strategies can also look to capture alternative risk premiums. such as liquidity risk, natural disaster risk (e.g., insurance-linked securities, such as catastrophe bonds and quota shares), volatility risk, or some combination of these premiums (e.g., distressed strategies seek to capture credit and liquidity risk premiums).

Active strategies seek to capture return by exploiting market inefficiencies. These opportunities typically arise when market behavior deviates from the manager's assumptions. Generally speaking, inefficiencies can be categorized as behavioral or structural.

- *Behavioral inefficiencies* are perceived mispricings created by the actions of other market participants, usually associated with biases, such as trend following or loss aversion. These inefficiencies are temporary, lasting long enough for the manager to identify and exploit them before the market price and perceived intrinsic value converge.
- *Structural inefficiencies* are perceived mispricings created by external or internal rules and regulations. These inefficiencies can be long lived and assume a continuation of the rules and regulations rather than a convergence.

It is important to evaluate these assumptions and the role they play in the investment process to understand how the strategy will behave through time and across market environments.

- Can the manager clearly and consistently articulate their investment philosophy? It is hard to have confidence in the repeatability and efficacy of an investment process when the manager, and investment personnel, cannot explain the assumptions that underpin the process. This clarity also provides a consistency check that the investment process and personnel are appropriate for the stated philosophy.
- Are the assumptions credible and consistent? That is, does the decision maker agree with the assumptions underlying the strategy, and are these assumptions consistent with the investment process? A decision maker who believes a market is efficient would likely not find the assumptions of an active manager in that market credible. In the decision maker's judgment, the assumptions must support a repeatable and robust investment process.
- How has the philosophy developed over time? Ideally, the philosophy is unchanged through time, suggesting a repeatable process. If philosophy has evolved, it is preferred that changes are judged to be reasonable responses to changing market conditions rather than a series of ad hoc reactions to performance or investor flows. Such changes suggest a lack of repeatability and robustness.
- Are the return sources linked to credible and consistent inefficiencies? The decision maker must judge whether the investment philosophy is based on an inefficiency that is based on an informational advantage, likely a behavioral inefficiency by interpreting information better than other market participants, or a structural inefficiency that suggests the investment process is repeatable.

If the source of return is linked to a credible inefficiency, there is the additional issue of capacity. Capacity has several related aspects, such as the level of assets the strategy or opportunity can absorb without a dilution of returns, the number of opportunities or securities available, and the ability to transact in a timely manner at or near the market price—that is, liquidity. Overall, capacity is the level, repeatability, and sustainability of returns that the inefficiency is expected to support in the future.

- Does the inefficiency provide a sufficient frequency of opportunity and level of return to cover transaction costs and fees? If so, does this require leverage?

- Does the inefficiency provide a repeatable source of return? That is, can the opportunity be captured by a repeatable process, or is each opportunity unique, requiring a different process of skill set to exploit?
- Is the inefficiency sustainable? That is, at what asset level would the realized return from the inefficiency be unacceptably low? Sustainability will be a function of the market's depth and liquidity, as well as how much capital is allocated, either by the manager or competitors, to the inefficiency.

EXAMPLE 9

Investment Philosophy

1 Which of the following is **not** an important consideration when evaluating a manager's investment philosophy?
   - A What are the compensation arrangements of key employees?
   - B Are the investment philosophy assumptions credible and consistent?
   - C Can the manager clearly and consistently articulate their investment philosophy?

2 Generally speaking, inefficiencies can be categorized as:
   - A large and small.
   - B internal and external.
   - C structural and behavioral.

3 Which of the following is **not** an important consideration when evaluating the capacity of an inefficiency?
   - A Does the strategy rely on unique information?
   - B Does the inefficiency provide a repeatable source of return?
   - C Does the inefficiency provide a sufficient frequency of opportunity and level of return to cover transaction costs and fees?

Solution to 1:

A is correct. Employee compensation is a legal and compliance issue considered as part of operational due diligence.

Solution to 2:

C is correct. Behavioral inefficiencies are created by the actions of other participants in the market. These inefficiencies are temporary, lasting long enough for the manager to identify and exploit them before the market price and perceived intrinsic value converge. Structural inefficiencies are created by external or internal rules and regulations. These inefficiencies can be long lived and assume a continuation of the rules and regulations rather than a convergence.

Solution to 3:

A is correct. The uniqueness of information used by the manager is a consideration when evaluating the assumptions of the investment process.

3.3.2 *Investment Personnel*

Before discussing the investment process, we first explore the subject of investment personnel. An investment process can only be as good as the people who create and implement it, and even the best process can be compromised by poor execution by the people involved. This view is not a question of liking the manager or team but of trusting that they possess the expertise and experience to effectively implement the strategy.

- Does the investment team have sufficient expertise and experience to effectively execute the investment process? The need for expertise is self-evident. The greater the experience, particularly managing the current strategy across market environments, the greater the confidence in the manager's ability to effectively execute the investment process. As noted with drawdowns, it is especially instructive to see how the manager responded to stressed markets and poor performance.
- Does the investment team have sufficient depth to effectively execute the investment process? A strategy that focuses on a small universe of publicly traded stocks might not require a large investment team. A global macro or multi-strategy fund, which holds positions across numerous global markets, likely requires a large team with expertise and experience supporting the manager.
- What is the level of key person risk? A strategy that is overly dependent on the judgment or particular skills of an individual or small team of people faces **key person risk**, an overreliance on an individual or individuals whose departure would negatively affect the strategy's performance.
- What kinds of agreements (e.g., non-compete) and incentives (ownership, bonus, pay) exist to retain and attract key employees to join and stay at the firm?
- What has been the turnover of firm personnel? High personnel turnover risks the loss of institutional knowledge and experience within the team.

3.3.3 *Investment Decision-Making Process*

The investment decision-making process has four elements: signal creation, signal capture, portfolio construction, and portfolio monitoring.

3.3.3.1 Signal Creation (Idea Generation) An investment signal is a data point or fact that can be observed early enough to implement as an investment position. The basic question is, how are investment ideas generated? The efficient market hypothesis posits that the key to exploiting inefficiencies is to have information that is all of the following:

- **Unique:** Does the strategy rely on unique information? If so, how is this information collected, and how is the manager able to retain an informational edge, particularly in a regulatory environment that seeks to reduce informational symmetries?
- **Timely:** Does the strategy possess an information timing advantage? If so, how is this information collected, and how is the manager able to retain a timing edge, particularly in a regulatory environment that seeks to reduce informational symmetries?
- **Interpreted differently:** Interpretation is typically how managers seek to differentiate themselves. Does the manager possess a unique way of interpreting information? Or does the manager claim their strategy possesses a "secret sauce" component or that its team is simply smarter than other managers?

3.3.3.2 Signal Capture (Idea Implementation) The second step is signal capture, translating the generated investment idea into an investment position.

- What is the process for translating investment ideas into investment positions?
- Is this process repeatable and consistent with the strategy assumptions?

- What is the process, and who is ultimately responsible for approving an investment position?

The Investment Process

One of the first indications that something was amiss at Bernard L. Madoff Investment Securities was Harry Markopolos's inability to reconcile the return track record with the investment process. In addition to observing the unrealistically consistent nature of the claimed returns, Markopolos concluded that there was no way to generate the returns legally using the claimed investment process. Further analysis convinced him that Madoff's returns resulted not from front running—that is, taking positions to exploit knowledge of investor trade flows—but rather from fraud.

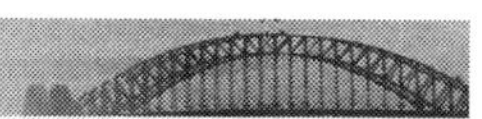

Self-Reported Risk Factors

Requesting and obtaining self-reported risk factors not only is important for understanding the manager's investment process but also provides an interesting operational check. A manager should readily comply with all requests for risk reporting. If not, it suggests a lack of transparency that may become challenging for monitoring the manager and strategy in the future. Additionally, it might indicate an inability to generate essential reports, which raises questions about the firm's policies and procedures.

All risk reporting should be meaningful, consistent, accurate, and timely. A lack of meaningful reporting indicates that the reports are not useful in monitoring the manager and that there is a lack of transparency. In the worst case, the manager does not understand the risk exposures or does not want to disclose them.

A lack of consistent reporting also reduces the usefulness of the reporting. Inconsistent reports preclude the ability to track levels and trends of important risk factors. The manager may be choosing to selectively report particular risks that they deem important or interesting. In the worst case, it may mean that the manager is selectively reporting in order to hide risks created by deviations from the stated investment process.

A lack of accuracy suggests that the manager cannot properly measure portfolio risks or is intentionally misreporting results. A lack of timeliness reduces the reports' usefulness and suggests either inefficient procedures or attempts to manipulate the flow of information. In all of these cases, poor risk reporting, at a minimum, suggests a reevaluation of the manager and, if issues are identified, potential termination.

3.3.3.3 Portfolio Construction The third element is portfolio construction; how investment positions are implemented within the portfolio. This element begins to capture the manager's risk management methodology. Good investment ideas need to be implemented properly to exploit opportunities and capture desired risk premiums. It is also important that portfolio construction is consistent with the investment philosophy and process as well as the expertise of the investment personnel.

- How are portfolio allocations set and adjusted? The allocation process should be consistent with investment philosophy and process. For example, if the portfolio is actively managed, its turnover should agree with the frequency of signals generated and the securities' liquidity. The allocation process should be well-defined and consistently applied, supporting the repeatability of the investment process. For example, are allocations made quantitatively or qualitatively?
- Are portfolio allocations based on the manager's conviction? In other words, do the positions the manager believes will most likely outperform or exhibit the greatest outperformance receive the largest active overweighting, and the securities the manager believes will underperform receive the largest active underweighting?
- How have the portfolio characteristics changed with asset growth? Has the number and/or characteristics of the positions held changed to accommodate a larger amount of AUM?
- Does the portfolio use **stop-losses** to manage risk? If so, are they hard (positions are automatically sold when the loss threshold is reached) or soft (positions are evaluated when the loss threshold is reached)? Although stop-losses represent a clear risk management approach, the goal of protecting against large losses must be balanced with the risk of closing positions too frequently.
- What types of securities are used? Does the manager use derivatives to express investment ideas? What experience does the manager have investing in these securities? The manager should be sufficiently well-versed and experienced with the securities used to understand how they will behave in different market environments.
- How are hedges implemented? What security types are used? How are hedge ratios set? Consider a manager that focuses on stock selection to generate alpha and hedges to reduce or remove market risk. The hedges must be sized correctly, or they can be ineffective (underhedged) or they can overwhelm stock selection (overhedged), with performance driven more by beta than by alpha.
- How are long and short ideas expressed? Are they paired—that is, each long position has a corresponding short position—or are long and short positions established independently? How long and short positions are allocated is important for understanding the portfolio's overall exposure. If long and short positions are paired, with the idea of capturing alpha as prices converge while offsetting market risk, the positions must be well-matched and sized correctly.

An important risk is liquidity. Strategies that are not intending to capture a liquidity risk premium must be aware of portfolio liquidity in terms of adapting to changing information, changing market conditions, and changing investor liquidity demands. An existing portfolio consisting of illiquid securities will be more costly to change, not only to take advantage of new opportunities but also to trade because of higher transaction costs. There is the additional cost of having to sell positions at inopportune times as a result of market events or investor liquidity demands. When assessing security liquidity, it is important to consider all of the assets under management for that particular manager and investment process.

- What percentage of the portfolio can be liquidated in five business days or less? What percentage requires more than 10 business days to liquidate? The less liquid the portfolio, the higher the transaction costs if the manager is forced to sell one or more positions. A more liquid portfolio offers flexibility if the manager faces unexpected investor liquidity demands or rapidly changing market conditions.

- What is the average daily volume weighted by portfolio position size?
- Have any of the portfolio holdings been suspended from trading? If so, what is the name of the company, and what are the circumstances pertaining to the suspension?
- Are there any holdings in which ownership by the firm across all portfolios collectively accounts for more than 5% of the market capitalization or float of the security?
- What is the firm's trading strategy? Does the investment manager tend to provide liquidity or demand it? Has the trading strategy changed in response to asset growth?

3.3.3.4 Monitoring the Portfolio The investment decision-making process is a feedback loop that consists of ongoing monitoring of the portfolio in light of new information and analysis. This monitoring includes an assessment of both external and internal considerations. External considerations include the economic and financial market environments. Has anything meaningful occurred that might affect the manager's ability to exploit the market inefficiency that is the strategy's focus? Internal considerations include the portfolio's performance, risk profile, and construction. Has anything changed that might signal potential style drift or other deviations from the investment process? Ongoing monitoring and performance attribution help to ensure that the manager remains appropriate for the clients' mandates.

3.3.4 *Operational Due Diligence*

Performance appraisal assumes that reported returns are accurate and fully reflect the manager's risk profile. Unfortunately, as we have seen, this assumption is not always true. Although investment due diligence is one step toward understanding these risks, one must remember that investment managers are real businesses, and in many cases they are small businesses with a high degree of risk. Regardless of the strength of the investment process or the historical investment results, investment management firms must be operated as a successful business in order to ensure their sustainability. This requirement creates the potential for business risk, a misalignment of interests between the manager and the investor, and weaknesses in the firm's infrastructure that represent latent risks to the investor. Operational due diligence analyzes the integrity of the business and seeks to understand and evaluate these risks by examining and evaluating the firm's policies and procedures.

A strong back office (support staff) is critical for safeguarding assets and ensuring that accurate reports are issued in a timely manner. The manager should have a robust trading process that seeks to avoid human error. A repeatable process requires consistent implementation. The allocator needs to understand the following:

- What is the firm's trading policy?
- Does the firm use soft dollar commissions? If so, is there a rigorous process for ensuring compliance?
- What is the process for protecting against unauthorized trading?
- How are fees calculated and collected?
- How are securities allocated across investor accounts, including both pooled and separately managed accounts? The allocation method should be objective (e.g., based on invested capital) to avoid the potential to benefit some investors at the expense of others.

- How many different strategies does the firm manage, and are any new strategies being contemplated? Is the firm's infrastructure capable of efficiently and accurately implementing the different strategies?
- What information technology offsite backup facilities are in place?
- Does the firm have processes, software, and hardware in place to handle cybersecurity issues?

An important constituent of the infrastructure is third-party service providers, including the firm's prime broker, administrator, auditor, and legal counsel. They provide an important independent verification of the firm's performance and reporting.

- Are the firm's third-party service providers known and respected?
- Has there been any change in third-party providers? If so, when and why? This information is particularly important with regard to the firm's auditor. Frequent changes of the auditor is a red flag and may mean the manager is trying to hide something (see the story about Bayou Group LLC in Section 4.3).

The risk management function should be viewed as an integral part of the investment firm and not considered a peripheral function. The extent to which integration exists provides insight into the firm's culture and the alignment of interests between the manager and the investor. The manager should have a risk manual that is readily available for review:

- Does the portfolio have any hard/soft investment guidelines?
- How are these guidelines monitored?
- What is the procedure for curing breaches?
- Who is responsible for risk management?
- Is there an independent risk officer?

3.3.5 *Firm*

An investment management firm must operate as a successful business to ensure sustainability. A manager that goes out of business does not have a repeatable investment process. An important aspect of manager selection is assessing the level of business risk.

- What is the ownership structure of the firm?
- What are the total firm AUM and AUM by investment strategy?
- What is the firm's breakeven AUM (the asset base needed to generate enough fee revenue to cover total firm expenses)?
- Are any of the firm's strategies closed to new capital?
- How much capital would the firm like to raise?

A firm that is independently owned may have greater autonomy and flexibility than a firm owned by a larger organization, but it may have a higher cost structure and lack financial support during market events, raising potential business risks. Outside ownership could create a situation in which the outside owner has objectives that conflict with the investment strategy. For instance, the outside owner might want to increase the asset base to generate higher fee revenue, but this action could prevent the portfolio from holding lower-capitalization stocks. Ideally, ownership should be spread across as many employees as is feasible and practical. A firm managing a smaller asset base may be more nimble and less prone to dilution of returns but will likely have lower revenues to support infrastructure and compensate employees. At a minimum, the asset base needs to be sufficient to support the firm's current expenditures.

Last, and by no means least important, are legal and compliance issues. It is critical that the firm's interests are aligned with those of the investor.

- What are the compensation arrangements for key employees? For example, are any people compensated with stock in the firm, and if so, what happens to this stock when they leave the firm?
- Do employees invest personal assets in the firm's strategies? As with most elements, a balance is required. Having some "skin in the game" (investing their own money) is likely to motivate the manager, but too much may lead the manager to be overly concerned with personal/business risk rather than investment risk.
- Does the firm foster a culture of compliance?
- What is covered in the compliance manual?
- Has the firm or any of its employees been involved with an investigation by any financial market regulator or self-regulatory organization?
- Has the firm been involved in any lawsuits?
- Are any of the firm's employees involved in legal actions or personal litigation that might affect their ability to continue to fulfill their fiduciary responsibilities?

Hiring a manager requires trust. A firm's culture as expressed by its compliance policies and procedures should provide a level of confidence that the manager's and investor's interests are aligned.

Warning Signs

Bernard "Bernie" L. Madoff ran one of the biggest frauds in Wall Street history. In hindsight, there were many red flags over the years that indicated there was something wrong with his investment management process. The firm claimed to generate steady returns in every market environment. Mr. Madoff was known to disregard questions about his strategy, arguing that his business was too complicated for outsiders to understand. He ran a secretive business and kept his financial statements locked up. He also operated as a broker/dealer with an asset management division, profiting from trading commissions rather than the investment management fees that hedge funds charged.

The structure seemed odd to other investment professionals, raising concerns about the firm's legitimacy. A large conflict of interest arises when a manager uses a related-party broker/dealer. A manager that owns a broker/dealer loses the incentive to use other brokers that offer better execution for the investors. Another large red flag was raised when it was determined that the firm used a small, unknown auditor with only three employees. It soon became clear that if Mr. Madoff claimed the strategy was so complex that no one could understand it, a small, three-person audit firm would not be able to audit the financial statements (Zuckerman 2008).

3.3.6 *Investment Vehicle*

There are two broad options for implementing investment strategies: individual separate accounts and pooled (or commingled) vehicles. An additional operational consideration is evaluating whether the investment vehicle is consistent with the investment process and suitable for the investor IPS. Separate accounts offer additional control, customization, tax efficiency, reporting, and transparency advantages, but these come at a higher cost. The question is whether the benefit to the investor is larger than the additional cost.

In a pooled or commingled vehicle, the money from multiple investors is held as a single investment and managed to a particular mandate without potential customization for any investor. All accounts are managed the same or *pari passu* (on equal footing). Such vehicles include open-end funds, closed-end funds, exchange-traded funds, exchange-traded notes, and hedge funds. As the name infers, a separately managed account (SMA) vehicle holds the money in a segregated account in the investor's name. The funds are managed to a particular mandate with the potential to customize the strategy for each investor. The advantages of SMA vehicles include the following:

- **Ownership:** In an SMA, the investor owns the individual securities directly. This approach provides additional safety should a liquidity event occur. Although the manager continues to make investment decisions, these decisions will not be influenced by the redemption or liquidity demand of other investors in the strategy. An SMA also provides clear legal ownership for the recovery of assets resulting from unforeseen events, such as bankruptcy or mismanagement.
- **Customization:** SMAs allow the investor to potentially express individual constraints or preferences within the portfolio. SMAs can thus more closely address the investor's particular investment objectives.
- **Tax efficiency:** SMAs offer potentially improved tax efficiency because the investor pays taxes only on the capital gains realized and allows the implementation of tax-efficient investing and trading strategies.
- **Transparency:** SMAs offer real-time, position-level detail to the investor, providing complete transparency and accurate attribution to the investor. Even if a pooled vehicle provides position-level detail, such information will likely be presented with a delay.

The investment due diligence process is used to evaluate pooled and separate account vehicles. If the manager has a single mandate, all investor assets within the pool and across the SMAs are managed *pari passu*, and the investment due diligence process can cover both vehicles. If the SMA is customized, separate investment due diligence may be required to account for differences in security selection or portfolio construction. In addition, there are operational due diligence considerations.

- **Cost:** Separate accounts represent an additional operational burden on the manager, which translates into potentially higher costs for the investor. SMAs do not scale as easily as pooled vehicles. Once a pooled investment is established and the fixed costs paid, the cost of each new investor is largely the incremental costs of custody, trading larger positions, and generating an additional report. With an SMA, a new account must be established for each investor. In addition, SMAs are likely to face higher transaction costs to the degree that trades cannot be aggregated to reduce trade volumes. These costs are a function of the extent to which the strategy is customized or traded differently to accommodate different investor needs.
- **Tracking risk:** Customization of the strategy creates tracking risk relative to the benchmark, which can confuse attribution because performance will reflect investor constraints rather than manager decisions.
- **Investor behavior:** Transparency, combined with control and customization, allows for potential micromanagement by the investor—that is, the investor attempting to manage the portfolio. Such an effort not only negates the benefit of hiring a manager but is particularly problematic if these changes decrease

the portfolio's value. Potential investor behaviors include performance chasing, familiarity bias (being overly averse to unfamiliar holdings), and loss aversion (a tendency to disaggregate the portfolio and not appreciate the value of hedging).

The allocator's goal is to evaluate the costs and benefits of the vehicle used and judge its suitability for the IPS:

- Is the vehicle structure consistent with the investment process?
- Does the manager have the operational infrastructure necessary to manage the SMA?
- Is there a benefit to holding the securities in a separate account? If so, are these benefits sufficient to compensate for additional costs?
- Is tax efficiency an important objective of the IPS?
- Are there concerns that the available transparency and ability to customize will result in decisions by the investor that do not add value?

EXAMPLE 10

Pooled Investments and Separate Accounts

Which of the following are advantages of separately managed accounts compared with pooled investments?

A Typically lower cost

B Potential management of the portfolio by the investor

C Ability to take close account of individual client constraints or preferences

Solution:

C is correct. With SMAs, the investor owns the individual securities directly and can potentially express individual constraints or preferences within the portfolio. In particular, SMAs offer potentially improved tax efficiency because the investor pays taxes only on the capital gains realized and allows the implementation of tax-efficient investing and trading strategies.

3.3.7 *Evaluation of the Investment's Terms*

An additional and important aspect of manager selection is understanding the terms of the investment as presented in the prospectus, private placement memorandum, and/or limited partnership agreement. These documents are, in essence, the contract between the investor and the manager, outlining each party's rights and responsibilities. Although these documents cover numerous topics, this section focuses on liquidity and fees. The objective of the decision maker is to determine whether the liquidity and fee structure make the manager suitable for the investor's needs and the "best" manager for expressing a particular portfolio need.

3.3.7.1 Liquidity Different vehicles provide different degrees of liquidity. Liquidity is defined as the timeliness with which a security or asset can be sold at or near the current price. The same criteria can be applied to managers.

The most liquid vehicles are closed-end funds and ETFs. As listed securities, they can be bought and sold intra-day, and the price received will depend on the trading volume and depth of the fund. The obvious advantage of these funds is ease of trading, although there can be some price uncertainty for less liquid funds, particularly when trying to buy or sell a large number of shares.

Open-end funds are slightly less liquid, providing daily liquidity but also price certainty; shares are bought and sold at the end-of-day NAV. As noted in Section 3.2.1, mutual funds often charge a fee if the fund is sold shortly after purchase, creating a gap between the sales price and NAV. Regardless, in most cases, mutual funds provide sufficient liquidity.

Unlike open-end funds, ETFs, or closed-end funds, limited partnerships, such as hedge funds, venture capital funds, and private equity funds, typically require investors to invest their money for longer periods. Hedge fund liquidity has four basic features: redemption frequency, notification period, lockup, and gates. Redemption frequency indicates how often an investor can withdraw capital from the fund, and the notification period indicates how far in advance of the redemption investors must tell the fund of their intention to redeem. A lockup is the initial period, after making an investment, during which investors cannot redeem their holding. Lockups have two types: a hard lock, which allows for no redemptions, and a soft lock, which charges a fee, paid into the fund, for redemptions. A mutual fund redemption fee is equivalent to a hedge fund soft lock. Gates limit the amount of fund assets, or investor assets that can be redeemed at one redemption date.

Private equity and venture capital funds provide the least liquidity. Investors are committed to contribute specific amounts over time, or capital calls, during the investment phase and then receive distributions and capital as investments are divested during the remaining term of the fund. Funds can have up to 5-year investment phases and 10-year terms, as well as the option to extend the term.

The obvious disadvantage of partnership liquidity terms is the reduced flexibility to adjust portfolio allocations in light of changing market conditions or investor circumstances, as well as the reduced ability to meet unexpected liquidity needs. The advantage of such terms is that they do lock up capital for longer horizons, allowing funds to take long-term views and hold less liquid securities—such as start-up companies, buyouts, turnarounds, real estate, or natural resources—with reduced risk of having to divest assets at inopportune times in response to redemption requests. An additional advantage, which was apparent during the 2008 financial crisis, is that limited liquidity imposes this long horizon view on investors, reducing or removing their ability to overreact.

Because SMA assets are held in the investor's name, the securities in the portfolio can be sold at any time. As a result, an SMA's liquidity will depend on the liquidity of the securities held. An SMA holding listed large-cap stocks will likely be highly liquid, whereas an investor in an SMA that holds unlisted or illiquid securities will have to accept a discount when selling.

3.3.7.2 Fees and Expenses The evaluation of expenses in investment performance appraisal is best understood in the context of the efficient market theory. The traditional perspective on market efficiency asserts that an asset's market price is the best available estimate of its true or intrinsic value. An advanced and more modern formulation—rational efficient markets (Grossman and Stiglitz 1980)—is based on observations that

- passive investors can, without cost, accept the market price of an asset as an estimate of its intrinsic value, and
- active investors can, at a cost, gather and analyze information in an attempt to improve on market prices as indicators of value.

Therefore, rational investors would not incur the expenses of information gathering and analysis if they did not expect to be rewarded by earning higher gross-of-expenses returns. According to this argument, in equilibrium, active investors should, at the margin, earn just sufficient extra returns to cover their additional expenses. As a result, performance appraisal should be conducted using net returns:

- The investor's wealth is affected only by net returns. For a given level of risk, the investor benefits only if, net of expenses, an active manager earns positive incremental returns relative to a passive alternative.
- The level of expenses affects the level of realized returns.
- The structure of the expenses affects the measured volatility of realized returns.

Fees typically have two components:

- **Management fee:** A fixed percentage fee based on assets under management.
- **Incentive fee:** A fee charged as a percentage of net returns above a specified hurdle rate, also known as a preferred return, and above a high-water mark (HWM).[3] A hurdle rate is the minimum return below which the incentive fee is not charged. The HWM is the highest cumulative return attained by the fund, net of fees, and the incentive fee is paid only for returns above the HWM.

The Impact of Fee Structure on Net Returns

Consider four fee structures applied to the same 12-month return series gross of fees:

- 0.50% management fee, 0% performance fee
- 0.50% management fee, 15% performance fee
- 1.50% management fee, 0% performance fee
- 1.50% management fee, 15% performance fee

The fees are accrued at the end of each month. This example is a simplification but illustrates the important effects of fee level and structure on net performance. As Exhibit 15 shows, the average monthly gross return is 0.72% with a 1.37% monthly standard deviation. Not surprisingly, charging a management fee (MF) lowers the level of realized return without affecting the standard deviation of the series. The management fee is a constant shift in the level and thus does not affect volatility. The addition of a performance fee (PF) also lowers the level of realized returns but has the added effect of lowering the realized standard deviation. This dynamic occurs because in up months, the performance fee is accrued, and in down months, it is subtracted from the accrual balance to reflect the appropriate fee for the cumulative performance. This accounting has the effect of adjusting the monthly returns toward zero and lowering the measured volatility. The larger the performance fee, the more pronounced this effect. Exhibit 16 shows a graph of the cumulative returns for each fee structure.

3 This discussion of incentive fees does not cover fulcrum fees; the topic is beyond the scope of this reading.

Exhibit 15 Effects of Expense on Portfolio Performance

		Monthly Gross Return												Avg.	
MF	PF	1	2	3	4	5	6	7	8	9	10	11	12	Ret.	S.D.
0.0%	0.0%	2.00%	3.00%	−0.20%	−0.50%	0.50%	0.90%	1.00%	−2.00%	1.50%	2.00%	−0.50%	1.00%	0.72%	1.37%
0.5%	0.0%	1.96%	2.96%	−0.24%	−0.54%	0.46%	0.86%	0.96%	−2.04%	1.46%	1.96%	−0.54%	0.96%	0.67%	1.37%
0.5%	15.0%	1.66%	2.51%	−0.21%	−0.46%	0.39%	0.73%	0.81%	−1.74%	1.24%	1.66%	−0.46%	0.81%	0.57%	1.16%
1.5%	0.0%	1.88%	2.88%	−0.32%	−0.62%	0.37%	0.77%	0.88%	−2.12%	1.37%	1.88%	−0.62%	0.88%	0.59%	1.37%
1.5%	15.0%	1.59%	2.44%	−0.28%	−0.53%	0.32%	0.66%	0.74%	−1.81%	1.17%	1.59%	−0.53%	0.74%	0.50%	1.16%

Exhibit 16 Cumulative Return

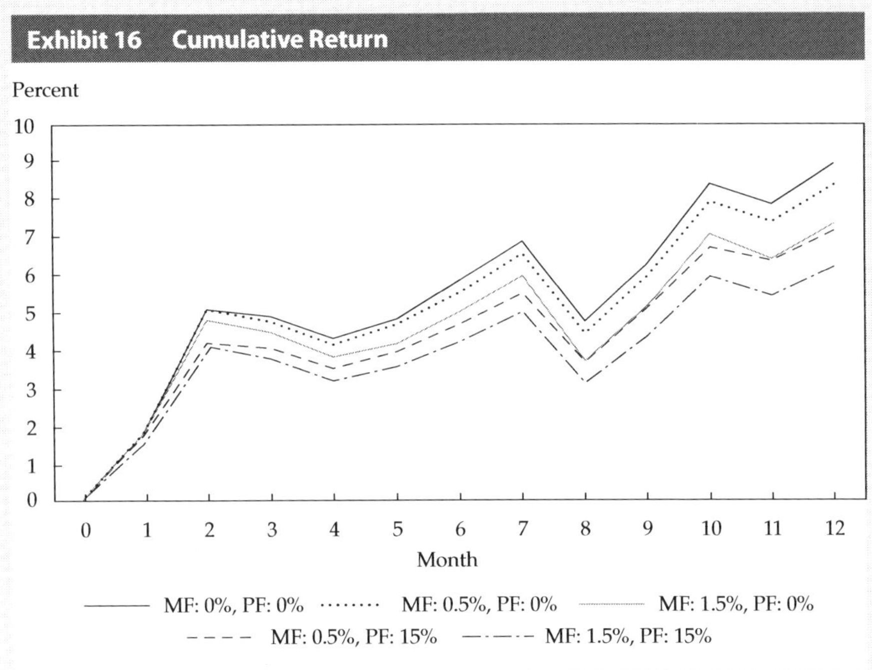

Given the potentially significant effect of expenses, a clear distinction must be drawn between performance analysis based on gross returns and net of expenses returns.

An additional consideration is the different degree of uncertainty between expenses and the potential added value of the active portfolio manager. Expenses are paid for certain, whereas the added value of the active strategy compared with the passive strategy is uncertain. For example, suppose an active strategy is expected to generate a gross return that is 2% greater than the passive strategy, but the cost of the active strategy is 2% greater than the passive strategy. A risk-averse investor would likely prefer the passive strategy; although the expected net return of the strategies is the same, the uncertainty of the outperformance would be unappealing. The riskier the active strategy, the greater the return volatility and the greater the volatility of the added value relative to the passive strategy. The significance is, the added value of the active strategy has to be sufficiently large and certain to justify the higher cost of the strategy.

In sum, the presence of positive significant average excess return is evidence for manager skill. This excess return, however, must be net of fees and expenses for the benefit of this skill to accrue to the investor.[4] The preference is for more linear compensation to the manager to reduce the incentives to change the portfolio's risk profile at inflection points, as discussed in the style drift section.

4 INVESTMENT MANAGER CONTINUANCE

The evaluation of a manager does not end with their initial engagement. Investment managers must be monitored on an ongoing basis to confirm that they retain the integrity of their investment process and remain suitable for their role in managing the investor's portfolio. Many changes can take place within the firm that can either erode or enhance the integrity of the investment process as well as the firm's sustainability. Even if the manager is no longer the "best," there is a balance between the opportunity cost of not replacing a manager and the actual cost of replacing a manager.

In the following, we examine selected issues that arise in deciding whether to retain or dismiss an investment manager that was previously hired, beginning with the principle for rationally updating the evaluation of manager skill based on new information. This concept is variously called the manager continuance decision or the manager retention decision.

4.1 Adherence to Investment Philosophy and Process

Monitoring investment managers is essentially ongoing investment and operational due diligence. The objective is to confirm that the rationale for selecting a manager remains in place. As with a security, if you would not buy it today, would you want to continue to hold it in your portfolio? Typically, monitoring follows a regular schedule (quarterly or annual), but there are triggers that indicate a review should be done.

Often the first indication for many investors to replace a manager is lagging performance, but performance can often be a delayed indicator of a lack of skill or operational problem at the firm—or simply "noise." As such, relying on performance as a signal might not be timely or useful. In some ways, it is also the least desirable reason to terminate a manager because of the risk of performance chasing. Performance-based termination should result from a reason that brings into doubt the skill of the manager or makes the manager unsuitable. Lagging performance can be a signal to reevaluate the manager but should have an identifiable source or be sufficiently sustained to lead to doubts about the manager's skill.

One potential reason for lagging returns is dilution, the decline in skill (lower alpha for active, higher tracking risk for passive) because of external competition or growth in strategy AUM. This situation is a particular problem for active managers. The underlying assumption is that markets tend toward efficiency. As more investors identify or become aware of an inefficiency, more capital is directed to exploit it. Even if the inefficiency does not disappear, the proceeds are shared by more managers, thus reducing the alpha available to each. This dynamic creates a constant challenge for manager selection, because great performance begets large asset growth, which entails the potential risk of changes to the investment process and personnel to accommodate this growth.

4 Ultimately, the net return to the investor accounts not only for fees and expenses but also for taxes. This more complex issue is beyond the scope of this reading.

An additional concern is large idiosyncratic drawdowns. If the manager cannot explain or suffers from multiple events, it becomes difficult for investors to form expectations for future performance. Repeated events can also signal a non-repeatable or inconsistently implemented investment process.

4.2 Style Drift

An important aspect of selection and manager continuance is determining whether the manager continues to adhere to the stated investment philosophy and decision-making process. Style drift is a deviation from the stated risk factor exposures, identified using RBSA or HBSA, that underpin the investment philosophy and process. For managers whose investment process is expected to consistently adhere to a particular investment style, style drift undermines confidence in the repeatability of the investment process and compromises confidence in the manager's ability to repeat past performance in the future. Style drift may also suggest that the manager is no longer suitable for the investor and may be detrimental to portfolio asset allocation. The manager was hired to fill a particular role within the overall portfolio, and deviations from this role can expose the investor to unwanted risks.

Style drift should be viewed as a relative rather than an absolute concept. Thus, it is important to be clear on how style is measured and what might signal that style drift has occurred.

- **Measurement:** Style is measured as the risk factor exposures that explain the manager's performance. This attribution requires a benchmark, and so style drift is often considered to be deviations from the benchmark. This view has its limitations.
- **Skew versus drift:** Some manager investment processes are broad in nature and will naturally deviate from a stated benchmark. This deviation can be more of a benchmarking issue than a style drift issue and might reflect the lack of a precise benchmark rather than style drift.
- **Cyclical versus structural:** A manager's risk factors will naturally fluctuate through time. The key question is whether these differences represent a short-term deviation of the strategy or a longer-term change in the investment process and/or its implementation.

One method of determining and screening for style drift are **snail trail charts**.[5] A snail trail chart displays information about the manager's return characteristics through time. Exhibit 17 displays the rolling 36-month returns and standard deviations for an enhanced equity index portfolio relative to the Russell 1000 benchmark. The larger the symbol, the more recent the observation.

5 Examples are from Meier 2009.

Exhibit 17 Manager Risk/Return, January 2001–December 2007

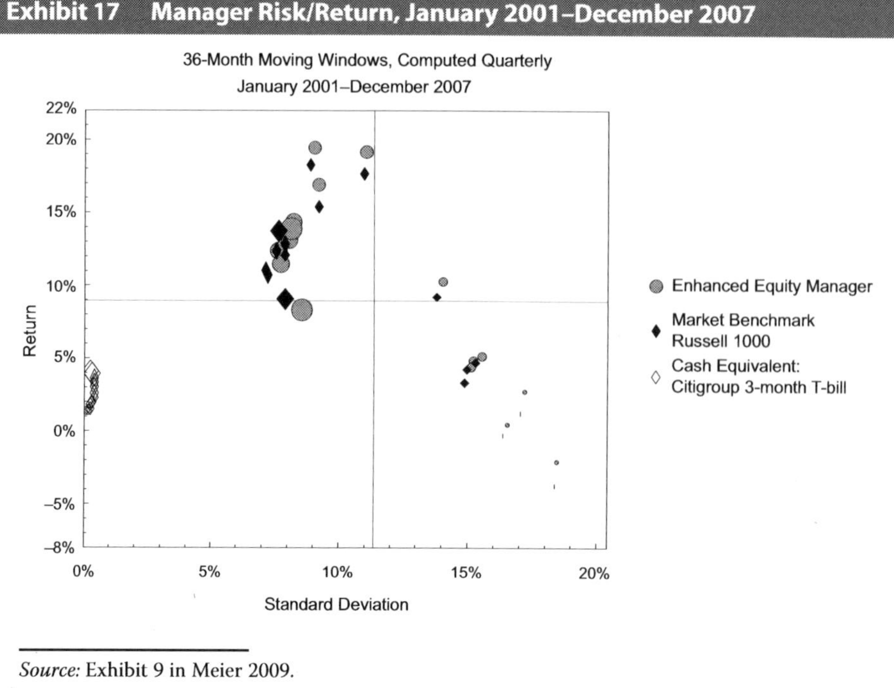

Source: Exhibit 9 in Meier 2009.

The trail shows that the manager's standard deviation initially declined and has been between 7.5% and 10% for the most recent windows. The manager's return initially increased but has declined through the most recent windows.

Notice that the return and standard deviation of the benchmark follows a similar pattern. To examine the manager's alpha and tracking risk, the graph can be recast to display the rolling 36-month relative returns (portfolio returns in excess of the benchmark return) and relative risk (tracking risk). Exhibit 18 displays the rolling 36-month excess returns and tracking risk for the enhanced equity index portfolio relative to the Russell 1000 benchmark. Again, the larger the symbol, the more recent the observation.

Exhibit 18 Manager Risk/Return, January 2001–December 2007

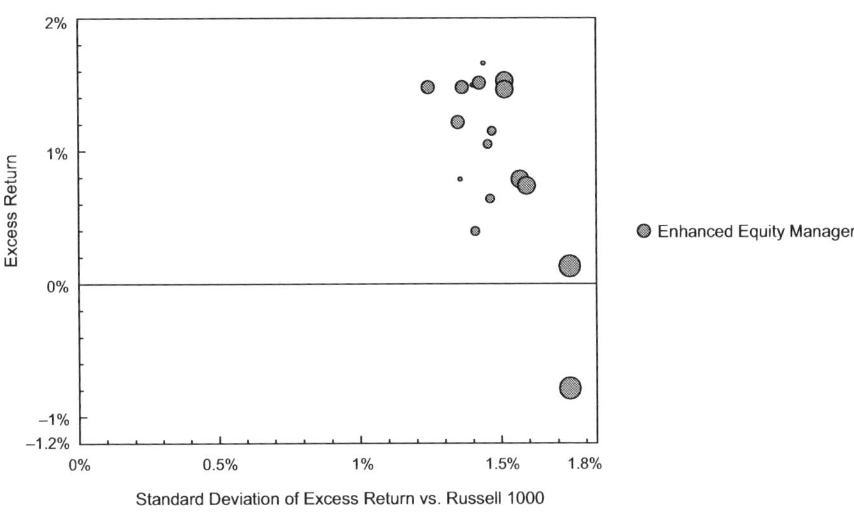

Source: Exhibit 10 in Meier 2009.

In this case, we are interested in the level and consistency of the realized tracking risk. As an enhanced index strategy, the goal is consistent positive excess return with limited and consistent tracking risk. Consistent performance through time would result in all of the dots falling on top of, or in close proximity to, each other. In this case, the manager has generated consistent tracking, and although there has been a slight increase through time, the overall level of tracking risk has not increased substantially. Excess return, however, has declined noticeably for the most recent windows and is now negative. Such a pattern signals the need for further investigation into the underlying causes of the underperformance.

Snail trail plots can also be used to track the evolution of other portfolio characteristics. For example, we could plot the weighted average market capitalization on the *y*-axis (small-cap to large-cap) relative to a weighted average style on the *x*-axis (value to growth) for an equity portfolio manager. A consistent pattern of shifting market capitalization or value/growth tilt would signal potential style drift and the need for further investigation into the portfolio's changing risk exposures.

A consistent deviation, or strong trend away, from the risk factor exposures indicated by the investment philosophy and process is a signal of style drift. Style drift can happen for a variety of reasons. The evaluator must determine whether the deviations represent a long-term change in the manager's investment philosophy and process rather than the result of short-term market movements. An example would be a temporary over-allocation to larger-capitalization stocks because of price appreciation that is subsequently remediated, versus the holding of internet stocks by value funds during the dot-com markets. The allocator needs to understand and evaluate the following:

- Did the manager deviate from their investment process to chase returns in any given quarter or year?
- Did the manager engage in trading that is excessive relative to the investment process?

- Did the manager buy securities that do not fit the parameters of the investment process?
- Does the manager have, and implement, a credible process for remediating breaches of the portfolio investment guidelines?

The allocator also needs to evaluate whether the deviation represents internal issues, such as a potential misalignment of interests.

- **Compensation:** Managers that are just below the threshold for earning a performance-based fee have the incentive to increase portfolio risk as the end of the evaluation period approaches.
- **Business risk:** Managers that have suffered large losses may no longer focus on investment risk but focus solely on maintaining AUM by reducing portfolio risk at the expense of return.
- **Dilution:** The reduction in available investment opportunities may lead a manager to strategies outside of the stated investment philosophy and process (and potentially outside their area of expertise) in an attempt to find additional sources of return.
- **Portfolio construction:** Changing risk exposures can signal potential implementation issues, such as poorly constructed hedges or poorly constructed trades. As noted, asset growth and the need to allocate a larger portfolio can result in changes to the number and characteristics of positions held.

Any evidence of an apparently permanent change in the investment philosophy or process, evidence of internal issues or a misalignment of interests, or inadequate policies and procedures to remediate style drift warrants re-evaluation and potential termination.

The Importance of Monitoring

As yields reached historic lows in 2012 and 2013, many bond funds used new and creative ways to boost paltry performance. Morningstar reported in 2013 that 352 funds that it tracks that are classified as bond funds actually held stock as well (Light 2013). The bond managers likely bought stock because the dividend yields on the stocks they purchased were higher than the current yield they could obtain on bonds. But such news can come as a real surprise to investors. Morningstar reported that a large percentage of the bond funds that were investing in stocks actually compared their funds against a bond benchmark. This scenario is a clear example of style drift that investors should avoid. The investor has no certainty about how large the allocation to stocks might become, which could bring about a huge deviation from the target asset allocation. Investors need to control the asset allocation decision by moving funds out of pure bond funds rather than accepting style drift within their bond funds.

EXAMPLE 11

Style Analysis in Continuation Decisions

1 Which of the following is **not** a reason why style drift is an important aspect of monitoring?

A Style drift might signal that the vehicle structure is not consistent with the investment process.

B Style drift might suggest the manager is no longer suitable for the investor and may be detrimental to portfolio asset allocation.

C Evidence of style drift undermines confidence in the repeatability of the investment process and compromises confidence is the manager's ability to repeat past performance in the future.

2 Which of the following is a sign of alignment of manager and client interests?

A The manager closes a strategy to new money.

B The manager consistently raises or lowers risk exposures toward the end of the year.

C The manager significantly lowers the portfolio risk exposure in response to a sharp decline in the market.

3 Style analysis does **not** include:

A understanding how the risk exposures evolve through time.

B determining whether a manager has lost key personnel.

C understanding the manager's risk exposures relative to the benchmark.

4 Style analysis that is **not** consistent with the philosophy and investment process can suggest that:

A the manager has a high batting average.

B the manager's return profile is asymmetrical.

C the investment process is not repeatable or is not consistently implemented.

Solution to 1:

A is correct. An important aspect of monitoring is determining whether the manager continues to adhere to the stated investment philosophy and decision-making process. Style drift is the deviation from the stated risk factor exposures that underpin the investment philosophy and process. Style drift may also suggest the manager is no longer suitable for the investor and be detrimental to portfolio asset allocation.

Solution to 2:

A is correct. Consistent year-end changes in risk exposures may be the result of compensation issues. Reducing risk after suffering a large loss may indicate business risk is dominating investment risk and a focus on maintaining AUM at the expense of return. A manager should close a strategy if it believes that adding new capital could dilute returns

Solution to 3:

B is correct. Although a firm can be only as good as the people running it, evaluating personnel turnover is a consideration of operational due diligence, not style analysis.

Solution to 4:

C is correct. Style analysis should be consistent with the manager's philosophy and the investment process. If it is not, the process might be unrepeatable or inconsistently implemented. Or, if the risk exposures deviate through time, such an inconsistency may indicate style drift.

EXAMPLE 12

Adherence to Stated Investment Philosophy

Which of the following is consistent with a manager adhering to a stated investment philosophy and process?

A Style drift

B Increasing leverage

C Occasional underperformance

Solution:

C is correct. Terminating a manager because of lagging short-term performance runs the risk of performance chasing, although sustained underperformance can lead to doubts about the manager's skill. Increasing leverage can indicate dilution and an attempt to maintain a sufficient level of return in response to declining opportunities. As noted, style drift undermines confidence in the repeatability of the investment process and compromises confidence in the manager's ability to repeat past performance in the future. If the manager cannot explain or suffers from multiple drawdowns, it becomes difficult to form expectations for future performance. Repeated events can also signal a non-repeatable or inconsistently implemented investment process.

4.3 Operational Monitoring

Operational monitoring entails confirming the integrity of the business by reviewing a firm's policies and procedures and understanding any changes.

A firm can be only as good as the people running it. It is essential to understand the firm's organization. Changes in the organization can be positive or may reflect internal turmoil and instability. As such, it is important to understand the context and reason behind personnel changes. All else being equal, personnel continuity is a sign of stability. Unexpected departures or high personnel turnover do not necessarily suggest immediately firing the manager, but continued issues can distract individuals from focusing on the investment process and are likely to negatively affect performance.

- Has there been any loss of key personnel without a clear and credible succession plan? The more senior the people leaving, the more problematic.
- Has there been any turnover among investment or operational staff? An inability to retain staff may signal potential cultural or compensation issues and increases investment and operational risks because of inexperience.
- Have there been new hires, and what are the roles of any new hires? The expertise and experience of an individual must be suitable for the role he or she plays.
- High turnover among sales and investor service may indicate that the firm's future business prospects have dimmed.
- All else being equal, it is of greater concern if the departed personnel take similar positions at competing companies and of less concern if they leave for roles that have greater responsibility. Conversely, it is of even less concern if they leave for a completely different vocation—for instance, running a charitable foundation or opening an art gallery.

Legal and compliance issues should be reviewed to confirm that the firm's interests remain aligned with those of the investor.

- Have there been any changes in third-party service providers? A potential red flag is a change in prime broker, auditor, or administrator. Third-party service providers independently verify manager performance. Changes can signal attempts to reduce transparency or hide potential issues.
- Have there been any changes in the compensation arrangements of key employees?
- Have there been any changes in the way employees invest personal assets in the firm's strategies?
- Have there been any changes in the compliance manual?
- Has the firm or any of its employees been involved in an investigation by any regulator or self-regulatory organization?
- Has the firm been involved in any lawsuits?
- Are any of the firm's employees involved in legal actions or personal litigation that might affect their ability to continue to fulfill their fiduciary responsibilities?

Bayou Group LLC

Bayou Group LLC was founded in 1995 by Samuel Israel III and James Marquez. In 2008, Israel and Daniel Marino were charged with defrauding investors of $450 million and sentenced to 20 years in jail. Israel received an additional two-year sentence after attempting to fake his own death. Only $100 million was recovered for investors. Bayou's story is not new or original; rather, it is a representative case that displayed several red flags that are important for recognizing and identifying potential operational issues:

- **Change in auditor:** In 1998, Bayou changed auditors from Grant Thornton to a small, little-known firm. The firm, Richmond–Fairfield Associates, was founded by Bayou's CFO Daniel Marino. Bayou fired its independent auditor and created its own accounting firm with the intent of issuing fraudulent statements to hide losses. Documents given to prospective investors in 2003 stated Bayou Funds was founded in 1997, editing out the poor returns from 1996. The firm lost 12% that year, according to Grant Thornton's audit.
- **Affiliated broker/dealer:** All of the fund's trades were executed by Bayou Securities, a brokerage firm owned by Mr. Israel. As noted, this affiliation created a conflict of interest. Bayou Securities and Israel continued to earn commissions even as the fund was losing money. Furthermore, it removed an independent source of information about the veracity of the fund's actual trading results and returns. In 1998, as part of an attempt to recoup losses, Israel planned to credit commissions back to the fund to offset trading losses.
- **Inconsistent transparency:** Although investors liked Mr. Israel's frequent and plain spoken commentary, one investor noticed communication was less frequent when the fund was down and redeemed.

- **Unconfirmed work history:** Israel reported that he was the head trader at Omega Advisors, a multi-billion-dollar hedge fund run by former Goldman Sachs partner Leon Cooperman. It was later reported that Israel worked at Omega for only 18 months, and although he executed orders on behalf of senior partners, he was not the head trader.
- **Legal issues:** Bayou was subject to a breach of contract lawsuit in 2003 in which a former employee alleged Bayou had possibly violated US SEC regulations governing the operation of hedge funds. The case went to arbitration, and the outcome is not publicly available. Samuel Israel was arrested in 1999 for DUI and criminal possession of a controlled substance. It was later revealed that Israel relied heavily on painkillers.

Several investors and consultants who had recommended the fund to their investors appeared to become wary of Bayou's operations in 2002 and 2004 and recommended investors redeem.

This review of legal or compliance issues also includes new revelations about previous but unreported cases. There is a large presumption of trust when hiring a manager, and anything that violates that trust—particularly withholding of material information—is unacceptable and grounds for termination.

Monitoring growth in AUM is important because a dilution of skill is possible as more capital is directed to a particular opportunity. As noted, one risk is that the manager exhibits style drift in an attempt to maintain performance or implement the strategy with a larger asset base. Ideally, the manager can identify new opportunities. Alternatively, the manager can close the strategy to maintain performance for current investors. Closing a fund or strategy shows desirable discipline and alignment of interests by the manager but raises issues for a decision maker that uses the manager for multiple investors. Preferably, the firm has a clearly stated policy and process for closing funds, but in all cases, such a policy must be applied consistently across strategies and investors.

- **Hard close:** The manager closes to all investors. Although this arrangement protects current investors, it presents a problem to the allocator. If a comparable replacement can be found, there is the added operational cost of maintaining two managers for the same role in the portfolio with higher name count and due diligence costs. If no comparable can be found, there is the problem of basis risk—that is, different investors in the same model realizing different returns. Firing the manager to create a common model, however, penalizes those investors that held the closed manager (opportunity cost of holding a less skillful manager). A hard close can also result in hesitancy to fire the manager for fear of losing access to the manager. For capacity-constrained mandates, it is generally a good practice to negotiate a paid-in-capital capacity amount with the manager before engaging with them.
- **Soft close:** The manager closes to new investors but remains open to current investors. Although this arrangement also protects current investors, it increases the risk that the fund eventually undertakes a hard close.

The decision of whether closure requires terminating a manager requires balancing these issues.

In addition to the level of AUM, it is important to understand the composition of the firm's investor base. A higher concentration in a limited number of investors increases **liquidity risk**, the potential for redemptions that negatively affect the portfolio's value. A potentially unstable investor base warrants reevaluating the manager.

- What is the investor breakdown (e.g., percentage endowment/foundation, high net worth /family office, pensions, and individuals)? A broader, more diverse investor base is less susceptible to large, concentrated outflows.

EXAMPLE 13

Adherence to Stated Investment Philosophy

1 Objectives of investment due diligence include:

A the qualitative evaluation of the portfolio construction process and the manager's operational efficiency to determine the manager's ability to precisely trade at low cost with minimal cash.

B the examination and evaluation of the firm's policies and procedures to identify potential risks that may not be captured in historical performance and assess the firm's sustainability.

C understanding whether the investment philosophy, process, people, and portfolio construction satisfy the assumption that past performance provides some guidance for expected future performance.

2 Objectives of operational due diligence include:

A the qualitative evaluation of the portfolio construction process and the manager's operational efficiency to determine the manager's ability to precisely trade at low cost with minimal cash.

B the examination and evaluation of the firm's policies and procedures to identify potential risks that may not be captured in historical performance and assess the firm's sustainability.

C understanding whether the investment philosophy, process, people, and portfolio construction satisfy the assumption that past performance provides some guidance for expected future performance.

Solution to 1:

C is correct. Investment due diligence examines and evaluates the qualitative considerations that the manager's investment process is repeatable and consistently implemented. This procedure entails understanding whether the investment philosophy, process, people, and portfolio construction satisfy the assumption that past performance provides some guidance for expected future performance.

Solution to 2:

B is correct. Regardless of the strength of the investment process or historical performance, investment management firms must be operated as successful businesses to ensure sustainability. Operational due diligence examines and evaluates the firm's policies and procedures to identify potential risks that may not be captured in historical performance and assess the firm's sustainability.

EXAMPLE 14

Manager Continuance

1 Which of the following are considerations in manager continuation?

I. Adherence to the investment philosophy and process

II. Operational due diligence

III. The costs and benefits of replacing the manager

A I and II

B II and III

C I, II, and III

2 Which of the following are considerations in investment manager continuation?

I. Confirming that the manager retains the integrity of their investment process

II. Confirming that the manager remains suitable for their role in the portfolio

III. Confirming the sustainability of the firm

A I and II

B II and III

C I, II, and III

Solution to 1:

C is correct. Monitoring is essentially ongoing investment and operational due diligence. The objective is to confirm that the rationale for selecting a manager remains in place. Even if the manager is no longer the "best," there is a balance between the opportunity cost of not replacing a manager and the actual cost of replacing a manager.

Solution to 2:

C is correct. It is essential that investment managers be monitored on an ongoing basis to confirm that the manager retains the integrity of their investment process and remains suitable for their role in the portfolio. Many changes can take place within the firm that can either erode or enhance the integrity of the investment process and sustainability of the firm.

5 PASSIVE MANAGER SELECTION

The framework and discussion has largely focused on active manager selection. Although much of the discussion can be applied to selecting a passive manager, there are differences, particularly in the importance of components examined and their interpretation. The differences are driven by the decision maker's assumption that the expected benefit of identifying alpha is insufficient to cover the associated costs. The reason for this assumption is either because the decision maker believes markets are efficient and positive alpha is not available; positive alpha is available but the decision maker lacks the ability to identify skilled managers; or positive alpha is available and the decision maker can identify skilled managers, but the level of alpha available is insufficient to cover the costs after accounting for manager's costs and the decision maker's costs, time, and effort. The manager's ability to capture the appropriate risk premiums of the benchmark thus becomes important.

Tracking tolerance is the manager's tracking risk target. If the manager replicates the benchmark's risk premiums, the result should be low active share, low alpha, and systematic risk exposures close to one.

The qualitative considerations concern the appropriateness of the portfolio construction process and the manager's operational efficiency.

There are two approaches to passive management construction:

- **Full replication** entails holding all of the constituents in the index at the same weight as the index. This approach is appropriate for large portfolios or indexes with a limited number of constituents. It would work for the FTSE 100 Index or FTSE 500 Index but would be difficult for the Russell 2000 Index or bond indexes.
- **Sampling** involves holding a subset of the benchmark universe weighted so that the risk premiums of the portfolio match the risk premiums of the benchmark within tolerances. Sampling works for even large indexes and can limit the number of portfolio holdings while optimizing to match risk premiums. Sampling has potential basis risk, which is the risk that the realized risk factors of the portfolio do not equal those of the benchmark.

Regardless of the passive management construction approach used, the manager's operational efficiency key to success is precise trading at low cost with minimal cash.

- Is the index and manager portfolio conducive to full replication? As noted, full replication is practical for large asset levels and indexes with few constituents. That is, the implied portfolio position sizes must be sufficiently large to support efficient trading. Numerous small position sizes would result in higher transaction costs and greater tracking risk.
- Is the sampling process robust and able to consistently replicate the key risk factors?
- Does the manager's infrastructure support precise trading at low cost for the necessary volume?

A passive manager's quantitative goal is to replicate a benchmark's returns. This process entails the following:

- **Low tracking risk:** If the manager replicates the risk premiums of the benchmark, the result should be low active share (see Example 15), zero alpha, and systematic risk exposures close to one.
- **Replicate the benchmark risk factor exposures:** Full replication by design should closely replicate the benchmark's risk factors. Sampling techniques typically seek to replicate the benchmark factors by constraining the expected portfolio risk factors to equal those of the benchmark. Whether sampling technique is able to replicate the risk factors can be determined by using style analysis techniques.
- **Low premium/discount:** Premium/discount (the difference between the fund's NAV and its market price) represents potential tracking risk as the premium/discount changes through time based on investor demand. Typically, this risk relates to closed-end funds but also applies to ETFs that have suspended the

creation and redemption of shares.[6] Even if premium/discount is expected to be zero in the long term, basis risk exists if the premium/discount fluctuates. Lee, Shleifer, and Thaler (1991) propose that premiums and discounts are driven by changes in investor sentiment.

EXAMPLE 15

Passive Managers

1 Tracking tolerance is:
  - A the manager's tracking risk target.
  - B the difference in return between the manager and the benchmark.
  - C calculated as the standard deviation of the return difference between the manager and the benchmark.

2 A sampling approach to passive management involves:
  - A actively selecting securities that are perceived to be mispriced.
  - B holding all of the constituents within the index at the same weight as the index.
  - C holding a subset of the benchmark universe weighted so that the portfolio's risk premiums match the benchmark's risk premiums.

3 The quantitative goal of replicating the benchmark does **not** entail:
  - A low tracking risk.
  - B high premium/discount.
  - C replicating the benchmark risk factors.

Solution to 1:

A is correct. Tracking tolerance is the manager's tracking risk target. Tracking risk is the difference in return between the manager and the benchmark, calculated as the standard deviation of the return difference between the manager and the benchmark.

Solution to 2:

C is correct. Full replication involves holding all of the constituents within the index at the same weight as the index. Active management seeks to select securities that are perceived to be mispriced.

Solution to 3:

B is correct. A quantitative goal of passive management is a low premium/discount to reduce potential tracking risk as the premium/discount changes through time.

6 Suspending the creation and redemption of shares can result in premiums and discounts because the ability to arbitrage, which works to limit the spread between the market price and NAV, is removed. For example, if an ETF is trading at a premium, an investor could buy the underlying components at roughly the NAV and then exchange the basket for a share of the ETF, which is trading at the higher market price.

SUMMARY

Evaluating an investment manager is a complex and detailed process. It encompasses a great deal more than analyzing investment returns. A manager's investment results are historical, and as we know, past performance does not guarantee future performance. In conducting investment manager due diligence, the focus is on understanding how the investment results were achieved and assessing the likelihood that the manager will continue to follow the same investment process that generated these returns. This process also entails operational due diligence, including an evaluation of the integrity of the firm, its operations, and personnel, as well as evaluating the vehicle structure and terms. As such, due diligence involves both quantitative and qualitative analysis.

The purpose of this reading is to provide a framework that introduces and describes the important elements of the manager selection process:

- Investment manager selection involves a broad set of qualitative and quantitative considerations to determine whether a manager displays skill and the likelihood that the manager will continue to display skill in the future. Although performance appraisal is necessary, it is insufficient for manager selection.
- Manager continuance requires ongoing monitoring to confirm that the manager adheres to their investment philosophy and process and remains suitable for their role in portfolio, as well as to confirm that no operational issues have arisen.
- For a manager to be the "best" choice, they must be suitable for the investor. The IPS captures the investor's objectives, constraints, and preferences, thereby providing the criteria for determining suitability.
- The selection of active and passive investment managers differs in the importance of components examined and their interpretation. The differences are driven by the decision maker's assumption that the expected benefit of identifying alpha is insufficient to cover the associated costs.
- Passive managers are evaluated on their ability to capture the appropriate risk premiums of the benchmark. If the manager replicates the benchmark's risk premiums, the result should be low tracking risk, low active share, low alpha, and systematic risk exposures close to one. The qualitative considerations concern the appropriateness of the portfolio construction process and the manager's operational efficiency.
- The qualitative analysis consists of investment due diligence, which evaluates the manager's investment process, investment personnel, and portfolio construction; and operational due diligence, which evaluates the manager's infrastructure.
- A Type I error is hiring or retaining a manager who subsequently underperforms expectations—that is, rejecting the null hypothesis of no skill when it is correct. A Type II error is not hiring or firing a manager who subsequently outperforms, or performs in line with, expectations—that is, not rejecting the null hypothesis when it is incorrect.
- The manager search and selection process has three broad components: the universe, a quantitative analysis of the manager's performance track record, and a qualitative analysis of the manager's investment process. The qualitative analysis includes both investment due diligence and operational due diligence.
- Batting average measures the frequency of positive outcomes that can be used to measure the consistency of performance. The limitation is that batting average does not measure the magnitude of returns. As such, it is best used in combination with other measures.

- Capture ratio measures the asymmetry of returns, and a ratio greater than 1 indicates that the attractive characteristic of greater participation in rising versus falling markets. Drawdown is the loss incurred in any continuous period of negative returns. An asymmetrical return profile or avoiding large drawdowns can result in higher risk-adjusted returns caused by the proportionally larger gain needed to recover from increasingly large losses. In addition, a manager that experiences larger drawdowns may be less suitable for investors closer to the end of their investment horizons.
- The investment philosophy is the foundation of the investment process. The philosophy outlines the set of assumptions about the factors that drive performance and the manager's beliefs about their ability to successfully exploit these sources of return. The investment manager should have a clear and concise investment philosophy. It is important to evaluate these assumptions and the role they play in the investment process to understand how the strategy will behave over time and across market environments. The investment process has to be consistent and appropriate for the philosophy, and the investment personnel need to possess sufficient expertise and experience to effectively execute the investment process.
- The prospectus, private placement memorandum, and/or limited partnership agreement are, in essence, the contract between the investor and the manager, outlining each party's rights and responsibilities. The provisions are liquidity terms and fees. The obvious disadvantages of limited liquidity terms are the reduced flexibility to adjust portfolio allocations in light of changing market conditions or investor circumstances, as well as the reduced ability to meet unexpected liquidity needs. The advantage is that it allows the funds to take long-term views and hold less liquid securities with reduced risk of having to divest assets at inopportune times in response to redemption requests. A management fee lowers the level of realized return without affecting the standard deviation, whereas a performance fee has the added effect of lowering the realized standard deviation. The preference is for more-linear compensation to reduce the incentives to change the portfolio's risk profile at inflection points.
- Style analysis, understanding the manager's risk exposures relative to the benchmark, is an important component of performance appraisal and manager selection, helping to define the universe of suitable managers.
- Returns-based style analysis is a top-down approach that involves estimating the risk exposures from an actual return series for a given period. Although RBSA adds an additional analytical step, the analysis is straightforward and should identify the important drivers of return and risk factors for the period analyzed. It can be estimated even for complicated strategies and is comparable across managers and through time. The disadvantage is that RBSA is an imprecise tool, attributing performance to an unchanging average portfolio during the period that might not reflect the current or future portfolio exposures.
- Holdings-based style analysis is a bottom-up approach that estimates the risk exposures from the actual securities held in the portfolio at a point in time. HBSA allows for the estimation of current risk factors and should identify all important drivers of return and risk factors, be comparable across managers and through time, and provide an accurate view of the manager's risk exposures. The disadvantages are the additional computational effort, dependence on the degree of transparency provided by the manager, and the possibility that accuracy may be compromised by stale pricing and window dressing.
- Style drift is the deviation from the stated risk factor exposures that underpin the investment philosophy and process. It undermines confidence in the repeatability of the investment process and compromises confidence in the manager's

ability to repeat past performance in the future. Style drift may also suggest the manager is no longer suitable for the investor and may be detrimental to portfolio asset allocation.

- The objective of investment manager monitoring is to confirm that the rationale for selecting the manager remains in place. As such, termination should result from a reason that brings into doubt the manager's skill or makes the manager unsuitable. Deviations from the investment philosophy and investment process can signal a potential decline in skill, a non-repeatable or inconsistently implemented investment process, or misalignment of incentives.
- The comparison of individual separate accounts relative to pooled (or commingled) vehicles evaluates whether the vehicle is consistent with the investment process, whether it is suitable for the investor IPS, and whether the benefits outweigh the additional costs.

REFERENCES

Constable, Neil, and Jeremy Armitage. 2006. "Information Ratios and Batting Averages." *Financial Analysts Journal*, vol. 62, no. 3 (May/June):24–31.

DALBAR. 2005. *QAIB 2005: Quantitative Analysis of Investor Behavior*. Boston: DALBAR, Inc.

Grossman, Sanford, and Joseph Stiglitz. 1980. "On the Impossibility of Informationally Efficient Markets." *American Economic Review*, vol. 70, no. 3 (June):393–408.

Khandani, Amir E., and Andrew W. Lo. 2011. "What Happened to the Quants in August 2007? Evidence from Factors and Transactions Data." *Journal of Financial Markets*, vol. 14, no. 1 (February):1–46.

Lee, Charles M.C., Andrei Shleifer, and Richard Thaler. 1991. "Investor Sentiment and the Closed-End Fund Puzzle." *Journal of Finance*, vol. 46, no. 1 (March):75–109.

Light, Joe. 2013. "Bond Funds Running Low on...Bonds." *Wall Street Journal* (1 May 2013).

Meier, John. 2009. "Investment Performance Appraisal." In *Investment Performance Measurement: Evaluating and Presenting Results*, Philip Lawton and Todd Jankowski. Hoboken, NJ: John Wiley & Sons, Inc.

Stewart, Scott D. 1998. "Is Consistency of Performance a Good Measure of Manager Skill?" *Journal of Portfolio Management*, vol. 24, no. 3 (Spring):22–32.

Stewart, Scott D. 2013. "Manager Selection." Charlottesville, VA: Research Foundation of CFA Institute.

Stewart, Scott D., John J. Neumann, Christopher R. Knittel, and Jeffrey Heisler. 2009. "Absence of Value: An Analysis of Investment Allocation Decisions by Institutional Plan Sponsors." *Financial Analysts Journal*, vol. 65, no. 6 (November/December):34–51.

Zuckerman, Gregory. 2008. "Fees, Even Returns and Auditor All Raised Red Flags." *Wall Street Journal* (13 December 2008).

PRACTICE PROBLEMS

1 Which of the following considerations would *most likely* be part of both the manager selection process and the performance appraisal process?

A Verifying risk metrics such as standard deviation

B Determining if the investment process can be consistently applied

C Assessing the likelihood that the investment organization will be a stable on-going firm

2 An investment policy statement that stipulates a need for short-term liquidity *most likely* rules out a manager whose portfolio is largely invested in:

A real estate.

B US short-term securities.

C exchange-traded securities.

3 Which of the following qualitative considerations is *most* associated with determining whether investment manager selection will result in superior repeatable performance?

A Transparency

B Investment process

C Operational process

4 A passive manager is more suitable than an active manager when an investor desires:

A low tracking risk.

B a highly skilled manager.

C significant positive alpha.

5 Which of the following statements about active and passive management is *most* accurate?

A Low tracking risk is consistent with an investor's assumption of market efficiency.

B Positive alpha is more likely achieved when a manager invests in an efficient market.

C Generally, there is an inverse relationship between tracking risk and attainable alpha.

6 Which of the following is *most likely* a key consideration in investment due diligence?

A Suitability of the investment vehicle

B Back office processes and procedures

C Depth of expertise and experience of investment personnel

7 When manager performance is mean reverting, a Type I error occurs when the investor:

A avoids hiring managers with weak short-term track records.

B does not fire a strong performing manager with a short-term track record.

C fires a poor performing manager and performance improves after the firing.

8 A decision-making investor is *most likely* to worry more about making a Type I error than a Type II error because:

A Type II errors are errors of commission.

B Type I errors are more easily measured.

C Type II errors are more likely to have to be explained as to why a skilled manager was fired.

9 An investor is considering hiring three managers who have the following skill levels:

Manager	Large-cap skill level	Small-cap skill level
1	Skilled	Unskilled
2	Skilled	Skilled
3	Unskilled	Unskilled

Type I and Type II errors both occur when the investor is:

A hiring Manager 1 for large-cap stocks and not hiring Manager 3 for small-cap stocks.

B hiring Manager 3 for large-cap stocks and not hiring Manager 2 for small-cap stocks.

C hiring Manager 3 for large-cap stocks and not hiring Manager 1 for small-cap stocks.

10 Suppose that the results of a style analysis for an investment manager are not consistent with the stated philosophy of the manager and the manager's stated investment process. These facts suggest the:

A absence of style drift.

B investment process may not be repeatable.

C manager should be included in the universe of potential managers.

11 Compared with holdings-based style analysis (HBSA), a returns-based style analysis (RBSA):

A is subject to window dressing.

B requires less effort to acquire data.

C is more accurate when illiquid securities are present.

12 A manager whose relative performance is worse during market downturns *most likely* has a capture ratio that is:

A less than one.

B equal to one.

C greater than one.

13 An investor gathers the following data about an investment manager:

Time	Manager Returns (%)	Benchmark Returns (%)
1	2.0	1.5
2	-1.0	-2.0
3	-0.5	-1.3
4	1.2	0.5
5	1.7	1.2
6	-2.0	-1.1
7	2.5	1.8
8	-0.6	-0.9
9	1.3	1.4
10	3.0	2.5

The downside capture is *closest* to:

A 0.77.

B 0.78.

C 1.31.

14 When an investment strategy generates many small gains with an occasional large loss in a generally rising market, the manager's absolute batting average will *most likely* be:

A less than the relative batting average.

B the same as the relative batting average.

C greater than the relative batting average.

15 Which of the following is consistent with the expectation that exploiting a structural inefficiency is repeatable?

A The inefficiency is a unique event that occurs infrequently.

B The level of gross return is equal to the amount of transaction costs and expenses.

C The aggregate value of all assets affected by the inefficiency is larger than the AUM of the manager and its competitors.

16 Which of the following is **not** a reason that an investor might favor a separately managed account rather than a pooled vehicle? The investor:

A is tax exempt.

B requires real-time details on investment positions.

C has expressed certain constraints and preferences for the portfolio.

17 Which of the following investment vehicles provide investors with the highest degree of liquidity?

A Open-end funds

B Private equity funds

C Limited partnerships

18 Which of the following statements is consistent with the manager adhering to a stated investment philosophy and investment decision-making process?

A Senior investment team members have left to form their own firm.

B A senior employee has been cited by the SEC for violating insider trading regulations.

C A large drawdown occurs because of an unforeseen political event in a foreign country.

19 A manager has a mandate to be fully invested with a benchmark that is a blend of large-cap stocks and investment-grade bonds. Which of the following is **not** an indication that style drift has occurred? The manager:

A initiates an allocation to small-cap stocks.

B decreases investments in investment-grade corporate bonds.

C increases allocation to cash in anticipation of a market decline.

20 Which of the following would *most likely* trigger a review of a manager's adherence to investment philosophy and process?

A The manager is inundated with a significant increase in assets under management.

B A snail trail chart shows 36-month excess returns fall on top of or close proximity to each other.

C The manager's chief investment officer retires and is replaced by the head of the investment team.

21 If the manager replicates the risk premiums of a passive benchmark, this should result in:

A high alpha.

B low active share.

C systematic risk exposure close to zero.

22 Which of the following investment policy statement (IPS) features would *most likely* prevent the investment committee of a socially responsible investment fund from selecting a manager that invests in weapon manufacturers or tobacco companies?

A Risk tolerance

B Return objectives

C Unique circumstances

23 The manager selection process begins by defining the universe of feasible managers. When defining this manager universe, the selection process should avoid:

A excluding managers based on historical risk-adjusted returns.

B identifying the benchmark against which managers will be evaluated.

C using third-party categorizations of managers to find those that might fill the desired role in the portfolio.

24 A passive manager and an active manager have the same benchmark. The passive manager will *most likely* have a:

A lower tracking risk than the active manager.

B higher management fee than the active manager.

C greater opportunity to generate alpha than the active manager.

25 An investor hires manager A and does not hire manager B. The investor has committed both Type I and Type II errors if:

A both manager A and B are unskillful.

B manager A is skillful and manager B is unskillful.

C manager A is unskillful and manager B is skillful.

26 Which of the following statements with respect to Type I and Type II errors in the manager selection process is correct?

A Type I errors create explicit costs.

B Type I errors are errors of omission.

C Type II errors are errors of commission.

27 A return distribution of skilled managers that is highly distinct from the return distribution of unskilled managers, *most likely* implies a:

A highly efficient market.

B low opportunity cost of not hiring a skilled manager.

C high opportunity cost of not hiring a skilled manager.

28 An advantage of a returns-based style analysis is that such analysis:

A is comparable across managers.

B is suitable for portfolios that contain illiquid securities.

C can effectively profile a manager's risk exposures using a short return series.

29 Which of the following types of style analysis use(s) a bottom-up approach to estimate the risk exposures in a portfolio?

A Returns-based style analysis only

B Holdings-based style analysis only

C Both return-based and holdings-based style analysis

30 In a quarter, an investment manager's upside capture is 75% and downside capture is 125%. We can conclude that the manager underperforms the benchmark:

A only when the benchmark return is positive.

B only when the benchmark return is negative.

C when the benchmark return is either positive or negative.

31 A manager's monthly returns for the second quarter are presented in Exhibit 1.

Exhibit 1

Month	Return
April	0.4%
May	–5.9%
June	–2.7%

The drawdown for the second quarter is *closest* to:

A –8.6%.

B –8.4%.

C –8.2%.

32 Which of the following is an accurate interpretation of a manager's 90% relative batting average?

A The manager had positive returns on 90% of the investment decisions.

B The manager's cumulative return was 90% of the benchmark's return.

C The manager matched or underperformed the benchmark in 10% of the periods.

33 Passive strategies seek to capture return through:

A exploiting behavioral inefficiencies.

B exposure to systematic risk premiums.

C exploiting mispricing created by rules and regulations.

34 Which of the following fee structures *most likely* decreases the volatility of a portfolio's net returns?

A Incentive fees only

B Management fees only

C Neither incentive fees nor management fees

35 An investor should prefer a pooled investment vehicle to a separately managed account when she:

A is cost sensitive.

B focuses on tax efficiency.

C requires clear legal ownership of assets.

36 Which of the following investment types is the most liquid?

A ETFs

B Hedge funds

C Private equity funds

37 Which of the following *most likely* indicates a lack of skill for a passive investment manager? The manager:

A exhibits high tracking risk.

B replicates the benchmark's risk factors closely.

C uses sampling rather than full replication for portfolio construction.

SOLUTIONS

1 A is correct. Performance appraisal is primarily a quantitative process that systematically evaluates the investment performance of a fund. This process would include using such risk metrics as standard deviation. In addition to qualitative considerations, manager selection includes assessment of the amount of risk assumed by the manager to generate results.

2 A is correct. An investor with shorter-term liquidity needs should not hold less liquid long-term assets, such as private equity or real estate.

3 B is correct. A critical element of manager selection is to assess if the investment process is superior, repeatable, and can be consistently applied.

4 A is correct. Low tracking risk of the benchmark is more consistent with the assumption of market efficiency, making a passive manager more suitable. A highly skilled manager would add more value and justify fees when acting in an active management role. Significant positive alpha for a passive manager suggests high tracking risk and potential for unintended risk exposures.

5 A is correct. Close tracking of the benchmark is consistent with an assumption of market efficiency. In an efficient market it is difficult to earn alpha and positive alpha is less likely to be achieved. In general, there is a direct, not an inverse, relationship between tracking risk and alpha.

6 C is correct. Experienced investment personnel is a key aspect of investment due diligence. A strong back office and suitable investment vehicles are key aspects of operational due diligence.

7 C is correct. A Type I error would be hiring a strong performer or firing a poor performer only to see a reversion in performance. Choices A and B describe Type II errors.

8 B is correct. Type I errors are more easily measured than Type II errors. In addition, Type I errors may be linked to the compensation of the decision maker. Type I errors are errors of commission, whereas Type II are errors in omission. Firing a skilled manager is less transparent to the investor.

9 B is correct. Hiring unskilled Manager 3 for large-cap stocks is an error of commission or Type I error, whereas not hiring skilled Manager 2 for small-cap stocks is an error of omission or Type II error.

10 B is correct. The results of the returns-based style analysis and the holdings-based style analysis should be consistent with the philosophy of the manager and the investment process. If this is not the case, it may suggest that the process is not repeatable or not consistently implemented. For these results the manager should not be included in the universe of potential managers, whereas if the results track over time they may suggest style drift.

11 B is correct. RBSA typically does not require a large amount of additional, or difficult to acquire, data. HBSA requires data on each security in the investment portfolio. HBSA is a snapshot of the portfolio at a single point of time and thus is subject to window dressing. Both HBSA and RBSA are subject to difficulties in interpreting returns when illiquid securities are present.

12 A is correct. A capture ratio less than one indicates the downside capture is greater than upside capture and reflects greater participation in falling markets than in rising markets.

13 A is correct. The downside capture is 0.77. The downside returns are:

Time	R(*m*) (%)	R(*B*) (%)
2	−1.0	−2.0
3	−0.5	−1.3
6	−2.0	−1.1
8	−0.6	−0.9
Geo. Avg.	−1.03	−1.33
Downside Capture = 0.77		

14 C is correct. The absolute batting average includes all positive returns, even those less than the benchmark return, which would not be included when computing the relative batting average.

15 C is correct. Given the amount of inefficient assets compared with the AUM of managers likely to exploit them provides some assurance that the inefficiency is repeatable. It would likely take some time for the inefficiency to converge to efficient valuation. The infrequent nature of the inefficiency and the zero marginal return suggest that the inefficiency is probably not worthwhile to pursue.

16 A is correct. The tax advantages to separately managed accounts do not accrue to a tax exempt investor. Choices B and C are considerations that reflect the investor's preferences and could be better satisfied using a separately managed account.

17 A is correct. Open-end funds provide daily liquidity; shares are bought and sold at the end-of-day NAV. Limited partnerships and private equity funds typically require investors to invest their money for longer periods.

18 C is correct. A large drawdown that results from an unforeseen event is explainable as a single isolated event that does not prohibit the manager from adhering to its investment philosophy and process. The events of senior team members leaving to form their own investment firm and an insider trading investigation by the SEC call into question the ability of the firm to adhere to its philosophy and decision-making process.

19 B is correct. In the normal course of business, the manager conforms to its style by reducing exposure to some class of investment grade bonds. Increasing allocation to cash and small-cap stocks is in violation of the mandate to be fully invested with equity exposure to large-cap stocks.

20 A is correct. As more funds are available to the manager, monitoring the growth in assets under management is important because a dilution of skill is possible as more capital is directed to a particular opportunity. A snail chart with data points on top of each other indicates consistent adherence to philosophy and process. Retirement of the CIO and replacement by head of the investment team would not trigger much concern if the replacement had worked closely with the retiring CIO.

21 B is correct. The manager replicating the risk premiums of the benchmark results in low active share, low alpha, and systematic risk exposures close to one.

22 C is correct. An investor's IPS will generally outline any unique circumstances that apply to their assets. Unique circumstances may include such factors as allowable investments and the types of risk exposures permitted. A socially responsible investment policy may prohibit investments in weapon manufacturers or tobacco companies. A and B are incorrect because an investment in weapons manufacturers or tobacco companies does not necessarily present higher risk or higher returns.

23 A is correct. The focus of the initial screening process is on building a universe of managers that could potentially satisfy the identified portfolio need and should not focus on historical performance. Identifying a benchmark is a key component of defining the manager's role in the portfolio, and third-party categorizations are an efficient way to build an initial universe which can then be further refined.

24 A is correct. Effective passive managers have low tracking risk relative to active managers, indicating that the portfolio's returns closely approximate the returns on the benchmark. As passive managers seek to closely match the risk and return characteristics of the benchmark rather than to outperform the benchmark, they have fewer opportunities to generate alpha than do active managers. Passive managers typically charge a lower fee than active managers within the same investment universe.

25 C is correct. Hiring an unskillful manager is a Type I error; rejecting a skillful manager is a Type II error. Therefore, both Type I and Type II errors are committed. Hiring a skillful manager and not hiring an unskillful manager are not errors.

26 A is correct. Hiring an underperforming manager (a Type I error—choosing a manager who underperforms expectations) creates an explicit, identifiable cost.

27 C is correct. When the two distributions are highly distinct, the unskilled managers are expected to significantly underperform the skilled managers, implying a high opportunity cost of not hiring the skilled managers. Efficient markets are likely to exhibit smaller differences of returns between skilled and unskilled managers.

28 A is correct. Returns-based style analysis on portfolios of liquid assets is generally able to identify the important drivers of return and the relevant risk factors for the period analyzed, even for complicated strategies. In addition, the process is comparable across managers and through time. If the portfolio contains illiquid securities, the lack of current prices on those positions may lead to an underestimation of the portfolio's volatility in a returns-based style analysis. Longer return series generally provide a more accurate estimate of the manager's underlying standard deviation of return.

29 B is correct. Holdings-based style analysis estimates the portfolio's risk exposures using the securities held in the portfolio (a bottom-up approach), whereas returns-based style analysis uses portfolio returns to estimate a portfolio's sensitivities to security market indexes (a top-down approach).

30 C is correct. Upside capture of 75% suggests that the manager only gained 75% of benchmark increase when the benchmark return was positive. Downside capture of 125% suggests that the manager lost 125% as much as the benchmark when the benchmark return was negative. Therefore, the manager underperformed the benchmark in both scenarios.

31 B is correct. To calculate drawdown—the cumulative peak-to-trough loss during a particular period—consecutive negative returns are geometrically linked:

$$
\begin{aligned}
(1 - 0.059) \times (1 - 0.027) - 1 &= (0.941 \times 0.973) - 1 \\
&= 0.9137 - 1 \\
&= -0.0844 \text{ or } -8.4\%
\end{aligned}
$$

A is incorrect because the monthly returns must be geometrically linked, not added. C is also incorrect because the positive April return should not be included when calculating the drawdown.

32 C is correct. A 90% relative batting average implies that the manager outperformed the benchmark in 90% of return periods; in other words, the manager matched or underperformed the benchmark in 10% of return periods.

33 B is correct. Passive strategies seek to capture return through exposure to systematic risk premiums, such as equity risk, duration risk, or credit risk. Active strategies seek to exploit inefficiencies in the market; such inefficiencies may be either behavioral inefficiencies or structural (created by internal or external rules and regulations) inefficiencies.

34 A is correct. Because incentive fees are fees charged as a percentage of returns (reducing net gains in positive months and reducing net losses in negative months), its use lowers the standard deviation of realized returns. Charging a management fee (a fixed percentage based on assets) lowers the level of realized return without affecting the standard deviation of the return series.

35 A is correct. Pooled investment vehicles are typically operated at a lower cost than separately managed accounts because operational costs can be spread among multiple investors. An investor who is focused on tax efficiency would prefer a separately managed account because a separate account allows the implementation of tax-efficient investing and trading strategies, and the investor pays taxes only on capital gains realized. If the investor requires clear legal ownership, they would prefer a separately managed account in which the investor owns the individual security directly.

36 A is correct. ETFs, as listed securities that can be bought and sold intra-day, are the most liquid vehicles. Hedge fund liquidity features—such as redemption frequency, notification period, lockup, and gates—limit the liquidity of hedge funds. Private equity funds return capital and make profit distributions to investors only as investments are sold during the life of the fund, which is often 10 years and may be extended.

37 A is correct. A passive manager is expected to replicate the risk profile of the benchmark using either sampling or full replication. If done successfully, they will achieve low tracking risk. Therefore, a high tracking error would suggest an unskillful passive manager.

READING

11

The Role of Investment Philosophy in Evaluating Investment Managers

A Consultant's Perspective on Distinguishing Alpha from Noise

by John R. Minahan, PhD, CFA

John R. Minahan, PhD, CFA, is an independent consultant (USA).

LEARNING OUTCOMES

Mastery	The candidate should be able to:
☐	a. describe defining characteristics of an investment philosophy;
☐	b. describe investment manager characteristics that increase the likelihood that a manager is an alpha generator;
☐	c. evaluate whether specific managers pass the "investment philosophy test."

It has long been noted that investment returns have a substantial random element, and that this elevates the importance of investment philosophy in evaluating investment managers.[1] Despite this seeming consensus on the centrality of investment philosophy to the task of evaluating managers, it is rare that I encounter a manager that can articulate a compelling investment philosophy. While most managers have an "investment philosophy statement," in my experience these statements are more often marketing slogans or product positioning statements than they are thoughtful encapsulations of the investment insights an investment process is designed to exploit.

I have come to the view that many investment managers are "alpha-pretenders." That is, I believe that generating positive ex-ante alpha is a secondary consideration for many investment management firms. The primary concern for such firms appears to be exploiting the fact that randomness in returns will at times cause a mediocre

The author would like to thank Alison Ballard, Brian Bruce, Mike Manning, Alan Spatrick, Jeff Vivian, Barton Waring, and the participants of the Boston QWAFAFEW seminar for helpful comments and discussion. The views expressed in this paper are those of the author, and may or may not be those of New England Pension Consultants.

1 See Brinson [2005] for a recent articulation of this point.

investment process to exhibit positive ex-post alpha. Pretending to be an alpha-generator while in fact selling noise can be a successful business strategy because it is very difficult for a prospective investor to sort out whether ex-post alpha was generated by ex-ante alpha or noise. Consequently, investors overweight the importance of past performance, and often select managers whose future alpha-generation prospects are no better than chance.

Yet it is reasonable to assume that not all investment managers are pretenders. If one wishes to retain a true alpha-generator—a manager that can reasonably be expected to generate alpha in the future—how does one use the concept of investment philosophy to distinguish the alpha-generator from the pretender?[2] This article addresses the question by defining the concept of investment philosophy and discussing, with illustrations from my consulting experience, how the concept can be applied to evaluating investment managers. The paper concludes that investment managers and consultants are both underutilizing the investment philosophy concept, and that many true alpha-generators—by not articulating their investment philosophies more explicitly—are passing up an opportunity to differentiate themselves from alpha-pretenders.

WHAT IS AN INVESTMENT PHILOSOPHY?

In a sense, successful active management is simple. All one has to do is discount the cash flows of an asset by an appropriate discount rate, compare the resulting value to the asset's price, buy if the price is below the value, and sell if the price is above the value. If the investors using this process produced reasonably consistent and positive results, investing wouldn't need to be a philosophical endeavor.

But failure breeds introspection, and, it turns out, successful investment isn't so simple after all. The following turns out to be important:

- No one knows what the cash flows of a risky asset will be.
- No one knows the right discount rate for a risky asset.
- Market prices tend to reflect information and points of view as that information and those points of view are traded upon.

These facts reframe the problem of active management, and make central the following question: Why has the market not discounted the information or point of view on which cash flow projections and discount rates are based?[3]

Answering this question requires that a manager have points of view (implicit or explicit) on how the market prices—and sometimes misprices—securities, and on what the manager's competitive advantage is in identifying and exploiting such mispricings. These points of view frame the problem of designing an investment process, and provide guiding principles for the execution of the investment process.

With this background, we can define an investment philosophy as follows:

- A set of beliefs regarding the security pricing mechanism and what it is about that mechanism that sometimes causes securities to be mispriced.

2 There are, of course, quantitative approaches to distinguishing alpha from noise, including measuring the consistency of ex-post post alpha through time and across a firm's products. This article, however, is focused on using a manager's investment philosophy to assess that manager qualitatively.

3 Some managers argue it does not matter why the market has not discounted the manager's point of view so long as it, in fact, has not. This is a little like not asking why a chess master has offered you a piece. It seems more prudent to assume that the winner's curse—the tendency of the highest bidder on an item of unknown value to be the bidder with the highest misestimate of value—is alive and well.

- A set of beliefs regarding the manager's competitive advantage in exploiting these mispricings.
- A thesis about how these beliefs can be exploited to generate alpha (an "alpha thesis").

We might go further and define a *sound* investment philosophy as one that:

- Knows where it stands with respect to capital market theory and evidence.
- Is *living*; that is, it wrestles with confirmation and disconfirmation as it is used in practice, and adapts as necessary.
- Has deep enough core principles that adaptation does not result in total change.

HOW DOES ANALYSIS OF A MANAGER'S INVESTMENT PHILOSOPHY AID IN DISTINGUISHING ALPHA FROM NOISE?

I am not aware of any empirical studies establishing a link between investment philosophy and performance. Yet, there is broad acceptance of the idea that a sound investment philosophy is critical to generating ex-ante alpha. I look forward to future research on this topic, but in the meantime I will take on faith the idea that a well-thought out active management strategy is more likely to generate alpha than is a haphazard approach.[4]

The investment philosophy concept suggests that managers are more likely to generate alpha if they:

1 ***Have a clear thesis of how they generate alpha***. Managers are not likely to generate ex-ante alpha without having a very clear idea of what they do that generates alpha, what it is about the markets they invest in that provides the opportunity to generate alpha, and what their competitive advantage is in exploiting that opportunity.
2 ***Put significant effort into understanding where their performance comes from***. Good managers recognize that they have as much at stake as anybody in understanding whether their performance is due to successful execution of the alpha thesis, benchmark misfit, or luck, and are therefore very thoughtful about evaluating their own performance.
3 ***Have thought about whether their alpha-generation process will need to change over time***. In competitive capital markets, alpha-generation sources tend to be arbitraged away. Good managers understand this, and therefore monitor whether or not it is happening, and have a process for seeking out new alpha sources which lever the manager's competitive advantage.

4 A valid criticism of this article is that I assert that investment philosophy can be used to identify alpha-generators, yet offer no evidence. It appears that I am failing to practice what I preach. My response to this criticism is: I agree that evidence would make my argument stronger. Yet, the idea that investment philosophy is important has a strong theoretical basis. Consider the alternative—that knowledge of how securities market work is of no relevance in generating alpha. This borders on nihilism.

This suggests a set of questions to which an evaluator should seek answers when striving to judge whether positive ex-post alpha was generated by positive ex-ante alpha or noise. Together, these questions comprise what can be called the "investment philosophy test":

- What is the thesis (or theses) of how the product generates alpha?
- What is the conceptual basis of the alpha thesis? What is the manager's view about the security pricing mechanism that underlies the thesis?
- What is the relationship of this view to capital market theory?
- What is the manager's competitive advantage in executing the thesis?
- What is the evidence that alpha has been generated by successful execution of the alpha thesis and not a mismatched benchmark or luck? If evidence is lacking, how does the manager convince him- or herself that the thesis is sound?
- How does the manager think about the possible need for the alpha thesis to change over time?

It is not always fruitful to ask a manager these questions directly, particularly if the manager doesn't think in these terms. Yet, an evaluator should strive to be able to answer these questions for him- or herself by the end of an evaluation.

COMMON WAYS OF FAILING THE INVESTMENT PHILOSOPHY TEST

The majority of managers I interview do not pass the investment philosophy test. Following are examples of common failings:

1 ***Managers that don't have an alpha thesis.***

Many managers present themselves by describing what they do without ever offering an argument why one should expect the process to add value relative to a passive alternative. Perhaps these managers think that, if they have good performance, consultants will just assume that the performance came from ex-ante alpha rather than noise. Perhaps they are right in some cases. However, consultants following the approach outlined in this paper will assume the good performance is noise unless the manager can present a credible case otherwise. A key component of such a case is being able to articulate a thesis of how the investment process generates alpha.

Sometimes it is possible to tease an alpha thesis out of a manager who hadn't thought to articulate one; these are sometimes the clearest ones, since they are composed of the manager's real thoughts rather than a script. However, just as often, the manager gets uncomfortable and sometimes even defensive. It is not unusual for managers in such situations to accuse the evaluator of trying to oversimplify their investment process.

2 ***Managers that have an alpha thesis that isn't conceptually grounded.***

I am amazed at all the managers that make an assertion of the type: "In the long run X always wins," where X could be dividend yield, earnings growth, quality of management, a quantitative factor or mix of factors, etc.—yet are unable cite a reason why X should be systematically underpriced by the market. The managers may be able to point to data suggesting that X has been associated with excess returns in the past, but without a plausible explanation of *why* X should outperform, such data do not convince me that X is likely to outperform in the future.

Sometimes managers present data purportedly in support of an alpha thesis, but the data doesn't connect with the thesis. My favorite example of this is when managers claim that because over half of the total return of the S&P 500 since 1926 has come from reinvested dividends, one should expect high dividend-paying stocks to outperform low dividend-paying stocks over long time periods. I don't know whether the managers making this argument really believe it or just think it sounds good, but either way, the argument is a testament to the low quality of thinking one sometimes finds in manager–consultant meetings.

3 ***Managers that don't think very deeply about where their performance comes from.***

I also find it striking that many managers with good performance don't put much thought into figuring out whether their performance came from ex-ante alpha or noise. They seem to think that good performance speaks for itself, as if they didn't understand that the consultant's job is to figure out whether the good performance came from alpha or noise, and as if they didn't have an interest in knowing themselves where their performance comes from.

A good example of this is a manager that selects securities from a universe that is different than the market benchmark to which the manager is compared. There is nothing wrong with this, per se, as there is no reason to expect the universe within which a manager can add value to exactly coincide with a market benchmark. However, benchmark misfit adds an extra step to performance evaluation. The manager's alpha should be calculated relative to the selection universe, so in order to even know what the manager's ex-post alpha is, not to mention evaluate it, one needs to know the performance of the manager's selection universe.[5]

In my experience, most managers with benchmark misfit don't even think about the performance of their selection universes. This makes it difficult for them to convince me that they will add value relative to it.

4 ***Managers that don't think about whether their alpha generation process is based on temporary characteristics of the markets.***

A good example is a currency manager I once interviewed who used technical analysis to ride currency trends. The manager's thesis seemed to be: "Currencies trend: Certain technical trading rules have successfully exploited trends in the past, therefore those rules should be expected to work in the future." The manager was unable to satisfactorily answer the questions: Why do currencies trend? Might the underlying cause of trending change over time? How do you monitor whether or not the underlying cause is still present? Why do your trading rules work? Why are they not arbitraged away?

I was open to being convinced of the manager's process, but not if the manager didn't have a thoughtful perspective on these questions. I was even willing to leave some questions unanswered as long as the manager had wrestled with them. But in this case and many others, managers seem to have a predisposition against really thinking through why their processes should be expected to add value in the future. This makes me wonder if these managers are afraid of something. Perhaps deep down they understand that they are not really alpha-generators, but pretenders hoping that they can hook enough clients before luck turns against them.

5 See Kuenzi [2003] for a detailed discussion of this point.

UNCOMMON WAYS OF PASSING THE INVESTMENT PHILOSOPHY TEST

Managers that have good answers to all the questions of the investment philosophy test are very rare. Less rare, but still uncommon, are managers that cannot answer all the questions, but who do have a sound investment philosophy underlying their investment process.

To avoid inadvertently eliminating managers that have solid alpha-generation processes but haven't thought in terms of the investment philosophy test, an evaluator needs to let managers tell their stories on their own terms. By listening first, an evaluator may find ways to ask the investment philosophy questions that flow naturally from the way a manager thinks about adding alpha. In other words, the questions should not be seen as a checklist, but as a tool for opening windows into a manager's thought process and game plan for adding value.

Following are examples of manager characteristics that make it more likely for me to get comfortable with a manager's investment philosophy, even when the manager is unable to articulate his or her philosophy in the terms I have laid out in this article:

1 ***Managers that measure the success of the steps of the process and not just the ultimate outcome.***

   For example, consider a bond manager that makes the claim that his or her credit research not only predicts upgrades and downgrades, but makes those predictions before the expectation of a rating change is reflected in the market price. This manager tracks every prediction to see if the market consensus (as reflected by price) and rating agencies come around to his or her view. I get comfort from the facts that (1) such managers know their views only have value if they are not only correct but different than consensus, and (2) they track how prices eventually come to reflect, or not reflect, their views. Similarly, managers that evaluate their own performance with strategy benchmarks designed to replicate their selection universe demonstrate they understand the importance of attempting to differentiate alpha from noise (see Kuenzi [2003]).

2 ***Managers that recognize that every strategy they come up with is potentially subject to being arbitraged away.***

   For example, consider a quantitative equity manager that that plays many themes at once. Each theme is viewed as having a finite life, and the performance of each theme is isolated and monitored so as to observe the decay in the value of the theme. The manager considers his or her competitive advantage to be in the identification of new themes, and in the technology for measuring the contribution of each theme to performance. A similar idea is presented in the adaptive market hypothesis of Lo [2004], where the market is always tending toward efficiency, but the types of trades needed to move it towards efficiency rotate and evolve over time.

3 ***Managers that claim they exploit inefficiencies, and identify the specific inefficiency they are exploiting with every position they take.***

   Most managers that say they exploit inefficiencies use this claim as a broad justification for their investment process, but are unable to identify the specific inefficiency they are exploiting in any given decision they make. Those that routinely specify how their information or point of point differs from that reflected in price are much more credible.

4 ***Managers that know their companies so well that they are quicker to interpret change, even though they have no explicit alpha thesis.***

There is always an exception to the rule. Sometimes a manager is simply talented and cannot articulate an alpha thesis.

Despite examples such as these, it remains frustratingly difficult to distinguish between true alpha-generators and alpha-pretenders. I believe there is more that alpha-generators can do to distinguish themselves, and that consultants should be more insistent that they do it.

CONCLUDING THOUGHTS: IMPLICATIONS FOR MANAGERS AND CONSULTANTS

The investment philosophy test is not easy for a manager that doesn't have answers. Even if a marketer were very creative in reverse engineering a story that seemed to answer the questions, it would be very unlikely for such a story to hold up under cross examination, especially if the evaluator cross-references the story with analysis of the manager's holdings.

Therefore, a good way for alpha-generators to differentiate themselves from alpha-pretenders is to develop answers to the investment philosophy questions. Or, if the questions seem to not be on-target, given the manager's particular approach, the manager should reframe the questions in a way that they can be answered. However the questions are framed, it ought to be the case that true alpha-generators find it easier to come up with coherent answers than do alpha-pretenders.

For several years I worked as a freelance consultant to investment managers, providing a variety of services related to product management, including helping managers prepare for consultant evaluations. My approach in helping a manager prepare started with trying to get the manager to answer the investment philosophy questions. I generally found managers resistant to engaging these questions, not because they disagreed with them in any fundamental sense, but because they didn't believe that consultants really thought in terms of these questions. They would say to me things like: "John, the objective is not to prepare us for an evaluation by you, but for evaluations by the consulting community at large, which, as far as we can tell, does not employ the investment philosophy approach."

I agree that the investment philosophy approach as I have laid it out is not widely used by consultants, but not because consultants disagree with it. Rather, I believe it is not used because it is very difficult to get answers to the investment philosophy questions from managers. Thus, we appear to be in a situation where consultants don't use the approach because managers don't think in terms of it, and managers don't think in terms of it because consultants don't use it.

This situation does not serve clients well. Nor does it serve the interests of consultants or alpha-generators. The only group that benefits from consultants not being able to get answers to the investment philosophy questions are alpha-pretenders. How the rest of us let the pretenders get the upper hand I do not know. But it is time for clients and consultants to more forcefully insist that alpha-generators distinguish themselves from the pretenders. I would think that managers that really believe they have an alpha-generation process would support and encourage this development.

REFERENCES

Brinson, Gary P. 2005. "The Future of Investment Management." *Financial Analysts Journal*, vol. 61, no. 4 (July/August): 24–28.

Kuenzi, David E. 2003. "Strategy Benchmarks." *Journal of Portfolio Management*, vol. 29, no. 2 (Winter): 46–56.

Lo, Andrew W. 2004. "The Adaptive Markets Hypothesis: Market Efficiency From An Evolutionary Perspective." *Journal of Portfolio Management*, vol. 30, no. 5 (30th Anniversary): 15–20.

PRACTICE PROBLEMS

1 Hugh Weatherby is a Principal in Global Performance Analytics, an investment consulting firm that serves a wide range of institutional investors. Weatherby is interviewing Henley Townsend, the managing partner of Townsend & Griffin Investment Managers, commonly known as T&G.

- Townsend points to the firm's track record, saying, "We've outperformed the Russell 3000® Index, a broad US equity market benchmark, by 375 basis points on average over the past 5 years and by 250 basis points on average over the past 10. We think our record speaks for itself."
- Weatherby asks Townsend to describe T&G's investment philosophy, to which Townsend replies, "We scour the globe for undervalued securities. Our research analysts are the best in the business and have an average of 20 years experience in the industry." Townsend continues, "It's well known that value investing beats the market in the long run, and our performance history is ample proof of the enduring dependability of that philosophy. We see no reason to believe that the long-term relationship between value investing and the overall market will change in the future."
- When Weatherby asks Townsend how T&G determines that a security is undervalued, Townsend replies, "Our analysts screen thousands of securities. We're able to find the best bargains in the marketplace."

Determine if Townsend's explanation of T&G's investment philosophy answers or leaves unanswered each of the questions below:

Question	Answered	Not Answered
What is the thesis of how the product generates alpha?		
What view of the security pricing mechanism underlies the thesis?		
What is the relationship of this view to capital market theory?		
What is the evidence that alpha has been generated by successful execution of the alpha-thesis and not a mismatched benchmark or luck?		
How does the manager think about the possible need for the alpha-thesis to change over time?		

The following information relates to Questions 2–5

Carlos Pinheiro is an analyst in the manager research department of an investment consulting firm. Pinheiro is preparing for a meeting with Differential Asset Management to discuss Differential's enhanced international equity indexing strategy. After examining

Differential's historical performance, Pinheiro turns his attention to the firm's investment philosophy. He finds the following statements in marketing materials, research papers, and journal articles posted on Differential's website:

- Differential's international equity investment strategy is to systematically identify and exploit investor mistakes resulting from human bias such as overconfidence. The composite's objective is to outperform its benchmark, the MSCI EAFE® Index, while maintaining tracking error within a prescribed tolerance range.
- Differential assumes that, for the most part, share prices reflect the discounted value of expected future cash flows. However, the firm also assumes that there are, for example, enough overconfident investors to systematically but temporarily bias the prices of individual stocks away from fundamental value.
- The firm uses a proprietary model to rate the stocks in their research universe according to the valuation criteria found to be the most effective predictors of mispricing. The portfolio construction process overweights stocks with high ratings and underweights stocks with low ratings while minimizing other sources of risk relative to the benchmark.
- In addition to monitoring tracking error, Differential employs a security-level performance attribution model that reflects the firm's investment decision process. The firm also conducts ongoing research in an effort to discern behavioral shifts, to identify emerging anomalies, and to test new hypotheses about the price impact of investors' biases.

While waiting for Differential's head of consultant relations to arrive, Pinheiro reviews a list of specific questions he has prepared for the meeting. His questions focus on explaining the past performance of the enhanced international equity indexing composite in light of the firm's investment philosophy.

2 Pinheiro sees his task as differentiating true alpha-generators from alpha-pretenders. Which of the following statements is *most likely* to characterize true alpha-generators? They have:

A positive *ex-post* alpha.

B an investment philosophy statement.

C a conceptually grounded alpha-thesis.

3 Which statement *best* describes Differential's alpha-thesis?

A Investors typically misestimate future cash flows.

B Dividend discount rates reflect individual investors' required returns.

C Psychological factors cause individual stocks to be temporarily misvalued.

4 Differential's active return is *least likely* to result from:

A luck.

B benchmark misfit.

C successful execution of the alpha-thesis.

5 Does Differential appear to recognize that the market might arbitrage away the alpha-generation sources that the firm is currently exploiting?

A Yes.

B No; the strategy is based on a settled view of human nature.

C No; the strategy assumes that pricing anomalies are predictable.

SOLUTIONS

1

Question	Answered	Not Answered
What is the thesis of how the product generates alpha?	✓	
What view of the security pricing mechanism underlies the thesis?		✓
What is the relationship of this view to capital market theory?		✓
What is the evidence that alpha has been generated by successful execution of the alpha-thesis and not a mismatched benchmark or luck?		✓
How does the manager think about the possible need for the alpha-thesis to change over time?	✓	

2 C is correct. True alpha-generators are most likely to have an alpha-thesis that is conceptually grounded, that is, based upon a view of the security pricing mechanism and plausibly supported by pertinent data. A is incorrect because alpha-pretenders may have positive ex post alpha caused by noise. B is not the best answer because managers' "investment philosophy statements" may prove to be no more than marketing slogans or product positioning statements.

3 C is correct. Differential's alpha-thesis is that, due to behavioral biases such as overconfidence, some investors systematically but temporarily bias the prices of individual stocks away from fundamental value. Although A and B may be reasonable statements, they are not the best choices because they do not express Differential's distinctive alpha-thesis.

4 B is correct. Benchmark misfit may be ruled out because the portfolio is managed in accordance with an enhanced indexing strategy, one of whose objectives is to maintain tracking error within a prescribed tolerance range.

5 A is correct. Differential engages in performance attribution analysis to evaluate the sources of returns; conducts ongoing research to identify changes in investors' behavior; watches for emerging anomalies; and tests new hypotheses about exploitable patterns of mispricing. These facts strongly suggest that Differential recognizes the possibility that the investment strategy will have to be adapted in the future. B is not the best answer because Differential conducts ongoing research to discern behavioral shifts. Although C is a true statement, it does not mean that Differential believes that specific patterns of mispricing that have generated alpha in the past will persist indefinitely. The firm seeks to identify new sources of mis-valuation that might be exploited in the future.

Investment Performance Presentation

Study Session 7 Investment Performance Presentation

TOPIC LEVEL LEARNING OUTCOME

The candidate should be able to explain the needs served by various kinds of investment performance presentation, and explain the need for global investment performance presentation standards.

INVESTMENT PERFORMANCE PRESENTATION

STUDY SESSION 7

Investment Performance Presentation

Investment performance presentation (IPP) is a specific type of investment reporting that typically focuses on the presentation of investment performance as the outcome of investment management decisions. As discussed in the first reading, four factors determine in detail the type of investment performance presentation: The investment performance information to be communicated; the intended user of the presentation; the intended use of the presentation; and the preparer of the presentation.

Where the preparer of an IPP is an investment manager competing for clients and the intended user is a prospective client—by definition without first-hand experience with the manager—the potential for unfair or biased IPP would be substantial in the absence of compliance by managers with a set of investment performance presentation standards. The second reading explores the motivation for and value of Global Investment Performance Standards (GIPS®). The third and fourth readings provide further orientation to GIPS.

READING ASSIGNMENTS

12 Investment Performance Presentation: An Introduction
by Stefan J. Illmer, PhD

13 Beyond GIPS Compliance: Maximizing Value
by Iain W. McAra

14 Introduction to the Global Investment Performance Standards (GIPS)

15 Global Investment Performance Standards (GIPS)

READING

12

Investment Performance Presentation: An Introduction

by Stefan J. Illmer, PhD

Stefan J. Illmer, PhD, is at Illmer Investment Performance Consulting AG (Switzerland)

LEARNING OUTCOMES

Mastery	The candidate should be able to:
☐	a. describe factors that determine the properties of an investment performance presentation;
☐	b. describe steps of an investment performance presentation process;
☐	c. describe the content and purposes of investment performance presentations when these presentations are classified by (i) type of process and (ii) type of performance evaluation information;
☐	d. explain differences between internal and external investment performance presentations.

INTRODUCTION

1

An investment performance presentation, in general, is the presentation of investment performance information. Specifically, it is the presentation of the returns achieved and the risks taken within an investment portfolio over some specified measurement period(s). Investment performance presentation is a specific type of investment reporting that focuses on the analysis and the presentation of the performance of an investment portfolio.

This reading provides an introduction to investment performance presentation and is organized as follows: Section 2 explains its defining factors and describes the processes by which such presentations are designed and produced. Section 3 describes types of investment performance presentations. Section 4 provides conclusions and a summary.

2 OVERVIEW OF INVESTMENT PERFORMANCE PRESENTATION

In the following, we define investment performance presentation as a specific type of investment reporting, discuss the different determining factors of investment performance presentations, and outline the generic investment performance presentation process.

2.1 Investment Performance Presentation: A Specific Type of Investment Reporting

Investment reporting is defined as the presentation of investment information and includes information on the investments made, the results achieved, and the risks taken.

Investment performance presentation (IPP) is a specific type of investment reporting that typically focuses on the presentation of investment performance as the outcome of investment management decisions. An IPP may be a stand-alone presentation or part of a broader presentation such as a marketing presentation (pitch book). In contrast, investment reporting may contain additional information and may present performance information within a much broader context, including holding or transaction analytics, accounting or tax related information, compliance and monitoring information, market commentaries, and other items. Investment reporting and IPP are important activities within investment management and are integral components of the investment management process.

Exhibit 1 illustrates investment management as an integrated set of activities or a process aiming toward the attainment of investor objectives. The exhibit shows a sequence of activities that begin with understanding investor objectives and constraints. Portfolio policies and strategies combine with capital market expectations to determine the asset allocation and portfolio construction. Performance measurement—understood to include investment reporting and investment controlling[1]—provides a feedback mechanism as adjustments are made to align portfolio characteristics with investor objectives. Depending on the investment management philosophy, variations in the process are possible but generally will include the steps illustrated. Investment reporting and presentation play key roles in informing investors and other stakeholders—such as investment managers or compliance officers—about the results and consequences of investment decisions.

1 In general, investment controlling is defined as the (independent) monitoring of the performance (quality) of investment management decisions with the aim of ensuring that investment objectives are reached.

Exhibit 1 The Portfolio Construction, Monitoring, and Revision Process

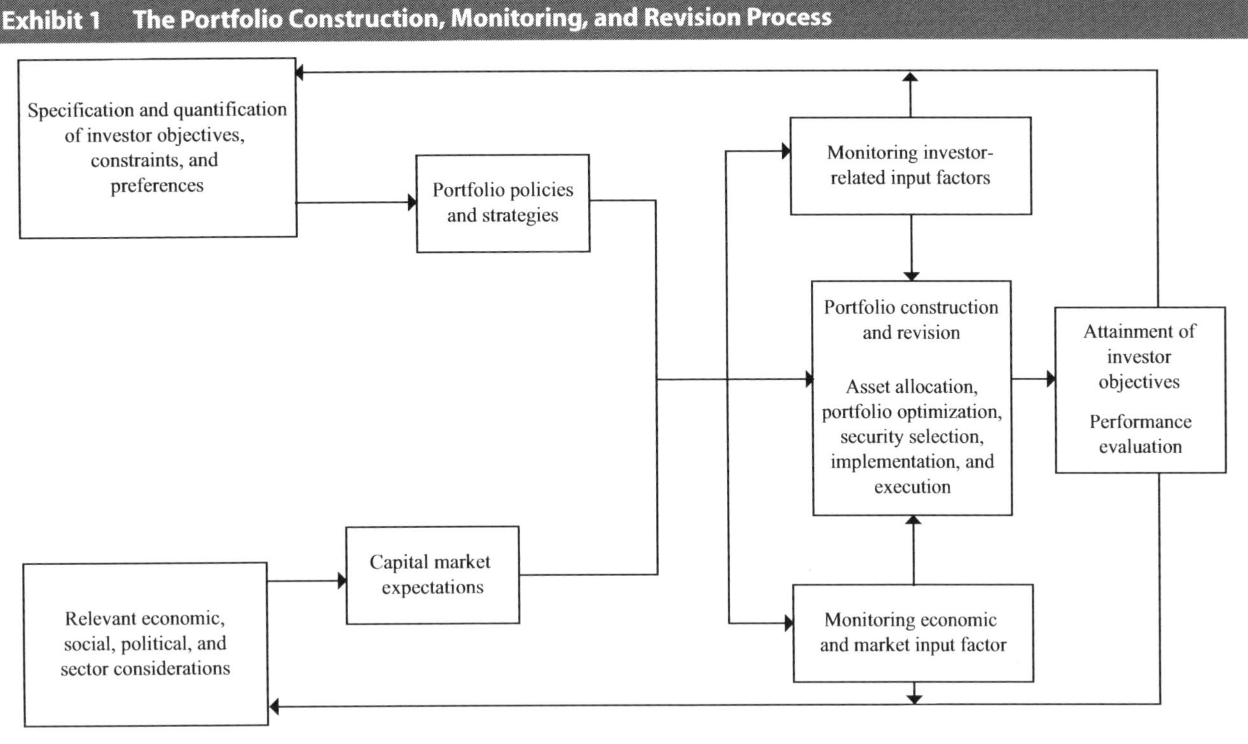

Source: John L. Maginn, Donald L. Tuttle, Dennis W. McLeavey, and Jerald E. Pinto, "The Portfolio Management Process and the Investment Policy Statement," Chapter 1 in John L. Maginn, Donald L. Tuttle, Dennis W. McLeavey, and Jerald E. Pinto, eds., *Managing Investment Portfolios: A Dynamic Approach* (CFA Institute, 2007), p. 6.

2.2 Defining Factors of Investment Performance Presentations

In general, reporting as a process is defined as the transfer of any information or data in any form and format from the preparer of the information to the intended user(s). Investment performance presentation covers every type of reporting of investment performance information or data—whether via file, online display, or paper. Exhibit 2 diagrams four factors that determine the type of IPP:

- the investment performance information to be communicated,
- the intended user of the presentation,
- the intended use of the presentation, and
- the preparer of the presentation.

Exhibit 2 Factors that Determine Investment Performance Presentations

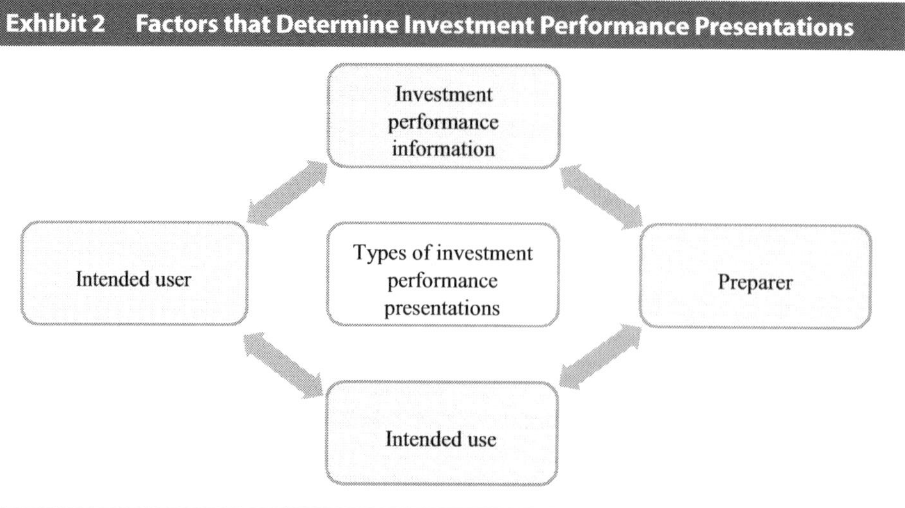

The variations of the determining factors are manifold. Examples of each are provided below:

- Investment performance information: Profit and loss figures; performance figures (return and risk), ex-ante (forward looking) and ex-post (historical) performance figures; portfolio, benchmark, composite, and peer group performance figures; or performance analytics including performance attribution.
- Intended user: Prospective or existing clients, marketing, control or compliance officers, portfolio managers, investment committee members, senior management, investment consultants, regulators, or tax authorities.
- Intended use: Determination of the sources of the absolute or relative return and risk, monitoring the implementation of the investment strategy, monitoring the agreed risk limits, product review, performance appraisal,[2] or peer group comparisons.
- Preparer of presentation: (Global) custodian, investment management company, broker, financial analyst, investment advisor, investment consultant, investment controller, or the investor.

Different types of investment performance presentations can be characterized along these dimensions. For example, consider the return attribution report for a multi-asset class portfolio illustrated in Exhibit 3.[3] It consists of information analyzing the sources of investment returns in terms of investment management decisions—in particular, asset allocation and stock selection.[4] The preparer of the presentation may be the investment manager or a consultant hired by the investor, and the end user may be the investment manager (for control purposes) or the investor (for monitoring purposes and performance appraisal). Other sets of characteristics can define other kinds of IPPs such as risk analysis, composite presentations, performance watch lists, or peer group comparisons.

2 In general, performance appraisal is defined as the evaluation of performance for evidence of investment skill.

3 "Return attribution" is frequently referred to as "performance attribution."

4 The management effects illustrated in Exhibit 3 were calculated using the Brinson, Hood, and Beebower methodology.

Exhibit 3 Sample Return Attribution Report

	Portfolio			Benchmark			Management Effects			
	Return	Weight	Contribution	Return	Weight	Contribution	Asset allocation	Stock picking	Interaction	Total
Cash	0.50%	10.00%	0.05%	0.10%	6.00%	0.01%	0.00%	0.02%	0.02%	0.04%
Domestic bonds	1.50%	22.00%	0.33%	0.50%	20.00%	0.10%	0.01%	0.20%	0.02%	0.23%
Foreign bonds	3.00%	10.00%	0.30%	4.50%	15.00%	0.68%	−0.23%	−0.23%	0.08%	−0.38%
Domestic equities	2.00%	17.00%	0.34%	2.50%	14.00%	0.35%	0.08%	−0.07%	−0.02%	−0.01%
Foreign equities	0.50%	12.00%	0.06%	−2.00%	16.00%	−0.32%	0.08%	0.40%	−0.10%	0.38%
Mortgages	0.50%	5.00%	0.03%	0.50%	3.00%	0.02%	0.01%	0.00%	0.00%	0.01%
Real estate	2.00%	16.00%	0.32%	1.50%	20.00%	0.30%	−0.06%	0.10%	−0.02%	0.02%
Commodities	6.00%	4.00%	0.24%	3.00%	4.00%	0.12%	0.00%	0.12%	0.00%	0.12%
Private equity	2.00%	3.00%	0.06%	0.50%	1.00%	0.01%	0.01%	0.02%	0.03%	0.06%
Hedge funds	1.00%	1.00%	0.01%	−1.50%	1.00%	−0.02%	0.00%	0.03%	0.00%	0.03%
Total	**1.74%**	**100.00%**	**1.74%**	**1.24%**	**100.00%**	**1.24%**	**−0.10%**	**0.59%**	**0.01%**	**0.50%**

2.3 General Investment Performance Presentation Process

Investment performance presentation is often perceived as the business card of an investment firm because it reflects the quality of the whole value chain of the firm's investment management process. Investment performance presentation is more than the mere illustration of numbers and figures. This section will make the point in more detail before we turn to discussing the different types of IPPs in Section 3.

In the extreme, an IPP may consist of just one number—for example, the absolute return of a portfolio over some period. That one number would still reflect the results of hundreds or even thousands of activities within the investment management firm. These activities include sub-processes such as asset allocation, benchmark selection, portfolio construction, security and cash transactions, rebalancing of the portfolio, settlement, corporate actions, recovery of taxes, and the payment of management and custody fees. Investment performance presentation is affected by nearly every process of investment management.

Investment performance presentation is a recurring communication process which uses feedback generated from the different participants and stakeholders of the investment management process. In practice, this process is not standardized because it depends on specific organizational characteristics and on the historical development of the performance measurement department and its related sub-processes.[5] Nevertheless, there is a common view regarding the main steps of the generic IPP process. The individual implementation can vary, mainly because of the size of the organization, the level of centralization within the organization, the number and types of IPPs that the firm must develop, and the complexity of the performance analytics contained in the presentations.

Exhibit 4 illustrates the generic IPP process. It is usually split into three sub-processes: data management, production, and support. Although the arrow diagram suggests that the sub-processes are sequential, in practice this might not be the case because of feedback loops and variations in how organizations operate. Many investment performance presentations are updated monthly, although daily updates are becoming more common especially as a result of the introduction of online tools (e.g., online reporting and online management information systems).

Exhibit 4 Generic Investment Performance Presentation Process

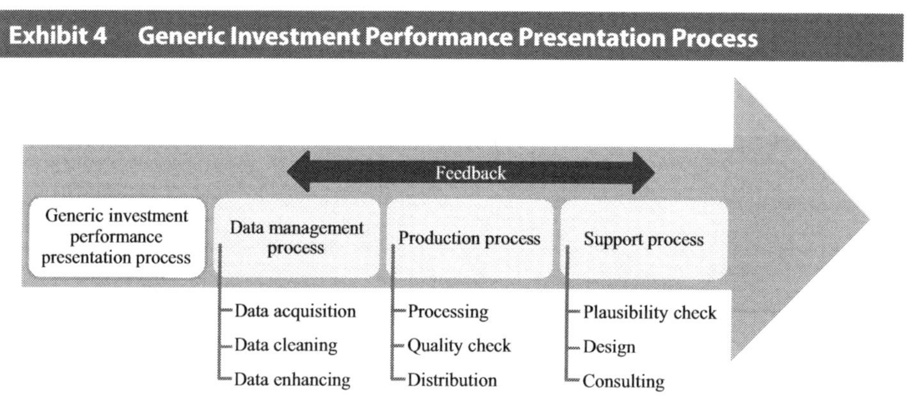

The data management process contains different sub-processes to ensure that the required data are available with the necessary quality for the subsequent production process. Generally speaking, data management covers all methodical, conceptual,

5 For example, at one extreme, performance measurement, performance attribution, performance presentation, and data management may be centralized for all types of investment products or client segments and managed within one department. At the other extreme, all of these processes might be separately managed and uncoordinated.

organizational, and technical methods applied to data with the objective of using the information to its maximum potential within the relevant business processes. Following this general definition, data management can be split into the following three connected sub-processes:

- Data acquisition: This deals with activities—such as data searches, data buying, data contracting, data gathering, data import, data input, data changes, and data re-runs—that get the required and necessary data into investment performance systems. For example, data import and data input involve the daily upload of price or reference data for indexes and portfolios from provider systems into the performance database. The objective is for all required data to be available to subsequent processes.
- Data cleaning: This covers activities—such as data monitoring, data verification, and data correction—that ensure that required data are complete, correct, available, timely, and up-to-date before they are processed further. Examples of data monitoring include a daily check of whether all required price data are in the performance database or a daily check of whether required reference data for new securities are missing or have been changed.
- Data enhancing: This involves activities—such as data changes, data improvements, and data adjustment—that ensure that data of the required quality are input into investment performance systems. An example of data improvement and adjustment is the correction of a misclassification of the industry membership of a security.[6] Another example is working with a data vendor to improve the timeliness of data delivery to allow an IPP to be produced earlier in the reporting cycle. This sub-process is very important for the quality of IPPs.

The production process—the second step of the IPP process illustrated in Exhibit 4—involves activities to ensure the IPPs are processed and disseminated to users. The production process can be split into the following three connected sub-processes:

- Processing: This refers to activities—such as setup, queuing, calculations and processing, monitoring, and re-runs—that produce presentations using IPP systems in a pre-defined way. The objective is that all presentations are available and ready for use by the subsequent processes. An example of setup is collecting and inputting client reference data into or defining the report frequency in the IPP system.
- Quality check: This is concerned with activities—such as checking and change requests—that ensure all presentations produced by the IPP systems are correct and fulfill the agreed-upon and committed reporting requirements. The objective is that all presentations be complete with respect to the specifications, errorless, available, timely, and up-to-date for use within the subsequent processes. Depending on the desired level of quality, complexity, performance period (1 month versus 3 year period), and frequency of reporting (daily versus

6 In general, classifications of securities should reflect the investment strategy or the investment style of the specific investment portfolio. An example is the investment in a stock exchange traded real estate investment trust (REIT) which may be classified as equity for a US equity portfolio and as real estate for a multi-asset class portfolio.

quarterly reporting), different layers of quality checks are defined and implemented.[7] This step is very important for the quality of the investment performance presentation.

- Distribution: This involves activities—such as administration of mailing lists and preparation of the respective cover letters, printing, and actual mailing via mail or email—that ensure that all required IPPs are printed and mailed to the users in a timely way; or, if not sent out at this stage, that the presentations are available for use within subsequent processes.

The support process—the third step of the IPP process in Exhibit 4—is concerned with all activities that assure the IPPs are understood by their users and fit their requirements and needs. The support process can be split into the following three connected sub-processes:

- Plausibility check: This involves activities—such as confirmation of holdings, reference data, cash flows, prices or returns, and report comparisons—that ensure that all items in an IPP make sense and are relevant to the presentation's intended use.
- Design: This covers activities—like setup and change of templates—to ensure that all IPPs are designed to meet the user's requirements and needs. The objective is to ensure that the content and the structure of the IPPs are appropriate and relevant for the intended user(s). The design process is especially important for very demanding users, because the respective IPPs may contain tailor-made solutions addressing individual needs for layout, content, or structure. For every user there may be a specific template that is tailor-made to meet individual needs and requirements or regulatory requirements.[8]
- Consulting: This involves activities such as explanations and support for the users of IPPs, user training, and advising for tailor-made solutions. The objective is for the presentation to be useful, relevant, and suitable for users. The consulting process aims to inform and help the user set requirements with respect to performance measurement, analysis, and presentation. Consulting may be necessary for complex investment management processes, if complex financial instruments are used, or if new or not-yet-available reporting features or performance analytics are required.

In addition to the three main sub-processes mentioned above, other activities may be relevant and integrated into the overall IPP process. Such additional activities could include, for example:

- Compliance: Ensuring that all IPPs comply with the most stringent relevant requirements whether they are local laws and regulations or organizational policies.
- Auditing and verification: Investigating whether all IPPs are produced according to industry best practices or in accordance to internal policies and procedures.
- Quality management: Ensuring efficient processing with a very low error frequency.
- Product development: Ensuring that all IPPs and the respective analytics are designed to fit the requirements and needs of the users.

---

7 For example, in an investment management firm the first layer is covered by the report processing team checking the content and layout, the second control might be executed by the team responsible for the plausibility checks, and the final check might be done by staff within the investment management team—often the portfolio manager.

8 Here we do not distinguish between external and internal users. An internal user—like the portfolio manager or the marketing department—is normally treated like any external user.

- Data provider management: Ensuring that all necessary data and information delivered meet quality standards.

EXAMPLE 1

The Steps of the Investment Performance Presentation Process

1 The steps in a generic IPP process include:

   A data analysis and presentation.

   B data management and return appraisal.

   C data management, production, and support.

2 Official mutual fund returns are found not to reconcile to the returns reported as part of an investment performance presentation to an investor. The presentation process is *most likely* deficient in the:

   A support process.

   B production process.

   C data management process.

3 What support sub-process works with the user to ensure that the investment performance presentations are useable, relevant, and suitable for the intended use?

   A Design process.

   B Consulting process.

   C Plausibility check process.

Solution to 1:

C is correct. As illustrated in Exhibit 4, the generic IPP process is usually split into the three sub-processes: data management, production, and support.

Solution to 2:

C is correct. A failure in data cleaning—a sub-step of the data management process—is the most likely cause of the error.

Solution to 3:

B is correct. The consulting process aims to help the user articulate and formulate requirements with respect to performance measurement, analysis, and presentation so that the presentation becomes useful, relevant, and suitable for users.

The IPP process is complex and involves many different sub-processes. But this process itself is part of an even more comprehensive process which, among others, covers additional data management related (sub-)processes. The preceding data-related processes generate or calculate many of the data and information needed to produce an investment performance presentation. These processes are important for the outcome and the quality of the investment performance presentations and can be distinguished as follows:

- Data creation process: This process generates or gathers data and information to be provided to subsequent processes within the whole organization—and not just to the IPP process. Data creation deals with all types of data and information from inside or outside the investment management organization. Data types might include reference data, index data, price data, research information, and any other data and information required or needed to build an IPP. An example is a centralized reference data management process that collects reference data from different internal or external data providers.

- Source data process: Data and information from different (internal or external) providers are collected and—in contrast to the data creation process—also improved and enhanced for use in subsequent processes within the whole organization—and not just in the IPP process. Source data processes provide processed, pre-calculated, or derived data such as reference and pricing data, payment and tax data, index and benchmark data, and transaction and corporate action data. An example is a centralized index and benchmark data management process collecting index data, maintaining the constituencies of benchmarks, and providing the respective performance data for (customized) benchmarks. Another example is a centralized pricing process generating and providing valuations or model prices for illiquid securities.

3 TYPES OF INVESTMENT PERFORMANCE PRESENTATIONS

This section explains different types of investment performance presentations in more detail by highlighting the purpose, scope, and basic components of each.[9] Section 3 ends with a discussion of the differences between internal and external IPPs.

3.1 Process-related Investment Performance Presentations

As discussed in Section 2, the specific IPP is determined by the information presented, by the intended user, the intended use, and the preparer of the presentation. As illustrated in Exhibit 5, we identify three process-related types of IPPs, classified by intended use: sales-oriented presentations, management-oriented presentations, and monitoring-oriented presentations.

Exhibit 5 Process-related Investment Performance Presentations Classified by Intended Use

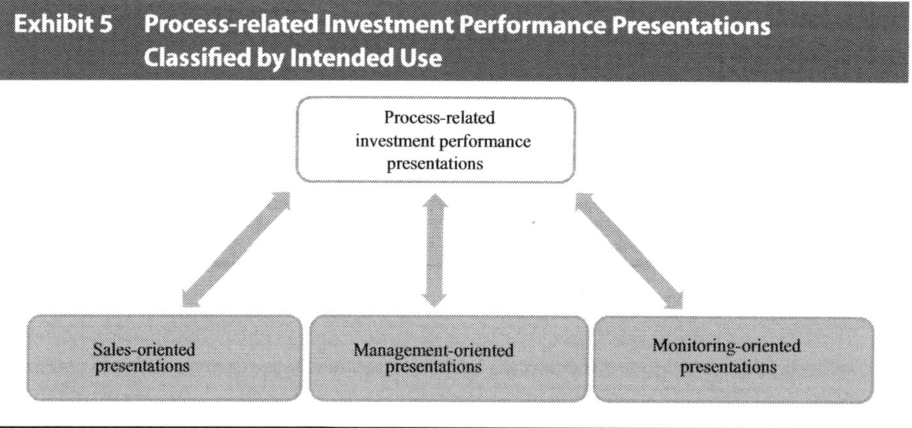

9 Here we focus on presentations prepared by investment management organizations. With minor adjustments, the explanations that follow also apply to other preparers, such as custodians or consultants.

A sales-oriented investment performance presentation is a specific type of presentation used in the sales process of an investment management organization. Here we distinguish between pre-sales, time-of-sales, and after-sales processes, each having distinct characteristics:

- In the pre-sales process, IPPs normally cover more general, aggregated, and/or high level information about the investment product. These presentations often focus on time-series performance analytics such as rolling or period returns and risk metrics. Furthermore, the time series data may be associated with high-level holdings or portfolio information that provides a better sense of the (proposed) investment strategy and investment portfolio. This investment performance presentation is designed to lead prospective clients into a deeper discussion of the investment information. Exhibit 6 provides an example of such a presentation commonly used in the investment management industry—a GIPS standards compliant composite presentation.[10]

Exhibit 6 Sample GIPS Standards Compliant Composite Presentation

Investment Firm Balanced Growth Composite

1 January 2002 through 31 December 2011

Year	Composite Gross Return (%)	Composite Net Return (%)	Custom Benchmark Return (%)	Composite 3-Yr St Dev (%)	Benchmark 3-Yr St Dev (%)	Number of Portfolios	Internal Dispersion (%)	Composite Assets ($ M)	Firm Assets ($ M)
2002	−10.5	−11.4	−11.8			31	4.5	165	236
2003	16.3	15.1	13.2			34	2.0	235	346
2004	7.5	6.4	8.9			38	5.7	344	529
2005	1.8	0.8	0.3			45	2.8	445	695
2006	11.2	10.1	12.2			48	3.1	520	839
2007	6.1	5.0	7.1			49	2.8	505	1,014
2008	−21.3	−22.1	−24.9			44	2.9	475	964
2009	16.5	15.3	14.7			47	3.1	493	983
2010	10.6	9.5	13.0			51	3.5	549	1,114
2011	2.7	1.7	0.4	7.1	7.4	54	2.5	575	1,236

Investment Firm claims compliance with the Global Investment Performance Standards (GIPS®) and has prepared and presented this report in compliance with the GIPS standards. Sample 1 Investment Firm has been independently verified for the periods 1 January 2000 through 31 December 2010. The verification report is available upon request. Verification assesses whether (1) the firm has complied with all the composite construction requirements of the GIPS standards on a firm-wide basis and (2) the firm's policies and procedures are designed to calculate and present performance in compliance with the GIPS standards. Verification does not ensure the accuracy of any specific composite presentation.

10 From Appendix A of *Global Investment Performance Standards*, 2010.

Notes:

1 Sample 1 Investment Firm is a balanced portfolio investment manager that invests solely in US-based securities. Sample 1 Investment Firm is defined as an independent investment management firm that is not affiliated with any parent organization. Policies for valuing portfolios, calculating performance, and preparing compliant presentations are available upon request.

2 The Balanced Growth Composite includes all institutional balanced portfolios that invest in large-cap US equities and investment-grade bonds with the goal of providing long-term capital growth and steady income from a well-diversified strategy. Although the strategy allows for equity exposure ranging between 50–70%, the typical allocation is between 55–65%. The account minimum for the composite is $5 million.

3 The custom benchmark is 60% YYY US Equity Index and 40% ZZZ US Aggregate Bond Index. The benchmark is rebalanced monthly.

4 Valuations are computed and performance is reported in US dollars.

5 Gross-of-fees returns are presented before management and custodial fees but after all trading expenses. Composite and benchmark returns are presented net of non-reclaimable withholding taxes. Net-of-fees returns are calculated by deducting the highest fee of 0.83% from the monthly gross composite return. The management fee schedule is as follows: 1.00% on the first $25 million; 0.60% thereafter.

6 This composite was created in February 2000. A complete list of composite descriptions is available upon request.

7 Internal dispersion is calculated using the equal-weighted standard deviation of annual gross returns of those portfolios that were included in the composite for the entire year.

8 The three-year annualized standard deviation measures the variability of the composite and the benchmark returns over the preceding 36-month period. The standard deviation is not presented for 2002 through 2010 because monthly composite and benchmark returns were not available and is not required for periods prior to 2011.

- During the time-of-sales process, investment performance presentations may cover more detailed information on the specific investment product under consideration to even better understand its return and risk characteristics—such as a performance attribution or a risk analysis. The level of detail depends on the technical possibilities, on the system capabilities, and more importantly on the level of sophistication of the client. This investment information and the respective presentation are designed to convince the potential or prospective client that the considered investment product is of great value, managed professionally, and that it fits the investment requirements.
- In the after-sales process, investment performance presentations normally cover more detailed investment information not on a specific investment product, but on the individual client investment portfolio. In addition to time series performance analytics and high level investment information, this type of presentation often contains detailed information on the sources of the absolute and excess return or risk and may be associated by more detailed information

on the transactions and current holdings of the portfolio.[11] This investment information and the respective presentation are designed to get a better view on the implemented investment strategy and the recent investment portfolio. The objective is to prove that the proposed investment strategy was actually implemented and to illustrate the quality of the respective investment management decisions. These presentations are often the input for the regular performance review meetings between the investment management organization and the existing client.

A management-oriented IPP is a specific type of presentation used in the investment management process. Here we distinguish between presentations used for investment reporting and for investment controlling:[12]

- Similar to the before mentioned after-sales process, the investment reporting process deals with IPPs designed for use outside of the investment management organization and focuses on client investment portfolios. The content of these presentations depends very much on the level of sophistication of the client or user and the importance of the client for the investment management organization. Here, the IPP is normally part of a broader and more extensive investment report containing additional information like market commentary, detailed asset allocations, or transaction overviews.

  Depending on the level of detail, we distinguish different types of investment reports containing distinct kinds of IPPs. A standard investment report may contain a simple IPP illustrating some performance numbers such as return and excess return for a specific reporting period. In contrast, a comprehensive investment report may contain a very detailed IPP covering multiple aspects of performance analysis from a detailed time series analysis to a client-specific tailor-made performance attribution. Between these two extreme types of investment reports, one can find endless variations. The objective should be to illustrate the return and risk characteristics of the investment portfolio as well as the results of the implemented investment strategy.

- In the investment controlling process, the content of the IPP depends on the intended use and the intended user (often from within the investment management organization). The presentation may refer to investment portfolios, to investment products, or to investment strategies and, depending on the specific purpose, may contain more or less detailed investment information or purpose-oriented performance analytics. For example, a peer group comparison may cover a time series analysis focusing on the absolute and excess return of the different investment products used to analyze the competitiveness of the investment management company. Another example would be a presentation featuring detailed return and risk attribution analytics that are relevant to evaluating the implementation of an investment strategy. Exhibit 7 provides an example of an investment controlling report containing different analytics illustrating return and risk statistics and return decompositions.

A monitoring-oriented IPP is a specific type of presentation used in the monitoring process. The monitoring may be done from inside or from outside the investment management organization. The focus of such investment performance presentation is often on investment management policies or guidelines and on regulatory requirements. The presentation may refer to investment portfolios, to investment products, to

11 In the after-sales process, there is only a fine line between an investment performance presentation and an investment report—and it is the latter that existing clients normally receive from their investment managers.

12 Investment performance presentations or respective analytics may be used within other investment management sub-processes. For example, performance analytics like ex-ante risk attribution used for asset allocation or portfolio construction decision making.

Exhibit 7 Sample Investment Controlling Report

- FORKE INTERNAL USE ONLY -

BM KE Basic CHF Equity - SAA
PF KE BASIC CHF Equity - TAA

Period Start: 31.12.2006
End: 14.08.2007

Performance Table

	PF	BM	Rel.
Explicit Periods			
Specified	2.01	2.02	-0.01
MtD	-2.85	-2.76	-0.09
YtD	2.01	2.02	-0.01
Rolling Periods			
1M	-7.28	-7.08	-0.20
3M	-5.39	-5.23	-0.16
6M	-2.65	-2.58	-0.08
1Y			
3Y			
5Y			

Performance Trend
from 31.12.2006 to 14.08.2007 In %

Rel. PF BM

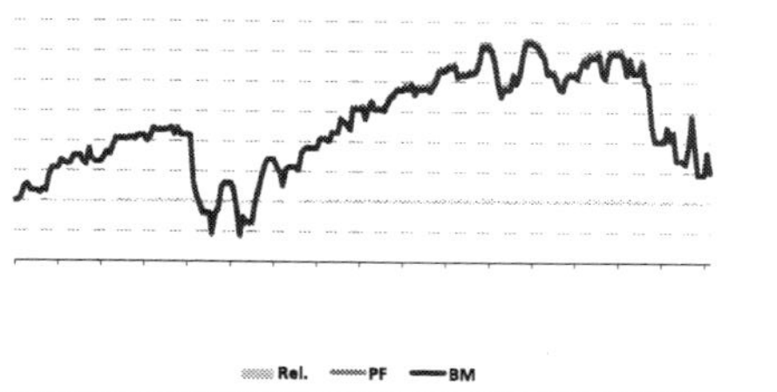

Module Performance (unweighted Asset-Sub-Class Performance)
from 31.12.2006 to 14.08.2007 In %

PF BM Rel.

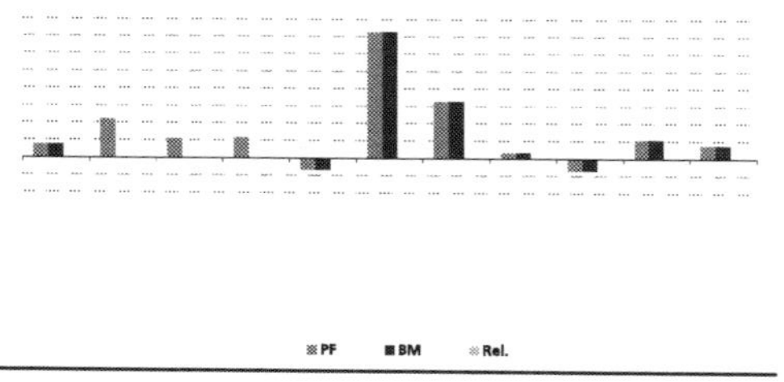

Attribution BHB - Model by Asset-Sub-Class
from 31.12.2006 to 14.08.2007 In %

Timing Selection Interaction

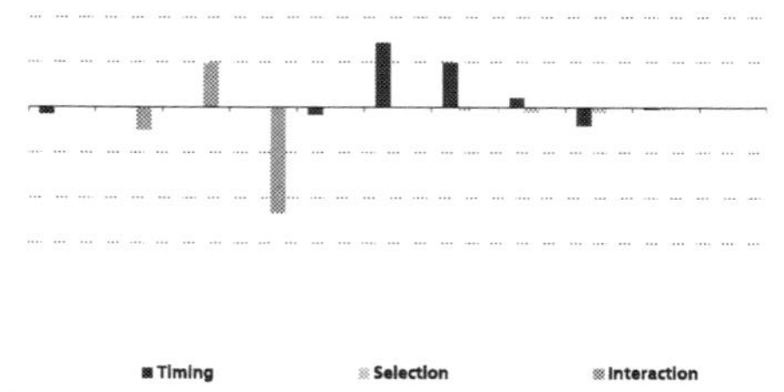

Contribution by Asset Class

	PF	BM	Rel.
Total Portfolio	**2.01**	**2.02**	**-0.01**
Liquidity	-0.02	0.07	-0.10
Equities	1.96	1.87	+0.09
Alternative Investments	0.08	0.07	+0.00

Contribution by Asset-Sub-Class
from 31.12.2006 to 14.08.2007 In %

PF BM Rel.

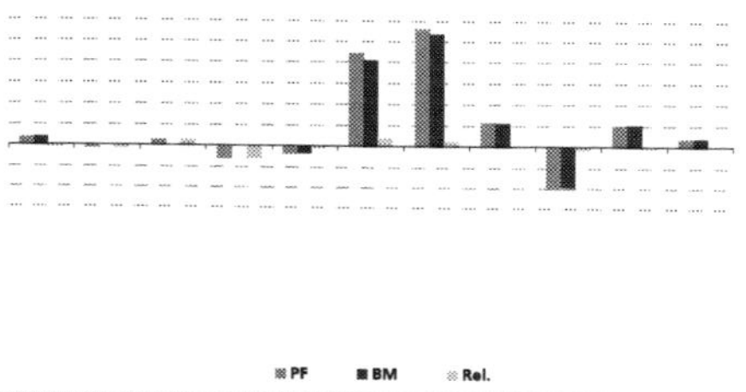

Impact on Instrument Selection

		Inv.?	Avg. Wgt.	Abs. Return	Rel. Return	Abs. Contr.	Rel. Contr.
Strongest Contributors							
(1)	MSCI Emerging Markets	I	5.92	14.49	-0.00	0.89	+0.07
(2)	Asia Currency Index 09.03.06	I	1.20	2.21	-	0.05	+0.05
(3)	MSCI EMU	I	17.24	6.51	+0.00	1.12	+0.05
(4)	MSCI USA	I	29.78	0.66	+0.00	0.22	+0.01
(5)	JPM Cash Index CHF 3M	I	5.00	1.44	-0.00	0.08	+0.00
Weakest Contributors							
(1)	JPM Cash Index USD 3M	I	-2.51	2.36	-	-0.12	-0.12
(2)	MSCI Switzerland	I	25.19	-1.35	+0.00	-0.40	-0.02
(3)	JPM Cash Index EUR 3M	I	-0.73	4.38	-	-0.02	-0.02
(4)	MSCI Japan	I	5.41	-1.28	-0.00	-0.07	-0.01
(5)	JPM Cash Index CHF 3M	I	4.49	1.44	-0.00	0.07	-0.01

Attribution BF - Model by Asset-Sub-Class
from 31.12.2006 to 14.08.2007 In %

Timing Selection

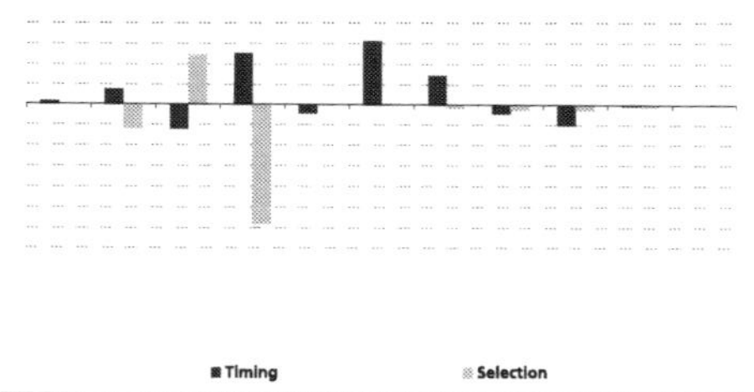

Risk & Return Statistics

	PF	BM	Rel.
Annualized figures			
ann. Ret.	2.83	2.88	-0.05
Volatility	10.48	10.19	+0.30
TE	0.32		
IR	-0.15		
Value-at-Risk (1 week, 5% Prob.)	3.13	3.05	+0.08
Period statistics			
Correl.	1.00	R2	1.00
Alpha (%)	0.00	N (#)	32
Beta (x)	1.03		
Downside Risk		Start	End

Risk & Return Chart (based on weekly data)
from 31.12.2006 to 14.08.2007 In %

PF BM

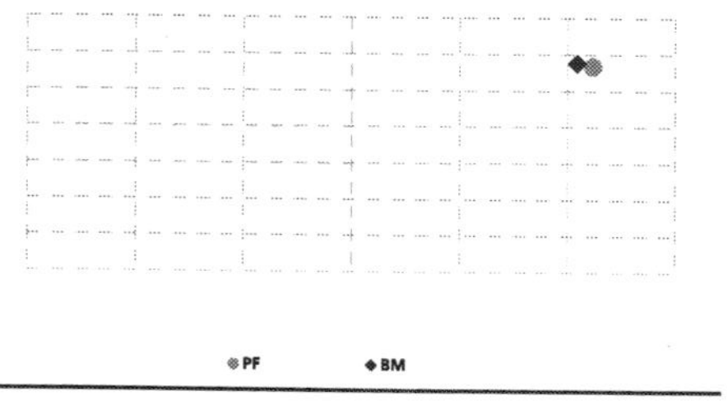

Downside Risk
from 31.12.2006 to 14.08.2007 In %

Time under water Start Max drawdown Recovery

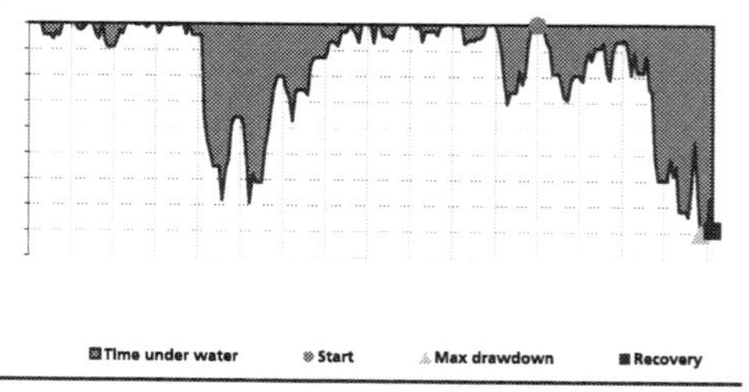

Weekly Return Distribution (Non-parametric Kernel Density Function)
from 31.12.2006 to 14.08.2007 In %

PF
PF VaR
BM
BM VaR
Norm. Dist.

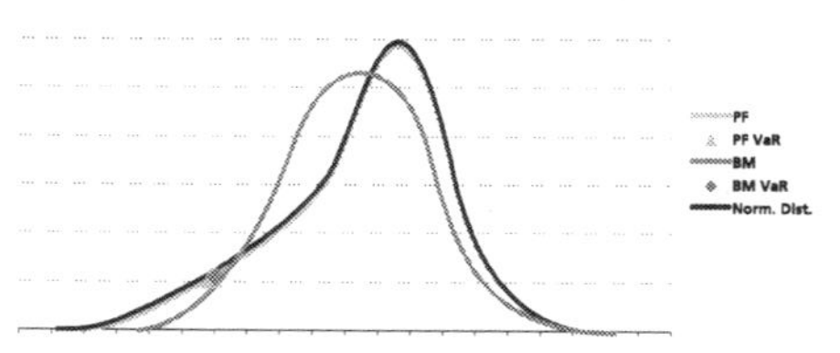

investment strategies, or to a total investment management organization. The objective of monitoring-oriented presentations is to provide certain investment performance information—often exposure and risk figures—to show that the investment mandate, strategy, or company was in compliance with investment policies or guidelines and regulatory requirements, or in compliance with specific transparency requirements. Depending on the individual guidelines or regulations, the performance analytics used can be manifold and complex. In addition, for more complex organizational setups such as pension funds, monitoring-oriented presentations are becoming more important over time as internal investment guidelines are becoming more detailed and as decision-oriented performance analytics are seen as fundamental for the future success of an organization. The objective of monitoring-oriented presentations is to increase transparency of activities as well as return and risk contributions resulting from individual decisions.

EXAMPLE 2

Process-related Investment Performance Presentations

1 Sales-oriented investment performance presentations are used for:
   - **A** existing clients.
   - **B** prospective clients.
   - **C** prospective as well as existing clients.

2 After-sales investment performance presentations focus on:
   - **A** investment products or composites.
   - **B** portfolio managers' individual performance.
   - **C** existing clients' individual portfolios.

3 Pre-sales presentations normally do not contain:
   - **A** performance comparison against the benchmark.
   - **B** detailed information on the sources of the excess return.
   - **C** general information about the investment management organization.

Solution to 1:

C is correct. Pre-sales and time-of-sales presentations are prepared for prospective clients and after-sales presentations are prepared for existing clients.

Solution to 2:

C is correct. In contrast to pre-sales and time-of-sales presentations, after-sales presentations are designed for existing clients especially presenting the performance of the client's individual investment portfolio.

Solution to 3:

B is correct. Detailed performance information, like a performance attribution analysis, is normally added to a pre-sales presentation only if the prospective client specifically asked for it.

Despite the fact that the three different types of process-related IPPs may vary depending on the intended user and use, all types of presentation share the same overall purpose: creating or increasing transparency concerning the investments made, the results achieved, and the risks taken. Investment performance presentations are important components of the overall investment management process and are often used for investment reporting and controlling. In this respect, the objective of IPPs consists in arranging the presentation and the included analyses—within the framework of the investment management process—in such a way that the processes (e.g., forecasting, decision making, and implementation), their quality, results (e.g., returns), risks (e.g., of using derivatives), and costs (e.g., transaction fees) become more transparent. The investment management process shown in Exhibit 1 may in reality be highly complex because of the large number of possible financial instruments and the number of decision makers involved (e.g., research team, asset allocation team, and specialists in the various investment categories). The effect of this complexity is that the results of the investment management process and the factors that affect it are not always apparent. In this context, effective IPPs help users understand the contributions of the individual decisions of the investment management process, especially with respect to return and risk, and to allocate them to the responsible decision makers. The figures and measures illustrated and the conclusions drawn from the IPP provide important feedback and input into the investment management process which can enhance the quality and future performance of the investment managers.

3.2 Analytics-related Investment Performance Presentations

Four important analytics-related types of investment performance presentations are:

- performance report;
- return attribution report;
- risk report; and
- portfolio holdings report.

A performance report is the presentation of the return of the investment portfolio or product during the measurement period, on a stand-alone basis or against the benchmark or peer group. Performance reporting contains investment information mainly based on time series analysis. Such information normally includes absolute and excess return for different fixed or rolling periods as well as the cumulative absolute and excess return over the measurement period. The possibilities for illustrating such information are manifold: They can range from tables to graphics, where the chosen design and format supports a better understanding and use of the investment information. In summary, a performance report helps the user obtain a better view of the portfolio or product's historical absolute and excess returns. In addition, performance appraisal measures—such as the Sharpe ratio or the information ratio—are sometimes included to provide a better understanding of performance in relation to historical risk.[13]

Exhibit 8 provides an example of a performance report illustrating the absolute and excess return of a multi-asset class portfolio and its asset classes for different measurement periods.

13 There is no common view in the industry whether the risk-adjusted figures belong to performance or to risk reporting.

Exhibit 8 Sample Performance Report

Panel A

	Portfolio			Benchmark			Excess Return		
	1 Month	6 Month	12 Month Portfolio	1 Month	6 Month	12 Month Benchmark	1 Month	6 Month	12 Month Excess
Cash	0.05%	0.15%	0.50%	0.05%	0.20%	0.10%	0.00%	−0.05%	0.40%
Domestic bonds	0.30%	0.60%	1.50%	0.20%	0.80%	0.50%	0.10%	−0.20%	1.00%
Foreign bonds	−0.50%	−0.20%	3.00%	−0.25%	0.20%	4.50%	−0.25%	−0.40%	−1.50%
Domestic equities	−5.00%	−1.00%	2.00%	−4.00%	−1.50%	2.50%	−1.00%	0.50%	−0.50%
Foreign equities	−3.50%	−2.00%	0.50%	−4.00%	−3.00%	−2.00%	0.50%	1.00%	2.50%
Mortgages	0.10%	0.25%	0.50%	0.15%	0.30%	0.50%	−0.05%	−0.05%	0.00%
Real estate	0.30%	0.80%	2.00%	0.50%	1.00%	1.50%	−0.20%	−0.20%	0.50%
Commodities	1.50%	−2.00%	6.00%	2.00%	1.50%	3.00%	−0.50%	−3.50%	3.00%
Private equity	−2.00%	−3.00%	2.00%	−1.00%	−1.00%	0.50%	−1.00%	−2.00%	1.50%
Hedge funds	0.50%	−1.00%	1.00%	2.00%	1.00%	−1.50%	−1.50%	−2.00%	2.50%
Total	**−1.20%**	**−0.32%**	**1.74%**	**−1.00%**	**−0.22%**	**1.24%**	**−0.20%**	**−0.10%**	**0.50%**

Panel B

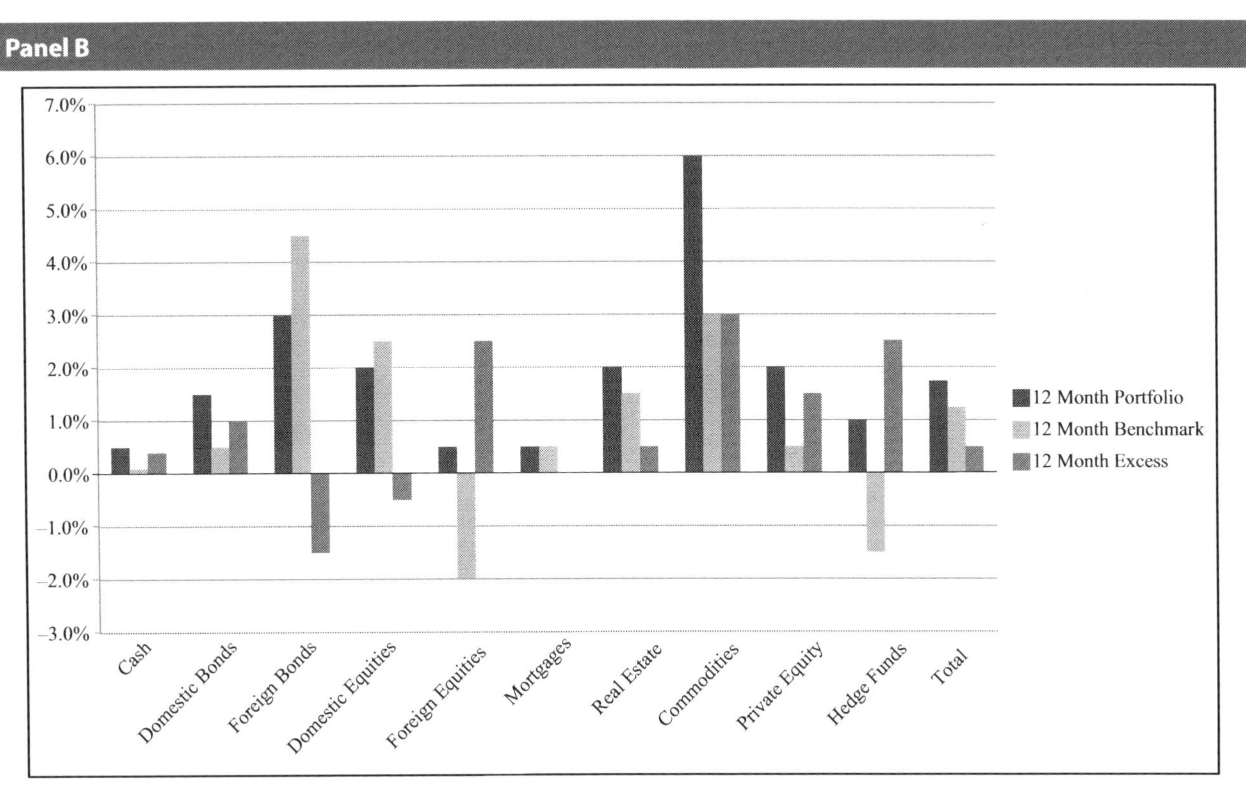

A return attribution report is a presentation of the different contributions to the (excess) return of the investment portfolio or product during the measurement period as a result of decisions to depart from the benchmark. Contribution analysis, which is concerned with how holdings or asset classes contributed to total return on a stand-alone basis, may also be presented. The decomposition of the (excess) return should reflect the investment management process. Return attribution helps the user to better understand the sources of (excess) return. This information, as input or feedback into the investment management process, has great value because it helps monitor whether the proposed investment strategy was really implemented and identifies how investment management decisions contributed to the overall (excess) return.

Exhibit 9 provides an example of a return attribution report for a multi-asset class portfolio illustrating the decomposition of the investment portfolio's absolute and excess return segregated by asset class.

Exhibit 9 Sample Return Attribution Report

Panel A

	Portfolio			Benchmark			Management Effects			
	Return	Weight	Contribution	Return	Weight	Contribution	Asset allocation	Stock picking	Interaction	Total
Cash	0.50%	10.00%	0.05%	0.10%	6.00%	0.01%	0.00%	0.02%	0.02%	0.04%
Domestic Bonds	1.50%	22.00%	0.33%	0.50%	20.00%	0.10%	0.01%	0.20%	0.02%	0.23%
Foreign Bonds	3.00%	10.00%	0.30%	4.50%	15.00%	0.68%	−0.23%	−0.23%	0.08%	−0.38%
Domestic Equities	2.00%	17.00%	0.34%	2.50%	14.00%	0.35%	0.08%	−0.07%	−0.02%	−0.01%
Foreign Equities	0.50%	12.00%	0.06%	−2.00%	16.00%	−0.32%	0.08%	0.40%	−0.10%	0.38%
Mortgages	0.50%	5.00%	0.03%	0.50%	3.00%	0.02%	0.01%	0.00%	0.00%	0.01%
Real Estate	2.00%	16.00%	0.32%	1.50%	20.00%	0.30%	−0.06%	0.10%	−0.02%	0.02%
Commodities	6.00%	4.00%	0.24%	3.00%	4.00%	0.12%	0.00%	0.12%	0.00%	0.12%
Private Equity	2.00%	3.00%	0.06%	0.50%	1.00%	0.01%	0.01%	0.02%	0.03%	0.06%
Hedge Funds	1.00%	1.00%	0.01%	−1.50%	1.00%	−0.02%	0.00%	0.03%	0.00%	0.03%
Total	**1.74%**	**100.00%**	**1.74%**	**1.24%**	**100.00%**	**1.24%**	**−0.10%**	**0.59%**	**0.01%**	**0.50%**

Panel B

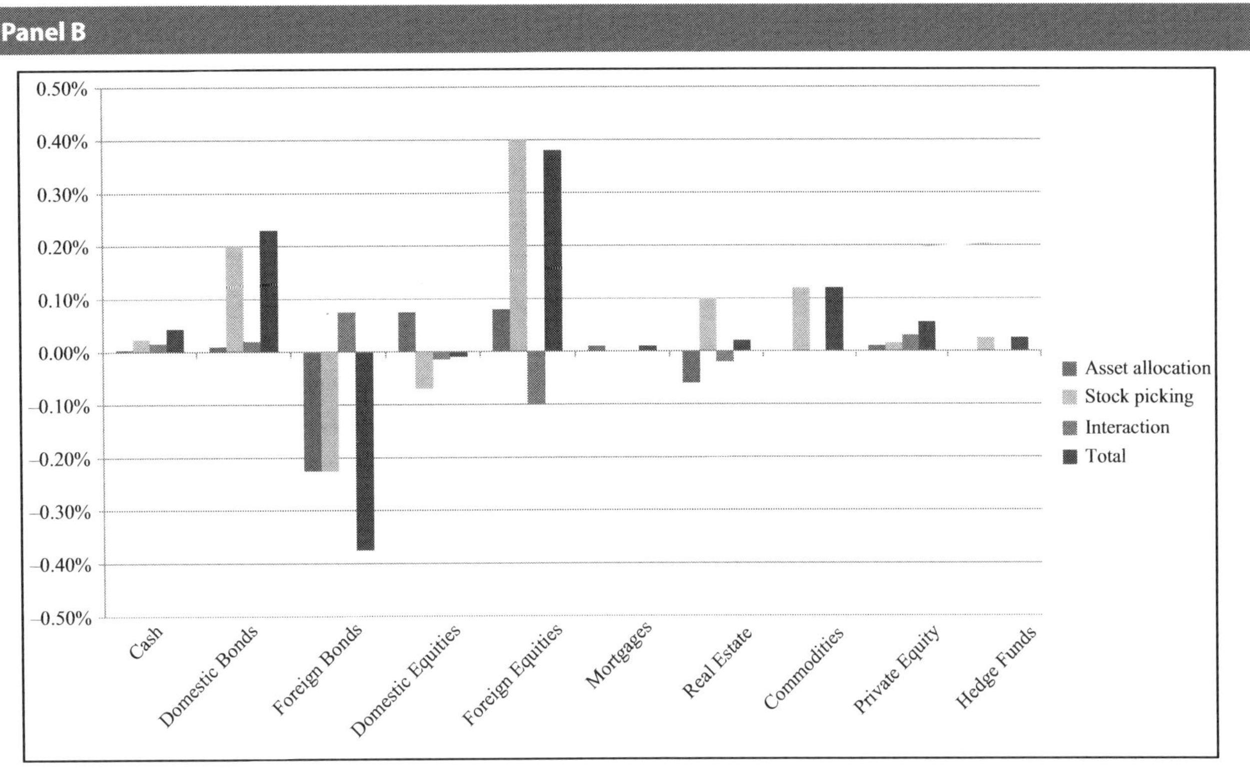

A risk report is the presentation of the historical dispersion and distribution of the return of the investment portfolio or product during the measurement period—on either a stand-alone basis or against the portfolio manager's benchmark or peer group. A risk report contains investment information mainly based on time series analysis, such as statistical risk figures over different fixed or rolling time periods or risk break down analysis. The possibilities of illustrating such information are manifold and can include tables, graphics, dispersion measures, and figures describing the return distribution. The chosen design, format, and methodology should support a better understanding of risk and risk-related investment information. In summary, risk reporting helps the user gain a better view on the past development of the fluctuations of the absolute and excess returns of the investment portfolio or product being considered. In addition, ex-ante risk analytics afford a better understanding of what the expected absolute and excess risk could be and where it might come from.

Exhibit 10 provides an example of a risk report illustrating the absolute and excess risk of a multi-asset class portfolio and its asset classes for different measurement periods, as well as the respective contributions to volatility and tracking risk.

Exhibit 10 Sample Risk Report

Panel A

	Portfolio			Benchmark			Contribution to Portfolio Risk		
Annualized	**1 Year**	**3 Years**	**5 Years**	**1 Year**	**3 Years**	**5 Years**	**1 Year**	**3 Years**	**5 Years**
Bonds									
Volatility	6.50%	5.50%	6.10%	6.40%	6.00%	5.60%	35.03%	34.34%	35.39%
Tracking error	0.50%	0.90%	1.50%				15.30%	16.23%	25.36%

(continued)

Exhibit 10 (Continued)

Annualized	Portfolio 1 Year	Portfolio 3 Years	Portfolio 5 Years	Benchmark 1 Year	Benchmark 3 Years	Benchmark 5 Years	Contribution to Portfolio Risk 1 Year	Contribution to Portfolio Risk 3 Years	Contribution to Portfolio Risk 5 Years
Equities									
Volatility	17.50%	16.20%	16.80%	17.40%	16.80%	16.40%	59.13%	62.03%	59.14%
Tracking error	1.50%	0.90%	2.00%				63.21%	68.45%	64.23%
Alternative Investments									
Volatility	5.20%	3.50%	4.70%	5.00%	4.00%	6.00%	5.85%	3.63%	5.48%
Tracking error	2.50%	1.30%	1.60%				21.49%	15.32%	10.41%
Total									
Volatility	5.16%	4.41%	4.82%	5.21%	4.87%	4.78%	100.00%	100.00%	100.00%
Tracking error	0.68%	1.04%	0.85%				100.00%	100.00%	100.00%

Panel B

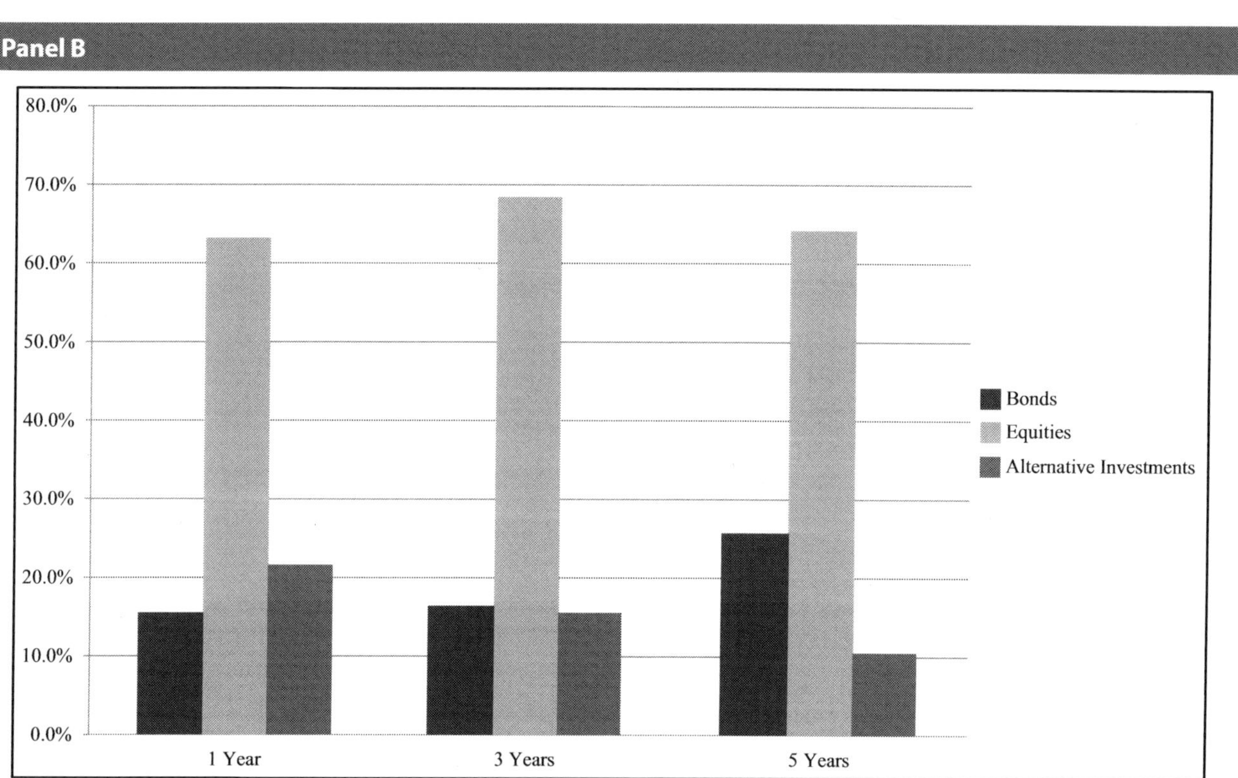

A portfolio holdings report is the presentation of the investments made within the investment portfolio in which typically the holdings or exposures are as of the end of the measurement period. Holdings may be presented on a stand-alone basis or against the respective benchmark. Portfolio holdings may be presented as a list (one-dimensional) or as a matrix (two-dimensional) where the classification scheme should be purpose-specific or risk-oriented.[14] A transactions analysis may be added to support a better understanding of the changes to the investment portfolio's risk profile during the measurement period. Portfolio holdings and transactions analysis helps the user gain a better view of the past and current risk exposures in the investment portfolio.

Exhibit 11 provides an example of a portfolio holdings report illustrating the portfolio and benchmark asset allocation of a multi-asset class portfolio segregated by asset class in percent and in EUR terms.

Exhibit 11 Sample Portfolio Holdings Report

Panel A

	Portfolio		Benchmark		Relative	
	Weight	million EUR	Weight	million EUR	Weight	million EUR
Cash	10.00%	15.00	6.00%	9.00	4.00%	6.00
Domestic bonds	22.00%	33.00	20.00%	30.00	2.00%	3.00
Foreign bonds	10.00%	15.00	15.00%	22.50	–5.00%	–7.50
Domestic equities	17.00%	25.50	14.00%	21.00	3.00%	4.50
Foreign equities	12.00%	18.00	16.00%	24.00	–4.00%	–6.00
Mortgages	5.00%	7.50	3.00%	4.50	2.00%	3.00
Real estate	16.00%	24.00	20.00%	30.00	–4.00%	–6.00
Commodities	4.00%	6.00	4.00%	6.00	0.00%	0.00
Private equity	3.00%	4.50	1.00%	1.50	2.00%	3.00
Hedge funds	1.00%	1.50	1.00%	1.50	0.00%	0.00
Total	**100.00%**	**150.00**	**100.00%**	**150.00**	**0.00%**	**0.00**

14 The holdings analysis of a portfolio may only be purpose-specific or risk-oriented if the classification of individual securities are reflective of the investment style—for example, for an equity portfolio following a sector timing approach, only the sector allocation is useful.

Panel B

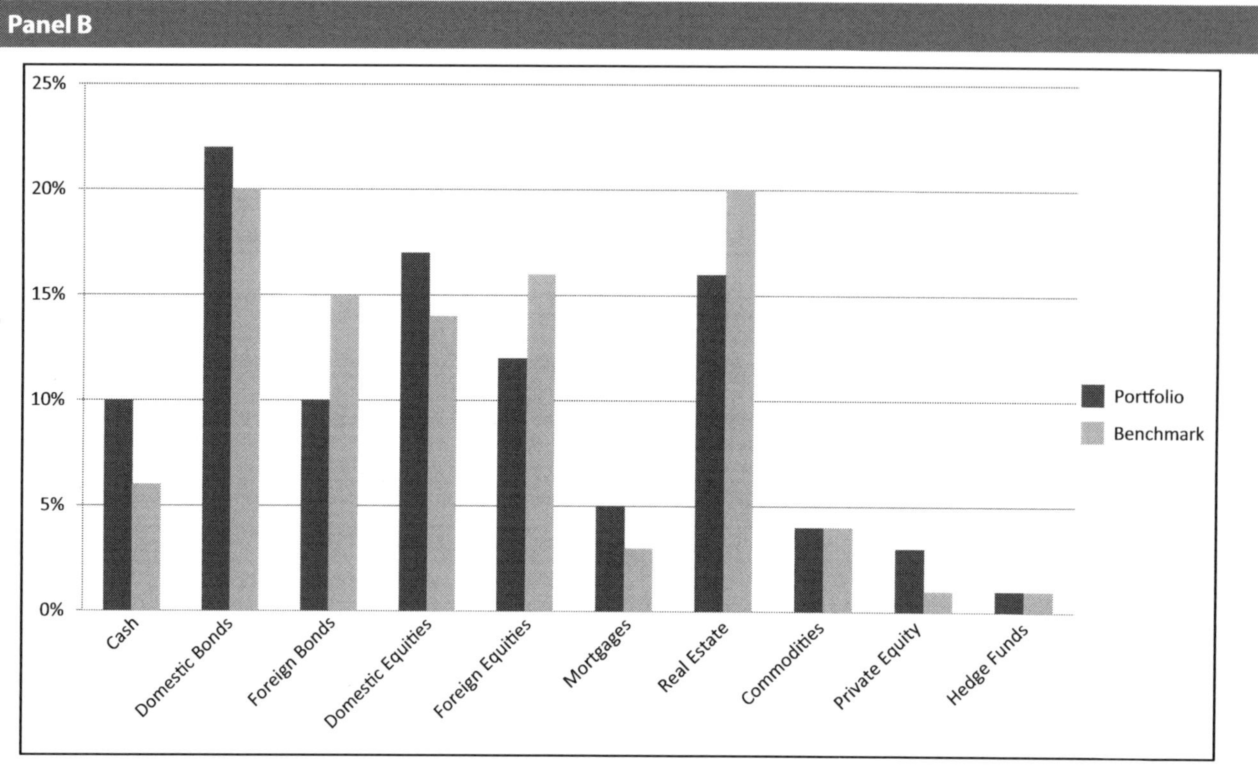

The performance and holdings analytics discussed above are normally not presented in isolation but are instead grouped together to form a comprehensive investment performance presentation. To make the presentation complete, investment management companies can supplement the analytics mentioned with other components. Supplemental materials can include the following:

- A cover page
- Sections with general information about the investment portfolio, the investment strategy or product, the fund manager, and the investment management company
- A performance explanation
- A market outlook
- A section with disclosures explaining methodologies or data used
- A legal disclaimer

3.3 Internal versus External Investment Performance Presentations

It is important to highlight and discuss the distinction between internal and external investment performance presentations:

- External investment performance presentations are reports prepared by an investment management organization intended for distribution outside the firm to external users such as prospective or existing clients, shareholders, and the general public. External presentations normally do not contain sensitive organizational or investment information unless it is necessary to comply with local laws and regulations, to adhere to respective industry best practices, or to achieve a particular purpose. These external reports are prepared to disclose appropriate investment information to satisfy the information needs of the external users.

We further distinguish between voluntary and mandatory external IPPs: Voluntary external reporting is based on the investment management organization's mission, as well as self-imposed transparency and accountability. Here, self-regulation comes into place and gives guidance on best practices with respect to the calculation, the analysis, and finally the presentation of investment performance to external users.[15] Mandatory external reporting is based on local laws and regulations or on client agreements and contracts.[16]

- In contrast, internal investment performance presentations are reports prepared by an investment management organization intended for inside distribution, circulation, and use by portfolio managers, risk managers, compliance officers, marketing officers, boards of trustees, and/or senior management. Internal presentations may contain sensitive or confidential organizational or investment information and are therefore not designed to be made public. These internal reports are prepared to disclose appropriate investment information to satisfy the information needs of the internal users. Furthermore, these presentations are expected to be less formal than those that might be sent out to external users. Internal presentations may include information on portfolios, products, employees, departments, or on the whole investment management organization.[17] These presentations can discuss revenues, market share, efficiency, performance, risk, and other aspects relevant for the future organizational success.[18] A basic internal presentation may provide just factual information which has been collated into a single document. Others may include certain commentary and conclusions on how well the organization or parts of it are doing versus defined targets or objectives. Internal IPPs can often be accompanied by emotional discussions between the different stakeholders. To limit such discussions, internal IPPs should follow some guiding principles or best practices:[19]
  - The purpose for the IPP and the reasons for its creation and content are transparent and clear.
  - The type of the intended user or the audience in mind and their expected use of the investment information are taken into account when designing the IPP.
  - The IPP is a fair representation of the investments made, results achieved, and the risks taken.
  - The IPP is relevant and appropriate for the presented asset classes, investment strategies, and investment product.
  - The IPP complies with all applicable laws and regulations.

---

15 The GIPS standards are a good example for such an industry best practice.

16 The local laws and regulations for IPPs are manifold and are available for specific types of investment products or client segments—for example in Europe the MiFID (Markets in Financial Instruments Directive) and the UCITS (Undertakings for Collective Investment in Transferable Securities Directive) or in the United States, various Federal public laws and related implementing regulations (see www.sec.gov/about/laws.shtml).

17 For example, the head of portfolio management might be interested in the performance of an individual portfolio manager or a specific portfolio management team.

18 Examples for such internal IPPs are controlling-type reports on the performance and the quality of the offered investment products presented and discussed at senior management meetings or reports on the performance of individual investment portfolios or products discussed during performance appraisals.

19 In general, these principles are also relevant for external IPPs but, if not explicitly required by regulations or best practices, may not be followed.

- The policies and procedures for investment performance presentation are documented and available upon request.
- The policies and procedures for investment performance presentation are reviewed regularly by an independent (third) party.

4 CONCLUSIONS AND SUMMARY

This reading describes different types of investment performance presentation and outlines the preparation and uses within investment management organizations and processes. Among the points made are the following:

- An IPP is the illustration of investment information, the presentation of the results achieved, and the risks taken within a portfolio.
- An IPP is a specific type of investment reporting. As an integrated part of the investment management process, it provides all stakeholders with information and feedback that can enhance future decisions and activities.
- The different types of IPP can be described by the presented information, the intended user, the intended use, and the report preparer.
- The IPP process is a recurring communication process between the different participants and stakeholders of the overall investment management process.
- The generic IPP process is split into three sub-processes: data management, production, and support.
- The data management process contains activities to ensure that data are available and of sufficient quality for the subsequent report production.
- The production process involves activities to ensure that the required IPP is processed and disseminated to users.
- The support process is concerned with all activities to ensure that the IPP is understood by and meets the requirements of users.
- The three process-related types of IPPs are sales-oriented, management-oriented, and monitoring-oriented presentations.
- A sales-oriented IPP is a specific type of presentation used in the individual steps of the sales process of an investment management organization.
- A management-oriented IPP is a specific type of presentation used in the investment management process especially for investment reporting and for investment controlling.
- A monitoring-oriented IPP is a specific type of presentation used for certain monitoring purposes, often focusing on investment management policies and guidelines or on regulatory requirements.
- Important and often used analytics-related IPPs include (a) portfolio holdings report, (b) performance report, (c) return attribution report, and (d) risk report. In addition, presentations may be accompanied by a cover page, general information, disclosures, or a disclaimer.
- External IPPs are reports prepared by an investment management organization intended for outside distribution, circulation, and use by external users such as prospective or existing clients, shareholders, and the general public.

- Internal IPPs are reports prepared by an investment management organization intended for inside distribution, circulation, and use by internal users such as portfolio managers, risk managers, compliance officers, marketing officers, board of trustees, and/or senior management.
- IPPs should be a fair representation of the investments made, the results achieved, and the risks taken and therefore should be designed following respective industry best practices.

PRACTICE PROBLEMS

1 The manager of the equity portfolio of a pension plan asks a performance analyst to prepare the annual investment performance presentation of a client's portfolio. Which of the following topics should have the *highest* priority in the presentation?

A Return attribution

B Market commentary on asset classes

C Effect of taxation on portfolio returns

2 An individual owns a portfolio of €3 million that he has invested himself in passively managed exchange-traded funds according to the following precise asset allocation: 40% diversified stocks, 40% long-term bonds, and 20% short-term securities. He asks a consultant to prepare a performance presentation of his investments that covers the period of the last five years. Which of the following information is *most* relevant to the requested presentation?

A Tracking risk

B Return attribution

C Peer group comparison

3 An investment management firm has been asked to submit a proposal to an endowment fund to manage the fund's bond portfolio. The performance analyst responsible for preparing the presentation on historical performance intends to make available the GIPS standards presentation that is given to all prospective clients. However, he would like to personalize the presentation by presenting additional relevant information. The department involved with which of the following processes in investment performance presentation is *best* equipped to design the personalized presentation?

A Support

B Production

C Data management

4 According to Provision 2.A.2 of the GIPS standards, "Firms must calculate time-weighted rates of return that adjust for external cash flows." Which of the following sub-processes within the investment performance presentation process is *most* relevant to presenting accurate calculations?

A Consulting (within support process)

B Quality check (within production process)

C Data enhancing (within data management process)

5 To evaluate the implementation of an investment strategy, a performance analyst prepares an investment performance presentation (IPP) that features detailed return and risk attribution analytics. Such an IPP is *best* classified as:

A sales-oriented.

B monitoring-oriented.

C management-oriented.

6 The sponsor of a pension plan is surprised when he receives a preliminary performance report from his investment manager for the most recent fiscal year. The investment manager had been given the mandate to actively manage the asset allocation but not the securities within each asset class. The investment policy called for a long-term strategic asset allocation of 50% long-term

domestic bonds, 40% domestic stocks, and 10% money market securities. The report that the sponsor has just received shows an 8% return for the whole portfolio with no further decomposition. Because the sponsor knows that the return on the portfolio benchmark is around 6%, he suspects that the investment policy has not been followed. In order to quickly check that his suspicion is well founded, what *minimum* information should the sponsor request from the investment manager?

A A return attribution report showing the excess return by asset class.

B A portfolio holdings analysis showing the holdings of each asset class.

C A risk attribution report showing the contribution to portfolio risk by asset class.

7 A performance analyst is preparing external investment performance presentations for the ten largest equity portfolios that his firm manages. His supervisor has asked that these presentations contain as little information as possible that is taken from the internal presentations of the firm. Which of the following pieces of information, specifically classified as internal by the supervisor, should the analyst still mention in the presentations because of its relevance to the investment management process?

A The use of a sub-advisor to manage the equity portfolios.

B A peer group comparison of the amounts of similar equity portfolios managed by other firms.

C The fraction of the total revenues of the firm originating from the management of equity portfolios.

SOLUTIONS

1 A is correct. The investment performance information "typically focuses on the presentation of the performance as the outcome of investment management decisions." Of the three topics mentioned, return attribution is the only one related to investment management decisions.

   B is incorrect because the preparer here is the investment manager of the equity portfolio and market commentary on asset classes is not relevant to the decisions of the equity portfolio manager. This does not preclude the presentation of market commentary as supplemental information. C is incorrect because the intended user is the sponsor of the pension plan and the pension plan is not taxable. Therefore the taxation aspect is not relevant.

2 A is correct. Tracking risk is most relevant to evaluating how well this individual investor's strategic investment decision was executed.

   B is incorrect because return attribution aims to indicate how the investment results compare to the benchmarks in terms of sector allocation and security selection. None of these variables is important in the present situation since (i) the investment strategy is precisely defined in terms of asset class weights, and (ii) the investor uses passively managed exchange-traded funds within each asset class. C is incorrect because although peer group comparison may be useful in indicating the historical results of a set of managers with the same investment strategy, here the strategy is unique to the individual who owns the portfolio.

3 A is correct. The support process "is concerned with all activities that assure that investment performance presentations are understood by their users and fit their requirements and needs." In particular, the people in the design sub-sector will be able to consider "tailor-made solutions addressing individual needs for layout…"

   B is incorrect because the production process will ensure that the "presentations are processed and disseminated to users" but will not assist with the design of the new presentation. C is incorrect because the data management process will ensure that the required data are available for the production process but only after the production process is known.

4 B is correct. Quality checks will ensure that all presentations "fulfill the agreed-upon and committed reporting requirements."

   A is incorrect because consulting deals with helping "the user to articulate and formulate requirements." Here the requirements are already well defined. C is incorrect because data enhancing deals with the quality of data. Here, we are dealing with a calculation formula that uses existing data.

5 C is correct. The IPP is management-oriented and fulfills a control function in checking on the implementation of an investment strategy.

   A is incorrect because sales is not involved. B is not correct because the purpose is best described as management oriented.

6 B is correct. The sponsor simply wants to know to what extent the investment manager has dissociated from the long-term investment strategy of 50% bonds/40% stocks/10% short-term. The portfolio holdings will indicate just that.

A is incorrect because the excess return from the benchmark for each asset class is more than what is needed by the sponsor. C is incorrect because the contribution to portfolio risk by asset class is more than what is needed by the sponsor. Indeed, at this stage, the sponsor has expressed no concern over the risk taken by the investment manager.

7 A is correct. The use of a sub-advisor is an important element of the investment management process that will affect the return/risk profile of the portfolio.

B is incorrect because the market share of the firm is not an important element in the investment management process. C is incorrect because the relative source of revenues of the firm, among the different asset classes managed, does not affect the investment management process.

READING

13

Beyond GIPS Compliance: Maximizing Value

by Iain W. McAra

Iain W. McAra is at CFA Institute (United Kingdom).

LEARNING OUTCOMES

Mastery	*The candidate should be able to:*
☐	**a.** explain the value added from being a GIPS compliant firm with respect to investors, intermediaries, and regulators;
☐	**b.** explain the benefits to the firm of complying with the GIPS standards.

Investors, intermediaries, and regulators each benefit from a firm's claim of compliance with the GIPS standards. Compliance, however, yields benefits to the firm that go far beyond the ability to claim compliance. The processes that support claims of compliance can enhance productivity, improve product management and governance, and increase cross-functional collaboration. This use of the Standards can add value to the firm, clients, prospective clients, intermediaries, regulators, and the industry as a whole.

The resources required to achieve and maintain compliance with the GIPS standards are not insignificant, but there are many ways in which these efforts can be leveraged beyond just making the claim of compliance. That is the focus of this reading—"Beyond GIPS Compliance: Maximizing Value."

MISSION STATEMENT OF THE GIPS EXECUTIVE COMMITTEE

The GIPS standards are maintained by the GIPS Executive Committee, a nine-member committee of senior investment industry professionals. The Executive Committee's mission statement is as follows:

This presentation comes from the GIPS Standards Annual Conference held in Chicago on 27–28 October 2011.

> Promote ethics and integrity and instill trust through the use of the Global Investment Performance Standards by achieving universal demand for compliance by asset owners, universal adoption by asset managers, and universal support from regulators for the ultimate benefit of the global investment community.

In aligning with a group that pursues this mission, an investment management firm announces to clients, prospective clients, employees, and regulators that the firm embraces the elements of ethics, integrity, and trust inherent in the mission statement.

WHAT COMPLIANCE MEANS: OVERVIEW OF THE GIPS STANDARDS

The GIPS standards contain both *requirements* that must always be followed and *recommendations* that are optional. Firms that adhere to the GIPS standards must follow the same set of fundamental rules relating to underlying input data, time-weighted rate of return calculations, composite construction, disclosures, and presentation. To claim compliance with the GIPS standards, a firm must, at the very minimum, meet every requirement of the standards, without exception. When a claim of compliance is made, knowledgeable users of the information, such as plan sponsors and investment consultants, can assume that

- the investment management firm maintains documented policies and procedures for performance reporting;
- any allowable deviations from the requirements of the Standards are disclosed;
- the universe of client portfolios included in the definition of the firm is described and disclosed;
- all actual, fee-paying, discretionary portfolios are included in at least one composite; and
- the firm is not excluding poorly performing portfolios.

Investors should be able to see that they are getting everything, good performance and not-so-good performance, according to the definition of the firm.

A firm must initially present 5 years of compliant annual returns (or since inception, if fewer than 5 years old), building up over time to 10 years of consecutive annual returns. The GIPS standards prohibit annualizing partial-year performance. Beyond presenting returns, the GIPS standards include risk measures, such as the 36-month rolling standard deviation of returns of both the composite and its benchmark.

The GIPS standards promote genuine cross-border comparability of performance between countries and across strategies. As of April 2016, there are 36 endorsed GIPS country sponsors (organizations CFA Institute partners with to promote and develop the Standards) and five endorsed translations of the 2010 GIPS standards—in German, Japanese, Korean, Spanish, and Russian. Country sponsors promote the GIPS standards locally and provide input on the global development of the GIPS standards. Cross-border comparability aids both the investor and the investment management firm.

Because prospective clients can now compare like with like, they are able to make truly informed decisions. Required disclosures regarding fees, returns, dispersion of accounts within each composite, and the use of leverage, among others, are part of the Standards. By adhering to the Standards, investment managers increase the level of transparency and consistency in the industry, contributing to the mission of promoting ethics and integrity and instilling trust.

BENEFITS OF THE GIPS STANDARDS

A firm's compliance with the Standards benefits many parties—the investor; intermediaries, such as consultants and other advisers; and regulators, as well as the investment management firm itself.

Value to Investors

Compliance with the GIPS standards enables investors to more readily compare the performance of investment strategies among managers. The returns are not only comparable, but information regarding the consistency and quality of the data, the frequency and types of valuations, the handling of accruals, and the treatment of large cash inflows and outflows are also accessible. As an example, according to the Standards, large external cash flows trigger a revaluation of portfolio holdings. However, there is no universally accepted measure of what constitutes a large cash flow; each firm has discretion to define it as appropriate to its business. All such discretionary determinations must be either disclosed or made available upon request if a firm claims compliance with the GIPS standards.

The required disclosures enable the investor to ask the investment manager more informed questions. A few of the possible areas for discussion include composite inception dates, composite dispersion, and key personnel changes. We will discuss these three briefly, but there are other required disclosures, such as changes to the composite definition and changes to the benchmark, that are also helpful to the investor.

When evaluating a manager, investors are presented with the track record of the manager's strategies. Many composites have creation dates (which must be disclosed) a long time after the inception date of the strategy. Observing the gap between the inception of the strategy and the inception of the composite, investors should seek to understand the manager's rationale. Were the early returns sub-standard? Did the strategy evolve as assets under management grew? Understanding the information in a manager's presentations and the data behind it, investors can ask management relevant questions to enhance their understanding of the strategy.

Composite dispersion statistics provide another avenue for inquiry. There are multiple ways in which composite dispersion characteristics may be presented. It is often presented as the maximum and minimum returns of portfolios in the composite, or as the standard deviation of portfolio returns. A narrowly defined composite should probably have a tight dispersion measure; a broad definition can be expected to have a wider dispersion. A wide range should be evaluated further, particularly if the composite has been described as having a tightly defined and implemented strategy.

All significant events that would assist a prospective client in interpreting the GIPS-compliant presentation must be disclosed. The departure of key investment personnel is one such event, as is the acquisition of another firm. The investor should understand what the manager considers to be a significant event. The disclosure of significant events can also lead to a discussion of other events that occurred but that the manager did not think were significant.

A GIPS-compliant presentation also includes information regarding the relative importance of the strategy to the firm's overall business. The investment manager must report, either in absolute dollar amounts or relative to total-firm assets, the proportion of firm-wide assets the strategy represents. It must also report the number of accounts invested in the strategy. A list of all of the firm's composites must be made available upon request so that clients can assess how large the composite is in relation to other composites and strategies pursued by the firm. This information often leads to an important question: Is this particular composite or strategy really getting enough of management's attention?

Insights such as these can be valuable in developing a qualitative understanding of the investment management firm. The key is for investors to look behind the numbers and disclosures and to ask questions that are prompted by what has been presented as well as what has been excluded.

Value to Intermediaries

Intermediaries, such as investment consultants, also benefit from these same GIPS disclosures, but dealing with GIPS-compliant investment managers yields an additional benefit to intermediaries. They are able to receive and process *standardized* information more quickly and, therefore, focus their efforts on the higher value-added elements of their services to clients.

The data-gathering process is an aspect of a consultant's manager evaluation services that is low-margin but has a high potential for error. In requesting GIPS-compliant performance records, the consultant can be assured of the quality and the consistency of the data underlying the information and thereby avoid the need to validate the returns themselves, moving immediately to the *evaluation* of the firms. In much the same way that the investor benefits from the GIPS standards, the intermediary can use the disclosures to ask pertinent questions, recognize anomalies, and conduct more in-depth due diligence.

The intermediary might also request that firms that are not claiming compliance provide the same set of information for comparison purposes. In some cases, a GIPS-compliant performance presentation becomes a criterion on which the consultant will filter the universe of eligible managers. There is information in those firms' responses—or lack of response.

Value to Regulators

Regulators are concerned with a firm's compliance—with the GIPS standards, whether the firm claims GIPS compliance, and with local regulatory requirements, such as those that govern advertising. If a firm claims to be compliant with the GIPS standards, regulators can expect that the firm has policies and procedures that support the production of investment performance results; the examiners will then evaluate the firm's adherence to the Standards as well as to the firm's own policies and procedures. If they find that the firm is *not* following these guidelines, the firm may be accused of falsely advertising its abilities.

LEVERAGING THE EFFORTS REQUIRED TO COMPLY WITH THE GIPS STANDARDS

As illustrated above, GIPS compliance is likely to aid an investment manager in building its client relationships. In addition to this most obvious benefit, compliance can enhance productivity and provide many ancillary benefits to the investment manager. The robust data collection processes and formal policies and procedures necessary to claim GIPS compliance can be leveraged throughout the firm.

Defining "the Firm"

The GIPS standards must be applied on a firm-wide basis. Fundamental to the GIPS standards is the premise that all actual, fee-paying, discretionary portfolios must be included in at least one composite. As the first step in complying with the GIPS standards, the firm must be defined fairly and appropriately. Firms should adopt the broadest, most meaningful definition of the firm and consider how it is held out to the public. The scope of this definition should include all offices, regardless of geographical distinctions, operating under the same brand name regardless of the actual name of the individual investment management company.

For the purposes of the GIPS standards, a "firm" is an investment firm, subsidiary, or division held out to clients or prospective clients as a distinct business entity—that is, a business unit that

1 is organizationally and functionally segregated from other units, divisions, departments, or offices;
2 retains discretion over the assets it manages; and
3 has autonomy over the investment decision-making process.

The GIPS standards recommend that if a parent company contains multiple firms, each firm within the parent company should disclose a list of the other firms contained within the parent company.

Source: GIPS Standards Firm Definition Guidance Statement.

Productivity

GIPS compliance simplifies performance reporting through the reduction of customized reporting requests. In the 1980s, well before the introduction of the GIPS standards as we know them today, firms generated multiple investment performance presentations, each relevant to a specific geographic location and prepared in accordance with each country's preferred practices.[1] The same data might be reworked several times for the firm to present a given strategy in the various locales where it planned to do business. Now, with one global performance standard, the one set of data can be presented and accepted in multiple countries—a savings in time and effort that, at least in part, offsets the time and effort invested in becoming GIPS compliant.

Many professionals within the investment firm often request unique data items or custom reports to serve a very specific need. For example, the finance department wants to aggregate assets under management by strategy or based on the use of performance fees to anticipate management fee income; the legal department wants data to complete a new regulatory requirement involving performance data; or the internal audit function wants performance information to ensure that fund performance and individual account performance are not biased in any way.

Supporting these unique requests can be an expensive and inefficient use of firm resources. The effort to achieve and maintain GIPS compliance requires a very robust data management system. With this system, numerous reports are produced to maintain the claim of compliance; it is quite likely that these reports contain all the information the managers need. Leveraging this data management system allows accurate reports to be produced quickly using consistent data across the firm and reduces the time spent on manual manipulation of spreadsheets.

1 The founding document that would eventually become today's GIPS standards first appeared in the September/October 1987 issue of the *Financial Analysts Journal*.

To maximize the use of the data internally, it is important to involve each of the strategy, product, and asset groups in the development of the data management system.

Product Management and Oversight

Compliance with the GIPS standards introduces practices that facilitate track record transparency and the ability to conduct a full and fair internal review of products, strategies, and individual accounts. Developing a detailed understanding of the data being presented can prompt internal discussions concerning risks and opportunities.

By examining the composite reporting, managers can identify outlier portfolios—those whose performance places them at either extreme of the composite's returns. Although the outliers may be within the tolerance of the composite definition, an examination of them can provide insights into the effect of cash flows or the performance of individual portfolio managers.

The dispersion measure can also be used in cross-product evaluation and internal control. A composite dispersion that is noticeably broader than others or that exhibits material changes over time may signal something about that strategy's management processes or internal controls that requires attention. An investigation into the causes of the dispersion can lead to detailed questions that may reveal other characteristics or cause for concern with respect to the strategy.

Firm Governance

A GIPS compliance committee is an important first step toward successful GIPS compliance. To ensure success of the effort to achieve and maintain compliance, it is important that senior management serve as members of this committee. Senior management has a broad understanding of the firm's products, goals, and objectives. Their participation in the committee signals to the rest of the firm that senior management is invested in the success of GIPS compliance.

An investment management firm claiming GIPS compliance must have documented policies and procedures that are adhered to consistently. Developing and maintaining comprehensive policies and procedures entails a significant commitment. Although there is not a one-size-fits-all set of policies and procedures, the Standards provide a clear structure within which the firm-specific policies and procedures can be collected.

Documented policies and procedures are an essential element of good governance and they can be leveraged in many ways—risk management, internal control and audit, and training. Once documented, policies must be kept current to reflect prevailing industry practice. In a dynamic environment, such as the investment industry, there will be frequent policy changes driven by regulation, systems capabilities, and product development. All policy changes must be tracked so that an audit will reveal what policy was in force at the time of a given report or event under examination. The policy document becomes a valuable archive of the history of the firm and serves to preserve institutional memory.

The documentation should capture the evolution of policies and procedures in response to industry dynamics, including the decisions taken and the justification behind those decisions. If a similar scenario is encountered again, it is then possible to refer back to the earlier decisions and confidently follow the same procedure, ensuring a speedy response and consistent approach.

Policies and procedures become a valuable training resource. New employees are easily oriented to the firm's processes, and employees transferring among responsibilities can refer to the applicable policies and procedures to quickly come up to speed. GIPS policies and procedures are a valuable training manual not only for performance staff, but also for marketing, compliance, and anyone who produces reports for clients.

Even if a firm's client-reporting team has primary responsibility for producing the reports in compliance with the Standards, others in the firm who discuss how past performance is represented to prospective clients must also understand the Standards. As an example, a firm may determine from its assessment of GIPS reporting that change is required to minimize the impact of large external cash flows on investment performance. This may, in turn, lead to changes in the way in which flows are communicated and processed among the various internal groups. In a Six Sigma environment,[2] policies and procedures should dovetail into the business production process flows.

Cross-Functional Collaboration

Preparation of performance presentations that are compliant with the Standards relies on information from multiple business units. A large investment management organization may be spread out not only across buildings, but also across states and even countries. Today, some of the largest firms outsource some or all of their functions to third parties or affiliated offshore entities within their firm. The need to communicate across the divisional and geographical entities to maintain GIPS compliance helps to keep regular communications channels open and active.

Keeping the policies and procedures up-to-date requires collaboration among legal and compliance, finance and audit, information services, portfolio management, client service and marketing, and the performance reporting team. Input data and calculation methodology, valuation policies and sources, information technology for accounting processes, the asset classification system, mandate information, fee data, and assets under management all must be kept up-to-date to maintain compliance with the Standards.

Benchmark selection for a composite also often entails collaboration across functional teams. The investment teams' internal reviews of their products and accounts often use the composites produced by the performance team, and the understanding of both groups is enhanced when they discuss the creation and maintenance of the composites or the suitability of a particular benchmark.

The legal, performance, investment, and marketing teams must also collaborate to ensure that the marketing literature appropriately reflects the underlying information.

Verification

Verification is a recommended, not mandatory, provision of the GIPS standards. Verification is an assessment of firm-wide composite-construction requirements and proper documentation of GIPS policies and procedures by a qualified and independent third party. This third-party verification, in and of itself, is a useful independent audit of the effectiveness of the firm's policies and procedures. If an investment management firm chooses to pursue verification, it can leverage the verifier's expertise in many ways.

Verifiers, because of the work required in a verification, must understand the structure of each client's firm, the processes and procedures it follows, its valuation basis, its performance calculations, its product base, and other information that is relevant to the claim of GIPS compliance. Verification firms, through the knowledge that they acquire from visiting different companies, can guide firms toward best practices by sharing their opinions and views about what solutions are available, as well as approaches to maintaining, monitoring, and reporting the necessary information. Once a verification is complete, the verification firm may provide a recommendation

---

2 Six Sigma is a business management strategy that seeks to improve the quality of output and customer outcomes by identifying and improving processes that generate errors and defects. Originally applied to the manufacturing sector in the 1980s, Six Sigma is widely used today in other industries, including financial services.

letter describing the findings and may include recommendations or suggestions for improvement, such as improvement in production processes or software enhancements to reduce the risk of errors and reduce time spent on certain tasks.

The policies and procedures required by the Standards aid the business recovery function. An independent third-party review of these policies and procedures, which must be done as part of a verification, can provide an objective assessment of the ability of the policies to fulfill the business continuity objective.

At the same time, the verifier's work of collecting, analyzing, and testing the policies and procedures from other business units to ensure that the claim is maintained correctly can help those business units identify areas for improvement. Such an evaluation will highlight areas where beneficial changes can or should occur, where inconsistencies may exist, where tightening can benefit throughput and accuracy, and where a policy or procedure is documented but not actually followed or cannot be demonstrated as being followed. These all add value beyond just making the claim of compliance.

Performance Examination

In addition to firm-wide verification, an optional performance examination determines whether a specific composite is in compliance with the GIPS standards. A performance examination report cannot be issued unless a verification report has also been issued. In a composite-specific performance examination, verifiers investigate the way in which the composite is constructed, including the data used to create a composite return stream, the inclusion or exclusion of client accounts in a composite, the valuation methodology used and its consistency, the performance calculation, the completeness of the compliant presentation, and the availability of the supporting documentation.

A firm will not necessarily have every composite examined; the selection of composites to be examined is often based on which strategies are popular and where interest from prospects is likely to be. Verification and performance examinations not only signal to prospects the quality of the compliance claim, but may be used by the firm's enterprise risk management function to identify areas that can be strengthened or where additional checks and balances, documentation, and process improvements could be beneficial.

CONCLUSION

The investment industry—by its very nature—exists on a system of checks and balances; transactions are confirmed on every single trade, daily reconciliations are performed on accounts, and a lot of time and money is spent on confirming investment decisions as well as monitoring and maintaining records. GIPS compliance is one step on the road to a robust system of checks and balances.

OPTIONAL SEGMENT

QUESTION AND ANSWER SESSION

Iain W. McAra

Question: How willing are portfolio managers to use the GIPS standards as a tool for self-improvement?

McAra: They are always seeking self-improvement. They may not be explicitly aware that the information they require comes from the ideas behind GIPS compliance, but if they are looking at the distribution of the returns for the month, quarter, or full year and trying to determine why a particular portfolio consistently underperforms or outperforms, then they are implicitly using the structure in place for supporting GIPS compliance.

That fact illustrates my point that it is important to educate people about what performance specialists do and what information they have readily available. One report widely used by investment managers shows, for multiple time periods, exactly how each portfolio is doing in relation to all the others.

The legal department also appreciates that report to make sure there is no front-running of the firm's own account before clients' accounts. So, although colleagues may not realize up front what is coming out of GIPS compliance process, there are great benefits from using that information as a monitoring tool that leads to self-improvement.

Question: How can investment management firms educate investment consultants on the right questions to ask in (requests for proposals) RFPs?

McAra: If intermediaries ask the wrong question and the firm cannot answer it, then the intermediary will not learn anything. For example, an intermediary might ask whether a particular composite is AIMR-PPS verified. As performance experts, we know that it is an inappropriate question because the Association for Investment Management and Research Performance Presentation Standards (AIMR-PPS) were dissolved and merged with the GIPS standards in 2006. So, do I educate the intermediary that verification is done on a firm-wide basis, that performance experts have moved away from AIMR-PPS to GIPS standards, and that single composites are not verified?

We miss out on the benefits of standardized procedures if intermediaries do not ask the correct questions. Intermediaries also miss out on the advances that the Standards include because they are dynamic, which could point intermediaries to ask for the most relevant information and also to know when a response requires further investigation.

It seems that there is an ongoing need to educate intermediaries on the correct use of the GIPS standards. Through our outreach initiative, we have produced a guide for plan sponsors and investment consultants—"Why Compliance Matters"—which is available on the GIPS website. There probably are some common miscommunications that need to be corrected. The investor consultant subcommittee of the GIPS Executive Committee is working with a number of intermediaries to restructure some of the questions that are in consultants' databases.

Eventually, fixing these questions will be a benefit to everyone concerned. But these things take time to move forward, and it all needs the appropriate support from information technology departments in terms of programming and software.

Question: Is there momentum for formal performance attribution standards?

McAra: No, it is not in the top five priorities of the GIPS Executive Committee's strategic plan.

Question: In the midst of global consolidation of investment management firms, what are the key features with respect to portability of performance history that is GIPS compliant?

McAra: In general, performance is the record of the firm, not an individual, so changes to a firm's personnel may not lead to an alteration of historical composite performance.

The Guidance Statement on Performance Record Portability (available on the GIPS website) describes how performance of a past firm or affiliation must be linked to or used to represent the historical performance of a new or acquiring firm on a composite-specific basis. Three conditions must be satisfied:

1 Substantially all of the investment decision makers are employed by the new or acquiring firm, such as research department staff, portfolio managers, and other relevant staff.

2 The decision-making process remains substantially intact and independent within the new or acquiring firm.

3 The new or acquiring firm has records that document and support the performance.

Of the three, the last condition is the most difficult to satisfy; 90% of the records is not good enough. It must be all the records necessary to support the performance.

Question: Are the GIPS standards exactly the same in each of the countries that have adopted them so far?

McAra: The GIPS standards are the same, but there may be deviations among countries where there is a conflict between local applicable laws pertaining to investment performance and the GIPS standards. When there is a conflict, the 2010 edition of the GIPS standards requires that firms adhere to the local applicable performance law and disclose how it differs from the Standards.

END OPTIONAL SEGMENT

PRACTICE PROBLEMS

1 An investor reading a performance report from a GIPS-compliant firm can assume that:

A the firm has been in existence for at least five years.

B the firm follows all requirements and recommendations of GIPS.

C the firm maintains documented policies and procedures for performance reporting.

2 Bluewater Creek Investments claims GIPS compliance for the first time effective 31 December 2015. Bluewater Creek has a Long–Short equity composite with an inception date of 1 January 2003. As of 31 December 2015, the firm must present the performance report for the Long–Short equity composite starting at a minimum from:

A 1 January 2006.

B 1 January 2011.

C 1 January 2015.

3 Which of the following is a benefit that GIPS-compliant firms offer to investors?

A Large cash flows are measured consistently across composites.

B The same measure of internal portfolio return dispersion is presented for all composites.

C An event such as the resignation of key investment personnel is disclosed in a presentation.

4 Which of the following *best* represents a benefit that a GIPS-compliant firm can provide to an investment consultant?

A Ready access to non-standardized information

B Assurance that the performance records have been verified

C Confidence in the quality and consistency of the data provided

5 A GIPS-compliant firm *must*:

A be defined by a distinct geographical boundary.

B include only marketed composites in the firm definition.

C retain autonomy over the investment decision-making process.

6 Which of the following would represent an operational benefit that a firm would gain from GIPS compliance? GIPS compliance:

A prevents outlier portfolios from becoming part of the firm's track record.

B provides a specific set of policies and procedures that a company must adopt.

C allows for one set of performance data to be presented and accepted in multiple countries.

7 GIPS compliance *best* promotes collaboration by:

A encouraging communication across geographical entities.

B specifying the functional teams for creating portfolio composites.

C prohibiting the outsourcing of firm performance functions to third parties.

8 A firm that pursues GIPS verification:

A is likely to obtain knowledge of industry best practices from the verification firm.

B will obtain a recommendation letter describing the verification firm's findings.

C must prepare GIPS-compliant presentations only for a sample of its composites.

9 A performance examination:

A must cover all of a firm's composites.

B can be issued independent of a verification report.

C signals to prospects the quality of the compliance claim.

SOLUTIONS

1 C is correct. When a claim of compliance is made, knowledgeable users of the information can assume that the investment management firm maintains documented policies and procedures for performance reporting.

2 B is correct. A firm must initially present five years of compliant annual returns for the Long–Short equity composite (or since inception, if less than five years old), building up over time to 10 years of consecutive annual returns. Since the firm claims GIPS compliance on 31 December 2015, the initial minimum starting period of compliance for the Long–Short equity composite would be 1 January 2011.

3 C is correct. The resignation of key investment personnel would represent a significant event. All significant events must be disclosed in a GIPS-compliant presentation.

4 C is correct. In requesting GIPS-compliant performance records, the consultant can be assured of the quality and the consistency of the data underlying the information.

5 C is correct. For the purposes of the GIPS standards, a firm is an investment firm, subsidiary, or division held out to clients or prospective clients as a distinct business unit that retains discretion over the assets it manages.

6 C is correct. With one global performance standard, one set of data can be presented and accepted in multiple countries—a savings in time and effort that is expected to, at least in part, offset the time and effort invested in becoming GIPS compliant.

7 A is correct. The need to communicate across divisional and geographical entities to maintain GIPS compliance helps keep regular communication channels open.

8 A is correct. Verification firms, through the knowledge that they acquire from visiting different companies, are likely to guide firms toward best practices by sharing their opinions and views about what solutions are available, as well as approaches to maintaining, monitoring, and reporting the necessary information.

9 C is correct. Verification and performance examinations signal to prospects the quality of the compliance claim.

READING

14

Introduction to the Global Investment Performance Standards (GIPS)

LEARNING OUTCOMES

Mastery	The candidate should be able to:
☐	a. explain why the GIPS standards were created, what parties the GIPS standards apply to, and who is benefitted by the Standards;
☐	b. explain the construction and purpose of composites in performance reporting;
☐	c. explain benefits of verification.

The objective of this reading is to orient the candidate approaching the assigned sections of the GIPS standards. It explains why the GIPS standards were created, who can claim compliance, and who benefits from compliance. It also introduces the key notion of composites, states the purpose of verification, and previews the structure of the Standards.

1. WHY WERE THE GIPS STANDARDS CREATED?

Institutions and individuals are constantly scrutinizing past investment performance returns in search of the best manager to achieve their investment objectives.

In the past, the investment community had great difficulty making meaningful comparisons on the basis of accurate investment performance data. Several performance measurement practices hindered the comparability of performance returns from one firm to another, while others called into question the accuracy and credibility of performance reporting overall. Misleading practices included:

- Representative Accounts: Selecting a top-performing portfolio to represent the firm's overall investment results for a specific mandate.

- Survivorship Bias: Presenting an "average" performance history that *excludes* portfolios whose poor performance was weak enough to result in termination of the firm.
- Varying Time Periods: Presenting performance for a selected time period during which the mandate produced excellent returns or out-performed its benchmark—making comparison with other firms' results difficult or impossible.

Making a valid comparison of investment performance among even the most ethical investment management firms was problematic. For example, a pension fund seeking to hire an investment management firm might receive proposals from several firms, all using different methodologies for calculating their results.

The GIPS standards are a practitioner-driven set of ethical principles that establish a standardized, industry-wide approach for investment firms to follow in calculating and presenting their historical investment results to prospective clients. The GIPS standards ensure fair representation and full disclosure of investment performance. In other words, the GIPS standards lead investment management firms to avoid misrepresentations of performance and to communicate all relevant information that prospective clients should know in order to evaluate past results.

II. WHO CAN CLAIM COMPLIANCE?

First, any investment management firm may choose to comply with the GIPS standards. Complying with the GIPS standards is voluntary. Compliance with the GIPS standards is not typically required by legal or regulatory authorities.

Second, only investment management firms that *actually manage* assets can claim compliance with the Standards. Plan sponsors and consultants cannot make a claim of compliance unless they actually manage assets for which they are making a claim of compliance. They can claim to endorse the Standards and/or require that their investment managers comply with the Standards. Similarly, software (and the vendors who supply software) cannot be "compliant." Software can assist firms in achieving compliance with the GIPS standards (e.g., by calculating performance in a manner consistent with the calculation requirements of the Standards) but only an investment management firm can claim compliance once the firm has satisfied all requirements of the Standards.

Third, compliance is a firm-wide process that cannot be achieved on a single product or composite. A firm has only two options with regard to compliance with the GIPS standards: fully comply with *all* requirements of the GIPS standards and claim compliance through the use of the GIPS Compliance Statement; or not comply with all requirements of the GIPS standards and not claim compliance with, or make any reference to, the GIPS standards.

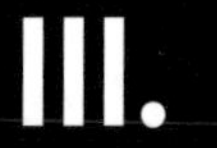

III. WHO BENEFITS FROM COMPLIANCE?

The GIPS standards benefit two main groups: investment management firms and prospective clients.

- By choosing to comply with the GIPS standards, investment management firms assure prospective clients that the historical "track record" they report is both complete and fairly presented. Compliance enables the GIPS-compliant firm to participate in competitive bids against other compliant firms throughout the world. Achieving and maintaining compliance may also strengthen the firm's internal controls over performance-related processes and procedures.

- Investors have a greater level of confidence in the integrity of performance presentations of a GIPS-compliant firm and can more easily compare performance presentations from different investment management firms. While the GIPS standards certainly do not eliminate the need for in-depth due diligence on the part of the investor, compliance with the Standards enhances the credibility of investment management firms that have chosen to undertake this responsibility.

COMPOSITES

IV.

One of the key concepts of the Standards is the required use of composites. A composite is an aggregation of one or more portfolios managed according to a similar investment mandate, objective, or strategy. A composite must include all actual, fee-paying, discretionary portfolios managed in accordance with the same investment mandate, objective, or strategy. For example, if a GIPS-compliant firm presents its track record for a Global Equity Composite (the Composite), the Composite must include all portfolios that are managed, or have historically been managed, in the firm's Global Equity strategy. The firm may not subjectively select which Global Equity portfolios will be included in or excluded from the calculation and presentation of the Global Equity Composite. The determination of which portfolios to include in the Composite should be done according to pre-established criteria (i.e., on an ex-ante basis), not after the fact. This prevents a firm from including only their best-performing portfolios in the Composite.

VERIFICATION

Firms that claim compliance with the GIPS standards are responsible for their claim of compliance and for maintaining that compliance. That is, firms self-regulate their claim of compliance. Once a firm claims compliance with the Standards, they may voluntarily hire an independent third party to perform a verification in order to increase confidence in the firm's claim of compliance. Verification may also increase the knowledge of the firm's performance measurement team and improve the consistency and quality of the firm's compliant presentations.

Verification is performed with respect to an entire firm, not on specific composites. Verification does not ensure the accuracy of any specific composite presentation. Verification tests:

- whether the investment firm has complied with all the composite construction requirements of the GIPS standards on a firm-wide basis, and
- whether the firm's policies and procedures are designed to calculate and present performance in compliance with the GIPS standards.

Verification must be performed by an independent third party. A firm cannot perform its own verification.

Third-party verification brings additional credibility to a firm's claim of compliance. A verified firm may provide existing and prospective clients with greater assurance about its claim of compliance with the GIPS standards. Verification may also provide improved internal processes and procedures as well as marketing advantages to the firm.

VI. THE STRUCTURE OF THE GIPS STANDARDS

The provisions within the 2010 edition of the GIPS standards are divided into nine sections: Fundamentals of Compliance, Input Data, Calculation Methodology, Composite Construction, Disclosure, Presentation and Reporting, Real Estate, Private Equity, and Wrap Free/Separately Managed Account (SMA) Portfolios. The provisions are further categorized into requirements and recommendations.

READING

15

Global Investment Performance Standards (GIPS)

LEARNING OUTCOMES

Mastery	The candidate should be able to:
☐	a. describe the key features of the GIPS standards, the fundamentals of compliance, and the requirements and recommendations for input data;
☐	b. describe the scope of the GIPS standards with respect to an investment firm's definition and historical performance record;
☐	c. explain how the GIPS standards are implemented in countries with existing standards for performance reporting and describe the appropriate response when the GIPS standards and local regulations conflict;
☐	d. describe the nine sections of the GIPS standards.

PREFACE

OPTIONAL SEGMENT

CFA Institute is a global not-for-profit association of investment professionals with the mission of leading the investment profession globally by setting the highest standards of ethics, education, and professional excellence. CFA Institute has a long-standing history of and commitment to establishing a broadly accepted ethical standard for calculating and presenting investment performance based on the principles of fair representation and full disclosure. The goals in developing and evolving the Global Investment Performance Standards (GIPS) are to establish them as the recognized standard for calculating and presenting investment performance around the world and for the GIPS standards to become a firm's "passport" to market investment management services globally. As of January 2010, CFA Institute has partnered with organizations in 32 countries that contribute to the development and promotion of the GIPS standards.

History

In 1995, CFA Institute, formerly known as the Association for Investment Management and Research (AIMR), sponsored and funded the Global Investment Performance Standards Committee to develop global standards for calculating and presenting investment performance, based on the existing AIMR Performance Presentation Standards (AIMR-PPS®).

In 1998, the proposed GIPS standards were posted on the CFA Institute website and circulated for comment to more than 4,000 individuals who had expressed interest. The result was the first Global Investment Performance Standards, published in April 1999.

The initial edition of the GIPS standards was designed to create a minimum global investment performance standard that would:

- Permit and facilitate acceptance and adoption in developing markets;
- Give the global investment management industry one commonly accepted approach for calculating and presenting performance; and
- Address liquid asset classes (equity, fixed income, and cash).

In 1999, the Global Investment Performance Standards Committee was replaced by the Investment Performance Council (IPC) to further develop and promote the GIPS standards. The development of the GIPS standards was a global industry initiative with participation from individuals and organizations from more than 15 countries.

The IPC was charged with developing provisions for other asset classes (e.g., real estate, private equity) and addressing other performance-related issues (e.g., fees, advertising) to broaden the scope and applicability of the GIPS standards. This was accomplished when the second edition of the GIPS standards was published in February 2005.

With the release of the 2005 edition of the GIPS standards and growing adoption and expansion of the GIPS standards, the IPC decided to move to a single global investment performance standard and eliminate the need for local variations of the GIPS standards. All country-specific performance standards converged with the GIPS standards, resulting in 25 countries adopting a single, global standard for the calculation and presentation of investment performance.

In 2005, with the convergence of country-specific versions to the GIPS standards and the need to reorganize the governance structure to facilitate involvement from GIPS country sponsors, CFA Institute dissolved the IPC and created the GIPS Executive Committee and the GIPS Council. The GIPS Executive Committee serves as the decision-making authority for the GIPS standards, and the GIPS Council facilitates the involvement of all country sponsors in the ongoing development and promotion of the GIPS standards.

To maintain global relevance, and in recognition of the dynamic nature of the investment industry, the GIPS standards must be continually updated through interpretations, guidance, and new provisions. In 2008, the GIPS Executive Committee began its review of the GIPS standards in an effort to further refine the provisions as well as eliminate provisions that are no longer necessary and add new requirements and recommendations that promote best practice. The GIPS Executive Committee worked in close collaboration with its technical subcommittees, specially formed working groups, and GIPS country sponsors. These groups reviewed the existing provisions and guidance and conducted surveys and other research as part of the efforts to produce the 2010 edition of the GIPS standards.

END OPTIONAL SEGMENT

INTRODUCTION

Preamble—Why Is a Global Investment Performance Standard Needed?

Standardized Investment Performance Financial markets and the investment management industry have become increasingly global in nature. The growth in the types and number of financial entities, the globalization of the investment process, and the increased competition among investment management firms demonstrate the need to standardize the calculation and presentation of investment performance.

Global Passport Asset managers and both existing and prospective clients benefit from an established global standard for calculating and presenting investment performance. Investment practices, regulation, performance measurement, and reporting of performance vary considerably from country to country. By adhering to a global standard, firms in countries with minimal or no investment performance standards will be able to compete for business on an equal footing with firms from countries with more developed standards. Firms from countries with established practices will have more confidence in being fairly compared with local firms when competing for business in countries that have not previously adopted performance standards. Performance standards that are accepted globally enable investment firms to measure and present their investment performance so that investors can readily compare investment performance among firms.

Investor Confidence Investment managers that adhere to investment performance standards help assure investors that the firm's investment performance is complete and fairly presented. Both prospective and existing clients of investment firms benefit from a global investment performance standard by having a greater degree of confidence in the performance information presented to them.

Objectives

The establishment of a voluntary global investment performance standard leads to an accepted set of best practices for calculating and presenting investment performance that is readily comparable among investment firms, regardless of geographic location. These standards also facilitate a dialogue between investment firms and their existing and prospective clients regarding investment performance.

The goals of the GIPS Executive Committee are:

- To establish investment industry best practices for calculating and presenting investment performance that promote investor interests and instill investor confidence;
- To obtain worldwide acceptance of a single standard for the calculation and presentation of investment performance based on the principles of fair representation and full disclosure;
- To promote the use of accurate and consistent investment performance data;
- To encourage fair, global competition among investment firms without creating barriers to entry; and
- To foster the notion of industry "self-regulation" on a global basis.

Overview

Key features of the Global Investment Performance Standards include the following:

- The GIPS standards are ethical standards for investment performance presentation to ensure fair representation and full disclosure of investment performance. In order to claim compliance, firms must adhere to the requirements included in the GIPS standards.
- Meeting the objectives of fair representation and full disclosure is likely to require more than simply adhering to the minimum requirements of the GIPS standards. Firms should also adhere to the recommendations to achieve best practice in the calculation and presentation of performance.
- The GIPS standards require firms to include all actual, discretionary, fee-paying portfolios in at least one composite defined by investment mandate, objective, or strategy in order to prevent firms from cherry-picking their best performance.
- The GIPS standards rely on the integrity of input data. The accuracy of input data is critical to the accuracy of the performance presentation. The underlying valuations of portfolio holdings drive the portfolio's performance. It is essential for these and other inputs to be accurate. The GIPS standards require firms to adhere to certain calculation methodologies and to make specific disclosures along with the firm's performance.
- Firms must comply with all requirements of the GIPS standards, including any updates, Guidance Statements, interpretations, Questions & Answers (Q&As), and clarifications published by CFA Institute and the GIPS Executive Committee, which are available on the GIPS website (www.gipsstandards.org) as well as in the *GIPS Handbook*.

The GIPS standards do not address every aspect of performance measurement or cover unique characteristics of each asset class. The GIPS standards will continue to evolve over time to address additional areas of investment performance. Understanding and interpreting investment performance requires consideration of both risk and return. Historically, the GIPS standards focused primarily on returns. In the spirit of fair representation and full disclosure, and in order to provide investors with a more comprehensive view of a firm's performance, the 2010 edition of the GIPS standards includes new provisions related to risk.

Historical Performance Record

- A firm is required to initially present, at a minimum, five years of annual investment performance that is compliant with the GIPS standards. If the firm or the composite has been in existence less than five years, the firm must present performance since the firm's inception or the composite inception date.
- After a firm presents a minimum of five years of GIPS-compliant performance (or for the period since the firm's inception or the composite inception date if the firm or the composite has been in existence less than five years), the firm must present an additional year of performance each year, building up to a minimum of 10 years of GIPS-compliant performance.
- Firms may link non-GIPS-compliant performance to their GIPS-compliant performance provided that only GIPS-compliant performance is presented for periods after 1 January 2000 and the firm discloses the periods of non-compliance. Firms must not link non-GIPS-compliant performance for periods beginning on or after 1 January 2000 to their GIPS-compliant performance. Firms that manage private equity, real estate, and/or wrap fee/separately

managed account (SMA) portfolios must also comply with Sections 6, 7, and 8, respectively, of the Provisions of the GIPS standards that became effective as of 1 January 2006.

Compliance

Firms must take all steps necessary to ensure that they have satisfied all the requirements of the GIPS standards before claiming compliance. Firms are strongly encouraged to perform periodic internal compliance checks. Implementing adequate internal controls during all stages of the investment performance process—from data input to preparing performance presentations—will instill confidence in the validity of performance presented as well as in the claim of compliance.

Firms may choose to have an independent third-party verification that tests the construction of the firm's composites as well as the firm's policies and procedures as they relate to compliance with the GIPS standards. The value of verification is widely recognized, and being verified is considered to be best practice. The GIPS Executive Committee strongly recommends that firms be verified. In addition to verification, firms may also choose to have specifically focused composite testing (performance examination) performed by an independent third-party verifier to provide additional assurance regarding a particular composite.

Effective Date

The effective date for the 2010 edition of the GIPS standards is 1 January 2011. Compliant presentations that include performance for periods that begin on or after 1 January 2011 must be prepared in accordance with the 2010 edition of the GIPS standards. Prior editions of the GIPS standards may be found on the GIPS website (www.gipsstandards.org).

Implementing a Global Standard

The presence of a local sponsoring organization for investment performance standards is essential for effective implementation and ongoing support of the GIPS standards within a country. Such country sponsors also provide an important link between the GIPS Executive Committee, the governing body for the GIPS standards, and the local markets in which investment managers operate.

The country sponsor, by actively supporting the GIPS standards and the work of the GIPS Executive Committee, ensures that the country's interests are taken into account as the GIPS standards are developed. Compliance with the GIPS standards is voluntary, and support from the local country sponsor helps to drive the adoption of the GIPS standards.

The GIPS Executive Committee strongly encourages countries without an investment performance standard to promote the GIPS standards as the local standard and translate them into the local language when necessary. Although the GIPS standards may be translated into many languages, if a discrepancy arises, the English version of the GIPS standards is the official governing version.

The GIPS Executive Committee will continue to promote the principles of fair representation and full disclosure and develop the GIPS standards so that they maintain their relevance within the changing investment management industry.

The self-regulatory nature of the GIPS standards necessitates a strong commitment to ethical integrity. Self-regulation also assists regulators in exercising their responsibility for ensuring the fair disclosure of information within financial markets. The GIPS Executive Committee encourages regulators to:

- Recognize the benefit of voluntary compliance with standards that represent global best practices;
- Give consideration to taking enforcement actions on firms that falsely claim compliance with the GIPS standards; and
- Recognize and encourage independent third-party verification.

Where existing laws, regulations, or industry standards already impose requirements related to the calculation and presentation of investment performance, firms are strongly encouraged to comply with the GIPS standards in addition to applicable regulatory requirements. Compliance with applicable law and/or regulation does not necessarily lead to compliance with the GIPS standards. In cases in which laws and/or regulations conflict with the GIPS standards, firms are required to comply with the laws and regulations and make full disclosure of the conflict in the compliant presentation.

OPTIONAL SEGMENT

Sponsors

The presence of a local sponsoring organization for investment performance standards, known as a "sponsor," is essential for effective implementation of the GIPS standards and ongoing support within a local market. Sponsors collectively form the GIPS Council, which provides a formal role in the ongoing development and oversight of the GIPS standards. Country sponsors:

- Promote the GIPS standards locally;
- Provide local market support and input for the GIPS standards;
- Present local market–specific issues to the GIPS Executive Committee; and
- Participate in the governance of the GIPS standards via membership in the GIPS Council and Regional Investment Performance Subcommittees.

Each organization undergoes a formal review before being endorsed as a sponsor. Additional information and a current list of sponsors can be found on the GIPS website (www.gipsstandards.org).

Endorsed GIPS Sponsors **(as of 1 January 2010)**

Australia	Investment and Financial Services Association Limited—Performance Analyst Group
Austria	1) Österreichische Vereinigung für Finanzanalyse und Asset Management and 2) Vereinigung Österreichischer Investmentgesellschaften
Belgium	Belgian Asset Managers Association
Canada	Canadian Investment Performance Committee
Denmark	The Danish Society of Financial Analysts and CFA Denmark
France	1) Société Française des Analystes Financiers and 2) Association Française de la Gestion Financière
Germany	German Asset Management Standards Committee: 1) Bundesverband Investment und Asset Management e.V., 2) Deutsche Vereinigung für Finanzanalyse und Asset Management, and 3) German CFA Society

Greece	Hellenic CFA Society
Hong Kong	Local Sponsor: The Hong Kong Society of Financial Analysts
Hungary	1) CFA Society of Hungary and 2) the Association of Hungarian Investment Fund and Asset Management Companies
Ireland	Irish Association of Investment Managers
Italy	Italian Investment Performance Committee: 1) L'Associazione Bancaria Italiana, 2) L'Associazione Italiana degli Analisti Finanziari, 3) Assogestioni, 4) Sviluppo Mercato Fondi Pensione, 5) Assirevi, and 6) Italian CFA Society
Japan	The Security Analysts Association of Japan
Kazakhstan	Kazakhstan Association of Financial and Investment Analysts
Liechtenstein	Liechtenstein Bankers' Association
Micronesia	Asia Pacific Association for Fiduciary Studies
The Netherlands	The Netherlands Beroepsvereniging van Beleggingsprofessionals
New Zealand	CFA Society of New Zealand
Norway	The Norwegian Society of Financial Analysts
Pakistan	CFA Association of Pakistan
Portugal	Associação Portuguesa de Analista Financeiros
Russia	National League of Management Companies
Singapore	Investment Management Association of Singapore
South Africa	Association for Savings and Investment, South Africa
South Korea	Korea GIPS Committee
Spain	Asociación Española de Presentación de Resultados de Gestión
Sri Lanka	CFA Sri Lanka
Sweden	Swedish Society of Financial Analysts
Switzerland	Swiss Bankers Association
Ukraine	The Ukrainian Association of Investment Business
United Kingdom	UK Investment Performance Committee: 1) Association of British Insurers, 2) Investment Management Association, and 3) National Association of Pension Funds
United States	CFA Institute—US Investment Performance Committee

END OPTIONAL SEGMENT

PROVISIONS OF THE GLOBAL INVESTMENT PERFORMANCE STANDARDS

I.

The provisions within the GIPS standards are divided into the following nine sections: Fundamentals of Compliance, Input Data, Calculation Methodology, Composite Construction, Disclosure, Presentation and Reporting, Real Estate, Private Equity, and Wrap Fee/Separately Managed Account (SMA) Portfolios.

The provisions for each section are categorized into requirements and recommendations. Firms must meet all the requirements to claim compliance with the GIPS standards. Firms are encouraged to implement as many of the recommendations as possible. These recommended provisions are considered to be industry best practice and assist firms in fully adhering to the spirit and intent of the GIPS standards.

0 **Fundamentals of Compliance:** Several core principles create the foundation for the GIPS standards, including properly defining the firm, providing compliant presentations to all prospective clients, adhering to applicable laws and

regulations, and ensuring that information presented is not false or misleading. Two important issues that a firm must consider when becoming compliant with the GIPS standards are the definition of the firm and the firm's definition of discretion. The definition of the firm is the foundation for firm-wide compliance and creates defined boundaries whereby total firm assets can be determined. The firm's definition of discretion establishes criteria to judge which portfolios must be included in a composite and is based on the firm's ability to implement its investment strategy.

1 **Input Data:** Consistency of input data used to calculate performance is critical to effective compliance with the GIPS standards and establishes the foundation for full, fair, and comparable investment performance presentations. For periods beginning on or after 1 January 2011, all portfolios must be valued in accordance with the definition of fair value and the GIPS Valuation Principles.

2 **Calculation Methodology:** Achieving comparability among investment management firms' performance presentations requires uniformity in methods used to calculate returns. The GIPS standards mandate the use of certain calculation methodologies to facilitate comparability.

3 **Composite Construction:** A composite is an aggregation of one or more portfolios managed according to a similar investment mandate, objective, or strategy. The composite return is the asset-weighted average of the performance of all portfolios in the composite. Creating meaningful composites is essential to the fair presentation, consistency, and comparability of performance over time and among firms.

4 **Disclosure:** Disclosures allow firms to elaborate on the data provided in the presentation and give the reader the proper context in which to understand the performance. To comply with the GIPS standards, firms must disclose certain information in all compliant presentations regarding their performance and the policies adopted by the firm. Although some disclosures are required for all firms, others are specific to certain circumstances and may not be applicable in all situations. Firms are not required to make negative assurance disclosures (e.g., if the firm does not use leverage in a particular composite strategy, no disclosure of the use of leverage is required). One of the essential disclosures for every firm is the claim of compliance. Once a firm meets all the requirements of the GIPS standards, it must appropriately use the claim of compliance to indicate compliance with the GIPS standards. The 2010 edition of the GIPS standards includes a revised compliance statement that indicates if the firm has or has not been verified.

5 **Presentation and Reporting:** After constructing the composites, gathering the input data, calculating returns, and determining the necessary disclosures, the firm must incorporate this information in presentations based on the requirements in the GIPS standards for presenting investment performance. No finite set of requirements can cover all potential situations or anticipate future developments in investment industry structure, technology, products, or practices. When appropriate, firms have the responsibility to include in GIPS-compliant presentations information not addressed by the GIPS standards.

6 **Real Estate:** Unless otherwise noted, this section supplements all of the required and recommended provisions in Sections 0–5. Real estate provisions were first included in the 2005 edition of the GIPS standards and became effective 1 January 2006. The 2010 edition of the GIPS standards includes new provisions for closed-end real estate funds. Firms should note that certain provisions of Sections 0–5 do not apply to real estate investments or are superseded by provisions within Section 6. The provisions that do not apply have been noted within Section 6.

7 **Private Equity:** Unless otherwise noted, this section supplements all of the required and recommended provisions in Sections 0–5. Private equity provisions were first included in the 2005 edition of the GIPS standards and became effective 1 January 2006. Firms should note that certain provisions in Sections 0–5 do not apply to private equity investments or are superseded by provisions within Section 7. The provisions that do not apply have been noted within Section 7.

8 **Wrap Fee/Separately Managed Account (SMA) Portfolios:** Unless otherwise noted, this section supplements all of the required and recommended provisions in Sections 0–5. Firms should note that certain provisions in Sections 0–5 of the GIPS standards do not apply to wrap fee/SMA portfolios or are superseded by provisions within Section 8. The provisions that do not apply have been noted within Section 8.

Defined Terms: Words appearing in capital letters in the GIPS standards are defined in the GIPS Glossary, which is located at the end of this reading.

0 Fundamentals of Compliance

Fundamentals of Compliance—Requirements

0.A.1 FIRMS MUST comply with all the REQUIREMENTS of the GIPS standards, including any updates, Guidance Statements, interpretations, Questions & Answers (Q&As), and clarifications published by CFA Institute and the GIPS Executive Committee, which are available on the GIPS standards website (www.gipsstandards.org) as well as in the *GIPS Handbook.*

0.A.2 FIRMS MUST comply with all applicable laws and regulations regarding the calculation and presentation of performance.

0.A.3 FIRMS MUST NOT present performance or performance-related information that is false or misleading.

0.A.4 The GIPS standards MUST be applied on a FIRM-wide basis.

0.A.5 FIRMS MUST document their policies and procedures used in establishing and maintaining compliance with the GIPS standards, including ensuring the existence and ownership of client assets, and MUST apply them consistently.

0.A.6 If the FIRM does not meet all the REQUIREMENTS of the GIPS standards, the FIRM MUST NOT represent or state that it is "in compliance with the Global Investment Performance Standards except for . . ." or make any other statements that may indicate partial compliance with the GIPS standards.

0.A.7 Statements referring to the calculation methodology as being "in accordance," "in compliance," or "consistent" with the Global Investment Performance Standards, or similar statements, are prohibited.

0.A.8 Statements referring to the performance of a single, existing client PORTFOLIO as being "calculated in accordance with the Global Investment Performance Standards" are prohibited, except when a GIPS-compliant FIRM reports the performance of an individual client's PORTFOLIO to that client.

0.A.9 FIRMS MUST make every reasonable effort to provide a COMPLIANT PRESENTATION to all PROSPECTIVE CLIENTS. FIRMS MUST NOT choose to whom they present a COMPLIANT PRESENTATION. As long as a PROSPECTIVE CLIENT has received a COMPLIANT PRESENTATION within the previous 12 months, the FIRM has met this REQUIREMENT.

0.A.10 FIRMS MUST provide a complete list of COMPOSITE DESCRIPTIONS to any PROSPECTIVE CLIENT that makes such a request. FIRMS MUST include terminated COMPOSITES on the FIRM's list of COMPOSITE DESCRIPTIONS for at least five years after the COMPOSITE TERMINATION DATE.

0.A.11 FIRMS MUST provide a COMPLIANT PRESENTATION for any COMPOSITE listed on the FIRM's list of COMPOSITE DESCRIPTIONS to any PROSPECTIVE CLIENT that makes such a request.

0.A.12 FIRMS MUST be defined as an investment firm, subsidiary, or division held out to clients or PROSPECTIVE CLIENTS as a DISTINCT BUSINESS ENTITY.

0.A.13 For periods beginning on or after 1 January 2011, TOTAL FIRM ASSETS MUST be the aggregate FAIR VALUE of all discretionary and non-discretionary assets managed by the FIRM. This includes both fee-paying and non-fee-paying PORTFOLIOS.[1]

0.A.14 TOTAL FIRM ASSETS MUST include assets assigned to a SUB-ADVISOR provided the FIRM has discretion over the selection of the SUB-ADVISOR.

0.A.15 Changes in a FIRM's organization MUST NOT lead to alteration of historical COMPOSITE performance.

0.A.16 When the FIRM jointly markets with other firms, the FIRM claiming compliance with the GIPS standards MUST be sure that it is clearly defined and separate relative to other firms being marketed, and that it is clear which FIRM is claiming compliance.

Fundamentals of Compliance—Recommendations

0.B.1 FIRMS SHOULD comply with the RECOMMENDATIONS of the GIPS standards, including RECOMMENDATIONS in any updates, Guidance Statements, interpretations, Questions & Answers (Q&As), and clarifications published by CFA Institute and the GIPS Executive Committee, which will be made available on the GIPS website (www.gipsstandards.org) as well as in the *GIPS Handbook.*

0.B.2 FIRMS SHOULD be verified.

0.B.3 FIRMS SHOULD adopt the broadest, most meaningful definition of the FIRM. The scope of this definition SHOULD include all geographical (country, regional, etc.) offices operating under the same brand name regardless of the actual name of the individual investment management company.

0.B.4 FIRMS SHOULD provide to each existing client, on an annual basis, a COMPLIANT PRESENTATION of the COMPOSITE in which the client's PORTFOLIO is included.

1 Input Data

Input Data—Requirements

1.A.1 All data and information necessary to support all items included in a COMPLIANT PRESENTATION MUST be captured and maintained.

1.A.2 For periods beginning on or after 1 January 2011, PORTFOLIOS MUST be valued in accordance with the definition of FAIR VALUE and the GIPS Valuation Principles.[2]

---

1 For periods prior to 1 January 2011, TOTAL FIRM ASSETS MUST be the aggregate of the MARKET VALUE of all discretionary and non-discretionary assets under management within the defined FIRM.

2 For periods prior to 1 January 2011, PORTFOLIO valuations MUST be based on MARKET VALUES (not cost basis or book values).

1.A.3 FIRMS MUST value PORTFOLIOS in accordance with the COMPOSITE-specific valuation policy. PORTFOLIOS MUST be valued:

- **a** For periods beginning on or after 1 January 2001, at least monthly.[3]
- **b** For periods beginning on or after 1 January 2010, on the date of all LARGE CASH FLOWS. FIRMS MUST define LARGE CASH FLOW for each COMPOSITE to determine when PORTFOLIOS in that COMPOSITE MUST be valued.
- **c** No more frequently than required by the valuation policy.

1.A.4 For periods beginning on or after 1 January 2010, FIRMS MUST value PORTFOLIOS as of the calendar month end or the last business day of the month.

1.A.5 For periods beginning on or after 1 January 2005, FIRMS MUST use TRADE DATE ACCOUNTING.

1.A.6 ACCRUAL ACCOUNTING MUST be used for fixed-income securities and all other investments that earn interest income. The value of fixed-income securities MUST include accrued income.

1.A.7 For periods beginning on or after 1 January 2006, COMPOSITES MUST have consistent beginning and ending annual valuation dates. Unless the COMPOSITE is reported on a non-calendar fiscal year, the beginning and ending valuation dates MUST be at calendar year end or on the last business day of the year.

Input Data—Recommendations

1.B.1 FIRMS SHOULD value PORTFOLIOS on the date of all EXTERNAL CASH FLOWS.

1.B.2 Valuations SHOULD be obtained from a qualified independent third party.

1.B.3 ACCRUAL ACCOUNTING SHOULD be used for dividends (as of the ex-dividend date).

1.B.4 FIRMS SHOULD accrue INVESTMENT MANAGEMENT FEES.

2 Calculation Methodology

OPTIONAL SEGMENT

Calculation Methodology—Requirements

2.A.1 TOTAL RETURNS MUST be used.

2.A.2 FIRMS MUST calculate TIME-WEIGHTED RATES OF RETURN that adjust for EXTERNAL CASH FLOWS. Both periodic and sub-period returns MUST be geometrically LINKED. EXTERNAL CASH FLOWS MUST be treated according to the FIRM'S COMPOSITE-specific policy. At a minimum:

- **a** For periods beginning on or after 1 January 2001, FIRMS MUST calculate PORTFOLIO returns at least monthly.
- **b** For periods beginning on or after 1 January 2005, FIRMS MUST calculate PORTFOLIO returns that adjust for daily-weighted EXTERNAL CASH FLOWS.

2.A.3 Returns from cash and cash equivalents held in PORTFOLIOS MUST be included in all return calculations.

2.A.4 All returns MUST be calculated after the deduction of the actual TRADING EXPENSES incurred during the period. FIRMS MUST NOT use estimated TRADING EXPENSES.

2.A.5 If the actual TRADING EXPENSES cannot be identified and segregated from a BUNDLED FEE:

3 For periods prior to 1 January 2001, PORTFOLIOS MUST be valued at least quarterly.

a When calculating GROSS-OF-FEES returns, returns MUST be reduced by the entire BUNDLED FEE or the portion of the BUNDLED FEE that includes the TRADING EXPENSES. FIRMS MUST NOT use estimated TRADING EXPENSES.

b When calculating NET-OF-FEES returns, returns MUST be reduced by the entire BUNDLED FEE or the portion of the BUNDLED FEE that includes the TRADING EXPENSES and the INVESTMENT MANAGEMENT FEE. FIRMS MUST NOT use estimated TRADING EXPENSES.

2.A.6 COMPOSITE returns MUST be calculated by asset-weighting the individual PORTFOLIO returns using beginning-of-period values or a method that reflects both beginning-of-period values and EXTERNAL CASH FLOWS.

2.A.7 COMPOSITE returns MUST be calculated:

a For periods beginning on or after 1 January 2006, by asset-weighting the individual PORTFOLIO returns at least quarterly.

b For periods beginning on or after 1 January 2010, by asset-weighting the individual PORTFOLIO returns at least monthly.

Calculation Methodology—Recommendations

2.B.1 Returns SHOULD be calculated net of non-reclaimable withholding taxes on dividends, interest, and capital gains. Reclaimable withholding taxes SHOULD be accrued.

2.B.2 For periods prior to 1 January 2010, FIRMS SHOULD calculate COMPOSITE returns by asset-weighting the individual PORTFOLIO returns at least monthly.

3 Composite Construction

Composite Construction—Requirements

3.A.1 All actual, fee-paying, discretionary PORTFOLIOS MUST be included in at least one COMPOSITE. Although non-fee-paying discretionary PORTFOLIOS may be included in a COMPOSITE (with appropriate disclosure), non-discretionary PORTFOLIOS MUST NOT be included in a FIRM'S COMPOSITES.

3.A.2 COMPOSITES MUST include only actual assets managed by the FIRM.

3.A.3 FIRMS MUST NOT LINK performance of simulated or model PORTFOLIOS with actual performance.

3.A.4 COMPOSITES MUST be defined according to investment mandate, objective, or strategy. COMPOSITES MUST include all PORTFOLIOS that meet the COMPOSITE DEFINITION. Any change to a COMPOSITE DEFINITION MUST NOT be applied retroactively. The COMPOSITE DEFINITION MUST be made available upon request.

3.A.5 COMPOSITES MUST include new PORTFOLIOS on a timely and consistent basis after each PORTFOLIO comes under management.

3.A.6 Terminated PORTFOLIOS MUST be included in the historical performance of the COMPOSITE up to the last full measurement period that each PORTFOLIO was under management.

3.A.7 PORTFOLIOS MUST NOT be switched from one COMPOSITE to another unless documented changes to a PORTFOLIO'S investment mandate, objective, or strategy or the redefinition of the COMPOSITE makes it appropriate. The historical performance of the PORTFOLIO MUST remain with the original COMPOSITE.

3.A.8 For periods beginning on or after 1 January 2010, a CARVE-OUT MUST NOT be included in a COMPOSITE unless the CARVE-OUT is managed separately with its own cash balance.[4]

3.A.9 If the FIRM sets a minimum asset level for PORTFOLIOS to be included in a COMPOSITE, the FIRM MUST NOT include PORTFOLIOS below the minimum asset level in that COMPOSITE. Any changes to a COMPOSITE-specific minimum asset level MUST NOT be applied retroactively.

3.A.10 FIRMS that wish to remove PORTFOLIOS from COMPOSITES in cases of SIGNIFICANT CASH FLOWS MUST define "significant" on an EX-ANTE, COMPOSITE-specific basis and MUST consistently follow the COMPOSITE-specific policy.

Composite Construction—Recommendations

3.B.1 If the FIRM sets a minimum asset level for PORTFOLIOS to be included in a COMPOSITE, the FIRM SHOULD NOT present a COMPLIANT PRESENTATION of the COMPOSITE to a PROSPECTIVE CLIENT known not to meet the COMPOSITE's minimum asset level.

3.B.2 To remove the effect of a SIGNIFICANT CASH FLOW, the FIRM SHOULD use a TEMPORARY NEW ACCOUNT.

4 Disclosure

Disclosure—Requirements

4.A.1 Once a FIRM has met all the REQUIREMENTS of the GIPS standards, the FIRM MUST disclose its compliance with the GIPS standards using one of the following compliance statements. The claim of compliance MUST only be used in a COMPLIANT PRESENTATION.

For FIRMS that are verified:

> "[Insert name of FIRM] claims compliance with the Global Investment Performance Standards (GIPS®) and has prepared and presented this report in compliance with the GIPS standards. [Insert name of FIRM] has been independently verified for the periods [insert dates]. The verification report(s) is/are available upon request.
>
> Verification assesses whether (1) the firm has complied with all the composite construction requirements of the GIPS standards on a firm-wide basis and (2) the firm's policies and procedures are designed to calculate and present performance in compliance with the GIPS standards. Verification does not ensure the accuracy of any specific composite presentation."

For COMPOSITES of a verified FIRM that have also had a PERFORMANCE EXAMINATION:

> "[Insert name of FIRM] claims compliance with the Global Investment Performance Standards (GIPS®) and has prepared and presented this report in compliance with the GIPS standards. [Insert name of FIRM] has been independently verified for the periods [insert dates].

4 For periods prior to 1 January 2010, if CARVE-OUTS were included in a COMPOSITE, cash MUST have been allocated to the CARVE-OUT in a timely and consistent manner.

> Verification assesses whether (1) the firm has complied with all the composite construction requirements of the GIPS standards on a firm-wide basis and (2) the firm's policies and procedures are designed to calculate and present performance in compliance with the GIPS standards. The [insert name of COMPOSITE] composite has been examined for the periods [insert dates]. The verification and performance examination reports are available upon request."

For FIRMS that have not been verified:

> "[Insert name of FIRM] claims compliance with the Global Investment Performance Standards (GIPS®) and has prepared and presented this report in compliance with the GIPS standards. [Insert name of FIRM] has not been independently verified."

4.A.2 FIRMS MUST disclose the definition of the FIRM used to determine TOTAL FIRM ASSETS and FIRM-wide compliance.

4.A.3 FIRMS MUST disclose the COMPOSITE DESCRIPTION.

4.A.4 FIRMS MUST disclose the BENCHMARK DESCRIPTION.

4.A.5 When presenting GROSS-OF-FEES returns, FIRMS MUST disclose if any other fees are deducted in addition to the TRADING EXPENSES.

4.A.6 When presenting NET-OF-FEES returns, FIRMS MUST disclose:

- **a** If any other fees are deducted in addition to the INVESTMENT MANAGEMENT FEES and TRADING EXPENSES;
- **b** If model or actual INVESTMENT MANAGEMENT FEES are used; and
- **c** If returns are net of any PERFORMANCE-BASED FEES.

4.A.7 FIRMS MUST disclose the currency used to express performance.

4.A.8 FIRMS MUST disclose which measure of INTERNAL DISPERSION is presented.

4.A.9 FIRMS MUST disclose the FEE SCHEDULE appropriate to the COMPLIANT PRESENTATION.

4.A.10 FIRMS MUST disclose the COMPOSITE CREATION DATE.

4.A.11 FIRMS MUST disclose that the FIRM's list of COMPOSITE DESCRIPTIONS is available upon request.

4.A.12 FIRMS MUST disclose that policies for valuing PORTFOLIOS, calculating performance, and preparing COMPLIANT PRESENTATIONS are available upon request.

4.A.13 FIRMS MUST disclose the presence, use, and extent of leverage, derivatives, and short positions, if material, including a description of the frequency of use and characteristics of the instruments sufficient to identify risks.

4.A.14 FIRMS MUST disclose all significant events that would help a PROSPECTIVE CLIENT interpret the COMPLIANT PRESENTATION.

4.A.15 For any performance presented for periods prior to 1 January 2000 that does not comply with the GIPS standards, FIRMS MUST disclose the periods of non-compliance.

4.A.16 If the FIRM is redefined, the FIRM MUST disclose the date of, description of, and reason for the redefinition.

4.A.17 If a COMPOSITE is redefined, the FIRM MUST disclose the date of, description of, and reason for the redefinition.

4.A.18 FIRMS MUST disclose changes to the name of a COMPOSITE.

4.A.19 FIRMS MUST disclose the minimum asset level, if any, below which PORTFOLIOS are not included in a COMPOSITE. FIRMS MUST also disclose any changes to the minimum asset level.

4.A.20 FIRMS MUST disclose relevant details of the treatment of withholding taxes on dividends, interest income, and capital gains, if material. FIRMS MUST also disclose if BENCHMARK returns are net of withholding taxes if this information is available.

4.A.21 For periods beginning on or after 1 January 2011, FIRMS MUST disclose and describe any known material differences in exchange rates or valuation sources used among the PORTFOLIOS within a COMPOSITE, and between the COMPOSITE and the BENCHMARK.[5]

4.A.22 If the COMPLIANT PRESENTATION conforms with laws and/or regulations that conflict with the REQUIREMENTS of the GIPS standards, FIRMS MUST disclose this fact and disclose the manner in which the laws and/or regulations conflict with the GIPS standards.

4.A.23 For periods prior to 1 January 2010, if CARVE-OUTS are included in a COMPOSITE, FIRMS MUST disclose the policy used to allocate cash to CARVE-OUTS.

4.A.24 If a COMPOSITE contains PORTFOLIOS with BUNDLED FEES, FIRMS MUST disclose the types of fees that are included in the BUNDLED FEE.

4.A.25 For periods beginning on or after 1 January 2006, FIRMS MUST disclose the use of a SUB-ADVISOR and the periods a SUB-ADVISOR was used.

4.A.26 For periods prior to 1 January 2010, FIRMS MUST disclose if any PORTFOLIOS were not valued at calendar month end or on the last business day of the month.

4.A.27 For periods beginning on or after 1 January 2011, FIRMS MUST disclose the use of subjective unobservable inputs for valuing PORTFOLIO investments (as described in the GIPS Valuation Principles) if the PORTFOLIO investments valued using subjective unobservable inputs are material to the COMPOSITE.

4.A.28 For periods beginning on or after 1 January 2011, FIRMS MUST disclose if the COMPOSITE'S valuation hierarchy materially differs from the RECOMMENDED hierarchy in the GIPS Valuation Principles.

4.A.29 If the FIRM determines no appropriate BENCHMARK for the COMPOSITE exists, the FIRM MUST disclose why no BENCHMARK is presented.

4.A.30 If the FIRM changes the BENCHMARK, the FIRM MUST disclose the date of, description of, and reason for the change.

4.A.31 If a custom BENCHMARK or combination of multiple BENCHMARKS is used, the FIRM MUST disclose the BENCHMARK components, weights, and rebalancing process.

4.A.32 If the FIRM has adopted a SIGNIFICANT CASH FLOW policy for a specific COMPOSITE, the FIRM MUST disclose how the FIRM defines a SIGNIFICANT CASH FLOW for that COMPOSITE and for which periods.

4.A.33 FIRMS MUST disclose if the three-year annualized EX-POST STANDARD DEVIATION of the COMPOSITE and/or BENCHMARK is not presented because 36 monthly returns are not available.

4.A.34 If the FIRM determines that the three-year annualized EX-POST STANDARD DEVIATION is not relevant or appropriate, the FIRM MUST:

a Describe why EX-POST STANDARD DEVIATION is not relevant or appropriate; and

5 For periods prior to 1 January 2011, FIRMS MUST disclose and describe any known inconsistencies in the exchange rates used among the PORTFOLIOS within a COMPOSITE and between the COMPOSITE and the BENCHMARK.

b Describe the additional risk measure presented and why it was selected.

4.A.35 FIRMS MUST disclose if the performance from a past firm or affiliation is LINKED to the performance of the FIRM.

Disclosure—Recommendations

4.B.1 FIRMS SHOULD disclose material changes to valuation policies and/or methodologies.

4.B.2 FIRMS SHOULD disclose material changes to calculation policies and/or methodologies.

4.B.3 FIRMS SHOULD disclose material differences between the BENCHMARK and the COMPOSITE's investment mandate, objective, or strategy.

4.B.4 FIRMS SHOULD disclose the key assumptions used to value PORTFOLIO investments.

4.B.5 If a parent company contains multiple firms, each FIRM within the parent company SHOULD disclose a list of the other firms contained within the parent company.

4.B.6 For periods prior to 1 January 2011, FIRMS SHOULD disclose the use of subjective unobservable inputs for valuing PORTFOLIO investments (as described in the GIPS Valuation Principles) if the PORTFOLIO investments valued using subjective unobservable inputs are material to the COMPOSITE.

4.B.7 For periods prior to 1 January 2006, FIRMS SHOULD disclose the use of a SUB-ADVISOR and the periods a SUB-ADVISOR was used.

4.B.8 FIRMS SHOULD disclose if a COMPOSITE contains PROPRIETARY ASSETS.

5 Presentation and Reporting

Presentation and Reporting—Requirements

5.A.1 The following items MUST be presented in each COMPLIANT PRESENTATION:

a At least five years of performance (or for the period since the FIRM's inception or the COMPOSITE INCEPTION DATE if the FIRM or the COMPOSITE has been in existence less than five years) that meets the REQUIREMENTS of the GIPS standards. After a FIRM presents a minimum of five years of GIPS-compliant performance (or for the period since the FIRM's inception or the COMPOSITE INCEPTION DATE if the FIRM or the COMPOSITE has been in existence less than five years), the FIRM MUST present an additional year of performance each year, building up to a minimum of 10 years of GIPS-compliant performance.

b COMPOSITE returns for each annual period. COMPOSITE returns MUST be clearly identified as GROSS-OF-FEES or NET-OF-FEES.

c For COMPOSITES with a COMPOSITE INCEPTION DATE of 1 January 2011 or later, when the initial period is less than a full year, returns from the COMPOSITE INCEPTION DATE through the initial annual period end.

d For COMPOSITES with a COMPOSITE TERMINATION DATE of 1 January 2011 or later, returns from the last annual period end through the COMPOSITE TERMINATION DATE.

e The TOTAL RETURN for the BENCHMARK for each annual period. The BENCHMARK MUST reflect the investment mandate, objective, or strategy of the COMPOSITE.

f The number of PORTFOLIOS in the COMPOSITE as of each annual period end. If the COMPOSITE contains five or fewer PORTFOLIOS at period end, the number of PORTFOLIOS is not REQUIRED.

g COMPOSITE assets as of each annual period end.

h Either TOTAL FIRM ASSETS or COMPOSITE assets as a percentage of TOTAL FIRM ASSETS, as of each annual period end.

i A measure of INTERNAL DISPERSION of individual PORTFOLIO returns for each annual period. If the COMPOSITE contains five or fewer PORTFOLIOS for the full year, a measure of INTERNAL DISPERSION is not REQUIRED.

5.A.2 For periods ending on or after 1 January 2011, FIRMS MUST present, as of each annual period end:

a The three-year annualized EX-POST STANDARD DEVIATION (using monthly returns) of both the COMPOSITE and the BENCHMARK; and

b An additional three-year EX-POST risk measure for the BENCHMARK (if available and appropriate) and the COMPOSITE, if the FIRM determines that the three-year annualized EX-POST STANDARD DEVIATION is not relevant or appropriate. The PERIODICITY of the COMPOSITE and the BENCHMARK MUST be identical when calculating the EX-POST risk measure.

5.A.3 FIRMS MUST NOT LINK non-GIPS-compliant performance for periods beginning on or after 1 January 2000 to their GIPS-compliant performance. FIRMS may LINK non-GIPS-compliant performance to GIPS-compliant performance provided that only GIPS-compliant performance is presented for periods beginning on or after 1 January 2000.

5.A.4 Returns for periods of less than one year MUST NOT be annualized.

5.A.5 For periods beginning on or after 1 January 2006 and ending prior to 1 January 2011, if a COMPOSITE includes CARVE-OUTS, the FIRM MUST present the percentage of COMPOSITE assets represented by CARVE-OUTS as of each annual period end.

5.A.6 If a COMPOSITE includes non-fee-paying PORTFOLIOS, the FIRM MUST present the percentage of COMPOSITE assets represented by non-fee-paying PORTFOLIOS as of each annual period end.

5.A.7 If a COMPOSITE includes PORTFOLIOS with BUNDLED FEES, the FIRM MUST present the percentage of COMPOSITE assets represented by PORTFOLIOS with BUNDLED FEES as of each annual period end.

5.A.8 a Performance of a past firm or affiliation MUST be LINKED to or used to represent the historical performance of a new or acquiring FIRM if, on a COMPOSITE-specific basis:

i. Substantially all of the investment decision makers are employed by the new or acquiring FIRM (e.g., research department staff, portfolio managers, and other relevant staff);

ii. The decision-making process remains substantially intact and independent within the new or acquiring FIRM; and

iii. The new or acquiring FIRM has records that document and support the performance.

b If a FIRM acquires another firm or affiliation, the FIRM has one year to bring any non-compliant assets into compliance.

Presentation and Reporting—Recommendations

5.B.1 FIRMS SHOULD present GROSS-OF-FEES returns.

5.B.2 FIRMS SHOULD present the following items:

a Cumulative returns of the COMPOSITE and the BENCHMARK for all periods;

b Equal-weighted mean and median COMPOSITE returns;

c Quarterly and/or monthly returns; and

d Annualized COMPOSITE and BENCHMARK returns for periods longer than 12 months.

5.B.3 For periods prior to 1 January 2011, FIRMS SHOULD present the three-year annualized EX-POST STANDARD DEVIATION (using monthly returns) of the COMPOSITE and the BENCHMARK as of each annual period end.

5.B.4 For each period for which an annualized EX-POST STANDARD DEVIATION of the COMPOSITE and the BENCHMARK are presented, the corresponding annualized return of the COMPOSITE and the BENCHMARK SHOULD also be presented.

5.B.5 For each period for which an annualized return of the COMPOSITE and the BENCHMARK are presented, the corresponding annualized EX-POST STANDARD DEVIATION (using monthly returns) of the COMPOSITE and the BENCHMARK SHOULD also be presented.

5.B.6 FIRMS SHOULD present additional relevant COMPOSITE-level EX-POST risk measures.

5.B.7 FIRMS SHOULD present more than 10 years of annual performance in the COMPLIANT PRESENTATION.

5.B.8 FIRMS SHOULD comply with the GIPS standards for all historical periods.

5.B.9 FIRMS SHOULD update COMPLIANT PRESENTATIONS quarterly.

6 Real Estate

Unless otherwise noted, the following REAL ESTATE provisions supplement the REQUIRED and RECOMMENDED provisions of the GIPS standards in Sections 0–5.

REAL ESTATE provisions were first included in the GIPS standards in 2005 and became effective 1 January 2006. All COMPLIANT PRESENTATIONS that included REAL ESTATE performance for periods beginning on or after 1 January 2006 were REQUIRED to meet all the REQUIREMENTS of the REAL ESTATE provisions of the 2005 edition of the GIPS standards. The following REAL ESTATE provisions are effective 1 January 2011. All REAL ESTATE COMPOSITES that include performance for periods beginning on or after 1 January 2011 MUST comply with all the REQUIREMENTS and SHOULD adhere to the RECOMMENDATIONS of the following REAL ESTATE provisions.

The following investment types are not considered REAL ESTATE and, therefore, MUST follow Sections 0–5 in Provisions of the Global Investment Performance Standards:

- Publicly traded REAL ESTATE securities;
- Commercial mortgage-backed securities (CMBS); and
- Private debt investments, including commercial and residential loans where the expected return is solely related to contractual interest rates without any participation in the economic performance of the underlying REAL ESTATE.

Real Estate—Requirements

Input Data—Requirements (the following provisions do not apply: 1.A.3.a, 1.A.3.b, and 1.A.4)

6.A.1 For periods beginning on or after 1 January 2011, REAL ESTATE investments MUST be valued in accordance with the definition of FAIR VALUE and the GIPS Valuation Principles.[6]

6.A.2 For periods beginning on or after 1 January 2008, REAL ESTATE investments MUST be valued at least quarterly.[7]

6.A.3 For periods beginning on or after 1 January 2010, FIRMS MUST value PORTFOLIOS as of each quarter end or the last business day of each quarter.

6.A.4 REAL ESTATE investments MUST have an EXTERNAL VALUATION:

- **a** For periods prior to 1 January 2012, at least once every 36 months.
- **b** For periods beginning on or after 1 January 2012, at least once every 12 months unless client agreements stipulate otherwise, in which case REAL ESTATE investments MUST have an EXTERNAL VALUATION at least once every 36 months or per the client agreement if the client agreement requires EXTERNAL VALUATIONS more frequently than every 36 months.

6.A.5 EXTERNAL VALUATIONS must be performed by an independent external PROFESSIONALLY DESIGNATED, CERTIFIED, OR LICENSED COMMERCIAL PROPERTY VALUER/APPRAISER. In markets where these professionals are not available, the FIRM MUST take necessary steps to ensure that only well-qualified independent property valuers or appraisers are used.

Calculation Methodology—Requirements (the following provisions do not apply: 2.A.2.a, 2.A.4, and 2.A.7)

6.A.6 FIRMS MUST calculate PORTFOLIO returns at least quarterly.

6.A.7 All returns MUST be calculated after the deduction of actual TRANSACTION EXPENSES incurred during the period.

6.A.8 For periods beginning on or after 1 January 2011, INCOME RETURNS and CAPITAL RETURNS (component returns) MUST be calculated separately using geometrically LINKED TIME-WEIGHTED RATES OF RETURN.

6.A.9 COMPOSITE TIME-WEIGHTED RATES OF RETURN, including component returns, MUST be calculated by asset-weighting the individual PORTFOLIO returns at least quarterly.

Disclosure—Requirements (the following provisions do not apply: 4.A.5, 4.A.6.a, 4.A.15, 4.A.26, 4.A.33, and 4.A.34)

6.A.10 The following items MUST be disclosed in each COMPLIANT PRESENTATION:

- **a** The FIRM's description of discretion;
- **b** The INTERNAL VALUATION methodologies used to value REAL ESTATE investments for the most recent period;
- **c** For periods beginning on or after 1 January 2011, material changes to valuation policies and/or methodologies;

6 For periods prior to 1 January 2011, REAL ESTATE investments MUST be valued at MARKET VALUE (as previously defined for REAL ESTATE in the 2005 edition of the GIPS standards).

7 For periods prior to 1 January 2008, REAL ESTATE investments MUST be valued at least once every 12 months.

d For periods beginning on or after 1 January 2011, material differences between an EXTERNAL VALUATION and the valuation used in performance reporting and the reason for the differences;

e The frequency REAL ESTATE investments are valued by an independent external PROFESSIONALLY DESIGNATED, CERTIFIED, OR LICENSED COMMERCIAL PROPERTY VALUER/APPRAISER;

f When component returns are calculated separately using geometrically LINKED TIME-WEIGHTED RATES OF RETURN; and

g For periods prior to 1 January 2011, if component returns are adjusted such that the sum of the INCOME RETURN and the CAPITAL RETURN equals the TOTAL RETURN.

6.A.11 For any performance presented for periods prior to 1 January 2006 that does not comply with the GIPS standards, FIRMS MUST disclose the periods of non-compliance.

6.A.12 When presenting GROSS-OF-FEES returns, FIRMS MUST disclose if any other fees are deducted in addition to the TRANSACTION EXPENSES.

6.A.13 When presenting NET-OF-FEES returns, FIRMS MUST disclose if any other fees are deducted in addition to the INVESTMENT MANAGEMENT FEES and TRANSACTION EXPENSES.

Presentation and Reporting—Requirements (the following provisions do not apply: 5.A.1.i, 5.A.2, and 5.A.3)

6.A.14 FIRMS MUST present component returns in addition to TOTAL RETURNS. COMPOSITE component returns MUST be clearly identified as GROSS-OF-FEES or NET-OF-FEES.

6.A.15 FIRMS MUST NOT LINK non-GIPS-compliant performance for periods beginning on or after 1 January 2006 to their GIPS-compliant performance. FIRMS may LINK non-GIPS-compliant performance to their GIPS-compliant performance provided that only GIPS-compliant performance is presented for periods beginning on or after 1 January 2006.

6.A.16 The following items MUST be presented in each COMPLIANT PRESENTATION:

a As a measure of INTERNAL DISPERSION, high and low annual TIME-WEIGHTED RATES OF RETURN for the individual PORTFOLIOS in the COMPOSITE. If the COMPOSITE contains five or fewer PORTFOLIOS for the full year, a measure of INTERNAL DISPERSION is not REQUIRED.

b As of each annual period end, the percentage of COMPOSITE assets valued using an EXTERNAL VALUATION during the annual period.

The following provisions are additional REQUIREMENTS for REAL ESTATE CLOSED-END FUND COMPOSITES:

Calculation Methodology—Requirements

6.A.17 FIRMS MUST calculate annualized SINCE INCEPTION INTERNAL RATES OF RETURN (SI-IRR).

6.A.18 The SI-IRR MUST be calculated using quarterly cash flows at a minimum.

Composite Construction—Requirements

6.A.19 COMPOSITES MUST be defined by VINTAGE YEAR and investment mandate, objective, or strategy. The COMPOSITE DEFINITION MUST remain consistent throughout the life of the COMPOSITE.

Disclosure—Requirements

6.A.20 FIRMS MUST disclose the FINAL LIQUIDATION DATE for liquidated COMPOSITES.

6.A.21 FIRMS MUST disclose the frequency of cash flows used in the SI-IRR calculation.

6.A.22 FIRMS MUST disclose the VINTAGE YEAR of the COMPOSITE and how the VINTAGE YEAR is defined.

Presentation and Reporting—Requirements

6.A.23 The following items MUST be presented in each COMPLIANT PRESENTATION:

- **a** FIRMS MUST present the NET-OF-FEES SI-IRR of the COMPOSITE through each annual period end. FIRMS MUST initially present at least five years of performance (or for the period since the FIRM's inception or the COMPOSITE INCEPTION DATE if the FIRM or the COMPOSITE has been in existence less than five years) that meets the REQUIREMENTS of the GIPS standards. Each subsequent year, FIRMS MUST present an additional year of performance.
- **b** For periods beginning on or after 1 January 2011, when the initial period is less than a full year, FIRMS MUST present the non-annualized NET-OF-FEES SI-IRR through the initial annual period end.
- **c** For periods ending on or after 1 January 2011, FIRMS MUST present the NET-OF-FEES SI-IRR through the COMPOSITE FINAL LIQUIDATION DATE.

6.A.24 If the GROSS-OF-FEES SI-IRR of the COMPOSITE is presented in the COMPLIANT PRESENTATION, FIRMS MUST present the GROSS-OF-FEES SI-IRR of the COMPOSITE for the same periods as the NET-OF-FEES SI-IRR is presented.

6.A.25 FIRMS MUST present, as of each annual period end:

- **a** COMPOSITE SINCE INCEPTION PAID-IN CAPITAL;
- **b** COMPOSITE SINCE INCEPTION DISTRIBUTIONS;
- **c** COMPOSITE cumulative COMMITTED CAPITAL;
- **d** TOTAL VALUE to SINCE INCEPTION PAID-IN CAPITAL (INVESTMENT MULTIPLE or TVPI);
- **e** SINCE INCEPTION DISTRIBUTIONS to SINCE INCEPTION PAID-IN CAPITAL (REALIZATION MULTIPLE or DPI);
- **f** SINCE INCEPTION PAID-IN CAPITAL to cumulative COMMITTED CAPITAL (PIC MULTIPLE); and
- **g** RESIDUAL VALUE to SINCE INCEPTION PAID-IN CAPITAL (UNREALIZED MULTIPLE or RVPI).

6.A.26 FIRMS MUST present the SI-IRR of the BENCHMARK through each annual period end. The BENCHMARK MUST:

- **a** Reflect the investment mandate, objective, or strategy of the COMPOSITE;
- **b** Be presented for the same time period as presented for the COMPOSITE; and
- **c** Be the same VINTAGE YEAR as the COMPOSITE.

Real Estate—Recommendations

Input Data—Recommendations (the following provision does not apply: 1.B.1)

6.B.1 For periods prior to 1 January 2012, REAL ESTATE investments SHOULD be valued by an independent external PROFESSIONALLY DESIGNATED, CERTIFIED, OR LICENSED COMMERCIAL PROPERTY VALUER/APPRAISER at least once every 12 months.

6.B.2 REAL ESTATE investments SHOULD be valued as of the annual period end by an independent external PROFESSIONALLY DESIGNATED, CERTIFIED, OR LICENSED COMMERCIAL PROPERTY VALUER/APPRAISER.

Disclosure—Recommendations

6.B.3 FIRMS SHOULD disclose the basis of accounting for the PORTFOLIOS in the COMPOSITE (e.g., US GAAP, IFRS).

6.B.4 FIRMS SHOULD explain and disclose material differences between the valuation used in performance reporting and the valuation used in financial reporting as of each annual period end.

6.B.5 For periods prior to 1 January 2011, FIRMS SHOULD disclose material changes to valuation policies and/or methodologies.

Presentation and Reporting—Recommendations (the following provisions do not apply: 5.B.3, 5.B.4, and 5.B.5)

6.B.6 FIRMS SHOULD present both GROSS-OF-FEES and NET-OF-FEES returns.

6.B.7 FIRMS SHOULD present the percentage of the total value of COMPOSITE assets that are not REAL ESTATE as of each annual period end.

6.B.8 FIRMS SHOULD present the component returns of the BENCHMARK, if available.

The following provision is an additional RECOMMENDATION for REAL ESTATE CLOSED-END FUND COMPOSITES:

Calculation Methodology—Recommendations

6.B.9 The SI-IRR SHOULD be calculated using daily cash flows.

7 Private Equity

Unless otherwise noted, the following PRIVATE EQUITY provisions supplement the REQUIRED and RECOMMENDED provisions of the GIPS standards in Sections 0–5.

PRIVATE EQUITY provisions were first included in the GIPS standards in 2005 and became effective 1 January 2006. All COMPLIANT PRESENTATIONS that included PRIVATE EQUITY performance for periods ending on or after 1 January 2006 were REQUIRED to meet all the REQUIREMENTS of the PRIVATE EQUITY provisions of the 2005 edition of the GIPS standards. The following PRIVATE EQUITY provisions are effective 1 January 2011. All PRIVATE EQUITY COMPOSITES that include performance for periods ending on or after 1 January 2011 MUST comply with all the REQUIREMENTS and SHOULD comply with the RECOMMENDATIONS of the following PRIVATE EQUITY provisions.

The following are provisions that apply to the calculation and presentation of PRIVATE EQUITY investments made by fixed life, fixed commitment PRIVATE EQUITY investment vehicles including PRIMARY FUNDS and FUNDS OF FUNDS. These provisions also apply to fixed life, fixed commitment SECONDARY FUNDS, which MUST apply either the provisions applicable to PRIMARY FUNDS or the provisions applicable to FUNDS OF FUNDS depending on which form the SECONDARY FUND uses to make investments. PRIVATE EQUITY OPEN-END and EVERGREEN FUNDS MUST follow Sections 0–5 in the Provisions of the Global Investment Performance Standards. REAL ESTATE CLOSED-END FUNDS MUST follow Section 6 in the Provisions of the Global Investment Performance Standards.

Private Equity—Requirements

Input Data—Requirements (the following provisions do not apply: 1.A.3.a, 1.A.3.b, and 1.A.4)

7.A.1 For periods ending on or after 1 January 2011, PRIVATE EQUITY investments MUST be valued in accordance with the definition of FAIR VALUE and the GIPS Valuation Principles.[8]

7.A.2 PRIVATE EQUITY investments MUST be valued at least annually.

Calculation Methodology—Requirements (the following provisions do not apply: 2.A.2, 2.A.4, 2.A.6, and 2.A.7)

7.A.3 FIRMS MUST calculate annualized SINCE INCEPTION INTERNAL RATES OF RETURN (SI-IRR).

7.A.4 For periods ending on or after 1 January 2011, the SI-IRR MUST be calculated using daily cash flows. Stock DISTRIBUTIONS MUST be included as cash flows and MUST be valued at the time of DISTRIBUTION.[9]

7.A.5 All returns MUST be calculated after the deduction of actual TRANSACTION EXPENSES incurred during the period.

7.A.6 NET-OF-FEES returns MUST be net of actual INVESTMENT MANAGEMENT FEES (including CARRIED INTEREST).

7.A.7 For FUNDS OF FUNDS, all returns MUST be net of all underlying partnership and/or fund fees and expenses, including CARRIED INTEREST.

Composite Construction—Requirements (the following provision does not apply: 3.A.10)

7.A.8 COMPOSITE DEFINITIONS MUST remain consistent throughout the life of the COMPOSITE.

7.A.9 PRIMARY FUNDS MUST be included in at least one COMPOSITE defined by VINTAGE YEAR and investment mandate, objective, or strategy.

7.A.10 FUNDS OF FUNDS MUST be included in at least one COMPOSITE defined by VINTAGE YEAR of the FUND OF FUNDS and/or investment mandate, objective, or strategy.

Disclosure—Requirements (the following provisions do not apply: 4.A.5, 4.A.6.a, 4.A.6.b, 4.A.8, 4.A.15, 4.A.26, 4.A.32, 4.A.33, and 4.A.34)

7.A.11 FIRMS MUST disclose the VINTAGE YEAR of the COMPOSITE and how the VINTAGE YEAR is defined.

7.A.12 FIRMS MUST disclose the FINAL LIQUIDATION DATE for liquidated COMPOSITES.

7.A.13 FIRMS MUST disclose the valuation methodologies used to value PRIVATE EQUITY investments for the most recent period.

---

8 For periods ending prior to 1 January 2011, PRIVATE EQUITY investments MUST be valued according to either the GIPS Private Equity Valuation Principles in Appendix D of the 2005 edition of the GIPS standards or the GIPS Valuation Principles in the 2010 edition of the GIPS standards.

9 For periods ending prior to 1 January 2011, the SI-IRR MUST be calculated using either daily or monthly cash flows.

7.A.14 For periods ending on or after 1 January 2011, FIRMS MUST disclose material changes to valuation policies and/or methodologies.

7.A.15 If the FIRM adheres to any industry valuation guidelines in addition to the GIPS Valuation Principles, the FIRM MUST disclose which guidelines have been applied.

7.A.16 FIRMS MUST disclose the calculation methodology used for the BENCHMARK. If FIRMS present the PUBLIC MARKET EQUIVALENT of a COMPOSITE as a BENCHMARK, FIRMS MUST disclose the index used to calculate the PUBLIC MARKET EQUIVALENT.

7.A.17 FIRMS MUST disclose the frequency of cash flows used in the SI-IRR calculation if daily cash flows are not used for periods prior to 1 January 2011.

7.A.18 For GROSS-OF-FEES returns, FIRMS MUST disclose if any other fees are deducted in addition to the TRANSACTION EXPENSES.

7.A.19 For NET-OF-FEES returns, FIRMS MUST disclose if any other fees are deducted in addition to the INVESTMENT MANAGEMENT FEES and TRANSACTION EXPENSES.

7.A.20 For any performance presented for periods ending prior to 1 January 2006 that does not comply with the GIPS standards, FIRMS MUST disclose the periods of non-compliance.

Presentation and Reporting—Requirements (the following provisions do not apply: 5.A.1.a, 5.A.1.b, 5.A.1.c, 5.A.1.d, 5.A.1.e, 5.A.1.i, 5.A.2, and 5.A.3)

7.A.21 The following items MUST be presented in each COMPLIANT PRESENTATION:

- **a** FIRMS MUST present both the NET-OF-FEES and GROSS-OF-FEES SI-IRR of the COMPOSITE through each annual period end. FIRMS MUST initially present at least five years of performance (or for the period since the FIRM'S inception or the COMPOSITE INCEPTION DATE if the FIRM or the COMPOSITE has been in existence less than five years) that meets the REQUIREMENTS of the GIPS standards. Each subsequent year, FIRMS MUST present an additional year of performance. COMPOSITE returns MUST be clearly identified as GROSS-OF-FEES or NET-OF-FEES.
- **b** For periods beginning on or after 1 January 2011, when the initial period is less than a full year, FIRMS MUST present the non-annualized NET-OF-FEES and GROSS-OF-FEES SI-IRR through the initial annual period end.
- **c** For periods ending on or after 1 January 2011, FIRMS MUST present the NET-OF-FEES and GROSS-OF-FEES SI-IRR through the COMPOSITE FINAL LIQUIDATION DATE.

7.A.22 For periods ending on or after 1 January 2011, for FUND OF FUNDS COMPOSITES, if the COMPOSITE is defined only by investment mandate, objective, or strategy, FIRMS MUST also present the SI-IRR of the underlying investments aggregated by VINTAGE YEAR as well as other measures as REQUIRED in 7.A.23. These measures MUST be presented gross of the FUND OF FUNDS INVESTMENT MANAGEMENT FEES and MUST be presented as of the most recent annual period end.

7.A.23 FIRMS MUST present as of each annual period end:

- **a** COMPOSITE SINCE INCEPTION PAID-IN CAPITAL;
- **b** COMPOSITE SINCE INCEPTION DISTRIBUTIONS;
- **c** COMPOSITE cumulative COMMITTED CAPITAL;
- **d** TOTAL VALUE to SINCE INCEPTION PAID-IN CAPITAL (INVESTMENT MULTIPLE or TVPI);

- **e** SINCE INCEPTION DISTRIBUTIONS to SINCE INCEPTION PAID-IN CAPITAL (REALIZATION MULTIPLE or DPI);
- **f** SINCE INCEPTION PAID-IN CAPITAL to cumulative COMMITTED CAPITAL (PIC MULTIPLE); and
- **g** RESIDUAL VALUE to SINCE INCEPTION PAID-IN CAPITAL (UNREALIZED MULTIPLE or RVPI).

7.A.24 FIRMS MUST present the SI-IRR for the BENCHMARK through each annual period end. The BENCHMARK MUST:

- **a** Reflect the investment mandate, objective, or strategy of the COMPOSITE;
- **b** Be presented for the same time periods as presented for the COMPOSITE; and
- **c** Be the same VINTAGE YEAR as the COMPOSITE.

7.A.25 For FUND OF FUNDS COMPOSITES, if the COMPOSITE is defined only by investment mandate, objective, or strategy and a BENCHMARK is presented for the underlying investments, the BENCHMARK MUST be the same VINTAGE YEAR and investment mandate, objective, or strategy as the underlying investments.

7.A.26 For periods ending on or after 1 January 2011, for FUND OF FUNDS COMPOSITES, FIRMS MUST present the percentage, if any, of COMPOSITE assets that is invested in DIRECT INVESTMENTS (rather than in fund investment vehicles) as of each annual period end.

7.A.27 For periods ending on or after 1 January 2011, for PRIMARY FUND COMPOSITES, FIRMS MUST present the percentage, if any, of COMPOSITE assets that is invested in fund investment vehicles (rather than in DIRECT INVESTMENTS) as of each annual period end.

7.A.28 FIRMS MUST NOT present non-GIPS-compliant performance for periods ending on or after 1 January 2006. For periods ending prior to 1 January 2006, FIRMS may present non-GIPS-compliant performance.

Private Equity—Recommendations

Input Data—Recommendations (the following provision does not apply: 1.B.1)

7.B.1 PRIVATE EQUITY investments SHOULD be valued at least quarterly.

Calculation Methodology—Recommendations (the following provision does not apply: 2.B.2)

7.B.2 For periods ending prior to 1 January 2011, the SI-IRR SHOULD be calculated using daily cash flows.

Composite Construction—Recommendations (the following provision does not apply: 3.B.2)

Disclosure—Recommendations

7.B.3 FIRMS SHOULD explain and disclose material differences between the valuations used in performance reporting and the valuations used in financial reporting as of each annual period end.

7.B.4 For periods prior to 1 January 2011, FIRMS SHOULD disclose material changes to valuation policies and/or methodologies.

Presentation and Reporting—Recommendations (the following provisions do not apply: 5.B.2, 5.B.3, 5.B.4, and 5.B.5)

7.B.5 For periods ending on or after 1 January 2011, for FUND OF FUNDS COMPOSITES, if the COMPOSITE is defined only by VINTAGE YEAR of the FUND OF FUNDS, FIRMS SHOULD also present the SI-IRR of the underlying investments aggregated by investment mandate, objective, or strategy and other measures as listed in 7.A.23. These measures SHOULD be presented gross of the FUND OF FUNDS INVESTMENT MANAGEMENT FEES.

7.B.6 For periods ending prior to 1 January 2011, for FUND OF FUNDS COMPOSITES, FIRMS SHOULD present the percentage, if any, of COMPOSITE assets that is invested in DIRECT INVESTMENTS (rather than in fund investment vehicles) as of each annual period end.

7.B.7 For periods ending prior to 1 January 2011, for PRIMARY FUND COMPOSITES, FIRMS SHOULD present the percentage, if any, of COMPOSITE assets that is invested in fund investment vehicles (rather than in DIRECT INVESTMENTS) as of each annual period end.

8 Wrap Fee/Separately Managed Account (SMA) Portfolios

The following provisions apply to the calculation and presentation of performance when presenting a COMPLIANT PRESENTATION to a WRAP FEE/SMA PROSPECTIVE CLIENT (which includes prospective WRAP FEE/SMA sponsors, prospective WRAP FEE/SMA clients, and existing WRAP FEE/SMA sponsors). Unless otherwise noted, the following WRAP FEE/SMA provisions supplement all the REQUIRED and RECOMMENDED provisions of the GIPS standards in Sections 0–5.

Although there are different types of WRAP FEE/SMA structures, these provisions apply to all WRAP FEE/SMA PORTFOLIOS where there are BUNDLED FEES and the WRAP FEE/SMA sponsor serves as an intermediary between the FIRM and the end user of the investment services. These provisions are not applicable to PORTFOLIOS defined as other types of BUNDLED FEE PORTFOLIOS. These provisions are also not applicable to model PORTFOLIOS that are provided by a FIRM to a WRAP FEE/SMA sponsor if the FIRM does not have discretionary PORTFOLIO management responsibility for the individual WRAP FEE/SMA PORTFOLIOS. Similarly, a FIRM or overlay manager in a Multiple Strategy Portfolio (MSP) or similar program is also excluded from applying these provisions to such PORTFOLIOS if they do not have discretion.

All WRAP FEE/SMA COMPLIANT PRESENTATIONS that include performance results for periods beginning on or after 1 January 2006 MUST meet all the REQUIREMENTS of the following WRAP FEE/SMA provisions.

Wrap Fee/SMA Requirements

Composite Construction—Requirements

8.A.1 FIRMS MUST include the performance record of actual WRAP FEE/SMA PORTFOLIOS in appropriate COMPOSITES in accordance with the FIRM's established PORTFOLIO inclusion policies. Once established, these COMPOSITES (containing actual WRAP FEE/SMA PORTFOLIOS) MUST be used in the FIRM's COMPLIANT PRESENTATIONS presented to WRAP FEE/SMA PROSPECTIVE CLIENTS.

Disclosure—Requirements (the following provision does not apply: 4.A.15)

8.A.2 For all WRAP FEE/SMA COMPLIANT PRESENTATIONS that include periods prior to the inclusion of an actual WRAP FEE/SMA PORTFOLIO in the COMPOSITE, the FIRM MUST disclose, for each period presented, that the COMPOSITE does not contain actual WRAP FEE/SMA PORTFOLIOS.

8.A.3 For any performance presented for periods prior to 1 January 2006 that does not comply with the GIPS standards, FIRMS MUST disclose the periods of non-compliance.

8.A.4 When FIRMS present COMPOSITE performance to an existing WRAP FEE/SMA sponsor that includes only that sponsor's WRAP FEE/SMA PORTFOLIOS (resulting in a "sponsor-specific COMPOSITE"):

- **a** FIRMS MUST disclose the name of the WRAP FEE/SMA sponsor represented by the sponsor-specific COMPOSITE; and
- **b** If the sponsor-specific COMPOSITE COMPLIANT PRESENTATION is intended for the purpose of generating WRAP FEE/SMA business and does not include performance net of the entire WRAP FEE, the COMPLIANT PRESENTATION MUST disclose that the named sponsor-specific COMPLIANT PRESENTATION is only for the use of the named WRAP FEE/SMA sponsor.

Presentation and Reporting—Requirements (the following provision does not apply: 5.A.3)

8.A.5 When FIRMS present performance to a WRAP FEE/SMA PROSPECTIVE CLIENT, the COMPOSITE presented MUST include the performance of all actual WRAP FEE/SMA PORTFOLIOS, if any, managed according to the COMPOSITE investment mandate, objective, or strategy, regardless of the WRAP FEE/SMA sponsor (resulting in a "style-defined COMPOSITE").

8.A.6 When FIRMS present performance to a WRAP FEE/SMA PROSPECTIVE CLIENT, performance MUST be presented net of the entire WRAP FEE.

8.A.7 FIRMS MUST NOT LINK non-GIPS-compliant performance for periods beginning on or after 1 January 2006 to their GIPS-compliant performance. FIRMS may LINK non-GIPS-compliant performance to their GIPS-compliant performance provided that only GIPS-compliant performance is presented for periods beginning on or after 1 January 2006.

GIPS VALUATION PRINCIPLES II.

The GIPS standards are based on the ethical principles of fair representation and full disclosure. In order for the performance calculations to be meaningful, the valuations of PORTFOLIO investments must have integrity and fairly reflect their value. Effective 1 January 2011, the GIPS standards REQUIRE FIRMS to apply a FAIR VALUE methodology following the definition and REQUIREMENTS listed below. The GIPS Valuation Principles, including the definition of FAIR VALUE, were developed with consideration of the work done by the International Accounting Standards Board (IASB) and the Financial Accounting Standards Board (FASB) as well as other organizations.

The shift to a broader FAIR VALUE REQUIREMENT has implications for all FIRMS claiming compliance with the GIPS standards. For liquid securities in active markets, the change to FAIR VALUE from MARKET VALUE will typically not result in a change to valuations. FIRMS MUST use the objective, observable, unadjusted quoted market prices for identical investments on the measurement date, if available.

Markets are not always liquid and investment prices are not always objective and/or observable. For illiquid or hard to value investments, or for investments where no observable MARKET VALUE or market price is available, additional steps are necessary. A FIRM's valuation policies and procedures MUST address situations where the market prices may be available for similar but not identical investments, inputs to valuations are subjective rather than objective, and/or markets are inactive instead of active. There is a RECOMMENDED valuation hierarchy in Section C below. FIRMS MUST disclose if the COMPOSITE's valuation hierarchy materially differs from the RECOMMENDED valuation hierarchy.

Although a FIRM may use external third parties to value investments, the FIRM still retains responsibility for compliance with the GIPS standards, including the GIPS Valuation Principles.

FIRMS claiming compliance with the GIPS standards MUST adhere to all the REQUIREMENTS and SHOULD comply with the RECOMMENDATIONS below.

A. Fair Value Definition

FAIR VALUE is defined as the amount at which an investment could be exchanged in a current arm's length transaction between willing parties in which the parties each act knowledgeably and prudently. The valuation MUST be determined using the objective, observable, unadjusted quoted market price for an identical investment in an active market on the measurement date, if available. In the absence of an objective, observable, unadjusted quoted market price for an identical investment in an active market on the measurement date, the valuation MUST represent the FIRM's best estimate of the MARKET VALUE. FAIR VALUE MUST include accrued income.

B. Valuation Requirements

FIRMS MUST comply with the following valuation REQUIREMENTS:

1 For periods beginning on or after 1 January 2011, PORTFOLIOS MUST be valued in accordance with the definition of FAIR VALUE and the GIPS Valuation Principles (Provision 1.A.2).

2 FIRMS MUST value investments using objective, observable, unadjusted quoted market prices for identical investments in active markets on the measurement date, if available.

3 FIRMS MUST comply with all applicable laws and regulations regarding the calculation and presentation of performance (Provision 0.A.2). Accordingly, FIRMS MUST comply with applicable laws and regulations relating to valuation.

4 If the COMPLIANT PRESENTATION conforms with laws and/or regulations that conflict with the REQUIREMENTS of the GIPS standards, FIRMS MUST disclose this fact and disclose the manner in which the laws and/or regulations conflict with the GIPS standards (Provision 4.A.22). This includes any conflicts between laws and/or regulations and the GIPS Valuation Principles.

5 FIRMS MUST document their policies and procedures used in establishing and maintaining compliance with the GIPS standards, including ensuring the existence and ownership of client assets, and MUST apply them consistently (Provision 0.A.5). Accordingly, FIRMS MUST document their valuation policies, procedures, methodologies, and hierarchy, including any changes, and MUST apply them consistently.

6 FIRMS MUST disclose that policies for valuing PORTFOLIOS, calculating performance, and preparing COMPLIANT PRESENTATIONS are available upon request (Provision 4.A.12).

7 For periods beginning on or after 1 January 2011, FIRMS MUST disclose the use of subjective unobservable inputs for valuing PORTFOLIO investments (as described in the GIPS Valuation Principles) if the PORTFOLIO investments valued using subjective unobservable inputs are material to the COMPOSITE (Provision 4.A.27).

8 For periods beginning on or after 1 January 2011, FIRMS MUST disclose if the COMPOSITE's valuation hierarchy materially differs from the RECOMMENDED hierarchy in the GIPS Valuation Principles (Provision 4.A.28).

Additional Real Estate Valuation Requirements:

9 REAL ESTATE investments MUST have an EXTERNAL VALUATION (Provision 6.A.4).

10 The EXTERNAL VALUATION process MUST adhere to practices of the relevant valuation governing and standard setting body.

11 The FIRM MUST NOT use EXTERNAL VALUATIONS where the valuer's or appraiser's fee is contingent upon the investment's appraised value.

12 EXTERNAL VALUATIONS must be performed by an independent external PROFESSIONALLY DESIGNATED, CERTIFIED, OR LICENSED COMMERCIAL PROPERTY VALUER/APPRAISER. In markets where these professionals are not available, the FIRM MUST take necessary steps to ensure that only well-qualified independent property valuers or appraisers are used (Provision 6.A.5).

13 FIRMS MUST disclose the INTERNAL VALUATION methodologies used to value REAL ESTATE investments for the most recent period (Provision 6.A.10.b).

14 For periods beginning on or after 1 January 2011, FIRMS MUST disclose material changes to valuation policies and/or methodologies (Provision 6.A.10.c).

15 For periods beginning on or after 1 January 2011, FIRMS MUST disclose material differences between an EXTERNAL VALUATION and the valuation used in performance reporting and the reason for the differences (Provision 6.A.10.d).

16 FIRMS MUST present, as of each annual period end, the percentage of COMPOSITE assets valued using an EXTERNAL VALUATION during the annual period (Provision 6.A.16.b).

Additional Private Equity Valuation Requirements:

17 The valuation methodology selected MUST be the most appropriate for a particular investment based on the nature, facts, and circumstances of the investment.

18 FIRMS MUST disclose the valuation methodologies used to value PRIVATE EQUITY investments for the most recent period (Provision 7.A.13).

19 For periods ending on or after 1 January 2011, FIRMS MUST disclose material changes to valuation policies and/or methodologies (Provision 7.A.14).

20 If the FIRM adheres to any industry valuation guidelines in addition to the GIPS Valuation Principles, the FIRM MUST disclose which guidelines have been applied (Provision 7.A.15).

C. Valuation Recommendations

FIRMS SHOULD comply with the following valuation RECOMMENDATIONS:

1 **Valuation Hierarchy**: FIRMS SHOULD incorporate the following hierarchy into the policies and procedures for determining FAIR VALUE for PORTFOLIO investments on a COMPOSITE-specific basis.

 a Investments MUST be valued using objective, observable, unadjusted quoted market prices for identical investments in active markets on the measurement date, if available. If not available, then investments SHOULD be valued using;

 b Objective, observable quoted market prices for similar investments in active markets. If not available or appropriate, then investments SHOULD be valued using;

 c Quoted prices for identical or similar investments in markets that are not active (markets in which there are few transactions for the investment, the prices are not current, or price quotations vary substantially over time and/or between market makers). If not available or appropriate, then investments SHOULD be valued based on;

 d Market-based inputs, other than quoted prices, that are observable for the investment. If not available or appropriate, then investments SHOULD be valued based on;

 e Subjective unobservable inputs for the investment where markets are not active at the measurement date. Unobservable inputs SHOULD only be used to measure FAIR VALUE to the extent that observable inputs and prices are not available or appropriate. Unobservable inputs reflect the FIRM's own assumptions about the assumptions that market participants would use in pricing the investment and SHOULD be developed based on the best information available under the circumstances.

2 FIRMS SHOULD disclose material changes to valuation policies and/or methodologies (Provision 4.B.1).

3 FIRMS SHOULD disclose the key assumptions used to value PORTFOLIO investments (Provision 4.B.4).

4 For periods prior to 1 January 2011, FIRMS SHOULD disclose the use of subjective unobservable inputs for valuing PORTFOLIO investments (as described in the GIPS Valuation Principles) if the PORTFOLIO investments valued using subjective unobservable inputs are material to the COMPOSITE (Provision 4.B.6).

5 Valuations SHOULD be obtained from a qualified independent third party (Provision 1.B.2).

Additional Real Estate Valuation Recommendations:

6 Although appraisal standards may allow for a range of estimated values, it is RECOMMENDED that a single value be obtained from external valuers or appraisers because only one value is used in performance reporting.

7 It is RECOMMENDED that the external appraisal firm be rotated every three to five years.

8 FIRMS SHOULD explain and disclose material differences between the valuation used in performance reporting and the valuation used in financial reporting as of each annual period end (Provision 6.B.4).

9 For periods prior to 1 January 2011, FIRMS SHOULD disclose material changes to valuation policies and/or methodologies (Provision 6.B.5).

Additional Private Equity Valuation Recommendations:

10 FIRMS SHOULD explain and disclose material differences between the valuations used in performance reporting and the valuations used in financial reporting as of each annual period end (Provision 7.B.3).

11 For periods prior to 1 January 2011, FIRMS SHOULD disclose material changes to valuation policies and/or methodologies (Provision 7.B.4).

12 The following considerations SHOULD be incorporated into the valuation process:

- **a** The quality and reliability of the data used in each methodology;
- **b** The comparability of enterprise or transaction data;
- **c** The stage of development of the enterprise; and
- **d** Any additional considerations unique to the enterprise.

GIPS ADVERTISING GUIDELINES

A. Purpose of the GIPS Advertising Guidelines

The GIPS Advertising Guidelines provide FIRMS with options for advertising performance when mentioning the FIRM's claim of compliance. The GIPS Advertising Guidelines do not replace the GIPS standards, nor do they absolve FIRMS from presenting a COMPLIANT PRESENTATION as REQUIRED by the GIPS standards. These guidelines only apply to FIRMS that already satisfy all the REQUIREMENTS of the GIPS standards on a FIRM-wide basis and claim compliance with the GIPS standards in an advertisement. FIRMS that choose to claim compliance in an advertisement MUST follow the GIPS Advertising Guidelines or include a COMPLIANT PRESENTATION in the advertisement.

Definition of Advertisement

For the purposes of these guidelines, an advertisement includes any materials that are distributed to or designed for use in newspapers, magazines, FIRM brochures, letters, media, websites, or any other written or electronic material addressed to more than one PROSPECTIVE CLIENT. Any written material, other than one-on-one presentations and individual client reporting, distributed to maintain existing clients or solicit new clients for a FIRM is considered an advertisement.

Relationship of GIPS Advertising Guidelines to Regulatory Requirements

FIRMS advertising performance MUST adhere to all applicable laws and regulations governing advertisements. FIRMS are encouraged to seek legal or regulatory counsel because additional disclosures may be REQUIRED. In cases where applicable laws and/or regulations conflict with the REQUIREMENTS of the GIPS standards and/or the GIPS Advertising Guidelines, FIRMS are REQUIRED to comply with the law or regulation.

The calculation and advertisement of pooled unitized investment vehicles, such as mutual funds and open-ended investment companies, are regulated in most markets. The GIPS Advertising Guidelines are not intended to replace applicable laws and/or regulations when a FIRM is advertising performance solely for a pooled unitized investment vehicle.

Other Information

The advertisement may include other information beyond what is REQUIRED under the GIPS Advertising Guidelines provided the information is shown with equal or lesser prominence relative to the information REQUIRED by the GIPS Advertising Guidelines and the information does not conflict with the REQUIREMENTS of the GIPS standards and/or the GIPS Advertising Guidelines. FIRMS MUST adhere to the principles of fair representation and full disclosure when advertising and MUST NOT present performance or performance-related information that is false or misleading.

B. Requirements of the GIPS Advertising Guidelines

All advertisements that include a claim of compliance with the GIPS standards by following the GIPS Advertising Guidelines MUST disclose the following:

1 The definition of the FIRM.

2 How a PROSPECTIVE CLIENT can obtain a COMPLIANT PRESENTATION and/or the FIRM's list of COMPOSITE DESCRIPTIONS.

3 The GIPS compliance statement for advertisements:

> "[Insert name of FIRM] claims compliance with the Global Investment Performance Standards (GIPS®)."

All advertisements that include a claim of compliance with the GIPS standards by following the GIPS Advertising Guidelines and that present performance MUST also disclose the following information, which MUST be taken or derived from a COMPLIANT PRESENTATION:

4 The COMPOSITE DESCRIPTION.

5 COMPOSITE TOTAL RETURNS according to one of the following:

- a One-, three-, and five-year annualized COMPOSITE returns through the most recent period with the period-end date clearly identified. If the COMPOSITE has been in existence for less than five years, FIRMS MUST also present the annualized returns since the COMPOSITE INCEPTION DATE. (For example, if a COMPOSITE has been in existence for four years, FIRMS MUST present one-, three-, and four-year annualized returns through the most recent period.) Returns for periods of less than one year MUST NOT be annualized.
- b Period-to-date COMPOSITE returns in addition to one-, three-, and five-year annualized COMPOSITE returns through the same period of time as presented in the corresponding COMPLIANT PRESENTATION with the period end date clearly identified. If the COMPOSITE has been in existence for less than five years, FIRMS MUST also present the annualized returns since the COMPOSITE INCEPTION DATE (For example, if a COMPOSITE has been in existence for four years, FIRMS MUST present one-, three-, and four-year annualized returns in addition to the period-to-date COMPOSITE return.) Returns for periods of less than one year MUST NOT be annualized.
- c Period-to-date COMPOSITE returns in addition to five years of annual COMPOSITE returns (or for each annual period since the COMPOSITE INCEPTION DATE if the COMPOSITE has been in existence for less than five years) with the period end date clearly identified. The annual returns MUST be calculated through the same period of time as presented in the corresponding COMPLIANT PRESENTATION.

6 Whether returns are presented GROSS-OF-FEES and/or NET-OF-FEES.

7 The TOTAL RETURN for the BENCHMARK for the same periods for which the COMPOSITE return is presented. FIRMS MUST present TOTAL RETURNS for the same BENCHMARK as presented in the corresponding COMPLIANT PRESENTATION.

8 The BENCHMARK DESCRIPTION.

9 If the FIRM determines no appropriate BENCHMARK for the COMPOSITE exists, the FIRM MUST disclose why no BENCHMARK is presented.

10 The currency used to express performance.

11 The presence, use, and extent of leverage, derivatives, and short positions, if material, including a description of the frequency of use and characteristics of the instruments sufficient to identify risks.

12 For any performance presented in an advertisement for periods prior to 1 January 2000 that does not comply with the GIPS standards, FIRMS MUST disclose the periods of non-compliance.

13 If the advertisement conforms with laws and/or regulations that conflict with the REQUIREMENTS of the GIPS standards and/or the GIPS Advertising Guidelines, FIRMS MUST disclose this fact and disclose the manner in which the laws and/or regulations conflict with the GIPS standards and/or the GIPS Advertising Guidelines.

VERIFICATION IV.

VERIFICATION is intended to provide a FIRM and its existing clients and PROSPECTIVE CLIENTS additional confidence in the FIRM's claim of compliance with the GIPS standards. VERIFICATION may increase the knowledge of the FIRM's performance measurement team and improve the consistency and quality of the FIRM'S COMPLIANT PRESENTATIONS. VERIFICATION may also provide improved internal processes and procedures as well as marketing advantages to the FIRM. Verification does not ensure the accuracy of any specific COMPOSITE presentation.

The GIPS standards RECOMMEND that FIRMS be verified. VERIFICATION brings additional credibility to the claim of compliance and supports the overall guiding principles of fair representation and full disclosure of a FIRM's investment performance.

The VERIFICATION procedures attempt to strike a balance between ensuring the quality, accuracy, and relevance of performance presentations and minimizing the cost to FIRMS.

A. Scope and Purpose of Verification

1 VERIFICATION MUST be performed by a qualified independent third party.

2 VERIFICATION assesses whether:

- a The FIRM has complied with all the COMPOSITE construction REQUIREMENTS of the GIPS standards on a FIRM-wide basis, and
- b The FIRM's policies and procedures are designed to calculate and present performance in compliance with the GIPS standards.

3 A single VERIFICATION REPORT is issued with respect to the whole FIRM. VERIFICATION cannot be carried out on a COMPOSITE and, accordingly, does not provide assurance about the performance of any specific COMPOSITE. FIRMS MUST NOT state that a particular COMPOSITE has been "verified" or make any claim to that effect.

4 The initial minimum period for which VERIFICATION can be performed is one year (or from FIRM inception date through period end if less than one year) of a FIRM's presented performance. The RECOMMENDED period over which VERIFICATION is performed is that part of the FIRM's performance for which compliance with the GIPS standards is claimed.

5 A VERIFICATION REPORT MUST opine that:

a The FIRM has complied with all the COMPOSITE construction REQUIREMENTS of the GIPS standards on a FIRM-wide basis, and

b The FIRM's policies and procedures are designed to calculate and present performance in compliance with the GIPS standards.

The FIRM MUST NOT state that it has been verified unless a VERIFICATION REPORT has been issued.

6 A principal verifier may accept the work of another verifier as part of the basis for the principal verifier's opinion. A principal verifier may also choose to rely on the audit and/or internal control work of a qualified and reputable independent third party. In addition, a principal verifier may choose to rely on the other audit and/or internal control work performed by the VERIFICATION firm. If reliance on another party's work is planned, the scope of work, including time period covered, results of procedures performed, qualifications, competency, objectivity, and reputation of the other party, MUST be assessed by the principal verifier when making the determination as to whether to place any reliance on such work. Reliance considerations and conclusions MUST be documented by the principal verifier. The principal verifier MUST use professional skepticism when deciding whether to place reliance on work performed by another independent third party.

7 Sample PORTFOLIO Selection: Verifiers MUST subject the entire FIRM to testing when performing VERIFICATION procedures unless reliance is placed on work performed by a qualified and reputable independent third party or appropriate alternative control procedures have been performed by the verifier. Verifiers may use a sampling methodology when performing such procedures. Verifiers MUST consider the following criteria when selecting samples:

a Number of COMPOSITES at the FIRM;

b Number of PORTFOLIOS in each COMPOSITE;

c Type of COMPOSITE;

d TOTAL FIRM ASSETS;

e Internal control structure at the FIRM (system of checks and balances in place);

f Number of years being verified; and

g Computer applications, software used in the construction and maintenance of COMPOSITES, the use of external performance measurers, and the method of calculating performance.

This list is not all-inclusive and contains only the minimum criteria that MUST be considered in the selection and evaluation of a sample. For example, one potentially useful approach would be to include in the sample a PORTFOLIO that has the largest impact on COMPOSITE performance because of its size or because of extremely good or bad performance. Missing or incomplete documents, or the presence of errors, would normally be expected to warrant selecting a larger sample or applying additional VERIFICATION procedures.

8 After performing the VERIFICATION, the verifier may conclude that the FIRM is not in compliance with the GIPS standards or that the records of the FIRM cannot support a VERIFICATION. In such situations, the verifier MUST issue a

statement to the FIRM clarifying why a VERIFICATION REPORT could not be issued. A VERIFICATION REPORT MUST NOT be issued when the verifier knows that the FIRM is not in compliance with the GIPS standards or the records of the FIRM cannot support a VERIFICATION.

9 The minimum VERIFICATION procedures are described below in Section B. The VERIFICATION REPORT MUST state that the VERIFICATION has been conducted in accordance with these VERIFICATION procedures.

B. Required Verification Procedures

The following are the minimum procedures that verifiers MUST follow when conducting a VERIFICATION. Verifiers MUST complete the VERIFICATION in accordance with these procedures prior to issuing a VERIFICATION REPORT to the FIRM:

1 Pre-VERIFICATION Procedures:

- **a** Knowledge of the GIPS Standards: Verifiers MUST understand all the REQUIREMENTS and RECOMMENDATIONS of the GIPS standards, including any updates, Guidance Statements, interpretations, Questions & Answers (Q&As), and clarifications published by CFA Institute and the GIPS Executive Committee, which are available on the GIPS standards website (www.gipsstandards.org) as well as in the *GIPS Handbook*.
- **b** Knowledge of Regulations: Verifiers MUST be knowledgeable of applicable laws and regulations regarding the calculation and presentation of performance and MUST consider any differences between these laws and regulations and the GIPS standards.
- **c** Knowledge of the FIRM: Verifiers MUST gain an understanding of the FIRM, including the corporate structure of the FIRM and how it operates.
- **d** Knowledge of the FIRM's Policies and Procedures: Verifiers MUST understand the FIRM's policies and procedures for establishing and maintaining compliance with all the applicable REQUIREMENTS and adopted RECOMMENDATIONS of the GIPS standards. The verifier MUST obtain a copy of the FIRM's policies and procedures used in establishing and maintaining compliance with the GIPS standards and ensure that all applicable policies and procedures are properly included and adequately documented.
- **e** Knowledge of Valuation Basis and Performance Calculations: Verifiers MUST understand the policies, procedures, and methodologies used to value PORTFOLIOS and compute investment performance.

2 VERIFICATION Procedures:

- **a** Fundamentals of Compliance: Verifiers MUST perform sufficient procedures to determine that:
  - **i.** The FIRM is, and has been, appropriately defined;
  - **ii.** The FIRM has defined and maintained COMPOSITES in compliance with the GIPS standards;
  - **iii.** All the FIRM's actual, fee-paying, discretionary PORTFOLIOS are included in at least one COMPOSITE;
  - **iv.** The FIRM's definition of discretion has been consistently applied over time;
  - **v.** At all times, all PORTFOLIOS are included in their respective COMPOSITES and no PORTFOLIOS that belong in a particular COMPOSITE have been excluded;

vi. The FIRM's policies and procedures for ensuring the existence and ownership of client assets are appropriate and have been consistently applied;

vii. The COMPOSITE BENCHMARK reflects the investment mandate, objective, or strategy of the COMPOSITE;

viii. The FIRM's policies and procedures for creating and maintaining COMPOSITES have been consistently applied;

ix. The FIRM's list of COMPOSITE DESCRIPTIONS is complete; and

x. TOTAL FIRM ASSETS are appropriately calculated and disclosed.

b Determination of Discretionary Status of PORTFOLIOS: Verifiers MUST obtain a list of all PORTFOLIOS. Verifiers MUST select PORTFOLIOS from this list and perform sufficient procedures to determine that the FIRM's classification of the PORTFOLIOS as discretionary or non-discretionary is appropriate by referring to the PORTFOLIO's investment management agreement and/or investment guidelines and the FIRM's policies and procedures for determining investment discretion.

c Allocation of PORTFOLIOS to COMPOSITES: Verifiers MUST obtain lists of all open (both new and existing) and closed PORTFOLIOS for all COMPOSITES for the periods being verified. Verifiers MUST select PORTFOLIOS from these lists and perform sufficient procedures to determine that:

i. The timing of inclusion in the COMPOSITE is in accordance with policies and procedures of the FIRM.

ii. The timing of exclusion from the COMPOSITE is in accordance with policies and procedures of the FIRM.

iii. The PORTFOLIO's investment mandate, objective, or strategy, as indicated by the PORTFOLIO's investment management agreement, investment guidelines, PORTFOLIO summary, and/or other appropriate documentation, is consistent with the COMPOSITE DEFINITION.

iv. PORTFOLIOS are completely and accurately included in COMPOSITES by tracing selected PORTFOLIOS from:

a The PORTFOLIO's investment management agreement and/or investment management guidelines to the COMPOSITE(S); and

b The COMPOSITE(S) to the PORTFOLIO's investment management agreement and/or investment guidelines.

v. PORTFOLIOS sharing the same investment mandate, objective, or strategy are included in the same COMPOSITE.

vi. Movements from one COMPOSITE to another are appropriate and consistent with documented changes to a PORTFOLIO's investment mandate, objective, or strategy or the redefinition of the COMPOSITE.

d Data Review: For selected PORTFOLIOS, verifiers MUST perform sufficient procedures to determine that the treatment of the following items is consistent with the FIRM's policy:

i. Classification of PORTFOLIO flows (e.g., receipts, disbursements, dividends, interest, fees, and taxes);

ii. Accounting treatment of income, interest, and dividend accruals and receipts;

iii. Accounting treatment of taxes, tax reclaims, and tax accruals;

iv. Accounting treatment of purchases, sales, and the opening and closing of other positions; and

v. Accounting treatment and valuation methodologies for investments, including derivatives.

e Performance Measurement Calculation: Recognizing that VERIFICATION does not provide assurance that specific COMPOSITE returns are correctly calculated and presented, verifiers MUST determine that the FIRM has calculated and presented performance in accordance with the FIRM's policies and procedures. Verifiers MUST perform the following procedures:

i. Recalculate rates of return for a sample of PORTFOLIOS, determine that an acceptable return formula as REQUIRED by the GIPS standards is used, and determine that the FIRM's calculations are in accordance with the FIRM's policies and procedures. The verifier MUST also determine that any fees and expenses are treated in accordance with the GIPS standards and the FIRM's policies and procedures.

ii. Take a sample of COMPOSITE and BENCHMARK calculations to determine the accuracy of all required numerical data (e.g., risk measures, INTERNAL DISPERSION).

iii. If a custom BENCHMARK or combination of multiple BENCHMARKS is used, take a sample of the BENCHMARK data used by the FIRM to determine that the calculation methodology has been correctly applied and the data used are consistent with the BENCHMARK disclosure in the COMPLIANT PRESENTATION.

f COMPLIANT PRESENTATIONS: Verifiers MUST perform sufficient procedures on a sample of COMPLIANT PRESENTATIONS to determine that the presentations include all the information and disclosures REQUIRED by the GIPS standards. The information and disclosures MUST be consistent with the FIRM's records, the FIRM's documented policies and procedures, and the results of the verifier's procedures.

g Maintenance of Records: The verifier MUST maintain sufficient documentation to support all procedures performed supporting the issuance of the VERIFICATION REPORT, including all significant judgments and conclusions made by the verifier.

h Representation Letter: The verifier MUST obtain a representation letter from the FIRM confirming that policies and procedures used in establishing and maintaining compliance with the GIPS standards are as described in the FIRM's policies and procedures documents and have been consistently applied throughout the periods being verified. The representation letter MUST confirm that the FIRM complies with the GIPS standards for the period being verified. The representation letter MUST also contain any other specific representations made to the verifier during the VERIFICATION.

C. Performance Examinations

In addition to a VERIFICATION, a FIRM may choose to have a specifically focused PERFORMANCE EXAMINATION of a particular COMPOSITE COMPLIANT PRESENTATION. However, a PERFORMANCE EXAMINATION REPORT MUST NOT be issued unless a VERIFICATION REPORT has also been issued. The PERFORMANCE EXAMINATION may be performed concurrently with the VERIFICATION.

A PERFORMANCE EXAMINATION is not REQUIRED for a FIRM to be verified. The FIRM MUST NOT state that a COMPOSITE has been examined unless the PERFORMANCE EXAMINATION REPORT has been issued for the specific COMPOSITE.

Please see the Guidance Statement on PERFORMANCE EXAMINATIONS for additional guidance.

END OPTIONAL SEGMENT

V. GIPS GLOSSARY

ACCRUAL ACCOUNTING — The recording of financial transactions as they come into existence rather than when they are paid or settled.

ADDITIONAL INFORMATION — Information that is REQUIRED or RECOMMENDED under the GIPS standards and is not considered SUPPLEMENTAL INFORMATION.

ADMINISTRATIVE FEE — All fees other than TRADING EXPENSES and the INVESTMENT MANAGEMENT FEE. ADMINISTRATIVE FEES include CUSTODY FEES, accounting fees, auditing fees, consulting fees, legal fees, performance measurement fees, and other related fees. (See "BUNDLED FEE")

ALL-IN FEE — A type of BUNDLED FEE that can include any combination of INVESTMENT MANAGEMENT FEES, TRADING EXPENSES, CUSTODY FEES, and ADMINISTRATIVE FEES. ALL-IN-FEES are client specific and typically offered in certain jurisdictions where asset management, brokerage, and custody services are offered by the same company.

BENCHMARK — A point of reference against which the COMPOSITE's performance and/or risk is compared.

BENCHMARK DESCRIPTION — General information regarding the investments, structure, and/or characteristics of the BENCHMARK. The description MUST include the key features of the BENCHMARK, or the name of the BENCHMARK for a readily recognized index or other point of reference.

BUNDLED FEE — A fee that combines multiple fees into one total or "bundled" fee. BUNDLED FEES can include any combination of INVESTMENT MANAGEMENT FEES, TRADING EXPENSES, CUSTODY FEES, and/or ADMINISTRATIVE FEES. Two examples of BUNDLED FEES are WRAP FEES and ALL-IN-FEES.

CAPITAL EMPLOYED (REAL ESTATE) — The denominator of the return calculations and is defined as the "weighted-average equity" (weighted-average capital) during the measurement period. CAPITAL EMPLOYED does not include any INCOME RETURN or CAPITAL RETURN earned during the measurement period. Beginning capital is adjusted by weighting the EXTERNAL CASH FLOWS that occurred during the period.

CAPITAL RETURN (REAL ESTATE) — The change in value of the REAL ESTATE investments and cash and/or cash equivalent assets held throughout the measurement period, adjusted for all capital expenditures (subtracted) and net proceeds from sales (added). The CAPITAL RETURN is computed as a percentage of the CAPITAL EMPLOYED. Also known as "capital appreciation return" or "appreciation return."

CARRIED INTEREST (REAL ESTATE and PRIVATE EQUITY) — The profits that GENERAL PARTNERS are allocated from the profits on the investments made by the investment vehicle. Also known as "carry" or "promote."

Carve-out	A portion of a PORTFOLIO that is by itself representative of a distinct investment strategy. It is used to create a track record for a narrower mandate from a multiple-strategy PORTFOLIO managed to a broader mandate. For periods beginning on or after 1 January 2010, a CARVE-OUT MUST be managed separately with its own cash balance.
Closed-end fund (REAL ESTATE and PRIVATE EQUITY)	A type of investment vehicle where the number of investors, total COMMITTED CAPITAL, and life are fixed and not open for subscriptions and/or redemptions. CLOSED-END FUNDS have a capital call (drawdown) process in place that is controlled by the GENERAL PARTNER.
Committed capital (REAL ESTATE and PRIVATE EQUITY)	Pledges of capital to an investment vehicle by investors (LIMITED PARTNERS and the GENERAL PARTNER) or by the FIRM. COMMITTED CAPITAL is typically not drawn down at once but drawn down over a period of time. Also known as "commitments."
Compliant presentation	A presentation for a COMPOSITE that contains all the information REQUIRED by the GIPS standards and may also include ADDITIONAL INFORMATION or SUPPLEMENTAL INFORMATION. (See Sample COMPLIANT PRESENTATIONS in Appendix A)
Composite	An aggregation of one or more PORTFOLIOS managed according to a similar investment mandate, objective, or strategy.
Composite creation date	The date when the FIRM first groups one or more PORTFOLIOS to create a COMPOSITE. The COMPOSITE CREATION DATE is not necessarily the same as the COMPOSITE INCEPTION DATE.
Composite definition	Detailed criteria that determine the assignment of PORTFOLIOS to COMPOSITES. Criteria may include investment mandate, style or strategy, asset class, the use of derivatives, leverage and/or hedging, targeted risk metrics, investment constraints or restrictions, and/or PORTFOLIO type (e.g., segregated or pooled, taxable versus tax exempt.)
Composite description	General information regarding the investment mandate, objective, or strategy of the COMPOSITE. The COMPOSITE DESCRIPTION may be more abbreviated than the COMPOSITE DEFINITION but MUST include all key features of the COMPOSITE and MUST include enough information to allow a PROSPECTIVE CLIENT to understand the key characteristics of the COMPOSITE'S investment mandate, objective, or strategy. (See the Sample List of Composite Descriptions in Appendix C)
Composite inception date	The initial date of the COMPOSITE'S performance record. The COMPOSITE INCEPTION DATE is not necessarily the same as the COMPOSITE CREATION DATE.
Composite termination date	The date that the last PORTFOLIO exits a COMPOSITE.

(continued)

Custody fee	The fees payable to the custodian for the safekeeping of PORTFOLIO assets. CUSTODY FEES are considered to be ADMINISTRATIVE FEES and typically contain an asset-based portion and a transaction-based portion. The CUSTODY FEE may also include charges for additional services, including accounting, securities lending, and/or performance measurement. Custodial fees that are charged per transaction SHOULD be included in the CUSTODY FEE and not included as part of TRADING EXPENSES.
Direct investments (PRIVATE EQUITY)	Investments made directly in PRIVATE EQUITY investments rather than investments made in fund investment vehicles or cash and/or cash equivalents.
Distinct business entity	A unit, division, department, or office that is organizationally and functionally segregated from other units, divisions, departments, or offices and that retains discretion over the assets it manages and that should have autonomy over the investment decision-making process. Possible criteria that can be used to determine this include: ■ being a legal entity, ■ having a distinct market or client type (e.g., institutional, retail, private client, etc.), and ■ using a separate and distinct investment process.
Distribution (REAL ESTATE and PRIVATE EQUITY)	Cash or stock distributed to LIMITED PARTNERS (or investors) from an investment vehicle. DISTRIBUTIONS are typically at the discretion of the GENERAL PARTNER (or the FIRM). DISTRIBUTIONS include both recallable and non-recallable DISTRIBUTIONS.
DPI (REAL ESTATE and PRIVATE EQUITY)	SINCE INCEPTION DISTRIBUTIONS divided by SINCE INCEPTION PAID-IN CAPITAL. (See "REALIZATION MULTIPLE")
Evergreen fund (PRIVATE EQUITY)	An OPEN-END FUND that allows for on-going subscriptions and/or redemptions by investors.
Ex-ante	Before the fact.
Ex-post	After the fact.
External cash flow	Capital (cash or investments) that enters or exits a PORTFOLIO.
External valuation (REAL ESTATE)	An assessment of value performed by an independent external third party who is a qualified, PROFESSIONALLY DESIGNATED, CERTIFIED, OR LICENSED COMMERCIAL PROPERTY VALUER/APPRAISER.

FAIR VALUE	The amount at which an investment could be exchanged in a current arm's length transaction between willing parties in which the parties each act knowledgeably and prudently. The valuation MUST be determined using the objective, observable, unadjusted quoted market price for an identical investment in an active market on the measurement date, if available. In the absence of an objective, observable, unadjusted quoted market price for an identical investment in an active market on the measurement date, the valuation MUST represent the FIRM's best estimate of the MARKET VALUE. FAIR VALUE MUST include accrued income.
FEE SCHEDULE	The FIRM's current schedule of INVESTMENT MANAGEMENT FEES or BUNDLED FEES relevant to the particular COMPLIANT PRESENTATION.
FINAL LIQUIDATION DATE (REAL ESTATE and PRIVATE EQUITY)	The date when the last PORTFOLIO in a COMPOSITE is fully distributed.
FIRM	The entity defined for compliance with the GIPS standards. (See "DISTINCT BUSINESS ENTITY")
FUND OF FUNDS (PRIVATE EQUITY)	An investment vehicle that invests in underlying investment vehicles. PRIVATE EQUITY FUNDS OF FUNDS predominately invest in CLOSED-END FUNDS and may make opportunistic DIRECT INVESTMENTS.
GENERAL PARTNER (REAL ESTATE and PRIVATE EQUITY)	A class of partner in a LIMITED PARTNERSHIP. The GENERAL PARTNER retains liability for the actions of the LIMITED PARTNERSHIP. The GENERAL PARTNER is typically the fund manager, and the LIMITED PARTNERS (LPs) are the other investors in the LIMITED PARTNERSHIP. The GENERAL PARTNER earns an INVESTMENT MANAGEMENT FEE that typically includes a percentage of the LIMITED PARTNERSHIP'S profits. (See "CARRIED INTEREST")
GROSS-OF-FEES	The return on investments reduced by any TRADING EXPENSES incurred during the period.
GROSS-OF-FEES (REAL ESTATE and PRIVATE EQUITY)	The return on investments reduced by any TRANSACTION EXPENSES incurred during the period.
INCOME RETURN (REAL ESTATE)	The investment income earned on all investments (including cash and cash equivalents) during the measurement period net of all non-recoverable expenditures, interest expense on debt, and property taxes. The INCOME RETURN is computed as a percentage of the CAPITAL EMPLOYED.
INTERNAL DISPERSION	A measure of the spread of the annual returns of individual PORTFOLIOS within a COMPOSITE. Measures may include, but are not limited to, high/low, range, or STANDARD DEVIATION (asset weighted or equal weighted) of PORTFOLIO returns.

(continued)

Internal valuation (real estate)	A firm's best estimate of value based on the most current and accurate information available under the circumstances. Internal valuation methodologies include applying a discounted cash flow model, using a sales comparison or replacement cost approach, or conducting a review of all significant events (both general market and asset specific) that could have a material impact on the investment.
Investment management fee	A fee payable to the firm for the management of a portfolio. Investment management fees are typically asset based (percentage of assets), performance based (see "performance-based fee"), or a combination of the two but may take different forms as well. Investment management fees also include carried interest.
Investment multiple (TVPI) (real estate and private equity)	Total value divided by since inception paid-in capital.
Large cash flow	The level at which the firm determines that an external cash flow may distort performance if the portfolio is not valued. Firms must define the amount in terms of the value of cash/asset flow or in terms of a percentage of the portfolio assets or the composite assets.
Limited partner (real estate and private equity)	An investor in a limited partnership. The general partner is liable for the actions of the limited partnership, and the limited partners are generally protected from legal actions and any losses beyond their committed capital.
Limited partnership (real estate and private equity)	The legal structure used by most private equity and real estate closed-end funds. Limited partnerships are usually fixed life investment vehicles. The general partner manages the limited partnership pursuant to the partnership agreement.
Link	1 *Mathematical Linking*: The method by which sub-period returns are geometrically combined to calculate the period return using the following formula: Period return = $[(1+R_1) \times (1+R_2)...(1+R_n)] - 1$ where R_1, R_2...R_n are the sub-period returns for sub-period 1 through n, respectively. 2 *Presentational Linking*: To be visually connected or otherwise associated within a compliant presentation (e.g., two pieces of information are linked by placing them next to each other).
Market value	The price at which investors can buy or sell an investment at a given time multiplied by the quantity held plus any accrued income.
Must	A provision, task, or action that is mandatory or required to be followed or performed. (See "require/requirement")
Must not	A task or action that is forbidden or prohibited.

Net-of-fees	The gross-of-fees return reduced by investment management fees (including performance-based fees and carried interest).
Open-end fund (real estate and private equity)	A type of investment vehicle where the number of investors and the total committed capital is not fixed and is open for subscriptions and/or redemptions. (See "evergreen fund")
Paid-in capital (real estate and private equity)	Capital inflows to an investment vehicle. Committed capital is typically drawn down from limited partners (or investors) over a period of time through a series of capital calls, which are at the discretion of the general partner or firm. Paid-in capital is equal to the amount of committed capital that has been drawn down since inception. Paid-in capital includes distributions that are subsequently recalled by the general partner or firm and reinvested into the investment vehicle.
Performance-based fee	A type of investment management fee that is typically based on the performance of the portfolio on an absolute basis or relative to a benchmark.
Performance examination	A detailed examination of a specific composite's compliant presentation by an independent verifier.
Performance examination report	A performance examination report is issued after a performance examination has been performed and opines that a particular composite's compliant presentation has been prepared and presented in compliance with the GIPS standards.
Periodicity	The length of the time period over which a variable is measured (e.g., a variable that is measured at a monthly periodicity consists of observations for each month).
Pic multiple (real estate and private equity)	Since inception paid-in capital divided by cumulative committed capital.
Portfolio	An individually managed group of investments. A portfolio may be an account or pooled investment vehicle.
Primary fund (private equity)	An investment vehicle that makes direct investments rather than investing in other investment vehicles.
Private equity	Investment strategies include, but are not limited to, venture capital, leveraged buyouts, consolidations, mezzanine and distressed debt investments, and a variety of hybrids, such as venture leasing and venture factoring.

(continued)

Professionally designated, certified, or licensed commercial property valuer/appraiser (real estate) — In Europe, Canada, and parts of Southeast Asia, the predominant professional designation is that of the Royal Institution of Chartered Surveyors (RICS). In the United States, the professional designation is Member [of the] Appraisal Institute (MAI). In addition, each state regulates real estate appraisers and registers, licenses, or certifies them based on their experience and test results.

Proprietary assets — Investments owned by the firm, the firm's management, and/or the firm's parent company that are managed by the firm.

Prospective client — Any person or entity that has expressed interest in one of the firm's composite strategies and qualifies to invest in the composite. Existing clients may also qualify as prospective clients for any strategy that is different from their current investment strategy. Investment consultants and other third parties are included as prospective clients if they represent investors that qualify as prospective clients.

Public market equivalent (PME) (private equity) — The performance of a public market index expressed in terms of an internal rate of return (IRR), using the same cash flows and timing as those of the composite over the same time period. A PME can be used as a benchmark by comparing the IRR of a private equity composite with the PME of a public market index.

Real estate — Investments in:

- Wholly owned or partially owned properties,
- Commingled funds, property unit trusts, and insurance company separate accounts,
- Unlisted, private placement securities issued by private real estate investment trusts (REITs) and real estate operating companies (REOCs); and
- Equity-oriented debt (e.g., participating mortgage loans) or any private interest in a property where some portion of return to the investor at the time of investment is related to the performance of the underlying real estate.

Realization multiple (DPI) (real estate and private equity) — Since inception distributions divided by since inception paid-in capital.

Recommend/Recommendation — A suggested provision, task, or action that should be followed or performed. A recommendation is considered to be best practice but is not a requirement. (See "should")

Require/Requirement — A provision, task, or action that must be followed or performed. (See "must")

Residual value (private equity and real estate) — The remaining equity that limited partners (or investors) have in an investment vehicle at the end of the performance reporting period.

RVPI (REAL ESTATE and PRIVATE EQUITY)	RESIDUAL VALUE divided by SINCE INCEPTION PAID-IN CAPITAL. (See "UNREALIZED MULTIPLE")
SECONDARY FUND (PRIVATE EQUITY)	An investment vehicle that buys interests in existing investment vehicles.
SETTLEMENT DATE ACCOUNTING	Recognizing the asset or liability on the date when the exchange of cash and investments is completed.
SHOULD	A provision, task, or action that is RECOMMENDED to be followed or performed and is considered to be best practice, but is not REQUIRED. (See "RECOMMEND/RECOMMENDATION")
SIGNIFICANT CASH FLOW	The level at which the FIRM determines that a client-directed EXTERNAL CASH FLOW may temporarily prevent the FIRM from implementing the COMPOSITE strategy. The measure of significance MUST be determined as either a specific monetary amount (e.g., €50,000,000) or a percentage of PORTFOLIO assets (based on the most recent valuation).
SINCE INCEPTION (REAL ESTATE and PRIVATE EQUITY)	From the initial cash flow of a COMPOSITE.
SINCE INCEPTION INTERNAL RATE OF RETURN (SI-IRR) (REAL ESTATE and PRIVATE EQUITY)	The internal rate of return (IRR) is the implied discount rate or effective compounded rate of return that equates the present value of cash outflows with the present value of cash inflows. The SI-IRR is a special case of the IRR that equates the present value of all cash flows (capital calls and DISTRIBUTIONS) with the period end value. The SI-IRR is always annualized except when the reporting period is less than one year, in which case the SI-IRR is not annualized.
STANDARD DEVIATION	A measure of the variability of returns. As a measure of INTERNAL DISPERSION, STANDARD DEVIATION quantifies the distribution of the returns of the individual PORTFOLIOS within the COMPOSITE. As a measure of historical risk, STANDARD DEVIATION quantifies the variability of the COMPOSITE and/or BENCHMARK returns over time. Also referred to as "external STANDARD DEVIATION."
SUB-ADVISOR	A third-party investment manager hired by the FIRM to manage some or all of the assets for which a FIRM has investment management responsibility.
SUPPLEMENTAL INFORMATION	Any performance-related information included as part of a COMPLIANT PRESENTATION that supplements or enhances the REQUIRED and/or RECOMMENDED provisions of the GIPS standards.

(continued)

Temporary new account	An account for temporarily holding client-directed EXTERNAL CASH FLOWS until they are invested according to the COMPOSITE strategy or disbursed. FIRMS can use a TEMPORARY NEW ACCOUNT to remove the effect of a SIGNIFICANT CASH FLOW on a PORTFOLIO. When a SIGNIFICANT CASH FLOW occurs in a PORTFOLIO, the FIRM may direct the EXTERNAL CASH FLOW to a TEMPORARY NEW ACCOUNT according to the COMPOSITE'S SIGNIFICANT CASH FLOW policy.
Time-weighted rate of return	A method of calculating period-by-period returns that negates the effects of EXTERNAL CASH FLOWS.
Total firm assets	All discretionary and non-discretionary assets for which a FIRM has investment management responsibility. TOTAL FIRM ASSETS includes assets assigned to a SUB-ADVISOR provided the FIRM has discretion over the selection of the SUB-ADVISOR.
Total return	The rate of return that includes the realized and unrealized gains and losses plus income for the measurement period.
Total return (REAL ESTATE)	The rate of return, including all CAPITAL RETURN and INCOME RETURN components, expressed as a percentage of the CAPITAL EMPLOYED over the measurement period.
Total value (REAL ESTATE and PRIVATE EQUITY)	RESIDUAL VALUE plus DISTRIBUTIONS.
Trade date accounting	Recognizing the asset or liability on the date of the purchase or sale and not on the settlement date. Recognizing the asset or liability within three days of the date the transaction is entered into (trade date, T+1, T+2, or T+3) satisfies the TRADE DATE ACCOUNTING REQUIREMENT for purposes of the GIPS standards. (See "SETTLEMENT DATE ACCOUNTING")
Trading expenses	The actual costs of buying or selling investments. These costs typically take the form of brokerage commissions, exchange fees and/or taxes, and/or bid–offer spreads from either internal or external brokers. Custodial fees charged per transaction SHOULD be considered CUSTODY FEES and not TRADING EXPENSES.
Transaction expenses (REAL ESTATE and PRIVATE EQUITY)	All actual legal, financial, advisory, and investment banking fees related to buying, selling, restructuring, and/or recapitalizing PORTFOLIO investments as well as TRADING EXPENSES, if any.
TVPI (REAL ESTATE and PRIVATE EQUITY)	TOTAL VALUE divided by SINCE INCEPTION PAID-IN CAPITAL. (See "INVESTMENT MULTIPLE")
Unrealized multiple (RVPI) (REAL ESTATE and PRIVATE EQUITY)	RESIDUAL VALUE divided by SINCE INCEPTION PAID-IN CAPITAL.

VERIFICATION	A process by which an independent verifier assesses whether 1) the FIRM has complied with all the COMPOSITE construction REQUIREMENTS of the GIPS standards on a FIRM-wide basis and 2) the FIRM'S policies and procedures are designed to calculate and present performance in compliance with the GIPS standards.
VERIFICATION REPORT	A VERIFICATION REPORT is issued after a VERIFICATION has been performed and opines that the FIRM has complied with all the COMPOSITE construction REQUIREMENTS of the GIPS standards on a FIRM-wide basis and that the FIRM'S policies and procedures are designed to calculate and present performance in compliance with the GIPS standards.
VINTAGE YEAR (REAL ESTATE and PRIVATE EQUITY)	Two methods used to determine VINTAGE YEAR are: **1** The year of the investment vehicle's first drawdown or capital call from its investors; or **2** The year when the first COMMITTED CAPITAL from outside investors is closed and legally binding.
WRAP FEE	WRAP FEES are a type of BUNDLED FEE and are specific to a particular investment product. The WRAP FEE is charged by a WRAP FEE sponsor for investment management services and typically includes associated TRADING EXPENSES that cannot be separately identified. WRAP FEES can be all-inclusive, asset-based fees and may include a combination of INVESTMENT MANAGEMENT FEES, TRADING EXPENSES, CUSTODY FEES, and/or ADMINISTRATIVE FEES. A WRAP FEE PORTFOLIO is sometimes referred to as a "separately managed account" (SMA) or "managed account."

APPENDIX A: SAMPLE COMPLIANT PRESENTATIONS

SAMPLE 1 INVESTMENT FIRM BALANCED GROWTH COMPOSITE

1 January 2002 through 31 December 2011

Year	Composite Gross Return (%)	Composite Net Return (%)	Custom Benchmark Return (%)	Composite 3-Yr St Dev (%)	Benchmark 3-Yr St Dev (%)	Number of Portfolios	Internal Dispersion (%)	Composite Assets ($ M)	Firm Assets ($ M)
2002	−10.5	−11.4	−11.8			31	4.5	165	236
2003	16.3	15.1	13.2			34	2.0	235	346
2004	7.5	6.4	8.9			38	5.7	344	529
2005	1.8	0.8	0.3			45	2.8	445	695
2006	11.2	10.1	12.2			48	3.1	520	839
2007	6.1	5.0	7.1			49	2.8	505	1,014
2008	−21.3	−22.1	−24.9			44	2.9	475	964
2009	16.5	15.3	14.7			47	3.1	493	983
2010	10.6	9.5	13.0			51	3.5	549	1,114
2011	2.7	1.7	0.4	7.1	7.4	54	2.5	575	1,236

Sample 1 Investment Firm claims compliance with the Global Investment Performance Standards (GIPS®) and has prepared and presented this report in compliance with the GIPS standards. Sample 1 Investment Firm has been independently verified for the periods 1 January 2000 through 31 December 2010. The verification report is available upon request. Verification assesses whether (1) the firm has complied with all the composite construction requirements of the GIPS standards on a firm-wide basis and (2) the firm's policies and procedures are designed to calculate and present performance in compliance with the GIPS standards. Verification does not ensure the accuracy of any specific composite presentation.

Notes:

1 Sample 1 Investment Firm is a balanced portfolio investment manager that invests solely in US-based securities. Sample 1 Investment Firm is defined as an independent investment management firm that is not affiliated with any parent organization. Policies for valuing portfolios, calculating performance, and preparing compliant presentations are available upon request.

2 The Balanced Growth Composite includes all institutional balanced portfolios that invest in large-cap US equities and investment-grade bonds with the goal of providing long-term capital growth and steady income from a well-diversified strategy. Although the strategy allows for equity exposure ranging between 50–70%, the typical allocation is between 55–65%. The account minimum for the composite is $5 million.

3 The custom benchmark is 60% YYY US Equity Index and 40% ZZZ US Aggregate Bond Index. The benchmark is rebalanced monthly.

4 Valuations are computed and performance is reported in US dollars.

5 Gross-of-fees returns are presented before management and custodial fees but after all trading expenses. Composite and benchmark returns are presented net of non-reclaimable withholding taxes. Net-of-fees returns are calculated by deducting the highest fee of 0.83% from the monthly gross composite return. The management fee schedule is as follows: 1.00% on the first $25 million; 0.60% thereafter.

6 This composite was created in February 2000. A complete list of composite descriptions is available upon request.

7 Internal dispersion is calculated using the equal-weighted standard deviation of annual gross returns of those portfolios that were included in the composite for the entire year.

8 The three-year annualized standard deviation measures the variability of the composite and the benchmark returns over the preceding 36-month period. The standard deviation is not presented for 2002 through 2010 because monthly composite and benchmark returns were not available and is not required for periods prior to 2011.

SAMPLE 2 ASSET MANAGEMENT COMPANY ACTIVE WORLD EQUITY COMPOSITE

Creation Date: 1 July 2005
Reporting Currency: EUR

Year	Gross Return (%)	XYZ World Index Return (%)	Dispersion (Range) (%)	# of Portfolios	Composite Assets (€ M)	% of Firm Assets (%)
2011	−1.9	−0.5	0.2	6	224.9	2.1
2010	16.3	13.5	0.7	8	256.7	2.0
2009	29.0	25.8	1.5	8	205.6	1.9
2008	−39.8	−36.4	1.3	7	164.1	1.5
2007	−2.8	−2.7	n/a	≤ 5	143.7	1.2
2006	9.3	7.5	n/a	≤ 5	62.8	0.4
2005*	14.2	12.6	n/a	≤ 5	16.1	< 0.1

* Returns are for the period from 1 July 2005 (inception date) through 31 December 2005.

Compliance Statement

Sample 2 Asset Management Company claims compliance with the Global Investment Performance Standards (GIPS®) and has prepared and presented this report in compliance with the GIPS standards. Sample 2 Asset Management Company has not been independently verified.

Definition of the Firm

Sample 2 Asset Management Company is an independent investment management firm that was established in 1997. Sample 2 Asset Management Company manages a variety of equity, fixed-income, and balanced assets for primarily European clients.

Policies

Sample 2 Asset Management Company's policies for valuing portfolios, calculating performance, and preparing compliant presentations are available upon request.

Composite Description

The Active World Equity Composite includes accounts whose objective is to exceed the XYZ World Index by 2% over a rolling three-year period. Securities are selected using the firm's proprietary analytics tool, which selects securities expected to be the top performers from within the XYZ World Index universe. Portfolios are more concentrated, typically holding approximately 100–120 securities, versus the benchmark, which reflects the performance of more than 500 holdings. Composite returns may, therefore, have a lower correlation with the benchmark than a more diversified global equity strategy.

Benchmark

The benchmark is the XYZ World Index, which is designed to measure the equity market performance of developed market countries. The benchmark is market-cap weighted and is composed of all XYZ country-specific developed market indexes. Sources of foreign exchange rates may be different between the composite and the benchmark; however, there have not been material differences to date. Benchmark returns are net of withholding taxes.

Fees

Returns are presented gross of management fees, custodial fees, and withholding taxes but net of all trading expenses.

List of Composites

A list of all composite descriptions is available upon request.

Fee Schedule

The standard fixed management fee for accounts with assets under management of up to €50 million is 0.35% per annum; 0.25% thereafter.

Minimum Account Size

The minimum portfolio size for inclusion in the composite is €1 million.

Internal Dispersion

Internal dispersion is calculated using the asset-weighted standard deviation of annual gross-of-fees returns of those portfolios that were included in the composite for the entire year. For those years when less than six portfolios were included in the composite for the full year, no dispersion measure is presented.

Ex-Post Standard Deviation

The three-year annualized ex-post standard deviation of the composite and benchmark as of each year end is as follows:

Year	Composite 3-Yr St Dev (%)	Benchmark 3-Yr St Dev (%)
2011	12.9	14.6
2010	13.2	14.1
2009	17.0	16.3
2008	15.6	14.2

SAMPLE 3 REAL ESTATE: OPEN-END FUNDS/SEPARATE ACCOUNTS

Real Estate Advisors Value-Added Strategy Composite
Schedule of Performance Results 1 January 2002 through 31 December 2011

	Composite Gross-of-Fees Returns					Composite Net-of-Fees Returns	Value-Added Benchmark Returns (Open-End Funds/ Separate Accounts)			Composite Statistics at Year End				
Year	Income Return (%)	Capital Return (%)	Total Return (%)	Low (%)	High (%)	Total Return (%)	Income Return (%)	Capital Return (%)	Total Return (%)	# of Portfolios	Composite Assets (HKD Million)	External Appraisal % of Composite Assets	Total Firm Assets (HKD Million)	Non-Real Estate % of Composite Assets
2002	7.9	1.9	9.9	n/a	n/a	8.8	8.4	−1.6	7.1	≤ 5	3,085	25	13,919	0
2003	8.5	2.9	11.7	5.8	20.4	10.5	8.0	1.0	9.2	6	3,294	25	14,911	0
2004	8.2	2.6	10.9	5.5	19.2	8.3	7.5	6.7	14.4	7	3,348	44	15,144	0
2005	6.6	11.2	18.1	9.0	31.6	16.6	6.8	12.7	19.7	7	3,728	72	19,794	0
2006	6.1	7.9	14.2	7.1	24.9	12.5	6.2	9.9	16.3	8	4,022	46	20,482	0
2007	5.4	8.0	13.7	6.8	23.9	11.8	5.6	9.9	15.6	7	4,348	33	24,219	0
2008	5.2	−11.4	−6.6	−9.8	−1.6	−8.2	5.1	−11.1	−5.9	7	3,836	100	21,447	0
2009	7.5	2.7	10.3	5.2	18.1	7.4	7.3	3.2	10.8	7	3,371	52	16,601	0
2010	7.2	1.7	9.0	4.2	19.5	6.9	7.8	3.1	11.1	7	2,852	38	4,516	0
2011	7.2	2.8	10.2	5.1	17.8	8.1	7.1	3.2	10.6	7	3,457	50	17,414	5
	Annualized Returns (%)													
3 Year	7.3	1.9	9.8			7.5	7.4	3.2	10.8					
5 Year	6.5	2.9	7.1			5.0	6.6	1.4	8.2					
7 Year	6.4	2.6	9.6			7.6	6.6	4.2	10.9					
10 Year	7.0	11.2	10.0			8.1	7.0	3.5	10.7					
Since Inception	7.0	7.9	10.0			8.1	7.0	3.5	10.7					

Disclosures

Compliance Statement

Sample 3 Real Estate Advisors claims compliance with the Global Investment Performance Standards (GIPS®) and has prepared and presented this report in compliance with the GIPS standards. Sample 3 Real Estate Advisors has been independently verified for the periods 1 January 2006 through 31 December 2011. The verification reports are available upon request.

Verification assesses whether 1) the firm has complied with all the composite construction requirements of the GIPS standards on a firm-wide basis and 2) the firm's policies and procedures are designed to calculate and present performance in compliance with the GIPS standards. Verification does not ensure the accuracy of any specific composite presentation.

The Firm

Sample 3 Real Estate Advisors (the "Firm"), a subsidiary of Sample 3 Capital, Inc., is based in Hong Kong and manages international real estate strategies. A list of the Firm's composite descriptions is available upon request.

The Composite

The Value-Added Strategy Composite consists of all discretionary open-end funds and separate accounts managed by the Firm using a value-added investment strategy with an equal income and appreciation focus and having a minimum portfolio size of HKD 10 million. Portfolio management will invest in only Asian multi-family, office, industrial, and retail property types that require correction or mitigation of the investments' operating, financial, redevelopment, and/or management risk (s). A moderate level of leverage ranging between 30% and 40% is used. Real estate investments are generally illiquid, and the investment outlook may change given the availability of credit or other financing sources.

The composite was created on 1 January 2006. The returns presented for periods prior to 2006 are not in compliance with the GIPS standards. Annual internal dispersion is presented using the high and low gross total returns for those portfolios that have been in the composite for the entire year.

Description of Discretion

The Firm has responsibility for sourcing, valuing, and managing the acquisition and disposition of assets. Although some of the Firm's separate accounts require client approval for the acquisition and disposition of assets, the Firm defines such portfolios as discretionary because its recommendations are consistent with the investment strategy and such client approvals are typically perfunctory.

Valuation

Real estate assets are internally valued by the Firm quarterly. For periods prior to 1 January 2011, assets were externally appraised by an independent appraiser at least every 36 months. Beginning 1 January 2011, assets are externally appraised annually unless client agreements stipulate otherwise, in which case such assets are appraised at least every 36 months or per the client agreement if the client agreement requires external valuation more frequently than every 36 months. The percentage of composite assets valued using an external valuation is shown for each annual period. When market circumstances dictate, the Firm may increase the frequency of external appraisals. All valuations are performed as of calendar quarter-ends.

Internal property valuations are determined by applying market discount rates to future projections of gross cash flows and capitalized terminal values over the expected holding period for each asset. To the extent leverage (debt) is used, the debt is valued separately from the real estate. Property mortgages, notes, and loans are marked to market using prevailing interest rates for comparable property loans if the terms of existing loans preclude the immediate repayment of such loans. Due to the nature of real estate investments, valuations are based upon subjective unobservable inputs.

Basis of Accounting

All funds in the composite report their assets and liabilities on a fair value basis using International Financial Reporting Standards (IFRS).

Calculation of Performance Returns

Returns are presented in Hong Kong dollars and are net of leverage. Net-of-fee returns are net of actual investment management fees including incentive fees, which are recorded on an accrual basis. Returns include cash and cash equivalents and related interest income.

Capital expenditures, tenant improvements, and lease commissions are capitalized, included in the cost of property, and reflected in the capital return component. Income and capital returns may not equal total returns due to the compounding linking of quarterly returns. Composite returns are calculated quarterly on an asset-weighted basis using beginning-of-period values. Annual returns are calculated by linking quarterly composite returns.

Policies for valuing portfolios, calculating performance, and preparing compliant presentations are available upon request.

Investment Management Fees

Some of the funds in the composite pay incentive fees ranging between 10% and 20% of profits in excess of a targeted SI-IRR. The standard annual investment management fee schedule for separately managed institutional accounts is as follows:

Up to HKD 30 million:	1.6%
HKD 30–50 million:	1.3%
Over HKD 50 million:	1.0%

Benchmark

The benchmark is the Value-Added Open-End Fund/Separate Account Index (the "Benchmark"). The Benchmark returns have been taken from published sources. The Benchmark is leveraged, includes various real estate property types, and excludes cash, cash equivalents, and other non-property-related assets, liabilities, income, and expenses. The extent of leverage used by the Benchmark may be different from that of the portfolios in the composite. As of 31 December 2011, the Benchmark leverage was 52%.

SAMPLE 4 REAL ESTATE: CLOSED-END FUND

2006 Value-Added Strategy Closed-End Fund Composite
Schedule of Performance Results 1 April 2006 through 31 December 2011

	Composite Gross TWR			Composite NET TWR	Benchmark			Composite at Year-End						
Year	Income Return (%)	Capital Return (%)	Total Return (%)	Total Return (%)	Income Return (%)	Capital Return (%)	Total Return (%)	# of Portfolios	Composite Assets (U.S. Million)	Leverage (%)	External Appraisal % of Composite Assets	Total Firm Assets (U.S. Million)	% of Firm Assets	Non-Real Estate % of Composite Assets
4/06–12/06	−3.2	0.8	−2.5	−4.0	4.9	2.2	7.2	1	70	40	35	2,641	20	0
2007	2.5	3.4	6.0	4.5	5.8	1.1	7.1	1	164	45	28	3,125	18	0
2008	6.2	1.9	8.2	6.7	6.9	3.8	10.9	1	215	50	100	2,754	18	0
2009	7.4	30.7	38.6	36.1	7.0	10.2	17.4	1	256	53	44	2,142	21	0
2010	6.6	−13.7	−7.3	−8.8	6.1	−8.8	−2.5	1	111	57	28	1,873	19	0
2011	5.8	−1.5	4.3	2.8	5.4	−2.6	3.0	1	112	60	85	2,247	20	15

Year	Gross SI-IRR	Net SI-IRR	Total Committed Capital (U.S. Million)	Paid-In Capital (U.S. Million)	Cumulative Distributions (U.S. Million)	TVPI Multiple	DPI Multiple	RVPI Multiple	PIC Multiple
4/06–12/06	−2.3	−3.1	250	71	0	0.99	0.00	0.99	0.28
2007	3.7	2.2	250	161	1	1.02	0.01	1.02	0.64
2008	5.8	4.2	250	226	26	1.07	0.12	0.95	0.90
2009	18.5	15.2	250	236	76	1.41	0.32	1.08	0.94
2010	11.5	9.8	250	240	201	1.30	0.84	0.46	0.96
2011	10.8	9.1	250	245	208	1.31	0.85	0.46	0.98

TVPI (investment multiple) = total value to paid-in capital
DPI (realization multiple) = cumulative distributions to paid-in capital
RVPI (unrealized multiple) = residual value to paid-in capital
PIC (PIC multiple) = paid-in capital to committed capital

Disclosures

Compliance Statement

Sample 4 Real Estate Managers claims compliance with the Global Investment Performance Standards (GIPS®) and has prepared and presented this report in compliance with the GIPS standards. Sample 4 Real Estate Managers has been independently verified for the periods 1 January 2006 through 31 December 2011. The verification reports are available upon request.

Verification assesses whether 1) the firm has complied with all the composite construction requirements of the GIPS standards on a firm-wide basis and 2) the firm's policies and procedures are designed to calculate and present performance in compliance with the GIPS standards. Verification does not ensure the accuracy of any specific composite presentation.

The Firm

Sample 4 Real Estate Managers (the "Firm") is a registered investment adviser under the Investment Advisers Act of 1940. A list of the Firm's composite descriptions is available upon request.

The Composite

The 2006 Value-Added Strategy Closed-End Fund Composite includes a single closed-end commingled fund managed by the Firm using a value-added investment strategy with a focus on both income and appreciation. Portfolio management intends to invest in properties located in major markets within the United States with higher operational risk than traditional property types. The target level of leverage is 50% with a maximum allowable level of 60%. Real estate investments are generally illiquid, and the investment outlook may change given the availability of credit or other financing sources. If investment opportunities and/or exit strategies become limited, the life of the fund may be extended and capital calls and distributions may be delayed. The composite was created on 1 January 2006. The composite vintage year is 2006, which was determined based on the fund's first capital call in April 2006.

Description of Discretion

The Firm has complete discretion for all investment activities within the fund.

Valuation

Real estate investments are internally valued by the Firm quarterly. For periods prior to 1 January 2011, investments were externally appraised by an independent appraiser at least every 36 months. Beginning 1 January 2011, assets are externally appraised annually. The percentage of composite assets valued using an external valuation is shown for each annual period. When market circumstances dictate, the Firm may increase the frequency of external appraisals. All valuations are performed as of calendar quarter-ends. Internal investment valuations are determined by applying market discount rates to future projections of net cash flows (gross real estate cash flows less debt service) and capitalized terminal values over the expected holding period for each asset. Due to the nature of real estate investments, valuations are based upon subjective unobservable inputs.

Basis of Accounting

All assets and liabilities are reported on a fair value basis using US Generally Accepted Accounting Principles for non-operating companies.

Calculation of Performance Returns and Metrics

Returns are presented in US dollars and are net of leverage. Net-of-fee returns are net of actual investment management fees, including incentive fees, which are recorded on an accrual basis.

Capital expenditures, tenant improvements, and lease commissions are capitalized, included in the cost of property, and reflected in the capital return component. Income and capital returns may not equal total returns due to the compounding linking of quarterly returns. Composite time-weighted returns are calculated quarterly on an asset-weighted basis using beginning-of-period values. Annual returns are calculated by linking quarterly composite returns.

SI-IRRs are calculated using quarterly cash flows through 2010 and daily cash flows starting in 2011.

Policies for valuing portfolios, calculating performance, and preparing presentations are available upon request.

Investment Management Fees

The fund pays an incentive fee of 15% of profits if the SI-IRR exceeds a preferred return to investors of 11%. The incentive fee is calculated annually. The standard annual investment management fee schedule for separately managed institutional accounts is as follows:

Up to $100 million: 1.50%

Over $100 million: 1.25%

Benchmark

The benchmark is the Value-Added Closed-End Fund Index (the "Benchmark"). The Benchmark is a time-weighted return index and returns have been taken from published sources. The Benchmark is leveraged and includes various real estate investment and property types, cash and other non-property-related assets, liabilities, income, and expenses. The extent of leverage used by the Benchmark may be different from that of the fund in the composite. As of 31 December 2011, the Benchmark leverage was 60%. There is no SI-IRR benchmark available for the 2006 vintage year.

SAMPLE 5 PRIVATE EQUITY: FUND OF FUNDS BY INVESTMENT STRATEGY

ABC Fund of Funds Manager, LLC
2006 Buyout Strategy Fund of Funds Composite
Results Reported as of Calendar Year End

Year End	# of Portfolios	Gross-of-Fees SI-IRR (%)	Net-of-Fees SI-IRR (%)	Benchmark SI-IRR (%)	Composite Assets ($ Mil)	Composite % of Firm Assets
2006*	8	26.9	26.4	17.2	2,336	80.8
2007	10	18.5	17.8	10.2	2,512	83.6
2008	11	18.7	18.1	11.0	3,227	84.2
2009	13	19.6	18.9	11.5	4,518	84.8
2010	13	20.7	20.1	11.8	6,330	85.2
2011	13	21.9	21.3	11.8	9,269	86.0
2012	14	22.2	21.7	12.3	12,286	86.4
2013	14	15.1	14.4	9.6	12,346	87.7

* Partial year from 15 April 2006 (inception) through 31 December 2006.

Year End	Paid-In Capital ($ Mil)	Cumulative Committed Capital ($ Mil)	Since Inception Distributions	Investment Multiple (TVPI)	Realization Multiple (DPI)	Unrealized Multiple (RVPI)	PIC Multiple (PIC)
2006	1,556	3,177	1,205	1.5	0.8	0.7	0.48
2007	1,908	3,675	1,341	1.3	0.7	0.6	0.51
2008	2,371	5,166	1,623	1.4	0.7	0.7	0.45
2009	3,254	6,401	2,186	1.4	0.7	0.7	0.50
2010	4,400	8,370	2,950	1.4	0.7	0.8	0.51
2011	6,303	11,344	4,138	1.5	0.7	0.8	0.54
2012	8,167	13,713	6,513	1.5	0.8	0.7	0.69
2013	9,651	15,290	7,091	1.3	0.7	0.5	0.71

Aggregate Performance of Underlying Investments by Vintage Year
Results Reported as of 31 December 2013

Vintage Year	Gross-of-Fees Annualized SI-IRR (%)	Benchmark SI-IRR (%)
2006	22.3	2.5
2007	13.4	1.9
2008	26.0	7.1
2009	18.1	3.9
2010	0.7	1.0
2011	–16.2	–7.5
2012	–25.6	–19.9
2013	–49.9	–40.3

Vintage Year	Paid-In Capital ($ Mil)	Cumulative Committed Capital ($ Mil)	Since Inception Distributions ($ Mil)	Investment Multiple (TVPI)	Realization Multiple (DPI)	Unrealized Multiple (RVPI)	PIC Multiple (PIC)
2006	731	724	939	3.0	1.3	1.7	1.0
2007	710	234	294	1.8	0.4	1.3	3.0
2008	1,475	1,220	1,442	2.0	1.0	1.0	1.2
2009	1,640	1,048	1,156	1.9	0.7	1.2	1.6
2010	1,896	3,695	1,124	1.9	0.6	1.4	0.5
2011	1,984	4,518	1,100	2.1	0.6	1.5	0.4
2012	680	1,998	938	2.2	1.4	0.8	0.3
2013	535	1,853	100	1.1	0.2	0.9	0.3

TVPI (investment multiple) = total value to paid-in capital
DPI (realization multiple) = cumulative distributions to paid-in capital
RVPI (unrealized multiple) = residual value to paid-in capital
PIC (PIC multiple) = paid-in capital to committed capital

Compliance Statement

ABC Fund of Funds Manager, LLC, claims compliance with the Global Investment Performance Standards (GIPS®) and has prepared and presented this report in compliance with the GIPS standards. ABC Fund of Funds Manager, LLC, has been independently verified for the periods 15 April 2006 through 31 December 2012.

Verification assesses whether 1) the firm has complied with all the composite construction requirements of the GIPS standards on a firm-wide basis and 2) the firm's policies and procedures are designed to calculate and present performance in compliance with the GIPS standards. Verification does not ensure the accuracy of any specific composite presentation. The verification report is available upon request.

The Firm

ABC Fund of Funds Manager, LLC, is an independent private equity investment firm with offices in New York, London, and Tokyo. The firm's list of composite descriptions, as well as information regarding the firm's policies for valuing investments, calculating performance, and preparing compliant presentations, are available upon request.

The Composite

The 2006 Buyout Strategy Fund of Funds Composite includes primary and secondary partnership investments with strategies focused on leveraged and growth-oriented buyouts primarily in the United States. Managers of partnerships are expected to focus on reducing costs, preparing companies for downturn, and providing operational improvement rather than financial engineering. Investments may be in small, medium, and large buyout partnerships, aiming to make selective commitments diversifying across stages, industries, and vintage years. Secondary deals take advantage of distressed primary partnership sales providing access to an increased mix of assets. The underlying funds are leveraged between 100–300%. Private equity investments are illiquid and, therefore, if investment opportunities and/or exit strategies become limited, the life of the fund may be extended and capital calls and distributions may be delayed. The composite was created on 31 December 2006. The vintage year is 2006 and was determined by the initial subscription date of the fund of funds.

Valuation

The firm uses valuations reported by the general partner of the investment partnerships. Given the nature of the investments, all valuations are determined using both subjective observable and subjective unobservable inputs.

Calculation of Performance Returns

The fund's SI-IRR calculation uses daily cash flows. All cash flows and values used to calculate returns are in, or have been converted to, US dollars. Gross returns are net of all underlying investment partnership expenses, management fees, and carried interest but gross of ABC Fund of Funds Manager's management fees. Net returns are net of all underlying partnership fees and expenses, including ABC Fund of Funds Manager's management fees.

Investment Management Fee

ABC Fund of Funds Manager's management fee varies based on the size of the commitment and structure of the program. The management fee is 100 basis points, based on the total commitment to a fund of funds, plus a 10% carry on total gains. Net returns are calculated using actual management fees of the fund of funds and underlying funds, including performance fees.

Benchmark

The benchmark is derived from private equity dollar-weighted IRRs, and the calculation is based on the overall market return for buyout fund of funds as determined by benchmark provider GHI. Individual vintage year benchmarks are the median SI-IRR for the applicable vintage years, at 31 December 2013.

SAMPLE 6 PRIVATE EQUITY: FUND OF FUNDS BY VINTAGE YEAR

Investments 2002 Fund of Funds Composite
Results Reported as of Calendar Year End

Calendar Year	Gross-of-Fees SI-IRR (%)	Net-of-Fees SI-IRR (%)	Benchmark SI-IRR (%)	Composite Assets ($ Mil)	Total Firm Assets ($ Mil)	# of Portfolios
2002*	2.5	–5.5	8.5	2.6	250	≤ 5
2003	–4.2	–12.3	–3.8	4.7	300	≤ 5
2004	12.5	6.5	14.4	7.5	350	≤ 5
2005	45.8	40.8	42.7	24.2	400	≤ 5
2006	35.6	31.5	30.2	21.6	450	≤ 5
2007	22.2	19.3	13.5	14.7	500	≤ 5
2008	17.4	15.5	8.1	11.8	550	≤ 5
2009	17.3	15.3	7.5	11.0	600	≤ 5
2010	16.5	14.8	8.0	9.3	650	≤ 5
2011	15.9	13.5	8.5	8.1	700	≤ 5
2012	16.8	14.0	10.3	6.5	750	≤ 5

* Returns are for the period from 1 May 2002 (inception date) through 31 December 2002.

Calendar Year	Cumulative Committed Capital ($ Mil)	Paid-In Capital ($ Mil)	Cumulative Distributions ($ Mil)	DPI	RVPI	TVPI	PIC
2002	20	3	0	0.00	1.04	1.04	0.15
2003	20	5	0	0.00	0.93	0.93	0.25
2004	20	8	2	0.22	0.94	1.16	0.40
2005	20	15	4	0.23	1.62	1.85	0.75
2006	20	17	12	0.71	1.25	1.96	0.85
2007	20	18	16	0.89	0.82	1.71	0.90
2008	20	19	17	0.89	0.62	1.51	0.95
2009	20	19	19	0.99	0.57	1.56	0.96
2010	20	20	23	1.18	0.47	1.65	0.98
2011	20	20	25	1.25	0.41	1.66	1.00
2012	20	20	29	1.45	0.33	1.78	1.00

Underlying Partnership Investments by Strategy
Results Reported as of 31 December 2012

Investment Strategy	SI-IRR Gross-of-Fees (%)	Benchmark Return (%)	Committed Capital ($ Mil)	Paid-In Capital ($ Mil)	Cumulative Distributions ($ Mil)	Assets ($ Mil)	TVPI Multiple	DPI Multiple	RVPI Multiple	PIC Multiple
Venture Capital	65.3	32.6	8.0	8.0	16.0	2.0	2.3	2.0	0.3	1.0
Buyout	11.3	10.2	12.0	12.0	13.0	4.5	1.5	1.1	0.4	1.0

Disclosures

Sample 6 Investments claims compliance with the Global Investment Performance Standards (GIPS®) and has prepared and presented this report in compliance with the GIPS standards. Sample 6 Investments has not been independently verified.

Sample 6 Investments is an independent private equity manager of fund of funds strategies with offices in Zurich, Menlo Park, New York, and Hong Kong. The composite was created in May 2002 and includes one closed-end fund that invests in buyout and venture capital funds. The fund of funds has an 8–10 year investment time horizon, but it may be longer based on the life of the underlying funds, which may be extended due to changes in investment and/or exit opportunities. As more fully described in the fund's offering memorandum, primary risks include industry and geographic concentration depending on investment opportunities, and liquidity risks due to the nature of the fund's investments.

The composite's vintage year is 2002, which was determined using the date of the initial capital call of the fund of funds. Returns are presented in US dollars.

The 2002 Fund of Funds Composite complies with PQR's valuation guidelines, which are consistent with the GIPS Valuation Principles. Valuations are normally based on valuations provided by the manager of the underlying investments' partnerships. Because fund investments are not publicly traded, all investments are considered to be valued using subjective unobservable inputs.

All returns for the 2002 Fund of Funds Composite reflect the deduction of administrative expenses (legal, auditing, etc.) of the closed-end fund. Gross returns do not reflect the deduction of Sample 6 Investments' management fees. Net returns reflect the deduction of actual management fees and accrued carried interest, if any.

The fund's SI-IRR calculation incorporates daily cash flows. Sample 6 Investments' annual management fee is 1% on the total committed capital.

The Vendor ABC Private Equity Fund of Funds Index (vintage year 2002) is used as the benchmark.

A complete list of the firm's composite descriptions is available upon request, as are policies for valuing portfolios, calculating performance, and preparing compliant presentations.

SAMPLE 7 PRIVATE EQUITY: PRIMARY FUND VEHICLE

Private Equity Capital Management
2001 Venture Capital Composite
Results Reported as of 31 December

Year End	Paid-In Capital (AUD Mil)	Since Inception Distributions (AUD Mil)	Cumulative Committed Capital (AUD Mil)	Composite Assets (AUD Mil)	% of Firm Assets
2001*	40.3	0.0	175.0	38.5	64.2
2002	82.3	1.0	175.0	78.8	52.5
2003	129.5	29.9	175.0	105.0	58.3
2004	143.5	42.3	175.0	120.8	41.6
2005	157.5	97.0	175.0	119.0	37.8
2006	166.2	129.3	175.0	112.0	31.1
2007	171.5	184.7	175.0	98.0	28.0
2008	182.5	184.7	175.0	78.8	21.0
2009	182.5	184.7	175.0	49.0	11.9
2010	182.5	184.7	175.0	31.5	7.5
2011	182.5	205.8	175.0	5.2	1.1

* Returns are for the period from 3 February 2001 (inception date) through 31 December 2001.

Year End	TVPI	DPI	RVPI	PIC	Composite Gross-of-Fees SI-IRR (%)	Composite Net-of-Fees SI-IRR (%)	Benchmark SI-IRR (%)
2001	0.96	0.00	0.96	0.23	−7.5	−9.5	−12.5
2002	0.97	0.01	0.96	0.47	0.3	−1.6	−3.5
2003	1.04	0.23	0.81	0.74	4.1	2.3	1.2
2004	1.14	0.29	0.84	0.82	8.2	6.4	7.4
2005	1.37	0.62	0.76	0.90	11.0	9.3	8.2
2006	1.45	0.78	0.67	0.95	13.0	10.1	9.7
2007	1.65	1.08	0.57	0.98	18.1	12.3	11.4
2008	1.44	1.01	0.43	1.04	16.9	10.4	10.1
2009	1.28	1.01	0.27	1.04	14.9	8.7	7.2
2010	1.18	1.01	0.17	1.04	14.0	7.7	6.8
2011	1.16	1.13	0.03	1.04	11.2	6.2	5.5

TVPI = Total Value to Since Inception Paid-In Capital
DPI = Since Inception Distributions to Since Inception Paid-In Capital
PIC = Since Inception Paid-In Capital to Cumulative Committed Capital
RVPI = Residual Value to Since Inception Paid-In Capital

Disclosures

Compliance Statement

Private Equity Capital Management claims compliance with the Global Investment Performance Standards (GIPS®) and has prepared and presented this report in compliance with the GIPS standards. Private Equity Capital Management has been independently verified for the periods 3 February 2001 through 31 December 2010.

Verification assesses whether 1) the firm has complied with all the composite construction requirements of the GIPS standards on a firm-wide basis and 2) the firm's policies and procedures are designed to calculate and present performance in compliance with the GIPS standards. The 2001 Venture Capital Composite has been examined for the periods 1 January 2005 through 31 December 2010. The verification and performance examination reports are available upon request.

Firm & Composite

Private Equity Capital Management ("PECM") is an independent private equity investment firm with offices in New York, London, and Sydney. The 2001 Venture Capital Composite includes one fund, whose objective is to seek long-term capital appreciation by acquiring minority interests in early-stage technology companies. The fund invests in technology companies in Europe, Asia Pacific, and emerging markets. European venture investments are more concentrated than in the other regions and are focused in a few high quality companies. Exit opportunities include IPOs, trade sales, and secondary sales. Opportunities in China and India will be targeted for investment, and an allocation to Chinese high-tech will be at least 10% of the invested capital over the life of the fund. International venture capital investments are generally illiquid and are subject to currency risk. If investment opportunities and/or exit strategies become limited, the life of the fund may be extended and capital calls and distributions may be delayed. The 2001 Venture Capital Composite was created in 2001. The vintage year of the composite is 2001 and was determined by the year of the first drawdown. The firm's list of composite descriptions and the firm's policies for calculating performance and preparing compliant presentation are available upon request.

Input Data & Calculation

The 2001 Venture Capital Composite complies with the LMN Venture Capital Association's valuation guidelines as well as the GIPS Valuation Principles. Valuations are prepared by PECM's valuation committee and reviewed by an independent advisory board. All investments within the composite are valued using either a most recent transaction or an earnings multiple. Policies for valuing investments are available upon request. Due to the nature of private equity investments, all investments are valued using subjective unobservable inputs.

The SI-IRR calculation incorporates monthly cash flows for periods prior to 31 December 2009 and daily cash flows thereafter. Performance is expressed in Australian dollars (AUD).

Gross returns are net of transaction expenses and all administrative expenses. Net returns are net of transaction expenses, administrative expenses, management fees, and carried interest. The standard fee schedule currently in effect is as follows:

> The manager will receive an annual management fee equal to 2% of capital commitments. The manager's participation in profits (carried interest) begins after the limited partners have been provided an 8% preferred return. The manager collects 20% of the distributed profits from that point forward. Subsequently, if the amount of cumulative

carried interest exceeds 20% of the net cumulative gains, the manager will repay the excess amount to the fund for distribution to the limited partners.

There is only one fund in the composite for all periods; therefore, the internal dispersion of portfolio returns is not applicable.

Benchmark

The benchmark return is derived from private equity dollar-weighted IRRs, and the calculation is based on the overall market return for international venture capital funds as published by Benchmark Provider GHI. Vintage year benchmarks are median returns for the applicable vintage year, as of each year end.

SAMPLE 8 INVESTMENTS LARGE-CAP SMA COMPOSITE

1 January 2001 through 31 December 2010

				As of 31 December			
Year	Net Return (%)	XYZ Index Return (%)	Internal Dispersion (%)	Number of Portfolios	Composite Assets ($ Millions)	Firm Assets ($ Millions)	% of SMA Portfolios
2010	8.4	10.2	0.7	1,834	2,125	18,222	100
2009	21.1	21.1	1.1	1,730	2,130	17,635	100
2008	–39.7	–39.8	1.0	1,631	2,141	19,246	100
2007	1.4	6.2	1.2	1,532	2,127	14,819	100
2006	11.4	10.5	0.9	1,428	2,116	12,362	100
2005	1.0	4.3	0.8	68	1,115	12,051	0
2004	6.8	4.9	1.0	52	1,110	13,419	0
2003	23.9	27.0	1.1	46	990	10,612	0
2002	–24.4	–19.1	0.9	38	975	9,422	0
2001	–17.7	–12.8	0.8	41	870	8,632	0

Notes:

1 Sample 8 Investments claims compliance with the Global Investment Performance Standards (GIPS®) and has prepared and presented this report in compliance with the GIPS standards. Sample 8 Investments has been independently verified for the period from 1 April 1996 through 31 December 2009.

Verification assesses whether 1) the firm has complied with all the composite construction requirements of the GIPS standards on a firm-wide basis and 2) the firm's policies and procedures are designed to calculate and present performance in compliance with the GIPS standards. The Large Cap SMA Composite has been examined for the period from 1 January 2006 through 31 December 2009. The verification and performance examination reports are available upon request.

2 Sample 8 Investments is an independent investment adviser registered under the Investment Advisers Act of 1940, was founded in March 1996, and manages global large-cap equity, fixed-income, and balanced strategies.

3 Beginning 1 January 2006, the composite includes only wrap fee (SMA) portfolios benchmarked to the XYZ Index. Performance results prior to 2006 are based on the Large-Cap Institutional Composite returns.

4 The Large-Cap SMA Composite is comprised of portfolios invested in US equities which have a market capitalization greater than $5 billion.

5 The composite was created in February 2006. A list of composite descriptions is available upon request.

6 All returns are expressed in US dollars. Policies for valuing portfolios, calculating performance, and preparing compliant presentations are available upon request.

7 The XYZ Index returns are provided to represent the investment environment existing during the time periods shown. For comparison purposes, the index is fully invested and includes the reinvestment of income. The returns for the index do not include any trading costs, management fees, or other costs. Index returns have been taken from published sources.

8 "Pure" gross returns, presented below as supplemental information, from 2006 through 2010 do not reflect the deduction of any trading costs, fees, or expenses and are presented for comparison purposes only. "Pure" gross returns prior to 2006 reflect the deduction of trading costs. The SMA fee includes all charges for trading costs, portfolio management, custody, and other administrative fees. Net returns are calculated by subtracting the highest applicable SMA fee (2.50% on an annual basis, or 0.21% monthly) on a monthly basis from the "pure" gross composite monthly return. The standard fee schedule in effect is as follows: 2.50% on total assets.

9 The dispersion is measured by the equal-weighted standard deviation of annual returns of those portfolios that are included in the composite for the full year.

10 At 31 December 2010, the three-year annualized ex-post standard deviation of the composite and the benchmark are 12.3% and 13.2%, respectively.

11 Past performance is not an indicator of future results.

Supplemental Information

Year	"Pure" Gross Return* (%)	Net Return (%) Assuming 3% SMA Fees	Net Return (%) Assuming 2% SMA Fees
2010	11.1	7.9	9.0
2009	24.0	20.5	21.7
2008	−38.0	−40.1	−39.4
2007	4.0	0.9	2.0
2006	14.1	10.8	11.9
2005	3.5	0.5	1.5
2004	9.5	6.3	7.4
2003	26.9	23.3	24.5

(continued)

(Continued)

Year	"Pure" Gross Return* (%)	Net Return (%) Assuming 3% SMA Fees	Net Return (%) Assuming 2% SMA Fees
2002	−22.3	−24.8	−23.9
2001	−15.5	−18.1	−17.2

* "Pure" gross-of-fees returns do not reflect the deduction of any expenses, including trading costs. "Pure" gross-of-fees returns are supplemental to net returns.

OPTIONAL SEGMENT

APPENDIX B: SAMPLE ADVERTISEMENTS

1. SAMPLE ADVERTISEMENT WITHOUT PERFORMANCE

Generic Asset Management

Generic Asset Management is the institutional asset management division of Generic Inc. and is a registered investment advisory firm specializing in qualitative growth-oriented investment management.

Generic Asset Management claims compliance with the Global Investment Performance Standards (GIPS®). To receive a list of composite descriptions of Generic Asset Management and/or a presentation that complies with the GIPS standards, contact Jean Paul at (123) 456-7890, or write to Generic Asset Management, 123 Main Street, Returnsville 12345, or jpaul@genericasset-managment.com.

2. SAMPLE ADVERTISEMENT INCLUDING ONE-, THREE-, AND FIVE-YEAR ANNUALIZED RETURNS

Generic Asset Management: Global Equity Growth Composite

	Ending 31 Mar 2012		
	1-Year	3-Year Annualized	5-Year Annualized
Global Equity Growth Composite	−0.3%	13.7%	0.1%
XYZ World Index	−0.5%	13.8%	−0.6%

Note: Returns are shown in US dollars net of fees.

Generic Asset Management is the institutional asset management subsidiary of Generic Inc. and is a registered investment adviser specializing in qualitative growth-oriented investment management. The Global Equity Growth strategy focuses on earnings, growth of earnings, and key valuation metrics. The benchmark is the XYZ World Index, which is designed to measure the equity market performance of developed market countries. The benchmark is market-cap weighted and is composed of all XYZ developed market indexes.

Generic Asset Management claims compliance with the Global Investment Performance Standards (GIPS®). To receive a list of composite descriptions of Generic Asset Management and/or a presentation that complies with the GIPS standards, contact Jean Paul at (123) 456-7890, or write Generic Asset Management, One Plain Street, Returnsville 12345, or jpaul@genericassetmanagement.com.

3. SAMPLE ADVERTISEMENT INCLUDING PERIOD-TO-DATE AND ONE-, THREE-, AND FIVE-YEAR ANNUALIZED RETURNS

Generic Asset Management: Global Equity Growth Composite

	Ending 31 Mar 2012	Ending 31 Dec 2011		
	Period to Date (3 months)	1-Year	3-Year Annualized	5-Year Annualized
Global Equity Growth Composite	–3.84%	1.3%	15.0%	–1.2%
XYZ World Index	–4.94%	1.5%	14.1%	–0.7%

Note: Returns are shown in US dollars net of fees.

Generic Asset Management is the institutional asset management subsidiary of Generic Inc. and is a registered investment adviser specializing in qualitative growth-oriented investment management. The Global Equity Growth strategy focuses on earnings, growth of earnings, and key valuation metrics. The benchmark is the XYZ World Index, which is designed to measure the equity market performance of developed market countries. The benchmark is market-cap weighted and is composed of all XYZ developed market indexes.

Generic Asset Management claims compliance with the Global Investment Performance Standards (GIPS®). To receive a list of composite descriptions of Generic Asset Management and/or a presentation that complies with the GIPS standards, contact Jean Paul at (123) 456-7890, or write Generic Asset Management, One Plain Street, Returnsville 12345, or jpaul@genericassetmanagement.com.

4. SAMPLE ADVERTISEMENT INCLUDING FIVE YEARS OF ANNUAL RETURNS

Generic Asset Management: Global Equity Growth Composite

	Period to Date (3 months to 31 Mar 2012)	Annual Returns Periods Ended 31 December				
		2011	2010	2009	2008	2007
Global Equity Growth Composite	–3.84%	1.3%	13.0%	33.0%	–40.6%	9.6%
XYZ World Index	–4.94%	1.5%	11.8%	30.8%	–40.3%	9.6%

Note: Returns are shown in US dollars net of fees.

Generic Asset Management is the institutional asset management subsidiary of Generic Inc. and is a registered investment adviser specializing in qualitative, growth-oriented investment management. The Global Equity Growth strategy focuses on earnings, growth of earnings, and key valuation metrics. The benchmark is the XYZ World Index, which is designed to measure the equity market performance of developed market countries. The benchmark is market-cap weighted and is composed of all XYZ developed market indexes.

Generic Asset Management claims compliance with the Global Investment Performance Standards (GIPS®).

To receive a list of composite descriptions of Generic Asset Management and/or a presentation that complies with the GIPS standards, contact Jean Paul at (123) 456-7890, or write to Generic Asset Management, 123 Main Street, Returnsville 12345, or jpaul@genericassetmanagment.com.

APPENDIX C: SAMPLE LIST OF COMPOSITE DESCRIPTIONS

Sample Asset Management Firm

List of Composite Descriptions

1 **Unconstrained Activist UK Equity Composite**

The Unconstrained Activist UK Equity Composite includes all institutional portfolios invested in both listed and unlisted UK equities that pursue an activist investment policy; there is no restriction on the market capitalization of companies held. Portfolios within this composite are highly concentrated, holding approximately 15 securities, so returns may have lower correlation with the benchmark than a fully diversified strategy. In times of increased market volatility, the composite characteristics may change significantly and stock liquidity could be reduced. Due to their more concentrated nature, portfolios will tend to have more stock-specific risk than a more diversified strategy. Portfolios can use both exchange-traded and OTC derivative contracts for efficient portfolio management, which may expose the strategy to counterparty risk. The benchmark is the FTSE All Share® Index.

2 **Emerging Market High Yield Fixed Income Composite**

The Emerging Market High Yield Fixed Income Composite includes all institutional and retail portfolios invested in high yield debt securities issued by countries outside the OECD. The strategy allows for investment in foreign currency denominated assets over which the manager has full discretion on hedging. The strategy aims to deliver a total return primarily through income but with some capital growth. High yield bonds carry increased levels of credit and default risk and are less liquid than government and investment grade bonds. Investment in less regulated markets carries increased political, economic, and issuer risk. The benchmark is the J.P. Morgan Emerging Market Bond Index (EMBI+).

3 **UK Liquidity Plus Composite**

The UK Liquidity Plus Composite includes all institutional portfolios invested in a broad range of short-dated interest-bearing deposits, cash equivalents, short-term commercial paper, and other money market investments issued by major UK clearing banks and lending institutions. The strategy has a targeted modified duration of less than one year. The principal investment objectives are preservation of capital, maintenance of liquidity, and provision of yield greater than that available for the benchmark, the three-month Libor rate. The UK Liquidity Plus strategy differs from more conventional cash strategies in that it additionally holds short-term commercial paper, which has a greater exposure to credit risk.

4 **Socially Responsible Investment (SRI) Composite**

The Socially Responsible Investment Composite includes all segregated institutional and pooled portfolios that invest in global equity securities issued by companies that make a positive contribution to society and the environment through sustainable and socially responsible practices. The strategy aims to provide long term capital appreciation together with a growing income stream through investment in a portfolio of core equity holdings diversified by economic sector, industry group, and geographic business concentration. All foreign currency exposures are fully hedged back to US dollars.

The SRI process tends to screen out certain companies and sectors, which may result in a more concentrated strategy than a fully diversified strategy. Changes in legislation, scientific thinking, national and supra-national policies, and behaviors could significantly affect the stocks of companies held within the strategy. The benchmark is the Morningstar Ethical/SRI Global GIF Sector peer group.

5 **Leveraged Bond Composite**

The Leveraged Bond Composite includes all institutional segregated portfolios invested in a diversified range of high yield corporate and government bonds with the aim of providing investors with a high level of income while seeking to maximize the total return. The portfolios are invested in domestic and international fixed income securities of varying maturities. The strategy allows investment in exchange-traded and OTC derivative contracts (including, but not limited to, options, futures, swaps, and forward currency contracts) for the purposes of risk, volatility, and currency exposure management. The strategy allows leverage up to but not exceeding twice the value of a portfolio's investments through the use of repurchase financing arrangements with counterparties. Inherent in derivative instrument investments is the risk of counterparty default. Leverage may also magnify losses as well as gains to the extent that leverage is employed. The benchmark is the Barclays Capital Global Aggregate Bond Index.

6 **Global Commodity Composite**

The Global Commodity Composite includes institutional portfolios that globally invest in a diversified range of companies that provide exposure to commodities, energy, and materials. Investment is primarily through the common or ordinary stock of these companies. Investment directly in raw materials is allowable to a maximum exposure of 10%. Exchange-traded funds and exchange-traded commodity securities up to a maximum 20% exposure are also allowed. The base currency is US dollars, and any or all of the currency risk associated with investments in currencies other than dollars may be hedged between 0% and 100% at the manager's discretion. The strategy cannot gear or otherwise deploy leverage but may use exchange-traded derivative instruments for efficient portfolio management.

Investments directly or indirectly in commodities may add to portfolio volatility. Global commodity prices can be affected by changes in legislation, national and supra-national policies, and behaviors. In times of commodity price volatility, the liquidity of directly held commodities and the correlation with the broad market can change quickly. The benchmark is the Dow Jones–UBS Commodity Index Total Return℠.

7 **Large Cap Equity Growth Composite**

The Large Cap Equity Growth Composite includes all institutional portfolios that invest in large capitalization US stocks that are considered to have growth in earnings prospects that is superior to that of the average company within the benchmark, the Russell 3000® Growth Index. The targeted tracking error between the composite and the benchmark is less than 3%.

8 **Balanced Growth Composite**

The Balanced Growth Composite includes all institutional balanced portfolios that invest in large-cap US equities and investment-grade bonds with the goal of providing long-term capital growth and steady income from a well-diversified strategy. Although the strategy allows for equity exposure ranging between 50–70%, the typical allocation is between 55–65%.

9 **Currency Overlay Composite**

The Currency Overlay Composite includes all institutional and retail portfolios invested in a broad range of foreign-currency-denominated deposits or instruments such as forward contracts, futures, or foreign exchange derivatives. The principal investment objective is alpha generation through currency appreciation and/or risk mitigation from adverse movements in exchange rates where the original currency exposure stems from a global or international portfolio. Hedging strategies may range from passive to fully active. Currency-related investing carries inherent risks due to changes in macroeconomic policy, which can be amplified in the case of emerging markets where political regime shifts and changes in the control of capital may be more prevalent. In volatile periods, liquidity and correlations between currencies may change expected returns drastically. Foreign exchange forwards and derivatives traded over the counter have counterparty default risk.

10 Asian Market Neutral Composite

The Asian Market Neutral Composite includes a single hedge fund with a market neutral strategy that invests in publically traded Asian equities with a market capitalization greater than $500 million. The strategy uses a risk controlled quantitative screening and optimization process that invests at least 85% of the net asset value in long equity positions and at least 85% of the net asset value in short equity positions. The long portion of the strategy will overweight those securities that have been quantitatively identified as potentially exhibiting superior and sustainable earnings growth compared with the market; conversely, the short portion of the strategy will consist of securities that have been identified as having inferior growth prospects or that may also be adversely affected by either specific events or by momentum considerations. The principal objective of the strategy is to outperform the return on three-month US Treasury Bills through active trading of long and short equity positions.

The Asian Market Neutral strategy seeks to dollar balance exposures between long and short positions so that broad market movements are neutralized. In certain market conditions, the investment process behind the strategy can give rise to unmatched country, sector, industry, market capitalization, and/or style bias exposures in the portfolio. The active trading strategy will involve significantly greater stock turnover when compared with passive strategies.

11 2001 Venture Capital Composite

The 2001 Venture Capital Composite includes one fund, whose objective is to seek long-term capital appreciation by acquiring minority interests in early-stage technology companies. The fund invests in technology companies in Europe, Asia Pacific, and emerging markets. European venture investments are more concentrated than in the other regions and are focused in a few high-quality companies. Exit opportunities include IPOs, trade sales, and secondary sales. Opportunities in China and India will be targeted for investment, and an allocation to Chinese high-tech will be at least 10% of the invested capital over the life of the fund. International venture capital investments are generally illiquid and are subject to currency risk. If investment opportunities and/or exit strategies become limited, the life of the fund may be extended and capital calls and distributions may be delayed.

12 2006 Buyout Strategy Fund of Funds Composite

The 2006 Buyout Strategy Fund of Funds Composite includes primary and secondary partnership investments with strategies focused on leveraged and growth-oriented buyouts primarily in the United States. Managers of partnerships are expected to focus on reducing costs, preparing companies for downturn, and providing operational improvement rather than financial engineering. Investments may be in small, medium, and large buyout partnerships, aiming to make selective commitments diversifying across stages, industries, and vintage years. Secondary deals take advantage of distressed primary partnership sales providing access to an increased mix of assets. The underlying funds are leveraged between 100–300%. Private equity investments are illiquid and, therefore, if investment opportunities and/or exit strategies become limited, the life of the fund may be extended and capital calls and distributions may be delayed.

13 Value-Added Strategy Non-Closed-End Real Estate Composite

The Value-Added Strategy Composite consists of all discretionary open-end funds and separate accounts managed by the Firm using a value-added investment strategy with an equal income and appreciation focus and having a minimum portfolio size of $10 million. Portfolio management will invest in multi-family, office, industrial, and retail property types only within Asia that require correction or mitigation of the investments' operating, financial, redevelopment, and/or management risk(s). A moderate level of leverage ranging between 30% and 40% is used. Real estate investments are generally illiquid, and the investment outlook may change given the availability of credit or other financing sources.

14 Value-Added Strategy Closed-End Real Estate Composite

The Value-Added Strategy Composite includes a single closed-end commingled fund managed by the Firm using a value-added investment strategy with a focus on both income and appreciation. Portfolio management intends to invest in properties located in major markets within the United States with higher operational risk than traditional property types. The target level of leverage is 50% with a maximum allowable level of 60%. Real estate investments are generally illiquid, and the investment outlook may change given the availability of credit or other financing sources. If investment opportunities and/or exit strategies become limited, the life of the fund may be extended and capital calls and distributions may be delayed.

15 US Core Equity Composite (Terminated Composites)

The US Core Equity Composite includes all institutional portfolios and pooled funds managed to a GARP (growth at a reasonable price) strategy through investment in a high-quality, focused portfolio of domestic, large capitalization stocks that are expected to generate returns above the S&P 500® Index over a market cycle. Sample Asset Management Firm uses a quantitative screening process together with fundamental research and then overlays macroeconomic factors and economic sector exposures to construct portfolios. The benchmark is the S&P 500 Index. Quantitative-driven investment screening relies on historical stock correlations, which can be adversely affected during periods of severe market volatility. The composite terminated in March 2009.

Detailed composite definitions are available upon request.

END OPTIONAL SEGMENT

PRACTICE PROBLEMS

1 One of the objectives of the Global Investment Performance Standards (GIPS) is:

   A to ensure fair representation and full disclosure of investment performance.

   B to ensure that firms have their investment performance verified by an independent third party.

   C to develop provisions that address the unique characteristics of each asset class in performance measurement.

2 With respect to the Global Investment Performance Standards, which of the following is one of the nine sections containing investment performance provisions?

   A Real Estate.

   B Derivatives.

   C Legal and Ethical Considerations.

3 According to the Fundamentals of Compliance section of the Global Investment Performance Standards, issues that a firm must consider when claiming compliance include all of the following *except*:

   A replicating performance.

   B properly defining the firm.

   C documenting firm policies and procedures used in establishing and maintaining compliance with the Standards.

4 A firm claims compliance with the GIPS standards as of 31 December 2014. All of the firm's portfolios are included in at least one of the composites presented in the following table:

Composite	Inception	GIPS-Compliant Performance
S&P Mid-Cap Value (MCV)	31 Dec 2008	All periods
Russell 2000 Value (R2V)	31 Dec 2003	Since 31 Dec 2005

   At a minimum, how many years of compliant performance must the firm present for each composite as of 31 December 2014?

   A Six years for MCV and nine years for R2V

   B Five years for MCV and five years for R2V

   C Six years for MCV and eleven years for R2V

5 G&F Advisors claims compliance with the Global Investment Performance Standards (GIPS) in its marketing materials. The compliant presentation includes a footnote which indicates that the firm has been verified by an independent third party. An additional note states that G&F is in compliance with the GIPS standards except for its private equity investments. It is *likely* that G&F violated the GIPS standards?

   A No, because the footnotes meet the requirements of the Standards.

   B No, because the provisions do not apply to the private equity investments.

   C Yes, because they cannot claim compliance unless all requirements of the Standard are met.

6 Company D has offices in London and Edinburgh. Although the individual investment managers in each office make the investment decisions, all the research and security trading are based in London. The Edinburgh office wants to define itself as a firm, "Firm D: Edinburgh," and claim compliance with the GIPS standards. Can that office define itself as a firm separate from the rest of Company D and claim compliance with the GIPS standards?

7 Walker, Pierce Corporation is a global financial services company. In addition to its London headquarters, the company has subsidiaries in New York, Frankfurt, and Hong Kong. Walker, Pierce Corporation has decided not to implement the GIPS standards. However, the head of marketing for its continental European subsidiary, Walker, Pierce & Company of Frankfurt, believes that the division would benefit by implementing the GIPS standards. Is it possible for Walker, Pierce & Company of Frankfurt to become GIPS-compliant even if Walker, Pierce Corporation does not implement the GIPS standards companywide?

8 Larson Dynamic Management claims to comply with the GIPS standards. At the time the firm first achieved compliance, trade-date accounting was recommended but settlement date accounting was acceptable. On 1 January 2005, trade-date accounting became mandatory. Larson Dynamic Management has been unable to reprogram its accounting system to produce statements on a trade-date basis. Larson Dynamic Management includes the following statement with composite performance presentations covering periods that began on or after 1 January 2005: "Larson Dynamic Management has prepared and presented this report in compliance with the Global Investment Performance Standards (GIPS®), except that settlement date accounting has been used as an acceptable alternative." Is this compliance statement allowable?

9 One of the stated goals of the GIPS Executive Committee is to encourage fair, global competition among investment management firms for all markets without:

A creating barriers to entry.

B increasing investment firms' compliance costs.

C constraining the development of new investment strategies.

10 A Guidance Statement that has been adopted by the GIPS Executive Committee is *best* described as setting forth:

A integral parts of the Standards.

B best practices in performance presentation.

C practical suggestions on interpreting and implementing the Standards.

11 A firm that claims compliance with the GIPS standards must be held out to clients or prospective clients as a distinct business entity. According to the GIPS Glossary, a distinct business entity must:

A be organized as a legal entity.

B retain discretion over the assets it manages.

C have a separate board of directors or equivalent governance body.

12 An investment consulting firm conducting a search for a custodian on behalf of a plan sponsor asks if the custodial division of New Fjord Bank and Trust complies with the GIPS standards. New Fjord's management believes that when the division prepares performance reports for institutional clients it meets all the requirements of the GIPS standards for input data and calculation methodology. The *most* appropriate response to the consultant's question is that the division:

A complies with applicable GIPS standards.

B cannot claim to be in compliance with the GIPS standards.

C calculates clients' returns in accordance with the GIPS standards.

13 According to the GIPS standards, firms must provide a list of composite descriptions to any prospective client who asks for this information. Terminated composites must:

A remain on the list indefinitely.

B be removed from the list promptly upon termination.

C remain on the list for at least five years after the composite termination date.

14 The GIPS standards do NOT require firms to document policies and procedures related to the:

A ownership of assets.

B correction of errors.

C confidentiality of information.

15 Firm B manages several portfolios according to a particular strategy; however, the firm does not ever plan to market the strategy. Do these portfolios have to be included in a composite?

16 Our firm definition includes both equity and fixed income products. Can we present only our equity products (strategies) in compliance with the Standards?

17 The GIPS standards state that composites must be defined according to investment:

A policies.

B mandate, objective or strategy.

C decision-making processes.

The following information relates to Questions 18–20

Seafarers Bank has two subsidiaries, Waterline Asset Management and Galiot Investments. The subsidiaries are held out to clients as two distinct business entities serving different types of clients.

Waterline, which complies with the GIPS standards, serves institutional investors through two divisions. The Fundamental Strategies Division actively manages equity and fixed-income portfolios, while the Quantitative Strategies Division manages global equity index and enhanced index funds.

Galiot, which does not claim to comply with the GIPS Standards, serves retail investors through two divisions. The Private Client Advisory Services Division manages portfolios for individuals with more than US $1 million in investable assets, and the Retail Brokerage Division provides investment research, portfolio administration, and trade execution services to individuals with smaller portfolios.

The following chart displays the organizational structure of Seafarers Bank.

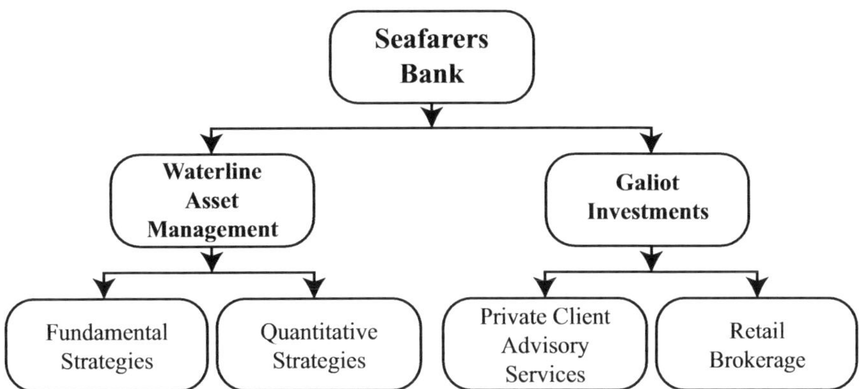

18 Hemant Choudry heads the performance analytics department of Waterline Asset Management. Choudry formulates the following definition of the firm: "Waterline Asset Management is the institutional investment management subsidiary of Seafarers Bank." Does Choudry's definition of the firm meet the requirements of the GIPS standards?

A Yes.

B No; it does not distinguish between Waterline's two divisions.

C No; it does not identify Galiot as another Seafarers subsidiary.

19 An unrelated investment management firm that claims to comply with the GIPS standards hires the Quantitative Strategies Division of Waterline Asset Management as a subadvisor to manage currency overlay portfolios. For the purposes of GIPS compliance, must Waterline include the sub-advised assets in total firm assets?

A Yes.

B No; they are not discretionary portfolios.

C No; they are included in the total firm assets of the hiring firm.

20 The Private Client Advisory Services Division of Galiot Investments comes into compliance with the GIPS standards and starts to hold itself out as a distinct business entity serving high-net-worth individuals. It is *most* appropriate to:

A define the firm as Seafarers Bank.

B define the firm so as to include Waterline Asset Management and the Private Client Advisory Services Division of Galiot Investments.

C keep the existing definition of Waterline and define the Private Client Advisory Services Division of Galiot Investments as a separate firm.

---

21 XYZ claims compliance with the GIPS standards. XYZ's firm assets include Composite Y, which was terminated on 31 December 2015. Under the GIPS standards, XYZ must include Composite Y in its list of composites until at least:

A 31 December 2015.

B 31 December 2020.

C 31 December 2025.

22 For periods starting on or after 1 January 2010, a GIPS-compliant firm must value portfolios within a composite at least monthly and on the dates of all:

A large cash flows.

B external cash flows.

C significant cash flows.

23 XYZ Capital intends to claim compliance with GIPS for all periods beginning 1 January 2012. XYZ invests in publicly traded equity securities and liquid corporate bonds. Which of XYZ's policies is *most likely* in compliance with the GIPS standards?

A Corporate bonds are valued on a cost basis.

B The valuation of corporate bonds excludes accrued interest.

C Trade date accounting is used for recording purchases and sales.

24 XYZ Capital is a GIPS-compliant firm with $10 billion in discretionary assets and $3 billion in non-discretionary assets. Of the firm's total assets, $1 billion are non-fee-paying. Under the GIPS standards, XYZ's total firm assets are:

A $10 billion.

B $12 billion.

C $13 billion.

25 ABC Partners has $500 million in assets managed directly, $200 million in assets managed by a selected sub-adviser, and $50 million in assets managed by a sub-adviser that the firm does not have discretion over selecting. Under the GIPS standards, ABC Partners' total firm assets are:

A $500 million.

B $700 million.

C $750 million.

26 Turquoise Capital started operations on 1 January 2008 and claimed compliance with the GIPS standards for the first time as of 31 December 2016 for the five-year period beginning 1 January 2012. Turquoise's Composite A has a creation date of 1 January 2010. When preparing the Composite A compliant presentation as of 31 December 2017, Turquoise must present Composite A's performance starting from:

A 1 January 2010.

B 1 January 2012.

C 1 January 2013.

27 Circle Capital Management began operations on 1 January 2002 and will initially claim compliance with GIPS as of 31 December 2016 for the 10-year period beginning 1 January 2007. Circle manages an equity composite that was created at the firm's inception. In the GIPS-compliant presentation of the equity composite, Circle:

A must not link performance prior to 1 January 2007 to performance beginning after that date.

B must link performance for all periods beginning 1 January 2002 and disclose that performance prior to 1 January 2007 is non-compliant.

C should, but is not required to, link performance for all periods beginning 1 January 2002 and disclose that performance prior to 1 January 2017 is non-compliant.

28 One of the roles of GIPS country sponsors is to:

A act as the governing body of the GIPS standards.

B support the GIPS standards and help drive adoption of the GIPS standards in their country.

C promote the principles of fair representation and full disclosure and develop the GIPS standards.

29 Forest Capital, a firm claiming compliance with the GIPS standards, is subject to the local laws and regulations of Country W. Forest determines that there are local regulations that conflict with requirements of the GIPS standards. Under the GIPS standards, Forest is required to:

A stop claiming compliance with the GIPS standards.

B adhere to local laws and regulations without additional disclosure.

C adhere to local laws and regulations and disclose the conflict with the GIPS standards in the compliant presentation.

30 Which of the following asset classes has separate provisions under the GIPS standards?

A Private equity

B Corporate bonds

C Mortgage-backed securities

31 Which of the following is excluded from the real estate provisions of the GIPS standards?

A A separate account investing in publicly traded REITs

B A closed-end fund investing in wholly owned properties

C A commingled fund investing in participating mortgage loans

32 Beacon Capital is a firm that claims GIPS compliance. Beacon's largest composite is a closed-end fund holding private equity investments. Which of the following *best* describes the provisions of the GIPS standards that apply to Beacon's private equity composite?

A The private equity provisions in Section 7 of the GIPS standards only

B All the provisions in Sections 0–5 as well as the private equity provisions if not superseded by the provisions in Sections 0–5

C All the private equity provisions as well as the provisions in Sections 0–5 if not superseded by the private equity provisions

SOLUTIONS

1 A is correct. Key features of the GIPS standards include fair representation and full disclosure of investment performance.

2 A is correct. Real Estate is one of the nine sections in the 2010 edition of the GIPS standards. Derivatives and Legal and Ethical Considerations are not sections of the Standards.

3 A is correct. Replication of performance is not included in the Fundaments of Compliance section within the GIPS standards.

4 B is correct. A firm is required to initially present, at a minimum, five years of annual investment performance that is compliant with the GIPS standards.

5 C is correct. Firms must meet all the requirements set forth in the GIPS standards and cannot claim partial compliance.

6 If the Edinburgh office of Company D is not held out to clients or potential clients as a separate entity, the Edinburgh office cannot define itself as a firm for the purposes of the GIPS standards.

7 The GIPS standards must be applied on a firm-wide basis, and the firm must be defined as an investment firm, subsidiary, or division held out to clients or potential clients as a distinct business entity (I.0.A.4). A "distinct business entity" is a unit, department, or office that is organizationally and functionally segregated from other units, divisions, departments, or offices and that retains discretion over the assets it manages and should have autonomy over the investment decision-making process (GIPS Glossary). If Walker, Pierce & Company of Frankfurt satisfies these criteria, it may define itself as a firm and undertake meeting all the requirements of the GIPS standards in order to claim compliance. The fact that Walker, Pierce & Company of Frankfurt has its own head of marketing suggests that it does hold itself out as a distinct business entity, and the fact that it is geographically separated from its parent company headquarters suggests that it may be organizationally and functionally segregated, but we lack sufficient information to determine if it retains discretion over the assets it manages and autonomy over the investment decision-making process.

8 The appropriate compliance statement must be included in compliant performance presentations prepared by firms claiming compliance with the GIPS standards. The firm must not represent or state compliance with the GIPS standards "except for" anything (I.0.A.6). In spite of the prior years' compliance with the then-prevailing Standards, Larson Dynamic Management may no longer claim compliance if it has failed to meet the 1 January 2005 deadline for trade-date accounting. The compliance statement may be used only if the firm complied with all requirements of the GIPS standards (I.0.A.1).

9 A is correct. One of the goals of the GIPS Executive Committee listed in the Introduction to the GIPS standards is "to promote fair, global competition among investment firms without creating barriers to entry". B and C are not stated goals of the GIPS Executive Committee.

10 A is correct. Provision I.0.A.1 states, "Firms must comply with all the requirements of the GIPS Standards, including any updates, Guidance Statements, interpretations, Questions & Answers (Q&As), and clarifications published by CFA Institute and the GIPS Executive Committee..."

11 B is correct. The GIPS Glossary in Chapter V. of the GIPS standards defines a distinct business entity as "A unit, division, department, or office that is organizationally and functionally segregated from other units, divisions, departments,

or offices and that retains discretion over the assets it manages and that should have autonomy over the investment decision-making process." Being a legal entity and using a separate and distinct investment process are possible criteria for determining an organization's status as a distinct business entity, but they are not requirements.

12 B is correct. Only investment management firms can claim to be in compliance with the GIPS standards, and they can do so only if they meet all the requirements of the GIPS standards. (Provisions I.0.A.1 and 0.A.12.) A is incorrect because a firm cannot claim only to comply with some of the GIPS standards. (Provisions I.0.A.1 & 6.) C is incorrect because Provision I.0.A.7 states, "Statements referring to the calculation methodology as being 'in accordance,' 'in compliance,' or 'consistent' with the Global Investment Performance Standards, or similar statements, are prohibited."

13 C is correct. Provision I.0.A.10 states in pertinent part, "Firms must include terminated composites on the firm's list of composite descriptions for at least five years after the composite termination date."

14 C is correct. The GIPS standards do not address confidentiality. Provision 1.0.A.5 states, "Firms must document their policies and procedures used in establishing and maintaining compliance with the GIPS standards, including ensuring the existence and ownership of client assets, and must apply them consistently."

15 Yes, these portfolios must be included in a composite if the portfolios are actual, fee-paying, discretionary portfolios. It is important to remember that the GIPS standards are not marketing or advertising standards, nor do they differentiate between "marketed" and "non-marketed" composites.

The requirement for firms to include all actual, fee-paying, discretionary portfolios in at least one composite ensures that a firm presents a complete picture of its entire performance record. Without this requirement, there is a potential for firms to exclude poor performing portfolios from composites. Because the intent of the Standards is to accurately and fairly represent firm performance, all actual, fee-paying, discretionary portfolios must be included in at least one of the firm's composites.

16 No, the claim of compliance is a firm-wide claim declared on the composite presentations, and, if the firm chooses, in advertisements. The firm described above has been defined to include both equity and fixed income products. As such, the firm must make the claim of compliance based on all of its actual, fee-paying, discretionary portfolios within the firm's defined boundaries— both the equity and the fixed income products— in composites. Additionally, the firm must ensure it has adhered to all the applicable requirements of the Standards prior to making the claim of compliance.

17 B is correct. Section IV of *Introduction to the Global Investment Performance Standards (GIPS)* states in part, "A composite must include all actual, fee-paying, discretionary portfolios managed in accordance with the same investment mandate, objective, or strategy."

18 A is correct. Waterline Asset Management is a subsidiary of Seafarers Bank and holds itself out to the public as a distinct business entity serving institutional investors. GIPS Provision I.0.A.12 states, "Firms must be defined as an investment firm, subsidiary, or division held out to clients or prospective clients as a distinct business entity." The GIPS Glossary defines distinct business entity as "a unit, division, department, or office that is organizationally and functionally segregated from other units, divisions, departments, or offices and that retains discretion over the assets it manages and that should have autonomy over the investment decision making process. Possible criteria that can be used to determine this include: being a legal entity; having a distinct market or client type (e.g., institutional, retail, private client, etc.); and using a separate and distinct investment process." In defining the firm for the purposes of the GIPS standards, Waterline is not required to identify its internal divisions or to identify other subsidiaries of its parent company.

19 A is correct. Waterline manages the sub-advised assets and must include them in total firm assets whether or not they are considered discretionary portfolios. In this case, both the hiring firm and the sub-advisor are able to claim the performance of the sub-advised assets as their own. GIPS Provision I.0.A.13 states, in part, "...Total firm assets must be the aggregate fair value of all discretionary and non-discretionary assets managed by the firm."

20 C is correct. Because Waterline and the Private Client Services Division of Galiot are held out to clients as two distinct business entities serving different client types, it is most appropriate to define them as separate firms. GIPS Provision I.0.A.12 states, "Firms must be defined as an investment firm, subsidiary, or division held out to clients or prospective clients as a distinct business entity." The GIPS Glossary defines distinct business entity as "a unit, division, department, or office that is organizationally and functionally segregated from other units, divisions, departments, or offices and that retains discretion over the assets it manages and that should have autonomy over the investment decision making process. Possible criteria that can be used to determine this include: being a legal entity; having a distinct market or client type (e.g., institutional, retail, private client, etc.); and using a separate and distinct investment process."

21 B is correct. Provision 0.A.10 requires that firms include terminated composites in the list of composite descriptions for at least five years after the composite termination date. Composite Y thus must be included in the list of composite descriptions until at least 31 December 2020.

22 A is correct. Provision 1.A.3 requires that portfolios be valued at least monthly on or after 1 January 2001 and on the dates of all large cash flows on or after 1 January 2010. A large cash flow is defined as an external cash flow at a level that the firm determines may distort performance if the portfolio is not revalued. It is a recommendation, not a requirement, to value portfolios on the dates of all external cash flows. A significant cash flow is defined as a client-directed external cash flow at a level that the firm determines may temporarily prevent the firm from implementing the composite strategy. Significant cash flows are related to a loss of discretion, whereas large cash flows are related to the prevention of performance distortions.

23 C is correct because trade date accounting is required for periods beginning on or after 1 January 2005 (Provision 1.A.5). This policy is in compliance with the GIPS standards. A is incorrect because for periods beginning on or after 1 January 2011, portfolios must be valued in accordance with the definition of fair value (Provision 1.A.2). B is incorrect because the value of fixed-income securities must include accrued income (Provision 1.A.6).

24 C is correct. Provision 0.A.13 states that total firm assets must be the aggregate fair value of all discretionary and non-discretionary assets managed by the firm, including both fee-paying and non-fee-paying portfolios. XYZ's total firm assets are thus calculated as the total of the \$10 billion in discretionary and \$3 billion in non-discretionary assets.

25 B is correct. Provision 0.A.13 requires the inclusion of all discretionary and non-discretionary assets in the total firm assets. Additionally, Provision 0.A.14 requires the inclusion of all assets assigned to sub-advisers provided the firm has discretion over the selection of those sub-advisers. Assets assigned to a

sub-adviser that the firm does not have discretion over selecting are not part of total firm assets. ABC Partners' firm assets are thus calculated as \$500 million + \$200 million = \$700 million.

26 B is correct. Turquoise Capital has applied the GIPS standards beginning 1 January 2012, bringing the minimum five years of initial performance into compliance as of 31 December 2016. The firm is required to present an additional year of performance each year until a minimum 10 years are included. As of 31 December 2017, the firm is required to show annual performance for the six-year period from 1 January 2012 to 31 December 2017.

27 A is correct. Firms are allowed to link non-compliant performance with compliant performance only for periods prior to 1 January 2000. Firms must not link non-GIPS-compliant performance for periods beginning on or after 1 January 2000 to their GIPS-compliant performance. In this case, Circle Capital Management must not link its non–GIPS-compliant performance for periods prior to 1 January 2007 to performance beginning 1 January 2007.

28 B is correct. One of the roles of GIPS country sponsors is to support the GIPS standards and help drive adoption of the GIPS standards in their country. The GIPS Executive Committee acts as the governing body of the GIPS standards, promotes the principles of fair representation and full disclosure, and develops the GIPS standards.

29 C is correct. In cases in which laws and/or regulations conflict with the GIPS standards, firms are required to comply with the laws and regulations and make full disclosure of the conflict in the compliant presentation.

30 A is correct. Private equity investments must adhere to the provisions of Sections 0–5 and Section 7 (Private Equity) within the GIPS standards. Neither corporate bonds nor mortgage-backed securities have separate provisions within the GIPS standards.

31 A is correct. Publicly traded REITs are not within the scope of the investments that must adhere to the real estate provisions within the GIPS standards; however, unlisted, private placement securities issued by private REITs must adhere to the real estate provisions.

32 C is correct. The private equity provisions in Section 7 of the GIPS standards supplement all of the required and recommended provisions in Sections 0–5. Certain provisions in Sections 0–5 do not apply to private equity investments or are superseded by provisions within Section 7, and these exceptions are noted within Section 7.

Glossary

Abnormal return The return on an asset that is in excess of its required rate of return. Often synonymous with *alpha*.

Absolute return attribution See *return contribution*.

Absolute return benchmark A minimum target return that an investment manager is expected to beat.

Absolute risk Risk without comparison with a benchmark.

Accounting risks Risks arising from uncertainty about how a transaction should be recorded and the potential for accounting rules to change.

Accrued interest The interest that has accumulated on a bond or other debt instrument since the most recent interest payment was made.

Active investment management skill The ability of a portfolio manager to add value on a risk-adjusted basis through investment analysis and insight.

Active investment strategies An approach to investing in which the portfolio manager seeks to outperform a given benchmark portfolio.

Active return Portfolio return in excess of the benchmark return.

Active risk The variability of a manager's deviations from the benchmark.

Active share A measure, ranging from 0% to 100%, of how similar a portfolio is to its benchmark. The measure is based on the differences in a portfolio's holdings and weights relative to its benchmark's holdings and their weights. A manager who precisely replicates the benchmark will have an active share of zero; a manager with no holdings in common with the benchmark will have an active share of one.

Adjusted beginning value Beginning value plus any beginning adjustment.

Adjusted ending value Ending value plus any ending adjustment.

Adjusted R^2 A measure of goodness-of-fit of a regression that is adjusted for degrees of freedom. Hence, it does not automatically increase when another independent variable is added to a regression.

Allocation In performance analytics, the decision to take sector weights in the portfolio different from the sector benchmark weights, and the value-added by such decisions.

Alpha The return on an asset in excess of the asset's required rate of return. Sometimes referred to as an *abnormal return*.

Annualized arithmetic mean rate of return The arithmetic mean rate of return stated on an annualized basis.

Annualized geometric mean rate of return The geometric mean rate of return stated on an annualized basis.

Appraisal The process of estimating the value of something; an estimate of value. *Note*: Often has the connotation of being done by an expert.

Appraisal ratio A measurement of the reward of active management relative to the risk of active management, calculated as the ratio of Jensen's alpha to the standard deviation of the portfolio's residual or non-systematic risk. Also referred to as the *Treynor–Black ratio*, the *Treynor–Black appraisal ratio*, and the *information ratio*.

Arithmetic difference A difference between two numbers a and b that is found as $a - b$.

Arithmetic mean rate of return The arithmetic mean of a set of holding period rates of returns.

Arithmetic mean return The sum of a set of returns divided by the number of returns summed.

Asset-grouping model An attribution model that isolates attribution effects by comparing the returns of variously constructed portfolios or groups of assets (example: the Brinson model).

Asymmetric risk Risk focusing on the part of variability that reflects losses rather than total variability.

Average drawdown The average of a specified number of the largest drawdowns over a given period.

BAI method See *linked IRR method*.

Base currency See *domestic currency*.

Basis points Hundredths of 1 percent.

Batting average A measure of investment performance consistency that reports (a) the percentage of investment decisions that result in a profit divided by the total number of investment decisions, or (b) the percentage of positive return periods relative to the benchmark or peers divided by the total number of return periods.

Beginning adjustment An adjustment to beginning portfolio value in order to better reflect the amount invested during a sub-period.

Benchmark In an investments context, a standard or point of reference for evaluating the performance of an investment portfolio.

Beta A measure of systematic risk that is based on the covariance of an asset's or portfolio's return with the return of the overall market; a measure of the sensitivity of a given investment or portfolio to movements in the overall market.

Book value The value of an asset recorded at the time it was purchased. Also known as *cost value* or *cost basis*.

bps See *basis points*.

Brinson model The approach to return attribution established in various papers co-authored by Gary Brinson; the Brinson–Hood–Beebower and Brinson–Fachler models viewed as a group.

Cap weighting See *capitalization weighting*.

Capital gains return See *price return*.

Capitalization weighting The most common security weighting scheme in which constituents are held in proportion to their market capitalizations, calculated as price times available shares. Also known as *market value weighting*, *market cap weighting*, or *cap weighting*.

Capture ratio A measure of the manager's gain or loss relative to the gain or loss of the benchmark.

Cash basis return The unleveraged return on an investment; the return on total capital invested including the amount financed by borrowing.

Chain linking With respect to returns, combining them using the linking formula. Also called *geometric compounding*.

Clean price Price quote on a bond that excludes the value of coupon interest accrued to the date of the quote; the price without accrued interest.

Coefficient of determination A measure of how well data points fit a linear statistical model, indicated in percentage terms from 0 to 100%. Also known as *R-squared* (R^2).

Composite An aggregation of one or more portfolios managed according to a similar investment mandate, objective, or strategy.
Compounding The calculation of interest on principal and accrued interest.
Confidence interval A range that has a given probability that it will contain the parameter it is intended to estimate.
Continuous compounding The compounding of continuously compounded returns (returns measured over infinitely small time intervals).
Contribution to VaR A measure of the relative volatility of the different segments compared to the volatility of the total fund.
Convexity An interest rate risk measure used in conjunction with duration; captures the degree of nonlinearity (curvature) in the relation between price change and yield change.
Correlation A measure of linear relationship calculated as covariance divided by the product of the individual asset standard deviations.
Cost basis See *book value.*
Cost value See *book value.*
Costly information efficient market hypothesis See *rational efficient markets hypothesis.*
Counterparty risk The risk of loss caused by a counterparty's failure to make a payment.
Coupon interest See *interest.*
Covariance A measure of how any two assets move together over time.
Credit risk The risk of loss caused by a counterparty or debtor's failure to make a promised payment.
Credit spread A premium over and above the current government bond yield.
Cross-sectional analysis Analysis over a group as of a given time.
Currency return The percentage change in the exchange rate over the period being considered (equivalently, the return from holding one unit of foreign currency).
Custom security-based benchmarks Benchmarks that are custom built to accurately reflect the investment discipline of a particular investment manager. Also called *strategy benchmarks* because they reflect a manager's particular strategy.
Day-weighted Dietz formula See *modified Dietz formula.*
Day-weighting fraction With reference to the calculation of a money-weighted rate of return, the fraction of a period over which a particular cash flow applies.
Deciles Values that divide a distribution ranked smallest to largest into 10 equal parts.
Direct quotation Exchange rate quotation of the form of the number of domestic-currency units per unit of foreign-currency. Also called *direct quote.*
Dirty price Price quote on a bond that includes the value of coupon interest; the value at which the asset can be exchanged for other assets in the market.
Discrete compounding The compounding of discrete returns.
Discrete returns A return measured over a finite time interval.
Dividends The investment income that may be received from ownership of common or preference shares.
Domestic asset An asset that trades in the investor's home (base) currency (e.g., in Swiss francs for a Swiss investor).
Domestic currency The currency an investor uses for consumption purposes (e.g., Canadian dollars for a Canadian investor is his domestic currency). Also called *base currency* or *home currency.*
Domestic-currency return The rate of return expressed in the investor's home currency.
Downside capture ratio A measure of capture when the benchmark return is negative in a given period; downside capture less (greater) than 100% generally suggests out (under) performance relative to the benchmark.
Downside risk The potential for loss.
Drawdown A decline in value (represented by a series of negative returns only) following a peak fund valuation. See *individual drawdown.*
Drawdown A decline in value (represented by a series of negative returns only) following a peak fund valuation. See *Individual drawdown.*
Drawdown duration The time it takes to experience and then recover from the maximum drawdown; time from peak to trough to peak.
Drawdown measures Measures that capture various aspects of peak-to-trough declines.
Due diligence Investigation and analysis in support of an investment action, decision, or recommendation.
Duration The percentage change in bond price given an unanticipated small change in interest rates.
Effective annual rate The amount by which a unit of currency will grow in a year, with interest on interest included.
Equal weighting Security weighting scheme in which all constituents are held at equal weights at specified rebalancing times.
***Ex ante* alpha** Alpha in a forward-looking sense. See *expected alpha.*
***Ex ante* risk** Risk looking to the future.
Ex-coupon date The first date that a bond trades without the coupon; date from which point forward a purchaser of a bond is not entitled to the coupon payment.
Ex-dividend date The first date that a share trades without the dividend; date from which point forward a purchaser of a share is not entitled to the dividend payment.
***Ex post* alpha** Historical alpha. See *realized alpha.*
***Ex post* risk** Risk in reference to a past record.
Excess return Used in various senses appropriate to context: 1) The difference between the portfolio return and the benchmark return, which may be either positive or negative; 2) The return in excess of the risk-free rate, thus representing the return for bearing risk.
Expected alpha The difference between the expected return and the required rate of return on an asset. Also called *ex ante alpha.*
External cash flows Deposits to or withdrawals from a portfolio.
F-test With reference to an estimated regression, tests the null hypothesis that all of the coefficient estimates are zero versus the alternative hypothesis that one or more of the coefficient estimates is not equal to zero.
Factor-model-based benchmarks Benchmarks constructed by examining a portfolio's sensitivity to a set of factors, such as the return for a broad market index, company earnings growth, industry, or financial leverage.
Financial risks Risks related to events in external financial markets.
Foreign assets An asset denominated in currencies other than the investor's home (base) currency. Also called *non-domestic asset.*
Foreign-currency return The return on an asset held in a foreign market; also called the *local currency return* or *local return* because it is the return of the asset expressed in local-currency terms.

Frequency distribution A tabular display of data summarized into a relatively small number of intervals.

Fund manager The professional manager of separate accounts or pooled assets structured in a variety of ways.

Fundamental law of active management The relation that the information ratio of a portfolio manager is approximately equal to the information coefficient multiplied by the square root of the investment discipline's breadth (the number of independent, active investment decisions made each year). The expression was later expanded to include a multiplicative term that reflects how effectively investment insights are transferred to the information ratio.

Fundamental weighting Patented by Research Affiliates LLC, this scheme uses company characteristics such as sales, cash flow, book value, and dividends to weight securities.

Funding risk The risk that funding cannot readily be obtained.

Geometric compounding See *chain linking*.

Geometric difference A difference between two numbers a and b that is found as $[(1 + a)/(1 + b)] - 1$.

Geometric mean rate of return The compound growth rate associated with a set of holding period rates of returns.

Gross-of-fee returns The returns based on portfolio values reduced by any trading expenses incurred during the period, but not reduced by investment management fees.

Histogram A bar chart of data that have been grouped into a frequency distribution.

Holding period An interval between two points in time over which an asset or portfolio is assumed to be held.

Holding period rate of return The percentage gain or loss in wealth resulting from holding some asset or portfolio over the stated holding period. Also known as *rate or return* or *return*.

Holdings-based style analysis A bottom-up style analysis that estimates the risk exposures from the actual securities held in the portfolio at a point in time.

Home currency See *domestic currency*.

Idiosyncratic risk Risk that is firm or security specific.

Income Sometimes called *investment income*, refers to cash payments made to owners of an asset.

Income return The component of rate of return that derives from investment income.

Indirect quotation Exchange rate quoted in terms of the number of foreign-currency units per unit of domestic currency.

Individual drawdown A decline in value (represented by a series of negative returns only) following a peak fund valuation.

Individual sector allocation Allocation referring to a single sector (e.g., energy).

Inflation rate The rate of change in the purchasing power of a currency unit over time.

Information ratio See *appraisal ratio*.

Interest The investment income that may be received from ownership of debt instruments; payment for lending funds. The interest income on bonds is also known as *coupon interest* or *coupon*.

Internal rate of return The constant rate of return that would produce the total ending value of a portfolio given the magnitude and timing of the cash flows. Also known as *money-weighted rate of return*.

Investment income See *income*.

Investment performance appraisal The systematic evaluation of the investment performance of a fund or strategy in order to understand and assess the past decisions and abilities of a portfolio manager. Concerned with distinguishing skill from luck.

Investment policy statement A written investment planning document that includes statements of a client's investment objectives and investment constraints.

Investment style A natural grouping of investment disciplines that has some predictive power in explaining the future dispersion of returns across portfolios.

Investment universe The set of assets that may be considered for investment.

Jensen measure See *Jensen's alpha*.

Jensen's alpha Measures the return of a portfolio in excess of the theoretical required return given the equilibrium model for asset returns known as the CAPM. Also called *Jensen measure*.

Key person risk The risk that results from over-reliance on an individual or individuals whose departure would negatively affect an investment manager.

Legal/contract risk Risk that arises from contract terms that are not clearly specified.

Leverage The use of borrowing or use of various financial instruments to magnify potential gains and losses relative to the investor's equity position.

Leveraged return With respect to a leveraged portfolio, the return achieved based on the capital invested. Also called *levered return*.

Levered return See *leveraged return*.

Liability return The return of a portfolio consisting only of liabilities.

Linked IRR method A method for calculating an approximate time-weighted rate of return that involves linking together internal rate-of-return estimates for sub-periods. Also known as *BAI method*.

Linked modified Dietz method The linked IRR method based on using the modified Dietz method for calculating sub-period returns.

Linking formula An expression for combining returns on a portfolio or asset over multiple periods so as to account for the cumulative effect on wealth.

Liquidity reserve Money held in cash and cash equivalents as a reserve.

Liquidity risk The risk that results from the inability to trade an asset quickly without a significant concession in price.

Local currency return See *foreign-currency return*.

M^2 An appraisal measure that indicates what a portfolio would have returned, assuming the same total risk as the market index.

M^2 alpha Difference between the risk-adjusted performance of the portfolio and the performance of the benchmark.

Macro attribution Attribution at the sponsor level.

Manager peer group See *manager universe*.

Manager universe A broad group of managers with similar investment disciplines. Also called *manager peer group*.

Margin With respect to trading, the use of borrowed money in making purchases; the collateral on deposit to meet potential performance obligations.

Marked to market A procedure used to revalue a financial asset or liability to its current market value.

Market cap weighting See *capitalization weighting*.

Market index Represents the performance of a specified security market, market segment, or asset class.

Market model A regression equation that specifies a linear relationship between the return on a security (or portfolio) and the return on a broad market index.

Market risk Risk related to market movements, e.g., unexpected changes in share prices, interest rates, currency exchange rates, and commodity prices.

Market value The price at which investors can buy or sell an investment in the marketplace.

Market value weighting See *capitalization weighting.*

Maximum drawdown The largest peak to trough loss within a period.

Mean absolute deviation A measure of dispersion calculated as the mean of the absolute values of deviations from the mean.

Median The "middlemost" observation; i.e., in a set of observations that has been ranked from highest to lowest, the median will lie in the middle.

Micro attribution Attribution at the portfolio manager level.

Model risk The risk that a model is incorrect or misapplied.

Modified Dietz formula With respect to the linked IRR method, a method for calculating sub-period returns that uses the actual dating of within-sub-period cash flows.

Money-weighted rate of return See *internal rate of return.*

Negative skewness The condition of being skewed towards smaller values; skewed to the left.

Net asset value The market value of assets minus the market value of liabilities, stated on a per-share or per-unit basis.

Net-of-fee return Investment return based on portfolio values, reduced by trading expenses and by the investment management fees; gross-of-fee returns reduced by investment management fees.

Nominal prices Actual transaction prices with no adjustment for inflation.

Nominal return The rate of return based on actual transaction prices.

Non-diversifiable risk See *systematic risk.*

Non-domestic assets See *foreign asset.*

Non-financial risks Includes operational risks, model risks, and settlement risks.

Off-benchmark decisions Decisions to invest in securities that are not included in the portfolio manager's benchmark.

Operational risk The risk of loss from failure in a company's systems or procedures or from external events such as acts of God, terrorist action, etc.

Optimization-based weighting Security weighting schemes using minimum-variance and efficiency.

Original Dietz formula With respect to the linked IRR method, a method for calculating sub-period returns that assumes that half of any within-sub-period cash flow is received at the beginning of the sub-period and half is received at the end.

P-value The smallest level of significance at which the null hypothesis can be rejected.

Passive investment strategies A buy-and-hold approach to investing in which an investor does not make portfolio changes based upon short-term expectations of changing market or security performance.

Pay date The date at which a declared dividend is acutally paid.

Percentiles Values that divide a distribution into 100 equal parts.

Performance appraisal The systematic evaluation of the investment performance of a fund or strategy in order to understand and assess the past decisions and abilities of a portfolio manager.

Performance attribution Attribution, including return attribution and risk attribution; often used as a synonym for return attribution.

Plan sponsor The trustee, company, or employer responsible for a public or private institutional investment plan.

Portfolio A collection of one or more assets.

Portfolio risk The risk of a collection of assets.

Positive skewness The condition of being skewed towards larger values; skewed to the right.

Price index A securities index that reflects price changes but not investment income.

Price return The return earned from changes in asset price; also called *capital gain return.*

Price weighting Security weighting scheme in which constituents are weighted in proportion to their prices.

Priced risks Risks for which investors demand compensation for bearing (e.g., equity risk, company-specific factors, macroeconomic factors).

Quartiles Values that divide a distribution into four equal parts.

Quintiles Values that divide a distribution into five equal parts.

R^2 See *coefficient of determination.*

Rate of return The percent gain or loss in wealth resulting from holding an investment over a specific period of time.

Rational efficient markets hypothesis The hypothesis that, on average, active investors earn just enough incremental returns to cover costs of information acquisition.

Real prices Nominal prices adjusted for inflation.

Real return The nominal rate of return adjusted for inflation.

Realized alpha The difference between the actual holding-period return and the contemporaneous required return. Also called *ex post alpha.*

Record date The date established by an issuer of a security for the purpose of determining the holders who are entitled to receive a dividend that has been declared; only owners as of the record date are entitled to receive the dividend.

Regulatory risk Risk of changes in regulations that adversely affect valuation.

Reinvested income Income that is received during a holding period and reinvested into a portfolio.

Relative risk Risk relative to some reference point.

Return attribution A set of techniques used to identify the sources of the excess return of a portfolio against its benchmark.

Return contribution Analysis of the contributions of portfolio components to the total return of a portfolio.

Return relative The ratio of ending value to beginning value of a portfolio or security. Also called *value relative* or *wealth ratio.*

Returns-based benchmarks Benchmarks constructed by examining a portfolio's sensitivity to a set of factors, such as the returns for various style indexes (e.g., small-cap value, small-cap growth, large-cap value, and large-cap growth).

Returns-based style analysis A top-down style analysis that involves estimating the sensitivities of a portfolio to security market indexes.

Reward-to-variability ratio See *Sharpe ratio.*

Risk Exposure to uncertainty.

Risk attribution The analysis of the sources of risk.

Risk premium An extra return expected by investors for bearing some specified risk.

Sector A grouping of assets that share some common characteristics.

Security market line The graphical representation of the CAPM formula, showing the relationship between expected return and beta.
Security specific Belonging to the security rather than to the market or to the sector.
Selection The value the portfolio manager adds by holding individual securities or instruments within the sector in different-from-benchmark weights.
Semi-standard deviation The square root of the semi-variance.
Semi-variance An asymmetric risk mean that is similar to the variance except that only deviations below the mean are measured.
Settlement date accounting Recognition of the value of assets and/or liabilities on the date when the actual exchange of cash and investments is completed.
Settlement risk Risk of a breakdown in the settlement of a trade.
Sharpe ratio The average return in excess of the risk-free rate divided by the standard deviation of return; a measure of the average excess return earned per unit of standard deviation of return. Also known as the *reward-to-variability ratio.*
Snail trail chart A method of determining and screening for style drift, a snail trail chart displays information about the manager's return characteristics through time.
Sovereign/political risk Risk related to potential government actions.
Specific asset selection The portion of excess return that is due to individual asset selection.
Spot exchange rate The rate at which one currency can be exchanged for immediate delivery of another currency.
Stand-alone risk Risk independent of the performance of other assets.
Stand-alone risk See *total risk.*
Standard deviation The positive square root of variance.
Stated annual rate The stated interest rate for a year ignoring the effect of any compounding; the periodic rate multiplied by the number of compounding periods per year.
Stop-losses A trading order that sets a selling price below the current market price with a goal of protecting profits or preventing further losses.
Strategy benchmarks *See custom security-based benchmarks.*
Surplus return The return on a portfolio of both assets and liabilities (i.e., the return on the portfolio's equity).
Surplus risk Risk related to the value of surplus (vales of assets minus the value of liabilities).
Symmetric risk Risk related to both upside and downside.
Systematic risk Risk originating from broad financial market conditions and the macroeconomy; also called *non-diversifiable risk.*
***t*-statistic** The ratio of the departure of the estimate of a parameter from its hypothesized value divided by the estimate's standard error.
Tail risk The possibility of extreme losses.
Tail value at risk Equal to VaR plus the expected loss in excess of VaR, given that such excess loss occurs.
Target semi-standard deviation A measure of downside risk that focuses on deviations below a target value. Also called *target semideviation.*
Target semi-variance The same as the semi-variance, except that a specified target return is used instead of the mean return.
Target semideviation See *target semi-standard deviation.*
Tax risk Risk of unexpected changes in tax rates or rulings.
Time-series analysis Analysis of where the returns for an asset were examined over time.
Total return Holding period return. *Note*: Used to emphasize that both the price and income components of return are being taken into account.
Total return index A securities index that reflects both reinvested income and price changes.
Total risk The sum of systematic risk and non-systematic risk; also called *stand-alone risk.*
Tracking risk The standard deviation of the differences between a portfolio's returns and its benchmark's returns. Also called *tracking error* and *active risk.*
Tracking tolerance The ex-ante tracking risk target or given threshold margin of an investment manager.
Treynor–Black appraisal ratio See *appraisal ratio.*
Treynor–Black ratio See *appraisal ratio.*
Treynor ratio A measure of risk-adjusted performance that relates a portfolio's returns in excess of the risk-free rate to a portfolio's beta.
Unit value pricing A method for accounting for ownership interests in pooled investments that lends itself to calculating time-weighted rates of returns.
Unrealized gain (loss) The difference between the market value and the cost basis of an asset.
Upside capture ratio A measure of capture when the benchmark return is positive in a given period; upside capture greater (less) than 100% generally suggests out (under) performance relative to the benchmark.
Value at risk An estimate of the loss that we expect to be exceeded with a given level of probability over a specified time period.
Value relative See *return relative.*
Variance The expected value or the mean of squared deviations from the mean.
Wealth ratio *See return relative.*
Zero-weight benchmark decisions See *off-benchmark decisions.*

Made in the USA
Middletown, DE
07 November 2017